The Piozzi Letters

Hester Lynch Piozzi in mourning for Gabriel Piozzi, portrait by John Jackson, 1810. Reproduction by the kind permission of The Hyde Collection, Four Oaks Farm, Somerville, New Jersey.

The Piozzi Letters

Correspondence of
Hester Lynch Piozzi, 1784–1821
(formerly Mrs. Thrale)

Volume 4
1805–1810

EDITED BY
Edward A. Bloom
AND
Lillian D. Bloom

NEWARK: University of Delaware Press
LONDON AND TORONTO: Associated University Presses

© 1996 by Associated University Presses, Inc.

All rights reserved. Authorization to photocopy items for internal or personal use, or the internal or personal use of specific clients, is granted by the copyright owner, provided that a base fee of $10.00, plus eight cents per page, per copy is paid directly to the Copyright Clearance Center, 222 Rosewood Drive, Danvers, Massachusetts 01923. [0-87413-393-9/96 $10.00 + 8¢ pp, pc.]

Associated University Presses
440 Forsgate Drive
Cranbury, NJ 08512

Associated University Presses
16 Barter Street
London WC1A 2AH, England

Associated University Presses
P.O. Box 338, Port Credit
Mississauga, Ontario
L5G 4L8 Canada

The paper used in this publication meets the requirements of the American National Standard for Permanence of Paper for Printed Library Materials Z39.48-1984.

Library of Congress Cataloging-in-Publication Data
(Revised for vol. 4)

Piozzi, Hester Lynch, 1741–1821.
  The Piozzi letters : correspondence of Hester Lynch Piozzi, 1784–1821 (formerly Mrs. Thrale).

  Includes bibliographical references and indexes.
  Contents: v. 1. 1784–1791—v. 2. 1792–1798—v. 3. 1799–1804—v. 4. 1805–1810.
  1. Piozzi, Hester Lynch, 1741–1821—Correspondence.
  2. Authors, English—18th century—Correspondence.
  3. London (England)—Intellectual life—18th century.
  I. Bloom, Edward Alan, 1914–1994. II. Bloom, Lillian D.
  III. Title.
  PR3619.P5Z48   1996   828'.609   87-40231
  ISBN 0-87413-115-4 (vol. 1 : alk. paper)
  ISBN 0-87413-360-2 (v. 2 : alk. paper)
  ISBN 0-87413-392-0 (v. 3 : alk. paper)
  ISBN 0-87413-393-9 (v. 4 : alk. paper)

PRINTED IN THE UNITED STATES OF AMERICA

Contents

List of Illustrations	7
Introduction	9
Short Titles for Major Manuscript Repositories	37
Short Titles for Hester Lynch Piozzi's Manuscripts and Books	39
Short Titles for Secondary Sources	43
Names and Abbreviations of Major Figures in the Piozzi Correspondence	51
Editorial Principles	53
Letters, 1805–1810	59
Index	325

Illustrations

Hester Lynch Piozzi, portrait by John Jackson   frontispiece

Dr. Charles Burney, portrait by Sir Joshua Reynolds   126

Sir George Colebrooke, portrait by Sir Joshua Reynolds   182

The Lady's Last Stake by William Hogarth,
   with the young HLP as the Lady   282

Introduction

Like all of Mrs. Piozzi's correspondence, that of the years 1805–1810 is notable for diversity and often trenchant opinion. Many of the letters—probably, indeed, those of most interest—become extensions in effect of her private journals, and in this spirit may be read as her affirmations of hope and ambition, as well as her declarations of frustration, grief, anger, and self-pity. She allows herself to be observed in her most personal and vulnerable states. In large blocks of letters she reveals the trauma that she has endured and yet, conversely, the independence of character that has made capitulation unthinkable.

Her days of authorship and private happiness now belong to the past and, sequentially, she is trapped in an atmosphere of loss and mourning. Literature has become secondary to her domestic obligations and to the stress engendered by Gabriel Piozzi's relentless decline and death. During this period also, the tacit feud waged by her daughters is underscored by their uncommonly cruel rejection of her. Rather than bend to this humiliation, however, she intensifies their resentment with steadily increasing attention to Salusbury, the adopted nephew whom she has destined to become her heir.

Thematically, then, the core of Volume 4 is particularly significant for its biographical implications as a kind of family portrait. At the same time and somewhat more externally, numerous letters not necessarily within the immediate range of these family tensions provide a continuum of another order. That is, many of Mrs. Piozzi's preoccupations from earlier years are still evident. At a practical level, for instance, she worries often about the management of affairs at Streatham and Brynbella, about the competence of the servants she has gathered about her, and about legal difficulties with tenants. Concerned about farming profits, she is constantly anxious about the weather. Other landed interests—her exclusion from the inheritance of her uncle's Offley estate and controversy about property rights in general—are matters of lasting vexation.

As a very social being, she has her share of friends and enemies (whether the latter are real or imagined) who figure in her correspondence. Public events—political and military—continue to engage her curiosity and interest. And even as in the past, though with less intensity, she retains her zest for subjects that are intellectual, sacred, or esthetic. Thus she likes to reflect on questions of religion and theology, on literature and art, on the theater, and on learning and educational theory. In the midst of her private anxieties, in short, she is always alert to ideas and happenings that might stretch her mind and her correspondents'.

I

By the year 1805, the vitality that had driven Mrs. Piozzi in her early and middle years was giving way to compulsive morbidity. She suffered frequent episodes of melancholia and imagined with dread the lonely prospect of existence without Gabriel Piozzi at her side. The comfortably framed, assured image of herself that she had once envisaged was blurring and at the age of sixty-four she reluctantly began to face an oppressive reality. Quite simply, no matter how aggressively she projected the engaging public manner, inwardly she was without joy. Since at least 1797, Piozzi had been subject to attacks of gout that lamed legs, feet, and hands. In the spring of 1803 she conceded that he was permanently disabled, capable of moving about only in "a borrowed Bath rolling chair." In this confined state he was afflicted by phlebitis, abscesses, ulcers, and gangrene. Further compounding his misery were a chronic deposit of chalkstones (uric acid), bronchitis, a fibroid disease of the heart accompanied by a strangling cough and a sluggish pulse.[1] Remission was infrequent and Piozzi's hold on life was tenuous, its ties fragile at best.

As for Mrs. Piozzi, she could hope only that his pain—thanks to a succession of sympathetic medical men—might be staved off or dulled by opiates. His desperate refuge in alcohol made matters worse until, almost at the end, she felt that she must deny him access to the bottle. Grimly, one year before his death, she wrote to the Reverend Thomas Sedgwick Whalley, "poor little Brynbella, which has so long been a *House of Mourning* for lost Health—it has nearly forgotten to be a *house of Feasting.*" With characteristic formal piety, she added, "We must not however choose our own Afflictions, but take with Patience those that we are sent by Heaven." Lamenting Piozzi's need to struggle against dreadful odds, she must on occasion have been fortified nevertheless by his stubborn vital force. Thus, even though "consolation [was] difficult" for her, she mustered whatever hope she could. Piozzi, she observed, has a "tolerable appetite, and no worse spirits than such a state of life and limbs must necessarily produce——so we must be contented I think, and pity those who are worse off than ourselves."[2] Ironically, he had even managed to rise above his own suffering and cry out, *"Bon Courage,"* in an attempt to buck up his "half-dead" wife during a competing moment of crisis.[3]

The rural splendors of North Wales were esthetically and spiritually invigorating, an enviable retreat from the tensions of English materialism. But even a setting as charming as Brynbella was hardly ideal for one whose health was as marginal as Piozzi's. No more than rudimentary medical care was to be had at nearby Denbigh. There the ever loyal apothecary Mr. Moore—father of the distinguished general John Moore—was always on call to dispense medication and diagnoses. He could be depended upon day and night to respond to urgent pleas for help, to offer advice, and even to share a friendly meal. For all his willingness, however, Moore had no qualifications perceptibly better than those of any reasonably competent, hard-working village apothecary. Given this kind of provincial expertise, he managed to alleviate sudden onsets of distress. Probably the result of opiates, the effects were only short term. For the nearest qualified practitioner, the Piozzis relied on Dr. William Makepeace Thackeray of Chester (grandfather of the novelist), who became a good friend as well as medical counselor. Thackeray came to Brynbella whenever he could, and his patients would sometimes journey to him from Wales.

Piozzi's condition was ameliorated enough to allow travel to spas or resorts. Mrs. Piozzi especially enjoyed bathing as a "cure," and whenever they could, they managed brief stays in Welsh seaside towns. More habitually, they observed an annual ritual—as socially correct as it was curative—of winter/spring residence in Bath. Unfailingly they would leave a card at the Assembly Room, drink the water at the Pump Room, socialize with friends, and when in need of medical assistance utilize the services of Mr. Bowen, another apothecary, and of Dr. Parry, a prominent physician. They were like two people constantly in flight from impending, inescapable danger. An anniversary visit to Prestatyn in North Wales was more like penance than celebration. "We have often kept our Wedding Day with the rich," she snobbishly confided to Lady Williams and her mother. But here "we are keeping it among the Poor . . . at Prestatyn; for 'tis a miserable Place sure, and no Fish: no, not a Net, nor a Notion of using one, as in other little Villages by the Seaside." If she had the dubious consolation of access to good bathing-machines, Piozzi took his comfort from resting his leg on a sofa transported for that purpose. She bathed "diligently every day to recruit her Spirits, Appetite and Strength which began Sensibly to feel the Wear and Tear of Time."[4] An excursion to another resort was equally disastrous, and they cut their visits short: seizures of gout among other disorders forced their return to Brynbella in August 1805: "God give us Strength & Ability for our Bath Journey—We shall there have some *help*, & some *Society* at hand; This is a dismal Life!" As she informed Queeney, the second of November 1805 "is the first Day [Piozzi] has got up to wash his Face, and put on the appearance of a human Creature since our Return."[5]

Within a few weeks both Piozzis had once again drawn upon resources of bodily will and sheer habit to prepare them for the arduous southward journey. Their experiences between December and March, when they resided in the house on Pulteney Street, were not particularly eventful. Mrs. Piozzi attended to her correspondence as usual, and both probably benefited from the water and the comparatively favorable climate of Bath, as well as from the *pro forma* rounds of social busyness and renewed friendships. Once returned to Wales, however, they had little access to amenities, other than neighborly good will, to distract them from their persistent health problems. Lady Williams, always a faithful friend and sympathetic listener, was told on 26 July 1806: "The Gout has partly forgotten Mr. Piozzi—or has changed his Mode of Attack: he is now subject to St. Anthony's Fire [i.e., erysipelas] more than to raging Pain——The Hands however go on enlarging, and the poor Piano e Forte is wholly out of favour." The anticipation of a jaunt to Chester should have been a source of pleasure. "There is no *present* Reason for supposing Mr. Piozzi will be incapable of receiving Amusement from such a Frolick." But there was never any real escape from the apprehension of imminent calamity. Gout, as Mrs. Piozzi wryly commented, "is a Fellow one cannot Answer for—out of one's Sight."[6]

The relative mildness of Piozzi's new affliction had encouraged his wife to mention it almost offhandedly as though it were a temporary but manageable nuisance. It is hard to believe, however, that she had not rationalized the situation, disguising from herself the fact of a false interlude. As 1806 drew to a close, they prepared for what was likely to be a "dreadful" journey to Bath. "Mr Piozzi has had another Fit of Gout—more dangerous, more cruel & oppressive than any he has yet endured, & leaving him more helpless: but then we have had longer Holydays than usual—longer Remission of these horrible Scenes—& Doctor Thackeray pulled us through most manfully."[7] This, however, was delusive optimism, for life in Bath was no kinder than it had been in Wales. Piozzi hardly ever left his room. "Never was Mortal Man so tortured surely, and the Gout driven from one Post resolutely attacks another, so that one feels less and less Confidence in Physic and Physicians every hour of one's Life."[8]

The last few years allotted to Piozzi were a death watch over which she presided with dwindling hope and mounting despair. Illness had become so intensely the center of her existence that, as she told Margaret Williams, "My poor Husband's Health will put me out of my Wits at last." A doctor—probably Parry—had "promised to come at a Moment's warning." Piozzi's cough was "beyond all things dreadful——attended with excessive Depression of Spirits, and total loss of Appetite." Ironically they lodged in a "*French* house, where the Cookery is so seducing, and the Kitchen removed to the Back Apartment . . . so that no Scent can be perceived." She no longer attempted to conceal the toll on her own emotional and physical being. "My Hopes are sadly kicked down Stairs, and so are *his* by this vile Relapse, if Relapse it can be called. Tell Bowen all I have told *you*, and tell him my Inside is very *unhappy*, but by dint of Temperance, Exercise, and forced Chearfulness, I keep it as quiet as I can. Oh my dear Miss Williams! nobody knows what my *Bowels* suffer on Account of my *Heart*——and none of these Anatomists or Surgeons can make them agree."[9]

Although Piozzi somehow endured his many afflictions for almost two more years, a diary entry of 12 June 1807 foreshadows the daily uncertainty that he faced. "Here we are, Thanks to Almighty God—once more returned from Bath & London, to lay our Bones quietly down at Brynbella. The Illness Mr Piozzi had to support in the first Named Place, this January & February; beat all I ever saw or read of:—on my Birthday 27th day of the new Year, Dr Parry was fetched at 2 or 3 o'Clock in the Morn^g, & between *then* & the first of May, my wretched Husband swallowed no fewer than 300 Medical Draughts.[10] Early in March we believ'd every Instant would have been his last, and I thought it Time to enquire if he would see a Romish Priest as Time seemed flying fast away. He cried No, No, No: with Earnestness.—a Protestant Clergyman? said I—by all means, was his Ans^r. Dear Mr Leman of the Crescent came at our Call, and my Piozzi is now a Member of our own Communion. He rec^d the Sacrament again according to *L'Eglise Anglicane* on Easter day; & his odd Dream at Milan is verified; how he took me by the Arm & walked out of their Church—resolving to walk in *no more.* See then what may be done by the old Method, suaviter in Modo, fortiter in re."[11]

The correspondence during the final fifteen or sixteen months of Piozzi's ordeal records virtually unremitting pain and crises. Her letters to Salusbury, especially, in which she seldom allows hope to punctuate a litany of anguish and inevitable dissolution, testify to a talent for graphic detail. She seems bent upon drawing images of the daily horrors that she has witnessed and shared with Salusbury's uncle. As time was to demonstrate, the nephew's memory was not as receptive or longlasting as Mrs. Piozzi would have hoped. For the moment, however, she had the gloomy satisfaction of commanding his attention to a catalogue of sad happenings. "I continue according to Promise," she assured him, "my melancholy Narrative."[12]

A dutiful memorialist, she had written shortly before: "Our Bulletin of Health here goes on very Ill. . . . Poor Uncle has been delirious now a whole Week. . . . complaining of no Pain at all, rather making odd Preparations for a Journey *in Italy,* for I understood he considered himself as now at *Milan.* The Attack on his Senses remitted however in due Time, and he conversed rationally with Mr. Oldfield the Attorney on *Wednesday* Morning. . . . *That* Night, notwithstanding we laid aside much of the Wine and Brandy; was passed wholly in delirious Raving. . . . Meanwhile Mr. Moore keeps on in his cold slow manner; assuring me there is *no cause* of *Alarm;* and *pledging his Life* there's *not an Atom* of *Danger.* But I have written for Doctor Thackeray again, and if *I* have not Cause of Alarm—I wonder who *has?* . . . whilst [Piozzi] was seeing Sights of Ladies, Processions, and I know not what Stuff——we shall have a shocking Place *there*——especially as the Supplies of Wine and Brandy *must* be cut off, or he must lose his Wits forever. . . . Nothing that *can* be *done* shall be left *un*done."[13]

In the midst of dealing with Piozzi's tribulations, Mrs. Piozzi was further saddened by the knowledge that Eleanor Williams, mother of Lady Williams, was dying of cancer of the throat. Her sympathy was genuine, even as was the compassion that she expressed for the "13 poor Women whose husbands were all destroyed at once Yesterday in the Coalpit at Mostyn!! Poor Creatures! I warrant they are made of the same Flesh and Blood as *we* are—created and Redeemed by the same Almighty Power: in whose Sight they are as *good*—perhaps *better* than we, who have more Words to lament our Fate with."[14] If there is a hint of condescension here, it may be attributed both to impersonal distance and formal Christian piety. Much more subjectively, however, she could not help mingling admiration with pity for her ailing friend and husband. Neither invalid, she marveled, would be deflected even by terminal illness from the niceties of social appearance. Mrs. Williams, as she observed, "dresses, dines at Table &c.—so does Mr. Piozzi: whose Torments I *trust,* even more than equal hers."[15]

With the sands truly running out, Mrs. Piozzi seized what solace she could from Dr. Thackeray's ministrations and from Moore's bumbling optimism. Piozzi's paranoid rages were almost as hard to bear as his lapses into delirium. "[As] soon as he was put to Bed—he *stormed* away with Anger, directed chiefly against *me* who he said had always used him very Ill, and worse now than Ever, so he fell asleep: and waked in an hour, and eat his Dinner with Appetite. . . . He is the Strongest Man ever under the hand of a Physician, and Mr. Moore says that Ill Humour and *Crossness* such as *his,* are certainly Pledges that he will get well."[16] Mrs. Piozzi wished to believe that, even though the following day she observed that her "Friends and Servants are even now enraged because they see I *think* my husband will recover."[17]

But Mrs. Piozzi could no longer will the continuation of Piozzi's life. Neither love nor stubborn denial could possibly alter the finality of the long, destructive battle. All through her daily "Pocketbooks" she had meticulously recorded the stages of decay until, on 23 March 1809, she tersely noted the inevitable: "Sleeps perpetually. Life ebbing out." Three days later: "All hope extinguished. All *Life* extinguished." On that day she wrote to Lady Williams: "Nothing can be exaggerated Dearest Madam: Mr. Piozzi's Sufferings far exceed whatever can be *said*.

"I will bear mine how I can. Thankful to my Friends; and Submissive to God's Will——but we are best alone; at such Times there is no Consolation but from above.

"We hope his Sufferings begin to remit now: Nature is nearly exhausted. . . ."

And then the poignantly bare conclusion: "Mr. Piozzi expired at 2 o'Clock."[18]

Preoccupied as she had been for several years with Piozzi's steadily failing health, since mid-May of 1805 she confided perceptibly fewer of her private thoughts to *Thraliana*. There was a fatal portent, she intimates, in that she was left with only "30 Pages more to fill" of the six red folios given her by Henry Thrale in 1776; "and now my Books, & Hopes, and Prospects—are all closing round me, what have I learned since I began the World?" Her foreboding was justified and on 30 March 1809 she closed still another chapter. "Every thing most dreaded *has* ensued,—all is over; and my second Husbands Death is the last thing recorded in my first husband's Present! Cruel Death!"[19]

On Monday, 3 April 1809, Gabriel Piozzi was interred in the vault of the Tremeirchion church. "The dismal Day," she wrote in her pocketbook, "last, last, last." On 7 April: "Blank Sorrow. Thankful for Salusbury's Company and Shephard's." Three days later, Salusbury and his companion departed from Wales and Mrs. Piozzi was left "All alone." In the dry entry of the "Tremeirchion Parish Burial Register, 1761–1810": "Gabriel Piozzi Esq. of Brynbella died on the 26th of March and was buried on the 3rd of April 1809. Aged 69."[20] The *North Wales Gazette* for 30 March published a similar obituary notice.

The medical and funeral expenses underscored the harsh aftermath. Thus on 14 April she complained that "Mr. Moore's Bill [was] dreadful," and on 17 April she paid Evans the undertaker £157.0.2. In the gloomy days following Piozzi's death and burial, she informed Queeney that the Anglican priest Dr. Myddelton had "read the Commendatory Prayer over my wretched Husband a full Week before his Release—but whether he *quite knew* what past—Poor Soul! I have never felt convinced. He administered the Sacrament to us all in our Drawing Room about a *Twelvemonth* ago, when Mr. Piozzi was in full Possession of his mental Powers—made his Will &c."[21]

These early days of mourning magnified in Mrs. Piozzi's thoughts not only the loss of a husband but the isolation experienced through the absence of her daughters. Instinctively, consistent with an abiding sense of maternal dominance, she cast herself as the mother figure at the head of a loyal staff of household servants. They served her domestic needs, to be sure, but at least equally important during this bleak time, they comprised her "family" (as in the original meaning of that word), but a family *manqué* in effect that supplanted the blood ties denied by her daughters. Eliciting sympathy—and possibly an edge of guilt—from Salusbury, she wrote: "It was such dreadful Weather on Sunday none of the Servants could go to Church;—still less durst I venture, and God forgive me I felt half glad to escape the black Pew &c. So I called my Family and read Prayers to them in the Drawing Room at Night;—to beg a Blessing both on the goers away and the Stayers-behind.———It was a melancholy Meeting—all in our Dismal Dresses so, but I got through it somehow; and Allen-Jones [her personal maid and confidante] and I had a good Hysterical Cry after all was over.———Her poor Husband gets gradually worse and worse. . . . What do You think Mr. Moore's Bill was for these last Two Years? Guess first, and then I'll tell you."[22]

A few days later Mrs. Piozzi was on her way to London, unable for the time being to remain at Brynbella with the burden of her memories. By the end of the month—29 April—she signed her will, which was witnessed by Smythe, a perfumer; Fell, a bookseller; and a Mr. Day.[23]

II

For Mrs. Piozzi, as for most of her contemporaries in an era of problematic medical science, existence took on the trappings of uneven combat; it was an age in which illness and the shadow of death were constant threats to happiness and achievement. Her first traumatic awareness of a finite state probably occurred in December of 1762 when her father died unexpectedly. Less than a year later a loveless match with Henry Thrale initiated a sequence of pregnancies fraught with the anxieties of infant maladies and the tragedy of premature deaths. "The Thrale family," as Mary Hyde has aptly remarked, was indeed "plagued . . . by medical problems."[24] Mrs. Piozzi had been harried by the depressive and physical complaints of Johnson from about 1766 to 1784. Domestic demands were further exacerbated by the ailments (compounded by financial worries) and death of Henry Thrale in 1781. Most affective of all had been the loss of her mother, Hester Maria Cotton Salusbury, in 1773, the pain of which is articulated in a journal entry dated 18 June: "On this day She died, & left me destitute of every *real* every *natural* Friend: for Sir Thos Salusbury has long ago cast me off, & Mr Thrale & Mr Johnson are the mere Acquisitions of Chance; which chance, or change of Behaviour, or Intervention of new Objects or twenty Things besides Death can rob me of. One solid Good I had & that is gone——my Mother!"[25]

Since 1784 she had reason to expect little but resentment from her four surviving daughters, the eldest of whom especially felt betrayed, if not indeed abandoned when she married Piozzi. Although all observed the prescribed decorum of family, the tensions between daughters and mother would never be resolved.

Maternally Mrs. Piozzi could worry about the health of her children or of her grandchildren; she could express polite interest in marriages, pregnancies, and spouses. But the calculated ways in which she was excluded from the traditional intimacies of family matters stung cruelly. A favorite sobriquet of hers, "the Ladies," at once playful in tone and ironic, serves to emphasize the mutual coolness that kept them apart in any genuine familial sense.

Death and illness relentlessly punctuate many passages in the letters and journals, sometimes with an excess of dramatic particularity that verges on the morbid. Some weeks after the Piozzis had returned from Bath in 1806, an entry in *Thraliana* denotes a mood that was somber, memories etched with thoughts of loss and impermanence, resignation and emptiness. "Here I am then once more," Mrs. Piozzi began, "*ripatriata* as the Italians express it—after our excursion to England: Piozzi and his Wife alive after so many Deaths dropping on every Side us. & if People are not *called* out of Life, they *run,* they *rush* out of it. Anne Lee at the beginning——John Edwd Madox At the End of the Winter! Two Suicides among one's own not numerous Acquaintance. Mrs Hanbury Williams, & Mr Bathurst Pye frighted all the *fine* People at Bath by their almost *public Exits;* they scarcely got into their own Bedrooms to expire; while Warren the Cheese Monger, the deaf & dumb Fish Boy, with poor Mrs Cooper who sold Greens——shall I see no more at the Market in *that* City;—here too in Wales we have lost Mr Wynne of Plasnewydd,—our Postmaster at Denbigh, cum multis aliis——& Cecy Mostyn says that Robin Jones [the apothecary] *says* that her showy young Husband is a dying Man.

"Oh Frightful Times! Oh horrible Occurrences!

"Cator & Crutchley likewise, once my Copartners—Coexecutors; Friends, Enemies, Indifferents—but gone!! no longer Friends *or* Enemies. Sweet M^{rs} De Luc lost from the Society of Wise & Good—The Duchess of Devonshire departed from amidst the Gay & Great; & Pitt pursued out of the World by fast-following Care, like a tormenting Wife seated on the Pillion, & goading him along."[26]

Inevitably, Gabriel's helpless detachment from most mental and social pursuits, Hester's age and ailments, the expanding register of dead and dying acquaintances, all of these could not but fix in her fertile imagination an assumption of impending dissolution. Happy memories of previous anniversaries gave way to gloom and foreboding. Thus, the sole entry in *Thraliana* under 25 July 1806, anything but celebratory in tone and substance, memorializes twenty-two years of marriage in a handful of verses that muse upon "Some silly Spite, some empty Sneers. . . /Could we but credit what appears / While Envy's Course now backward steers./ Did not Fate stand with ready Sheers / To cut off Joy from future Years."[27] The following day, in a letter to Lady Williams, Mrs. Piozzi was more explicit: "We had a dying Cook and an empty Table of *Course* yesterday; and we made melancholy Reflexions, calling to mind that all who dined with us in *1784* to the Number of eight or nine Friends, *on the like Occasion* were dead and gone; leaving only the Clergyman who maried us—*alive.*"[28] Her bills of mortality during this five-year run of correspondence included names of servants, of public figures, of friends and relatives. Some were distant, others—Gabriel Piozzi foremost, Eleanor Williams, even (grudgingly) her son-in-law

John Meredith Mostyn—were affectively close. Wryly truthful, she could see herself among the progression of "old Acquaintance dropping round [her]—like Ninepins."[29] Above all, in this long season of gloom, death was the inexorable enemy. A full year after Piozzi's tortured life had ended, she warned his adolescent nephew to "reflect how very necessary it is to keep the White Plumage in full Gloss ready for *sudden Flight*."[30]

Given the fatalistic pall that hung over the Piozzi household so steadily during these days, it is no wonder that she was becoming neurotic, afflicted with recurrent infirmities that varied in kind and degree of seriousness—from unidentifiable aches and pains to diarrhea, from "nerves" to depression and "low spirits." She cultivated for her own needs the services of medical practitioners in Wales, Chester, Bath, and London who were trying to slow Piozzi's deterioration. And yet she was by nature buoyant, vivacious, gregarious. "You know my Character exactly," she once reminded Queeney. "I never want for Amusement when thrown upon Society, and tho' we go out very *very* seldom at Night, I pick up some entertaining Chat in my Morning Rambles—and often think how pretty you are all looking in these new-fashioned Caps of Brown Ribbon, which on the fair-haired Lasses like yourself are *beautiful*."[31]

Although there was never any question of her devotion to Piozzi, her wifely perceptions were markedly different from those that distinguished her union with Henry Thrale. From 1762 to 1781 she had been conventionally loyal as mate, mother, hostess. She had been expected to subordinate herself to her husband's domestic well-being, his financial and extramarital excesses, and his political ambitions. She had had the duty of providing an atmosphere of social grace, charm, and conviviality. All of these she had fulfilled in exemplary fashion. In return she enjoyed the privileges of upper middle class affluence, such as comfort without burdensome responsibility (except for child rearing), or association with accomplished individuals to whom Thrale had offered hospitality. Following his death, however, she began to sag under fiscal encumbrances that Gabriel Piozzi was ill equipped to share. Their marriage—at least after the prolonged Continental honeymoon—tested her practical capabilities and exposed her shortcomings. As for him—and with her prodding—he tried hard to be a proper English squire. But this too was a way of life for which he was not well suited, either by culture or health. In a reversal of tradition, thus, she became the energizing partner. The creative precocity that had engaged her in childhood and adolescence promised to attain fruition with the *Anecdotes*, and she hoped to be identified as one who was more than a mere gifted female amateur. And indeed she had experienced a mix of notoriety and fame as an author until the publication of *Retrospection* in 1801 brought the collapse of her dreams.

Inescapably the failure of her personal ambition damaged her self-esteem. Yet resilience bolstered by egoism was a partial armor. Habitually, thus, she shielded herself against hostile reviewers with rationalized indignation and contempt; nor was she ever really prepared to acknowledge her limitations as a published author. Above all, she convinced herself that critics were the spawn of a breed beyond forgiveness. It is easy enough to complain about her intellectual vanity and occasional arrogance. But it is also well to be reminded that she was an exceptionally complex, utterly human creature who should not be defined solely by the evidence of externalized conduct. There were periods when the wrenching pain of her husband's illness was almost overwhelming. At such times she pitied herself as one who had been cast off by daughters and friends and fate. Still, as she perceived herself, she was "no *Whimperer,*"[32] and she usually emerged from dejection with renewed optimism. Some thirty years earlier Samuel Johnson had entreated her, "Be not solitary; be not idle," a maxim that had often helped him in his own struggles against the guilt of imagined unfulfilled obligation. For Mrs. Piozzi the same words could be a comforting reminder that her salvation lay in action, not despair.[33]

Nevertheless, strong-willed as she was, she often needed assurance that was more practical than philosophical or abstract. During these final years of his uncle's life, Salusbury was too young to offer much solace, let alone advice. But that was less important to his aunt than the fact that her letters to him conveyed maternal attitudes not readily shared with her daughters. Although Salusbury was still only an immature schoolboy, she reached out to him for sympathetic understanding. Symbolically, at least, he was an ally. So she thought, certainly, when she described hers as "indeed a melancholy Life."[34] How profoundly he absorbed the implications of her complaint can only be speculated upon. What mattered to her always, nevertheless, was a need for a receptive audience. To this end, among her most revealing letters were those that disclosed her fluctuating moods. An avid reader of newspapers, she reacted subjectively to daily events as though they were of personal consequence. Extraneous occurrences, even long stretches of unpleasant weather, magnified unwelcome feelings of loneliness and depression.

"Dear Mr. Chappelow," she implored, "reflect how we are Shut up here [in Brynbella] to read Thomson's Winter and Cowper's Task for four or five Months. . . . the Newspapers . . . I think *teem with Horrors* this Year more than I can remember. New and prodigious Crimes, portentous Meteors—We had one *here*, an Arrow all of Fire;——sudden Deaths—Suicides: or perhaps living alone and reading old Romances leads us to Dream of Murders &c."[35] Newspapers had long been her link with a world quite remote from the restrictive society of North Wales. During the annual visits to Bath and London, news of wars and politics, unabashed gossip about persons in high places, sensational accounts of violent breaches of law and decency, all such public events enlivened gatherings at dinner tables and assembly rooms. Despite her partiality for Brynbella, she missed the vivacity of those interludes. Her letters, consequently, drew upon topics that friends in other parts of the kingdom were also reading (and presumably also discussing). An epistolary exchange was for her, after all, essentially a dialogue, a reshaping of conversation, more notable in her current mood, probably, for inwardness rather than spontaneity. It was in this spirit, for instance, that she wrote to the Reverend Robert Gray (10 August 1808): "Our three times o-week newspaper [the *London Evening Mail*] gives us so many sudden deaths, so many accidents, so many thunder storms, it's like reading the casualties at the end of the old kings' reigns in a folio history."[36]

Among those deaths was that of Daniel Lyson's wife in 1808. Yet despite Mrs. Piozzi's warm regard for Lyson's, she was too dispirited to offer condolences directly. Rather, she renewed correspondence with his brother and her one–time confidant Samuel Lysons, requesting that he be an emissary. "Tell him yourself, my good Friend, and assure [him] yourself that the Accounts of his Wife's Death in the Papers gave me a Sensation beyond what my Acquaintance with her called for. . . . Well: you who live among the Records of past Life will bear these Things better; my Spirits are much depressed by Mr. Piozzi's miserable State of Health, nor can the Gayeties I hear of, draw my Attention from the Sorrows that I *see*."[37] With the passing months Mrs. Piozzi was unable to shake off for long her absorption in illness and her black moods. She experienced no lasting relief from anxiety about Piozzi's condition and concern about the effect on her own health of the prolonged, futile nursing. Sadly she admitted to one of her closest friends that she was coping badly with her lonely depression.[38]

By the following spring prophecy was fulfilled, for Brynbella had indeed become a "House of Mourning." Her doctors advised a regimen of good living —nourishment, exercise, and travel. She understood their good intentions but, in effect, dismissed them. "Ah—little do they know what my poor Nerves have suffered—from the Contemplation of Disease, Delirium, and Inevitable Death for Three sad Melancholy Moons—all in a solitary Country Seat too."[39] Intimate asides like these, for all their emphasis upon her "poor Nerves," signal the beginning of liberation from grief and guilt. That is not to say that she had ceased mourning for her husband. Yet one month after his death, a temporary change of environment and a perfunctory reunion with her daughters helped her to focus with renewed clarity of self-appraisal upon her situation. "My Nerves," she informed Lady Williams (1 May 1809), "did certainly use me ill enough upon *the Road:*—and the first Time I went to Church here at London, feeling myself one Solitary Soul among a *Thousand* human creatures assembled for Service at St. Martin's large, spacious Temple—The loud Organ pealing in my Ears, who have not heard a Musical Note or seen 25 People together for 25 Months; affected me too strongly: and I was very near fainting away.

"These delicate Feelings will however wear down by Degrees, and leave my Mind dull and *blunted* as an old Woman's *ought to be:* and when I return to Brynbella in July, I hope your Ladyship will do me the honour to come and *witness the Improvement.*

"My Daughters give me as much of their Time as I *possibly expect,*——more perhaps; and the Husbands of the married ones [Hoare and Lord Keith] are exceedingly civil and polite."[40]

Life would never again hold the rich quality for Mrs. Piozzi that she had enjoyed during the years with Gabriel, in sickness and in health, but she was once more prepared to face whatever reality lay ahead. Saddened, to be sure, but no longer distraught with self-pity, she was ready to deal with her widowed existence.

III

Near the close of 1798, Gabriel Piozzi's five-year-old nephew had left his home in Brescia to become a permanent ward of the Piozzis in Wales and England.

Eventually he would be adopted as Mrs. Piozzi's heir, a status that she appears to have had in mind for him from the beginning. The relationship, founded more on expedience than affection, afforded Mrs. Piozzi the opportunity to shape a male child of her own in a mold of English gentlemanliness. Giovanni Salusbury quickly became anglicized as John Salusbury, making even more explicit than his baptismal record a linkage with Mrs. Piozzi's family line. Vicariously he was to be the son denied her by the deaths of Harry and Ralph. Further, she hoped to exact from him the filial devotion, or at least loyalty, that her daughters had so long withheld. As she observed on 17 January 1798: "Italy is *ruined*, & England *threatened:* I have sent for one little Boy from among my husband's Nephews, he was christened *John Salusbury:* he shall be Naturalized, & we will see if He will be more grateful, & rational, & comfortable than Miss Thrales have been to the Mother they have at length *driven to Desperation.*"[41]

Pique, defiance, and autocracy are self-evident as she almost instantly set in place a methodical scheme of child–rearing. Little more than an infant, Salusbury was assumed to be a malleable subject for transformation from an Italian culture. To insure compliance with her aims, she delegated responsibility to professional educators in private schools. Piozzi, who left such decisions in her hands, probably recalled that his own anglicization—barring linguistic competence—had been shaped by the energy of her will and intelligence. Now, equally, he relied upon her to organize the course of Salusbury's prospects. The child's first mentor was the Reverend Reynold Davies, a Streatham tenant–neighbor, who implanted in him the basics of English learning and decorum. Then, in 1806, Salusbury moved on to the tutelage of the Reverend Thomas Shephard and other private instructors at Enborne in Berkshire. Following the gentry tradition, he underwent a rigorous program of education designed to prepare him for admission to Christ Church, Oxford, an event that took place in 1811.

But while Oxford was still a relatively distant goal, boarding school life limited normal family intercourse, except for annual holidays in Wales and Bath. Even from afar, Mrs. Piozzi kept a close epistolary check on the youth's progress in a manner reminiscent of Chesterfield's cautionary maxims on his son's moral and intellectual growth; or on much of the sententiae Johnson had addressed to her in the Thrale years. Surviving letters to Salusbury touch upon household gossip, various bits of trivia likely to interest him, and medical reports about his uncle. These letters are also catchalls of dicta on such matters as virtue, education, the use of talents, social propriety, and the like. Dutifully—almost certainly at her prompting—Salusbury penciled on the cover sheets of her letters dates of receipt and response. In answering his letters, she treated them as though they were measurable gauges of an evolving personality. A zealous correspondent in her own right, she hoped that Salusbury would become equally diligent—and informative. The lesson that she wished to pass on to him, she probably had learned from Johnson: "The importance of writing letters with propriety, justly claims to be considered with care, since next to the power of pleasing with his own presence, every man would wish to be able to give delight at a distance. . . . every man has frequent occasion to state a contract, or demand a debt, or make a narrative of some minute incidents of common life. On these subjects, therefore, young persons should be taught to think justly, and write clearly, neatly, and succinctly."[42]

Mrs. Piozzi, the self-appointed monitor, closely followed his development through the reports of his tutors, and she left no doubt that she expected him to heed her exacting if benevolent admonitions. "Let us do the *best*, and enjoy the *most* we can with Innocence and a clear Conscience," she urged. Nonetheless, she did not wish to provoke his resentment by an undue show of officiousness, denying that she was a "Cynical old Monitress."[43] Rather, as she always insisted, she was the "Dear Lad's ever affectionate Aunt." Characteristically, she pressed upon him "good Resolutions of increasing in Knowledge <and> Virtue: and when Mr. Shephard reads or talks to you seriously—listen to what he says, and do not *try* to keep your Head upon something else. . . . Be prudent my dear Salusbury, and do yourself all the Good you can, and gain all the Instruction in your Power."[44]

In a birthday letter whose spirit was more hortatory than festive, she chided him for his dilatory study habits. *"Your Uncle,"* she fretted, "has no Taste to see *You* Ignor<ant>. He will be very angry if you do not Study hard." There must have been little joy for him in the stern reminder: "And You my Dear have now but Seven Years left for Study, and *Hope* bids me expect that you will use them diligently. If you are to learn either Books or Life, it must be in these next Seven Years; for after that Period is past; you must be *living*, not *learning*: and in order that we may rationally wish you Joy of arriving safely at the Age of 21, You must resolve to *know* something, and be able to *do* something when that Time— now not far off—arrives." Whether the fourteen-year-old Salusbury was ripe enough to absorb the practical concerns of his tutors and guardians one may only guess. From an adult perspective, however, the sharp division between *living* and *learning* accentuates Mrs. Piozzi's realistic assumption that the boy was not a candidate for one of the learned professions. He was being trained, rather, to take his place in the world of affairs. He was to obviate "the Future Pain and Disgrace of being out of Countenance for want of knowing the History of Greece, Rome, and England;—They are *Indispensable* to a Gentleman's appearance in proper Company:——so are the Classics, so is the Heathen Mythology. A Lad who has not these Old Stories in His head—may as well have *no Head.*"[45]

At the same level of urgency, she admonished: "get the common Classical Knowledge driven deep into your Head—*now* whilst you are young, and it will *stick* there. What one reads after 18 Years old glides out of the Mind much easier than what is sown in the early Season, and as to the Necessity of Classic Knowledge,—a Man who tries to go thro' Life without it, resembles one who sits all Night at a Whist Table, playing every hand against the Ace of Trumps turned up—Certain to lose the one grand Trick——and conscious that every body knows it."[46] Appearance, privilege, and status, all these were inseparable in the world of gentry that was her legacy. As a woman, of course, and especially as one whose marriage to Piozzi set her apart, she had been denied full participation. She was determined, however, that Salusbury should not falter or stray from her expectations.

In a mix of lofty rhetoric and scriptural platitude she attempted to impress on him the gravity of self-realization. "Every Man in England makes and finds his proper Rank in Society; The Greatest Persons may lose, the Noblest may forfeit their Situations——and after a Man has been well educated, the World expects him to answer that Education. . . . allow me to remind you of God's Punishments denounced in the Gospel against the *unprofitable Servant* who having received a Talent from his Lord—gave it him back at the great Day of Account, laid up in a Napkin;—*and never used.*" By now, however, Mrs. Piozzi thought it prudent to desist. "But you begin to grow weary of these Admonitions," she rightly concluded, "and to be thinking of something else to divert Attention from my Preachment."[47]

Meanwhile she rationalized as a boon his inadequate preparation for admission to Eton. "Much Vice and Folly will certainly be escaped . . . I hope you will gain Virtue and Knowledge where you are, and such a *Love* of both will keep you out of Mischief when you enter into the World." Even more to his advantage, the Reverend Mr. Shephard was prepared to instruct Salusbury in the rituals of conversion to Anglicanism. This was particularly pleasing to the boy's aunt as a symbol of his expanding investment in British mores. The act of conversion, she wrote, is a way in "which a Man ratifies, and gives his *own* Consent, to his *own* Christianity—originally imposed on us in Infancy when we know not the Vow we are making. I shall be glad when you have been, by Imposition of a Bishop's hand,——*fixed* and *confirmed* in our *Anglican Church:* The superior Excellencies of which no one knows better than Mr. Shephard."[48]

She never tired of impressing upon him the values of religion and moral rectitude, and she went so far as to represent herself as a model worthy of emulation. In this personal context she paraphrased the admonition of Dr. Randolph, a clerical friend, "that the Nation like its Individuals has spent its Youth in Prodigality—its mature Age in Pride——that it even now dotes on the Dregs of Vice, and depends at last upon a *Death Bed* Repentance. This is bad news indeed—and is so near to true, It frights one. Keep *your* self dearest Salusbury an Exception to this general Corruption, and make *my Name* quoted as an Example of Excelling Virtue. Can there be a greater *honour* either to you or Me? . . . *This* Happiness 'tis in your Power to *bestow* on her who *I will say* best deserves it *from* You, even your old Aunt H:L:P.—who when She has seen her own Family *forced* to confess that her favours to You have been well deserved,—will die content, and sing *Nunc dimittis.*"[49]

Through Salusbury's repudiation of his Catholic origins, he demonstrated to his aunt's satisfaction how well he had responded to her influence as well as to that of his tutors. The boy's conversion, further, betokened for her the degree to which he was on his way toward becoming a true English gentleman, one who merited his branch on the Salusbury family tree. Another significant link in that process was the formality of British naturalization. This, with customary determination, Mrs. Piozzi began to advance about one month after Piozzi's death. Through her attorneys, she declared an intent of denization: a "Memorial and Petition of Hester Lynch Piozzi to the Secretary of State Lord Liverpool, in behalf of an Infant John Salusbury Piozzi, known by the Name of John Piozzi

Salusbury; whose request it is That the King will give him leave to . . . enjoy the Privileges of English Birth, for the Preservation of his Property; and to entitle him to accept, receive, and enjoy whatever Land or Money may be given or bequeathed him by the Memorialist."[50] On 30 June 1809 Salusbury, by decree no longer an Italian subject, had become a "faithful liege Subject" of the British Crown. Within a few months thereafter his aunt in effect severed all connection with the Brescian line when she paid the remainder of Piozzi's bequests to the boy's kin. Contemptuously she acknowledged "a heap of *Italian* Letters full of Stuff and Nonsense—and calling aloud" for an unpaid balance of £2,400. She was so eager to have done with the obligation that she divested herself of a "little Stock and Savings . . . for Purpose of Sending to Italy."[51]

The matter continued to rankle, and when she next wrote she hoped that the boy had "long since recovered the Good Humour which our Italian Letters recently disturbed. Relations always *do* disturb one's Good humour: I have often wished myself as far removed from *mine* as Providence has placed Yours from *You*. . . . Let us pay these People to the last Penny, and then wash our Heads clear of them."[52] Virtually at one stroke, thus, she dissociated him from a troublesome relationship and, by intimation, drew him into an alliance against her daughters. On the other side of the coin, she relished the breeding that she habitually identified with privileged family status—her own included. Consequently, she was convinced that association with well-born individuals must surely be advantageous in the mannered community wherein she expected Salusbury to prosper one day. Among the benefits that she had counted upon from his residence in the school at Enborne was his daily association with a select company of fellow students. One of the friendships especially agreeable to her was that with Edward Pemberton. Indeed, Salusbury became intimate enough for visits to the family estate in Longnor, Shropshire. And there too he met his future wife, Harriet.

Meanwhile, Mrs. Piozzi did not allow her interest in his educational opportunities to pass without judgment. Ever the vigilant schoolmistress, she rebuked him for grammatical imperfections. "Indeed," she complained, "I *do* wish that you would be pleased to *Anglify* your Style a little, and not write as the Foreigners do that You arrived *to* Enborne instead of *at* Enborne: how is it possible meanwhile for you to find Difficulty in learning *French?* . . . Here's Schooling enough however; I am as tired on't as you can be."[53] The pride that she had experienced as the discriminating author of *British Synonymy* was residual, and she did not surrender old habits gladly. Thus, even while praising a letter from Salusbury as "quite *lovely*," she could not forbear adding, "if you would only remember that *were* is A Verb, and *where* is an adverb; you never could mistake and spell the last without the Aspirate.—How the Women manage who *never* know one part of Speech from another,—They must tell; but certain it is, the Well-bred ones never miss."[54] Mrs. Piozzi was hardly reluctant to admit that she was one of "the Well-bred ones." Her impatience with Salusbury's awkward grammar extended to his slow grasp of English nuance. Vain of her own wit, which her friends generally acknowledged, she lamented his inability "to take a Silly Joke. . . . learn to know Jest from Earnest: and do not be such a mere

Matter of Fact Fellow, though I shall ever rejoyce in your Spirit of Virtue and Prudence."[55]

The condescension of such remarks, probably not lost on Salusbury, does not lessen her good intentions. But it does coincide with an impression of her office as benefactress. Alerting him to a proposed visit to Enborne, she reminds him that he "has cost [her] so much Money and Care in these Dozen Years of his British Life, that a little more may be willingly *thrown* in." During a subsequent leisurely journey to Wales, she charges him to stand "in Place both of *Protector* and *Protégé* united towards your truly Affectionate H:L:Piozzi."[56] By and large, in the days and weeks immediately following the demise of Piozzi, she grew perceptibly closer to Salusbury. There is a curious unfolding in her attitude that attests not only to a benign continuation of duty but also to a mellowing fondness. The affection that she could no longer lavish on Piozzi she began transferring to the boy. "Pray for *me* now dearest Salusbury, that I may do my Duty in this Life, so as to escape beating with *very many Stripes* in the next. See St. Luke 12th Chapter 47th Verse.——All that I do for *You* is prompted by *Affection* and will be compleatly rewarded in *this* World by your good Conduct, and continued Esteem."[57] Subsequently she confided to Lady Williams, "My Excursions into the living World are chiefly for purposes of Setting [Salusbury] *afloat* on't. Your Ladyship and Dear Sir John know my Intentions for him, and we must make early Friends and good Connexions as soon as we can; but . . . there must be a little Christ Church first; and he cannot get in before next Year. May I *but* live to launch him! He will in *me* lose a Parent, let my departure be soon or late."[58]

Mrs. Piozzi campaigned for him as vigorously as she once had for Henry Thrale in his parliamentary ambitions, soliciting letters of recommendation from prestigious individuals who might help to guarantee a place in Christ Church College. Her earlier reservations about the moral climate of Eton she put aside when a friend told her about comparable laxity in Christ Church. Suddenly, in the name of expedience, these were issues to be judged discretely. Nor did she have any qualms about quoting the friend's caution to Salusbury: "Oh now for Pity do not put that fine–pure hearted Boy to Christ Church; it is the wickedest College in Oxford——or any other College, Oh *any* Place but Christ Church, although my dear Doctor [Dean Charles Henry] Hall does purpose a restoration of that Discipline and an Encouragement of those good Morals, which the late Dean [Cyril Jackson] *wholly despaired of,* and by so doing, helped drive them away."[59] Whatever scruples Mrs. Piozzi may have harbored, she obviously was not prepared to resist the patently upper-class appeal of a Christ Church connection.

Indeed, she made her point so insistently that Salusbury, to her delight, offered "to forsake a [holiday] jaunt" and remain at Enborne, "studying Greek with Mr. Shephard" as further insurance for admission to Christ Church. "I cannot help forming good Expectations of *this* Creature," she bragged to the Reverend Mr. Whalley; "and with *your* Blessing, which I receive as you bestow it, in all true Kindness:——I am strong in the <Per>swasion he will be every thing his dear, *dear* Uncle wished."[60] Finally her importunities succeeded and she could jubilantly advise Salusbury: "Well! here is the desired Letter come from Doctor Hall, as kind as one *can* desire; and so your Fortune is fixed, and my Child must be launched into Life, The second Week after Good Friday next——I feel all over Goose-Skin at the Thought on't——knowing as I do, how sharp Folks are looking to see whether You make slips or no,—That they may be ready to push you quite down. As for the Letter I will copy it on the other Side—Tho' I could have written as good a Letter myself, *without* University Education."[61] The battle, in short, was as much hers as Salusbury's—a vindication of pride, an engagement that was a part of her ongoing defiance of the many persons whom she suspected—with cause—of being no well-wishers. On the face of it, she was oblivious to the pressure to prove himself that she was imposing on this unscholarly young man.

Even as Salusbury was nearing the end of his Enborne schooldays and about to venture on a university education, his aunt continued to pepper him with odds and ends of learning. Portentously, thus, she urged him to read Johnson's final, melancholy *Idler* essay.[62] She gave him a gratuitous lesson on British terms of hunting and cooking that had been derived from French etymology. Wistfully she rounded out her correspondence for the year 1810 with an analogy that was meant to be a reminder of her benevolent guardianship. "Young Trees," she wrote, "should be fenced in while *Young* with *Thorns:* and so perhaps Young *Minds* should. What will become of Dearest Salusbury—when the Cattle begin to browze—The Weather to beat *hard* on him!—will he blame my Care to keep all the Thorns away? I hope not."[63] It was in her nature to nurture as well as dominate. But like a veil that may be lifted on occasion, these attributes did not always conceal the profundity of her loneliness. With almost startling pathos, she pleaded that he "take all *four Wings* Duty, Fear, Interest and Affection and fly [to her bedside] the Moment Illness seizes" her. "Dear Love! when will you come home? I am very tired of sitting *alone.*"[64]

IV

From the time of Mrs. Piozzi's second marriage, the "Ladies," manifestly hostile, remained aloof. The choice was theirs, and though outwardly civil, interaction between mother and daughters was strained and sporadic. Queeney's, the most numerous of the known letters from the sisters, may be said to have set the tone. More like the effusions of a learned, prim acquaintance than of a blood connection, they avoid any real show of intimacy. Even as Lady Keith, Queeney continued to hold her mother in low esteem. With unusual candor, she confided to Mme D'Arblay, (Mrs. Piozzi's former protégée): "To others she can say what she pleases, & no doubt as she has invariably done, will ever continue to justify herself, in every Particular, at our expence."[65] Still, in any exchange of letters with her mother, Queeney concealed such overt antagonism. Mrs. Piozzi, for her part, did what she could to convey a semblance of maternal warmth. When writing to friends about her daughters, however, even though she asserted affection, an adversarial temper was generally close to the surface. This was true whether she openly criticized their conduct or, more subtly, affected an air of ironic detachment to obscure conflicting emotions of resentment and attachment.

If she was willful, the daughters were equally so, neither side allowing much if any latitude for compromise. The antagonisms that had been building for so many years finally became permanent when Hester and Gabriel adopted Salusbury. "As can be imagined, the taking on of Piozzi's nephew astonished the four Thrale sisters. They felt embarrassment, as well as anxiety about their inheritance. His intrusion into the family put an end to any hope of a true reconciliation between Mrs. Piozzi and her daughters."[66]

The breach dividing them appears to have made Mrs. Piozzi especially sensitive to familial relationships in general. Almost vicariously, she allied herself with other parents who had been affected by the failings of their children. When word reached her that the son of a friend suffered from a mysterious ailment, Mrs. Piozzi was compassionate, but she was also suspicious enough to hint: ". . . if his disorder is not a cancer or a pulmonary Consumption brought on by what oldfashioned People call *Vice* and new fashioned People call *Dissipation* he *may* Recover." Immediately following this uncharitable surmise, she described the sorrow of "Poor Mr. Wynn of Plasnewydd . . . said to be dying of a broken Heart at 41 Years old——his Sons have grieved him more by their Conduct than he *could* have grieved at their loss. The 1st went to School, and at 17 years old run away with his Master's Daughter of 35 Years old. The 2d. married at Liverpool—not a Mopsqueezer, but a Wench with whom Mopsqueezers will not associate." Indignantly, Mrs. Piozzi added: "I see nothing so likely as his own Death from distress of Mind. Ainsi va le Monde: By the Time he has fretted himself into the Grave the last young Bridegroom not yet 18 years old will possibly return rich from India and purchase the Freedom of the Family."[67]

Mrs. Piozzi was partial to gossip like this, which added spice to her letters. But also, without indulging in psychoanalysis, one may reasonably speculate that sharing the accounts with Queeney of other errant children was the implied reproach of a mother who believed herself wronged by her own brood. Reunions were infrequent and uncomfortable for both parent and children. During a brief visit of the Piozzis to London, as an instance, "The Ladies called [at their hotel in Leicester Square] very politely, and told in general Terms how they had passed their Time—no more."[68] The strained occasion, obviously ceremonial and unwished, typifies the unnatural distance that would always keep them apart, except for a deathbed reunion.

As far back as 1795, after a family gathering at Brynbella, Mrs. Piozzi privately characterized the personalities of her offspring. "On this Day [25 November] our fair Daughters are all gone away together: They have behaved very well; not loving Piozzi, nor liking Mostyn, nor approving the Connexion Cæcilia has made with one—and I with the other, it was no easy task to behave very well, yet all went as it should do without fawning & without Rudeness—with no assumed Transports of Delight, and no expressions or even Appearance of Disgust: Of so much Use is Good Breeding. I really delight unfeignedly in the Company of [Queeney]: She is a person greatly to my Taste, independent of relationship or Vanity:—not so my sweet Susette, though very amiable; Sophia

& I have more Ground in common that *She* or Cæcilia have, and Cecy is so *very* self-sufficient;—She is an *offensive* companion to any one—or I should think so."[69] Subsequently, Mrs. Piozzi emended the bland appraisal of Queeney with a tart judgment: "Altho we lived together civilly, & parted prettily, I never spoke a Word about any thing like Business to any One of them. It was often at my Tongue's end to talk to Miss Thrale concerning her Father's Contract with Government, & concerning his being bound for Mr Nesbitt &c but I always checked myself wth the Certainty that She has no Confidence in *me*, & y^t I ran risks by trusting *her;* beside that holding one's Tongue seldom does any harm, & Speaking frequently produces mischief. We are friends now—or at least Acquaintance: ripping up old stories might lessen her Pleasure in my Company perhaps—& what Good c^d it do?"[70]

Except for the youngest daughter, Cecilia, the Thrale girls had long remained unmarried, "but this was not for lack of opportunity. . . . 'The Ladies' were handsome and rich, and society respected them."[71] Susanna at the age of thirty-seven began living with a recently widowed artist, William Frederick Wells, and his seven children at "Ashgrove Cottage" in Kent. A displeased Mrs. Piozzi, who had learned about the liaison only indirectly from her maid and Piozzi's valet, commented: "Suzette leaves Town tomorrow if I am right, and consummates her marriage With Mr. *Ashgrove:* If like Many Modern Couples they should be soon tired of the binding Words *to have and to hold,* She may get a Divorce any Day." The terms "marriage" and "divorce" are intended as no more than euphemisms. In all likelihood she was already aware that no legal or church ceremony had sanctified the union, and so she resorted to language that connoted disparaging denial. Several months later, she openly conceded: "And so my sweet *Susette* has lost her Christian Name—*without* being married."[72]

The affair, if such it was, endured for perhaps a dozen years, after which Wells settled in Mitcham, Surrey. Susanna, who had once complained that *"there was not a tolerable Man* left in the County of Sussex,"[73] obviously preferred her unmarried state, and for the remainder of her life in "Ashgrove Cottage" gave herself over to good works. Mrs. Piozzi, who visited her occasionally in later years, remembered Susanna as a child of beauty and bright promise, but also as one who had long ago rejected her.[74] Susanna's independence was beyond her comprehension or tolerance, as can be seen by her ironic remark to Queeney: "So you all leave Susette in the Lurch! Poor Susette! But I think she will not stay starving in a Cottage this Weather without a Companion."[75]

As represented in Mrs. Piozzi's journals and letters, Queeney invariably emerges as the sibling with the most incisive and dominant personality. From the start her parents and Johnson had favored her by virtue of her seniority and learning. Ever the practical mother, Mrs. Thrale had once characterized Queeney's prospects as those of "a lovely Girl; gentle, soft, mild: & handsome enough for a Creature that will I verily think if the World holds firm, & does not crumble about us—carry twenty Thousand Pounds to whoever She marries, besides my own Estate which is entailed on her now, if I should not wish to revoke it; as I certainly shall not, unless something very singular happens indeed."[76] Lacking the gift of prophecy, she could not foresee that "something very singular" would occur with the arrival of Salusbury. Nor did she correctly estimate the firmness of will that would one day alienate Queeney, whose maturity always seemed far more advanced than the six or seven years that separated her from Susanna and Sophia, and of course the thirteen between her and Cecilia.

After 1784 Queeney was the bonding force to whom her sisters always looked for guidance and decisions. Mrs. Piozzi, often reproachfully, assumed this to be the case during the years of the second marriage. As Mrs. Thrale she had recognized some fundamental distinctions between her middle children: "My second Daughter Susan has a surprising Turn for Letter-writing; her Compositions are really elegant, & She delights—odd enough—in reading Voiture & Sevigné. Sophia, who is a more natural Character, finds no Entertainment in writing at all; but works hard at her Needle, and Harpsichord, and gets to spouting Fingal for her Diversion.—they both have obtained the French Accent very completely, considering they have never been out of England. I should like to treat them with a Run to the Continent."[77] That token of maternal affection was never to be. When Mrs. Piozzi did go abroad in 1784, she went not to reward her daughters but to escape with her new husband the malice of the gossip mongers at home.

The disappointment of Susanna's unconventional behavior was still fresh when Mrs. Piozzi learned that Sophia was about to marry (13 August 1807). The news was bittersweet. On the one hand she had the satisfaction of knowing that the match was to be a proper one with a man of social and financial substance who had courted Sophia for some six years. Only one year older, Henry Merrick Hoare was a partner in a well-placed London banking firm. The pleasure, nevertheless, was diminished. Sophia, like Susanna before her, neither troubled to discuss the marriage plans with her mother until the last moment, nor to let her believe that she would be a welcome member of the wedding. This came as a shock to Mrs. Piozzi, even though she knew that she was no longer the exemplary parent of the Thrale years. Her attachment to the sisters had been genuine even as late as 1783, when she was struggling with her crisis of passion. In November of that year Sophia had become so ill in Bath that Mrs. Piozzi, fearing her death was imminent, wrote in her journal: "Hester has behaved inimitably . . . *all* our Tenderness was called out on this Occasion: dear Creatures! they see I love them, that I would willingly *die* for them; that I *am* actually dying to gratifie their Humour at the Expence of my own Happiness: they can *but* have my Life—let them take it!"[78]

Dramatic as usual, she mistakenly expected gratitude and reciprocal sensitivity. Even in 1790 she could write: "Was ever Child more bound to a Parent than Sophy Thrale?"[79] The reality, unhappily, was far wide of the sentiment, as she herself admitted two years later in a mixture of recrimination and implied guilt. On the occasion of Sophia's coming of age, Mrs. Piozzi mused about the tensions that she chose to blame for the separation from the sisters. "Sophia Thrale is this Day emancipated by Law from that Governance & Tuition She withdrew herself from on the 27: June 1784 without Provocation on my Part, or Quarrel on hers. Compliance with her eldest Sister took her from my House first,—at least I suppose so: for she urged no Reason, and I hope had none to urge—'Tis a great Blessing that I should live to see her of Age; her Illness and my own when we were in Bath together in 1784 gave me small hopes or Expectation of so transcendent a Mercy: little merited by me God knows—perhaps her *Virtues*, perhaps *her Prayers* have obtained it. I hear an admirable Character of all my dear Girls from every one who speaks of them—and if they have but *one* Fault, that of not loving their Mother, who can help Taste? I may not be amiable—probably to my Children *am* not. . . . Mrs Cochran [the girls' companion] said they all did *esteem* me, and think well of my Abilities—that may be *honouring* their Mother perhaps: I would rather at any rate be in Fault myself, than find *them* so. and for keeping away, it was no such great matter, if they had not pecked at my Reputation—but *that* was cruelly done, and vainly;—for my Fame was never hurt by them at last, thank God;—Innocence always comes out clean after every attempt to stain it, and having *done* no harm—why I *suffered* none—in earnest:—a few horrid Pangs at the Moment of Infliction, but all is heal'd now, and if the Scars are gone, so should be the Remembrance of *the Wounds*."[80]

In November of 1807 Mrs. Piozzi wrote: "The *Thraliana* is coming fast to an End, so are the *Thrales*: The eldest is married now——Admiral Lord Keith the Man: a good Man for ought I hear, a rich Man for ought I am told, a brave Man we have always heard——and a wise Man I trow *by his Choice.*" As she intimates in her journal, the engagement was not altogether a surprise—Queeney and Keith had in fact first met in 1791. Barred as always from sharing the intimacies of her daughters' aspirations and relationships, Mrs. Piozzi even from afar reacted favorably to such a substantial mate. Nostalgically, on the third of December 1807, she wrote to Susanna: "Your eldest Sister and I having passed *Twenty Years* closely united, & never three Days out of each other's Sight.——Some Castles in the Air would now and then rise up in a Musing Hour,—as if we might *once more* meet in a like familiar Manner;—Those Misty Fabricks now are quite dissolved—and She has fixed *her* Castle—*in the Rock.*" The playful pun on Keith's family name (Elphinstone) implies Mrs. Piozzi's regret of the inevitable transition from childlike fantasy to mature reality.[81]

The marriage took place in Ramsgate on 10 January 1808 when Queeney was forty-three and the admiral—widowed since 1789 and father of a twenty-year-old daughter—sixty-two. Although Queeney did inform her mother that the wedding was to be celebrated, she withheld details and still precluded a meeting with the groom. More gracious than her daughter, Mrs. Piozzi expressed pleasure that her "dearest Girl will be so richly rewarded for all her numerous and various Virtues." She was "delighted too that a *British Admiral* [was] to be made happy by accepting her pretty little White Hand." The news, she added, had "put quite new Life" in Gabriel Piozzi, who began "rummaging over Music" as a gift for Queeney.[82] In the following year, Mrs. Piozzi carried out her husband's wish that Queeney be given "his little Piano Forte made in Form of a Coach Seat by Pohlman, and of most elegant *Tone.*" Because it could not be transported to London in her own chaise, "it must abate its *Dignity* poor Dear! and travel in a Waggon some Time, when you have done it the honour to promise it house Room and Patronage. You are to have Choice of Musick whatever you like best."[83]

Queeney's marriage to Keith gave Mrs. Piozzi fresh personal matter for her correspondence, and in anticipation she quipped to her friend the Reverend Leonard Chappelow: "If *any* body is safe, those are safe that anchor under Protection of a brave British Admiral." Less given to pleasantry than to pragmatism, Keith soberly assured his future mother–in–law that he realized "the approbation of a parent is a matter of essential consequence to the General comfort of such a Union." He reassured her, further, that he had "enough for all the Reasonable Comforts of Life, which he had "fully explained to Miss Thrale," and which she had "approved."[84]

Abetted by Queeney, the admiral kept Mrs. Piozzi at a formal distance. "With Regard to Lord Keith," she complained to Margaret Williams, "I never saw him, or ever heard—but by common Report (which of Course always exaggerates)— any one Word spoken concerning his Fortune and Affairs. We all heard when he captured the Dutch Fleet off the Cape of Good Hope:—and some one Said he was a Widower, whose Daughter had an Independent Estate of her own— but I know precisely nothing beyond Mr. Piozzi's sick Room, and my own little Study."[85] As one who could speak with authority about the hazards of birth, she was concerned about Queeney's pregnancy at the age of forty–five. Her daughter, however, solicited neither her help nor advice for the lying–in (12 December 1809) at her Harley Street residence. Only months after the event was she allowed to see for the first time her granddaughter, Georgina Augusta Henrietta Elphinstone.[86] Stung by Queeney's neglect, Mrs. Piozzi felt somewhat vindicated when Lady Kirkwall extended the hospitality of a stay in her "Nutshell" of a London house: "This is an offer I never had—no nor a *Hint* of any such Offer from any of Mr. Thrale's Daughters in Town or Country—Tho' I have slept I suppose six Times in my Life at *Segroid* [Cecilia's Welsh residence]; but I mean the two Married Ladies in London, or Susan Thrale who has a Country Seat 16 Miles off."[87]

Although Cecilia was the youngest of the surviving Thrale daughters, she had been the first to marry, eloping to Gretna Green in 1795 with John Meredith Mostyn of neighboring Llewesog Lodge. Both were underage. The initial Piozzi/ Thrale family reaction had been one of shock and irritation: Gabriel feared that his honor was compromised; Mrs. Piozzi feared that Cecilia had been seduced by a former suitor; Susanna and Sophia feared the loss of their legacies. The frosty "Miss Thrale behaves best, & I suffer most—on Acc^t of her Health & Youth & Inexperience—Oh my poor Cecy!"[88] But once all were convinced that the resolution was honorable, relief prevailed. Of the four daughters left to the care of chaperones and schoolmistresses in 1784, the eleven-year-old Cecilia doubtless had been the most vulnerable. Queeney, the self-appointed surrogate mother—in conjunction with Susanna and Sophia—had become an officious, even sinister, influence. So Mrs. Piozzi was convinced, and with cause. As a blatant instance: "While I was at Bath [in 1787] Miss Thrale wrote me a strange Letter thanking me for my *polite Attentions* to Cæcilia, but observing that they were superfluous, for that *She* intended removing her from the School She is in, to another *further from me;* and that She should take her immediately away to the Isle of Wight. I sent such an Ans' as the Letter deserved, & received a Reply which must I think have been dictated by *Baretti* and so it probably was: it would have been scarce justifiable to send such a one to the last Woman who was hanged. . . .

"I have got the Child home to us however, & Piozzi doats on her. . . . if they steal her away from me now, I shall lose my life: 'tis so very comfortable to have *one* at least saved out of *twelve.*

"The Harrass of these Letters made me miscarry tho'; and that was a bad Thing; we laid the Blame on a fall, but external Causes affect my health but little; if I *did* miscarry, (and all the Doctors say I did,) the Letters caused the misfortune."[89]

When Piozzi in 1789 proposed visiting Italy, Mrs. Piozzi demurred: "if I go with him I lose Cecilia; & for every Reason am *sure* to lose her: the moment we are off, Cator sends for her, which as he is her Guardian, I have no right to hinder; the Sisters seize her *Person,* & her *Mind,* & by the Time we return back, *both* will be alienated, & *She* will treat us as *they* do:—with as good Reason certainly, for they have none at all. I must not stir from my Post if I mean to defend it—*He may* come again to me, but *She never can:* 'tis Time enough however to think of all this." A few years later Piozzi renewed the possibility of a visit to Italy, and again she vetoed the idea because of his poor health and "on Cecilia's Acc'."

In the same journal entry she set down some revealing impressions of Cecilia, who had by then almost attained the age of fourteen. "Every body tells me that Cæcilia Thrale improves, & so I think She does; tho' not because they say so: were She less altered for the better, no less would be said about her perfections I suppose. but She has lost much of the savage Manners She brought from School: is tamer, & handsomer, and grows very like what her Sisters were when they lived with me.—The Exterior is best tho' with Cecilia; her Mind recovers more slowly than her Person, from a severe Shock certainly given to Both in the Year 1783 by the Hooping Cough & Measles together, when her younger Sister [Henrietta Sophia] lost that Life which was preserved to this Girl only by Sir Lucas Pepys's extreme Skill & Care. She will however be a fine Woman, with Accomplishments & Beauty & Virtue enough to accompany forty or fifty Thousand Pounds—although her Memory is far from strong, and her Spirit of Application to any Study much too weak ever to attain at Eminence I think.

"Her Temper when unthwarted is sweet, but She arms against opposition even instinctively; and will do nothing because She is commanded, but the contrary, while the same surly Independent Soul inhabits her Bosom with equal Rapacity to obtain, and Rage to appropriate, as in the hearts of any of her Family. Cecilia seems however to love M' Piozzi—in her way of loving—but no one accuses her of partiality towards *me* I believe, whose Company She studiously avoids; & I therefore say nothing, but provide Refuges for her to recur to, that are no less improving Companions than myself. . . . She can hear of nothing but Literature, so I care not."[90]

With near paranoid conviction, Mrs. Piozzi assured herself that Queeney "wanted always to separate Cecilia from *me* & now [in 1799] we *are* separated—Susan & Sophy wanted to separate Cecilia from Mostyn's Mother,—If we could but get her from *that* Mrs Wynne they said I remember. Well now Cecilia never sees either Mrs Wynne or Mrs Piozzi, they should be happy & not *fret*."[91] Thanks probably to their geographical proximity, Mrs. Piozzi was even more conscious of Cecilia's failings as a daughter than she was of those of the elder sisters. The articulate mother who had carped so frequently about the child's escapades and extravagances, now found her more seriously wanting as a wife who was indifferent to her husband's infidelities. "Cecy Mostyn is a foolish Girl, & cannot rule her own Household—all our unfashionable Neighbours cry Shame! to see Mason her Maid with Child by the Master of the Mansion—& the Gay Mistress protecting this Partner in her Husband's Person because *it is the Way* She says; & all those who understand *genteel Life* think lightly of such Matters. When I offered to speak my *antiquated* Sentiments upon the Subject, She *forbid* me (smartly) to say another Word about it; & told my Maid that if Mrs Piozzi plagued her any more concerning such Nonsense She would leave the House—into wch She never came to say the Truth—except for mere Conveniency.... Strange conduct!"[92] Mrs. Piozzi, whose marriage to Henry Thrale had taught her to accept society's expectations of wifely duty, was baffled by Cecilia's rebelliousness, by her graceless refusal to subordinate herself. The young woman, in the eyes of her parent, had no more regard for Mostyn than she would have had for a suitor or a lap dog. "She could set them *all three* to *snap* at, and *bite* her Mother, *for her Sport*.... Let them do their own Way—I have *done* with them."[93]

Both of them immature and willful, the young Mostyns resented Mrs. Piozzi's disapproval of their reckless lives, and they had no qualms about letting their harsh reactions be known. From her censorious perspective they were no better than "A pretty *Nest* of Wasps." She disliked John Mostyn because of his arrogance and disrespect, as well as his amorality; but she blamed Cecilia for being the *provocatrice*. The mutual distrust between the Mostyns and Mrs. Piozzi was exacerbated by Cecilia's thoughtless gossip to strangers about her parents' financial affairs, by fabrications about her mother's opinions, and even by tales about her sister Susanna. Cecilia, according to Mrs. Piozzi, complained of Mostyn's "gross Avarice and rough Behaviour.... yet something says to my heart that half of this is a *Fable*, & spoken with Design of some sort to dig out how far I should grieve at, or resent his Treatment of her if it was absolutely & truly what She represents." Cecy, she said flatly, "is as false as Water.... & what this fashionable Lady says, must be taken with a Grain of Salt."[94] Setting aside the possible justice of such recriminations, neither Cecilia nor her partner seemingly had the temperament for a successful marriage, and theirs certainly had been deteriorating for some time. One element to be taken into account is Mostyn's poor health. Hence, in September 1805, suffering from tuberculosis (probably aggravated by dissipation), he went alone to Bath while Cecilia retreated to Cheltenham. Later she joined him. But in the following year they separated once again, this time placing their young sons in the care of Reynold Davies at his school in Streatham.[95]

Writing at Brynbella on 11 May 1806, Mrs. Piozzi lamented the number of "Deaths dropping on every Side [of] us," from prominent suicides to humble individuals such as a cheese monger, a greengrocer, a "deaf & dumb Fish Boy." At the end of a lugubrious bill of mortality, she commented almost as an afterthought, "& Cecy Mostyn says that Robin Jones [the apothecary] *says* that her showy young Husband is a dying Man." Her cynicism about Cecilia's capacity for truth–telling surfaces a few weeks later: "I believe less and less of every thing—every day—and very little *indeed* of Mr. Mostyn's Danger," although she conceded "that his Mind and Body both have more need of Exercise than Medicine." Finally, however, she must have considered as objective and credible the words of John Gillon (28 September 1806) about Mostyn's "precarious State of Health. I have heard that he is not careful enough, as to Regimen. It will be, indeed, an awkward Situation for a Young Widow, to be left with young Children to bring up and educate."[96] Mrs. Piozzi was little moved when she learned a month after the fact that Mostyn had died at Bath on 19 May 1807. Charitably one might say that constant anxiety about her own husband deadened any other sympathy. "Sophia Thrale is going to be married," she wrote by way of callous epitaph, "So I shall have a Son in Law again, notwithstanding the Death of Mr Mostyn." With a hint of remorse, to be sure, she inserted a belated note: "*We are alive* after so dreadful a Winter. Poor Mostyn is no longer so;—*his* Babes are Fatherless! *his* Wife a Widow!"[97]

During the immediate months and years following Mostyn's death, Mrs. Piozzi's correspondence reveals no significant revision in her attitude toward Cecilia, whom she found wanting in many respects. She complained to her other daughters, for instance, of Cecilia's cold indifference to her mother's illnesses. Pointedly Mrs. Piozzi remarked to Chappelow that "if She amuses herself as usual with painting Insects from Books of Natural History—She may perchance call to Mind that among the Hymenoptera are classed all those that wear Stings:—is not it *so*?"[98] Very few of Cecilia's traits and actions escaped Mrs. Piozzi's disapproval. By implication she accused the young woman of selfindulgence, supposing that "She will begin to enjoy herself [in London] towards May when her Mourning is over." In the same vein—overtly sarcastic—she punned with the sobriquet "Mousey Mostyn," who "will forget her Cares in the Crouds of London—unless Lady Keith should bring a Boy next Year—*That* Event would indeed affect her Good humour no little."[99]

This was not the first time that Mrs. Piozzi had pointed to Cecilia's jealousy of her eldest sister. Significantly, much of Mrs. Piozzi's fault–finding was recorded in letters to Salusbury (likewise a target of Cecilia's resentment), who by now was established as her principal beneficiary and favorite. "Mrs. Mostyn and Mr. Davies," she told him, "live in a constant Quarrel" over the education of the Mostyn boys. "It is a sad thing upon the Boys when Parents and Tutor do not agree." Conversely, she congratulated herself on the choice of Salusbury's tutor.[100] And similarly, in ridiculing Cecilia's extravagant improvements at Segroid, supposedly to enhance the value of the estate for the Mostyn heirs, Mrs. Piozzi implied the superiority of the prudential wisdom that she had been instilling in Salusbury. In so doing, she was deliberately charting the responsible course that she expected him to follow as the future squire of Brynbella. At the same time, she was in a sense warning him to be on guard against Cecilia's mercurial behavior. "No need," she cautioned, "of exciting *more* Jealousy or Malice."[101]

Notes

1. Clifford, p. 424 n. 1.
2. To TSW, 11 May 1808; to RG, 21 February 1805.
3. To the Miss Thrales, 8 June 1807.
4. To Ly W and Eleanor Williams, 26 July 1805.
5. *Thraliana* 2:1070; to Q, 2 November 1805.
6. To Ly W, 26 July 1806.
7. *Thraliana* 2:1081.
8. To Ly W, 10 February 1807.
9. To MW, [ca.11 April 1807].
10. *Thraliana* 2:1085 n. 2: "This Time last year [autumn 1806] Mr Piozzi was wild to go to Bath—for better help;—but those 300 Draughts washed his Regard for Bowen quite away. he will be content with Mr Moore This Winter I dare say—& perhaps do much better;—he *cannot do worse;* the Money (wch he likes best) will be saved for his Boy."
11. *Thraliana* 2:1081 and nn. 2 and 3.
12. To JSPS, 18 March 1809.
13. To JSPS, 5 March 1809.
14. To JSPS, 13–14 March 1809.
15. To MW, 18 February 1809.
16. To JSPS, 18 March 1809.
17. To Q, 19 March 1809.
18. N.L.W., MS.11099A, 11100A; Ly W, 26 March 1809.
19. *Thraliana* 2:1066, 1099.
20. C.R.O., Hawarden, Clywd, P/65/1/31.
21. To Q, 10 April 1809.
22. To JSPS, 19 April 1809.
23. "Pocket Books"; to JSPS, 1 May 1809; Clifford, pp. 426–27; Hyde, p. 283.
24. Hyde, p. ix.
25. Hyde, p. 65.
26. *Thraliana* 2:1071.
27. *Thraliana* 2:1077.
28. To Ly W, 26 July 1806; *The Piozzi Letters* 1:98–99 n.1.
29. To Dr. Caleb Hillier Parry, 15 July 1808.
30. To JSPS, 27 July 1810.
31. To Q, 6–7 March 1805.
32. To JSPS, 1 May 1809.
33. *Letters* 1:310 (30 March 1776); *The Piozzi Letters* 3:377 n.5.
34. To JSPS, 22 March 1808.
35. To LC, 21 November 1807.
36. To RG, 10 August 1808 and n.2.
37. To SL, 10 February 1808. Until his death (1819) Lysons was Keeper of the Records in the Tower of London.
38. To Ly W, 5 October 1808.
39. To MW, 26 April 1809.
40. To Ly W, 1 May 1809.
41. *Thraliana* 2:984; see also *The Piozzi Letters*, vols. 2 and 3.
42. SJ, "Preceptor," *Works* (Oxford, 1825) 5:236–37.
43. Years later she retrieved the ironical epithet for the benefit of the young actor William Augustus Conway (28 August 1819), to whom she had given "an Excellent Gold repeating Watch": "*Your* Monitress still, in this low-voic'd Repeater/ A useful Memento recorded may be;/ If wishing once more in the next Life to meet her/ You scorn not the Precepts of poor H:L:P.—"
44. To JSPS, 30 December 1807.
45. To JSPS, 9 September 1807.

Introduction

"I asked him if he really thought a knowledge of the Greek and Latin languages an essential requisite to a good education. JOHNSON. 'Most certainly, Sir; for those who know them have a very great advantage over those who do not. Nay, Sir, it is wonderful what a difference learning makes upon people even in the common intercourse of life, which does not appear to be much connected with it'" (*Boswell's Johnson* 1:457-58).

46. To JSPS, 28 January 1808.
47. To JSPS, 9 September 1807.
48. To JSPS, 26 September 1808; see also 14-15 October 1808.
49. To JSPS, 2 March 1810.
50. To JSPS, 6 May 1809.
51. To JSPS, 22 February 1810 and n. 7.
52. To JSPS, 2 March 1810.
53. To JSPS, 20 August 1808.
54. To JSPS, 14 March 1810.
55. To JSPS, 7 November 1808.
56. To JSPS, 7 June 1809.
57. To JSPS, 9 September 1809.
58. To Ly W, 5 March 1810.
59. To JSPS, 22 February 1810; see also 20 March 1810.
60. To TSW, 1 July, 1810.
61. To JSPS, 1 November 1810. He matriculated on 8 May 1811.
62. *Idler*, No. 103, an oddly morbid recommendation to a schoolboy: "This secret horrour of the last is inseparable from a thinking being, whose life is limited, and to whom death is dreadful."
63. To JSPS, 21 December 1810.
64. To JSPS, 16 July and 15 December 1810.
65. FBA, *Journals and Letters* 7:119n.
66. Hyde, p. 266.
67. To Q, 23 July 1805.
68. To MW, 28 May [1807].
69. *Thraliana* 2:946-47.
70. *Thraliana* 2:946-47 n.4; cf. 2:803-4.

For Mr. Nesbitt, see *Thraliana* 1:389 n.1, 2:803 etc., Hyde, pp. 52-54; for Thrale and politics, see Hyde, pp. 23, 107-8, 223-25, Clifford, pp. 35-36, etc.

71. Hyde, pp. 271, 274-76.
72. To the Miss Thrales, 8 June 1807; to SAT, 3 [December] 1807.
73. *Thraliana* 2:914.
74. *Thraliana* 1:394, 2:679.
75. To Q, 22 November 1807.
76. *Thraliana* 1:480.
77. *Thraliana* 1:468.
78. *Thraliana* 1:580; cf. SJ's cold reassurance, *Letters*, 27 November 1783.
79. *Thraliana* 2:772.
80. *The Piozzi Letters* 1:65-110; *Thraliana* 2:844.
81. *Thraliana* 2:1087; to SAT, 3 December 1807.
82. To Q, 22 November 1807.
83. To Q, 10 April 1809.
84. To LC, 1 December 1807; Lord Keith to HLP, 1 December 1807.
85. To MW, 17 February 1808.
86. Hyde, p. 287.
87. To Ly W, 11 December 1810.
88. *Thraliana* 2:931, 980.
89. *Thraliana* 2:685-86 and n.2.
90. *Thraliana* 2:721, 797-98.
91. *Thraliana* 2:998.
92. *Thraliana* 2:967-68.
93. *Thraliana* 2:985.
94. *Thraliana* 2:1062.
95. *Thraliana* 2:1062 n.3.
96. *Thraliana* 2:1071; to Q, 26 May 1806 and n. 19.
97. *Thraliana* 1081-82, 1081n.2. After Sophia's marriage, HLP remarked to LC (21 November 1807): "I have now Maids, Wife, and Widow Daughters; which do you think the happiest?"

"[On Tuesday last]," baldly announced *The Bath Chronicle* (Monday, 25 May 1807), "died at his house in Pulteney-st. J. Mostyn of Segroyt, Denbighshire."
 98. To LC, 1 December 1807.
 99. To JSPS, 1 March 1808; 14 March 1810.
100. To JSPS, 26 September 1808.
101. To JSPS, 27 July 1810; cf. 26 September 1808.

Short Titles for Major Manuscript Repositories

Barrett	The Barrett Collection of Burney Papers, British Library, London, 43 vols., Egerton [Eg.] 3690–3708
Berg	The Henry W. and Albert A. Berg Collection, New York Public Library, New York City
Bodleian	Bodleian Library, Oxford University
Bowood Collection	The Bowood Collection of Thrale-Piozzi letters in the possession of the marquis of Lansdowne, Bowood House, near Calne, Wilts.
Brit. Mus. Add. MSS	British Museum [now British Library] Additional Manuscripts
C.R.O.	County Record Office[s], England, Wales, and Ireland
Harvard University Library	Houghton Library at Harvard University
Historical Society of Pennsylvania	Historical Society of Pennsylvania, Philadelphia
Huntington Library	Henry E. Huntington Library, San Marino, California
Hyde Collection	The Donald and Mary Hyde Collection at Four Oaks Farm, Somerville, New Jersey; and at the Houghton Library, Harvard University
N.L.W.	National Library of Wales, Aberystwyth

N.P.G.	The National Portrait Gallery, Trafalgar Square, London
Osborn Collection	James Marshall and Marie-Louise Osborn Collection at the Beinecke Rare Book and Manuscript Library, Yale University
Peyraud Collection	The Paula F. Peyraud Collection of Piozzi letters and marginalia, Chappaqua, New York
Pforzheimer Library	The Carl H. Pforzheimer Library, New York City
The Pierpont Morgan Library	The Pierpont Morgan Library, New York City
Princeton University Library	Firestone Library at Princeton University
P.R.O.	Public Record Office, Chancery Lane, London
Ry.	The John Rylands University Library of Manchester, England
Victoria and Albert	Victoria and Albert Museum Library, London
Yale University Library	The Beinecke Rare Book and Manuscript Collection at Yale University

Locations of miscellaneous collections of Piozzi manuscripts not listed above are identified at the foot of each relevant letter under *"Text."*

Short Titles for Hester Lynch Piozzi's Manuscripts and Books

"Account Books"   "[Gabriel Piozzi's] Accounts, 1784– 1792," Drummond's Bank, Charing Cross, London

Anecdotes   *Anecdotes of the Late Samuel Johnson, LL.D., During the Last Twenty Years of His Life.* London: Printed for T. Cadell, 1786.

"Appeal"   "Mrs. Piozzi's Appeal against the *Critical Reviewers*," *Gentleman's Magazine* 71, pt. 2 (July 1801): 602–3.

British Synonymy   *British Synonymy: or, An Attempt at Regulating the Choice of Words in Familiar Conversation.* 2 vols. London: Printed for G. G. and J. Robinson, 1794.

"Children's Book"   For "The Children's Book or rather Family Book" from 17 September 1766 to the end of 1778 (Hyde Collection), see Hyde, Mary. *The Thrales of Streatham Park*. Cambridge and London: Harvard University Press, 1977.

"Commonplace Book"   "The New Commonplace Book." Random entries made by HLP after the completion of *Thraliana*, the first entry written at Brynbella in 1809 and the last in 1820 at Penzance (Hyde Collection).

Florence Miscellany   *Florence Miscellany*. Florence: Printed for G. Cam, Printer to His Royal Highness. With Permission, 1785. Hester Lynch Piozzi contributed the preface and nine poems.

French Journals	*The French Journals of Mrs. Thrale and Doctor Johnson.* Edited by Moses Tyson and Henry Guppy. Manchester: Manchester University Press, 1932. Hester Lynch Thrale's *French Journal* (1775) includes pp. 69–166; Hester Lynch Piozzi's *French Journey* (1784), pp. 191–213; Samuel Johnson's *French Journal* (1775), pp. 169–88.
"Harvard Piozziana"	"Poems and Little Characters, Anecdotes &c. Introductory to the Poems." 5 MS vols., 1810–14, for John Salusbury Piozzi Salusbury. Harvard University Library, MS Eng. 1280.
"Italian and German Journals"	"Italian and German Journals, from 5 September 1784 to March 1787," 2 MS notebooks (Ry. 618).
"Journey Book"	"Journey through the North of England and Part of Scotland, Wales, &c." 1789 (Ry. 623).
Letters	*Letters to and from the Late Samuel Johnson, LL.D.* 2 vols. London: Printed for A. Strahan and T. Cadell, 1788.
"Lyford Redivivus"	"Lyford Redivivus or A Grandame's Garrulity." [Signed by] "An Old Woman" [1809–15] (Hyde Collection).
"Memoirs"	Autobiographical Essays: For Sir James Fellowes, December 1815. Thirty-six MS pages bound into Johnson's *Letters.* Princeton University Library. For William Augustus Conway, May 1819. Eleven MS pages bound into *Observations.* Hyde Collection. See also Mrs. Piozzi to the Proprietors of the *Monthly Mirror,* 17 June 1798, Huntington Library, MSS 20831, and vol. 2, *The Piozzi Letters.*
"Memorial"	"Memorial of H. L. Piozzi against John Cator Esq." [autumn 1792]. John Rylands Library, MS. Ry. 611, and Appendix, vol. 2, *The Piozzi Letters.*

Merritt	*Piozzi Marginalia.* Edited by Percival Merritt. Cambridge: Harvard University Press, 1925.
"Minced Meat for Pyes"	"Minced Meat for Pyes" (1796–1820)," a collection of extracts, jottings, quotations, verses, &c. "Harvard University Library, MS Eng. 231F.
Observations	*Observations and Reflections made in the course of a Journey through France, Italy, and Germany.* 2 vols. London: Printed for A. Strahan and T. Cadell, 1789.
Old England	*Old England to her Daughters. Address to the Females of Great Britain.* [Signed by] "Poor Old England," penny broadside. London: Printed by J. Brettell for R. Faulder, ca. June 1803.
Retrospection	*Retrospection: or A Review of the Most Striking and Important Events, Characters, Situations, and their Consequences, which the last Eighteen Hundred Years have Presented to the View of Mankind.* 2 vols. London: Printed for John Stockdale, 1801.
"Thrale Estate Book"	"Accounts of the Estate of Henry Thrale, also Guardian Accounts with the four Thrale Daughters." MS in Hyde Collection.
Thraliana	*Thraliana: The Diary of Mrs. Hester Lynch Thrale (later Mrs. Piozzi), 1776–1809.* Edited by Katharine C. Balderston. 2d ed. 2 vols. Oxford: Clarendon Press, 1951. The original MS, 6 vols., is at the Huntington Library, San Marino, California.
Three Warnings	*The Three Warnings.* Kidderminster: Printed by John Gower, 1792. This work appeared originally in Anna Williams, *Miscellanies in Prose and Verse* (1766).
Three Warnings to John Bull	*Three Warnings to John Bull before He Dies. By an Old Acquaintance of the Public.* London: R. Faulder, 1798.

"Verses 1"   "Collection of Hester Lynch Piozzi's MSS Poetry." 140 leaves, of which 60, i.e., 120 pages, contain HLP's original poetry (Hyde Collection).

"Verses 2"   "Collection of Hester Lynch Piozzi's MSS Poetry." 34 pages of Hester Lynch Piozzi's verse plus 19 blank pages (Hyde Collection).

Welsh Tour   *Mrs. Thrale's Unpublished Journal of her Tour in Wales with Dr. Johnson, July–September, 1774.* In A. M. Broadley's *Doctor Johnson and Mrs. Thrale*, pp. 155–219. London and New York: John Lane, 1910.

Short Titles for Secondary Sources

We have used standard encyclopedias, school and university rosters, biographical dictionaries, law lists, peerages, armorials, baronetages, knightages, medical and clerical rosters, town and city directories, almanacs, and so forth. Along with these we have consulted annual army and navy lists; *Boyle's Court Guide: Royal Kalendar;* the Reverend William Betham, *The Baronetage of England,* 5 vols. (1801–5); the numerous editions of Burke's *Peerage and Baronetage* as well as Burke's *Landed Gentry;* Burke's *Royal Families of the World,* 2 vols. (1977); Burke's *Irish Family Records* (1976); George Edward Cokayne, *The Complete Peerage,* revised by Vicary Gibbs, et al., 13 vols. (1910–59); *The Complete Baronetage,* 6 vols. (1900–1909); W. A. Shaw, *The Knights of England,* 2 vols. (1906); Howard M. Colvin, *A Biographical Dictionary of British Architects, 1660–1840* (1954; 1978); Joseph Haydn and Horace Ockerby, *The Book of Dignities,* 3d ed. (1894); Gerrit P. Judd IV, *Members of Parliament, 1734–1832* (1955); Sir Lewis Namier and John Brooke, *The House of Commons, 1754–1790,* 3 vols. (1964).

These works will be cited only when specifically appropriate.

AR	*The Annual Register, or a View of the History, Politics, and Literature. 1758–.* (See Mrs. Piozzi to Mrs. Pennington, 4 August 1794, n. 10.)
Baronetage	Cokayne, George Edward, ed. *Complete Baronetage.* 6 vols. Exeter: W. Pollard, 1900–1909.
Bayle	*The Dictionary Historical and Critical of Mr. Peter Bayle.* 2d ed. 5 vols. London: Printed for J. J. and P. Knapton [etc.], 1734–38.
Boaden	Boaden, James. *Memoirs of Mrs. Siddons, Interspersed with Anecdotes of Authors and Actors.* 2 vols. London: Henry Colburn, 1827.
Boswell's Johnson	*Boswell's Life of Johnson.* Edited by George Birkbeck Hill and L. F. Powell. 6 vols. Oxford: Clarendon Press, 1934–64.

Broadley	Broadley, A. M. *Doctor Johnson and Mrs. Thrale.* London and New York: John Lane, 1910.
Brooke	Brooke, John. *King George III.* New York: McGraw-Hill, 1972.
Campbell	Campbell, Thomas. *Life of Mrs. Siddons.* 2 vols. London: Effingham Wilson, 1834.
Chandler	Chandler, David G. *The Campaigns of Napoleon.* London: Weidenfeld and Nicolson, 1966.
Chapman	Chapman, R. W., ed. *The Letters of Samuel Johnson, with Mrs. Thrale's Genuine Letters to Him.* 3 vols. Oxford: Clarendon Press, 1952.
Clifford	Clifford, James L. *Hester Lynch Piozzi (Mrs. Thrale).* 2d ed. Reprinted with corrections and additions. Oxford: Clarendon Press, 1968, 1987 (with a new introduction by Margaret Anne Doody).
Corr. George IV	*The Correspondence of George, Prince of Wales, 1770–1812.* Edited by A. Aspinall. 8 vols. New York: Oxford University Press, 1963–71.
Décembre-Alonnier	[Joseph] Décembre-[Edmond] Alonnier. *Dictionnaire de la Révolution française, 1789–1799.* 2 vols. Paris [1866–68].
Diary and Letters	*Diary and Letters of Madame d'Arblay.* Edited by Charlotte Barrett. 7 vols. [1842–46.] London: H. Colburn, 1854.
Dodsley	*A Collection of Poems in Six Volumes by Several Hands.* [Edited by Robert Dodsley.] London: Printed by J. Hughs, for J. Dodsley, in Pall-Mall, 1765.
Doody	Doody, Margaret Anne. *Frances Burney. The Life in the Works.* New Brunswick, New Jersey: Rutgers University Press, 1988.
Early Journals	*The Early Journals and Letters of Fanny Burney*, vol. 1 (1768–73). Edited by Lars E. Troide. Oxford and Montreal: Oxford University Press; McGill-Queens University Press, 1988–

English Poets	Johnson, Samuel. *Lives of the English Poets.* Edited by George Birkbeck Hill. 3 vols. Oxford: Clarendon Press, 1905.
Farington	*The Diary of Joseph Farington.* Vols. 1–6 edited by Kenneth Garlick and Angus D. Macintyre. Vols. 7–16 edited by Kathryn Cave. New Haven and London: Published for the Paul Mellon Centre for Studies in British Art, Yale University Press, 1978–84.
Genest	Genest, John. *Some Account of the English Stage, from the Restoration in 1660 to 1830.* 10 vols. Bath: Printed by H. E. Carrington and sold by Thomas Rodd, Great Newport Street, London, 1832.
GM	*The Gentleman's Magazine.* Edited by Sylvanus Urban. London, 1731–1907.
Hawkins	Hawkins, Sir John. *The Life of Samuel Johnson, LL.D.* 2d ed. Revised and corrected. London: J. Buckland, et al., 1787.
Hayward	Hayward, A., ed. *Autobiography, Letters and Literary Remains of Mrs. Piozzi (Thrale).* 2d ed. 2 vols. London: Longman, Green, Longman, Roberts, 1861.
Hazen	Hazen, Charles Downer. *The French Revolution.* 2 vols. New York: Henry Holt, 1932.
Hemlow	Hemlow, Joyce. *The History of Fanny Burney.* Oxford: Clarendon Press, 1958.
Highfill	Highfill, Philip H., Jr., Kalman A. Burnim, and Edward A. Langhans. *A Biographical Dictionary of Actors, Actresses, Musicians, Dancers, Managers & Other Stage Personnel in London, 1660–1800.* Carbondale and Edwardsville: Southern Illinois University Press, 1973–.
Hodson	Hodson, V. C. P. *List of the Officers of the Bengal Army 1758–1834.* 4 pts. London: Constable; Phillimore, 1927–47.

Howell	*Epistolae Ho-Elianae, The Familiar Letters of James Howell.* Edited by Joseph Jacobs. 2 vols. [1645–55.] London: David Nutt, 1892.
Hyde	Hyde, Mary. *The Thrales of Streatham Park.* Cambridge and London: Harvard University Press, 1977.
Hyde-Redford	The Hyde Edition of *The Letters of Samuel Johnson,* vols. 1–3. Edited by Bruce Redford. Princeton, N.J.: Princeton University Press, 1992–.
Idler	*The Idler and the Adventurer.* Edited by W. J. Bate, John M. Bullitt, and L. F. Powell. Vol. 2 of *The Yale Edition of the Works of Samuel Johnson.* New Haven and London, 1963.
Jerningham	*The Jerningham Letters (1780–1843).* Edited by Egerton Castle. 2 vols. London: Richard Bentley and Son, 1896.
Jesse	Jesse, J. Heneage. *Memoirs of the Life and Reign of King George the Third.* 2d ed. 3 vols. London: Tinsley Brothers, 1867.
Johns. Misc.	*Johnsonian Miscellanies.* Edited by George Birkbeck Hill. 2 vols. Oxford: Clarendon Press, 1897.
Johns. Shakespeare	*Johnson on Shakespeare.* Edited by Arthur Sherbo. Vols. 7–8 of *The Yale Edition of the Works of Samuel Johnson.* New Haven and London, 1968.
Journals and Letters	*The Journals and Letters of Fanny Burney (Madame d'Arblay).* Edited by Joyce Hemlow et al. 12 vols. Oxford: Clarendon Press, 1972–84. Especially vol. 7, edited by Edward A. Bloom and Lillian D. Bloom (1978); vol. 8, edited by Peter Hughes et al. (1980): vols. 9–10, edited by Warren Derry (1982).
Knapp	Knapp, Oswald G., ed. *The Intimate Letters of Hester Piozzi and Penelope Pennington 1788–1821.* London, Toronto, and New York: John Lane; Bell and Cockburn, 1914.
Lefebvre	Lefebvre, Georges. *The French Revolution.* Vol. 1, *From its Origins to 1793,* translated by Elizabeth

	Moss Evanson. Vol. 2, *From 1793 to 1799*, translated by John Hall Stewart and James Friguglietti. London: Routledge and Kegan Paul; New York: Columbia University Press, 1962–64.
Lloyd	Lloyd, J[acob] Y. *The History of the Princes, the Lords Marcher, and the Ancient Nobility of Powys Fadog, and the Ancient Lords of Arwystli, Cedewen, and Meirionydd.* 6 vols. London: T. Richards [Whiting], 1881–87.
London Stage	*The London Stage 1660–1800.* Edited by William Van Lennep, Emmett L. Avery, Arthur H. Scouten, et al. 5 vols. in 11 and index. Carbondale: Southern Illinois University Press, 1960–79.
McCarthy	McCarthy, William. *Hester Thrale Piozzi: Portrait of a Literary Woman.* Chapel Hill: University of North Carolina Press, 1985.
Mangin	[Mangin, Edward.] *Piozziana; or, Recollections of the Late Mrs. Piozzi, with Remarks.* London: Edward Moxon, 1833.
Manvell	Manvell, Roger. *Sarah Siddons: Portrait of an Actress.* London: Heinemann, 1970.
Marshall	Marshall, John. *Royal Naval Biography.* . . . 4 vols. London: Longman, Hurst, Rees, Orme, and Browne, 1823–35.
Nichols	Nichols, John. *Illustrations of the Literary History of the Eighteenth Century.* 8 vols. [7 and 8 by John Bowyers Nichols.] London: Nichols, Son, and Bentley, 1817–58.
Oxford Proverbs	*The Oxford Dictionary of English Proverbs.* 3d ed. Revised by F. P. Wilson [1970]. Oxford: Clarendon Press, 1982.
Parliamentary History	*The Parliamentary History of England from the earliest Period to the Year 1803, from which last-mentioned Epoch it is continued downwards in the work entitled "Hansard's Parliamentary Debates."* 36 vols. London: Printed by T. C. Hansard [etc.], 1806–20.

Pastor	Pastor, Baron Ludwig Friedrich August von. *The History of the Popes, from the Close of the Middle Ages*. 40 vols. London: J. Hodges et al., 1891–1953.
Peerage	Cokayne, George Edward. *The Complete Peerage of England, Scotland, Ireland, Great Britain and the United Kingdom*. 2d ed., rev. and enl. Edited by Vicary Gibbs et al. 13 vols. London: St. Catherine Press, 1910–59.
Poems	*Poems*. Edited by E. L. McAdam, Jr., with George Milne. Vol. 6 of *The Yale Edition of the Works of Samuel Johnson*. New Haven and London, 1964.
Prayers	*Diaries, Prayers, and Annals*. Edited by E. L. McAdam, Jr., with Donald and Mary Hyde. Vol. 1 of *The Yale Edition of the Works of Samuel Johnson*. New Haven and London, 1958.
Queeney Letters	*The Queeney Letters*. Edited by the marquis of Lansdowne. London: Cassell; New York: Farrar and Rinehart, 1934.
Rambler	*The Rambler*. Edited by W. J. Bate and Albrecht B. Strauss. Vols. 3–5 of *The Yale Edition of the Works of Samuel Johnson*. New Haven and London, 1969.
Rasselas	*Rasselas and Other Tales*. Edited by Gwin J. Kolb. Vol. 16 of *The Yale Edition of the Works of Samuel Johnson*. New Haven and London, 1990.
Redford	Redford, Bruce. *The Converse of the Pen*. Chicago and London: University of Chicago Press, 1986.
Repertorium	Winter, Otto Friedrich. Repertorium der diplomatischen Vertreter aller Länder seit dem Westfälischen Frieden (1648), vol. 3, 1764–1815. Graz-Köln: Verlag Hermann Böhlaus, 1965.
Rothenberg	Rothenberg, Gunter E. *Napoleon's Great Adversaries: The Archduke Charles and the Austrian Army, 1792–1814*. Bloomington: Indiana University Press, 1982.
Sale Catalogue	1. Streatham Park, Surrey. *A Catalogue of the . . . Household Furniture . . . a Collection of Valuable Paintings . . . also the Extensive and Well-Selected*

	Library . . . the genuine Property of Mrs. Piozzi . . . will be sold by Auction, by Mr. Squibb, on the Premises, on Wednesday the 8th of May, 1816, and Four following Days (Sunday excepted). 2. Collectanea Johnsoniana. Catalogue of the Library, Pictures, Prints, Coins, Plate, China, and other Valuable Curiosities, the Property of Mrs. Hester Lynch Piozzi, Deceased, to be sold by Auction, at the Emporium Rooms, Exchange Street, Manchester, by Mr. Broster, on Wednesday, [September 1823] the 17th instant, and [six] following days, Saturday and Sunday excepted. Chester.
Seward, *Anecdotes*	Seward, William. *Anecdotes of Some Distinguished Persons, Chiefly of the Present and Two Preceding Centuries.* 4 vols. and supplement. 2d ed. London: T. Cadell, Jr., and W. Davies, 1795–96.
Seward Letters	*Letters of Anna Seward: Written between the Years 1784 and 1807.* 6 vols. Edinburgh: Archibald Constable and Co.; London: Longman, Hurst, Rees, Orme, and Brown, William Miller, and John Murray, 1811.
Shakespeare	*The Riverside Shakespeare.* Boston: Houghton Mifflin, 1974.
Siddons Letters	Burnim, Kalman A. "The Letters of Sarah and William Siddons to Hester Lynch Piozzi in the John Rylands Library." *Bulletin of the John Rylands Library* 52 (1969–70): 46–95.
Spectator	*The Spectator.* 8 vols. London: Printed by H. Hughs for Payne, Rivington et al., 1789. This is Hester Lynch Piozzi's copy, bought in 1794, with her marginalia (Peyraud Collection).
Stanhope	Stanhope, Philip Henry, fifth earl. *Life of the Right Honourable William Pitt.* 4 vols. 3d ed. [1867]. New York: AMS Press, 1970.
Tilley	Tilley, Morris Palmer. *A Dictionary of the Proverbs in England in the Sixteenth and Seventeenth Centuries.* Ann Arbor: University of Michigan Press, 1950.
Walpole Correspondence	*The Yale Edition of Horace Walpole's Correspondence.* Edited by W. S. Lewis et al. 48 vols. in 49. New Haven, 1937–83.

Warton	Warton, Thomas. *The History of English Poetry, from the Close of the Eleventh to the Commencement of the Eighteenth Century.* 4 vols. London: J. Dodsley et al., 1774–81.
Watson	Watson, J. Steven. *The Reign of George III, 1760–1815.* Oxford: Clarendon Press, 1960.
Welsh Journey	Johnson, Samuel. *A Journey into North Wales, in the Year 1774.* In *Boswell's Johnson* 5:427–61.
Wheatley	Wheatley, Henry B. *London Past and Present.* 3 vols. London: John Murray; New York: Scribner and Welford, 1891.
Wickham	Wickham, The Reverend Hill, ed. *Journals and Correspondence of Thomas [Sedgwick] Whalley, D.D.* 2 vols. London: Richard Bentley, 1863.

Names and Abbreviations of Major Figures in the Piozzi Correspondence

AL	Alexander Leak (1776–1816)
CB	Charles Burney (1726–1814)
CMT } CMM }	Cecilia Margaretta Thrale (1777–1857); in 1795 Mrs. Mostyn
DL	The Reverend Daniel Lysons (1762–1834)
EM	The Reverend Edward Mangin (1772–1852)
FB } FBA }	Frances "Fanny" Burney (1752–1840); in 1793 Mme d'Arblay
GP	Gabriel Piozzi (1740–1809)
HLS } HLT } HLP }	Hester Lynch Salusbury (1741–1821); in 1763 Mrs. Thrale; in 1784 Mrs. Piozzi
HMP } HMS }	Harriet Maria Pemberton (1794–1831); in 1814 Mrs. Salusbury; in 1817 Lady Salusbury
HT	Henry Thrale (1728 or 1729–81)
JB	James Boswell (1740–95)
JF	James Fellowes (1771–1857); in 1809 Sir James, knight
JMM	John Meredith Mostyn (1775–1807)
JSPS	John Salusbury Piozzi Salusbury (1793–1858); in 1817 Sir John, knight
JW	John Williams (1794–1859); in 1830 Sir John, second baronet; in 1842 Sir John Hay-Williams
LC	The Reverend Leonard Chappelow (1744–1820)
Ly W	Margaret Williams (1768–1835) of Bodelwyddan; in 1798 Lady Williams
MF	Marianne Francis (1790–1832)
MW	Margaret Williams (1759–1823) of Bath
PSW } PSP }	Penelope Sophia Weston (1752–1827); in 1792 Mrs. Pennington
Q	Hester Maria "Queeney" Thrale (1764–1857); in 1808 Lady Keith
RD	The Reverend Reynold Davies (1752–1820)
RG	The Reverend Robert Gray (1762–1834)

SAT	Susanna Arabella Thrale (1770–1858)
SJ	Samuel Johnson (1709–84)
SL	Samuel Lysons (1763–1819)
SS	Sarah Siddons (1755–1831)
ST } SH }	Sophia Thrale (1771–1824); in 1807 Mrs. Hoare
TSW	The Reverend Thomas Sedgwick Whalley (1746–1828)
WAC	William Augustus Conway (1789–1828)

Genealogical Abbreviations

cr.	created
fl.	flourished
M.I.	monumental inscription

Editorial Principles

Manuscript Sources

All letters are arranged chronologically. Mrs. Piozzi's correspondence creates few textual problems since she prided herself on her penmanship and wrote with a strong hand. We have transcribed literally, changing only what we believe would detract from clarity. We have retained original spellings, capitalization, and punctuation. Certain accidentals—the omission of a period or a closing parenthesis—are silently emended. Superior letters are lowered. Her intermittent use of an elision to form a past tense—a usage that she came to see as outmoded—is normalized: e.g., "defer'd" becomes "deferred." Most abbreviations—except in a few instances or in addresses and postmarks—are expanded.

Mrs. Piozzi's paragraphing can puzzle. Occasionally she follows normal practice by dropping a line and then indenting. At other times to indicate a new paragraph she merely extends a space on the same line. Sense usually dictates where a visibly uncertain paragraph begins. Dashes, similarly, are hard to decipher since her lines for that mark can be of any length or even appear as a seemingly extended ellipsis. Dashes, consequently, are transcribed as "—" or, when elongated to suggest emotional response, as "——".

The writer's address is shown at the upper right of the letter along with the date. The complimentary close and signature for each letter are presented in run-on fashion with slash marks to indicate line breaks or divisions. At the foot of each letter are provided, where available, repository, address of recipient, and postmark. Franked letters are marked as such.

Pertinent complementary correspondence usually appears in notes in order to explain obscurities, clarify cryptic remarks, or solve problems. In a few instances, however, when Mrs. Piozzi answers a letter—say, of Sarah Siddons, Leonard Chappelow, Joseph Cooper Walker, or Daniel Lysons—point-for-point, we incorporate in the body of the text the letter that initiated or continued the correspondence.

Generally, square brackets "[ ]" signal such defects in the holographs as blots, tears, seals, oversights. In addition, when a date of composition is conjectural, it is enclosed in square brackets and annotated. Angle brackets "< >" indicate places where a printed date, as in a postmark, a word, or a phrase is blurred.

When warranted by the context, emendations are made within the appropriate square or angle brackets.

Printed Sources

Texts are reprinted literally although erroneous datings and obvious misprints are corrected with explanations when necessary, and certain typographical eccentricities, such as the arbitrary and inconsistent use of small capitals in words and phrases, are not reproduced.

We have consistently used the names of Welsh counties as HLP would have known them. Since 1974, however, following reorganization under the Local Government Act (1972), the new county of Clwyd, e.g., was created from Flintshire, most of Denbighshire, and the Edeyrnion district of Merioneth. Similarly, the new county of Gwynedd was formed out of Anglesey, Carnarvonshire (or Caernarfonshire), the rest of Merioneth, and the Conwy valley in Denbighshire.

The Piozzi Letters

Letters, 1805–1810

TO THE REVEREND ROBERT GRAY

Bath Thursday
21st: February 1805.

Young Roscius's premature powers attract universal attention, and I suppose that if less than an angel had told *his* parents that a bulletin of that child's health should be necessary to quiet the anxiety of a metropolis for his safety, they would not have believed the prediction.

Of Buonaparte's exaltation, still less appearance, still fewer traces could have been visible a dozen years ago; and how his family will support their new dignities remains yet to be seen.[1]

The Pope seems no more talked of. Is he gone home, or going? or will they set him down at Avignon, and secularize old Rome at once? *That* scheme is among the many one hears talked of.[2]

Mr. Piozzi's state of health is all this while nearer my heart than any of these things; it is not a good state of health, certainly, where frequent agony and continual lameness both of hands and feet preclude all possibility of enjoyment, and render even consolation difficult. Yet has Mr. Piozzi tolerable appetite, and no worse spirits than such a state of life and limbs must necessarily produce—— so we must be contented I think, and pity those who are worse off than ourselves.

Text: Hayward 2:263–64.

1. Joseph (1768–1844) and Louis Bonaparte (1778–1846) were each made *prince français* with the qualification of *imperial highness* on 18 May 1804. (Excluded from membership in the Imperial Family in 1804 were Lucien (1775–1840), who had to wait until 22 March 1815, and the underage Jérôme (1784–1860) who waited until 24 September 1806.)

Napoleon's sisters—Elisa (1777–1820), Pauline (1780–1825), and Caroline (1782–1839)—were each recognized as *princesse française* with the qualification of *imperial highness* on 18 May 1804.

For the first consul's earlier advancement of his brothers, see HLP to LC, 16 August 1802, n. 3.

2. HLP refers to the papal residence at Avignon from 1308/9 to 1376 or 1377. (Avignon then belonged to vassals of the Roman Church and was not on French soil.) Clement V (1264–1314), who ruled as pope from 1305 to 1314, installed the Holy See in Avignon (1309), assuming the papacy would be unable to stand firm in the revolt-torn Italian states. But the nearness of the French kings to the pope had created the historical impression that the kings ruled the popes.

TO HESTER MARIA THRALE

Bath Wednesday
6–7 March 1805
no, no: Thursday 7th.

My dearest Girl

I was glad to see your hand-writing and can easily resolve the enclosed Ænigma into a Press Error. *P. Piazzi* the famous Astronomer at Florence found a new Planet some Years ago, and called it the Ceres if I remember rightly; but it goes by the finder's Name, which is so like ours, that the Mistake is easy.[1]

You know my Character exactly; I never want for Amusement when thrown upon Society, and tho' we go out very *very* seldom at Night, I pick up some entertaining Chat in my Morning Rambles—and often think how pretty you are all looking in these new-fashioned Caps of Brown Ribbon, which on the fair-haired Lasses like yourself are *beautiful.*

Mr. Mostyn, and *his,* and *my* tall Cousin Thelwall have engaged to dine here next Sunday:[2] for tho' Mr. Piozzi was seized with a shivering Fit and Fever on the 2d. of March—last Saturday; and tho' a consequent Erysipelas broke out in the best Leg—Dr. Parry fought off the Enemy very handsomely indeed, and here we are again—not in a Bed—but on a Sopha. I am glad sweet Siddons does not pollute her noble Mind with Envy of an Infant's Excellence—[3]

> She, who should now with Laurels fairly won
> Sit smiling at the Goal whilst others run.[4]

The Boy I do believe is a sweet Creature:—Anstey—Writer of the Bath Guide,[5] at 87 Years old regrets his not coming to Bath. Mr. Anstey was related to Lady Salusbury, but obtained no Legacy; tho' he had been her Sweetheart he tells me, when both were Young.—He thought the Gentlemen who share her Fortune had been Sons to a Brother of my Uncle Thomas; and It is I find generally so supposed.[6]

Have you read Godwin's new Novel?[7] It is a very neat Key to the human heart, every dirty Corner and Sluts' Hole of which, he seems to have great delight in opening.—The *Wedding Supper* however is a Scene of horrible Sublimity, and kept me awake all Night.—This is his 3d. Performance, but I still prefer St. Leon.—You never say how you like Agrippina,[8] its Authour has got 100£ o'Year in present, and a Pension of 300£ o'Year in Prospect for superintending the Education of Lord Lucan's Family.[9] Poor Miss Seward is expecting her own death every day,[10] and I feel grieved for my old Acquaintance Mr. Richard Greatheed too. We are told here that he has a Cancer on his Face.[11]

This has been a calamitous Year to Individuals in every part of the World, and it is a vain thing to believe (whatever one may say) that there is not an uncommon Mortality upon our own Island. To chase such Anxieties away I have been to see Mr. Riddell's famous Picture representing all the high Mountains of the Globe——on one *Piece of Paper*—not Canvass for he paints in Acquatinta only, and in the most perfect Representer of Water in agitated Motion I ever yet have Seen.[12] His *Portrait* (such I must call it) of Staffa would delight you beyond Measure. Mr. Whalley has bought Fingal's Cave[13] but I prefer the *outside* of that strange *Mineral Honeycomb* with the Tossing Waves around. Oh pray *do* drive with Susan to see how well He has done what She herself did so excellently.— You have saved me all necessity of going to the Spot—My Heart tells me that I now know exactly *how it is*.

Mr. Riddell is Brother or Cousin to Sir James, but being *stone deaf*, resolves to sit Quiet and be a great Artist:[14] he has an agreable Friend with him who interprets. But we have a Miss Talbot here, a *Lady*, a Bath Belle; whose Performances in a very different way would I think *much amaze you*.[15] Such a Copyist I am confident exists not, and perhaps never did exist.—With the neatness of Vanderwerf[16] She repeats the Idea in small Coreggios, Albanos,[17] and little whole Length Parmegianos[18] to a Perfection I thought unattainable: and would deceive the Whole Royal Academy if She had a Mind.

But you will expect me to explain my own Expression when calling Staffa a Mineral Honeycomb, and if I can get this vile Pen to move along I will excuse the Notion it conveys by observing how oddly Nature loves to sport in Hexagonal or Pentagon Figures, wherever She does *quite her own Way*.—Within the Caves of Antiparos or Derby Peak[19]—or Gyants Causeway or Hebridian Isles—*those Forms prevail* as in a Wasp's or Bee's or Hornets Nest, which by the shortness of the Columns merely, makes a more smooth but scarcely a more regular Roof than Staffa bears in this Man's Portrait of its outside. But Adieu! I have scarce room to say how truly I am yours / and your Sisters ever H: L: P.

Text: Bowood Collection. *Address:* Miss Thrale / Great Cumberland Street / London. *Postmark:* BATH 8 MAR 1805.

1. Giuseppe Piazzi (1746–1826) entered the Theatine Order in 1764, accepted the chair of mathematics in the academy of Palermo in 1780, and had an observatory built there. On 1 January 1801 he discovered the first asteroid or minor planet, which he named Ceres, after the tutelary deity of Sicily.
2. The Reverend Edward Thelwall (d. ca. 31 October 1814) of Llanbedr Hall, Denbighshire, the rector of Trinity Church, Chester. See *GM* 84, pt. 2 (1814): 507.
3. HLP had obviously questioned SS about the worth of Master Betty. The actress answered through her companion, Patty Wilkinson, on [5 October 1804]: "All I know of *Master Betty* as you call him, is that he has electrified all the People at Edinbro, Dublin, Birmingham; and in short every place that he has shown his little person in—(he must be an astonishing Child) but that he can be a true portrait of Richard the 3d, Macbeth, Hamlet, &c—*is quite impossible;* it [tear: is?] expected by the people who has [sic] seen him perform to cause the same sensation of delight and astonishment as was excited at the appearance of Garrick, Siddons, Kemble, Cook &c.—Oh Lord—Oh Lord—*he* is only 13 years of age—Mrs. Sid. begs to know what she is to do with the Puppet—she thinks it will be quite absurd her playing with him & begs you will give your Opinion and advice" (*Siddons Letters,* p. 77).

Confidante and solace, Patty was the daughter of Tate Wilkinson (1739–1803), a comic actor and mimic as well as a self-admitted alcoholic (*Memoirs of his own Life,* 1790, as cited by Campbell 2: 227–28).

SS had importuned Tate on 29 May 1798 (the year of Maria's death): "It would *indeed* be a great comfort to us all, if you would allow our dear Patty to come to us, on our return to [London] in the autumn to stay with us a few months; I am sure it would do my Maria so much good; for the physician tells me she will require the same confinement and care the next winter. . . . Do, dear soul! grant my request." Campbell adds in his own voice: "Miss Wilkinson accepted the invitation, and became from that time a permament imate in the Siddons family. . . . Miss Wilkinson is still alive [1834]. She lived with the great actress till her last days. Besides the bland temper and disposition which attached Mrs. Siddons to her, she possessed a practical knowledge of the world, which made her a valuable inmate of the family."

For Master Betty (William Henry West Betty, 1791–1874), see HLP to LC, 17 November 1803, n. 2.

4. The lines (slightly altered) were originally written about William Congreve. See Edward Young, *Love of Fame, the Universal Passion*, Satire 1, lines 39–40.

5. The poet Christopher Anstey (1724–1805) is best known for the series of letters in rhyme called the *New Bath Guide* (1766). He had been a permanent resident of Bath for some thirty-five years.

6. "The bulk of Lady Salusbury's property is divided between her two nephews, Sir Robert Salusbury, of Llanwern, co. Monmouth, and the Rev. Lynch Salusbury, of Hitchin, Herts., who share a very considerable sum of ready money, and an income of at least £12,000 per annum." See *GM* 74, pt. 2 (1804): 687.

The Reverend Lynch Salusbury, later Burroughs (1763–1837), and Sir Robert Salusbury (1756–1817) were brothers. For the latter, see HLP to Q, 20 September 1803, n. 9.

Lady Salusbury exacted heavy tribute from her nephews for her bequests. See Farington 6:2370, 2373.

7. According to HLP, Godwin's "3d Performance" is *Fleetwood; or, The New Man of Feeling*, 3 vols. (London: Richard Phillips, 1805). She would regard as its predecessors *Things as They Are; or, The Adventures of Caleb Williams* (1794); and *St. Leon, a Tale of the Sixteenth Century* (1799). Apparently she did not associate the following works (printed anonymously) with his fiction: *Damon and Delia* (1784); *Imogen* (1784); and *Italian Letters; or, The History of the Count de St. Julian* (1785).

In Casimir Fleetwood, Godwin represents an extravagant fusion of Romantic sensibility and Othello-like moods of jealousy, unbridled rage, and other extremes of passion. The "Scene of horrible Sublimity" depicts Fleetwood's solitary, gruesomely evoked wedding anniversary. The "celebratory" atmosphere—dominated by waxen models of his innocent wife and an imagined lover, organ music, and a banquet—culminates in violent destruction and insanity (3: 247–53; chap. 15).

HLP would have admired Godwin's descriptions of Welsh scenery, and she had followed his career, often with approval, but sometimes with repugnance. She despised his revolutionary sympathies and radical associations. For her ambivalent feelings, see HLP to PSP, 1 August 1798, n. 7, and again to PSP, [6] September 1801; to Ly W, 24 February 1800. See also Peter H. Marshall, *William Godwin* (New Haven and London: Yale University Press, 1984), pp. 260–65.

8. Elizabeth Hamilton, *Memoirs of the Life of Agrippina, the wife of Germanicus*, 3 vols. (Bath, printed by R. Crutwell; for G. and J. Robinson, London, 1804).

9. (General) Richard Bingham (1764–1839), second earl of Lucan (1799), a representative peer for Ireland. He had married 26 May 1794 Lady Elizabeth Belasyse (d. 1819), the divorced wife of Bernard Edward Howard (1765–1842), later twelfth duke of Norfolk. Lord Lucan and Lady Elizabeth were the parents of four girls and two boys.

10. On 2 August 1803 John Saville (aged 68), a vicar-choral of the Lichfield cathedral, died. See *GM* 73, pt. 2 (1803): 793. For months a mourning Anna Seward would not leave her house, and she prepared for her own death (1809).

She described her physical symptoms to Walter Scott, 7 March 1805: "—a dizziness of head, in more or less degree, always upon me, and which has, since the 25th of October last, increased with dangerous force, amounting to sudden paroxysms, in which all the surrounding objects seem falling into chaos. . . . By this strange mysterious malady, which medicine has tried to combat in vain, the remnant of my days in destined to a gloomy suspension of every intellectual industry" (*Seward Letters* 6:207–8).

11. For Richard Wilson Greatheed, see HLP to Ann Greatheed, 2 April 1788^b, n. 3. He was to die in London in October 1832.

12. Robert Andrew Riddell (fl. 1793–99), a watercolorist whose art was inspired principally by natural settings in Scotland and Cheshire. His residence was Spreacombe House, Devon. In 1793 he exhibited at the Royal Academy a "South-East View of Dumfries." He also earned favorable attention in 1799 with "Travellers on a Hill in Cheshire." The picture that HLP mentions she probably saw at a public exhibition in the Saloon of Arts, No. 2, Union Passage, Bath (admission one shilling). See *Exhibition of the Royal Academy, M.DCC.XCIII. The Twenty-Fifth* [catalogue, no. 503] (London: T. Cadell, printer to the Royal Academy, 1793). See also *Bath Journal*, 4 and 11 March 1805.

13. Staffa was an uninhabited island of the Hebrides. While offering excellent pasturage, its coastline is dotted with basaltic caverns, the principal of which is Fingal's Cave.

14. The opaque reference to a "Brother or Cousin" encourages speculation. A likely candidate, whatever the relationship, is James Riddell (d. 1797) of Ardnamurchon and Sunart, county Argyll,

cr. baronet in 1778. A worldly individual, unlike Robert Andrew, Sir James (F.S.A. and LL.D.) had served as Superintendant-General to the British Fishery Society.

By his first wife (1754), Mary Milles of Durham, he had five children. A second marriage (1775), to the widowed Sarah Swinburne (1731–1817), née Burdon, produced no issue. She resided in Great Pulteney Street, Bath, until her death. On 16 June 1817 she was interred in Westminster Abbey.

Sir James's successor to the baronetcy was his grandson, James Milles Riddell (1787–1861). At the time of this letter the second baronet was a student at Christ Church College, Oxford.

15. Frances Talbot (1786–1857). On 23 August 1809 she would become the second wife of John Parker (1722–1840), Viscount Boringdon of North Molton and first earl of Morley (1815).

The daughter of Thomas Talbot, "a Surgeon & Apothecary" at Wymondham in Norfolk, Frances was praised by an acquaintance as a woman of "beauty, virtue, talents, and temper" (Farington 10: 3582–83, 12 October 1809).

16. Adriaen (or Adriaan) van der Werff (1659–1722) of Rotterdam. A painter-architect, he is best known for his design of the Merchants' Exchange of Rotterdam (1721–33) and oils on biblical subjects.

17. Francesco Albani, or Albano (1578–1660), was a Bolognese whose talent was encouraged by the Caraccis (Carraccis). He executed a number of large works on mythological and theological themes in a style described as more beautiful than grand.

For Correggio (i.e., Antonio Allegri, ca. 1494–1534), see HLP to SL, [5] July 1786, n. 5; the Caraccis: see HLP to Q, 4 June 1785, n. 19.

18. Girolamo Francesco Maria Mazzola, also Mazzolina or Mazzuola (1503–40), was a native of Parma known as Il Parmigiano and Parmigianino. A religious painter of the Mannerist school, he began as an imitator of Correggio. His talent and life were dissipated by an obsession with alchemy and a search for the philosophers' stone.

19. Antiparos is one of the Cyclades islands in the Aegean Sea, between Greece and Turkey. Its only remarkable feature is a stalactite Cavern.

Derby Peak is an area of millstone grit hills containing many caves, particularly near Castleton in northern Derbyshire.

The causeway is a promontory of columnar basalt along the northern coast of county Antrim, North Ireland. Folklore has it that the causeway was formed by a race of giants to provide access to Scotland.

TO THE REVEREND ROBERT MYDDELTON

Bath—Wednesday
28 [i.e., 27]: March 1805.

Dear Doctor Myddelton's

Letter is a very kind one, and I think the Blessing given at Mold, [Flintshire] has even now scarce finished its benign Operation; for I keep quite well myself and Mr. Piozzi is not yet confined tho' he lives in constant Preparation for the Enemy.

I tell nothing,—because there is nothing to tell; and because you will soon be at the Noisy Place of which this is the immediate—tho' faint Echo.

Your Business in its Environs is truly Interesting, and the lovely Boy carries with him thither my Sincerest Wishes that he may enter with due *Eclat* on his new Mode of Life.[1]

To the Spartans, War was a State of Relaxation we remember; and to a home-taught Child as he has been—School Lessons will be *light;* while his Companions feel them as a Burthen. *He* will have learned beside so to incorporate Book-

Knowledge with his whole System, that stated hours of Recreation will *not* drive all away which Study had sown into *his* Mind, as it commonly does from *theirs;* to whom Learning is a mere *Appliqué* of Show upon the Outside, never Embroidered *throughnthrough* as Workwomen justly phrase it. So here if you please I will end my happy Imitation of the military Lecture pronounced to Hannibal[2]—by no greater Blockhead than her who talks to Dr. Myddelton about Boy's Education.

We have had the Pleasure of seeing Mrs. Wyatt who looks very well indeed, and says She left all *safe* at dear Guaynynnog.[3]

Lord Kirkwall is Father of a Family now it seems, he must be grave and wise; it is to speak seriously a very great Blessing, and I rejoyce that his sweet Lady is safe.[4]

Mr. Thelwall and his young Folks afford a pleasing Picture of unexpected Felicity——the Reward of *cheerful* Endurance when Things went not so well.[5]

"Tis not for nothing that we Life pursue"[6] May yours and Mrs. Myddelton's Dear Sir, afford you every Year increasing Consolation prays / Your / Obliged and faithful Servant / H: L: Piozzi.

Text: Osborn Collection. *Address:* Rev: Dr. Myddelton / Gwaynnynog.

1. The Reverend Robert Myddelton was taking his eldest son to Harrow. Robert (1795–1876) was in 1813 to matriculate at Clare College, Cambridge, receiving his B.A. in 1818 and his M.A. in 1822. He was ordained a priest in 1822 and served at Gwaynynog after 1823.
2. Following the victory at the battle of Cannae (B. C. 216), "Hannibal's officers crowded round him with congratulations. . . . The others all advised him, now that he had brought so great a war to a conclusion, to repose himself and to allow his weary soldiers to repose for the remainder of that day and the following night. But Maharbal, the commander of the cavalry, held that no time should be lost. 'Nay,' he cried, 'that you may realize what has been accomplished by this battle, in five days you shall banquet in the Capitol! Follow after; I will precede you with the cavalry, that the Romans may know that you are coming!' To Hannibal the idea was too joyous and too vast for his mind at once to grasp it. And so, while praising Maharbal's goodwill, he declared that he must have time to deliberate regarding his advice. Then said Maharbal, 'In very truth the gods bestow not on the same man all their gifts: you know how to gain a victory, Hannibal; you know not how to use one.' That day's delay is generally believed to have saved the City and the empire." *Livy,* trans. B. O. Foster et al., 13 vols. (London: William Heinemann; New York: G. P. Putnam's Sons; Cambridge, Mass.: Harvard University Press, 1919–51), 22.51.1–4 (vol. 5, pp. 367–69). See also *Plutarch's Lives,* trans. Bernadotte Perrin, 11 vols. (London: William Heinemann; New York: Macmillan, 1914–26), "Fabius Maximus," 17.1 (vol. 3, p. 169). Mistakenly, Plutarch identifies the officer as Barca instead of Maharbal.
3. Godmother to Louisa Dorothea Myddelton in 1804, Mary Burberow had married in 1788 at the church of Saint Mary Magdalen, Richmond, John Wyatt (1764–1856), a barrister of the Inner Temple (1790), a bencher (1825), and attorney general for North Wales. See W. M. Myddelton, *Pedigree of the Family of Myddelton,* p. 53; *GM,* n.s., 1 (1856): 520; "Marriage Register," Saint Mary Magdalen, C.R.O., Surrey.
4. The Kirkwalls' second son, William Edward Fitzmaurice, was born 30 March.
5. The Reverend Edward Thelwall had married Mary Elizabeth, née Baldwyn (d. 1828), of Hoole, Cheshire. They had two daughters and four sons, two of whom had died young: Miles John and Richard. Their other two sons were Edward (1781–1870), destined to become rector of Llanbedr (1834–70), and Bevis (1783–post 1851), who was to attain the rank of commander, Royal Navy. See the "Llanbedr Baptism Records," C.R.O., Clwyd.
6. Dryden, *Aureng-Zebe,* 4.1.

TO LADY WILLIAMS

Bath Thursday
6 [i.e., 4]: April 1805.

My dear Lady Williams is not used to be so silent—and I hear of so many Changes and Chances in our little Vale that it makes me anxious concerning my best Friends and Neighbours.

The Poppyheads and Anodyne Balsam were sent with proper Directions—many *many* Weeks ago; and I have written Two Letters besides, and no Sign of one Scrap from dear Bodylwyddan: but I will *hope* all is pretty tolerable there *too,* or else the News would have reached me.

With regard to public Matters, People were weary of croaking, and of hearing *me* croak, before the really evil Days began: They are coming forward pretty fast now.[1]

East and West Winds all bring us in bad Tydings; and those who first leave the Stage, will soon be best off[2]——Tho' there are some merry Faces yet among us, and our Places of Entertainment have been greatly thronged: But next Week will give People Leisure f<or> Reflexion——perhaps for Repentance:[3] but it is not on *that* Side it seems to affect Folks:[4] There is more Grumbling than Reform, as far as I see.

But I will add no more except our truest Regards to the dear Family which has been ever kind to theirs / and Your Ladyship's Obliged / and Obedient / H: L: Piozzi.

Text: Ry. 2 (1802–6). *Address:* Lady Williams/Bodylwyddan/near St. Asaph. *Postmark:* DENBIGH 224.

---

1. News reports emanating from East and West gave HLP little comfort. Belated accounts from India supplied grim details of British encounters with the insurrectionary forces of Jaswant [also Jeswant; Jeswut Row] Ráo Holkar (d.1811). An illegitimate son of the ruling Tukaji family in Indore, Holkar had seized power in 1797 and thereafter aggressively opposed British interests. Particularly damaging to colonial prestige, in 1804 he turned a battle—albeit against a small force, led by Lieutenant Colonel William Monson (1760–1807)—into a demoralizing rout. In October, despite a "gallant defence" by the British, Holkar was able to deploy infantry and artillery in a nine-day siege of Delhi before being repulsed. Not until 13 November was he decisively defeated by General Gerard Lake [later first Viscount Lake of Delhi and Laswarree] (1744–1808). But news of that success would have been unknown to HLP until the end of April or early May. *The Times,* 12 October, 9 November, 10 December 1804; 4, 15, 19 March 1805; 17, 29 April; 2, 6, 17 May; *AR* 47 (1807): chaps. 16 and 17; *Cambridge Modern History* 9:727–28.

2. Additionally, a confident Bonaparte wrote to King George and, with beguiling reasonableness, declared that peace would be acceptable only under the terms of the treaty of Amiens, and that it would be in the best interest of England to agree to a cessation of hostilities. Lord Mulgrave responded to Talleyrand in February on behalf of his government. The British position was one of skepticism and, even, disbelief. "We find that rumours are now raised . . . that the Invasion of England is entirely abandoned. This, coupled with the pacific overture, confirms us in the suspicion that, finding his open attempts likely to prove impracticable, the enemy now wishes to lull our apprehensions to sleep, to enable him to assault us by a *coup-de-main.* We trust that Government will be sufficiently aware of this, not to relax a tittle in its vigilance. We trust that not a single ship,

nor even a boat less will be employed on the blockading station, and that not a single volunteer will desert his standard" (*The Times*, 5 February 1805; also 21 February; 15, 19, 21 May). Present fears notwithstanding, the possibility of French incursions onto British soil had been imminent since at least 1798. See *Thraliana* 2:989 n.2; HLP to LC, 24 February 1798; 30 July and 29 December 1803; to Ly W, 18 December 1798, n.4; Farington 6:2139. Cf. a vigorously antigallic broadside, *The Bishop of Llandaff's Thoughts on the French Invasion, Originally Addressed to the Clergy of his Diocese* (London, 1798).

3. In 1805 the six days of Easter began with Holy Wednesday on 10 April; Holy Thursday fell on the 11th and Easter Sunday on the 14th.

4. During the current session of parliament, an ailing William Pitt and his party were under continual attack: e.g., the ongoing Roman Catholic Question, the "Additional Force" Bill, Abolition of the Slave Trade, introduction of "Supplemental Taxes"—especially under the opposition leadership of Charles James Fox, Richand Brinsley Sheridan, and William Wilberforce, among others. The rhetoric of debate on both sides was more notable for heat than effect. See Stanhope 4:254–69.

TO THE REVEREND THOMAS SEDGWICK WHALLEY

Bath
24: April 1805.

My dear Mr. Whalley has been always so kind and so Friendly to us, that he will be half sorry I hope that he cannot this Year shew us his beautiful Seat, the much admired Mendip Lodge[1]——but we are called home earlier than Mr. Piozzi expected, and shall if alive set off from here upon the sixth of May, and be at little Brynbella on the Tenth without fail. Have you been at Cheltenham Dear Sir? The Report here is that you were so well there was no need of Water to mend your Health; good News indeed for all your friends.

Apropos to your friends, here is Sir Walter James come; and is watching a sick Aunt.[2] He has a Mind of a Residence in the Vale of Llwydd, and has made me write about Mr. Wynne's House called Plâsnewydd which you have seen advertised in the London Papers:[3] Yet I know not how it is, but my heart does not tell me that Sir Walter James will ever be our Neighbour——as he talks of buying the Estate——and having the house dropt him in—*for nothing:*—a *Price* our old Families will not relish the selling their Mansions for.

The Idea so long ago embodied in your own Mind, seems now to possess that of all Men: our Secret Expedition is sure enough intended for purpose of rescueing Sicily at least from the Tyrant Grasp of Buonaparte:[4] no other Potentate wishes us to save them——*They* resemble the drowning Boy in an old Newspaper, who when held out of Water by his Hair till more Help arrived—complained of the Head-Ach his Companion gave him, instead of returning any Thanks for his Assistance.

Adieu dear Sir present us respectfully to Mrs. Whalley,[5] and believe me with true Attachment Your ever Obliged and Faithful / H: L: Piozzi.

Text: Berg Collection +. *Address:* Rev: Thomas Sedgwick Whalley / Mendip Lodge / Bristol. *Postmark:* BATH.

1. Anna Seward described the renovated Mendip Lodge (Burrington, Somerset) to Mary Powys, 18 October 1804. The one-time cottage, she wrote, has been "transformed and enlarged [by TSW] . . . to an Italian villa, superbly furnished; [he] extended every way his steep and lawny walks; and placed before his house, and to its whole length, a Tuscan veranda. It is the loveliest architectural luxury I ever traversed." The floor-to-ceiling windows on the second floor opened onto the veranda. And on this floor were "two drawing-rooms and a boudoir. The arches of the veranda are light iron-work, painted green. Its breadth allows three to walk abreast. The shelving roof is also painted green, the floor a mosaic sale-cloth; the circular seats at the end have each a large pier-glass, reflecting a part of the beautiful vale below; the covered-sides are fine painted glass. Twenty-four large china jars were filled with autumnal flowers, and one of them placed under every arch. . . . To this villa urbana there is a villa rustica, which is the cook's region. It is placed sixty steps lower and hid amongst trees, a covered-way leading from it to the Arcadian palace above. . . . [Mendip Lodge] looks as if it had dropt from the clouds; and indeed when we stand in the veranda, or look from the bed-room windows on the third floor, we seem suspended between earth and heaven" (*Seward Letters* 6:202–3).

2. Sir Walter's aunt-in-law was Anna Maria Barrett-Lennard, née Pratt (d. 11 August 1806), widow of Thomas (1717–86), seventeenth baron Dacre, who had succeeded to the title in 1755.

3. See, e.g., the *Morning Post*, 15 April 1805: "An eligible Family Residence, called Plâsnewydd. The House is large and commodious, with all necessary attached and detached offices, stables, coach houses, farm yard, an excellent kitchen garden with very good walls covered with fruit trees, hot house, hot walls, ice house, nursery ground, orchard, pleasure grounds well laid out, two corn mills, and sundry farms, situate in the parish of Heullan, in which the house stands, and in the adjoining parishes of Llanyffydd, Llansannan, Llanrhaid, and Nantglyn, in the occupation of respectable tenants at will. The Mansion House is situated in the fertile vale of Clwydd, in an excellent sporting country, commanding an agreeable view of part of the vale, which is terminated by the Irish Sea."

As HLP suspected, Sir Walter James never bought Plâsnewydd.

4. On 1 April 1805 *The Times* wrote "Of the Expedition now about to take its departure" and remarked that "we have, for obvious reasons, always avoided to assign the probable object and destination. Circumstances, however, have disclosed themselves, which can leave little room for doubt, that the Mediterranean is the scene of its intended operation."

Yet by 18 April, according to *The Times*, "The Expedition which has so long been represented as upon the point of sailing from Portsmouth, is still at a stand. The troops, equipage, and every thing necessary have been on board more than a fortnight; but whether waiting for convoy, or favourable winds, they have been detained hitherto."

5. HLP refers to TSW's second wife, Augusta Utica, née Heathcote (d. 1807), wealthy and previously unmarried, who had resided in the Crescent, Bath.

TO THE REVEREND THOMAS SEDGWICK WHALLEY

Bath Monday
29: April 1805.

My dear Mr. Whalley

will now have Two Letters, instead of Two Friends: who would have liked the other way better: but hearing as I told you that Cheltenham Waters were superfluous to your health, we directed our last to Mendip Lodge; and told you how we were called off to Brynbella earlier than We hoped or wished.

Good News from the East must make us some Compensation, and tis pleasing to think that the Toulon Fleet are out, and Nelson at their Heels; We shall perhaps have a good Account of *them* at least.[1]

You will have the Malvern Hills[2] covered with Snow, as Winter seems to take a rough Farewell of us: its Spring will however prove Salubrious to your Constitution;³ and that is the best Thing for your Friends.

Mrs. Siddons seems as if detained in Town chiefly on her Children's Account: her husband has been (as we say) *poorly*——but mends, and will doubtless find his way to your beautiful Eagle's Nest.⁴

Sir Walter James considers Brynbella as *second best* to Mendip in point of Situation—and likes North Wales so well he has a Passion for Mr. Wynne's House there, just over against us.⁵ They are in actual Treaty about it now.⁶

But all this did I say before, and nothing new have I to add—It is no *new* Thing to say how sincerely I have the honour to / be Dear Sir yours and Mrs. / Whalley's Obliged Servant / H: L: Piozzi.

We set out for Wales directly.

Text: Berg Collection +. *Address:* Rev: Thomas Sedgwick Whalley / Cheltenham / Gloucesterhsire.

1. Having escaped the observation of Nelson, the Toulon fleet under the command of Admiral Pierre-Charles-Jean-Baptiste Silvestre de Villeneuve (1763–April 1806, a suicide) sailed to pick up reinforcements in Spain and then moved on to Martinique, where it was to rendezvous with squadrons from Rochefort and Brest. While the Rochefort fleet was able to follow orders, the more important fleet at Brest remained blockaded by Admiral William Cornwallis (1744–1819). According to the plan worked out by Napoleon and his high command: once the several fleets gathered together at Martinique, they were to be led to the Straits of Dover to secure the safe passage of the French army, already embarked at Boulogne on the flotilla. That is, 132,000 men and 15,000 horses were to be transported across the Straits and to invade England.
But the plan failed for two reasons: the Brest fleet was not able to run the blockade; and Villeneuve, in charge of the entire expedition, was to be thwarted by Admiral Sir Robert Calder (1745–1818) on 22 July 1805.
For Villeneuve, see HLP to LC, 4 June 1806, n.3.
2. The Malvern Hills constitute a watering spa on the border of Worcestershire and Herefordshire.
3. At this time TSW was suffering from recurrent bouts of fever and chills. See HLP to PSP, 3 June 1801, n. 2.
4. William Siddons's crippling "lumbago" was more serious than HLP would admit. By the autumn of 1804 he had retired to Bath, able to walk only with crutches. On 11 March 1808, (aged 67) he died unexpectedly. See Roger Manvell, *Sarah Siddons: Portrait of an Actress* (New York: G. P. Putnam's Sons, 1971), p. 284; Yvonne Ffrench, *Mrs. Siddons: Tragic Actress* (London: Derek Verschoyle, 1951), p. 221.
5. See HLP to TSW, 24 April 1805, n. 3.
6. Before the "Treaty" of ownership could be consummated, Robert Watkin Wynn (ca. 1754–1806) had died unexpectedly.

TO MARGARET OWEN

Monday—Rodbrough
6th of May 1805.

With the worst Inn's worst Pen, do I thank Dear Miss Owen for her most friendly Invitation.—We were stepping into the Carriage when your Letter was put into our hands—at Bath—and had I put my Answer into the Post Office there, you would have received it sooner.[1]

We are engaged to dine with the Ladies at Llangollen next Saturday[2]—and on Wednesday Evening—we must be at Shrewsbury of Course.[3] If you are in right earnest—as the Children say, we will drive up to your Door, Luggage and all—but if we are a *monstrous Inconveniency,* get us, kind Lady, Apartments at the Lyon. I would rather be with you of Course, but we *do* plead Invalids and must have the Man and Maid with us.——

You shall promise to return the Visit in Pultney Street, Bath next Winter. Mr. Piozzi has taken a House there from December 1805 to May 1806.[4]

Such a May as we have *now* is melancholy indeed, and I left long Faces in the public Rooms on account of our Fleets being at a Distance So: but we must leave These and many more Topics to discuss when we meet.[5]—If we arrive pretty well (like the Wild Creatures) on next Wensday, You shall shew us to Your Friends on *Thursday,* if it will be any Amusement to them or *you,*[6] / To whom I have been long and truly / an Obliged and faithful Servant / H: L: P.

We shall come only to Tea—not Dinner on Wednesday; but Thursday you shall *see* how we eat and drink, and you will I hope come over to Brynbella too, and partake our Wall Fruit.

This late Spring will save it whole.

Text: National Library of Wales: Brogyntyn MS. 38. *Address:* Miss Owen / at Mr. Eddowes's / Market Place / Shrewsbury.[7]

1. The Piozzis, having spent nearly three months in Bath between March and May 1805, were now returning to Brynbella where they arrived on 10 May (*Thraliana* 2:1069). Both GP and HLP, especially the latter, had hoped the visit to Bath would become an annual event, their health benefiting and their spirits reviving from "Chats," promenades (GP in a Bath chair), and an occasional evening out with friends.

2. The "Ladies of Llangollen" were Lady Eleanor Butler (ca. 1745–1829), sister of John Butler (1740–95), seventeenth earl of Ormonde [I.], and the Honorable Miss Sarah Ponsonby (ca. 1755–1831). The two women, about 1785, left their families and society to live in a cottage in the Vale of Llangollen (about fifteen miles southeast of Denbigh). Despite their vows of semiretirement, they maintained several friendships and occasionally made new ones. Celebrated as independent women, they were sought out by several intellectual ladies, particularly the Blue Stockings, and by curiosity seekers.

LC arranged meetings between the Ladies and the Piozzis, who were invited to visit Llangollen Vale on their travels between Brynbella and Bath. (Twenty-four letters from the Ladies of Llangollen were preserved by HLP; they are now at the John Rylands Library of the University of Manchester.)

LC not only introduced the Piozzis to the Ladies, who dubbed them Orpheus and Eurydice, but he also served as an intermediary. On 13 March 1796 (Ry. 562.31), he wrote to HLP: "Lady Eleanor

Butler and Miss Ponsonby present their best Compliments to Mr. and Mrs. Piozzi, and at any time will be extremely happy to see them at Llangollen Vale.—Mr. P. must bring his Piano Forte. Well *that is Charming. isn't it?*

"In short they said so many handsome things of you, that I should make you too vain was I to repeat them. You could not wish the dearest friends upon earth to speak better of you. . . . Their House is Literally a Cottage—so you must rest at the Inn nocturnally. . . . They have Lived 18 Years in their retreat having never been absent but 2 nights in all that time. They are indeed superior Beings and a happy mixture between mortal and immortality. I have a favour to beg of you.—tis this. They cannot any where get the Florence Miscellany.—May I give them mine? The Book in their Custody would meet with an Apotheosis."

3. The Piozzis planned a short visit to Margaret "Peggy" Owen. A distant relative of HLT and a trustworthy friend, she was the daughter of Lewys Owen (1696–1746) and Elizabeth, née Lyster, of Mongomeryshire, and Moynes Court, Monmouthshire.

Margaret Owen's father had been a Fellow of All Souls College; rector of Barking, Essex (1735–46), and of Wexham, Buckinghamshire (1742–46).

Margaret Owen had been born at Barking and was baptized there on 28 November 1742. Her mother died ca. 1756–58. Following the death of her father, she and her neurotic brother, John Owen (1741–1823), went to live with their maternal aunt, Susanna Lyster, in Shrewsbury.

Margaret Owen became part of the Johnson circle, having been introduced to its members by HLT. She died unmarried at Shrewsbury on 25 October 1816.

No jealousy existed between the two women. HLT, e.g., when thinking herself seriously ill, expected Margaret Owen to become the second wife of HT. The expectation, as we have seen, never became fact. See "The Children's Book," in Hyde, *The Thrales of Streatham Park*, p. 175; also HLP to Q, 17 August [1784], n. 9.

4. The Piozzis spent three separate winters and springs in Bath: from January 1805 to May or June 1805. In this same year "they went to Abergeley & Prestatyn . . . but could not stay ten Days at either: Mr Piozzi's sudden Seizure with Gout all over him drove us from ye last-named Place in August, & when we came home he was very bad indeed—"; from 1 December 1805 to 7 March 1806 they were again in their favorite house on Pulteney Street, Bath; and from December 1806 to June 1807—again in Bath. They rejoiced in the good weather and a plentiful harvest—"a quiet Autumn—so far; and Mr Piozzi [temporarily free] from Gout; his Hands feet & Voice are however wholly lost, & he is frighted at missing the Accustomed Fit of agonizing Pain, lest *worse*, that is more *dangerous* Consequences should be brought on." By 12 June 1807 the Piozzis were "once more returned from Bath & London, to lay our Bones quietly down at Brynbella." See *Thraliana* 2: 1065–67; 1070, n. 2; 1081.

5. The newspapers available to HLP were filled with accounts of British activities in remote places. Probably the most satisfying for jingoistic tastes was that of an engagement during the previous summer between a convoy of merchantmen, identified as the "China Fleet," and a French squadron commanded by Admiral Linois. The confrontation was glorified by the British as a triumphant "demonstration of gallantry and judgment. . . . That a small number of heavy laden merchantmen [in the vicinity of Batavia], carrying a comparatively light artillery should defeat and compel to flight a force consisting of one ship of the line, two heavy frigates, a corvette, and a brig, could scarcely have been deemed possible by any one, who was ignorant of what had been compassed by British valour. . . . the result of the affair is not less honourable to British valour, than it is disgraceful to the professional character of Linois. It is difficult to determine whether his cowardice or incapacity was most conspicuous" (*The Times*, 9 August 1804).

Belatedly, HLP learned also that merchantmen (or Indiamen) had arrived at Canton under naval escort and that an outward-bound China fleet had sailed from English ports in the spring of 1804. Currently, British vessels were in both Canton and Madras with orders to embark several regiments for destinations in the West Indies. Further reports confirmed naval support of military actions in India during the autumn and winter of 1804; and they described new sea engagements with Linois. See *The Times*, 18, 19 and 22 March 1805.

6. HLP's willingness to be displayed before Margaret Owen's friends is typical of her social self-assurance and her ability to engage in diverse and witty conversation.

7. Probably Joshua Eddowes (1724–1811), printer and bookseller at Shrewsbury. In 1788 he was joined in partnership by his son William (1754–1833). Together they published the *Salopian Journal*, the major newspaper of the county.

TO ISABELLA HAMILTON

> Brynbella, near Denbigh, N. Wales,
> Monday, 13th May 1805.

That my dear Miss Hamilton should wish to hear in our School Boy Phrase that I arrived Safe, is so good a thing for *me*, I hasten to tell it her, remembering the comfortable hope of seeing I received yours by return of Post.[1] We lingered on the Road visiting Miss Owen at Shrewsbury, and after that spending two or three Days with the Ladies of Llangollen Vale: and are now just sate down in our pretty house looking how the Sun sets in the Irish Sea, and thinking what charming Friends we have gained from the opposing Shore. It w^d not please me tho' that you should like my Letters as well as you do my Conversation. Doctor Johnson said of some Female Acquaintance who wrote agreeably. 'Now,' says he, if 'I were married to that Woman I would always live 200 Miles away from her, and make her write to me twice o'Week.'[2] But far from this, I am feeling awkward that instead of walking down the Hill only to walk up it again, as I shall surely do early to morrow Morning——I cannot walk to No. 41 and gain so many new and delightful Ideas——there w^d be no Need of Amusement to the Eyes——no desire of listening even to Woods full of Birds, while those Voices hung in one's Ear. Well! My Lord Chesterfield says the more Tastes people cultivate, the better for them;[3] I shall set about weaning my Calves, watching my young Plantations, reading with the Curate, and keeping clear of Complaints that may make it necessary to consult with the Apothecary. A little Scandal now and then with a female Neighbour will add to the Charms of rustic life.

> And thus do We
> By aid of Sugar sweeten Tea.[4]

but I had forgotten the Hour when Postman calls for the Brynbella Bag: oh may I once be able to teach my dear Miss Hamilton *that Hour!* 'tis all she will be able to learn from her's and her charming sister's[5] and her dear Mama's / Obliged and faithful servant / H: L: Piozzi.

Mr. Piozzi would have me stop the Man to scrawl his best Respects.

Text: Broadley, pp. 53–54. *Address:* Miss Hamilton, 41 Pulteney Street, Bath.

1. Isabella Hamilton (1777–1845) lived at 41 Pulteney Street, Bath, when the Piozzis rented a house in the same street during their 1805 spring holiday. Born in Armagh, Miss Hamilton was the younger daughter of Isabella, née Wood (1750–1834), who in 1772 had married Hugh Hamilton (1729–1805), bishop of Ossory (1799–1805). The Hamiltons had five sons and two daughters.
2. On 16 January 1816, HLP told JF that SJ's remark was directed against Elizabeth Abigail, née Cotton (1713–77), wife of Lynch Salusbury Cotton (ca. 1705–75), fourth baronet of Combermere (1748); M.P. for Denbighshire (1749–74), and HLP's uncle.
For the remark itself (with minor changes), see *Letters* 1:301–2 (HLT to SJ, 9 August 1775).
3. Chesterfield, in his letters to his son, treats taste, grace, and manners as though they were synonymous. See, e.g., in *The Letters of Philip Dormer Stanhope, 4th Earl of Chesterfield*, ed. Bonamy Dobrée, 6 vols. (London: Eyre and Spottiswoode; New York: Viking, 1932), 2:599; 4:1707.

4. Matthew Green, *The Spleen*, in Dodsley 1:129: "And thus in modish manner we / In aid of sugar sweeten tea."

5. Isabella Hamilton's sister was Frances (1775–1809), who had married in 1802 Michael Dodgson Madden (1777–1809) of county Kilkenny. A graduate of Trinity College, Dublin, he had been ordained a priest in the Church of Ireland on 24 August 1802 and served as vicar choral (chancellor) of Saint Canices (1801–3), chancellor of Ossory (1805–8). See the Reverend James B. Leslie, *Ossory Clergy and Parishes* (Enniskillen, 1933), pp. 87–88.

TO THE REVEREND LEONARD CHAPPELOW

Brynbella Thursday
23: May 1805.

We left the dear Ladies chearful, and well; and as usual well-informed of all that passes in the living world: every Trifling Circumstance had outrun me to Llangollen, which told us a Thousand Things we knew not till we called there. Of *your* Welfare Dear Sir we are ever most glad to be assured, and I thought it was *your* Fault not *mine,* that our Correspondence stagnated so——It shall flow brisker in future, notwithstanding these vile Ninepences, which cannot be avoided here, because the Bishop does not live among us as his Predecessor did;[1] and because Lord Kirkwall makes his Residence upon a Mile Stone: he is always on the high Road I think—not so his Lady—who has been confined with a Rheumatic Fever, and Deposit of Disease in her Leg, ever since the *last* Boy was born.[2]

Sorrows in private Life—and evil Expectancies with regard to public Affairs! I'm sorry Mr. Gillon looks serious, but no great harm will happen Westward—only a few piratical Depredations——and our kind Friends at home here, have scarcely even yet been able so to spread a Spirit of Discontent as to prepare us *this* Year for Invasion.[3] Buonaparte—like the Catholics of Ireland—must wait a while; it will do sometime, but it won't do yet.[4] London will see some more Masquerades first—more Young Rosciuses,—perhaps more Illuminations; I half hope for a Naval Victory gained by Lord Nelson, tho' the wisest People *do* wear the longest Faces.[5]

Mr. Piozzi proceeds as usual from sharp Pain to Convalescence, so on to Recovery; and *thence*——to sharp Pain again——as the Almanack used to say War begets Poverty,—Poverty Peace——Then grow Contentions and Quarrels Increase.

Here is a cruel Continuation of this vile Easterly Wind, my Trees are devouring with Caterpillars, and Winter lingering chills the Lap of May——but says dear Mr. Chappelow—"if People *will* live in Greenland" &c.

Well! really we have had a Greenland Winter for Tediousness, it began early in November and is scarce over now—not an Oak leaf to shade a King.[6] And Cecilia Mostyn I believe has found the Welsh Mountains dismal enough, for eleven Months constant Residence; without Carriage to drive, or Horse (except a blind and lame one) to ride on——The Husband however staid with her six or seven Weeks to *set her in*——and then to Bath and London—as I hear.

You say nothing of Lord Bradford; his charming Lady is always in Preparation for Heaven I know, but will I hope long remain on this Side the River that must be passed first——Of his Mama[7] I heard nothing at Bath, and conclude her Health reestablished for that reason. Doctor Thackeray is married and happy, except for this vile Lawsuit between his Brother and the College——a Case I understand not a Word of;—*You* can tell.[8] Are there any new Books come out worth buying? Mr. Southey's call upon his Readers in the First Page attracted Notice at Bath, but we left the Place before *Madoc* had been cut open and read by any one.[9] You are the Poet of *Nature*——did You like his *Thalaba?*[10] Write soon Dear Sir, You scarce can think how welcome Your kind Letters are to my Master and his H: L: P.

If you ever stumble on the Miss Thrales, tell how they look this Season.

If you see Dear Mr. Gillon coax him to write, for we are bursting in Ignorance[11] of many Things desirable to be known.

Text: Ry. 561.131. *Address:* Rev: Mr. Chappelow / No. 12 or 13 / Hill Street / Berkeley Square / London. *Postmark:* DENBIGH 224 May 25 1805.

1. Samuel Horsley (1733–1806), bishop of St. Asaph (1802–6). See HLP to Q, 7 November 1796, n. 14. Bishop Horsley's predecessor was Lewis Bagot (1740–1802).
2. Lady Kirkwall's second son was William Edward Fitzmaurice (born on 30 March 1805). On 4 May 1803, she had given birth to Thomas John. See HLP to PSP, 5 November 1803, n. 6.
3. John Gillon, who owned property in Dominica, worried about the military buildup of the French in the West Indies and, hence, about the area's instability. Thus, in the April issue of GM 75, pt. 1 (1805): 373, there was the threatening news "that a French squadron, consisting of five sail of the line (one a three decker), three frigates, and two brigs, had arrived at Martinique . . . and [21 February] landed 3000 troops in Prince Rupert's Bay." At the same time, however, "intelligence . . . [had] been received from Demarara, which announce[d] the retreat of the French from Dominica."
4. Roman Catholic activists, who sought increased political emancipation for their constituents, met several times in Dublin under the leadership of Arthur James Plunkett, eighth earl of Fingal (I., 1793). They voted to send a deputation of five to London with a petition for both houses of Parliament.
On 12 March the Irish deputies met Pitt, who refused to present their petition. They then appealed to Fox, who brought their petition to the Commons on 25 March, while Lord Grenville presented it on the same day to the Lords.
On 10 May, "Lord Grenville in the Peers, as on the 13th Mr. Fox in the Commons, moved to consider the petition so presented." After lengthy debate, "the division gave, including proxies, only 49 Peers in favour of the motion, and 178 against it."
The debate in the Commons lasted two nights. "Dividing at past four in the morning," those for Fox's motion were outnumbered almost three to one. See Stanhope 4:297–303.
5. Admiral Nelson planned to forestall Bonaparte's desire to gain control of the Channel by bringing into it the entire naval power of France and Spain. In late March or early April Nelson positioned his fleet west of Sicily and refused to move until he knew the precise location of the combined enemy fleet. By 16 April he knew that it had been sighted off Cape Gata. Although he was delayed by contrary winds, he managed to reach Gibraltar about 6 May. He pursued the French–Spanish fleet to Barbados, but it had already sailed to the West Indies, and thence back to Europe.
6. A half–serious comment about King Charles II's attempted refuge (1651) in an oak tree near Boscobel House, Salop. See HLP to LC, 31 March 1799, n. 11.
7. For dowager Lady Bradford, see HLP to LC, 23 August 1794, n. 4.
8. That is, Martin Thackeray (1783–1864), who in 1804 became a fellow of King's College, Cambridge, dean (1815–26), and vice provost (1826–34). He was involved not in a lawsuit but in a quarrel. "It is usual on granting a College Lease to take a fine from the tenant. One year there was a very

large one coming in of several thousand pounds. It was customary to divide such gains amongst the Society in certain proportions." But Martin Thackeray demurred, arguing "that these sums should be funded for the general benefit of the College." He carried his point against threats of legal suit. See Pryme and Bayne, *Memorials of the Thackeray Family*, p. 136.

9. In the dedication of *Madoc* to Charles Watkin Williams-Wynn (1775–1850), Robert Southey (1774–1843) called upon his readers:

> Come, listen to a tale of times of old!
> Come, for ye know me! I am he who sung
> The Maid of Arc; and I am he who framed
> Of Thalaba the wild and wonderous song.
> Come, listen to my lay, and ye shall hear
> How Madoc from the shores of Britain spread
> The adventurous sail, explored the ocean paths,
> And quelled barbarian power, and overthrew
> The bloody altars of idolatry,
> And planted in its fanes triumphantly
> The Cross of Christ. Come, listen to my lay!

10. *Thalaba the Destroyer* was published in 1801.
11. *Hamlet*; 1.4.46.

TO HESTER MARIA THRALE

Prestatyn[1]
23: July 1805.

From this savage Place—which Mr. Piozzi says *deve esser l'ultimo ch'Iddio ha creato*;[2] do I thank my dearest Girl for her Letter: if he had not been kind enough to leave his Hay and his Workmen, his Business and his Comforts to bring me Hither *now*, my Dips would have been lost, for He feels sure that Gout is coming, and we cannot expect it in Reason to stay away much longer. You was a wise Child not to direct to Lord Kirkwall; he is fishing in Water 3 Inches deep somewhere behind these Mountains, which whilst I write are reechoing to a ThunderStorm, very grand:—and I begin to think that *wherever* and *whenever* Nature puts on her noblest Appearance—her *Noblest* Work—a poor and honest Man makes his Meanest Figure. Mrs. Smyth shall not be blamed for hoping her Son's Recovery;[3] if his Disorder is not a cancer or a pulmonary Consumption brought on by what oldfashioned People call *Vice* and new fashioned People call *Dissipation* he *may* Recover.——Make my best Compliments and Respect to her with the Sincerest Wishes I can form for her *own* Health so likely to suffer from Affliction. Poor Mr. Wynn of Plasnewydd is said to be dying of a broken Heart at 41 Years old——his Sons have grieved him more by their Conduct than he *could* have grieved at their Loss.[4] The 1st went to School, and at 17 years old run away with his Master's Daughter of 35 Years old. The 2d. married at Liverpool—not a Mopsqueezer, but a Wench with whom Mopsqueezers will not associate;[5]—and to these Plagues when he has added that of owing 84000£ which his Estate would not quite discharge—could he get it sold—I see nothing so likely as his own Death from distress of Mind. Ainsi va le Monde: By the Time he has fretted himself into the Grave the last young Bridegroom not yet

18 years old will possibly return rich from India and purchase the Freedom of the Family.[6]

Sir Robert Salusbury is the Great Grandson of Colonel William Salusbury half Brother to my Father's Grandfather—and tho' very distant—as you see—is my Heir at Law;[7] had I never had Husbands and Children, and Power over my own Estate. My Father's Grandfather—married Bridget Percival daughter to Lord Egmont,[8] and *his* Son married Lucy Salusbury his own first Cousin[9]—but The Colonel, Issue of a second Marriage married meanly himself, and his Wife—*(if Wife)*—lay in distressfully in the Camp, where the Duke of Norfolk hearing their Situation took pity and took Charge of the Boy, who was christened *Norfolk Salusbury* and his Grace held him over the Font.[10] This Man married Jane Thelwall of Plas ŷ Ward—and his Son Thelwall Salusbury was Vicar at Offley—or his Grandson I am not sure which.[11] But there was I believe a second Norfolk Salusbury of whom little is known, for the family ran down to Misery apace, and the present Sir Robert's Mother was a rustic Wench known only by the Name of Gwendolen, and Cecy's Mother in Law Mrs. Wynn says they used to see her riding on Sacks to Denbigh Market when they were Children and that She was eminent for personal Beauty. Meanwhile my own Father and Uncle although apparently ashamed of his Progeny, were proud of their great great half Uncle old William; who having fought with King William in his Babydays, defending Holland from Louis Quatorze's Incroachments—was encouraged by the Prince to return with him to England, and offered a Regiment—but when he found *that* favour was to be purchased by acknowledgement of any other Sovereign during King James's Lifetime, he refused: and being unable to perswade his own Family to receive him, set out once more upon a Life of Adventure, which no doubt ended the sooner for all these Sorrows.[12]

Such and *not worse* is the Origin of Sir Robert Salusbury who has been persuaded I hear to send me my Father's Picture as a Present, but I have not yet received His Favours. I hear that his Son by Miss Van, a Lady of good Birth and Name is an exemplary Person;[13] but that He himself is intolerably proud and haughty—of all which I shall know *more too soon*.[14]—He found my Father's Picture at Offley; but strange to tell, That of my Uncle (Master of the House) is *lost*: altho a full Length in his Judge's Robes—by Hudson[15]—and his first Wife Miss Penrice—and her Father Old Sir Henry[16]—*all lost*—burned I suppose by the Honorable Mrs. King my Uncle's second Lady.—

Enough of old Friends.—Let me now say something of new Acquaintances, among whom, none are more valuable to me than those charming Miss Hamiltons of Bath.[17] I begged News from Isabella last Week. "News (She replies) I take to imply *Births, Deaths, Marriages* and *Scandal*—Take them all four in one Sentence. Miss < > has brought a *Child*, The Baby *died;* The Mother *marries* its Papa, who settles 4000£ o'Year on her;——and if this is not *Scandal* why 'tis Truth: and that's better." What say you to My Miss Hamilton?

The Account you transmit to me of the Opera and Amateur Concert Insolence, is wholly *new,* and very, *very* shocking. Porteus behaves like an Angel to stand all this ridicule of a World which I though he had respected more, but he is going to that where the Laugh is all on *his Side*.[18] Farewell! Sophia's little portable

Pens are nice things for squeezing much into a small Compass.—She sent me a Boxfull by Mrs. Wynn[19] and I sent her this Epigram in Exchange.

> To give my lovely Girl delight
> What with her Present must I write?
> What Character assume?
> A plodding Scholar best they'll fit;
> Since Foes to *feather*-headed Wit
> Are Pens without a *Plume*.[20]

Farewell! and write sometimes to your Exiled and Affectionate Mother / H: L: Piozzi.

I am out of the way of hearing *any* thing but by Charitable Subscribers.

You are a sly Rogue about these old Chaldaic Characters and will own nothing——but I will try to learn 'em in 'Spite of you.

Direct as usual tho' we are at this Place, the People come over every two or three Days with Letters &c. Mr. P. sends best remembrances.

Text: Bowood Collection. *Address:* Miss Thrale / Heath House / near Bristol. *Postmark:* ST ASAPH.

1. A popular bathing resort in Flintshire, North Wales.
2. ["This savage Place] must be the last that God has created."
3. Jane Smyth, née Whitchurch (1739–1819), and her husband Thomas (d. 1800) had two sons: Hugh (1772–1824), third baronet (1802), who inherited the title and estate of Ashton Court, Somerset, from his uncle Sir John Hugh Smyth (ca. 1735–1802), second baronet (1783). Upon the death of Sir Hugh in 1824, his younger brother John (1776–1849) became fourth baronet. The identity of the ailing son cannot be determined from the epistolary context. See the "Ashton Court Papers, Whitchurch Papers," in the City Record Office, Bristol; see also HLP to Q [23 May 1801], n. 14; [31 December 1804], n. 6.

   According to the Bristol archives, "the Smyths were the most prominent gentry family in the Bristol area between the seventeenth and nineteenth centuries."
4. Robert Watkin Wynn, or Wynne, and his wife Anne Sobieski, née Dod (d. 1818), had two daughters as well as five sons: Robert, who died young; John (1778–1836); Julius (d. 1832); Watkin (1786–1815, killed at Waterloo); Charles (d. 1851). See J. Y. Lloyd, *The History of the Princes*, 6:81–82; HLP to Q, 27 April 1796, n. 2.
5. The second but eldest surviving son of Robert Watkin Wynn was John (n. 4 above). For his elopement and unhappy marriage to Sarah Anne Parr (1772–1810), see HLP to LC, 1 February 1798, n. 8; also Warren Derry, *Dr. Parr A Portrait of the Whig Dr. Johnson* (Oxford: Clarendon Press, 1966), pp. 200–5, 249–50, 280–83, 344–46.

   For "mopsqueezer, a maid servant," see Grose, *A Classical Dictionary of the Vulgar Tongue* (1785).
6. Robert Watkin Wynn managed to retain his Garthmeilo estate, Merionethshire, that passed on to his son John. But Plasnewydd had to be sold to Richard Heaton (b. 1738) of Lleweny (or Lleweni; Llyweni Green) as a bequest to the latter's son, John Heaton (1787–1855). The estate was renamed Plas Heaton.

   For a description of Plasnewydd, see HLP to TSW, 24 April, 1805, n. 3.

   The prodigal son in India was either Watkin Wynn, aged seventeen, or Charles. Both are identified as minors in their father's will: P.R.O., Prob. 11/1453/974, proved 22 December 1806.
7. For Colonel William Salusbury (or Salesbury, d. ca. 1660) of Bachymbyd, halfway between Ruthin and Denbigh, see HLP to the *Monthly Mirror*, 17 June 1798, n. 18. In fact, Sir Robert Salusbury was the "Great Grandson" not of Colonel William but of Colonel Thomas (d. 1700).

   Sir Robert Salusbury (1756–1817) is identified with Cotton Hall and Llanwern, Monmouthshire.
8. We find no genealogical evidence that a Bridget Percival was HLS's great grandmother.

   In the interest of placing a member of her family in the peerage, she probably confused Bridget

Perceval (d. 1826), wife of John (1767–1835), fourth earl of Egmont, with Anne, the only daughter and heiress of Thomas Perceval, North Weston, Somerset. The widow of Evan Lloyd, Anne married Colonel Thomas Salusbury (d. 1700).

Colonel Salusbury had a brother, John, who married Mary Pennant of Bychton. One of their nine daughters was Lucy, née Salusbury (ca. 1667–1745), destined to become HLS's grandmother (n. 9). See HLP's "Harvard Piozziana," vol. 1.

9. Thomas Salusbury (d. 1714) married his cousin Lucy Salusbury. They became the parents of HLS's father John (1707–62) and her uncle Sir Thomas (1708–73), a judge of the Admiralty, for whom see HLP to SL, 23 April [1787], n. 3.

John Salusbury had been an administrative official of Nova Scotia in 1749 and again in 1752. See HLP to SL, 21 September 1785, n. 4.

10. The younger son of Colonel Thomas Salusbury (d. 1700), i.e., HLS's great uncle, was Norfolk (d. 1736), of Plas ŷ Ward, Ruthin, Denbighshire. He had married Elizabeth, née Williams (of Tynewydd, Denbighshire.

Apparently HLP refers to Thomas Howard (1683–1732), thirteenth duke of Norfolk (1701), although we cannot confirm the identification.

11. An elder son of Norfolk Salusbury was Robert (d. 1776) of Cotton Hall, Denbighshire. Robert married Gwendolen, née Davis (d. 1790), of Merionethshire. The biographical details of Norfolk's younger son, Thelwall, are elusive.

For the intricate Salusbury genealogy, we are indebted to William James Smith, ed. *Calendar of Salusbury Correspondence 1553–circa 1700*, tables 1–3 (Cardiff: University of Wales Press, 1954); J. Y. Lloyd, vol. 4; Henry Cotton Salusbury and Stephen Gibbon, *The Salusburies of Lleweni* (undated and unpaginated); the "Salusbury Pedigree" (ca. 1769), in an unknown hand (Ry. 530.3); Burke's *Landed Gentry* (1937); *Thraliana* 1:313–14 and n. 6.

12. Since Colonel William Salusbury died in 1660 and William (later William III of England) was born in 1650, HLP's claim to royal patronage is questionable. Nevertheless, it underscores the Salusbury allegiance to the Stuarts, an allegiance evident in William Salusbury's strenuous, if futile, effort to hold Denbigh Castle for Charles I and to prevent it from falling to the parliamentarians, as it did in October 1646.

13. On 16 May 1780 Sir Robert had married Catherine Van (or Vanne) of Llanwern, Monmouthshire. (She died in 1836.) They had three sons and two daughters: Thomas Robert (1783–1835), second baronet; the Reverend Charles John (1792–1868), third and last baronet; Henry Vanne. The daughters were Sarah Katherine and Charlotte Gwendolen (d. 1861).

14. The purpose of this genealogical outline was to identify Lady Salusbury's heirs—Sir Robert Salusbury and his brother, the Reverend Lynch Salusbury (later Burroughs) of Offley, Hertfordshire—for Q.

HLP in a previous letter to Q (dated "Solstice just ended 1805") had tried—without apparent success—to identify the heirs of Lady Salusbury.

"Sir Robert Salusbury is the very Man to whom my Uncle at his second Lady's Instigation, left Offley Place;—entailing it forward to many Collateral Branches of my Family, and to some People *no way* related to us at all; after which (says the Will) let it go to the right Heir. That right Heir [HLP] can never now within the Possibility of Things expect to enjoy it. Sir Robert Salusbury's eldest Son [Thomas Robert, now twenty-two] is come to Age, and has joined his Father in cutting the Entail off; so it fell to the Baronet's fair and free Disposal.—He with his Son's Approbation has therefore sold the same—*my* once dearly loved Hertfordshire Estate: and Sold it to *his own Brother,* who married a Miss [Jane] *Offley* with 15000£ Fortune,—and who inherits Lady Salusbury—my Uncle's Widow's enormous Legacies of House, Land, Jewels, Money &c. to the Amount of 20000£.—*That* Gentleman has taken I am told the Name of Burrows in honour of his Friend and Testatrix" (Bowood Collection).

15. Thomas Hudson (1701–79), a popular portrait artist of the day, specialized in depictions of the gentry.

16. For Anna Maria Penrice (1715–59), the first wife of Sir Thomas Salusbury (d. 1773), and her father Sir Henry Penrice (1677–1752), see HLP to the *Monthly Mirror*, 17 June 1798, n. 7.

17. See HLP to Isabella Hamilton, 13 May 1805, n. 1.

18. Beilby Porteus (1731–1809), awarded the B.A. degree in 1752 from Christ's College, Cambridge, was ordained deacon and priest in 1757. In 1776 he became bishop of Chester and in 1787 bishop of London. See *GM* 79, pt. 1 (1809): 485–86; pt. 2: 606, 675, 836–37.

HLP had first become interested in Bishop Porteus because of his commitment to improving the condition of slaves in the West Indies. As bishop of London he supported the evangelical party of the Anglican Church and befriended Hannah More during the Blagdon controversy. He had long

been the target of pamphleteers for different reasons, but in 1805 he was attacked for his opposition to the recently defeated Catholic Emancipation Bill.
    19. Anna Maria Wynn, née Meredith (d. 1828), wife of (1) John Mostyn of Segroid; (2) Major Edward Watkin Wynn (1755–1796) of Llewessog. See HLP to John Meredith Mostyn, 22 July 1795.
    20. *Thraliana* 2:1065.

TO LADY WILLIAMS AND ELEANOR WILLIAMS

Prestatyn
July 26: 1805.

How good is my dearest Lady Williams to remember her poor Friends at Prestatyn! Mr. Piozzi's Leg on the Sopha which we brought on purpose for it[1]——and his 21 Years old *Wife* bathing diligently every day to recruit her Spirits, Appetite and Strength which began Sensibly to feel the Wear and Tear of Time.

I believe in my heart that a positive Disease—such as dear Mrs. Williams or such as my Husband have laboured under for ten Years—contributes less to the shortening Life than does the mere *Living on*—a little worse and a little weaker every Day.—

She must not think of her Poppyheads except to use them when convenient, and the longer She can do without—the better: It is a foolish Measure *to take the Hill too soon* as Drivers say.[2] Here is wretched Weather—but very fine Corn: and the highest Tides ever known are expected—they are exceeding high now.

We have often kept our Wedding Day [23–25 July] with the rich, we are keeping it among the Poor here at Prestatyn; for 'tis a miserable Place sure,[3] and no Fish: no, not a Net, nor a Notion of using one, as in other little Villages by the Seaside: but we have good Machines for bathing, which are wanting at Abergeley.[4]

Is not Sir John Williams quite wearied with Expectation of News from Admiral Nelson?[5] I much fear he has been sent upon a Sleeve-less Errand,[6] and led out of his Way by every American he met——*All Friends to these charming French!*[7]

Adieu dear Ladies! and divert yourselves with your Buildings and think of your sweet Family, for whom you plunge thus into Brick and Mortar.[8]—Present us ever kindly to every Branch of it and believe me most faithfully Yours / H: L: Piozzi.

Text: Ry. 2 (1802–6).

    1. GP suffered from recurrent bouts of gout. From 1797 onward there was annually at least one critical attack that lamed legs, hands, and feet. By the spring of 1803 HLP acknowledged that GP was permanently crippled, able to move about only when he was in "a Bath rolling Chair." As of 1805 he had become a total invalid.
    2. Eleanor Williams, née Hughes (1755–1810), of Plas yn Rhoscolyn, Anglesey, had married Hugh Williams (1741–68), of Ty Fry, Anglesey. She became fatally ill in the early winter of 1808, suffering from a slowly developing cancer of the throat. She died at Bodelwyddan on 13 May 1810. (For her obituary, see the *North Wales Gazette*, 17 May 1810.)
    Poppyheads were the chief substance of an addictive opiate to deaden pain.

3. Ready access to the fine, sandy beaches of the Irish Sea, about six miles northeast of St. Asaph, attracted HLP to Prestatyn. But she was also, perhaps snobbishly, aware that the economy of this small Flintshire community was heavily dependent on the labors of the natives who worked in the productive lead mines of Talargoch. See also HLP's earlier comments on "melancholy . . . very romantic Prestatyn" (*Thraliana* 2:1028).

4. When SJ, accompanied by the Thrales and Q, traveled through North Wales in the summer of 1774, they visited Abergele (18 August). It was a small market town and watering place in north Denbighshire. HLP did not record her impressions, but SJ contemptuosly described Abergele as "a mean town, in which little but Welsh is spoken, and Divine Service is seldom performed in English."

Situated between Chester and Bangor, about one mile from the seashore, the town in 1774 consisted of a single long street, its population about 1,300 inhabitants, most of them engaged in mining and agriculture. It was established during the reign of Henry VIII.

See J. O. Halliwell-Phillips, *Notes of Family Excursions in North Wales:* printed for the author [1860], pp. 43–48; Thomas Roscoe, *Wanderings and Excursions in North Wales.* London: Henry G. Bohn [1836], 1853, pp. 57–58; *Boswell's Johnson* 5:446.

5. HLP refers to Admiral Nelson's inability to sight the Toulon fleet which, although sailing circuitously as far as the West Indies, planned an invasion of England.

6. An obsolete term meaning *futile* or *useless*.

7. In the spring of 1805 English newspapers often reported the arrival of French naval squadrons in the West Indies, where they were within easy range of the United States. Moreover, the English ministry was antiAmerican, recognizing the emergence of a new mercantile rival in the former colonies; a power able to negotiate diplomatically with the French, as in 1803; a country hospitable to England's traitors. E. g., as recently as June, HLP had read a "letter from Paris," which stated that "'many of the United Irish are quitting this country for America'" (*GM* 75, pt. 1 [1805]: 569).

8. In 1791 John Williams (1761–1830) married Margaret, née Williams (1768–1835) of Ty Fry, Anglesey. In 1798 he was created a baronet.

Situated about four miles from St Asaph, Bodelwyddan was architecturally renowned in the area. The mansion, under the ownership of Sir John Williams, was much enlarged and its former Grecian symmetry converted into a showplace that was medieval in appearance. The name signified "the abode of the chieftain." Built on an elevation, the castle-like building afforded from its turrets an extensive view of the sea and the vale of Clywd. The surrounding land, well stocked with deer, was heavily wooded and profuse with gardens and hothouses. As a public attraction, the estate had at one time admitted "respectable strangers on prescribed days." Access to the romanticized property was through a massive Gothic archway. The estate had been purchased from an ancient family named Humphreys by Sir William Williams (1634–1700), speaker of the House of Commons in 1680 and 1681. Subsequently, he was solicitor-general (knighted in 1687) and M. P. for Beaumaris (1689, 1695). See Roscoe, p. 57; *C. Black's Picturesque Guide to North Wales*, 19th ed. Edinburgh: Adam and Charles Black, 1886, p. 142.

TO THE REVEREND ROBERT GRAY

Brynbella
1st: August 1805.

A reading lady at Bath, not a writing lady,[1] told me that she opened an old book one day at an old friend's house, and found in it by mere accident whole pages of your predecessor Paley's Theology, particularly the passage about *finding a watch*.[2] She could not tell me the title of the book, but thought it was a *gentleman's religion* she said, or the religion of a *gentleman*, or some such title, but people, coming in, she was shy of further examination.[3] Can you guess what she *did* mean? I will answer for her veracity, *that* I would; and read nothing else but my Bible for as long as I have to live, unless it was your *Key*,[4] which first put such a thought into my head. My comfort is that *you* are young enough to be useful; and that every day sets you in some place whence you may more easily and with more power, as more dignity, dispense knowledge and practise virtue.[5]

Hannah More's hints for the education of a young princess is I fear but little read and tasted,[6] though a beautiful book; and attracts me oftener to open it (at least seldomer to shut it) than Mr. Roscoe's Leo X.[7] If I were but one dozen years younger than I am, I would learn Hebrew.[8]

Text: Hayward 2:264–65.

1. A whimsical allusion to an unidentified Bath acquaintance. The implication is that HLP's friends at Bath are learned ladies, whether readers or writers. The letter is in part ironic, since according to William Paley (1743–1805), nothing happens by accident, for that would be a violation of the divine plan. Yet the naive "reading lady" discovered Paley's *Natural Theology* and the pertinent page references quite by chance. Despite the modest comedy evident in the letter, HLP accepted as reasonable the premise of Paley's work.
2. The "reading lady" gave the wrong title to Paley's last book, *Natural Theology: or Evidences of the Existence and Attributes of the Deity, collected from the Appearances of Nature* (London: R. Faulder, 1802), especially chaps. 1, 2, 5. In this work, using the argument from design, Paley—then rector of Bishopwearmouth—hypothesized the discovery of a watch, its form and function. He concluded "that the watch must have had a maker; that there must have existed, at some time and at some place or other, an artificer or artificers who formed it for the purpose. . . . There cannot be a design without a designer; a contrivance without a contriver; order without choice; arrangement, without any thing capable of arranging."
3. The "reading lady" confused Paley's title and work with that of Edward Synge (1659–1741), archbishop of Tuam: *A Gentleman's Religion: In three Parts. The 1st contains the Principles of Natural Religion. The 2d. and 3d. the Doctrines of Christianity both as to Faith and Practice* (London: A. and J. Churchill, 1693–98).
4. For *A Key to the Old Testament and Apocrypha,* see HLP to Q, 12 February [1799], n. 11.
5. RG had been collated by Bishop Barrington in 1804 to the seventh stall in Durham Cathedral, and in 1805 to the rectory of Bishopwearmouth, where he succeded Paley. RG held this living until he became bishop of Bristol in 1827.
6. Hannah More, *Hints towards Forming the Character of a Young Princess,* 2 vols. (London: Cadell and Davies, 1805).
7. William Roscoe, *The Life and Pontificate of Leo the Tenth,* 4 vols. (Liverpool: J. M'Creery, 1805).
8. HLP had already begun the study of Hebrew, admitting to Q on 21 June 1805: "I told the Gentleman who assists me in learning the Rudiments, that I perceived Hebrew was a Gyant to be best conquered by the shepherd's Sling and smooth Stones from the Brook; a Coat of Mail and warlike Equipage is only an Incumbrance, as King Saul's Armour was to little David—nor should I have ventured to begin so late on a new Undertaking of such Magnitude, Had I not found out that the Illiterate and Itinerant Preachers of Methodism up and down, *all* study Hebrew, to torment the Clergy."
On 12 September she reported further difficulties to Q: "I am surrounded by no fewer than five Hebrew Grammars but all Syntax flies before a Language in which one never is to study Composition; so I have to learn new every day, concerning these Suffixes and Affixes and Prefixes which escape my Memory perpetually. But like Monsr. Jourdain I shall do better when I come *to read a Book.* Mean while the Alphabet is itself a Source of Devotional Amazement" (Bowood Collection).

TO HESTER MARIA THRALE

> Brynbella Saturday Morning
> 2d. November *1805*

Poor Mrs. Smyth! how I pity her. Do not dearest Girl leave her in such Distress[1]——but stay at Heathhouse till we come to Pultney [sic] Street, and then give *us one* Week at least of your Company. Whoever has a Claim upon your Kindness, I am Sure that Lady and I have Claim on your Compassion.[2]

Mr. Piozzi was brought back shrieking with Agony after being at Abergeley just Ten Days—Not so much with Gout then, as with a New Abscess in one Foot—which however healed up too Soon in my Opinion, and the Disorder threw itself upon His Throat, Ears and Head.[3] In a word this is the first Day he has got up to wash his Face, and put on the appearance of a human Creature since our Return, which was two days after I wrote that allegorical Sheet you speak so *truly* of; but it is very flattering to think you took the Scene for a real one.[4]

Lady Kirkwall was *more* pardonable in being deceived, because She knows the Characters of the simple Drama.——She still *persists* (comically enough) that there was *Some Truth in it.* Poor Dear Soul! I had not left her eight and forty hours, before The Cart came to carry *her* off—but Robin Jones[5] did give it a Turn somehow; and She is yet alive, covered as my Lord tells me with Jaundice and looking like a Kite's Claw——her Mother 200 Miles off—and her Sibyl as She calls *me* too much *employed in her own* house, to think of *Neighbours,* however interesting and amiable.

Indeed *Indeed* my heart has been much torne; and I am ready to write against Love and Friendship as against Study, or *Science never attained.*

What are any of them good for? but to wear out one's Health and Spirits.

Mr. Piozzi's own Room not being ready for him *this Time,* as our Distress came on unexpectedly——He *takes his Pains* to use the Midwive's Phrase, in my Bed chamber upstairs; and when I am not *closer* to him, the little Music Room with a Balcony, is *my* Apartment. *There* then was I sitting all alone, one of these rough Nights; the West Wind howling round the house, and a dead Silence within it:—when the Tempest ceased on a Sudden and every thing was *still.*

A deep-drawn Sigh, hollow, heavy, *long*—seized on my fatigued Attention at that Moment, and called me from my Book. I knew it was within two Yards of me by the Sound, and my first Reflexion was that I have *now* no favourite Dog—for the Breath was very like that of a large Greyhound composing himself to rest after a long Run. The Opiate held poor Mr. Piozzi quiet——and I looked whether an asthmatic Servant that we have, was panting at the Door in a Fit;—But no—There was nothing but pure Vacancy——so down I sate again to see if My sad Companion would return. In about ten Minutes more a Second Sigh *quite near* me; longer than the last, and towards the end broken and interrupted—gave me full Opportunity of Examination: and I found that it proceeded from the *Organ Pipes.*[6]

So now dear Soul if you thought my false Scene true, do not to make amends think this True Scene false: altho' I grant you it would make a figure under the hand of those writing Ladies who seek out for Mystery and Marvel, and put their Imagination on the Rack for Wonders, and Sorrows that sit close to them. So *True it was however*, that I felt it was my Turn to sigh *with* the Organpipes: which never—*never* more will feel the Hand of their Master—and certainly never *such* a hand; but Basta.

That Mr. Smyth has caught Cold surprizes me but little.[7] The Atmosphere affects every Place, short of an empty Receiver,—and I *have* heard it will affect even *that;* accelerating or retarding the Powers of an Air Pump.

My Invalid can bear *no* Clothes—no *Bed* Clothes but a Sheet, a Twenty Times scowered Blanket—Thin as a Shawl—and over them a Chintz Palampour[8]—— in Winter!! Yet he says if a Cough comes, 'twill *kill* him *with the Pain*. How *he* escapes is much more strange than how Mr. Smyth is catched. Of *him*,—If no Blood is thrown up, I have *yet* hopes; notwithstanding the Approach of a sharp Season: and if his Mother can but keep him till Spring is past——Je vous en repond.

Pray make her my respectful Compliments and thank Her for thinking amidst her own Afflictions on those of her Obedient Servant and / your Affectionate Mother / H: L: P.

Doctor Currie's *Death* grieves many People,[9] but Doctor Thackeray's *Life* ought to amaze *many more*. I wish he attended Mr. Smyth: He is married, and fat, and has a fine Girl born[10]—and was once in the Way of your Invalid exactly.

In the Cover—quite separate, come the *Kitchen*-Griefs;—Oh! they are many and various. We took in an additional House maid because our own were worried so, with my Master: and sure enough the Wench is dying up Stairs of a putrid Sore Throat and Fever,[11] which I expect we shall all catch, except Mr. Piozzi who is defended by *Ramparts of Lime Rock:* if he hears of it however, his Terror may throw the Gout into his Stomach; so I am at my Wit's end.

Meanwhile Ruth Watkins could scarce fling *our* Money about much;[12] for I am my own Market-Woman at London and Bath—and here we live wholly on our own Produce, of Fowls, Bacon, Pork, Mutton &c. no such Things being to be *bought here;* and they must be killed *when I please*——but we will talk further if we meet; and if we live over these *Horreurs*——The *Post Chaise* shall be our Mansion on Monday 3 Weeks 24: November.

Till then God bless my dearest, prays / her Affectionate / H: L: P.

The House at Bath is ours from 1st. of December to 7: March 1806.[13]

Text: Bowood Collection. *Address:* Miss Thrale / Heath House / Bristol. *Postmark:* franked by Lord Kirkwall, Abergele, November four 1805. ABERGELE 225.

1. See HLP to Q [31 December 1804], n. 6.
2. Between the letter to Q on 23 July and this, HLP sent three more: one on 10 August, which again discussed Lady Salusbury's heirs and HLP's renewed sense of disinheritance; another on 12 September; and the third on 6 October. These last two are short and describe her study of Hebrew.
3. The Piozzis had been at Prestatyn in July, returning after ten days to Brynbella. Early in

October, they went to Abergele, where they could stay for only ten days before GP's illness again forced them to retreat to Brynbella.

4. On Sunday, 6 October, HLP sketched a brief "allegory" for Q, who was visiting Mrs. Smyth at Heath House, near Bristol: "My dear Lady Kirkwall is so zealous to obtain *Literary* Knowledge for herself and her Sons, that she provoked me to tell her last Wednesday—when we celebrated my Lord's Birthday at Lleweney Hall; that the only Difference between Ignorance and Study is that of a Short Man sitting down, and a tall Man standing up: The last sees very little and the little— very imperfectly—; the other sees nothing, and concludes that there is nothing to be seen" (Bowood Collection).

John Hamilton Fitzmaurice, styled Viscount Kirkwall, was born on 9 October 1778. At Lleweni Hall in this year the birthday was celebrated one week early. See *Thraliana* 2:1045; HLP to PSP, 11 November 1798, n. 1.

5. Robert [Robin] Jones (fl. 1780–1837) was to become apothecary at the Denbighshire Infirmary from 1826 to 1836; shortly thereafter he disappears from the local trade and postal directories.

6. The incident is also recorded in *Thraliana* 2:1070–71.

7. Hugh (1772–1824), eldest son of Thomas and Jane Smyth. He became third baronet upon the death of his uncle, Sir John Hugh Smyth in March 1802.

8. A palampour (of unknown derivation) is a decorative, lightweight bedcover.

9. For Dr. James Currie, see HLP to Thomas Pennant, 24 December 1798, n. 4. In 1804 Dr. Currie began to ail seriously, went to Bath in hope of a cure, and decided to settle there. But growing worse, he went to Sidmouth, where he died of a degenerative heart ailment on 31 August. For his obituary, see *GM* 75, pt. 2 (1805): 885–86.

10. Dr. William Makepeace Thackeray had married in 1803 or 1804 Eliza, née Wilson (d. 8 September 1833), the widow of John Jones, esq., of Gelly-Gynan, Flintshire, by whom she had four children. When she died at Chester, she left two daughters by her second husband: Sarah Jane (1805–72) and Selina (1806–35).

11. *Thraliana* 2:1070 n. 3.

12. Presumably the current housekeeper of the Piozzis.

13. They rented their usual house on Pulteney Street in Bath from 1 December 1805 to 7 March 1806 (*Thraliana* 2: 1070 n. 2).

TO THE REVEREND LEONARD CHAPPELOW

Brynbella Thursday
14: November 1805.

You ask me dear Mr. Chappelow what my Opinion is of Anne Lee's disgraceful Exploit![1] My opinion is that careful as She used to be of her Toilette She misplaced her Garters terribly that fatal Morning,—and left the Sisterhood a bitter Legacy of Shame and sorrow.[2]

Our Critical Reviewers will *enlarge* the *Sisterhood,* and make all us demisçavantes look foolish on her Account I suppose:——stringing us up in a Row like Penelope's Maids at the End of Homer's Odyssey. I am very angry to be sure.[3]

And what say You will become of Buonaparte? Why if Buonaparte be the General he is reputed to be, and if he will take Example and Experience from those ancient Heroes he pretends to emulate; He must go strait forward, and without losing a Moment, to Vienna;[4] and he must frighten Francis out of his Empire, or into a Peace, which will virtually leave him *no* Empire:[5] If Buonaparte misses this one high Tide of Fortune—He's undone. Aut *Cæsar* aut nullus,[6] must be his Motto; and he must take it *ad Literam.*

Meanwhile our place of Dominion is the Ocean; and to obtain the Ships, and

Colonies and Commerce he desires, will require Time: The last Blow struck by Nelson and Collingwood on the French and Spanish Marine will be very long indeed in recovering:[7] how unlucky that the Admiral could not be prevailed on to change his Dress, and put aside those shining Distinctions which are always ill judged in a Battle

Pictus acu tunicas &c. &c.[8] and People are no wiser *now* you see, than Chlorius was in past Times.[9]

Lady Bradford will recover; She has a Strong Frame, and good Assistance: I love Doctor Parry and Mr. Bowen.[10] My Husband is just beginning to peep out of his last Months Confinement. He has had a miserable Summer of it upon the whole, but I hope the Winter with a little chearful Society will make amends——Last Year we did pretty well.

So I hear Jesse Foot the great Surgeon undertakes to write poor dear Murphy's Life—now he is *Tacitus* as you say:[11] Comical Mr. Chappelow! How does your own great Work go on?[12] Your Friends the *Swallows* staid most fashionably late upon their Summer Excursions among *us* this Season—I have seldom observed Swallows in October except A.D. 1805. You never told me what you thought of Young Roscius: I hope we shall have him at Bath after Christmas.[13] Every body and every Thing comes to Bath in Turn——I half expect Mrs. Siddons.

The Ladies of Llangollen are charming, but we go the Wrexham Road for Shortness——when there are so few hours in the Day. It will be very pleasant for me to be in the living World when we make the Rejoycing Day or Thanksgiving Day or whatever we are commanded to call it.[14] Sir Sydney Smith will perhaps give us still more Cause for Gratitude before the 4th of December but if he *does* blow up the Wasp's Nest at Boulogne,[15] I hope he will not be stung to Death like dear Nelson during the Operation——He is really a public Loss,—and Miss Thrales give a hint as if we were to have a publick Mourning.[16] They are already returned to their House in Great Cumberland Street: their Sister Mrs. Mostyn has left us, but She never did like Wales: and you care for nobody here, or I would tell you that we have lost the charming Blaquieres[17] from Denbigh, and that Lady Kirkwall has two pretty Boys,[18] but exceeding bad health and that Lady Williams—who never forgets you—has seven Children now—Three of them Sons;[19] and Sir John has so altered his house you would never know it.[20]

Adieu and accept the united Regards of my Master and your ever faithful &c. / H: L: P.

Doctor Thackeray is well, and happy, and fat, and has a beautiful Daughter:[21] he has likewise a mighty pretty Sister with one Black Eye and one blue one; I never saw such a Thing before, but there is no Deformity in it: The Lady is particularly handsome and pleasing.[22]

Once more Farewell! we set out for Winter Quarters next Monday *Sennight*.

Text: Ry. 561.132. *Address:* Rev: Mr. Chappelow / Hill Street / Berkeley Square / London. *Postmark:* DENBIGH 224; NOV 16 1805.

1. HLP replies to LC's letter, dated Bath, 5 November 1805 (Ry. 563.86).
2. HLP learned of Anna Lee's suicide in a letter from William Siddons, dated 29 October (Ry. 892.57): "On Wednesday last [23 October] Miss Ann Lee—was found suspended from the top railing of her Bed by a rope—quite dead, but warm. . . . She was called up to breakfast but begged they would let her lay a little longer being sleepy—upon which Mrs. Lee and Harriet after their breakfast walked into Bath for their marketing. On their return finding she was not up—went to call her—but found the door locked. Upon calling and receiving no answer, they were alarmed, got the Door forced, and there she was. . . . The Coronor sat and with great difficulty it seems brought in the Verdict Lunacy."

Anna Lee was not buried at St. Swithin's Church (Walcot), where she was a communicant, but "early on Sunday morning" (27 October) in St. Thomas à Becket churchyard (Widcombe), away from her own parish. No mention of suicide is made in the "Lyncombe and Widcombe Burial Register," C.R.O., Somerset.

3. Of Penelope's wicked maids, see Pope's *Odyssey* 22. 462–63, 498–504.
4. HLP was stunned by the news of Napoleon's victory over the British and Russians at Ulm in Germany. On 4 November 1805 the *Courier* reported that Ulm had surrendered——"General Mack has been taken prisoner, and his army has been annihilated." (*The Times* correctly reported that Ulm had fallen on 17 October. The road to Vienna, the British assumed, was now open.)

HLP's fear stemmed from Bonaparte's victories before and following that of Elchingen on 14 October. Within eight days, the day after Trafalgar, the remnant of the Austrian army, 23,000 strong, laid down their arms. Bonaparte, however, continued to march down the right bank of the Danube to Vienna, where he stopped to refit his army. Once that was done, he moved onward in preparation for the battle of Austerlitz in Moravia on 2 December 1805. The warring parties signed the treaty of Pressburg, (1 January 1806) by which Austria was to lose Venice and the Tyrol.

5. On 6 August 1806 Francis II formally abdicated the title and functions of Holy Roman Emperor. For Francis or Franz Joseph Karl (1768–1835), see HLP to PSP, 26 April 1794, n. 7; and 4 August 1794, nn. 10, 11; HLP to Q, 7 November 1796, n. 7. Francis had been crowned Roman Emperor (1792–1806), Emperor of Austria (1804–35), king of Hungary and Bohemia (1792–1835).
6. *Aut Cæsar, aut nihil,* the epithet by which Cæsar Borgia (1475–1507), younger son of Rodrigo Borgia (1431–1503), later Pope Alexander VI (1492–1503), boastfully lived and died. See HLP to LC, 14 July 1797, n. 4.
7. HLP refers to the battle of Trafalgar, south of Cadiz (21 October 1805). *The Times* on 6 November summed up the British emotional reaction to the event: "We know not whether we should mourn or rejoice. The country has gained the most splendid and decisive Victory that has ever graced the naval annals of England; but it has been dearly purchased. *The great and gallant* Nelson *is no more:* he was killed by almost the last shot that was fired by the enemy. . . . [who] were thirty-three sail of the line, Lord Nelson only twenty-seven."

Vice Admiral Cuthbert Collingwood (1750–1810) led the lee line at the battle of Trafalgar, and on Nelson's death, became the chief in command. His services were recognized immediately by his being created Baron Collingwood of Coldburne and Hethpoole in Northumberland; by an annual pension of £2,000 for life; by the thanks of Parliament; and by a sword from the duke of Clarence.

8. See Virgil, *Aeneid* XI. 777: "Pictus acu tunicas et barbara tegmina crurum."
9. For Chlorus (i.e., Aurelius Valerius Constantius Chlorus), see HLP to Q, 12 February [1799], n. 12.
10. Now a resident of Bath, the Dowager Lady Bradford, who would die on 6 March 1806, was—according to LC—ill and attended by Parry and Bowen. See LC's letter (dated 4 December 1798) to HLP.

For Caleb Hillier Parry, see HLP to PSW, 1 September [1789], n. 7; for William Bowen, see HLP to PSP, 14 April 1803, n. 2.

11. Jessé Foot (1744–1826) obtained his medical education in London, becoming a distinguished surgeon there. In 1811 his biography of Murphy appeared. Murphy had died 18 June 1805. Three days later HLP wrote to Q: "The Death of Dear Murphy was an Occurrence quite within *all our Ken;* yet when it came I felt very deeply affected: and am still wholly unable to dismiss his Figure from my Mind's Eye—his Voice from my Ear—Poor Poor Fellow! And how *did* he dye? Worne out perhaps, 'Taught half by Nature, half by mere decay / to welcome Death, and calmly pass away' [Pope, *An Essay on Man,* Epistle 2. 259–60]. Is he to be buried among the Romanists at Hammersmith? or does he go to the Parish Church or how? Father Hussey the late Catholic bishop of Waterford was inquisitive with me to know s'il y a voit quelque odeur de Saintete in his Conversation—perhaps they got round him at last: If you know, tell me" (Bowood Collection).

Reared in the Catholic faith, Murphy "never formally abjured [Catholicism as] . . . his original sect of Xtianity" (*Thraliana* 2: 1067–68). In his formative years he was educated at the English Jesuit

College of St. Omer, France (almost clandestinely under the name of "Arthur French"). Apparently, however, he had no profound sectarian conviction, divided as he must have been between the Catholicism of his mother Jane, née French (d. 1761), and the militant Anglicanism of both his brother James and his uncle Jeffrey French.

In his final years Murphy had lived in Brompton Row, Knightsbridge; earlier he had resided in the hamlet of Hammersmith, a part of Fulham Parish. Here, constructed under the aegis of Charles I in 1629 and consecrated by Archbishop Laud in 1631, a chapel had been dedicated to St. Paul. According to a written agreement between the vicar of Fulham and the principal inhabitants of the parish, "the rights of the Mother church were most strictly observed."

There were in Hammersmith at least two Roman Catholic chapels—as well as several non-Anglican meeting houses—yet Murphy chose the Anglican chapel of St. Paul for his mother's interment. And there, at his own request, he was buried on 26 June "near the remains of his mother, to whom, whilst living [in the words of Daniel Lysons], he had shown the highest degree of filial attachment. Under the west gallery is a tablet . . . with the following inscription: 'Sacred to the memory of Arthur Murphy Esq. a Barrister at Law, of distinguished character; a dramatic poet of great Celebrity; a classical scholar of rare attainments; a political writer of no common consideration; a loyal subject and a sincere Christian. This eminent man died on the 18th day of June 1805, in the 78th year of his age, and is interred in the same vault with his mother Mrs. Jane Murphy.'"

Ravaged by time and man-made pollution, the Hammersmith chapel of St. Paul was in the years 1882–9 replaced by another Anglican church.

Jessé Foot, *The Life of Arthur Murphy, Esq.* (London: J. Faulder, and John Nichols and Son, 1811), pp. 8–9, 443; *Thraliana* 2: 1067–68]); Daniel Lysons, *The Environs of London*, 2 vols., 2d ed. (London: T. Cadell and W. Davies, 1810) 2:260–66, 272–74; *The London Encyclopædia*, ed. Ben Weinreb and Christopher Hibbert (London, Macmillan, 1983).

Thomas Hussey (1741–1803) had been the Roman Catholic bishop of Waterford and Lismore (1795), F.R.S. (1792). Chaplain to the Spanish mission in London, he was a respected spokesman for English Catholics and also highly regarded in the Anglican community by such as George III, Edmund Burke, and SJ (*DNB* and *Boswell's Johnson* 4:411 and n. 2).

12. For LC's "great work," see HLP to LC, 3 June 1796, nn. 11, 15.

13. For William Henry West Betty, the boy-actor, see HLP to LC, 17 November 1803, n. 2.

14. The *London Gazette* (Saturday, 9 November) published a proclamation "giving directions for a general thanksgiving to Almighty God, on the 5th of December, 'for the recent and signal interposition of His good Providence . . . in the late . . . victories obtained by our fleet, under the command of the late Vice-admiral Lord Viscount Nelson, over the combined fleets of France and Spain.'" See *GM* 75, pt. 2 (1805): 1056.

15. According to *The Times*, 11 November, Sir Sidney Smith went aboard the *Diligence* sloop of war in Dover harbor. When the crew was mustered, he read to them the *Extraordinary Gazette*, which announced the victory at Trafalgar and Nelson's death. He went on to mention "to them, that an attack, under his direction, was to be made upon the enemy in one of their own harbours. . . . The project was openly avowed: and, although the particular point against which the attack is to be directed, was not mentioned by him, we have good reason for supposing, that the destruction of the flotilla in Boulogne harbour is to be attempted."

On 25 November *The Times* reported Sir Sidney's unsuccessful bombardment of Boulogne.

16. The public funeral for Lord Nelson, held on 9 January 1806 at St. Paul's, was preceded by a procession.

On 18 December *The Times* reviewed the order of events relevant to the funeral.

"The body of Lord Nelson, on its arrival at the Nore in the *Victory*, is to be removed into the yacht belonging to Commissioner Grey of Sheerness, for conveyance to Greenwich, where it is to lie in state. It will be removed from thence by water to Whitehall Stairs, and thence to the Admiralty Office, in the Hall of which it will remain all night, in a private manner; and, on the following morning, the procession to St. Paul's will commence. The Admiralty and Navy barges are to attend, as also those belonging to the several Public Offices."

17. For the "charming [De] Blaquieres," see HLP to Q [ca. 23 September] 1800, n. 7.

18. Lady Kirkwall's two sons were Thomas John Hamilton Fitzmaurice (1803–77), styled Viscount Kirkwall (1820); fifth earl of Orkney (1831). The second son was William Edward Fitzmaurice (30 March 1805–89). He served as major of the Denbighshire cavalry of Porthuca Tower, Conway; and of the Second Life Guards. From 1842–47 he represented Buckinghamshire in Parliament.

For Lord and Lady Kirkwall, see HLP to LC, 19 March 1799, n. 4.

19. The children of Sir John and Lady Williams were: John Hay (1794–1859), second baronet; Hugh (1802–76), third baronet; William (1805–92); Ellen (d. 1876); Mary Elizabeth (d. 1890); Margaret (1799–1880); the twins: Emma (1798–1889), and Harriet (1798–1885).

20. For a description of Bodelwyddan, see HLP to Ly W and Eleanor Williams, 26 July 1805, n. 8. The estate had been redone to justify Sir John's baronetcy in 1798 and to accommodate the growing Williams family.

21. Sarah Jane Thackeray, the first child, was born in 1805 and died a spinster in Chester, 1872. She bequeathed substantial sums of money to the Blue Coat Hospital of the city.

22. HLP refers to Jane Townley Thackeray (1788–ca. 1881). In September, she visited Denbigh, "where my Brother Martin had been passing part of the summer with Mrs. Heaton, whom I was also now to visit. . . . Mrs. Heaton took me to see Mrs. Piozzi . . . at Bryn Bella, a beautiful place on a hill so steep that we were all obliged to get out of the carriage and walk up to the house. She was very glad to see me, knowing my Brother William well. . . . She kissed me on parting and said, 'Now, my dear, you can say that you have been kissed by Mrs. Piozzi.' She was a very little talkative woman, and looked to me very ancient though she could not have been more than sixty-five years old. I recollect her dress which was a coloured print; her petticoats were very short, showing her white stockings and high-heeled shoes" (Pryme and Bayne, *Memorials of the Thackeray Family*, pp. 176, 178).

TO LADY WILLIAMS

Sunday 29: December 1805.

Being confined to the house with a Severe Cough and Cold—The Effect of these changes in the Atmosphere from Heat to Frost; What can I do so well as write to my dear Lady Williams and enquire for all our little darling Friends. Miss Williams has called on us very kindly, and made a good Report of Bodylwyddan;[1] and She was the first who informed me of the Happiness situate at good old Lleweney Hall. I fancy Peace and Reconciliation are *in* as the Boys say of their Games at School; Cricket is *in* &c.; I met Mr. and Mrs. Mostyn Arm in Arm at our Pump here one Morning when least expected,—and the self-same Day came lovely Mrs. Siddons driving hither to pass the merry Christmas and begin a happy New Year with Her truly good and amiable Husband.——[2]

Even Buonaparte strives for Peace, and in Peace at last must every human Dispute end—how foolish then it is ever to begin the War!

We are on Tip-toe for public Accounts confirming the Victory in Germany;[3] and those who do not expect a Cessation of Arms—as I do;—are preparing to hear how poor Vienna is burning to Ground by the French:[4] That would indeed be a new and dreadful Occurrence, and the Tyrant who should propose so horrible a Measure, would be deservedly hunted from the Face of the Earth. Meanwhile the Poor Duchess of Brunswick is dying.—She takes these Matters too seriously to heart I understand,[5] and our good Sovereign looks for Intelligence of his Sister's Death by every Messenger that comes.—

But your Ladyship's kind Friendship would prefer hearing about Mr. Piozzi: He really bore his journey surprizingly well, considering the State of Health he set out in; His looks are very good and we are never without some *Droppers-in* that contribute to his Amusement. I have been on the Invalide list only 3 or 4 Days, but know not when I shall be discharged Sound. My Companions in Affliction are numerous——it might be called an Influenza for its Frequency: but our Comfort here at Bath is, that things go worse at London.

No Loss of Ball or Theatre however: Such vile Dancing did I never see exhibited, and we have miserable Actors, because the new Playhouse fills its Manager's Pocket without their help on Account of its Beauty and freshness.[6] Much Pains have been taken to *write down* the Young Roscius in the Newspapers I am told, but Letters from London say 'tis all in vain, his Appearance still delights a discerning Audience. How lucky was my Dear Lady Williams in seeing him while yet a Child!—he will be a young Man before I get Sight of him certainly.[7]

The intolerable Cough which has kept me at home to write this Letter, has hindered me from writing it all at once; and really if these strange Transitions from hottest to coldest, and from coldest to hottest, again disturb all our Barometers;—few Constitutions will stand it.

How does the Building go on? and how do our dear Young People? Is the Cotillion Number likely to be completed in a few months more? I am sure that in seven Years the Dancing will be better at Bodylwyddan than at Bath, and Miss Williams will say the same. Her Report of the young Stranger makes me jealous lest Lady Kirkwall's Godson should rival mine.[8]

Dear Mrs. Williams will I fear find this odd Winter unfavourable to her painful Malady——has She recollection enough of her own Country I wonder, to be diverted with the strange Caricature of it called Castle Rackrent?[9] If She never read the book I will bring it to her. Adieu kind and amiable Ladies! and do not quite forget / Your ever faithful Servant / H: L: Piozzi.—

Text: Ry. 2 (1802–6). *Address:* Lady Williams / Bodylwyddan / St. Asaph / N. Wales. *Postmark:* BATH.

1. For Ly W's sister-in-law, Margaret Williams, see HLP's letter to the former, 18 December 1798, n. 1.
2. HLP mentions in succession those marriages which interested her if only because they were failures: Lord and Lady Kirkwall; JMM and CMM; William Siddons and SS. See *Thraliana* 2:1070 n. 1, 1084 and n.4.
3. HLP was still responding to "Hamburgh Mail" reports of 20 December that "Yesterday [3 December] a grand battle was fought between the Allied Forces and the French army . . . near Turas. It lasted until noon this day, and is stated to have been very bloody. The issue is still undecided."

On 21 December *The Times,* among others, recognized public anxiety while people awaited the outcome "of the late battle in Moravia," and it therefore reported from a variety of sources that "all concur in according the ultimate advantage in that desperate contest to the Combined Army. Government, we understand, entertain no doubts that the French were worsted in the engagement which began on the 2d, and was continued on the two following days."

Only on 31 December did *The Times,* quoting French and Dutch papers of the 15th, admit that the Allied Armies had surrendered to the French following the battle of Austerlitz on 2 December.

4. HLP anticipated an armistice between the Austrians and the French because she was aware of the dreadful losses suffered by the former in October and November.

The Times on 4 November had reported from French accounts that Napoleon "passed the Rhine on the 1st of October; the Danube the sixth, at five o'clock in the morning; the Lech the same day, at half past three; his troops entered Munich on the 12th; his advanced guard arrived on the Inn on the 15th. On the same day he was master of Memmingen, and on the 17th of Ulm.

"He took from the enemy, at the battles of Wertingen, Guntzburgh, Elchingen, the days of Memmingen and Ulm, and in the actions of Albreck, Langenau, and Neresheim, *forty thousand* men, infantry as well as cavalry, more than forty stand of colours, a great number of cannon, baggage waggons, &c. and to accomplish all this only marches and manœuvres were employed."

With his victory at Austerlitz a fact, Napoleon was able to impose the harsh treaty of Pressburg on Austria barely three weeks later.

5. Augusta, duchess of Brunswick (1737–1813), "is about a year older than the King, exceedingly resembles him in countenance, and still more in conversation and manner" (Jesse 3:518).
On 18 December, *The Times* reported that "The Duchess of Brunswick . . . was extremely ill at the date of our last advices from the Continent."
She would recover, only to be driven from her home by Napoleon's armies. On 7 July 1807 she arrived in England, setting up her establishment at 23 Hanover Square, London (*The Times*, 6, 14, 16 July).
6. The new theater in Beaufort Square, Bath, had opened 12 October with *King Richard the Third* and the farce, *The Poor Soldier*. The architecture was primarily the creation of John Palmer, the city architect, and the ornamentation that of George Dance. "There are three entrances in as many different directions. The grand front (for chairs) is in Beaufort-square; the carriage entrance in the Saw-close, and the remaining side, for pit, gallery, and stage. The extreme length is 125 feet, the width 60 feet, and the height 70; and the whole building is replete with conveniences of every possible description. . . . The ceiling has also been recently ornamented with some exquisite paintings, by Casali, which were purchased at the celebrated sale at Fonthill." See Roland Mainwaring, *Annals of Bath from the Year 1800* (Bath: printed by Mary Meyler and Son, 1832), pp. 45–46.
7. On 17 December *The Times* published an enthusiastic review of Betty's performance as Norval (in Home's *Douglas*) at the Drury Lane. He had made his first appearance of the season the night before. Although there was a hostile "cabal" in the audience, "an immense majority . . . immediately declared in favour of the boy." His adversaries were physically ousted from the theater.
He repeated the role of Norval on 19 December. On the 21st he played Frederick in *Lovers' Vows*, again at the Drury Lane. On the 27th he enacted Romeo at the Covent Garden; and the next day Gustavus Vasa in the "cold, monotonous play" of the same name (a new role for him), also at the Covent Garden. On 31 December he was scheduled to act in *Hamlet* at the Drury Lane.
8. The "young Stranger . . . Lady Kirkwall's Godson" was William Williams, third son of Sir John and Ly W, born on 20 September 1805.
9. Maria Edgeworth's *Castle Rackrent; an Hibernian Tale* was published in London by J. Johnson in 1800. (There was a Dublin edition in the same year.) The fourth English edition of the novel appeared in 1804.
We have not been able to document the Irish origins of Eleanor Williams, née Hughes. Before her marriage to Hugh Williams (1741–68), high sheriff of Anglesey (1766), she was the sole heiress of Hugh Hughes (d. 1810), of Plas yn Rhoscolyn, Anglesey. She and her husband were associated with Ty Fry, Anglesey (C. R. O, Gwynedd).

TO HESTER MARIA THRALE

Fryday Evening
17: January 1806.

Well! now My dearest Girl you have really made me amends—and You have told *told me Something*. My own Amour propre would not have said half as much from Mrs. Mackay;[1] The Blaquiere Family *do* love me a little I hope and believe. I have such a sincere Affection for Lady K————that my heart feels quite happy to hear of her,—pray does She drag the poor little Gambetta after her? or does it follow briskly as it should do?[2]

Old Mr. Jones has our best Wishes,[3] he is a Wonderful Mortal,—*if* Mortal; for he has kept the universal Enemy at Bay suprizingly to be sure. Should he die before me—which was once more likely than 'tis now;—Malherbe's Epitaph Sur un Octogenaire would come in my head to imitate for *him*.[4]

> N'attend, Passant que de ma Gloire
> Je te fasse une longue Histoire,
> Pleine de Langage Indiscret.
> Qui se loüe irrite L'Envie;
> Juge de moi par le Regret
> Qu'eut la Mort pour m'ôter la Vie.

> "No Battles won, or Captives taken"
>   This unassuming Stone records;
> Nor did these Limbs of Life forsaken
>   Compose a Man of many Words.
> Yet Fortune both her Eyes unbinding
>   Did at his Call her Gifts bestow;
> And Death—was five Score Years in finding
>   Where he could strike the fatal Blow.

The Device of making the dead Man speak Lines on his own Tomb, though a familiar Trick with other Nations, does not do in our Language. Ah me! What Language can describe my Amazement at all the Wonders that come crouding round me! and your Story of the French Emperor's *Name* is very striking even among that Multitude.[5] For tho' I cannot find the Mystery *myself*—no one would affirm so strange a Thing had *they* not found it, and my Fears prompt me to believe it true of *some* Language but not Greek. The Greek β is a numerical Letter certainly, and means *Two*; but when an Acute Accent is put under—means Two Thousand——I fancy Bis in Latin came from thence, but how we shall make six of it is hard to find. *Herein is Wisdom* as St. John says, but I possess it not.[6] The N or ν I can find no Account of as a Numeral except in the Barbarous Times, when it stood for 500, and with a Dash at Top Ā 5000. *"Possidet A numeros quingentos ordine recto."* But I will try again by and by.[7]

There was a Fasting Man some Thirty Years ago I recollect, who drew the Public Attention by declaring that he would fast the Forty Days of Lent in strict Imitation of the Abstinence practised by Moses, by Elias, and by our blessed Saviour: People watched him for one Week as I remember, and wondered at him a Second: but on the Monday following some Wag put it in the papers that whereas John Wilkins was supposed by some a Prophet and by some a Madman—he was only a Young Fellow qualifying himself to be my Lord Edgecumbe's Butler; as no Man could get anything to eat in that House but the Valet de Chambre.—It was not *the way* then to call that Nobleman Lord *Mount* Edgecumbe as it is now,[8] and we heard no more of the Lent-Keeper.

I think that of all human Impostures None can be more Mysterious than this supposititious Cousin of ours;[9] Miss Hinde is a live Lady, for I have at least dug *her* out; She is what She pretends to be, Daughter of a Hertfordshire Gentleman[10]—and She persists in saying that She knew the Boy's Mother, who married a Mr. Tench Son to Miss Mary Cotton—and a Surgeon[11]—That *he* died, and the Mother Miss Jones Sister to the Vicar of Offley[12] who succeeded that Mr. Thelwall Salusbury who I mentioned to you,——died also:[13] and left a Boy which Boy Mrs. Dimond is striving to find for me. When these Ænigmas can be discovered, you shall know――but Truth does live at the bottom of a Well as we have often heard,[14] and my Buckets have hitherto failed sadly in drawing her up; but I will have (as the Maids say) another Try at it.

Apropos to Maids we shall soon have none but new Faces round us, than which nothing in my Mind is less pleasing: but we seem to like the Housekeeper very well――it will be long before I can *expect* myself to find a Femme de Chambre agreeable, after being 15 Years accustomed to one Person.[15] Mrs. Mostyn seems very happy with the Servant I had bred up on purpose to succeed Miss Allen; and the Young Woman is delighted with her Place, and is useful about the Children, who tho' *larger* than other Babies, have doubtless inherited uncertain health from their Father: Harry in particular, who is my Favourite; seems very unlikely to *comb a Grey head* of his own, as the Nursery Phrase is.[16] Cæcilia looks beautifully, and they have a very pretty house at No. 42. I rejoyce that you did not go starving to Saint Paul's to see Lord Nelson's Funeral,[17] though few Shows ever made more lasting Impression on my Mind than did the little Black Chapel in Soho Square when the French Princes mourned le Duc D'Enghien's dreadful Death—but there may be *too much* done, as well as too little for purpose of *producing Effect*.[18]

I have often felt *that* upon the Continent, when devotional Processions were performing――My Devotion was lost in the *Show.*

Dear Siddons understood (instinctively) how much was necessary, and never stept beyond; till very lately when the large Theatres ruined fine Acting by forcing the Player's Voices and Expression. How little Roscius who you all describe a Boy, could fill such Theatres must remain ever an Amazement to *me*, and it does vex me I should lose so rare a Spectacle――I think it cruelly done to write the Child down so, for all the Evil falls personally upon *him* of Course;[19] the Harpy Relations will devour the *Good:* and when full 20 Years are past and over, William Henry West Betty will have to complain instead of to rejoyce, when reflecting on his Treatment by a British Public.

Nothing ends as one expects it to end.—This poor old Margrave of Anspach, who appeared to commit an Act of strange Imprudence in selling and quitting as he did his hereditary Possessions, secured an Independence by that very act; and saved himself from being trampled on or devoured:[20]—The only Choice left to the Duke of Wirtemberg.[21] I wonder where and how la belle Margravine will bury him![22]

But like Richard the 2d.s Queen one might do nothing else but *think on Testaments and talk of Wills:*[23] all my Contemporaries seem so dropping round me. Two Cousins, Companions of my Young Days, and poor Mr. Crutcheley the familiar Acquaintance of my maturer Years[24]—all gone! and the much more luckless King and Queen of Naples whom I have seen so playfully kind, and willingly mingling in English Society—*going*—and going to a dreadful End I greatly fear:[25]—it is difficult to look at high or low without feeling disposed to shudder.—The Wife of Mr. Perkins many a Time deemed by me too pert and showy; now moves up and down this Pump Room a perfect Shadow—quite Spectre-like; a tall Grandaughter dangling from her Arm.[26]

Mondo! Says Mr. Piozzi, when I talk to him of these Matters.

Well since my first Sheet was written, I have seen and conversed with Doctor Randolph, and told him (for a Wonder) about Buonaparte's Name making 666. And "have you" said he, "just found *that* out? Why Some of your Enemies the Scoffers printed it in an abusive Letter ridiculing Retrospection very early in 1801. And saying how could Mrs. Piozzi print those old Vagaries in her 2d. Volume concerning Lodovicus? when the same Thing might be predicated of a young Soldier just rising into Eminence—The Consul Buonaparte." For the *Fact is So*; the Letters *do* form the Number of the Anti Christ; and Doctor Randolph is easily perswaded to expect Events of yet uncalculated Magnitude.[27]

Mean while his most *immediate* Terror is for Ireland, whence the Bishop of Meath writes word that the French Emperor is adored by the low people,[28] as Defender of the Romish Faith, and hoped for *Protector* of its *Restoration* as an *Establishment*. All these Fears will I trust take still deeper Root in Doctor Randolph's heart, after the Catholic Emancipation Bill has been decided on; which will probably pass—this busy Year—with little Deliberation.

Were you acquainted with Miss Clarges?[29] and was She an agreeable Girl? I thought her Deafness kept her from Society, but People tell *me* She was a charmer of other Peoples Ears tho' her own were Stopt: I was sorrier by half for the Death of poor Doctor Naked as your Papa and Dr. Johnson used to call Tattersall the old Dipper of Brighton.[30] Smoaker has I trust, made his Exit long ago.—Some one told me if I remember rightly, that he died to save a drowning Female.

All this Stuff will be brought you by Mr. Whalley: our pleasant Friend M. P. Andrews met him here one Day at Dinner, and they liked each other much: It was pity that Parliament and Business called *him* away so soon, or Mr. Whalley would have shewn him Finery and Gayety in the Royal Crescent Bath, that needed envy nothing even at Cleveland Court.[31]

Mr. Whalley wishes to renew his Acquaintance with *You*, and is desirous of Introduction to Susan and Sophy; I hope he will catch Some of you at home.

Dear Dear! I have just discovered that my Voluminous Letter,—*Voluminous and vast!* has been written upon Paper of different Sizes; but I will not write it over again that is certain. So Adieu Sweet and fair Damsels, and remember that 107 Miles off lives Your Affectionate Mother H: L: Piozzi.

My Master says he is going to Bed with the Gout—but I believe him not. Mrs. Miles Our fine Fortepiano Player is dangerously ill,[32] She was just going to be happy; so I am Sadly afraid She will die. Mr. Mostyn is ill too, but not dangerously——he will not die I dare say.

Mr. Piozzi sends you 1000 Compliments!

Text: Bowood Collection.

1. For Lucy Mackay, née Jones, see HLP to PSW, 28 July [1791], n. 2.
2. At this time the Kirkwalls were the parents of two very young children, either of whom could have qualified as the frolicsome "little Gambetta": Thomas John Hamilton (b. 1803) and William Edward (b. 1805). See HLP to LC, 19 March 1799, n. 4, and 14 November 1805, n. 18; *Thraliana* 2:1045 and n. 3.

3. For John Jones, see HLP to Charlotte Lewis, 8 December 1790, n. 3. "Good old Mr. Jones" was in his eighty-ninth and final year. See *Thraliana* 2:999.

4. HLP enjoyed the poetry of François de Malherbe (1555–1628), which—according to Baudelaire—was "un vers . . . symétrique et carré de mélodie."
In this instance HLP cites "Épitaphe d'un Gentilhomme de ses Amis, qui mourut âgé de cent ans" from *Poésies de Malherbe* (Paris: Imprimé au Louvre par Didot L'Aîné, 1797). In line 1, read "N'attends" for "N'attend" (p. 324).

5. For HLP's vague statements about "the French Emperor's *Name,*" see n. 27.

6. Rev. 13:18. See HLP to Cadell and Davies, 11 January 1796, n. 2.

7. In *Retrospection* (2:538) HLP attributes the passage to Baronius, one of "his old technical verses, which explained the alphabet into numerals, as it seemed *then* merely for the amusement of young children."
An authority on the writings of the Italian ecclesiastical historian Cardinal Caesar Baronius (1538–1607), Professor Mario Borrelli (University of Naples) doubts the validity of the attribution. He is author of *Documenti sul Baronio presso la Bodleian Library* (1965) and *Richerchi sul Baronio,* in vols. 7 and 8, *Studi secenteschi* (1966, 1967).

8. The title earl of Mount Edgcumbe was granted to Admiral Lord George Edgcumbe (d. 1795) in 1789.
His predecessors were Richard Edgcumbe (d. 1758), first baron Edgcumbe (1742); and the second baron Edgcumbe, also named Richard, who died in 1761.

9. On 15 June 1805 (Ry. 555.98), HLP had received a letter from Mary Elizabeth Hinde: "The politeness and condescension predominant in the Mind of those; Who are placed in the most exalted Circles of Life, Will I hope *plead* for the *presumption* of an entire Stranger addressing herself to You . . . in behalf of the Unfortunate Widow, of the late Mr. Tench *(Grandson to Sir Lynch Salusbury Cotton own Brother to your Mother)* Who by a long Succession of Sickness and great Calamity died near four Years ago, leaving a Young family unprovided for, Two of them are still living. The most anxious Wish, of their Widowed Mother, is to implore Your Assistance in placing her Son upon some Charitable Foundation, or School till he arrives at an Age to be put in A Situation to provide for himself. He is near Eleven years old and appears of a Studious disposition—his Unfortunate Mother by supporting her Children is *now* so greatly reduced as to be under the Mortifying necessity of gaining their Subsistance by the *very Abject Situation* of *Common Service* in the Family of an Aged Gentleman—A *truly humiliating* one for the Niece of the late Revd. Mr. Jones *Vicar* of Offley."

10. Mary Elizabeth (d. 23 February 1816) was the daughter of Robert Hinde (d. 29 September 1786) of Hunsdown House in Hitchin parish, Hertsfordshire, and Mary, née Ball (d. 14 February 1819).
Robert Hinde, an eccentric, was purported to have modeled himself after Sterne's Uncle Toby. A one-time army officer, he indulged in war games, building fortifications, etc., in his gardens. On the king's birthday, he habitually had his servant ride horseback or march through the village of Hitchin, proclaiming the occasion. The family residence was Hunsdown House, but he preferred to live in a small house nearby, which he named "Preston Castle." See John Edwin Cussons, *History of Hertfordshire,* 3 vols. (London: Chatto and Windus, 1874–78), 2, pt. 1: 70–72.

11. The story of the Tenches begins with Mary Cotton, who on 29 October 1760 (Ry. 530.19) wrote to Hester Maria Salusbury: [I]magine you've heard that I was Marryed last Monday Morning at my own Parish Church in Chester, to the Reverend Mr. Tench of Wrenbury, I hope Madam I've not entirely lost your Favor by it."
For marrying the Reverend John Tench, curate of the parish church of Davenham, Mary was disinherited by her father, Sir Lynch Salusbury Cotton and ignored thereafter by most of her sisters and brothers. Nevertheless, the Tenches settled in Davenham and produced a sizable family: Philadelphia (b. 1761); Elizabeth (b. 1763); John (b. 1766); Thomas (b. 1767); Edward (b. 1774). See "Christenings, Davenham Parish," C.R.O., Cheshire.
Thomas Tench married Ann, née Jones (d. 1805). (For her death at Waltham Cross, Herts., see *Felix Farley's Bristol Journal,* 10 August 1805.) They in their turn went to live in Ludlow, where they had three children: John (1790–93); Mary Charlotte (b. 1792); Edward (b. 1793).
The "supposititious Cousin" was Edward, for whom Miss Hinde was asking help.

12. Gervas Jones (b. 1731) became vicar of the Offley parish church on 7 March 1775, when Thelwall Salusbury resigned. Jones continued at Offley until his death on 18 February 1784. See the manuscript compilation, "An Alphabetical List of Parochial Incumbents in the County of Hertford from the Lists compiled by the Rev. George L. Hennessey, with a continuation by H. R. Wilton Hall" (dated June 1918), in C.R.O., Hertfordshire.

13. For the Reverend Thelwall Salusbury, who died 14 February 1803, see HLP to Proprietors of the Monthly Mirror, 17 June 1798, n.15.

14. Tilley, T582.

15. Elener Allen was finally about to marry the Denbigh apothecary Robert (Robin) Jones; the marriage had been postponed some fifteen years. See *Thraliana* 2:1072n; HLP to PSW, 29 August [1791], n. 8.

16. Henry (Harry) Meredith Mostyn (1799–1840) was to have a distinguished career in the Royal Navy. He was the most notable of CMM's three children.

17. On 9 January "the burial of this illustrious warrior [Nelson] took place in St. Paul's Cathedral." For a description of the volunteer corps lining the streets from Saint Paul's Churchyard to the admiralty, the coaches of the nobility, the mourning coaches filled principally with naval officers, the regiments of cavalry and infantry quartered within one hundred miles of London who had served in the battle of the Nile, see *The Times*, 10 January, and HLP to LC, 14 November 1805, n. 16.

18. *The Times* on 27 April 1804 reported, "Yesterday morning a solemn Mass was performed at the Catholic Chapel, in Sutton-street, Soho-square, in memory of the late Duke D'Enghien" (Louis-Antoine-Henri de Bourbon [1772–1804]). See HLP to LyW, 12 April 1804, n. 2; also HLP to PSP, 16 April 1804, n. 10.

19. *The Times* (17 December 1805) was generally appreciative of the boy-actor although "[his tones] are intermixed, sometimes, by an infantine whine." On 30 December *The Times* noted that he performed in the role of Gustavus Vasa "as well as any boy of his years possibly could." Theatergoers were less enthusiastic than they had been and "the receipts of Drury-lane Theatre, on the last night of young Betty's performance there, amounted, we hear, to only £220."

20. For Christian Frederick, see HLP to Margaret Owen [ca. 12 February 1799], n. 3.
   In 1792 he had sold his principality to the king of Prussia and settled in England, having purchased Brandenburg House, Hammersmith, and the estate at Benham, Berks. He died on 5 January after an illness of only three days and left his wife an estate of almost £150,000. See *GM*, 76, pt. 1 (1806): 91–92.

21. HLP was concerned with Friedrich Wilhelm Karl (1754–1816), elector of Württemberg, because he took as his second wife Charlotte, princess royal of Great Britain and Ireland, and because Napoleon was victorious throughout most of Germany at this time. Her worry, however, was needless. The elector was able to work with Napoleon; his duchy increased in extent and his title was elevated to that of king (1806). Continuing to acquire more land so that his kingdom by 1809–10 was twice the size of his duchy, he abandoned Napoleon after the battle of Leipzig and switched to the Allies.

22. For Elizabeth, the margravine of Anspach, see HLP to Margaret Owen [ca. 12 February 1799], n. 3.
   The margrave's "remains were interred, in a sumptuous and splendid manner, the procession being very numerous and grand, in the church of Speen, near Newbury" (*GM*, 76, pt. 1: 92).

23. Wills and testaments are coupled at least three times in Shakespeare's plays: See *Timon of Athens*, 5.1.28; *Julius Caesar*, 3.2.154–59. In *Richard the Second*, the king himself remarks (3.2.148), "Let's choose executors and talk of wills." Richard's queen is a dramatic symbol of grief, of "woe . . . forerun with woe" (3.4.28), who lives in daily expectation of death.

24. Jeremiah Crutchley (or Crutcheley) had died on 28 December 1805. See HLT to Q, [27 June 1784], n. 12; 12 July [1784], n. 5.
   One of HLP's cousins, who died in 1805, was Henry Shelley (b. 1727), of Lewes; he had married Philadelphia, née Cotton (1738–1819). See *Thraliana* 1:298.

25. After their defeat at Austerlitz, the Austrians and Russians sued for peace, withdrawing their troops from the Austrian territories in Italy. The French almost immediately, under the command of General Laurent Gouvion-Saint-Cyr (1764–1830), began to march toward Naples. See HLP's next letter to Q, n. 19.

26. The second wife of John Perkins was the rich widow Amelia Bevan, née Mosely (1747–post 1816).
   Her grandchild was Amelia, the daughter of John (1775-ca. 1818) and Sarah Anne. See John Perkins to HLP, 1 October 1811.

27. It was probably not an abusive letter directly ridiculing *Retrospection* that HLP remembered (although there were enough of those); but as she later pointed out in the margin of WAC's copy of *Retrospection*: "A little Book written to ridicule [Comenius's *Lux e Tenebris*] early in 1803 says, Mrs. Piozzi believes Louis 14:th was 666; why Buonaparte's name makes 666:—She may as well believe it of *him*. & now all the Town does believe it of *him*; I never said I believed it of Louis Quatorze, 1812."
   HLP did indeed believe it of Louis, using Ludovicus to make 666 (*Retrospection* 2:408n.). On pp. 408 and 409 of WAC's copy, there are "three separate workings out of the number 666. . . . One produces Mahomet, another Bonaparte, both by use of Greek characters in spelling the names." The third is an elaborate equation of Napoleon Bonaparte and 666. See Merritt, pp. 194–98. For her association of Mahomet and 666, HLP was indebted to Bayle.

28. For Thomas Lewis O'Beirne, see HLP to PSP, 16 December 1802, n. 3.

29. On 11 January 1806 died Louisa Clarges, aged twenty-seven, the only daughter of Sir Thomas (1751–82), Third baronet, and Louisa, née Skrine (1760–1809).

She signed her will two days before she died, leaving a large fortune principally to her mother and her younger brother William (1782–1807). See P.R.O., Prob. 11/1436/19, proved 24 January 1806.

30. On 10 January 1806, "A man named Tattersal, well known (by the appellation of the Doctor) to the visitors of Brighthelmstone, where he had long been one of the principal male-bathers, fell over the Groyne, and was drowned, while endeavouring to fill a bucket with salt water." See *GM*, 76, pt. 1: 93.

31. Miles Peter Andrews lived near Cleveland Court, Saint James's. He occupied a mansion in Green Park, formerly owned by Lord Grenville. There Andrews held his lavish entertainments and gala nights for fashionable London.

For Andrews, see HLP to SL, 17 November 1787, n. 5.

32. Jane [Jenny] Mary Miles, née Guest (ca. 1765–ca. 1815) had been a child prodigy, appearing as a concert pianist in Bath before she was six. As Jenny Guest, she had been Q's singing teacher (*Thraliana* 1:455 n. 8). From 1779 onward, she often played in London. In the 1790s she performed under her married name in Rauzzini's concerts in Bath, where she was a prominent teacher at 7 Bathwick Street.

The happiness to which HLP alludes centers on an appointment as music instructor to Princess Charlotte in 1806, for which she received £300 annually (Farington 8:3051; 27–29 May 1807).

TO HESTER MARIA THRALE

Saturday Morning [25 January 1806][1]

You have indeed my dearest Girl told us Something, and Something very awful in my Mind—an Event not strange perhaps, but shocking enough, when we consider the Moment it arrives in. Who will be the Successor I wonder?[2] Lord Sidmouth is such a State Physician as good Mr. Moore of Denbigh makes to my poor Husband when delirious with Fever and Agony——yet may We fall into worse hands, whether speaking of Private Individuals, or Public Professors of Political Knowledge: Lord Sidmouth would do us no harm;[3] he would not sell the Nation to Buonaparte, he would not Set up O'Connor as King of Ireland.[4]

Mr. Pitt 'tis said, brought on a premature Old Age and an unconquerable Lethargy by too free an Exertion of Talents:[5] Mr. Mostyn is supposed to be bringing on himself a Nervous Debility which will perhaps *end no better*—by a resolute Determination to exert no Talents at all. How happy is it for those who remain in the middle way!

Medio tutissimus ibis.[6]

We saw a Man last Night whose Perfections are of the most dazzling kind, he looked like one indeed who had sacrificed all to Study—a Saxon Performer on the Piano e forte who so amazed our little Cluster of Knowing-ones—that all agreed on his undoubted Superiority to every thing yet exhibited. Rauzzini, Piozzi, Neild;[7] Miss Parkes, Miss Sharp and half a Dozen more competent Auditors expressed their Rapturous Wonder at his Powers, which really put me completely out of Breath, and sent me home fatigued as if I had been playing the Lesson over Myself. Wolfen or Wolveren is his Name I am told,[8] his Figure like an Actor dressed for the Part of the *Stranger*[9]—and a frightful Friend that *tends him i th'Eyes* as Shakespear says, who looks like a Jackall.[10]

So some new Marvel *springs* up almost Weekly, with this soft Weather, and takes off Attention from Matters of more Moment——although I do confess and willingly acknowledge, that on The Day your dear Scrap came—these Bath Folks Surrounded the Post-Office with Gestures of anxious Expectation—and many Letters bringing News to the same Tenor—I saw several Faces looking *avec un Air ebahi* in Marmontel's Phrase;[11] and Lady Melville has been no more seen since that hour, no not at the Pump.[12]

The World is certainly grown more serious since Seven or eight Years back, when I remember feeling much disgusted at hearing a beautiful Young Miss saying to some Man—"Lord! I wish there was neither Bread nor Seamen in the World for my Part; here's such an everlasting Clutter about the Poor and the Scarcity, and the Meeting and the Stuff." No Miss however charming, would charm by such Conversation in these Days; and they prudently do no longer *express* their Contempt of all but themselves and their Looking Glass.

I wonder if You have seen Mr. Whalley; he brought you a long Letter from me, and wished for Introduction to your Coteries—so do the Singing Miss Parkes.[13] We have an Invitation to hear *the Stranger* again in a larger Company next Sunday Evening, and on that Day Sennight Lady Anne Talbot's Daughter plays on the Piano e forte to a Select Party:[14] I think I have heard you extol *her* Performances——but my old Friend dear Mrs. Strickland's Grandaughter *Miss Stevenson,* carries the Applause away from many a fair Dilletante Player. Oh how was I oppressed by my own Feelings when first introduced to a tall young Woman and her Brother a wounded Officer shot in the Acheron Frigate[15]—that said they wished for my Acquaintance—having heard their Grand mother speak of me so highly—and the Grandame was poor Stricky![16] Why now thought I, it *is* Time to be gone, when the 3d. Generation is coming forward in somewhat like public characters—I shall believe *myself* Octogenaire by and by, and expect to hear of Lord Kirkwall's little Boy speaking in the house of Parliament, where his Uncle seems as if making no small Figure *now.*[17]

Augusta Coventry will soon be *Lady* Augusta Cotton, Sophy says; if these high Winds blow not her Lover away:[18] Buonaparte's permission of those Men's return, is one of the Mysteries I cannot fathom;—he might have insisted on Prussia's giving up the whole Army.[19]

Do you read Marmontel's Memoirs?[20] it is a Striking Contrast to the Life of Cumberland;[21] and shows the Difference—and the Resemblance too,——between a French Wit and an English one very prettily. They are the most entertaining Volumes in the World—just Incident enough, just Character enough; and so *very* interesting! It has been a famous Season for *pleasant* Publications, and one may justly expect *Instruction* from Faber's development of the Prophecies[22]——he is a deep Scholar, and his Knowledge in Mythological Studies scarce attainable in a long Life: witness his Bampton Lectures and his Dissertation on the Cabirs:[23] but here's the Paper out and no Frank appearing.—I will have a Stroke at Lord Tankerville[24] who will do it perhaps for your Sake.

Text: Bowood Collection.

1. HLP's letter was written on the 25th, after the death of Pitt, on 23 January, and before the new ministry (the Ministry of All the Talents) could be formed during the early days of February. See Stanhope 4:378-82.

2. The king had hoped "that, even without Mr. Pitt, his Ministers might stand their ground. He conveyed to them an offer to that effect through Lord Hawkesbury." But that scheme fell through and the scramble to create a ministry began. The king applied to Lord Grenville, who quickly undertook to form a government "comprising the chiefs of the three parties which had lately joined in opposition. Lord Grenville became First Lord of the Treasury, [Charles James] Fox Secretary of State for Foreign Affairs, and Lord Sidmouth Privy Seal." See Stanhope 4:390.

3. That Lord Sidmouth would gather his followers and lead a coalition ministry "patched up with the leaderless Pittites" appeared to many people the most logical and satisfactory solution to the crisis following the death of Pitt. See Philip Ziegler, *Addington* (London: Collins, 1965), p. 250.

For Henry Addington (1757–1841), first Viscount Sidmouth (1805), see HLP to James Robson, 17 June 1803; to PSP, 3 December 1803.

4. Roger O'Connor (1762–1834), the often imprisoned Irish nationalist.

5. The cause of Pitt's death was often attributed to gout and debility, aggravated by the Allied defeat at Austerlitz and the armistice that followed. *The Times* was dubious. On 27 January 1806 it commented: "The probable causes of his death have not, as far as we have observed, been stated with accuracy: they certainly existed previous to 1804; at which period it was the opinion of his medical advisers, that he could not return, without considerable hazard, to the labour and anxiety of an official life. Whether the rejection of this advice was fortunate for his own fame, and for the interests of his country, we will not presume to determine. Peace and honour to his memory!"

For several years prior to his death, he appeared ill: his hair had become white and his face showed marks of disease, anxiety, and alcoholism.

6. Ovid, *Metamorphoses*, 2.137.

7. Edward Neale (1770–1850), son of George Vansittart of Calcutta, was an Oxonian, who received his B.C.L. in 1796. He assumed the surname of Neale by royal license in 1803. A skilled musician, he served as rector of Taplow, Bucks., from 1803 until his death. See Farington 8:2878-79 (Sunday, 5 October 1806).

8. Joseph Wölfl (1773–1812), Austrian pianist and composer who in September 1801 moved to Paris and in May 1805 to London. Extremely tall and thin, he had huge hands that could stretch a thirteenth. In his own time he was considered second only to Beethoven as a pianist in Vienna and was admired by him.

9. The melodrama written by Kotzebue and altered for the English stage by Benjamin Thompson and Sheridan. See HLP to PSP, [29] April 1798, n. 2.

10. *Antony and Cleopatra*, 2.2.206–8 (slightly altered).

11. "Je ne puis me rappeler sans rire l'air ébahi qu'avaient mes Bernardins, et avec quelle estime profonde ils m'accueillirent lorsque je descendis de chaire." See *Mémoires: Oeuvres de Marmontel*, 7 vols. (Paris: A. Bellin, 1819–20), 1:50. For bibliographical details, see n. 20.

12. On 22 January Henry Dundas, first Viscount Melville (1802), pleaded in the Lords "not guilty" to articles of impeachment. See HLP to Q, 26 May 1806, n. 20.

Melville, having been divorced in 1779, married secondly on 2 April 1793 Jean, née Hope (d. 1829), daughter of the second earl of Hopetoun.

13. John Parke (1745–1829), the celebrated oboist of 90 Dean Street, had two daughters who performed musically. One was Frances Margaretta and the other—far more talented—was Maria Hester (1775–1822), singer, pianist, and composer. P.R.O., Prob. 11/1759/499, proved 18 August 1829. See also HLP to JSPS, 13 December 1809.

14. George Talbot (d. 1782), D.D., vicar of Guiting, County Gloucester (third son of Charles, first baron Talbot of Hensol [1685–1736/7]), had married on 3 January 1761 Anne (d. 1813), eldest sister of William Bouverie (1725–76), first earl of Radnor (1765).

Lady Anne had four children: two sons and two daughters—Cecil (d. 1832), the wife of Edmond John Chamberlayne; and Louisa, the wife of William Agar. For Lady Anne's will, see P.R.O., Prob. 11/1551/41, proved 22 January 1814.

15. Edward and Mary Cecilia Stephenson had four sons and three daughters. The two in Bath were Rowland (d. 1843), who later assumed the name of Standish, and Mary Eliza (1787–1821), who in 1807 was to marry her relative Rowland Stephenson (1782–1856).

See Henry Hornyold, *Genealogical Memoirs of the Family of Strickland of Sizergh, Kendal* (London: Titus Wilson and Son, Highgate, 1928; also HLP to Q, 3 July [1784]).

16. For Cecilia Strickland, see HLP to Q, 3 July [1784], n. 1.

17. HLP refers to Lord Kirkwall's cousin, Henry Petty-Fitzmaurice (1780–1863), third marquess of Lansdowne, M.P. for Calne (1802–6); Cambridge University (1806–7), Camelford (1807–9). He was

shortly to become chancellor of the exchequer in the Ministry of All the Talents (1806–7). See HLP to JSPS, 16 April 1811, n. 5.

18. The eldest daughter of the seventh earl of Coventry was Augusta Maria (1785–1865), who on 16 May 1806 was to marry Lieutenant General Sir Willoughby Cotton (1783–1860).

19. As early as 20 October 1805, the king of Prussia had "given leave to the Russians to march through his dominions" and prosecute the war against Napoleon. See *GM*, 75, pt. 2 (1805): 1064. Following the victory at Austerlitz, Napoleon allowed these Russians still in Prussian territory to return home. What amazed HLP was Napoleon's concession, since at this time the victorious French army was poised on the southern frontiers of Prussia, whose own army was demobilized.

20. *Mémoires d'un Père pour servir à l'instruction de ses enfans*, 4 vols. (Paris, 1804), translated as *Memoirs of Marmontel*, 4 vols. (London: Longman, Hurst, Rees, and Orme, 1805).
Jean-François Marmontel (1723–99), essayist and dramatist.

21. *Memoirs of Richard Cumberland. Written by himself, containing an Account of his Life and Writings, interspersed with Anecdotes and Characters of several of the most distinguished Persons of his Time, with whom he has had Intercourse and Connexion* (London: Lackington, Allen, 1806–7).

22. The Reverend George Stanley Faber (1773–1854), *A Dissertation on the Prophecies that have been fulfilled, are now fulfilling, or will hereafter be fulfilled, relative to the great period of 1260 years*, 2 vols. (London: F. C. and J. Rivington, 1806). Enlarged and revised, it went through five editions by 1814.

23. Faber's eight Bampton lectures delivered in 1801 were published as *Horæ Mosaicæ*, 2 vols. (Oxford, 1801).
See also his work entitled *A Dissertation on the Mysteries of the Cabiri* (Oxford: At the University Press for the Author, and sold by F. and C. Rivington, 1803).

24. Charles Bennet (1743–1822), fourth earl of Tankerville (1767).

TO LADY WILLIAMS

Bath
Monday 3: March 1806.

Your Ladyship's Letter my dear Madam gave me an Opportunity of contributing a *little* to Miss Williams's Pleasure by sending her the enclosed:[1] She kindly contributes a great deal to ours, and has behaved with true Friendship certainly, since we have been confined by this vexatious Influenza. I hope to be soon released tho' and go with her to Miss Sharpe's Benefit tho' that fine Singer has like her Auditors, suffered terribly this Year from Coughs, Colds, Tooth-aches— and a whole Train of Torments which People agree to call—*an Influenza*. North Wales does not by your Ladyship's Account wholly escape the Contagion, and our Irish Friends tell us that Dublin is full of a similar Complaint.

I am glad your Dean &c. like the new Ministry, I would fain have the People contented at *some time,* and *in some way.*[2] Mr. Wynne of Plâsnewydd used to break his heart for want of Mr. Fox, he will now enjoy the Thoughts of this happy Change.[3]

The Bishop delights himself still more rationally in my Mind, with the sight of a happy Family and promising Children willing to be diverted by Punch or Joan, altho' capable of the highest Instruction, and each in their separate Stations likely to obtain it.[4] What your Ladyship tells me of the Governante is very pleasing indeed.

Mrs. Williams has behaved *sweetly* to keep her good Looks through so trying a Winter, but the *rated* Invalides have suffered less than healthy Subjects upon the whole, and Mr. Hughes of Kinmael with his irregular Pulse,[5] makes Battle better than many Younger Fellows against the common Foe of Mankind.[6]—— That Expression though meant for Death, puts one in Mind of *Buonaparte,* who threatens and destroys at a great Rate, yet must suffer some Vexation too at this Capture of the Cape of good Hope.[7]—Private Letters read in this Town yesterday, tell that my Lord Lauderdale is going over to make Peace immediately, and stop an Invasion which he does not himself believe is coming.[8]

I see not why Lord Lauderdale who was so fond of the French Democrates,[9] should be any particular Favourite with Buonaparte, who is said to have been tampering with the French Emigrants now in London for facilitating his Projects against England.

Said I not well to Dear Mrs. Williams that She would yet live to see many wonderful Events? I did not however promise She should outlive Mahomet's Tomb,[10] or the Continuation of honours to his Shrine, but Things go on very rapidly—and the World seems running down hill as a Wheel does, increasing in velocity with every Rotation.[11] Some one speaking on the Subject said it was ending like a Game at Draughts—all who are *left*, are forced up and made *Kings of.* They are strange Times to be sure.

Meanwhile the new American War which frights so many People frights not *me:*[12] open Enemies are safer than Secret ones, and they are now playing us every treacherous Trick in their Power;—ensuring *here*, and loading with Goods they wish to have taken for purpose of supplying their French Allies—'tis better go to War with them at once; They can do us little more harm than they *have* done, when by false Intelligence they sent Lord Nelson to look for his Prey in wrong Places.

But we have not yet spoken of the Lleweney Family,[13] and for the best possible Reason *on my part*——because I never hear any thing of them or from them. *One* Letter I received from Lady de B———[14] since we left Wales, saying how happy She was with Her Children and her Friends, and dear Lady Orkney at Randalls: but that must have been Ten Weeks ago—and not a Breath concerning any of the family has ever reached me since.

Mr. William Clarges crossed me here one Night at an Assembly,[15] but I saw him no more; and to say true this is completely a moving Picture, a magic Lantern, like that which Mr. Leo[16] gave the Babies at dear Bodylwyddan and one set of Figures slide off, whilst another Set slide on. I hope it will not end exactly the same way as when little Miss Emma cried "Look sharp Mrs. Piozzi, for the Devil will come at the last."[17]

Farewell kind and lovely Lady; present me with affectionate Respects to Sir John and Mrs. Williams and Accept Mr. Piozzi's *hoarsely*-uttered Compliments with those of your ever faithful / H: L: P.

Text: Ry. 2 (1802–6). *Address:* Lady Williams / Bodylwyddan / near St. Asaph / Flintshire / North Wales. *Postmark:* BATH.

1. The enclosure is missing. For Margaret Williams, sister of Sir John of Bodelwyddan, see HLP to Ly W, 18 December 1798, no. 1.
2. For the Reverend William Davies Shipley, dean of Saint Asaph, see HLP to LC, 30 September 1796, nn. 9 and 10. HLP thought that the ministry had a Whiggish tint which would have appealed to the liberal dean.
3. Robert Watkin Wynne had little interest in the makeup of the Ministry of All the Talents or even in Fox as foreign secretary in Grenville's administration. For Wynne, see HLP to Q, 3 April 1796, n. 18; 14 March 1806, n. 4
For Charles James Fox (1749–1806), see HLP to John Ewen, November 1802, nn. 7, 9.
4. Horsley had but one son, Heneage (1776–1847), collated by the bishop to the valuable living of Gresford in Denbighshire and to a stall in the cathedral church of Saint Asaph. Young Horsley had married on 25 June 1801 the Limerick-born Frances Emma Bourke (d. 18 December 1821), who bore Frances on 4 December 1804 (baptized 1 January 1805). For the burial date of Mrs. Horsley, see *Pre-1855 Gravestone Inscriptions in Angus*, vol. 3, in the office of the Scottish Genealogical Society.
For Bishop Samuel Horsley, see HLP to Q, 7 November 1796, n. 14.
5. For the Reverend Hughes of Kinmel Park, see HLP to LC, 21 April 1800, n. 9.
6. Num. 16:29: "the common death of all men."
7. *The London Gazette Extraordinary* on 28 February announced the capitulation of the town and Dutch garrison of the Cape of Good Hope to Major General Sir David Baird (1757–1829). More specifically, he defeated General Jan Willem Janssens on 8 January; on 10 January Capetown surrendered, as did Janssens eight days later.
8. The Whig James Maitland (1759–1839), eighth earl of Lauderdale (S., 1789). *The Times* (17 February) reported that on 15 February "The King has been pleased to grant the dignity of a Baron of the United Kingdom of Great Britain and Ireland to the Right Hon. James Earl of Lauderdale . . . by the name, style, and title of Baron Lauderdale, of Thirlestane, in the county of Berwick." This honor preceded his appointment announced shortly thereafter as a joint commissioner to France (effective 1 August 1806).
9. From 1793 onward Lauderdale used the Lords to denounce England's war with France, and on one occasion he allegedly appeared in the House wearing a costume associated with Jacobinism. On 5 June 1795 he introduced a motion (which received only eight votes) in favor of concluding a peace with France.
10. Cf. HLP to Q, 14 March 1806, n. 8.
11. Cf. Horace, *Odes*, 3.10.10.
12. According to the *Courier*, 21 February: difficulties between the United States and Great Britain arose from what the Americans "related to the infringements of their rights, and of the impress made on their seamen by the English ships of war."
On 26 February the *Courier* made specific charges against the American bill on behalf of impressed seamen, which "has passed to a second reading." The newspaper concluded with a caveat: "The passing of such a Bill, we shall consider, as tantamount almost to a declaration of war against this country."
The *Courier* continued its attack on the United States and the bill respecting the impressment of seamen. The newspaper nevertheless hoped (3 March): "This dispute . . . may yet . . . be adjusted, without compromising the honour or the rights of either country."
13. Lord and Lady Kirkwall and their young sons.
14. For Eleanor De Blaquiere, see HLP to LC, 19 March 1799, n. 4; for Lady Orkney, HLP to LC, 5 October 1797, n. 3.
15. William (1782–1807), the son of Sir Thomas and Lady Clarges, was now a student at Christ Church, Oxford.
16. For Daniel Leo, see HLP to Q, 23 February 1794, n. 3.
17. Emma Williams (1798–1889) was one of five daughters of Ly W and Sir John.

TO HESTER MARIA THRALE

Bath Fryday
14: March 1806.

I take (as Mrs. Siddons says) this *Opportunity* of writing by Mr. Horace Twiss who is going to London and asked me for Commands;[1] tho' I really know nothing that requires telling of, except that Mrs. Mostyn with her Two Parrots, Three Children, a Tutor, and two Maids, set out on Monday Morning to pass the *Summer* at Segroid:[2] in and through such Storms of Snow and Hail as are Seldom seen even in January, with the keenest Frost we have witnessed since 1806 began to be our Date;—but never was Year so capricious with regard to Weather, so luckless with regard to Health. Since my last Letter poor Mrs. Ormsby,[3] and Mr. Wynne of Plâsnewydd[4] have swelled the List of Mortality among *my* Acquaintance; Hippisley Coxe was *every* body's Acquaintance. He died in this Town Three Days ago.[5] Like Richard the 2d:'s Queen in Shakespear's Play—we talk on Testaments and think on Wills alone; a propos Mr. Cator must have been a dilatory Friend not to have got you those unclaimed Dividends long ago——of which I wrote him word 3 or four Years past, and concerning which he must have been much better informed than me at all Times.[6]

Well! if we have outlived The Kingdom of Naples,[7] we have likewise outlived the Superstition of Mahomet and his Tomb:[8] Turcism will soon tumble when its Foundation is so sapped—and its Metropolis will doubtless be now of short duration——as Capital of the Ottoman Empire. Who are these *Warabees* as our Newspapers call them?[9] probably only *Arabies* with some aspirate which serves to confound Pronunciation, as my English Maid in Italy persisted to call *Morichelli* the great Singer *Molly Kelly* always:[10] and I am in my own Mind perswaded that the Difference between Languages has been so increased by each nation calling the same Thing *their own Way*—as to produce the apparent Impossibility of their ever being again recalled——*as they will be*——to their primitive and original Tongue. Doctor Randolph says truly, that my Hebrew Roots are all drying up now; but I must water and nurse them when we get back to Wales.[11] Here is a pretty Book come out called Christian Politics, I have read nothing so good a long Time:[12] and for Ladies who love Heart-breaking Fictions, Romance or Novel;—Mathilde beats them all.[13]

Lysons's great Work is not yet talked of, I dare say however that it will be very useful.[14] Authors are not to be despised because of their Tameness,——The Navigable Canal tho' neither sparkling from the Spring like Genius, nor rolling in deep and copious Torrents like Learning; is excellent for unloading heavy Luggage at our Doors, with Comfort and Convenience:——This has been a good Year for Books. I borrowed Cumberland's Memoirs when they first came out, and people snatched it from me in three Days; I borrowed it *again,* read it quite thro';—*and bought it after all.* It is the Writing of a Wit, a Scholar, and a Man of the World united.

Mr. Piozzi sends you many Compliments: he cannot yet speak to be heard for Cough and hoarseness; yet he *does* mend, or I *do* think so. Miss Sharp has 250£ offered her to sing at Liverpool, and we advise her to go, but Mr. Siddons says if She gets Colds, and loses Scholars, that Sum will make her no amends. He has been very bad Poor Fellow! but is Safe now.

Is it a Joke that Mr. Gillon is going to be married?—Governor Bruce told it *me*; but like his Cousin the Traveller he loves to talk *largely*, and I really could not find out at the Close of our Conversation whether it was Jest or Earnest.[15]

Miss Caldwell told me today that we should see Lady Orkney here, but *that* Intelligence seems too good to be true.[16] Let me know about Mr. Gillon before I write, because one shall be deficient in good Manners either way, if one takes such a Tale up *wrong*, and I would not offend him for the World.

Isabella Hamilton hopes you don't forget her. She is violently éprise de Mrs. Mostyn, and seeks all She can to drive away the Thought of losing her Sister—— but it will persue her: That hapless Girl with the fine Teeth who we saw playing on the Piano e forte, is in a deep Decline, *and die She must.*[17]

Adieu! keep yourselves *well*, and be thankful that You can do So.—We stand as in a Battle, and the Ranks are thinning upon every Side. It quite alarms your truly / Affectionate Mother / H: L: P.

Text: Bowood Collection. *Address:* Miss Thrale / Great Cumberland Street / London / No. 13. *Postmark:* 17 MR 1806.

1. Horace Twiss (1787–1849), nephew of SS; eldest son of Frances and Francis Twiss. See LC to HLP, 7 July 1812, n. 2.
2. The children of CMM and JMM were: John Salusbury (1798–1827); Henry (Harry) Meredith (1799–1840); Thomas Arthur Bertie (1801–76). For their later schooling, see HLP to JSPS, 22 February 1808. When they were pupils at RD's "university," the schoolmaster found them bright enough, but distracted by CMM. See also HLP to Q, 22 November 1807; to JSPS, 16 July 1810, and 1 July 1813.
3. For Margaret Ormsby, of Porkington, Salop, see PSP to PSP [ca. 26 July 1800], n. 5.
4. HLP had learned of the death of "poor Robert Watkin Wynne, aged fifty" (b. ca. 1754), from the Denbigh attorney John Oldfield (1760–1841), who had written on 14 March 1806 (Ry. 608.42): "His remains were interred on Monday last [the 10th]. Thank God he had made a Will and the best arrangements he was able to for the good of his Creditors and the benefit of his numerous Family."
Wynne, ill for some time, had signed his will on 15 October 1805. He was able to arrange for the payment of most of his debts and for a major bequest to his wife, Ann Sobieski Wynne. See P.R.O., Prob. 11/1453/974; HLP to Q, 27 April 1796, n. 2.
5. HLP has confused the names of John Hippisley Coxe (d. 1782) and Charles Westley Coxe (d. 10 March 1806) of Kemble, Wiltshire. For many years the latter had been a magistrate and deputy lieutenant of Wiltshire (*Bath Chronicle,* 20 March 1806). For John Hippisley Coxe, see HLP to Sophia Byron, 24 June 1788, n. 4.
6. On 27 March HLP wrote to Q on the subject of the dividends. "I will not however be a *dilatory Friend;* and as I hastened to tell you the *first* Instant I was informed of those unclaimed Dividends, so will I tell you of the last Conversation held by me in the Pumproom. It was with Mr. Perkins who came to Bath to fetch away his sick wife.

"'So Mr. Cator is dead, Sir'—bawld I in his deaf Ears. 'Yes,' replied he, 'I put into *his* Hands some Time ago all the Documents left in *my* hands concerning old Lemon's Money.' 'Old Lemon's Money! why was it ever *found?*' says I; 'No; only that 8000£ which we always knew of,' answered Perkins; 'for which the Wolravens and Chapmans maintained a long Suit at Law, and *with our help* Chapman's People were victorious. 'Mr. Thrale,' continued he, 'assisted that Family with Money and Advice for purpose of enabling them to gain the Cause, having previously bound them to entail the 8000£: on him and his Heirs for ever, after *their* Deaths: and,' added Mr. Perkins, 'I saw the last of the Chapmans drunk and dashing away on the Top of a Coachbox some Months past, from whence I think somebody told me that he fell—and if so, that eight Thousand Pounds must now belong to the Ladies'" (Bowood Collection).

7. *The Times* on 3 February reported that "the French army under the command of St. Cyr was advancing upon Naples, in three columns, which City, notwithstanding the preparations that were making to resist the enemy, is, probably, in their possession before now." Early in March *The Times* announced that Joseph Bonaparte, as "the future King was to make his solemn entry into the capital of the two Sicilies." Previously he had designated himself "Governor of the Kingdoms of Naples and Sicily."

General Laurent de Gouvion Saint-Cyr (1764–1830) was superseded by General André Masséna for the conquest of Naples.

8. As early as 1589 Sir Henry Wotton in one of his letters alluded to the popular supersitition of Mahomet's tomb being suspended between heaven and earth. Milton converted the legend to political use in *Eikonoklastes,* and Prior in *Alma* (2. 198–99) predicted "The balance always would hang even, / Like Mahomet's tomb, 'twixt earth and heaven."

9. HLP misspelled the name of the Wahhabis, who constituted a Muslim primitive movement founded by Mohammed ibn 'Abd al-Wahhab (1703–92) in the central part of Arabia (now Saudi Arabia).

But HLP was responding to reports of their fighting against Turkish rule, which appeared, e.g., in *The Times,* 22 February 1806.

"Intelligence . . . has been received from . . . the East India Company's Resident at Bagdad, containing an account of the capture of Medina by the Wahabees, whose army, having been reinforced from the desert, has overwhelmed the adjacent country, and taken the city by assault, with infinite bloodshed and devastation. They set fire to Medina, in various places, destroyed the mosques, after having ransacked them of their valuable shrines and treasures, and completely demolished the tomb of the Prophet."

(Turcism is an obsolete spelling of Turkism, i.e., Mohammedanism.)

10. For the soprano Anna (Reggio Emilia) Morichelli–Bosello, see HLP to Q, 4 March 1786, n. 12. (The "English Maid" was Mary Johnson.)

11. HLP's knowledge of Hebrew depended on her being tutored by the Reverend John Roberts.

12. Ely Bates, *Christian Politics* (London: Longman, et al., 1806).

13. The anonymous *Matilda; or the Adventures of an Orphan. An Interesting Tale,* published in London, undated. (The British Library conjectures 1804.) A chapbook, it consists of thirty-six pages.

14. See HLP to LC, 30 September 1801, n. 8. The first volume of *Magna Britannia* appeared in 1806 and dealt with the counties of Bedford, Berkshire, and Buckinghamshire. Published by Cadell and Davies, the ten-volume commentary was completed in 1822.

15. For Charles Andrew Bruce, governor of Prince of Wales Island, see HLP to PSP, 22 May 1802, n. 2. HLP apparently knew Governor Bruce through John Gillon. The two men had been friends from their days in the Leeward Islands in the West Indies. See Gillon's letter to HLP (21 April 1806; Ry. 577.141).

For James Bruce, the African traveler, see HLP to Q [22–23 October 1796], n. 3. Farington (8:2894) described James Bruce's experiences. "Henry Salt [formerly Farington's pupil], called—He landed on Sunday last at Portsmouth from the Neptune Man of War in which he came with Lord Valentia a passenger: from Gibraltar. He had accompanied His Lordship in a very extensive tour in India. They left England in 1802 in the month of June. Salt was 6 months in *Abyssinia,* and met with several persons in that Country who remembered the Traveller Bruce. He said much of what Bruce published was *authentic* but he added a good deal of the *fabulous.*—He described Abyssinia to be in a true *Feudal* state but very barbarous—Perpetual Hostility is kept up by what in Scotland would be called *Clans,* who are constantly at war with each other."

Gillon never married his long-time mistress Eleanor Hochkins, by whom he had a daughter. He left 2,000 guineas to the child, if she married. The contested will was to be in chancery court from 1811 until the final decree and order, 26 July 1816. See Chancery Index, P.R.O., C/33/1759–61.

16. Probably Mary Anne Caldwell (1755–1841), eldest daughter of Sir James (ca. 1720–84), fourth baronet (1744). His other surviving daughters were: Amelia Alice (ca. 1765–1841) and Elizabeth Frances (1767–1854). All three, residents of Bath, were interred nearby in the Weston family vault.

Sir James, of Castle Caldwell, county Fermanagh, was socially prominent in Dublin, Bath, and London. Educated at Dundalk and Trinity College (B.A., 1740), he was created count of Milan (1749) in the Holy Roman Empire by the Empress Maria Teresa for military service to Austria. He was elected F.R.S. (1753) and given the freedom of Dublin (1764).

On 18 December 1753 he had married at St. Anne's, Dublin, Elizabeth (1729–78), eldest daughter of Josiah Hort, archbishop of Tuam.

See William H. G. Bagshawe, *The Bagshawes of Ford.* For private circulation (London: Mitchell and

Hughes, 140 Wardour St., W., 1886), pp. 289–302, and the inserted manuscript pedigree of the Caldwell family (Ry. R95014); Frank Taylor, *Johnsoniana from the Bagshawe Muniments in the John Rylands Library: Sir James Caldwell, Dr. Hawkesworth, Dr. Johnson, and Boswell's Use of the 'Caldwell Minute'* (Manchester: The John Rylands University Library, 1952).

17. See HLP to Isabella Hamilton, 13 May 1805, n. 5.

TO THE REVEREND JOHN ROBERTS

[Bath,
between Dec. 1805 and Apr. 1806][1]

Dear Sir

The Questions you gave me to answer would be better replied to—in Conversation than Writing, because so much depends upon pronouncing the Words. We will begin with the French however. I find them capricious in their spelling Hebrew Names.[2] Japhet the Son of Noah, and Jared Father of Enoch[3] they write with a long J consonant—pronouncing softer than we do the same Letter, and more like the English Name *Shirley* or the Welsh *Shore.* Yet Solomon *Iarchi* the famous Rabbi of the 10th Century is spelt—and doubtless pronounced Vowelwise.[4] Names of Greek Etymology—where o follows the I, are kept right:—*Io* the Cow, and *Ion* the Tragic Poet, and Ionia, which they write *Ionie*, have the Vowel preceding for Example:[5] while *Hebrew* Appellations, Joseph, Josaphat, and *Josuè* as they call the Jewish Leader, have the consonant.[6]

Jupiter et *Junon* follow the Latin Method; and Juda, Jerusalem, Jephtè are all with long Js or Jays as some People call them.[7]

So much for the *French.*

Italians, when they are baptized Joseph, write themselves Giuseppe; because their Language abhors both the long J and the Greek *Phi* ϕ, but they print the Name of the blessed Virgin's Husband, *Josef*—and pronounce it as a Vowel. Saint John however is always written and spoken San Giovanni—and I believe the name of our Lord would be invariably Giesù as it commonly is written, but that being accustomed to pray in *Latin,* they take the Orthography as it is found *there,* and not seldom print it Jesus.

The common Hebrew Names Jethro,[8] and Jehoiakin they spell steadily with an I Vowel—Ietro and Ioachine, though if they christen a Baby after the Name of the Madonna's Father, that Boy will always write himself *Gioachino* in his own Country.—Italians however detest Jewish Appellations—and liked me a little the less for not having as they said (truly enough) a *Christian* Name: Tho' I once knew a Milanese Lady called Signora *Giuditta,* and that was certainly a little worse than mine:

The Explanation of the Spanish Way is more difficult *on Paper* because the long Is or Jays are Guttural in that Language, and *San Juan* is a single syllable when rightly pronounced; I mean *Juan* is.

The sacred Name by which God calls *himself* in Hebrew יְהוָה is used perpetually in the Spanish Bible *Jehovah Dios*—The *Lord God*; and the first Syllable is guttural—for Job and Joel &c. they are pronounced and written with the Vowel I as Yob, Yoel &c.[9]

Text: Victoria and Albert Museum Library. *Address:* Rev: John Roberts / Dymerchion.

1. The evidence for dating depends on the fact that HLP had begun studying Hebrew in the summer of 1805 under the tutelage of the Reverend John Roberts, then curate of Tremeirchion (Dymerchion). Their language discussions were carried on by post when the Piozzis made their annual visits from Wales to Bath. There they resided at Pulteney Street (1 December 1805 to 7 March 1806) and some other unspecified address before returning to Brynbella about the end of April. See *Thraliana* 2:1070, n. 2; Clifford, p. 417.

2. HLP in a letter rudimentary fashion anticipates the historical and scholarly account with which the editor Sir James Murray introduces the letter *J* in *OED*.

She was aware that the Roman letter *I* had developed into two forms, one with a tail, which subsequently came to be considered a separate letter. She would have known, further, that SJ in the *Dictionary* had begun the section with the comment: "I, is in English considered both as a vowel and consonant; though, since the vowel and consonant differ in their form as well as sound, they may be more properly accounted two letters." SJ, nevertheless, did not treat them as two letters.

Although HLP was reasonably accurate in rendering pronunciations, she was limited by being without phonetic alphabets, which would have enabled greater precision.

"In general," Professor Nelson Francis of Brown University advises us, "I would think that Mrs. P. was ahead of her time; she might have been a good phonetician if she had had the apparatus to work with!"

3. Japheth was the son of Noah and the brother of Shem and Ham. See especially Gen. 5:29–30, 6:10, 7:13, 9:20–23, 27.

Jared was an antediluvian patriarch of the line of Seth; the father of Enoch. See Gen. 5:15–20; 1 Chron. 1:2; Luke 3:37.

4. Rabbi Solomon ben Isaac, or Shelomoh ben Yizhak (1040–1105) was familiarly known as *Rashi* (his acronym), a word derived from the Hebrew initials of his name. He was erroneously called Jarchi (or Yarhi) by some.

He was born, lived, and died in Troyes. One of the most studious of medieval biblical commentators, he was recognized particularly for his exegesis of the Pentateuch and Talmud.

5. The mythological Io was a priestess of Hera at Argos. Zeus was enamored of her but to conceal her from Hera gave her the shape of a heifer. For her suffering created by Hera, see Aeschylus, *Prometheus Bound*, ll. 561–905; Ovid, *Metamorphoses*, 1.583–694.

The Greek poet Ion (b. ca. 490 B.C.) of Chios and Athens.

Ionia refers to the central part of the west coast of Asia Minor, probably related to a section of the Greek people mentioned in the *Iliad* (13.685).

6. For the story of Joseph and his brothers, see Gen. 37; for that of Joseph in Egypt, see chaps. 39–48; for Joseph as a type of Christ, see HLP to the Ladies of Llangollen, 14 June 1801, and to Q, 21 June 1801.

Jehoshaphet was a recorder in the administrations of David and Solomon (2 Sam. 8:16, 20:24; 1 Kings 4:3; 1 Chron. 18:15).

Josué is the Douay version of Joshua. He was the son of Nun and the major figure in the Old Testament account of the conquest of Canaan. See particularly the Book of Joshua.

7. Juda or Judah perhaps originated as the name of a place or a region, later becoming a tribal name, and finally that of a person—the fourth son of Jacob and the virtually sanctified leader of the tribe of Judah. See Gen. 35:23, 46:12; Exod. 1:2; 1 Chron. 2:3, etc.

Jephté is the Douay version of Jephthah, the Gileadite warrior who as "ruler" or "judge" freed Israel from the Ammonites, sacrificed his daughter to fulfill a vow, and defeated the Ephraimites. See Judg. 11:1–15; 12:1–7.

8. Jethro was a priest of Midian; the father-in-law of Moses (Exod. 3:1; 4:18; 18:1–2, 5–6, 12).

His given name Eliakim (2 Kings 23:34–36; 2 Chron. 36:4) was changed by Pharaoh Neco to

Jehoiakim. The second son of Josiah, he succeeded to the throne of Israel; see 2 Kings 23 and 24; 2 Chron. 36.

9. For Job, the man of great wealth and well-being suddenly overtaken by misfortune, see the Book of Job.

See also the Book of Joel, the second of the twelve short prophetic books which make up the concluding section of the Old Testament.

TO HESTER MARIA THRALE

[Brynbella]
Monday 26: May 1806.

I feel quite Thankful for your friendly Letter my dearest Girl, and Mr. Piozzi is much obliged by your kind Remembrance—He keeps from Bed and is chearful; tho the poor Piano e forte no longer a Resource of Comfort to him, presents only a painful Retrospect of Times long past. Miss Parke sings and plays like a first rate Professor, whilst her Manners are those of a Well-bred Dilletant;[1] none of them all *love Music* as She does I think——The Sharpina as we call her, would consider herself as happy never to touch an Instrument again: *She* too is a sweet Performer; and will I hope call here as She goes back to Bath from *Ireland*.[2] Miss Ormsby's Resolution to settle *there* pleases nobody—I believe, except the Irish:[3] You are correct in your notions concerning her Father's Family and Origin but they have of late Years lived somewhat Splendidly I am told.[4]

Of Abbé Nicholls as we all love to term him, it is ever my delight to hear; and to hear Good:[5] if he wants for no Pleasures, but those Romantic Scenery can afford him, the Tour you propose will complete his Felicity: but though we should be too happy to welcome him here at Brynbella I shall most certainly send him back again if he has not visited Kader Idris in his way.[6]

Well! it is a very surprizing Truth—but a Truth it *is* that while whole Nations are suffering Oppressions *past Compute* as Cumberland says:[7] some Individuals among us are only distressed how and in what to find Amusement: A fine Man came into this Country last Summer in Search of Rural Beauty—he had bid high for Grongar Hill he told me, but a Flaw in the Title hindered his purchasing, and no Place ever pleased him after *that* till he lighted on Llanbedr here in our Vale;[8] The surrounding Mountains of which he is covering with Timber Trees, having planted 17000 near his House this last Season; and means to continue the truly patriotic Sport. A novus homo you may be sure he is—the name Ablett—"Well, Well, go to; no matter for his Name Man" as the Constable says in Shakespear.[9]

Your new Acquaintance Mathias if *ryghte I arede his Name*,[10] is the Nephew of an old Merchant: you have heard me speak of, who had a famous Base Voice, and was a great Musician.[11] My Father thought him friendly I believe, but he proved false to us who really loved him; and leagued with the Second Lady

Salusbury to procure my *Disinheritance* because I refused to marry young Clifford a Dutch Negotiant to whom he was Guardian,[12] and who was heir to the great Commercial House at Amsterdam—second to Hope alone.[13] The Ill will might however have ceased with the old Uncle; but this *Mathias* Son to *his* Brother Vincent of Scotland Yard,[14] burst out *My Enemy fierce and fell*[15]—and no Mr. Ray with his kind seven Guineas being at hand, he began his Career of Wit and Learning, both which he possesses in a very eminent Degree, by holding me up for a Scare Crow[16]—to which I only replied by quoting his Verses with Approbation—(not those against myself)—in my best and biggest Book.[17] Page 512—2d. Vol.

Apropos to dear Mr. Ray, I will try *my* Eloquence this Time next Year with him,—that is if he will permit—for last Time we were in London he nor his Lady would return our Visits. Capricious as he may be however, Mr. Ray is a Man of consummate Honour and unwarped Integrity—and if he will not accept my Kindness—because he can extort my Esteem—why with all my heart—Every one take their own Way.

I would love Mr. Mathias if he would let me; because he is a good Scholar, and a good Aristocrate, and because I do believe he once sate in my Lap when he was four years old perhaps, and I was fourteen.

Meanwhile 'tis a wondrous World is it not? And bello—as Mr. Piozzi says, perche e variabile. To be sure one has seen a Thing or Two since Dear Susanna first opened her Eyes upon the Ruins of Palmyra there,[18] over against our Nursery Windows in Southwark—and now I say She is six and Thirty Years old; but Mr. Piozzi says She is only 35—Good News indeed! but I cannot believe it. I believe less and less of every thing—every day—and very little *indeed* of Mr. Mostyn's Danger.[19] The People in Scotland, Wales, and Ireland think it *respectful* to make those they wish well to—fancy themselves ill. Alas! Alas! poor Mr. Such a one, they cry—Alas! Alas! see but how thin he grows &c. I am however all of your Opinion that his Mind and Body both have more need of Exercise than Medicine—had he Mr. Piozzi's Feet and Fingers for one Week only, he would know what ailed him, and be good humoured when the Pain should remit its violence. As for working with Lysons I think *his* Broom should be literal not figurative——Sweeping away some real Cobwebs off those old Heroe's Busts might be useful to him.

I thought my Lord Melvil must have been made to refund *something*, like Leeches put in Salt to disgorge before they *stick again*.—Will the World be content with his Acquittal?[20] Here is *tenpenny worth of Nought* sure enough—as a Woman in Yorkshire said when She shewed me a bit of Beef for our Dinners.—She meant *Neat* tho'; and I mean *nothing* but to wish Susan Joy and to say how sincerely I am hers and Yours / H: L: P.—

Fear no Phantoms, nor be perswaded to pay much for what is worth so little—but

Jog on Jog on the Footpath Way
And merrily over the Style a

The Piozzi Letters

A Cheerful heart wags many a day
But a sad one tires in a Mile a.²¹

Text: Bowood Collection. *Address:* Miss Thrale / No. 13. / Great Cumberland Street / London. *Postmark:* May 28 1806.

1. Maria Hester Parke (1775–1822) was the eldest daughter of John Parke (1745–1829), a celebrated oboist. She herself was a singer, pianist, and composer, trained primarily by her father. She appeared often in concerts as pianist and as the principal soprano. In 1815, she married John Beardmore and retired professionally. See also HLP to JSPS, 13 December 1809.
2. For Elizabeth Sharp (1793–1849), see HLP to PSP, 26 April 1801, n. 4.
3. Mary Jane Ormsby (1781–1869) moved between Porkington, Salop, and Dublin, marrying on 11 January 1815 William Ormsby–Gore (1779–1860), M.P. for the counties of Leitrim (1806–7), Carnarvon (1830–31), and North Salop (1835–57). See HLP to PSP [ca. 26 July 1800], n. 5.
4. Mary Jane Ormsby's fortune came to her through her mother Margaret (d. 1806), the heiress of William Owen of Porkington. See HLP to PSP [ca. 26 July 1800], n. 5; 30 November 1801, n. 9. Through her father Miss Ormsby inherited Willowbrook House near Sligo in Ireland.
5. For the Reverend Norton Nicholls (ca. 1742–1809) of Blundeston, Suffolk, see HLP to PSP, 11 May 1795, n. 1.
6. Cader (or Caider) Idris, "the chair of Idris," an imposing mountain in North Wales, frequently mentioned in Welsh literature.
7. In a letter to HLT on 4 April 1776, SJ wrote: "Every evil will be more easily born while you fondly love one another, and every good will be enjoyed with encrease of delight *past compute* to use the phrase of Cumberland" (Hyde-Redford 2:318). SJ refers to the merchant jargon used throughout the dramatist's *The West Indian* (1771). Cf. HLP to TSW, 30 December 1800, n. 3.
8. HLP's cousin, the Reverend Edward Thelwall of Llanbedr Hall, Denbighshire, sold the property in 1804 to Joseph Ablett (d. 1827), originally of Manchester. For the next several years Ablett continued to buy property adjoining his initial purchase. In "Letters Patent," dated 6 February 1809, he was appointed "custodian of county Denbigh, with responsibility for collecting rates and profits on behalf of the Crown" (item 310, "Schedule of Bathafarn and Llanbedr Deeds," N.L.W.).
HLP is as obscure about Ablett's identity as she is about the Welsh estate for which he negotiated. Grongar Hill, the subject of a well–known poem by John Dyer (1726), is a picturesque region of Carmarthenshire, near Llandilo, overlooking the vale of Towy.
9. HLP's variation of the dialogue between Angelo and Elbow in *Measure for Measure*, 2. 1. 45–46.
10. The satiric poet Thomas James Mathias (ca. 1754–1835) was the Queen's treasurer and librarian.
11. The merchant James Mathias (1710–82) "was eminently skilled in Musick I asked Dr Burney about that—Yes says he the Man has Knowledge enough, but no more taste than a Bull" (*Thraliana* 1:148).
12. During the reign of Charles II, a Clifford became the most considerable planter in Surinam and other islands in the West Indies. When Surinam was ceded to the Dutch "by a peace, as some sort of compensation for their valuable colony of New York," the descendants of the original Clifford "laid large claims upon the Dutch West–India company for the losses which they [had] then sustained, and which have never yet been properly adjusted." See *AR* 24 (1781): 103.
One of the present litigants and HLS's one-time suitor was George Clifford, described as "Dutch Merchant, Walbrook," in *The Universal Directory; or, the Nobleman and Gentleman's True Guide to the Masters and Professors of the Liberal and Polite Arts and Sciences* (1763).
See also *Thraliana* 1:32–33 and n. 3; Clifford, pp. 22 and 32.
13. At first glance, "Hope" implies a wistful metaphor for HLS's early matrimonial prospects. In fact, "Hope" is her anglicized rendering of "Hop," the name of a Dutch dynasty with mercantile and political influence. Although we find no evidence of a direct connection with HLS, the family line of Hop figured prominently in eighteenth and nineteenth century England during her lifetime.
Beginning with Jacob and Renogie Symens Fortuyn sometime in the late sixteenth century, the Hops—mainly identified with Amsterdam—had for their principal members:

a. Cornelis Hop (1620–1704), affluent merchant, public official, and lawyer.

b. Jacob Hop (1654–1725), prominent in the East India service.

c. Cornelis Hop (1685–1762), a director of the Society of Surinam; an officer of Amsterdam's East and West India Companies.

d. Baron Hendrik Hop (1687–1761), brother of the above, a lieutenant general posted to London (where he died) as envoy extraordinary; associated with the Prince of Orange.

e. Johan Hop (1709–72), affiliated with the Dutch treasury office; his mother was Sara Johanna Bailly.

f. Hendrik Hop (d. 1801), official in the Dutch ministry.

g. Baron Hendrik Hop (fl. 1768–1824), active in the diplomatic corps, including service in Great Britain (1813–24).

14. Vincent Mathias (ca. 1711–82), sub-treasurer in the Queen's household and treasurer of Queen Anne's Bounty. He was the father of Thomas James.

15. The combination of "fierce and fell" may be traced in poetic and rhetorical usage to the fourteenth century (OED).

16. See HLP to ST, 6 November 1796, n. 12.

17. HLP believed that the French Revolution was a calamity for taste and learning that caused demands "for German plays and novels of a new sort, filled with what the Parisians call, emphatically enough, *phantasmagorie.*" To clinch her point, HLP cited one of Thomas James Mathias's couplets from *The Pursuits of Literature*: "Was it for this, in Leo's fostering reign, / Learning uprose with tempests in her train." See *Retrospection* 2:512.

18. HLP's facetious analogy of Southwark and the remains of Palmyra which, with its great temple of Bel (or Baal), shrines, theaters, colonnaded streets, and monumental arches, stands today as one of the most imposing sights in the Syrian desert. Palmyra was captured and partly destroyed by Aurelian ca. 273 A.D.

SAT was born 23 May 1770 in Southwark.

19. John Gillon on 28 September 1806 (Ry. 579.148) "was very sorry to hear of Mr. Mostyn's precarious State of Health. I have heard that he is not careful enough, as to Regimen. It will be, indeed, an awkward Situation for a Young Widow, to be left with young Children to bring up and educate."

JMM died intestate in May 1807 of tuberculosis and, probably, dissipation.

20. Henry Dundas (1742–1811), cr. baron of Dunira, county Perth, and Viscount Melville of Melville, county Edinburgh (24 December 1802). The trial of Lord Melville, which began to take shape late in January 1806, stemmed from his role as first lord of the admiralty between May 1804 and April 1805. "In June 1806 he was impeached . . . by the House of Lords on 10 charges, but acquitted, 12 June 1806, on all, though it was but by small majorities (27 and 31), on the charge of having permitted his paymaster . . . to withdraw public money and to employ it for his (Melville's) use" (*Peerage*).

HLP vindicated her sympathy for Lord Melville with a defense provided by two politically conservative pamphlets: *An Address to the Public containing a Review of the Charges exhibited against Lord Viscount Melville* (1805), and *Exposure of the Persecution of Lord Melville* (1805).

21. Shakespeare, *The Winter's Tale*, 4. 3. 123–26.

TO THE REVEREND LEONARD CHAPPELOW

Brynbella
4th: of June 1806.

After so long Silence such a lowspirited Letter afflicts me seriously; Poor dear Mr. Chappelow! indeed I am very sorry.[1] Lord Bradford and his charming Family keep well I hope, and you must try and be chearful notwithstanding these public Vexations.² We are not Buonaparte's Subjects yet, I think few of us would outlive the day we were declared such;——it would kill *me* sooner than cold Water by half.

Are not you very sorry for his Admirals Villeneuve and Linois?—*one* forced on Suicide,³ and *one* plunged in disgraceful Penury⁴——Surely no *French*men will serve such a Master, and his new Slaves in Greece⁵ and Italy will get tired of the Yoke in Time.⁶ Nothing so terrifies me as the Dread of his getting over Land to India,⁷ and really if Alexander sits quiet to see him possessed of the old Græcian Peloponesus I know not where or how he can be stopt.⁸ Will Russia suffer such a dismemberment of the Turkish Empire? which all her Sovereigns for these last Hundred Years have considered as their own lawful Prey? 'Tis difficult to believe that a Lyon will stand still, while Wolves devour a fat Bullock before his Face.

You are perfectly correct about the Malignity of Reviewers; They fall upon Friend and Foe: and Joanna Baillie being ill-treated by her own Countrymen—— The Edinburghers may shew how Impossible it is for them to let *any* Work take its fair chance with the Public which comes not forth from their own Junto.⁹ Lock your Verses up therefore—if you are averse to running the Gauntlet, but don't *destroy* them; There is no Justice in such Conduct: wait till better Times, and amuse your Self at your Leisure without provoking their Envy, or suffering your Feelings to be wounded by their Malice. A Writer who faces the Reading World in these days, must be as callous as Sir Knight, who says——

> I have been beaten till I know
> What Wood the Cudgel's of, by th' Blow;
> And kick'd till I can tell you whether
> The Shoe were Spanish, or Neat's Leather.¹⁰

I never see any Review but when I am at Bath——and cannot hear how they have treated Cumberland's entertaining Work;¹¹ it is sweetly written sure—say what they will:—a most pleasing mixture of Fact and Sentiment—Seriousness and Levity—I read it over Three Times—borrowing it,—and bought it after all.

Mr. Piozzi sends you 1000 Compliments—he will not try to repel *his* Gout you may assure Yourself, and Doctor Kinglake seems no Perswasive Writer; I doubt his having done much harm to anybody—but one is so desirous of finding a *Reason* for Death always, as if Death waited for *Reasons*.¹² Many young People who never felt Gout have died suddenly this Year, and *very* many who never heard of Doctor Kinglake——I wonder you that are a Naturalist should express no Surprise at our Paucity of Rain these last 12 Months: The Springs are strangely low, the Ground parched and arid——and a tall Man—Lord Bulkeley for example might have walked over the Avon at Bath on the 1st of December 1805 or on the 1st of May 1806——when all Rivers are wont to be full from the Autumnal or Spring Rains.¹³ Our Wheat looks thin here, and poorly; and my new planted Shrubs are gasping for Thirst.

Lord and Lady Kirkwall and Countess of Orkney have left the Neighbourhood, so have the dear Blaquieres: poor Cecy Mostyn has a sad Loss of them——

her Husband is at Bath for his Health—She and her Boys at Segroid. It was Susanna you were walking with I believe, but tis no Matter——She was the Swinger[14] at least so many Years ago.

Convey this Letter free Cost to them Dear Mr. Chappelow and accept my good husband's best Wishes with those of / Yours ever / H: L: P.

Text: Ry. 561.134. *Address:* Rev: Mr. Chappelow.

1. Elizabeth, dowager Lady Bradford, had died on 6 March 1806 at Bath.
2. Napoleon's domination of Europe became a fact after the climactic battle of Austerlitz, 2 December 1805, and the subsequent treaty of Pressburg (now Bratislava, Slovak Republic), 26 December 1805. Franz II was left with little more than a hollow title, Holy Roman Emperor. Austria was stripped of all the Venetian territory that she had gained through the peace of Campo Formio, 17 October 1797. She lost additional possessions in south Germany, the Tyrol, and the Voralberg, although she was allowed to annex Salzburg. In effect, then, Austria was barred from Italy and Germany. France, meanwhile, acquired Piedmont, Parma, and Piacenza. England, for its part, was bound to confront France virtually alone. The possibility of such a condition had long troubled LC.
3. Pierre-Charles-Jean-Baptiste-Sylvestre de Villeneuve (1763–1806) was defeated at the battle of Trafalgar, where he was taken prisoner. Freed in 1806, he returned from England to France and there committed suicide.

See, e.g., the *Daily Advertiser, Oracle,* and *True Briton,* 12 May 1806: "Admiral Villeneuve has put an end to his existence at *Rennes*. It was said that he had been summoned to *Paris* to take his Trial before a Court Martial. He was in a state of great depression before quitting this country. . . . This unfortunate Officer has preferred falling by his own hands rather than by those of the Government Assassins, who, in the Wood of *Vincennes,* and at the hour of midnight, execute the bloody Decrees of its base and prostitute Tribunals."

4. Charles-Alexandre-Léon Durand (1761–1848), comte de Linois, had risen to the grade of contre-amiral in 1799.

"On the 13th of March [1806] sir John Borlase Warren had the good fortune to overtake the Marengo of eighty guns, and the Belle Poule of 40, the remainder of the French squadron, under admiral Linois, that had so long infested the Indian seas. An engagement ensued, which lasted from before day-light till near ten o'clock in the morning; the result of it was the surrender of the enemy" (*AR* 48 [1806]: 335). The French admiral became a British prisoner from this time until 1814. For Linois's anxiety and effort to explain his defeat, see Farington 8:2834.

5. HLP's premature response to a French report reproduced, e.g., by *The Times,* 2 June. "As soon as the Russians shall have evacuated Cattaro, Corfu, Zante, &c. [the Ionian Islands] will be attacked, as the Seven Isles formerly belonged to Venice [and hence, by the treaty of Campo Formio, were declared a French possession]; the productions of those islands will revive our commerce." Not until the signing of the treaty of Tilsit did the czar cede the Ionian Islands and other Mediterranean possessions in return for France aiding Russia against the Sultan if Turkey refused to make peace within three months, etc.

6. Napoleon had himself crowned as king of Italy in the cathedral of Milan on 26 May 1805. He annexed the Republic of Genoa to France. He gave Lucca as a fief to one of his sisters, the Princess Elisa Bacciocchi. The king and queen of Naples, having already fled to Sicily, were again prepared to run either to Malta or Spain in the event of a French invasion. Joseph Bonaparte had been named king of Naples and the Two Sicilies. And according to French journals cited in England, "the Pope has been *induced* to consent to resign his dignity, which will be bestowed on Cardinal Fesch, who will remove the Papal chair to Avignon, to make room for the new territorial arrangements, which are to comprise the antient capital of the world." See *GM* 76, pt. 1 (1806): 467.

7. HLP's dread of Napoleon's getting to India had been born in 1798. See her letters to DL, 9 July [1798], n. 13; to RG, 14 October 1798, n. 2.

Bonaparte made no effort to hide his consistent interest not only in India but in the East as a whole. At the height of his power, he liked to remember the events of 1798–99 and the victories of the Army of Egypt, which he once hoped would win him the wealth of the Indies and of India. Just before Austerlitz, "the lure of the Orient formed the main topic of conversation around the headquarters campfire." In the early months of 1808 he planned a threefold strategic offensive to destroy British interests in India and other parts of Asia. See *La Correspondence de Napoléon Iier,* 32 vols. (Paris: 1858–70), no. 12749, 15:330.

8. HLP was aware of Russian efforts to provoke the Peloponnesians to rise against the Turks, as in 1770. The Russians intended the uprising to serve as a diversion in the recurrent Russo–Turkish wars. But their aid to the Peloponnesians was too late and too meager so that the revolt was savagely suppressed. The Russians then abandoned the Greeks in order to pursue the war with Turkey elsewhere. As a result of the treaty signed by the belligerent powers in 1774, the Russians assumed a right "to make representations" on behalf of the sultan's Christian subjects, and this established the excuse for all future acts of Russian intervention in Greek affairs, as in 1786. HLP expected from Alexander diplomatic behavior comparable to that of Catherine the Great.

9. Joanna Baillie's *Miscellaneous Plays* (1804) had been judged by the *Edinburgh Review* 5 (January 1805): 405–21, which concluded: "Upon the whole, however, we are afraid that this volume will by no means add to Miss Baillie's reputation. A pretty large proportion of it is unequivocally bad, and those parts which might have appeared excellent in an unknown writer, make but an indifferent figure when contrasted with her known previous productions. . . . We earnestly exhort Miss Baillie to write no more comedies."

10. Samuel Butler, *Hudibras*, pt. 2, canto 1, lines 221–24.

11. His *Memoirs* was well treated by the reviewers. See, e.g., *AR* 48 (1806): 892–912.

12. Robert Kinglake (1765–1842) wrote a pamphlet entitled *A Dissertation on Gout; exhibiting a new view of the origin, nature, cause, cure, and prevention, of that . . . disease* (1804). It provoked the mocking response of Dr. W[illiam] Perry: *A Dialogue in the Shades, recommended to every purchaser of Dr. Kinglake's Dissertation [on Gout], etc., as an appropriate tailpiece* (1805).

13. For Thomas James Viscount Bulkeley, see HLP to LC, 13 May 1796, n. 9.

14. Swinger: obsolete for "one who acts vigorously or forcibly; a vigorous performer" *(OED)*.

TO JOHN BRITTON[1]

Brynbella
24: June 1806.

Mrs. Piozzi has the honour of presenting her best Compliments with expressions of Concern at not being able to comply with Mr. Britton's request.[2] Such requests have been frequently made, but neither She, nor her Husband nor their Tenant[3] can ever resolve to suffer those Pictures to be touched, while they can hinder it.[4]

Text: National Portrait Gallery, London

1. John Britton (1771–1857) was born in the village of Kington in Wiltshire. He described the people there as "rude and uncultured, like the land they occupied." He learned little at the village school and was in time sent to the Chippenham school which he "quitted . . . at the age of thirteen." When sixteen, he traveled to London to be apprenticed to an uncle, a wine dealer in Clerkenwall.

In 1799 he became connected with the London theater. Within a year, however, he turned to "the pursuits which he cultivated with such ardour and success for the last fifty years of his life." The *Beauties of Wiltshire*, his first significant topographical work, appeared in two volumes in 1801, a third some twenty–four years later.

"He continued to write voluminously, concentrating on the antiquities of Britain," and was active in the creation of literary and archeological associations, which preserved national antiquities.

See *GM* 202 [n.s. 1] (1847):185–92; also *The Autobiography of John Britton, F.S.A. In Three Parts* (London: Printed for the Author, as Presents to Subscribers To "The Britton Testimonial," 1850).

2. At the bottom of HLP's letter near the right edge is the following statement in an unknown, contemporary hand: "Mr. Britton had applied to have copies made by Jackson from some of the [Reynolds] Portraits at Streatham."

3. Since 1798 Streatham Park's tenant had been Peter Giles (d. 1830), a wealthy corn factor in Tower Street, London. See HLP to PSP, [29] April 1798, n. 15; to Thomas Bellamy [4 May 1798].

4. The thirteen portraits by Sir Joshua Reynolds that hung in the Streatham Park library were sold at auction in May 1816. The original printed auction lists (with the prices written in for each picture sold) are preserved at the John Rylands University Library of Manchester (Ry. 612). See also HLP to PSW, 21 [November 1792], n. 5.

TO LADY WILLIAMS

Brynbella
Saturday 26: July 1806.

My Dear Lady Williams
is too kind in remembering us so; The Gout has partly forgotten Mr. Piozzi—or has changed his Mode of Attack: he is now subject to St. Anthony's Fire[1] more than to raging Pain——The Hands however go on enlarging, and the poor Piano e Forte is wholly out of favour.

Miss Sharp lay ill at Bangor Ferry 14 or 15 Days, and then *crawled* (for she could scarcely go) across the Country *home* for better Advice. We had a dying Cook and an empty Tale of *Course* yesterday;[2] and we made melancholy Reflexions, calling to mind that all who had dined with us in 1784 to the Number of eight or nine Friends, *on the like Occasion* were dead and gone; leaving only ourselves and the Clergyman who married us—*alive*.[3] Your Ladyship says nothing of the dear Young ones who have I hope done Coughing now. We hear nothing pleasant from pretty Gwaynynnog, though Doctor Myddelton is very polite to us, and kind to our little Church.

Dear Sir John's Pink[4] sends her Duty, and wishes our Hay off the Ground that She and her Playfellows may all come and skip in the Park and show her *preeminent* Beauty.

The Noise concerning our Princess of Wales begins to die off[5] and other Tales take Turn:[6] but Mr. Thelwall told me that Fitzherbert had two resolute Centinels posted near her Door for many Nights and Days while the Ferment lasted——A Lady without one Natural Friend tho', will soon be forgotten in an Island divided like ours between Business and Pleasure, in neither of which She can take any Part.

Our Hopes of Pleasure in the Chester Scheme do *not* die off; There is no *present* Reason for supposing Mr. Piozzi will be incapable of receiving Amusement from such a Frolick; but Gout is a Fellow one cannot Answer for—out of one's Sight. My Dear Lady Williams may always answer for the grateful and respectful Attachment with which I shall ever remain / her truly faithful Servant / H: L: P.—

Text: Ry. 2 (1802–6). *Address:* Lady Williams / Bodylwyddan / near St. Asaph. *Postmark:* ST. ASAPH 248.

1. The popular name for erysipelas, associated with a religious order founded in France ca. 1095 for the care of those suffering from the disease. According to another assumption, Saint Anthony of Padua (1195–1231) was the benefactor of erysipelas victims (*Encyclopedia Brittanica*, 3rd ed., 1797). See HLP to Q, 4 June 1785, n. 13.
2. The Piozzis' wedding anniversary on 25 July.
3. For Father Richard Smith, who was to die in 1808, see HLP to Q, 25 July 1784, n. 1.
4. "Pink," a heifer calf, was a gift from Sir John Williams to HLP.
5. HLP refers to "The Delicate Investigation," i.e., to the work of a committee made up of Grenville (prime minister), Spencer (secretary of state), Erskine (lord chancellor), and Ellenborough (lord chief justice), "while Sir Samuel Romilly, Solicitor-General was so to speak master-of-the-ceremonies." The committee was to investigate whether Princess Caroline gave birth to an illegitimate child in 1802. The committee, which sat in June, concluded on 14 July "that there is no foundation whatever for believing that the child [William Austin] . . . is the child of her Royal Highness, or that she was delivered of any child in the year 1802." See E. E. P. Tisdall, *The Wanton Queen* (London: Stanley Paul, 1939), pp. 112–31.
6. Mary Georgianna Emma (1798–1847) was the youngest daughter of Admiral Lord Hugh (1759–1801) and Lady Anne Horatia, née Waldegrave, Seymour (1762–1801). Admiral Seymour was the fifth son of Francis (1718–94), first marquess of Hertford.

Known also as "Minny," the orphaned Mary after 1801 lived with Mrs. Fitzherbert, who was devoted to her, as was the Prince of Wales. About 1803, her aunt and uncle (Lord Francis and Lady Isabella Seymour) sought to remove the child from the care of her protectors. A three–year custody battle ended in favor of Mrs. Fitzherbert by the Lords on 14 June 1806.

In 1825 "Minny" married George Lionel Dawson–Damer (1788–1856). He was the third son of John, first earl of Portarlington.

See Christopher Hibbert, *George IV: Prince of Wales 1762–1811* (New York, Evanston, San Francisco, London: Harper and Row, 1972), pp. 237–42.

TO MARGARET WILLIAMS

Brynbella
31: July 1806.

My dear Miss Williams

I take this Opportunity of sending a Scrap Gratis by Mr. Thelwall;[1] who looks well, and keeps up the *Toujours Gai* Whether in large or in little Societies, beyond most people I know. He will tell you of our Disappointment in Miss Sharpe, and *I* will tell you how sincerely I was vexed by it, on account of your Brothers;[2] to whom we well knew no Entertainment could have been half so desirable. If She is seriously ill however, no Sentiment but those of Compassion can retain a Place in my heart, who love her very sincerely.

The noise concerning our Princess dies gradually away, and She will doubtless be soon forgotten: one extraordinary Occurrence treads in these latter times so very hard upon the Heels of another—that Leisure for short and sudden Astonishment is all that is left to Beholders. Do you see Doctor Halifax sometimes?[3] What does he say concerning these Cities discovered under Ground in a country where no one ever heard they existed—in Siberia?[4] It is a matter of very curious Speculation, if the Cities *above* Ground gave us Leisure to speculate on ought but *their* Excesses: It was very right however to drive Sir John Buller away.[5]

These Storms of Thunder and Lightning should affright such Fellows methinks; I never saw Newspapers so filled with Tales of tempestuous Weather since I can recollect; We have had scarce any here in our quiet Vale of Llwydd: and our Irish Correspondents say that all is peaceable there.[6]

God keep us from a general Election—it is a general Riot always, and would be worse now than ever.—Sir Watkin Williams[7] is considered as an *ill Man* at present, and that Event must end him. Old Mr. Hughes of Kinmael[8] struggles with his strange Complaint in a surprising Manner, but will not now struggle much longer. Mr. Piozzi keeps up to all our Delight and Comfort; and we have some Thoughts of making a merry Week at Chester next Michaelmas with your Family and the Myddeltons. That eldest Boy,[9]—that *only* Boy indeed at Gwaynynnog, has miserably weak Health; and all the Children in the County except those of Segroid, are in the hooping Cough.

So there is Tattle enough, and pray send me some *Street* News as I call it; *Field* News have I none, but that the Heifer Calf Sir John gave me is beautiful and her Name *Pink*.

Adieu dear Miss Williams and Give Compliments in due Proportions to all who remember / Your faithful / H: L: P.

Oh Dear! I forgot a famous Occurrence too: We had kind Mr. Mostyn Edwards's Band of Music up at little wretched Dymerchion,[10] and Dr. Myddelton came and preached a Charity Sermon for setting up a Sunday School—and I made the Hymn, and the Babies sung it; and the People came far and near, and we collected 16:0 = 0 last Sunday—no longer ago.—

Text: Ry. 7 (18 May 1806–19 May 1808). *Address* Miss Williams / Upper Park Street / St. James's Square / Bath. By favour of Mr. Thelwall.

1. For the Reverend Edward Thelwall of Llanbedr Hall, see HLP to MW, 6–7 March 1805, n. 2.
2. For MW of Bath, see HLP to Ly W, 18 December 1798, n. 1. MW's brothers were Sir John, Roger Hesketh Fleetwood, and the Reverend William Williams (later Williams-Edwards).
3. Robert Hallifax (1735–1810), M.D., was physician extraordinary to the Prince of Wales and physician to the household of H. R. H. Dr. Hallifax died in Bath on 17 September 1810. See William Munk, M.D., *The Roll of the Royal College of Physicians of London*, 2d ed. (London: Published by the College, 1878-) 2:336.
4. A geological topic of interest at this time concerned a recently discovered "mass of iron" in a Siberian cave, variously attributed to a fallen meteor, volcanic action, or human agency. HLP was intrigued by this last theory, with its implications of an "Under Ground" city. Among those whose opinion she shared was Jean André de Luc, the Swiss geologist and a Bath acquaintance. See his "Observations Sur la masse de fer de Sibérie," in *Journal des Mines*, 11, no. 63 (Year X): 213–20; "Suite aux Observations Sur la Masse de Sibérie, et sur les Pierres, supposées tombées de l'atmostphère," *Journal des Mines* 13, no. 74 (Year XI): 92–107. See also HLP to PSP, 13 June 1800, n. 3.
5. The gossipy mention of Buller, probably in response to a comment by MW in a missing letter, is perplexing, although it warrants speculation. Uncertain about the title preceding Buller's name, HLP presumably had in mind the wealthy John Buller (1771–1849), who occupied the ancestral mansion in Morval, Cornwall. Descendant of a family well known in both Cornwall and Devonshire, he served at various times as J.P., D.L., high sheriff, and M.P. for West Looe.

In 1798 he had married Elizabeth, née Yorke, daughter of James (1730–1808), bishop of Ely. She had died childless in 1802 and it may be mere coincidence that Buller, like the eldest Thrale daughters, would have been an eligible candidate for courtship. He married secondly—but not until 1814—Harriet, née Hulse (d. 1868), daughter of Sir Edward, third baronet.

See Daniel Lysons and Samuel Lysons, *Magna Britannia; being a Concise Topographical Account of the Several Counties of Great Britain*, 10 vols. (London: T. Cadell and W. Davies, 1806–22), 3 [Cornwall, 1814]: xciv, ci, clxxvi, 242; *Burke's Landed Gentry*, "Tremayne of Morval."

6. Throughout the summer months, the British press devoted much space to "Tales of Tempestuous Weather." For summaries, see *GM* 76, pt. 2 (1806): 767–68, 867–68.

7. See HLP to LC, 17 June 1798, n. 11.

8. For the Reverend Edward Hughes (1738–1815) of Kinmel Park, Denbighshire, see HLP to LC, 21 April 1800, n. 9.

9. The Reverend Dr. Robert Myddelton's son was Robert (1795–1876). After attending Harrow, he matriculated at Clare College, Cambridge, in 1813, receiving his B.A. in 1818 and M.A. in 1822. He was ordained a priest in 1822 and served at Gwaynynog after 1823.

10. Thomas Mostyn Edwards (d. 1832) was the son of the Reverend Samuel Edwards of Pentre Hall, Montgomeryshire, and Charlotte, eldest daughter of Roger Mostyn of Cilcain Hall, Flintshire, as identified in the *Guide to the Flintshire Record Office*.

TO MARGARET WILLIAMS

Monday
4: August 1806.

Mr. Thelwall being stolen away[1]—I send this Letter by the Hand of poor luckless Barnes our Cook and Housekeeper: who after exhausting Mr. Moore's Shop,[2] and Mr. Piozzi's Patience, returns to her Friends incapable of Service. She has spent most of her Time in Bed, so can tell but little of what passes in Wales. We shall tell more when we are returned from Llyn whither we bend our Course next Thursday.[3] But do not dearest Lady keep on directing to *St. Asaph* so: because Denbigh is our Post Town, and the Letters come one Day later, and one Twopence costlier by so doing.[4]

Look sharp for us towards November and Remember 68 and 77 as the desirable Houses; likewise one which belongs to an old Friend of mine opposite the China Shop in Pierpoint Street—but I forger *her* Name and her Mansion's Number.[5] It is in Pultney Street of course, when it pleases / Your / H: L: P.

Text: Victoria and Albert Museum Library. *Address:* Miss Williams / Upper Park Street / St. James's Square / Bath. *Postmark:* GLOUCESTER 111.

1 The Reverend Edward Thelwall of Llanbedr Hall.
2. John Moore's apothecary shop in Vale Street, Denbigh.
3. The Piozzis intended to spend about two weeks at the lakes in Carnarvonshire, "—to *revisit* my native Soil: after an Absence of 32 Years since I visited it with my first Husband—we left it in 1747 I think—& I went with Mr Thrale there in 1774. I am now going with Mr Piozzi, God send us safely back *1806.* 5: Aug:—Brynbella" (*Thraliana* 2:1078).
Llyn is in Carnarvonshire.
4. The parish of Tremeirchion (Dymerchion) lies between Denbigh and Saint Asaph. It is closer to the former by about one half mile.
5. HLP's perennial quest for house rentals in Bath.

11 October 1806 117

TO THE REVEREND LEONARD CHAPPELOW

> 11: October 1806.
> Brynbella Saturday

It is a long Time since we heard of or *from* dear Mr. Chappelow; and many Things good and bad have occurred since we last had Conversation together or Correspondence—Deaths of great Men in particular——our Bishop the latest to take Passage in Charon's Boat[1]——We are earnest to find out the Successor,[2] and canvass him for poor Mr. Roberts the Curate of Dymerchion. He really has a Claim on you good Men who make it a point to endeavour the propagation of Christian Knowledge because the Employment that Society has given *him*, takes him away to Oxford after Books, and puts the Person so employed to much Expense and Trouble.[3] Some nice Preferment having dropt the very Week of Horsley's Departure, makes *his* Friends active to learn who is likely to obtain Disposal of it[4]——

Let me know soon as You can Dear Sir, it will be a real Obligation; and in the mean while I wish you Joy of our Trans Atlantic Possessions.[5] Have you read the Miseries of Life? I have just caught my self in an Agony resembling those recorded in that Book——because having written on the wrong Way of my Paper I shall be distressed how to fold it——Sensitive and Testy never hit on such a Case——and no more Smooth Paper in the house!!![6]

I will direct this to Weston at a Venture; Lord Bradford—if one durst ask him, could tell one who is the new Bishop of Course, and who will be pushed up into St. Asaph——not Parr certainly, because *his* Patron went first.[7] Mr. Piozzi is list'ning for News of Calabria;[8] I should be glad to see our old Friend Ferdinand once more reinstated in his own Dominions,[9] and hear of his Fishing in Peace without Fear of a French Shark. The other People I care less about, but the honest Lazaroni deserve to have their original Master home again.[10]

We have no News here—how *should* we? and what comes from London is sure to arrive Musty—as Game does *to* London from a distant Province. You will not care about poor dear Old Jones's Death I suppose,[11] nor wonder at Mr. Mostyn's Illness, who has been ill so often and Ill so long.[12] My Master has kept the Gout off famously this Year, and every body says the Ladies at Llangollen grow Younger—notwithstanding the *Cotton Mill*,——for that was *their* Misery.[13] Farewell, and *do* accept our truest Regards and write presently to Yours / most Faithfully / H: L: Piozzi.——

We leave this Place the last Week of October or beginning of November so *do* write soon.

Text: Ry. 561.135. *Address:* Rev: Mr. Chappelow.

1. Samuel Horsley (b. 1733), bishop of Saint Asaph, died unexpectedly on 4 October "at Brighthelmstone, of a complaint in his bowels." See *GM* 76, pt. 2 (1806): 987.

2. Horsley's successor was William Cleaver (1742–1815), translated from Bangor.

3. For the Reverend John Roberts's efforts as a press corrector of the Society for the Propagation of Christian Knowledge, particularly its Welsh Bible and Prayer Book (published in 1799), see HLP to PSP, 31 July 1803, n. 4.

4. Cleaver obviously listened to the requests of Roberts's friends. The young clergyman was to become vicar of Tremeirchion (Dymerchion) in March 1807.

5. On 13 September 1806 a *London Gazette Extraordinary* announced the capture of Buenos Aires by Commodore Sir Home Riggs Popham (1762–1820) and Colonel William Carr Beresford (1768–1854), the latter in command of a small land force. The short-lived capture was regarded as "a great acquisition to Commerce" and the means of disseminating British "Manufactures into every corner of South America" (Farington 8:2877–78).

6. James Beresford (1764–1840), *The Miseries of Human Life; or, the Groans of Samuel Sensitive and Timothy Testy . . . In Twelve Dialogues* (London: W. Miller, 1806). The book was to sell "prodigiously, so as to produce to Beresford a profit of £1,000" (Farington 8:2969).

7. HLP assumed that Charles James Fox, who had died on 13 September 1806, was the Reverend Samuel Parr's patron.

8. See *The Times*, 3 September 1806: "We have been favoured with the Official account of the first military operations of the British in Calabria. . . .

"The principal disembarkation took place on the morning of the 1st of July, in the Bay of St. Euphemia, without any opposition on the part of the French. . . . At the same time that the landing was made at St. Euphemia, an attack was made by Sir Sidney Smith, possibly as a diversion, on the Castle of Amantea. . . . By the 4th, Gen. Regnier had collected all the French troops in that quarter, and advanced towards the Bay of St. Euphemia, with an intention to attack the British. In this he was anticipated by the vigorous and active gallantry of General Stuart, who attacked and entirely defeated him." See also *The Times* for 5, 6, and 23 September.

The Times on 10 October stated that "We entertain the most sanguine expectations, that the rumour of the French having been a second time defeated by our countrymen in Calabria, will prove to be well founded. . . . The action is reported to have been fought on the 26th of August."

9. HLP's hope for the restoration of Ferdinando was supported by *The Times* on 3 September. "It is deeply to be regretted, that the determination was ever taken to withdraw the Allied army from the Neapolitan territory. Thirty thousand Russians and British, in conjunction with the troops of his Sicilian Majesty, could have defended it against the whole force of the French; or at least would have enabled the legitimate Sovereign to divide the Peninsula with the Usurping Upstart who came to dispossess him. We are aware, that it was done in the hope of conciliating and disarming France; but those who counselled the measure should have better judged of the heart and disposition of Buonaparte."

10. From Giuseppe Gorani's *Mémoires . . . des Cours . . . de L'Italie* HLP learned of Ferdinando's delight in fishing, the catch of which he would sell to the people.

For the *lazzaroni*, their courage and loyalty to the royal cause, see HLP to Ly W, 10 February 1799, n. 8, and *AR* 41 (1799): 151–54.

11. When John Jones died in September 1806, he was almost ninety. HLP's translation of Malherbe's "Epitaphe d'un Gentilhomme" became an "Epitaph on old Mr. Jones of Cavendish Square." See HLP to Q, 17 January 1806, and "Verses 1," p. 85. She emended the penultimate line to: "And Death! was ninety years in finding. . . ."

12. John Meredith Mostyn was dying of tuberculosis, aggravated by dissipation.

13. Since its recent introduction, the manufacture of cotton flannel in Llangollen had annoyed the Ladies. See HLP to LC, 18 June 1804, n. 8; to Anna Maria Pemberton, [ca. 24 December 1814], n. 10.

THE REVEREND LEONARD CHAPPELOW TO HESTER LYNCH PIOZZI

October 20th 1806

Dear Madam—

I shall not delay a moment for a 100d reasons, one is that tomorrow I may not be able—for I have been for 15 days in the same <frenetic> state, I was in, when you so hospitabl<y> nursed me at Brynbella—I went into a warm sea bath, made here in my house, last night—or I could not have written today—but I have received great benefit from it, and can use my pen.—But I cannot be able to hold out long enough to tell you half I have to say.—Brevis esse Laboro,[1]—and I fear you will find me Like Professor < 's> candle,[2] You forget none of my stories I know, not that they are good, but that your memory never fails.

In the first place I must tell you that from the beginning of April, till July I was very ill in London—and have been 9 weeks at the sea side at Cromer in Norfolk by myself—and at Aldeburgh with Lady Bradford and her children,[3] whilst Lord B——— was playing at soldiers at the Garrison at Ipswich, which I left last fryday 7th.—I believe I got cold at the Review, it rained all the time—the Royal Dukes were there—Lord Bradford met them 2 days before the Duke of York reviewed the Garrison, at Lord Rendleshams—ci devant Peter Thelluson.[4]—All drunk—enthusiastically,—the King's Health was drunk 7 times—D. of Cambridge—who loves his father, and is his greatest comfort, declared so good a Man as our old King never before existed, he was continually in tears when he talked of him.—

I am very glad Mr. Piozzi has fought for once, successfully against the gout.—Gout and Rheumatism are our miseries.

You will long before this, have heard that Clever Bishop of Bangor, was gazetted last Saturday night, Bishop of St. Asaph[5]—Coach man Horseley—is now gone—he was more of a Bear than a Bishop—who pays his Sons Debts.[6]—You make me smile, when you talk of Mr. Roberts Friends enquiring about nice Preferment lately vacant.—You know little how many hundreds are continually making ridiculous pretentions and applications, for preferment.—All must of course go to the Cabinet Ministers—Mr. Allen who succeeded Dr. Cole,[7] the late prebendary of Westminster, was private Secretary to Lord Spencer,[8] and Tutor to Lord Althorpe his Son[9]—what Interest could beat his.—The Chaplain to the House of Commons—as is customary was recommended, some years ago, by the petition to the King, from the Commons requesting him to have a Dignity and the present Chaplain, is not provided for any more than the first—and now the parliament is going to be dissolved. There will be a third recommended to the King for Preferement.—Clever was Tutor to Lord Grenville, who disposes of all the preferment.[10]

But I will tell you what may possibly be done, to assist Mr. Roberts, pecuniarily—for I am as much a Friend to Literary Merit, particularly that of Divinity as you can possibly be.—

There never was, since the world was created, so good, and so kind a man as the Bishop of Durham[11]—he always assists merit—he told old Dr. Heberden once,[12] I have this morning given a living worth 1500d pounds per annum to a man whom I never saw, and for whom I had no application.—The Good and Great Paley—now succeed[ed] by our worthy little Friend, whose merit can only be estimated—religiously as well as Literally by putting gold into one scale, and Dr. Gray into the other.—He now [is] really a little Jewel[13]—with 3000d per Annum all given by good Durham—Write to him, and I shall hope, the Bishop will alleviate his pecuniary distresses.—Some years ago, when I was on visit to Lord Bath at Longleat—a Mr. Skurry,[14] Lord Baths Curate—wrote to Good Barrington—bad Barrington died at Botany bay[15]—(how droll is Mr. Chappelow) in behalf of a distressed Clergyman's widow, and he kindly sent her £30.—I have not the slightest Objection, to your telling our good Friend Gray—that I put you upon the scent—and if it succeeds—we all 3 shall be equally delighted.—But Dr. Gray will tell you his mind very openly, and amiably.—Our now Bishop of Norwich,[16] was one of his prebendarys, and we discoursed of the virtues of the good Bishop together last July.

You make me smile again, when you think Lord Bradford troubles himself about preferment, he has no Interest, or connection with ministers.—

I do indeed congratulate you, upon our acquisitions in South America. I have always—said that ultimately, all South America, must belong to England or France.—The infamous Tyrant's plan was this—a separate peace with England[17]—all Spain and Portugal—the Bourbons again dethroned to make another Kingdom for some of his Wretches.—But they were only to have the European Territories—England does prevent <him. There wanting> ships, colonies and commerce, take and annex all South America, with gold and silver mines to France.

But thank God we are going to unwind him.—I hope you take the Times as you used to do, tis the best morning paper published but you should make my Master compliment you with an evening paper also.—You know I always rave against your œconomy, as publications,—I would was I in your case—actually rebel, if I could not have my new books, &c.—

So poor Mr. Jones—if they had put a glass and a bottle of wine with him in his coffin—he would have been content.—My Compliments Mrs. P—your very good health—So Mr. Mostyn is going.—And your Titmouse will hot off to her sisters, with her brood—and they will live, old Maids—and leave all to titmouses mice.—

This Morning with yours brought a letter from Lady B.—which I epitomise—in short—dated at the garrison at Colchester last Sunday—and Yesterday.

Lord B. has been talking to a Hannoverian officer just landed from Harwich—on his way to Town.—Hostilities commenced—on <   > of posts—the French repulsed previous to the 9th of this month. He brings Prussian Declaration of War—expressed in the strongest terms—perfect Understanding subsists between Hesse and Prussia—Prussian Strength—230 Thousand.—All concentrated within 25 miles—French Strength only 180,000*d*—a general action was expected to take place, about the 15 or 16th[18]—The King of Prussia in the Center of his Army,[19] attended by [the] Duke of Brunswick[20]—General Mollendorf[21] &c.—The greatest spirit prevails all over Prussia—all Loyalists—The Russians in great force, had passed Warsaw—expected to join Prussia about the 26—General <Daken> is the Hannoverian Officer—General <Daken> says the Russians expect a Large reinforcement of troops from England—What glorious News this is—tis better than Cherry Brandy— / Adieu—&c. &c. L. C.—

Text: Ry. 563.87. *Address:* Mrs. Piozzi / Brynbella / Denbigh / North Wales. *Postmark:* OC A 20 806.

1. Horace, *Ars Poetica*, line 25.
2. The allusion to "Professor < 's> candle" was a well-known joke (the name often changing) which appears in Joe Miller's *Jest Book* under the title "The Candle and Lantern": "During the period Sir Buswick Harwood was Professor of Anatomy in the University of Cambridge, he was called in, in a case of some difficulty, by the friends of a patient, who were anxious for his opinion of the malady. Being told the name of the medical man who had previously prescribed, Sir Buswick exclaimed, 'He, if he were to descend into the patient's stomach with a *candle and lantern*, when he ascended he would not be able to name the complaint.'"
3. Both places are in North Norfolk, Aldborough, on the river Bure, and Cromer on the coast.
4. Royal Dukes: Frederick, Duke of York (1763–1827), Adolphus Frederick, Duke of Cambridge (1774–1850). Lord Rondelsham: Peter Isaac Thelluson (1761–1808), cr. Baron Rendlesham of Rendlesham (I., 1806), a director of the Bank of England (1787–1806) and a Tory M.P. for various constituencies (1795–1808).
5. That is, William Cleaver—probably one of LC's drolleries—similar to "Coach man Horseley."
6. Heneage Horsley was now vicar of Castle Caereinion, county Montgomery (1805). He was to become chaplain of the Episcopalian Church at Dundee (May 1809), dean of Brechin. The young Horsley "was so extravagant as to cause His living to be sequestered [in 1811] for the benefit of His Creditors and He now resides within the privileges of Holyrood House, Edinburgh, to avoid His Creditors" (Farington 11: 3992).
The bishop himself for some time before he died "adopted a rigid plan of œconomy, in order to liquidate some pecuniary burthens [about £14,000]. If he had lived a few years longer, he would have enjoyed an annual income of 7000 *l.* by the operation of his prudent measures." His family, therefore, was planning to publish a complete edition of his works. See *GM* 76, pt. 2 (1806): 990; Farington 8: 2950-51.
7. Joseph Allen (1770–1845), a Cantabrigian, had been ordained deacon in 1799 and priest in 1800, becoming prebendary of Westminster (1806–34), vicar of Battersea, Surrey (1808–29), of Saint Bride's, London (1829–34), bishop of Bristol (1834–36) and of Ely (1836–45).
William Cole (1753–1806), also a Cantabrigian, had served as assistant master at Eton (1778–79). Ordained a priest on 14 March 1779, he became chaplain to the duke of Marlborough and tutor to his two sons; rector of Waddesdon, Bucks. (1781–89), of Mersham, Kent (1788–1806); prebendary of Westminster (1792–1806); vicar of Shoreham (1796–1806).
8. George John Spencer (1758–1834), second earl Spencer (1783), secretary of state for home (1806–7), having been first lord of the admiralty (December 1794–February 1801).
9. John Charles Spencer (1782–1845), styled Viscount Althorpe (1783–1834), third earl Spencer (1834). Having been educated at Harrow and Cambridge, he was at this time a Whig M.P. for Oakhampton (1804–6) and for Northamptonshire (1806–32); lord of the treasury (1806–7).
10. William Wyndham Grenville (1759–1834), cr. baron Grenville (1790), politician and statesman. He led the war party in Pitt's ministry but broke with him over the question of Catholic emancipation in 1801. During Pitt's second ministry, Grenville refused to serve because Fox had not been offered ministerial status. In 1806 he headed the Ministry of All the Talents, which was to last for about a year.
Cleaver was tutor not to Lord Grenville but to his elder brother, George (1753–1813), later Nugent–Temple–Grenville, third earl Temple (1779), cr. marquess of Buckingham (1784).
11. For Shute Barrington, bishop of Durham, see HLP to the Ladies of the Williams Family, 27 March 1798, n. 5.
12. William Heberden, the elder (1710–1801), a graduate of Cambridge, was one of the most eminent physicians of the eighteenth century. He had been described by SJ as "ultimus Romanorum" (*Boswell's Johnson* 4:399, n. 4).
13. Another of LC's drolleries. RG was "a little Jewel" because his father, Robert (d. 1788) was a goldsmith and jeweler at 13 New Bond Street.
"The Good and Great Paley" was the theologian William Paley (1743–1805). As rector of Bishopwearmouth, Durham (1795–1805), he was succeeded by RG (1805–27).
14. Francis Skurray (1775–1848) was awarded an Oxford B.A. in 1796 and M.A. in 1798. He became perpetual curate at Imber, Wilts. (1804–6), rector of Lullington, Somerset (1806), perpetual curate of Horningsham, Wilts. (1806), and rector of Winterbourne Abbas cum Steepleton, Dorset (1823–48). Lord Bath: Thomas Thynne (1765–1837), second marquis of Bath.

122   *The Piozzi Letters*

15. For the pickpocket George Barrington, who had been transported to Botany Bay in 1790, see HLP to LC, 19 March 1799, n. 9.
16. Henry Bathurst (1744–1837) earned his several degrees at Oxford and served as bishop of Norwich from 1805 to 1837.
17. Napoleon, aware that a war with Prussia was inevitable, wished to make a separate peace with England. To achieve it, he was prepared for several sacrifices: that Hanover should be restored to King George; that the possession of Malta should be confirmed to Great Britain; that England was to have absolute sovereignty of the Cape and the tenure of Pondicherry, Chandernagore, Mahee, and other independent settlements; that England was to possess Tobago.
The peace negotiations were begun informally by an exchange of letters between Charles James Fox and Talleyrand late in March 1806. By July the British plenipotentiary—Lord Yarmouth—was in Paris and within a month he was joined by Lord Lauderdale. But negotiations broke down. See *AR* 48 (1806): 250–54.
18. Humiliated by France in the first half of 1806, Prussia began to seek allies, to support a series of treaties with Russia, and to sign an agreement with Great Britain. All this activity led to the formation of a new Coalition, effective from 6 October 1806, in essence Prussia's declaration of war against France. But Napoleon moved quickly, forcing Prussia's defeat at the battle of Jena-Auerstädt on 14 October. The Prussians as well as their Russian Allies fought on until early July 1807 when the treaties of Tilsit were signed.
19. Friedrich Wilhelm III (1770–1840), king of Prussia (1797–1840).
20. General Friedrich Wilhelm (1771–1815), duke of Brunswick, fourth son of Karl Wilhelm of Brunswick. Denied his inheritance in 1808, he became a foe of Napoleon and played a large part in the raising of the "Black Brunswickers" in 1809. After living in England and Portugal, he was restored to his duchy in 1813. Two years later he was killed at the battle of Quatre Bras at the head of his Brunswick corps in the sixth Division.
21. Field Marshal Richard J. H. von Möllendorf (1724–1816). In 1794, after much previous service, he had commanded the main Prussian army in the field against the French and defended Kaiserslautern from 23 May to 20 September in a notable siege. In 1806 he was senior commander in the field, participating in the battle of Auerstädt and becoming a French prisoner.

TO THE REVEREND ROBERT GRAY

No. 71 Pultney Street, Bath
Fryday, 12th: December 1806.

I have *not* read Mr. Faber's last publication:[1] it is a prodigious favourite with the public, and the booksellers write up in their windows, 'Here you may have *Faber's Supplement;'*[2] but if I do not find time to study *his* opinions, I do find time to read the Bible (with Gray's *Key*) and form *my* own.[3] It seems to me *just now particularly* observable with what peculiar tenderness Joseph treats his brother Benjamin *at* and after the grand reconciliation.[4] Has that behaviour any mystical reference, I wonder, to the modern Jews? born as Benjamin was, just on *borders* of Canaan?[5] for the others were all produced whilst old Israel was in a wandering state; and nineteen years did he wander. Now as 'Annus pro die imputabitur,'[6] forty days searching the land,[7] and forty years spent in punishing their conduct who refused to enter it,[8] &c. may not nineteen centuries be implied in Jacob's having lived a foreigner and servant before he reached *home*, the place of his inheritance?[9] If so, the destined hour is not far off when his children will indeed return, and every day gives me fresh hope for them.[10]

Text: Hayward 2:265–66.

1. The subject of HLP's letter has to do with the restoration of the Jews to Palestine, a topic discussed by Faber in *A Dissertation on the Prophecies*. See HLP to Q [25 January 1806], n. 22.

2. *A Supplement to the Dissertation on the 1260 years: containing a full reply to the objections and misrepresentations of the Rev. E. W. Whitaker; some remarks on certain parts of the author's own Dissertation; and a view of the present posture of affairs as connected with prophecy* (London: F. C. and J. Rivington, 1806).

3. HLP's sense of prophecy about to be fulfilled was aroused not merely by the Bible and Gray's *Key to the Old Testament* but by a remark made by RG in a letter of 16 June 1806 (Ry. 571.34): "What think you of the Council of Jews to be assembled at Paris, its [seal] the Moral Principle? It is certainly a singular <sign> if genuine."

4. Gen. 43:29–34, 45:22.

5. Gen. 35:16, 19.

6. Cf. Ezek. 4:6; Num. 14:34.

7. Moses sent Joshua and others to search out Canaan, a quest which took forty days. See Num. 13:17–18, 25.

8. Deut. 1:35.

9. Here HLP anticipates a second millennium, with Jacob as a type of Christ. See Rev. 20:4–6.

10. The theme of this letter is explained in "Harvard Piozziana," vol. 4: "We are now all gaping to see when the Jews will return to Palestine—The Turk has sate cross-legged so long he has got the Cramp I believe, for he scarce would now try to hinder them: and Mr. Frey is preaching and making Converts every Day. Doctor Gray says there is a rich Israelitish Lady now living at Mogadore, who spends her Fortune in fitting out Families for their Journey; and there is a Rumour of the Ten Tribes being discovered at Houssa or Tombuctoo, as indeed we have long expected. But who are the happy People designated by Benjamin in the Pathetic Story of the Brothers' Return when Joseph makes himself manifest to them?

"It is very observable with what peculiar Tenderness *he* is treated when all is over. He perhaps represents the native Jews who will enjoy some particular Privileges—*a double portion* of their Saviour's Kindness—as having least offended. For we may remark that Jacob's Sons were all born to him whilst he was *Wandering* for 19 Years except poor Benjamin, born on *the Borders* where his Mother—perhaps typefying *Judaism*——expired——in 19 Centuries I think they will come back Annus prodie imputabiture, and Benoni Son of Sorrow may be made—Ben *Imaan* The *Right Hand Man*.

"I wonder not the Jews do (like the Lepers at the Gate of Samaria) begin to say—'Why sit we here &c.' excluded as they are from Society——and perhaps that very Occurrence was a Type of their future Deliverance, which I am still inclined to think will be *Sudden* in *Some* Sense of the Word—and not very far distant——yet *I* thought the Papacy would die suddenly—and it did not."

See also HLP to PSP, 3 June 1801, n. 8.

CHARLES BURNEY TO HESTER LYNCH PIOZZI

Bath, South Parade
21: January 1807.

Dear Madam

I was so animated by the honour of your visit, after losing sight of each other for so many years, that I fear you thought me less an invalide than I really am, and must have imagined me rude and ungrateful for not returning your visit;[1] but as I came hither for warmth more than water, I have never *walked* off my African Parade, nor been *carried* but to the Pump of the old Corperation Bath. Indeed I had been prevailed on to try my strength in making some calls, and to dine out on the only two days of Winter which we have had; but I have had cause to rue it ever since, by grafting a terrible new cold on an old chronical Cough, which now is my greatest evil.

I begin to hope that I have been "more frightened than hurt" by the paralytic seizure in my hand;[2] but not knowing what may be behind, Damocles' sword seemed constantly suspended over my head; and I have always more dreaded a *partial death,* than total dissolution.[3] All my medical councellers bid me beware of cold, my greatest enemy.

As soon as I am able to go out like other Christians, with safety, be assured, dear Madam that nothing will afford me more pleasure than the renewal of old friendships, and the talking over old times; and I shall wait on my ingenious and worthy friend Mr. Piozzi with the utmost pleasure. He was the first who let me know what good singing was, and excited in me so strong a desire to hear Pacchierotti,[4] whose style he imitated beyond any other vocal performer. I am grieved that with his other blessings, he does not enjoy better health, without which all else is but "vanity and vexation of spirit";[5] but I, who have been permitted to extend longevity, more than ten years beyond the limits assigned to humanity, must not grumble at a few infirmities—for, except the rapid decay of sight, hearing, and memory, my state of health, before the torpor in my hand, was *charming.* You will excuse, it is to be hoped, the garrulity of an *Octogenaire,*[6] and believe me to be, with true respect and regard, / Dear Madam, / Your obedient / and obliged Servant / Charles Burney.

Text: Ry. 545.13. *Address:* To / Mrs. Piozzi.

1. The Piozzis had arrived at Bath in December 1806, desperate to secure relief for GP. Apparently, however, HLP attempted to visit CB only when she learned that he was ailing. Behind his somewhat apologetic letter lay a series of incidents: In September 1806 he had a mild paralytic seizure, which affected his left hand. Although the numbness quickly passed, he expected he would soon be overcome by a major stroke and he henceforth thought of himself as an invalid. More serious than his physical condition, he was gripped, as he said, by "the *foul fiend,* Hypochondria." He had come to Bath on 20 December 1806, expecting to die there. By March 1807, however, he had sufficiently recovered to return home to Chelsea. See Roger Lonsdale, *Dr. Charles Burney: A Literary Biography* (Oxford: Clarendon Press, 1965), pp. 460–61; *Thraliana* 2:1081.

2. Proverbial: cf. John Heywood, *A Dialogue of Proverbs* [1546], ed. Rudolph E. Habenknicht (Berkeley and Los Angeles: University of California Press, 1963), 1.4.225: "She hath been more fear'd than harm'd." See also John Palsgrave, *Lesclarcissement de la langue francoyse* (1530); Tilley, A55.

3. CB dwelled on the two images (Damocles's sword and "partial death"). He had, e.g., written to Edmond Malone in November 1806. "Yet in gloomy moments I cannot help imagining that Damocles' sword is . . . suspended over my head; wch is not a very exhilerating idea." And to Lady Bruce he commented, "a *partial death* has more terrors in it wth me than entire dissolution, though wth a rapid decay of sight, hearing, & memory, I am not tired of life" (Lonsdale, pp. 460–61).

4. For Gasparo Pacchierotti, see HLT to FB, 20 May 1784, n. 7. For a full discussion of his stylistic perfection, see CB, *A General History of Music* 4:509–13.

In listing the Italian theaters at which Pacchierotti performed, CB noted that "previous to his arrival in England, where his reputation had penetrated a considerable time, and where Signor Piozzi, who had heard him at Milan, sung several airs after his manner, in a style that excited great ideas of his pathetic powers" (4:510).

5. Eccles. 1:14.

6. CB was born in April 1726.

TO CHARLES BURNEY

> Bath Wednesday
> 21: January 1807.

Dear Doctor Burney

has no Reason to complain while he can write such Letters; The Sword hangs over *all* our heads, but Damocles alone was permitted to *see* it——May it but fall at *once* on You and on Myself!—When the Animal part of Human Nature survives the Intellectual, it is dreadful; but few are so likely to escape that Situation as we are: Temperance, Exercise, and Chearfulness are as Doctor Cadogan said long ago,[1] the Grand Supporters of health, Let us not neglect them.

My poor Husband *must* not be what I call Temperate—'twould kill him; he *cannot* use Exercise, that's impossible; he is more chearful than could be expected.——All Thanks for kind Enquiries and Adieu—If Sir Walter James[2] had not given me to understand that you went out in an Evening, You should have had another Call from your old Friend and ever / faithful Servant / H: L: P.

Text: Osborn Collection.

1. William Cadogan (1711–97), *A Dissertation on the Gout, and all Chronic Diseases, Jointly Considered, as proceeding from the same Causes; what those Causes are; and a rational and natural Method of Cure proposed. Addressed to all Invalids* (London: J. Dodsley, 1771). See especially pp. 68–69, wherein he recommends remedies for gout: "Activity, Temperance and Peace of Mind."
2. For Sir Walter James (d. 1829), see HLP to PSP, 27 March 1798, n. 2.

TO THE REVEREND CHARLES BURNEY

> Bath
> 24: January 1807.

Doctor Charles Burney's Letter is a very Flattering one,[1]—but "Hope *does* tell flattering Tales."[2] Mr. Piozzi suffers much from Weakness—and from a strangling Cough which keeps him in a State of perpetual Irritation; but the Pain from Gout is remitted—probably for some Months.

Your still—charming Father and I, compliment one another on our good Looks,——but they scarce satisfy ourselves I believe, so as to lead us much towards the Looking Glass.

My heart wishes him a long Continuance of Enjoyment in this World for all our sakes, and particularly for the Sake of Sir / Your most Obedient Servant / H: L: Piozzi.[3]

Text: Osborn Collection. *Address:* Rev: Doctor Charles Burney / York House.

1. For the causes of HLP's hostility toward the Reverend Charles Burney, see her letters to Sophia Byron, 8 June 1788, n. 6; 8 June [1789], n. 7.

The Streatham Park portrait of Dr. Charles Burney, painted by Sir Joshua Reynolds for Henry Thrale. Reproduced by the kind permission of the Ashmolean Museum, Oxford.

2. From an anonymous song. See HLP to the Ladies of Llangollen, 24 December 1804, n. 1.
3. HLP's cool letter replies to Burney's, dated York House, Bath—24 January 1807 (Ry. 545.27): "It is with deep regret, that I submit to the necessity of inquiring by letter, after the health of Mr. and Mrs. Piozzi.—It was my ardent wish to do it in person; and to express my hopes of improving the acquaintance which I was so fortunate to make with them, when I was last at Bath.—*Dies aliter visum est!* [Seneca, *Epistle* 98: "Heaven decreed it otherwise." Cf. Virgil, *Aeneid* 2:428.]

"For near a fortnight I have been confined to mine Inn . . . [because of] a most violent cold and cough. . . .

"I have deferred *writing* to my last day; but I may not walk abroad.—I shall however, leave my dear father, better than he left Chelsea, and than I found him, on my arrival. If you can send me good intelligence of your health, and of Mr. Piozzi's, I shall turn my Horses heads homeward, not without some consolation."

TO MARGARET WILLIAMS

30: January 1807.

My dear Miss Williams will be happy to hear that the Medicine *She* suggested answered best. The Night was less afflictive, and I slept some good hours not uncomfortably.

Forget us to day sweet Friend, and *tomorrow* think of nothing else—but come and share my Calves' Head, and come *early;* and rejoyce in your own good Deeds.

Even poor Dunscombe makes holyday *sometimes*[1]—take yours *to day* if you please; the Camphire Julep with Æther and *Laudanum* as I take it, did wonders as a Pacifier——We have had but one very rough Fit since you left your / gratefully Obliged / H: L: P.[2]

Text: Victoria and Albert Museum Library.

1. GP's valet.
2. Left unsaid here are GP's desperate illness, HLP's anxiety, and sleeplessness. As she wrote in *Thraliana* 2:1081: "The Illness M̄ʳ Piozzi had to support in [Bath], this January & February; beat all I ever saw or read of:—on my Birthday 27th day of the new Year, Dʳ Parry was fetched at 2 or 3 o'Clock in the Mornᵍ." So ill had GP become in this period that HLP suggested he receive the last rites.

TO THE REVEREND ROBERT GRAY

31st: January 1807.

That quack lady who magnetises the people in London is accused of her (a patient's) death I observe, and many patients *do* come here quite oppressed by the half-broiled beef and hot buttered ale with which physicians say that Miss Prescott loads those who place themselves under her care.[1] But poor Mr. Piozzi is as ill as *they* can be, though he prefers boiled mutton and macaroni to all that a table can offer him; and he is in bed now with gout on his breast, hands, arms, &c., a cough beside shaking his harrassed frame to pieces. You may be sure I never quit him except for an hour's walk o' mornings, when I go out to hear what passes, and bring him accounts how Buonaparte was first to turn about, and *Le Troisième des Fuyards* that got safe into Warsaw.[2] *That* expression was spoken of as used from a conspicuous character in the metropolis to Mrs. Fitzherbert who was here a week ago attending her dying mother;[3] and yet the news rather loses than gains credit, notwithstanding *that letter* on which people naturally thought they might rely;[4] but an impenetrable mist seems to surround public affairs, and what is discerned by glimpses thro' the fog is sure to be magnified.

> 'When will time the veil remove?
> When will light the scene improve?
> When will truth our doubts dispel?
> Awful period! Who can tell?'[5]

Text: Hayward 2:266.

1. Undoubtedly HLP heard or read rumors about Miss Prescott. No evidence, however, exists of civil or criminal proceedings against her. Between 1806 and 1807 the Old Bailey Sessions Papers and those of other London courts make no mention of her (Guildhall, London).

2. On 28 November 1806 the Russian General Levin A. T. Bennigsen, whose troops together with those of the Prussians had occupied Warsaw, abandoned the city to Murat. The retreat was strategic, Bennigsen awaiting reinforcements. On 17 or 18 December Napoleon reached Warsaw (*The Times*, 9, 12, 14 January 1807).

HLP responds in part to Napoleon's arrival in Warsaw and his military preparations there. More specifically, she responds to rumors set forth in *The Times*, e.g., on 26 January, that Napoleon "finds himself not capable of carrying on offensive operations. After various actions of different magnitude with the Russians from the 23rd to the 26th of December inclusive, he orders his army into winter quarters, and returns to Warsaw. What inferences are to be drawn from this, but that he obtained no advantages over the Russians and that the French suffered so much in the different affairs as to render all hopes of further successes quite desperate?"

3. Mary Smythe, *née* Errington, died on 26 January 1807 at her house in Pulteney Street, Bath.

4. *The Times* on 13 November 1806 printed a letter presumably written by Napoleon to Friedrich Wilhelm on 13 October—the day before the battle of Jena-Auerstädt. The letter, implicitly threatening, nonetheless uses language both reasonable and polite. It was interpreted by some as the Emperor's desire to avoid further bloodshed. Thus, "Let your Majesty believe me . . . why should we shed so much blood? For what purpose is it? I shall use to your Majesty the same language that I used to the Emperor Alexander, before the Battle of Austerlitz. May heaven grant, that corrupt men and fanatics, who are more the enemies of you and your throne, than they can be of me and my nation, may not give you the same advice to bring you to the same result! . . . I pray your Majesty to see in this letter only the desire I have to spare the effusion of human blood, and to save a nation, that, from its geographical position, cannot be an enemy to mine."

5. John Hawkesworth, "Life. An Ode," in *GM* 17, pt. 2 (1747): 337.

TO LADY WILLIAMS

Bath.
10: February 1807.

My dear Lady Williams never bade me write to her this Year; and though I have nothing upon Earth to say, I feel half displeased some how, with *myself* that is; as thinking my Letters grow less worth wishing for, altho' like Sibyl's Leaves they ought to become valuable in Proportion as they are likely to be less numerous.[1] Tyed up Knockers and passing Funerals indeed prompt none but sad Reflections—nor can I boast animation from my own Household, the Master of which has been so long a confined Sufferer, that we hardly *think* of his coming down to Dine with us, an Event that has happened only Twice since last Christmas Day.

Never was Mortal Man so tortured surely, and the Gout driven from one Post resolutely attacks another, so that one feals less and less Confidence in Physic and Physicians every hour of one's Life. Miss Williams uses neither, tho' her Health is far from good; but all She sees of poor Mr. Piozzi gives her confirmation, that Medicine does much less for Invalides than they, or their Friends expect from it.

Her Company is far more beneficial to *me* than all the Doctors have been to him. She goes among the Great and the Gay and brings me Intelligence of what passes, and we sometimes carry our Chat to the Bedside, and amuse our Sick Man with Stories of Suffering or Tales of Enjoyment as he can *take* and relish them.

Poor Mostyn is a rated Invalid likewise, for the Sick List here contains both old and Young; and my Friend Mr. Gillon (who is neither) told me this Moment he was come *here to die*.[2] Beautiful Mrs. Dutton—once Honor Gubbins—is already dead;[3] and here is such dispiriting Weather, one can scarce care whether one lives or no. The Public indeed are amused with Lies to keep Attention wakeful as to Public Matters, but no Truths from Lord Hutchinson are yet arrived, and from him alone we can hope for Accounts on which any Dependance may be placed.[4]

My own Sadness goes on increasing with Mr. Piozzi's ill Health every hour, nor can the sweet and Varied Expression of Kindness from every Friend calm what I feel this Moment.

Mr. Hughes's irregular Pulse I understand, beats *no more*.[5]

While *mine* plays, Sir John Williams and his Lady and his kind Sister shall command the best Affection / of their H: L: P.

Text: Ry. 3 (1807–11). *Address:* Lady Williams / Bodylwyddan / near St. Asaph / Flintshire / N. Wales. *Postmark:* BATH.

1. As told in one legend, the sibyl offered Tarquin II nine volumes of prophecies at a price which he refused. She burned three of the *Sibylline Books* and asked the same price for the remaining six. Again he rejected them and again she burned three. But now he bought the last three.
2. John Gillon was suffering from weight loss, debility, and what he called "Ptyalism." He

improved enough at Bath to return to the Adelphi, where by 30 January 1808 (Ry. 579.150) he was "recovering flesh, and gaining strength. In mild, fine, Weather, I now go out airing in the Carriage, in the Park."

3. For Honoria, or Honor, Dutton, see HLP to PSP, 17 July 1799, n. 6; 7 March [1803], n. 3. Mrs. Dutton died on 13 January at Bath.

4. John Hely-Hutchinson (1757–1832), cr. Baron Hutchinson (1801), second earl of Donoughmore (1825). Educated at Eton and Trinity College, Dublin, he entered the army in 1774 and by 1803 was a lieutenant general. In November 1806 he had been sent by the Grenville ministry on a mission to the Prussian and Russian courts (*The Times*, 19 November). The newspapers regularly reported his dispatches (ibid., 18 and 26 February, 7 March). His mission failed.

5. For the Hughes of Kinmel Park, see HLP to LC, 21 April 1800, n. 9. The Reverend Edward Hughes died in 1815, aged seventy-seven.

TO THE REVEREND JOHN ROBERTS

White Lion Bath
2: March 1807.

I write to dear Mr. Roberts[1]—in a small hand and upon this tiny paper because I can by that means send my compliments free cost enclosed to Lady K[irkwall]—towards Dr. G[ray] my scruples will not now find any place.[2] He is rich and I hope happy, he is at least very kind in never forgetting old friends. You should have told me whence he dated his letter. My date of this scrap is from an Inn. There is not a house or apartment to be had in this crowded Town for money but a little Interest in an old Friend of poor Johnson's, Dr. Maxwell, gives us hope of his Mansion in a week's time.[3]

My worst fear lest our good Master should be laid up again diminishes daily. The only Medical Man we have seen says he is not likely to be plagued with gout again soon.

The first place I went to was Laura Chapel[4] where the prayers were read by a voice and in a manner so impressive my curiosity was excited and I heard in answer to my enquiries that the Clergyman was a Mr. Salvador a converted Jew[5] but till I see dear Dr. Randolph and make him tell the Story I am as if wholly ignorant—for such half true Tales as those one hears at Bath are more fatal to information than silence itself.

The first book I borrowed was Killala's Isaiah but here is no room for discussions of such a length as such a work requires[6]—and till my next year's Studies of the great language with your assistance at B[rynbella] I have no right to say anthing on the subject.

From John Wilkes's letters more might be expected.[7] It is however pleasing to find a man of so very light a character so little reprehensible in his private transactions and familiar correspondence. One never can be sure how good or how wicked any body is except one's self and indeed hardly that.

Candour and charity and a tolerating spirit are to be warmly cherished for every Reason. Therefore yet need we Reasons, when we read injuctions? And without those good qualities how cruelly do people judge of each other. May such ready censurers learn at length to spare dear Mr. Roberts and his faithful / Servant / H: L: P.

Text: Victoria and Albert Museum Library. A copy. Enclosed in this letter is HLP's copy of a letter sent to Bishop Cleaver regarding John Roberts.

A COPY

I should not have presumed to trouble Lord Bishop of St. Asaph any more but that I have fears lest he should suspect either my Integrity or that of poor Mr. Roberts. My Letter referred to the Concern he had in the last Edition[8]—not the present one[9]—of our Welsh Bible; In Pages 156 and 157 of the annual Sermon and Report (1800) his Name, and the Occasion of my Statement are mentioned.[10] The Mr. Evans spoken of there, is dead;[11] and some one told me that the Work injured his Health: but of those Matters I know little or nothing.

Mr. Roberts's Expences during his two Years residence at Oxford on Account of that Business[12] *could not be less* than 200£: his Remuneration was 75 Guineas— 11 of which he paid away to others—as I have heard him tell in Conversation round our Table at Brynbella—*Years ago;* when we were improving our little Church, and hoping he might one Day be Vicar &c.

He is himself a most unobtrusive Person; happy in Your Lordship's Employment and Approbation, and would be very ill pleased with my forward Zeal if he knew how and to whom I was writing. Do not Dear My Lord let me injure this excellent Man by the unskilfulness of my own Application. I will say no more for fear of doing Mischief. The Living is not yet disposed of. Think only of his Merits, and forget the awkward Solicitress he has found in / Your Lordship's / most Obedient humble Servant / H: L: Piozzi.

This is the Copy of the Letter I have written this Instant to the Bishop—— God send Success and / believe me Yours truly / H: L: P.

Mr. Piozzi thanks you, he mends gradually——The Post waits.

Text: Victoria and Albert Museum Library. *Address:* Rev: John Roberts / Dymerchion / near / Denbigh / N: Wales. *Postmark:* Bath.

1. HLP's letter indicates her continuing efforts to secure preferment for the Reverend John Roberts.
2. RG had been requested to solicit the support of the bishop of Durham for Roberts.
3. William Maxwell (1732–1818) graduated from Trinity College, Dublin (B.A. 1752; M.A. 1755; D.D. 1777). He became reader of the Temple Church and in 1775 obtained the rectory of Mount Temple, Westmeath. He was "for many years the social friend of Johnson, who spoke of him with a very kind regard" (*Boswell's Johnson* 2:116).
   According to Bath directories, Maxwell lived at 2 Henrietta Street.
4. Laura Chapel was one of the so-called proprietary chapels in Bath. Though within the Anglican tradition and ministered by ordained clergymen (e.g., Randolph, and his successor, W. Grinfield), they were privately owned, and worshipers paid for their seats. Located on Henrietta Street

(at right angles from Pulteney), Laura Chapel was opened in 1796. It was designed by Thomas Baldwin (1750–1820) to seat one thousand and was unique in being totally devoid of ornamentation.

HLP was a regular worshiper, Sunday services being held at 11 A.M. and 6 P.M.; prayers on Wednesdays, Fridays, and Saints' days at 11:15 A.M.; sacrament first Sunday in the month. See Wilfrid J. Jenkins, "A History of the Proprietary Chapels of Bath" (an unpublished typescript in the Bath Reference Library, 1948).

5. John Lovell Salvador (1771–1836), originally of Twickenham, matriculated at Christ Church, Oxford, on 22 December 1788. He received his B.A. (1793), M.A. (1795), remaining a student until 1812. He became rector of Staunton-on-Wye, county Hereford, in 1810 and served there until his death. See *GM* 7, pt. 1, n.s. (1837): 216.

6. Joseph Stock (1740–1813), successively bishop of Killala, and of Waterford and Lismore. The allusion is to *The Book of the Prophet Isaiah: in Hebrew and English. The Hebrew text metrically arranged: the translation altered from that of Bishop Lowth, with notes critical and explanatory.* By Joseph Stock (Bath: Printed by R. Cruttwell; sold by Robinsons, London, 1803).

7. *The Correspondence of the Late J.[ohn] W.[ilkes], with his friends, printed from the original manuscripts, in which are introduced memoirs of his life*, by John Almon, 5 vols. (London: R. Phillips, 1805). For John Wilkes, see HLP to LC, 3 June 1796, n. 8.

8. *Y Bibl Sanctaidd* to which HLP alludes was that printed in Oxford in 1799. It was "published by the S.P.C.K., under the patronage of Richard Bagot, D.D., Bishop of Oxford, who instructed D. Davies, Vicar of Penegoes, Montgomeryshire, to adopt the orthography of No. 23 [the 1752 edition], and to correct any errors occurring in it. Davies, however, appointed Evan Evans, of Llanfihangel, then at Jesus College, Oxford, to give in his corrections to the printers. The proofs of the Pentateuch were read by Robert Hughes, a Fellow of Jesus College, assisted by E. Hughes of Caerwys; and the remainder by John Roberts, afterwards Vicar of Tremeirchion." See John Ballinger, *The Bible in Whales* (London: H. Sotheran, 1906), p. 19.

9. A new *Y Bibl Sanctaidd*, ed. Peter Williams, was printed by D. Humphreys in Caerfyrddin in 1807. It was actually a reprint of the 1770 edition.

10. That is, the *Sermon and Annual Report*, 1799–1800, of the Society for Promoting Christian Knowledge. The sermon was delivered by John Buchner, bishop of Chichester. Pages 156 and 157 form part of appendix 4 in the *Report* and give an account of the 1799 Welsh Bible and Book of Common Prayer.

Particularly relevant to HLP's plea for Roberts's preferment was the following: "Offers of literary assistance were received from some considerable Welch Scholars in the principality, by which many *errata* in former editions were corrected; and, on the recommendation of the Reverend Dr. *Hughes* Fellow of *Jesus* College, Oxford, the Reverend *Evan Evans*, and the Reverend *John Roberts*, both of the same College, were engaged by the Society, the former to examine and prepare the copy before it went into the hands of the printer, and the latter to revise the proof sheets, as they should issue from the press. These worthy young clergymen . . . received remuneration from the Society to the full extent suggested by the delegates of the *Oxford* press; and in the month of *November*, 1799, the Secretary was enabled to report to the Board that the work was completed" (p. 157).

11. Evan Evans (b. 1743) of "Llanfihangel, Geneu-r-Glyn," county Cardigan. Although he is listed as having been a student of Jesus College, ca. 1763, there is no record of his having taken any degree.

12. 1797 and 1798.

TO THE REVEREND JOHN ROBERTS

Bath
20: March 1807.

Dear [Mr. Roberts]

Your Anxiety is very kind, and Mr. Piozzi is better, and thanks you with all his heart. I hope we shall have a happy Meeting after all alarms, and that the Bishop will be pleased with what he has done &c.[1] His Brother is excessively good natured,[2] and 'tis most probable there is a resemblance between them.

Mr. L[loyd] of W[igfair] knows this World well enough to consider a rival Canvasser as only a momentary Antagonist—*his* Friend will have good luck another day.

People's minds here are much agitated about the Catholick Question,³ but whilst a change of Ministry affects *some* People,⁴ the panic terror taken concerning Canine Madness here and at London too—affects *us all*. No Dog is to be seen in the Streets, and Hysterical Women are fancying themselves hydrophobous now—till the hospitals are crowded with Patients.⁵ Mr. M[oore] will be diverted with this Intelligence, pray tell it him with my Compliments and give him the satisfaction of hearing how rapidly Mr. Piozzi goes on mending.

I have no favourable news to communicate with regard to poor M[ostyn]— but he has three tender Assistants with him, Mother, Wife, and Sister. Dr. Gibbes comes twice a day besides⁶—and while there is life, there is Hope—even for *this* World:—our Hope as to the *other* must soon be swallowed up in certainty, be our duration here what it may—Adieu my good Sir and believe me yours sincerely / H: L: P.

Text: Victoria and Albert Museum Library. A copy.

1. William Cleaver of Saint Asaph.
2. Euseby Cleaver (1746–1819) had been born in Twyford, Bucks., educated at Westminster School and Christ Church, Oxford. Tutor to Lord Egremont, he was presented to the rectories of Tillington and of Petworth, Sussex. Through the interest of his elder brother William, who had been tutor to the marquess of Buckingham, he was appointed chaplain to that nobleman and went with him to Ireland. (Buckingham in 1787 served a second time as viceroy for Ireland.)

In March 1789 Euseby Cleaver was promoted to the sees of Cork and Ross and in June of the same year translated to the sees of Ferns and Leighlin. In August 1809 he was to become archbishop of Dublin.

3. On 5 March 1807 Lord Howick (later Earl Grey), foreign secretary in the Grenville minstry, introduced the Roman Catholic Army and Navy Service Bill, which would open both services to Catholics and dissenters. On the 13th the king informed both Howick and Grenville that he would never consent to the bill. The minsters agreed not to push the bill any further but to speak openly in Parliament in behalf of Catholic claims. On the 17th the king demanded assurance that they would never again urge him to make concessions to Catholics. The next day Grenville informed the king that such assurances could not be given in good conscience.

Much of this maneuvering remained unknown to the public. On 14 March 1807 *The Times* merely reported that the debate on the Roman Catholic Army and Navy Service Bill had been postponed from the 13th to the 19th and indicated that the postponement was prompted by "a disagreement of opinion on this subject . . . among the leading members of Government."

4. On 19 March, *The Times* announced "that the second reading of the Bill for admitting Roman Catholics to hold Commissions in the Army is deferred *sine die.*"

On the 20th *The Times* wrote that the Grenville ministry had not resigned but that "Lord Eldon and Lord Hawkesbury were sent for on Wednesday night to Windsor, where they arrived yesterday morning, as it is supposed to receive his Majesty's commands for the forming of a new Administration."

It was not until 26 March 1807 that *The Times* reported the makeup of the new ministry, with the duke of Portland as the first lord of the treasury. See also Farington 8:2994 for public confusion as late as 24 March concerning these activities.

5. *The Times* through the second half of January reported incidents of mad dogs roving the streets of London. Thus, on 15 January: "A Correspondent wishes us again [as on the 13th] to notice the unusual prevalence of madness among dogs. In the vicinity of London several persons have been bitten, and have suffered the miserable consequences. So notorious is the circumstance, that in various places, the Magistrates have required all persons to confine their dogs for a certain period, on pain of having them shot if seen at liberty."

6. George Smith Gibbes (1771–1851), an Oxonian, received the B.A. in 1792, the M.B. in 1796,

and the M.D. in 1799. He settled at Bath and opened his practice there, after becoming a Fellow of the Royal College of Physicians. In 1804 he was elected physician to the Bath (Mineral Water) Hospital, and in time obtained the appointment of physician extraordinary to Queen Charlotte. In 1820 he was knighted by George IV. About 1835 he was to leave Bath and retire to Cheltenham and Sidmouth. His most important written work was *A Few Observations on the Component Parts of Animal Matters, and their Conversion into a substance resembling Spermaciti* (1796).

TO MARGARET WILLIAMS

[ca. Saturday,
11: April 1807].

My dearest Miss Williams

must not be offended that I draw on our common,—rather our *uncommonly* kind Friend Mr. Gillon for your £2.10.6——we *have no other Banker* at Bath and I hate for you to be (as we call it) out of your Money.

My poor Husband's odd State of Health will put me out of my Wits at last; would you believe it his Pulse is at 80 *now* Saturday Morning—Marshall called it a heavy, but a powerful Pulse; and promised to come at a Moment's Warning[1]—he recommends Dr. Vaughan as the Physician,[2] and so does Miss Sophia Thrale.

Our Lodgings are unexpectedly—I may say *uncommonly* commodious for Mr. Piozzi whose Cough is beyond all things dreadful——attended with excessive Depression of Spirits, and total Loss of Appetite, at a *French* House, where the Cookery is so seducing, and the Kitchen removed to Back Apartments like the Cellars at York House Bath, so that no Scent can be perceived.

My Hopes are sadly kicked down Stairs, and so are *his* by this vile Relapse, if Relapse it can be called. Tell Bowen all I have told *you*,[3] and tell him my Inside is very *unhappy*, but by dint of Temperance, Exercise, and forced Chearfulness, I keep it as quiet as I can. Oh my dear Miss Williams! nobody knows what my *Bowels* suffer on Account of my *Heart*[4]——and none of these Anatomists or Surgeons can make them agree.

Well! do write to me, and tell about Catalani,[5] or about any thing to divert Care: and do ask a Mr. Reynolds a Perfumer in Abbey Street[6]—right Hand as you go from the Abbey to the Parades—if he has many more of those long thin Bottles of real French Hungary Water which I saw unpacked at his Door. The great Mr. Smyth of Bond Street London says they are *inestimable; he has none.*[7] God bless you my dear Miss Williams and continue to love your poor / H: L: P.

I see nothing of Sir John[8]—Lady Killmorey has left her Card.[9]

I met Lady Newborough (not knowing her) at Salthill;[10] and kissed my young Cousins the dear little Wynnes quite unconsciously: They are beautiful Babies indeed.[11]

Text: Houghton Autograph File. *Address:* John Gillon Esq. / No. 10 / Bath Street / Bath. *Postmark:* B AP 11 807.

1. Andrew Marshall (1742–1813) received the M.D. at Edinburgh in 1782 and in the next year settled in London. There he taught anatomy and practiced medicine, concentrating on his practice almost exclusively after 1800.
2. For Dr. Henry Vaughan, see HLP to Q [31 December 1804], n. 16.
3. For the apothecary William Bowen, see HLP to PSP, 14 April 1803, n. 2.
4. HLP, always partial to word play, uses "bowels" in its now-archaic sense of "tenderness" or "pity," etc.
5. Angelica Catalani (1780–1849), an Italian soprano, made her debut in 1797 and within three years was singing at La Scala. She performed before Napoleon at St. Cloud in 1806 and on 13 December of the same year made her successful London debut at the King's Theatre. By 1807 she was earning £2,000 a season; she remained in England until her return to Paris in 1814. See Farington 8:2970, 3163.
6. James Reynolds (fl. 1771–1812), perfumer and "toy-man," 6 Kingston Buildings, Bath.
7. James Smyth and Nephews, perfumers to the Queen, at 110 New Bond Street (1795–1808) and later at 117 New Bond Street (1809–11).
8. Sir John Williams of Bodelwyddan was visiting at Bath.
9. In 1792 at Combermere Abbey, Frances (1769–1818), eldest daughter of Sir Robert Salusbury Cotton, fifth baronet, married Robert Needham (1746–1818), eleventh viscount Kilmorey (I., 1791).
10. The second wife of Thomas Wynn (1736–1807), cr. Baron Newborough (I., 1776), was born Maria Stella Petronilla Chiappini (1773–1843). They had been married 10 October 1786 in Florence. She styled herself "Marchesina of Modigliana." She married secondly in 1810 Baron Edward Ungern-Steinberg, a Russian.
11. HLP refers to the two youngest sons of Lord and Lady Newborough: Thomas John Wynn (1802–32) and Spencer Bulkeley Wynn (1803–1888).

The Wynns were related to HLP through their ancestor Catherine, daughter of Henry Salusbury of Llanrhaiadr, who had in the middle of the sixteenth century married Hugh ap John of Bodvil.

TO ROBERT RAY

Sabloniere's Hotel
Leicester Fields
Monday Morning
20: April 1807.

I leave this Note for Dear Mr. Ray to tell him we are in London, and wish earnestly to see him. Mr. Piozzi is confined by Ill health——a Gouty Man;—— and cannot call himself on *any* Friend;——hope his unfortunate Excuse may be accepted.

I go tomorrow to see Streatham Park,[1] but can do nothing without Mr. Ray——his Virtue will send him tho' his kindness may be withdrawn from her who has unvariably been his admiring Friend and / Obliged Humble Servant / H: L: Piozzi.

Come any Day but tomorrow.

Text: Yale University Library. *Address:* Robt. Ray, Esq.

1. HLP was going to Streatham Park not merely to look over her property but to meet her new tenant, Abraham Atkins. Negotiations over the lease had preoccupied him and John Gillon from early April 1806 to May 1807.
Peter Giles—according to Gillon on 5 April 1806—had planned to sell "the Remainder of his

Term in Streatham Park" to Abraham Atkins (d. ca. 1812) of Saint Katherine Coleman, London, and Clapham, Surrey. Giles's behavior had been "excited by the jealous and turbulent Conduct of Mrs. [Ann] Jones; who would not admit of his . . . *new Favorite*." Atkins offered "to take Streatham Park on Lease for *seven* Years, from the Expiration of Giles's Lease at £*500* a year, and to pay all Taxes, except the *Property* Tax. . . . Thus you would have a nett of £125 a Quarter: Out of which you would pay the Property or Income Tax only. . . . Mr. Atkins is a Merchant . . . in a considerable way; is . . . *a married Man* with a Family" (Ry. 579.138). For Giles's mistress Ann Jones, see HLP to LC, [18] May [1800], n. 18.

The lease seemed ready to be signed in June 1806. But by 13 August "an unlucky mistake about the Garden" had been discovered; i.e., all mention of the garden had been omitted from the lease. Gillon informed HLP of this latest misadventure on 13 August (Ry. 579.146). "Giles will most probably keep Possession of it, for the mere purpose of thwarting you and the new Tenant. And Atkins says that, without the Garden, the House will be of no Use to him, and if it cannot be so arranged that he may have Possession of both at the same Time, he thinks that he has a Right to consider his Bargain as *null* and *void*." Nevertheless, the lease was signed in May 1807.

In view of such complications and HLP's own fear of legal technicalities, she felt that her presence at Streatham Park had to be supported by an attorney. Moreover, she was suing Peter Giles for nonpayment of rent.

TO MARGARET WILLIAMS

21: May [1807]

My dearest Miss Williams
   will believe me when I say that I have had but Three Letters from my Three Daughters since We left Bath; nor did Sophia Thrale ever by any Accident shew me any Accounts She received of them of their Invalid.[1]

Such horrible Stories came to my Ears thro' Servants &c. that at last I wrote to Bowen, because *he* needed to have Scruples,[2] and you ought to keep out of all Family Bustles sure, who have suffered so much from your own.

At length he is dead poor Fellow! and I am dying to know who he has left Guardians to those 3 Children.[3] Write what you hear and write soon——for we shall leave London in ten or Twelve Days at furthest.

Lord bless me! I should be *so* shocked were we to be following that wretched Man's Hearse along the Road.[4]

I am far from well myself, and marvellously low-spirited; Dear Bowen predicted right of Mostyn, and I suppose he will not be very wrong about *me*.

Mr. Piozzi defies them all, and gains Health and Strength every Day.

Leak has long been sent off to Brynbella,[5] and we are under the Care and Tuition of Mr. Dunscombe and Mrs. Chancey; who likes her present Companion much better than the last, who locked the good Things all up tight.

Mr. Gillon is very well and very good, and calls on his Invalid Friends very kindly.

Sophia Thrale has never failed in Propriety or Punctilio. Her Sisters will be coming soon I suppose: Pick me up some News of what they do with the Dead Man and with the living Lady. Of Sir John Williams I know nothing: You are a dear Creature to say he lives *at Bob Hesketh's* but I have no means of knowing where Bob Hesketh as you call him—lives.[6]

I met dear Mr. Thelwall in the Street and he seemed low about *his* Son;[7] Lady Clarges has lost hers—of the same Complaint.[8]

Tis Melancholy to see Young Creatures go before one so; I do not like it: Yet am in no hurry to set out myself.

Adieu dear Miss Williams, this is a true Black-Letter Performance scrawled in haste and worthy your own hand or that / of Yours ever / H: L: Piozzi.

True Love to Mrs. Glover and her Family.[9]

Poor Allen Jones has been exceeding ill, and brought a dead Child.—I told you how *that* would be—no Comfort to be hoped there—but never mind: if my Piozzi will keep on mending, as he does now; I were ungrateful to fret about any thing else.

Yet *do* send me word concerning this Dear Widowed Monkey [CMM], and what Tricks She plays:——I am very, *very* sorry.

Oh dear Soul make Dr. Parry know how much I thank him for the kind Interest he takes in my happiness.

Text: Victoria and Albert Museum Library. *Address:* Miss Williams / Upper Park Street / St. James's Square / Bath. *Postmark:* A MA 21 807.

1. ST visited the Piozzis in London between 14 April and 27 May. See HLP to Q, 14 April; 12 May (Bowood Collection). HLP regarded ST as "exceeding *civil* and I may say *kind* when we were Sick at Sabloniere's Hotel in Leicester Fields this last Spring:—her Sisters went to comfort Cecilia, whose Husband lay expiring at Bath; whence *mine* escaped with *Life* after swallowing 300—25 Dozen I think, of Medical Draughts from Bowens Shop" (*Thraliana* 2:1082).
2. HLP's sole contact in Bath—however remote and indirect—with her dying son-in-law.
3. John Meredith Mostyn died intestate, aged thirty-one, on 19 May (presumably of tuberculosis as suggested by Clifford, p. 418). CMM, who coped with her husband's debts and tangled affairs, was guardian of their three children. See "Chronicle," *AR* (1807):577.
4. Mostyn was buried on 2 June in the churchyard of Llanrhaiadr, near Segroid, where CMM continued to live ("Llanrhaiadr Burial Register," C.R.O., Clwyd).
5. Alexander Leak (b. 1776) was HLP's "wise" and loyal steward at Streatham Park, replacing Jacob Weston (ca. 1806). While attending to her interests, he was to die unexpectedly at New King Street, Bath, and to be buried on 28 June 1816 in the churchyard of Saint Swithin's. See "Walcot Parish Burial Registers," C.R.O., Somerset.
6. Robert Hesketh (1765–1824), of Rossall and North Meols, and Heysham Hall, Lancs. He had matriculated at Brasenose College, Oxford, 31 January 1781, receiving a B.C.L. in 1789. In September 1790 he had married Maria, *née* Rawlinson (d. 1824).
7. The sick son was Bevis. See HLP to the Reverend Robert Myddelton, 28 March 1805, n. 5.
8. William Clarges (b. 1782) died at Falmouth 8 May 1807, of hæmoptysis [haemoptoe], on his return from Portugal, where he had been for his health. He had been a student of Christ Church, Oxford.
9. Lieutenant Colonel John Jackson Glover (d. ca. 1823) of the Eleventh Regiment of Foot (and subsequently colonel commandant of the Bath Loyal Volunteers) married in 1776 Frances, *née* Cook, or Cooke (d. 21 February 1846), of Kiltinane Castle, county Tipperary. They had five children: Anna, Frances, Henrietta, John Octavius Augustus, and Frederick Augustus.
See Glover's will, proved 5 February 1823 (P.R.O., Prob. 11/1666/80); *GM* 25, pt. 1, n.s. (1846): 444.

TO MARGARET WILLIAMS

Leicester Square
Thursday 28: May [1807].

I thank you very kindly for all your Letters dearest Miss Williams, you are very good to me indeed; and so is Mr. Bowen. What kind Advice he has given me! Pray tell him how truly I feel obliged, and how sincerely I esteem his Friendship.——I wonder what his Bill was, and who is to pay it? Mr. Mostyn busies *himself* no doubt, and does well to sleep at Llanrhaider.[1]

The Ladies called last night very politely, and told in general Terms how they had passed their Time—no more: We all dine with Mr. Gillon next Saturday, and on Monday set out for Wales. Mr. Piozzi is *now* very *little*, if *any* thing worse than he was last Summer; and I expect a comfortable Journey.

You would not think what numbers of Visitants we have had, though coming for so short a Time, and to such a Place as an Hôtel and bad health and all, we meant to see *no*body, and *no* thing.

Meanwhile I got one Look at the Somerset house Exhibition,[2] and one good View of the Marquis of Stafford's fine Pictures which amused me exceedingly[3]——and some Droppers-*in* have told me that Miss Blaquiere is going to be married to a rich Mr. Hankey[4] Nephew to the Gentleman who died the other Day a Martyr to Electioneering Business.[5]

But of Lady Kirkwall or Mrs. Bunnell[6]—The Child born last night knows as much as I do.

Streatham Park Affairs are settled at last, and Mr. Abram Atkins pays us 500£ o'year for it; without deduction for Taxes. I worked at arranging the Library with Fell a Bond Street Bookseller for two Whole Days,[7] and said last Night how I was fatigued. "Why *are* there any Books left? says Miss Thrale coldly; I thought they all belonged to Mr. Giles." I hope replied H:L:P that you will find 3468 if you look on the Shelves tomorrow Morning or I shall have lost much Labour. We have examined the Pictures too, and put every thing in Order: and Mr. Gillon shall make the new Tenant accept the Catalogue of Ornamental Furniture, Books &c. and give all up this Time seven Years, as he receives them now.

Adieu dear Miss Williams, and let me copy over to *You*, Mr. Bowen's Advice to *myself:* Do not agitate your Nerves too much about Worldly Matters—They must end soon with us all, and in the Course of Nature cannot long torment / Your faithful and Obliged / H: L: Piozzi.

Text: Victoria and Albert Museum Library. *Address:* Miss Williams / Upper Park Street / St. James's Square / Bath. *Postmark:* <A> MA 28 807.

1. Edward Mostyn (1785–1841), seventh baronet Mostyn (1823), of Talacre, was a distant relative of John Meredith Mostyn. Apparently he came to attend the funeral and to help CMM at Segroid.
2. HLP went with ST ca. 21 May to the Somerset House Exhibition; i.e., to the thirty-ninth exhibition of the Royal Academy. See HLP to Q, 21 May 1807 (Bowood Collection).
   The following works received newspaper attention: Beechey's portraits of Earl St. Vincent and another of Mary, countess of Breadalbane; paintings by Turner, Westall, and West; a small model for the statue of Sir Joshua Reynolds to be erected in Saint Paul's Cathedral, by John Flaxman.

The actual number of paintings, sculpture, and architectural sketches on exhibit was 1,113.

3. George Granville Leveson-Gower (1758–1833), second marquess of Stafford (1803) and first duke of Sutherland (1833). An art patron, he first opened his private art collection to the public in May 1806. According to *The Times*, 1 April: "The Marquis of Stafford, who certainly possesses one of the most valuable collections of ancient paintings in the world, is adding to his gallery several of the best performances of our living artists, chiefly selected from those now exhibiting at the British Institution, Pall Mall. This illustrious and accomplished amateur, for the very honourable purpose of accelerating the progress of Fine Arts in our island, sent cards of invitation and admission last year to most of the British Artists resident in this kindom, who were thereby enabled to contemplate in Cleveland row, the acknowledged excellencies of the ancient masters, without combatting the difficulties of visiting the Continent."

4. For Elizabeth de Blaquiere and John Bernard Hankey, see HLP to Elizabeth de Blaquiere [July 1803], n. 2.

They were married at Saint George's, Hanover Square, on 9 June 1807.

5. "At a quarter before six o'clock in the evening, of an inflammation in his bowels, aged 41, John-Peter Hankey, esq. banker, and alderman of the ward of Candlewick, in which he succeeded the late Alderman Perchard, who died January 21, 1806 . . . and in which he is succeeded by Samuel Birch, esq. deputy of the ward of Cornhill. The extreme fatigue which he had sustained during a canvas of 8 or 10 days for the City of London, produced a fever which terminated his life. The first symptoms of his complaint appeared about eight on the preceding evening, when he complained of great fatigue and extreme thirst." Leaving a wife and four children, "he would most likely have been one of the successful candidates, having on the day he died had the greatest shew of hands, and standing third on that day's poll."

See *GM* 77, pt. 1 (1807): 493; Farington 8:3039.

6. For a Mrs. Bunnell, Lady Orkney's housekeeper-companion, see HLP to MW, 5 July [1807].

7. Nornaville and Fell, booksellers and stationers located at 29 New Bond Street.

TO THE MISS THRALES

Monday 8: June 1807.
Brynbella.

My dear Girls

on the only Scrap of Paper left in the House—(for my own is not come—or not unpacked,)—do I write the History of my Travels from Salt hill; where I enjoyed the Company of Colonel Henry Barry and the *Green Pease Soup*—which we found so delicious: but by the Time we arrived at Woodstock, my Head seemed giddy; nor did our beautiful Drive thro' Blenheim Park quite settle it somehow—and at Chapel House!!

"No six Sycophants from Syracuse made sick with Camomile Tea"[1] ever equalled the Distress I was in all Night.

The next Day took us to Worcester, where I swallowed a few Drops of Laudanum which I suppose locked in what were left of the Enemy's Troops, and we ran forward to Ellesmere [Salop] the Day after—Mr. Piozzi crying *Bon Courage* to me, who was more than half dead.——On Sunday Morning or rather Saturday Night——The Enemy made another *sprightly Saillie*——and my old Experienced *General Moore*[2] has been obliging him to *evacuate* the Town ever since, till I am so weak I can scarce hold a Pen.

My Memory however serves me to recollect that on this Day dear Mr. Nicholls dines with you, (not on Green Pease Soup I hope;) and that His *Clothes, Chapeau-*

las &c. are all packed up and sent away for Blunston [Blundeston]. Suzette leaves Town tomorrow if I am right, and consummates her Marriage With Mr. *Ashgrove:* If like Many Modern Couples they should be soon tired of the binding Words *to have and to hold,* She may get a Divorce any Day:[3]——Those beautiful Places within 20 Miles of Town, are incessantly changing Possessors; and her Comfort may arise from the Reflexion that her Money will be paid her again——but here is Plasnewydd sold for only 56000£—!! a melancholy End to poor Mr. Wynne's Improvements.[4]

Dr. Myddelton's little Boy is come down *alive* to be Saved by his native Air; but unless they burn his Books, no Care can quite recover him. When he was 8 Years old it was his Sport to multiply 8 Figures by 3 without touching Pen and Ink——but it is the *Way* now—among a certain Sort of Boys and Girls,—— to kill Themselves by Study.[5]

Well! *That* was not poor Mostyn's Death I trow; Cecy wrote me a Cold Note when I was so Ill that all Denbigh said I was come home to die:——but that is so much the better; Widows are never censured for *Coldness;* but suspected of Warmth.—

The Measles are all over Wales this Year, and fatal almost every where;—Dear Sophia will remember the Fear She was in of the Measles a Month or two ago.

No Frankers yet, tho' the Spirit of Electioneering still agitates the Country round us; that heaves as one has seen the Sea do, after the Storm is called off[6]——No other News circulates but who had most Votes &c. and what I see most interesting in the Papers as private Intelligence—seems a Marriage between Sir John Shelley who his Father used to call Tib,—and a Lady said to bring him two or Three Hundred Thousand Pounds——I know not *whence* tho', for her Name is new to me.[7]

This is a joint Letter,—common Property; but I will send my dear Sophy a Copy of my Epitaph on Susan Adams when I can find it[8]——and find free cost Conveyance for the same——recollect my Account of her Mother's partial Fondness however, and the Difficulty of pleasing People who had suffered Panegyrics to be written on that Girl in the Irish Papers—which Isabella of Spain or Elisabeth of England could scarce have answered, had they been adorned with the Beauty of Mary Queen of Scots. But I am come to my last Line and must hastily pray God to bless you / as is wished by your Affectionate / H: L: P.

Mr. Piozzi is so much better than when he left Brynbella. The People are ready to make Bonfires. He sends you 1000 kind Regards, and says 'tis his Turn to take Care of Me now——so thinks me better to day.

Text: Hyde Collection. *Address:* Miss Thrales / Great Cumberland Street / No. 13. / London. / Single Sheet. *Postmark:* CHESTER 190 JUN 9 1807; JUN 11 1807.

1. The alliterative joke has Plautine overtones: the one sycophant of the *Menaechmi*—voracious Peniculus—is inflated to six, an echo of sick. HLP thus emphasizes her discomfort from the effects of overeating and nausea induced by camomile, a popular if repugnant home remedy.
  For a Shakespearian version, cf. the Dromio twins in *The Comedy of Errors.*

2. For John Moore, the "Surgeon of Vale Street," Denbigh, see HLP to PSW, 15 September [1792], n. 3.

3. In June 1807 SAT went to live with William Frederick Wells (1764–1836), a watercolorist, at his house Ashgrove Cottage in Kent. That she contributed to its maintenance is implied in the listing of her name and Wells's in the tax rolls for 1808 as "joint occupants."

There were no legal obstacles to the marriage of SAT and Wells, whose wife had died on 7 February. Neither wished to marry, although SAT assumed responsibility for his seven surviving children during the few years in which she lived with their father. By 1819, if not earlier, SAT became the sole occupant of Ashgrove Cottage, where she continued to live until her death in November 1858. For his part, Wells took up permanent residence in Mitcham, Surrey. See Hyde, pp. 334–35.

4. For the sale of Plâsewydd to the Heatons of Lleweny (or Lleweni) Green, see HLP to Q, 23 July 1805, n. 6.

5. For young Robert Myddelton, now a pupil at Harrow, see HLP to the boy's father, 28 March 1805.

6. The king on 27 April 1807 had unexpectedly prorogued Parliament. The next day *The Times* in its leading article referred to the speech delivered by the lord chancellor in the king's name: "It states, 'that his Majesty is anxious to recur to the sense of his people, while the events which have recently taken place were fresh in their recollection.' This is certainly placing the question upon its true grounds, and putting it fairly to the Country. The elective body, by this appeal, will have an opportunity of pronouncing on the respective merits and principles of the last and present administration. If 'the late unfortunate and uncalled for agitation of a question' [i.e., the Catholic bill] has cancelled all the good that the Ex-Ministers are allowed to have done, it will be for the Country to declare so. The Father of his people will, no doubt, abide by this result, whatever it may be."

By 30 April, electioneering began, and the voting continued all through May with *The Times*, e.g., reporting on the state of contested elections until at least 2 June. For HLP, the election which most "agitated the country" was the Westminster election when Lord Cochrane was returned at the head of the poll, Sir Francis Burdett being his colleague.

7. John Shelley (1772–1852), sixth baronet (1783), married at Saint George's, Hanover Square, on 4 June 1807 Frances (d. 1873), only daughter and heiress of Thomas Winckley of Brockholes, Lancs.

8. See HLP to PSP, 19 August 1804, n. 5.

TO MARGARET WILLIAMS

Brynbella Wensday Night
10: June 1807.

My dear Miss Williams

will be glad to hear that we are come home *alive* and *safe;* because saying we are come home *very well,* is the greatest of Nonsense, but I believe it is the Fasion to say so.

Mr. Piozzi has however undoubtedly gained Strength, or he could not have run 65 Miles in one Day with one pair of Horses from seven in the Morning till 10 at Night.—I was myself very much fatigued, having been ill (in *your* Way) *Diarrhœa;* at Chapelhouse[1] on the Wednesday—only one day before, and not half recovered;—when his Man Dunscombe called me up at 5—and said we were to drive on as far as Ellesmere from Worcester Town. Meeting Poor Mostyn's returned Hearse did not mend my Spirits, and dear Mr. Bowen will wonder there is any of his lean Countrywoman left by this Time.

Here however we are; as I may say for my own part—*completely knocked up.* My Master coughs and strangles, and laments the bad Taste in his Mouth; but his Pulse is strong and his Appetite restored.—I have very little of the *one* and scarce any of the *other*.

Mr. Moore is very angry, says I have stopt just short of Destruction, he gives *me* Tincture [of] Rhubarb and Columbo Root, and gives his Compliments with my own to Mr. Bowen.—You have my leave and Desire to shew him this Letter.

Now for our Welsh Affairs; the Report is that Mrs. Bunhall[2] is going to be married to Mr. Gough, a Young Upholsterer.——That the Family at Bodylwyddan are as well and happy as usual; That the Lleweney Folks expect their Lord home soon, but that Miss Elizabeth de Blaquiere's approaching Marriage and her own feeble Health, will delay Lady Kirkwall's return from Tunbridge Wells.

Mrs. Mostyn of Segroid sent me a Cold How d'ye do?—When the Denbigh People all said I was come Home to dye; but dear Mrs. Jones hastened hither, and has not left me Day or Night: You know I mean Allen who married to Pontriffith—and by the way She has had her Father and Mother here in Wales with her on a Visit, so *her* Spirits are a good Supply for mine. She is the happiest young Woman I know.[3]

I left my fair and deserving Daughters as dear Mr. Gillon calls them, in high health and Beauty; we made a gay Day at his London house, and a grand Dinner he did give us *surely*; and seemed as well as ever, and my Master very tolerably well too, and in Haste to begin his Journey. We left the Hotell in Leicester Fields however late on the Monday Evening—and slept no further off than Salthill; our next day's Drive ended at Chapel house, where I was very ill indeed; and on Wensday we got no further than Worcester, whence it was Time [to] hasten sick or well; and enjoy the fine new Inn at Ellesmere where we got in late o' *Thursday*. From thence home was scarce 39 Miles: so here is our History detailed in an 8 peny, or 18 peny Pamphlet, for no Frankers can I find tho' the Election, and Dean Shipley's Triumphant Conquest over the two prostrate Baronets fill every mouth,—he won it by 8 only.[4]

Our Compliments to very kind Inquirer shall employ what is left of this Paper which testifies the grateful Affection borne to Dear Miss Williams / by Her faithful / H: L: P.

Text: Victoria and Albert Museum Library. *Address:* Miss Williams / Upper Park Street / St. James's Square / Bath. *Postmark:* DENBIGH 224.

1. Chapelhouse was an inn in Chipping Norton, Oxon.
2. Apparently Mrs. Bunnell (or Bunhall) and Mr. Gough were not natives of North Wales; in any event, their marriage is not recorded in any known parish record of the area.
3. Elener (Allen) Jones added to the cover sheet the following comment:

My Dear Madam,
With Pleasure I can inform you We have Mr and Mrs Piozzi Safe at Pretty Brynbella Once a gain to my great Astonishment to see Poor Mr Piozzi a gain which Could not be Expected after the Verry Bad Account I had of him When at Bath and in Short London no Better But I have good hops of him once a gain—this Moment he is going out in his Chair Mr Moore Says if he can gett out in the Air the Cough will be better——I think Mrs Piozzi is or have been Worse than the *Squire*.

4. HLP confuses Dean William Shipley with his eldest son, William (d. 1829), a lieutenant colonel. The latter in the Flint Borough election of 27 May polled 129 votes against Sir Stephen Richard Glynne's 128 and Sir Edward Pryce Lloyd's 120.
Sir Stephen (1780–1815) was eighth baronet (1780) of Hawarden Castle, Flintshire.

TO MISS WILLIAMS

Brynbella
Sunday 5: July [1807][1]

I would not write to my Dear Miss Williams till I had something tolerably agreeable to tell her. I can now say that She has the most beautiful Set of Baby Nephews and Nieces that ever were boasted of by Maiden Lady. Sir John and Lady Williams dined here last Week, and kindly invited *us* Yesterday, and *our* Nephew; and Mr. Shepherd who is with him here for Holydays, to Dinner at Bodylwyddan:[2] where we had the honour of meeting our new Bishop and his Lady[3]—and we were the first Carriage-full, who ever were set down at the Entrance under the Doric Pillars, which now Sustain an Elegant Balcony filled with Flowers, and have a magnificent Appearance to the Front.

I hardly could find my Way in or about the house, every thing is so altered and improved, but as the Doge of Venice said when the French asked him what was most surprizing in all Paris?—I thought *Ourselves* the greatest Wonder, and so would you have thought too had you seen Mr. Piozzi walking in and out with little Assistance, and joining in Society as usual. Mrs. Williams could not sit down to dine, but She found her Place at the Teatable, and looked astonishingly well for so complete an Invalide.[4] They were all extremely obliging: and seemed strongly perswaded of our national Prosperity from their late Visit to Liverpool, whence the young Squire of the House was just come back with his Uncle William who is looking particularly well:[5] We had Turtle and Turbot and all the good Things for Dinner.

Miss Margaret is the Beauty amongst the young Ladies—decidedly; and is taller than Miss Emma *now*:[6] The Infant Boy talks and walks, I never saw such a forward Baby in my Life[7]——My own dear Godson as handsome as an Angel:[8] he is the same Age of Tommy Mostyn, but infinitely the finer Fellow, *he always was*.[9]—There was Talk of a Wax Doll you had sent, and Mr. Piozzi and I expressed our Gratitude for the Kindness you shewed us at Bath, in the best Manner we were able. Sir John appeared very comfortable, and says he was soon tired of London. Mrs. Lewis Hughes goes there tomorrow for the first Time in her Life.[10]

Lord Kirkwall is not come home yet: and Mrs. Bunnell have I no Chance for seeing; I never *did* see her to know her, and never *heard* of her till *you* Dear Lady told me of your Regard for her, which made her an Object of Enquiry——The report is *hereabouts* that She is to Marry Mr. Goff—or Gough; a Relation of Mr. Bradford's, who lived at Lleweney ever since my Lord was married,[11] and I fancy presided at fitting up the House——I recollect Dancing with him on Tenant's Day in the old Hall, when Young FitzMaurice was Christened.[12]

So here is a Letter full of Welsh News, we have no other here; the Kings and Emperors are fighting and assassinating whilst we confine our Cares to the Hay and the Taxes. You who live among a freer Circle of Conversers, must tell me what People are talking of, who have no *Hay* and few Taxes. The Dust in our Roads would choke any Inclination to Talk, before one arrives at the Visit; our Bishop and his Lady appear well disposed to please their Neighbors however, and those who wish to give Pleasure, seldom fail.

My Wish is to express how much I feel of grateful Affection to Dear Miss Williams and to say how / Sincerely I am her / faithful etc. / H: L: P.

Mr. Piozzi unites his truest regards; you will make our Compliments to all kind Enquirers.

Text: Victoria and Albert Museum Library. *Address:* Miss Williams / Upper Park Street / St. James's Square / Bath. *Postmark:* DENBIGH 224.

1. The letter may be dated 1807, when William Cleaver, who had been translated to Saint Asaph in October 1806, was still the new bishop.

2. JSPS was now a pupil at the school of Thomas Shephard at Enborne, Bucks. His son was Charles Mitchell Smith Shephard (1782–1841), educated at Eton and Jesus College, Cambridge, where he received the B.A. in 1805 (having been admitted to Gray's Inn on 22 May 1803). Becoming an attorney, he was ca. 1814 to go to the West Indies, and by 1816 to become attorney general of Saint Vincent in the Windward Islands.

3. About 1779 William Cleaver had married Anne, daughter of Ralph Assheton of Downham and Cuerdale, Lancs.

4. For Ly W's mother, Eleanor Williams, *née* Hughes, see HLP to the Ladies of the Williams Family, 3 May 1797, n. 1.

5. The squire was John II, now aged thirteen. His uncle was the Reverend William Williams, later Williams-Edwards (1774–1829), who had studied at Christ's College, Cambridge, receiving the B.A. in 1796 and M.A. in 1799. See the "Llanynys Burial Register," C.R.O., Clwyd. See also ALP to Ly W, 18 March 1802, n. 11.

6. Margaret Williams (b. 1799) and her elder sister Emma (b. 1798).

7. The "Infant Boy" was William Williams, not quite two.

8. Hugh Williams had been born on 8 January 1802.

9. Thomas Arthur Bertie Mostyn, CMM's third son, had been born 11 July 1801.

10. Charlotte Margaret Grey (d. 1835), of Backworth, county Northumberland, had married on 8 March 1804 William Lewis Hughes (1767–1852), cr. first baron Dinorben (1831). The family owned Kinmel Park near Abergele.

11. William Mussage Kirkwall Bradford (1774–post 1807) of Henley, Oxfordshire, had matriculated at Christ Church on 21 May 1791, receiving the B.A. in 1795 and the M.A. in 1798.

He was once the subject of gossip, as in 1801, when HLP had written in *Thraliana* 2:1032, n. 1: "Widowhood is unhappy even to poor Lady Orkney who had a wretched Husband—& who lives pleasantly & kindly with her only Child—yet the World will not *let her alone.* Example There is a Report here or a Surmise—or a somewhat, y^t Lady Orkney is secretly married to her Son's Companion a Lame Mr Bradford. I see no Sign of it—but then I am not quick sighted."

Two years later HLP repudiated the gossip as "Lyes" when Bradford married Mary Wharton, who reared Lord de Blaquiere's daughters. The marriage took place on 22 September 1803 in the Bodfari church. See the "Bodfari Parish Marriage Register," C.R.O., Clwyd.

12. Thomas John Hamilton Fitzmaurice had been christened in October 1803. See HLP to PSP, 5 November 1803, n. 6.

SOPHIA THRALE TO GABRIEL PIOZZI

Great Cumberland Street
21: July [1807]

My dear Mr. Piozzi[1]

I am just returned from Susan's pretty House in the Country, which will account to you for my not having immediately answered your very kind Letter; I assure you nothing would give me greater pleasure than to accept your obliging Invitation to Brynbella and Mr. Hoare[2] would I know be particularly delighted with the beautiful scenery of N. Wales, but unfortunately he has engaged himself for this year to His Brother's at Stourhead where more of his numerous Family have appointed to meet us.[3] From thence we purpose going into Devonshire to Mr. Charles Hoare (another Brother) who has a beautiful Seat near Dawlish, and a very amiable wife whose delicate Health does not a[llo]w her ever to quit the pure Air of that delightful Coast.[4] We shall I believe return early in the Winter to London where at present we are much engaged in House-hunting—no very pleasing occupation in the *Dog-days*, but necessary for future Comfort.[5]

The Account you give of the amended State of your health gave me sincere pleasure, and I assure you I read with amazement your well-penned Epistle, remembering the sad state of your poor Fingers—the Contents of it and the kind and affectionate Interest you appear to take in an Event so interesting to me cannot but be extremely grateful to my feelings, and I must commission you to express both mine and Mr. H's united Thanks to my Mother for her kindness—he would most willingly accelerate the Marriage as much as possible, but where Lawyers are concerned you know, that is not always to be done, and I should think some time in August would be the earliest time it could take place.[6] With all our best Wishes for your Health and Happiness, and best Love to my Mother believe me my dear Sir your obliged and Sincerely *Sophia Thrale*.

Text: Ry. 553.33.

1. This letter and the next by ST are merely alluded to by HLP in her own long but impersonal letter to Q, 11 August 1807. HLP used such impersonality to hide hurt.
ST's notes are, nevertheless, significant because they epitomize a muted suspicion of her mother. ST is polite but she does not want HLP at her wedding. She conceals the date and place of her marriage. HLP was not insensitive to ST's secrecy, distorting it in "Harvard Piozziana" (3:104–5) to claim that she did not know of the intended nuptials until a week before the event. Moreover, she was pained by ST's refusal of GP's invitation and, contrarily, of ST's plans to visit the Hoares.
2. As early as 1801, Henry Merrik Hoare (1770–1856) courted ST. See Gillon's letter to HLP, 24 August 1801 (Ry. 578.85).
Merrik was the third son of Richard Hoare (1734/35–1787), cr. baronet (1786), and his second wife, Frances Anne, née Acland (d. 1800). Just before his marriage in 1807, he lived at Adelphi Terrace and was a partner in Hoare's Bank.
3. Merrik Hoare had four brothers or, as HLP was to say, "there are so many Brothers I never know which is which."
Apparently, some of the brothers planned to meet at Stourhead, the estate of their widowed half-brother Richard Colt Hoare (1758–1838), second baronet (1787). Coming to Stourhead in Wiltshire

were not only the newlyweds but also Peter Richard Hoare (1772–1849) and his wife, Arabella Penelope Eliza, née Greene (1781–1865).

4. Charles Hoare (1767–1851), F.R.S., F.S.A., also a partner in the bank, had employed John Nash (1752–1835) as his architect and Humphry Repton (1752–1818) as his landscape gardener when he built Luscombe Castle near Dawlish in South Devon (1800–7). He had on 7 May 1790 married Frances Dorothea, née Robinson (1769–1853), originally of Cranford, Northants. See the parish records of Dawlish (Saint Michael's), in C.R.O., Devon.

5. The Hoares were to make their residence at 31 York Place, just off Regent's Park. The brick house, four storeys tall, was in a row between the Turnpike (now Marylebone Road) and Paddington Street.

6. ST and Henry Merrik Hoare were married on 13 August 1807 at Saint Mary le Bone.

SOPHIA THRALE TO HESTER LYNCH PIOZZI

Great Cumberland Street
1: August 1807

My dear Mother

You may suppose I am very much hurried or I should have written again before this time—I will let you know when the Day for my Marriage is fixed, but I think it will take place early in the Week after next, as the Writings[1] are nearly finished. It is impossible for any one to have behaved more liberally than Mr. Hoare has done, and I have every Reason to think myself highly fortunate in having gained the Affections of so amiable a Man. I think there is no doubt of our being happy and yet as the time approaches it is natural to feel a considerable degree of Anxiety. I mentioned to Mr. Piozzi our intended Tour into Devonshire and I hope next Summer we shall be able to accept your kind Invitation to Brynbella.[2] Immediately after the Ceremony we are to go to Mr. Hugh Hoares in Bedfordshire and from thence proceed upon our long Journey.[3] I hope Mr. Piozzi's health continues as well as when he wrote, and with many Apologies for this hasty Scrawl / believe me my dear Mother / Your Affectionate Daughter / *Sophia Thrale.*

Text: Ry. 553.34.

1. That is, provisions of the marriage settlement.
2. According to the entry under 12 August 1808 in *Thraliana* 2:1097: "M^r and Mrs Hoare have been here on a short Ten-day Visit, and are gone with Cecy Mostyn to make the fashionable Mountain Tour of N: Wales:—The Ton Folks *do* so now o' Days; that they may say next April in London, at what a *Distance* they pass'd their Summer from the Metropolis."
3. Henry Hugh Hoare (1762–1841), third baronet (1838) of Wavendon House, Bucks., had married on 25 August 1784 Maria Palmer, née Acland (d. 1845).

TO HESTER MARIA THRALE

> Brynbella Tuesday
> 11: August 1807.

My dearest Girl's magnificent Present—is arrived safe,—ponderous as you said, but to me very desirable. It is shameful to own that I never have read Lowth's Isaiah,[1] and I should have fallen instantly to work on it, had not that fascinating Book—the Life of Beattie by Sir William Forbes, accompanied the larger Work.[2] It is *so* seducing to see all one's old Friends and Foes,—Companions at *any* Rate;——over again in good Preservation, that I can no more quit Such reading now, than I could hasten from a Room where they should all be represented in Wax Figures as at Rackstraw's[3]—some chatting, some listening, and some taking Snuff &c. The present Mode of publishing Biographical Anecdotes—*begun by myself* is exquisitely pleasing in these Peoples hands.—*Once*, like the Melancholy Shepherd—I could have plaid the Trick as well, and saved *myself* as Cumberland has done, by telling my own Tale my own way: but

> Omnia fert aetas; animum quoque.— — — — — —
> — — — — — — — — — — — — — — —
> Nunc oblita mihi tot Carmina; vox quoque Mœrim
> Iam fugit ipsa.[4]—

My Husband has a better heart of Things; and I do verily believe will Sing a Song, and accompany himself this very Day to amuse the Bishop who dines here; and into whose Coat Pocket I shall convey this Letter—if I live so long: but les *Boyaux de Madame*, et le *Bas Ventre de Madame* are very rebellious. I put myself in Mind perpetually of the old Verses from Niceness to Newfangle where

> Once o'Week for fashion's Sake, my Lady *must be sicke*,
> No Meat but *Mutton, or at most* the *Pinion of a Chicke;*
> To day her owne Hayre best becomes, which yellow is as Golde,
> Tomorrowe in a Periwigge,—Blacke to be holde;
> Now is She bare-backed to be seene, now on her Muffler goes;
> Now is her Phỳznomie display'd, now nuzzled to the Nose.[5]

So went the World in Gammer Gurton's Days, and so goeth it still. The Post is not come yet, and we have no News of Sophia: or I should have a pleasanter Theme than myself to talk about, and should pity nobody but Mr. Hoare,[6] with whom I trust "Time goes on Crutches, as Count Claudio says; till Love have all his Rites."[7]

Cæcilia is not gone to Barmouth,—She will dine here, and meet Mrs. Cleaver, to whom *She wishes an Introduction*. Astonishing! after the Things one has heard her say of this Country, its Inhabitants, Neighbourhood &c. I expect to see Bonfires lighted in honour of her gracious though Tardy Condescension——but I would rather talk of Killala's Isaiah,[8] and how it differs from Dr. Lowth's; for tho' dear old Johnson said *that* Knowledge was the best, which treated of Things that before us lie in daily Life—⁹

I have always found it *easier* to comprehend Criticism, Astronomy, or even Explications of a Prophetic Writer; than to understand the Views, Intents, or Purposes of those with whom I lived in the most *familiar* Habits.—I use not the Word *Intimate*, because Long and Prosperous Lives may to my Knowlege be past in this World, without any *Intimacy* at all. So said King Solomon of old (you reply;) "The Heart knoweth its own Bitterness, and another meddleth not with his Joy."¹⁰ But now for the Prophecy of Isaiah.

When Dr. Stock the Bishop of Killala, lived in this Neighbourhood; ¹¹ and we conversed freely together,——When *I* knew not the Hebrew Characters for *my* Part,—, and he used to shew me his Critique on the 14th: Chapter It came into my Fancy that the End of the 14th Verse

How hath the Oppressor ceased! the *Golden City* ceased! was a mere Allusion to the popular Name of Babylon, which probably was called Babylon the *Golden* as Italians Say to this Hour Padua la Dotta, Roma la Santa &c. His Lordship was delighted with the Conceit, which *he* strengthened by observing that מדהבה being a Chaldaic Word, was sure enough the Epithet by which the proud Babylonians distinguished their magnificent Metropolis¹²——and he *might* have corroborated the Conjecture still stronger, by Nebuchadnezzar's Dream, where Daniel says to the King of Babylon *Thou art that Head of Gold,* alluding I suppose to what his Majesty knew was His Town's common Apellation.¹³

Diodati however,—is of *Lowth's* Opinion; and translates the Passage come è restato L' Oppressore! Come è *cessato il Tributo!* he considers as an *Exactress of Gold* completely, the Seat of that Monarch who made all Nations his Tributaries; and those who follow Diodati in general do quite right I believe.¹⁴ Arias Montanus renders it Aurea pensio desiit;¹⁵ *Exactor* cessavit. So I have little to uphold our Conceit with—as to Translations of other Tongues; tho' 'tis not impossible that when *Aur*elian named the Town he built in France—a *Golden* City, *Orl*eans encore;——he was not without Precedent;¹⁶ and that in the 17th. Chapter of the Revelations Babylon is discriminated as holding a Gold Cup in her hand¹⁷— does not the Greek call her Chrysa?——if *that* Epithet is *there* given to the City (as I believe it is,) and not the *Cup*; I shall hold fast by my Conjecture almost in Spite of Authorities.—The *Cup* might be to hold Exactions.

Apropos If you should ever light on Stock's Isaiah—remember that *I enter my Protest* against his Explanation of the 13th. Verse of the same Chapter¹⁸—I have not Paper *now,* and I am sure I have not *words* to express my Disapprobation of the whole Note——Tho' 'tis not all his own Idea, but *borrowed:*—not however from Your H: L: P who seems to have taken up her *Mashal* משל pretty insolently already.¹⁹

So Adieu dear Girls! and be married, and be merry; for the Time shortens, and the Plot thickens; and Sophia's Grand Children will I doubt not witness the winding-up.

When comes America against us with her little Navy of Blefuscu?²⁰ I should like that Collingwood or some of our Admirals should *tow* them all in together some Day *for a Frolic.*²¹ Once more Farewell! and forget not / Your Affectionate Mother / H: L: Piozzi.

The Jews you see have convened another Sanhedrim.²²

I am glad that the Story of a Claimant is not against any among my few Quality Friends after all. The Duke of Norfolk will stop this Man's Mouth I suppose and the Story will dye away.²³

Thanks for Ruspini's Styptic—I am horribly in your Debt:—but it is not *that* which makes me so lowspirited and Nervous. I believe it is seeing Mr. Piozzi exerting his odd Resolution to enjoy these next 3 Months when so *convinced* as he is that he shall never see the Year 1808.

Adieu and write soon for Pity—I shall go to the Sea next Monday or Monday sennight.

Text: Bowood Collection. *Address:* Miss Thrale / 13 Great Cumberland Street / London. *Postmark:* [franked by Cleaver] August twelfth. FREE 14 Au 1807.

1. Robert Lowth (1710–87), bishop of London (1777), *Isaiah. A New Translation; with a Preliminary Dissertation, and Notes Critical, Philological, and Explanatory* (London: J. Nichols; J. Dodsley; T. Cadell, 1778).

2. Sir William Forbes (1739–1806), *An Account of the Life and Writings of James Beattie, LL.D. . . . including many of his original Letters*, 2 vols. (Edinburgh: Archibald Constable and William Creech, 1806).

HLP owned the second edition of this work (3 vols.). It is now in the British Library (1085 b. ee. 9) and contains her marginalia.

3. According to advertisements, Rackstraw's Museum was located at "No. 197, Fleet Street, near Temple Bar. Established near Fifty Years; lately Improved, Enlarged, and Enriched with Many very valuable Articles.

"This Museum consists of most Curious Objects, no where else to be seen; it is an Assemblage of Wonders, in which, the Works of Art and Nature seem to vie with each other. . . . The View of the Anatomical Figures is solemn, delightful, interesting, and instructive, impressing the Beholders with Ideas of the Omnipotence of the Creator, and Condition of their own Existence. . . . even the most Delicate of the Fair-Sex daily crowd to see them. . . .

"Among its wonders: waxen figures to represent the dissected body of a woman who had been executed, a pregnant woman with embryo exposed; skeleton of a whale; Geo. II in full costume, jewels, etc.; rhinoceros & other animals, birds, etc.; Egyptian mummy; etc.etc."

See *Collectanea; or, a Collection of Advertisements and Paragraphs from the Newspapers, Relating to various Subjects* ([Title page] Printed at Strawberry-Hill, by Thomas Kirgate, for the Collector, Daniel Lysons [1661–1840];BL: c. 103. k. 11).

4. Virgil's *Bucolica*, eclogue 9, lines 51–54.

5. According to the original title page: *The Coblers Prophesie. Written by Robert Wilson. Gent. Printed at London by John Danter for Cuthbert Burbie: and are to be sold at his shop nere the Royall-Exchange. 1594.* We are indebted to Professor Albert Brownmiller, of U.C.L.A. for the Reference.

The lines quoted are spoken by Mars to Venus, sig. D3.

6. HLP still did not know precisely when ST would marry Henry Merrik Hoare and was awaiting news of the event.

7. *Much Ado About Nothing*, 2.1.357.

8. See HLP to John Roberts, 2 March 1807, n. 6, for *The Book of the Prophet Isaiah*, by Bishop John Stock.

9. The line is from *Paradise Lost*, 8.193 and is quoted by HLP in her preface to the *Letters* (1:ii) as a justification for the "domestick and familiar events" which alone "can be expected from a private correspondence."

10. Prov. 14:10.

11. The bishop of Killala lived in North Wales in the summer of 1803. See HLP to LC, 30 July 1803.

12. Stock's translation of this verse and its meaning were colored by HLP's assumptions. Thus, on p. 39, he wrote

> That thou shalt take up this parable
> Against the king of Babylon, and say:
> How hath the oppressor ceased! the
> golden city ceased!

To this he appended a note: "Babylon is said to be in the Revelations, xvii. 4 מדהבה, being a Chaldee word, was probably the epithet by which that people distinguished their capital, as the Italians say, Florence the fair, Padua the learned, &c. Of course it was not a name of reproach, which seems implied in Bishop Lowth's *exactress of gold.*"

13. Dan. 2:38.

14. See La Sacra Bibbia, che contiene il Vecchio, ed il Nuovo Testamento, tradotta in Lingua Italiana da Giovanni Diodati, di Nazion Lucchese, Riveduta di Nuovo Sopra Gli Originali, e corretta con ogni maggior' accuratezza da Giovanni David Muller ([1641] Leipzig: Apresso Giacomo Born, Libraio, 1744).

Giovanni Diodati (1576–1649) on p. 727 translated the passage as "Tu proverbierai cosi il rè di Babilonia, e dirai: come è restato l'esattore? *come* è cessato il tributo."

15. The Latin/Hebrew [Biblia Hebraica] Isaias, Ieremias, Ezechiel . . . Cum interlineari versione Xantis Pagnini; Ben. Ariae Montani, & aliorum collato studio, ad Hebraicam dictionem diligentissimè expensa (Ex Officina Plantiniana Raphelengii, 1610).

On p. 17 the translation is "Aurea pensio desiit, exactor cessavit Quomodo" with the gloss "oppressor, quicuit plene auro?" Benedictus Arias Montanus (1527–98).

16. That is, Lucius Domitius Aurelianus (ca. 212–275), Roman emperor (270–75 A.D.).

HLP referred to the fact that Orléans "was anciently called *Genabum,* or *Cenabum;* and afterwards denominated *Aurelia, Aureliae,* and *Aurelianum,* by the Emperor Aurelian," who virtually raised it from ruins left when Caesar massacred its inhabitants and reduced the city to ashes. Aurelian, or Aurélian, rebuilt its walls and considerably enlarged the city itself. See *Enc. Brit.,* 3d ed. S.V. Orleans.

17. HLP agrees with Lowth's interpretation of Isa., chaps. 13 and 14: namely, that a materially glorious but morally corrupt Babylon had to be destroyed. But HLP goes further to correlate these chapters with Rev. 17:4–6 and to suggest the equation of Babylon and the Beast (or the Antichrist). The destruction of the one demands the destruction of the other, and so prepares for the establishment of the New Jerusalem. HLP regards the prophecy of Isa. 14:4 as being repeated by Revelation, and hence the prophecy, suppported by the Old and New Testaments, had to be fulfilled.

18. HLP's disapprobation centers on Stock's explanation of Isa. 14:13 and his reading of the phrase "mount of the assembly" (or "congregation"). He wrote: "Not mount Moriah, nor any place of religious worship, either in Judea or elsewhere; for that would be a manifest anticlimax, to him who had already in imagination seated himself in the heavens. The mountain here pointed to is the Olympus of the Eastern nations, where they supposed their inferior gods to be met in council by the supreme. . . . It would of course be suppposed to sit on the greatest heights known to the Asiatics, which were the mountains of Armenia, to the north of their country. Hence this climber of heaven is set to get up *to the sides of the north,* the arctic regions" (*Book of the Prophet Isaiah,* p. 40).

19. To exemplify her "insolence," HLP borrows from Lowth the term *mashal,* which figures in his commentary upon Isa. 14:4. "The verb *mashal* signifies to rule, to exercise authority; to make equal, to compare one thing with another" (pp. 96–97).

20. HLP refers to the following incident reported in *The Times,* 27 July 1807: "We feel much concern in announcing that an engagement has been fought between one of our cruizers attached to the Halifax station, and an American frigate, which terminated in the capture of the latter. . . . The name of the American frigate is the *Constellation.* She is said to have had 15 Men killed, besides a considerable number wounded, before she struck to the *Leopard,* who engaged her. The action . . . took place off Sandy Hook."

On 8 August *The Times* printed the entire text of President Jefferson's proclamation (issued 2 July) which ordered out of all American harbors and waters "armed vessels bearing commissions under the government of Great Britain" (see also 10 August 1807).

Nothing more came of the incident.

21. HLP refers to Cuthbert Collingwood; see HLP to LC, 14 November 1805, n. 7.

22. On 6 October 1806, a French assembly of notables invited all Jewish communities in Europe to send delegates to the sanhedrim or sanhedrin (from Jewish antiquity: supreme council) in Paris on 20 October.

The opening of the sanhedrim, delayed until 9 February, was made up of seventy-one members, twenty-five laymen and forty-six rabbis. After a solemn religious service in the synagogue, the members met in the Hôtel de Ville.

The decisions of the sanhedrim, formulated in nine articles, were reached over two months and were written in French and Hebrew. The articles themselves were designed to integrate the Jews, without loss of piety, into the secular community.

23. LC dismisses HLP's query in a letter dated 26 November 1807 (Ry. 560.88). "The Howard story is a very old one and now quite forgotten—I never did know what it meant."
The "Tale" refers to Charles Augustus Ellis (b. 1799), the son of Charles Rose Ellis, cr. Baron Seaford (15 July 1826) and his first wife, Elizabeth Catherine Caroline (d. 1803), daughter and heir of John Augustus Hervey (d. 1796), styled Lord Hervey, himself the son of Frederick Augustus, fifth earl of Bristol (1799) and de jure Lord Howard (of Walden).
In February 1806, the child Charles Augustus petitioned for his right to the barony of Howard (of Walden), last held by his great-grandfather Frederick Augustus Hervey (d. 1803). His right to the barony was confirmed in February, and at that time he became Lord Howard of Walden.
He was to become a successful diplomat, dying 29 August 1868, at his château.

TO JOHN SALUSBURY PIOZZI SALUSBURY

Brynbella
9: September 1807.

My dearest Salusbury

I write to you on your Birthday to wish you Joy, and to say that it was very prettily done of you to let us know you returned safely and pleasantly to Enborne.¹ Mr. C. Shephard sent me a kind Letter too, but I dare say he is now in Somerset or Devonshire, so our Compliments will not reach *him* till Winter has called him to London.²

If Weather was to name the Seasons it is dead Winter now³——but brighter Days must be hoped for, or we should break our hearts before the Time.

Hope was left in Pandora's Box you may remember when all the Evils flew out. Poor Uncle has got a bad Foot again, a *very* bad Foot; but *Hope* tells me it is to mend.

And You my Dear have now but Seven Years left for Study, and *Hope* bids me expect that you will use them diligently. If you are to learn either Books or Life, it must be in these next Seven Years; for after that Period is past; you must be *living*, not *learning*: and in order that we may rationally wish you Joy of arriving safely to the Age of 21, You must resolve to *know* something, and be able to *do* something when that Time—now not far off—arrives.

In this World, or at least in this Island, The *fruges consumere nati* are the most despicable Description of Men:⁴ some Business must be followed, some Knowledge must be obtained, if we would be respected above our own Footmen——Every Man in England makes and finds his proper Rank in Society; The Greatest Persons may lose, the Noblest may forfeit their Situations——and after a Man has been well educated, the World expects him to answer that Education. Fortune is soon weary of following those who know not how to court her;—and lest you should think these Maxims too Selfish and worldly, allow me to remind you of God's Punishments denounced in the Gospel against the *unprofitable Servant* who having received a Talent from his Lord—gave it him back at the great Day of Account, laid up in a Napkin;—*and never used.*⁵ But you begin to grow weary of these Admonitions, and to be thinking of something else to divert Attention from my Preachment.

I will hasten to relieve it by telling you that Miss Sharpe is here,[6] who cultivates *her* Talents to our Delight, and that Mrs. Mostyn is gone to Barmouth with her Children; who I think She keeps much too long from School. But Ladies are very apt to think differently from me, and it is therefore lucky for Boys to have a Parent who feels desirous of their Improvement. *Your Uncle* has no Taste to see *You* Ignor<ant>. He will be very angry if you do not Study hard for these remaining Years; and let me beg of you not to give yourself the Future Pain and Disgrace of being out of Countenance for want of knowing the History of Greece, Rome, and England;—They are *Indispensable* to a Gentleman's appearance in proper Company:——so are the Classics, so is Heathen Mythology. A Lad who has not these Old Stories in His head—may as well have *no Head;* and so Mr. Charles Shephard and I have told you repeatedly.

So now farewell, and be good; and mind your Book, and your Business; and prepare yourself for being an Honour and Credit to your Instructors:——remembering that whatever Faults or Negligences may be committed *we* will endeavour to escape all future Censure on *our* Parts. As nothing is nearer than Your Improvement / to the Heart of Your Affectionate Aunt / H: L: Piozzi.

Text: Ry. 585.2. *Address:* Master Salusbury / at the Rev. T. Shephards / Enborne Cottage / near Newbury / Berks. *Postmark:* DENBIGH 224.

1. HLP drew a verbal portrait of JSPS at this time. "He is handsomer than any Boy I ever saw of his Age—else neither better nor worse than the next Boy. His Heart is wholly an Italian one: his Resemblance in Body & Mind strong to Mr Piozzi, for whom he has I think a much more sincere Affection & Partiality than *English* Lads ever feel towards an old Parent, who is commonly nothing in their Sight but an Obstacle to Pleasure,—an Object of Contempt. We must however recollect that young Salusbury Has no one else in the Island . . . to whom he can look up for Friendship or Suppoprt—& that may serve as a Reason" (*Thraliana* 2:1084).
2. Shephard studied at Gray's Inn.
3. HLP wrote in *Thraliana* 2:1083–84: "Every Thing has been *Early* this Year. The Harvest is particularly early; & very copious: All housed by the 1st of Septr 1807.—& now heavy Rains—& an *early* Anticipation of Winter."
4. Horace, *Epistles,* 1.2.27.
5. Matt. 25:18–19, 24–30.
6. Elizabeth Sharp, the musician.

TO HESTER MARIA THRALE

                                      Brynbella Saturday
                                      17: October 1807.

I was glad to see Your Letter my dearest Girl; I have had but one from Cecy since we parted, and that was such a disagreeable Recapitulation of *Faults,* where She and I ought to see only *Merits*—that it made me wretched. Lord Kirkwall dined here on Sunday last, meaning to tell his Tale I believe; but we had People with us who precluded Confidence, and gave no Entertainment;[1] and I was half glad to see the Comet when they were gone, as promoting a Change of Ideas. A propos 'tis neither Caudatus nor Barbatas nor even Crinitus as I can find; nor distant enough to delight my Imagination in any way——but like an artificial Meteor formed with Camphor so very *White* is its Lustre:[2] We have a good Ramsden Telescope with pretty strong Powers,[3] and thro' *that* the Appearance is not unlike Hershals Moon with a long Ridge of Mountains or rather a long Wall broke in Places—running obliquely across the Disk.[4]

It is apparently descending towards the Sun, and is I trust a new Acquaintance to the Astronomers, or Some of them would have calculated its Return, but I hear nobody speak of it here who knows any more than myself.

Susan's Cottage[5] Altho' clear of London Smoke is not far from the Seat of general Intelligence as Cumberland said when *he located* himself near Tunbridge.[6] Your Knockholt Beeches I remember well; We called them the Waggon and Horses from the Appearance of Some Trees latelier planted than the rest standing as it were before them; but they are grown out of *that* form of course long ago.[7] There was a Plane Tree at Knowle of uncommon Dignity 30 Years ago,[8] and I recollect Sacchini's Portrait prodigiously fine, but no other Picture *then* which greatly attracted my Attention.[9]

I have a beautiful Picture here which Mr. Piozzi and I mean As a Nuptial Present to Sophia when She will tell us where to Send it. She loves the modern Artists; This is a Gainsborough, scarce five Feet by four—The Subject Cattle driven down to drink, and the first Cow expresses something of Surprize as if an Otter lurked under the Bank.[10] It is A *naked* looking Landscape—done to divert *Abel* the Musician by representing *his* Country Bohemia in no favourable Light,[11] and the Dog is a favourite's Portrait[12]—so that it is more curious than a richer Subject when all the Story is told.

The *Bifolco* as Mr. Piozzi calls the looby Lad that conducts the Creatures to Water is admirable, and the Cattle *so* naturally done! But Basta.

I have been very ill indeed—not merely Face-Ach like the Prince of Wales, A Blister took that away: but Cholera Morbus—as poor Dr. Maclean said of the Influenza—"*In all its Horrors.*"[13] When just recovering, I saw Mr. Moore and Mr. Piozzi and half a Dozen Maids past and present Sitting as a Jury; and I think the Verdict was brought in *Pork Steaks*. The Master of the House continues as well as one could expect, indeed he has a bad Foot now—very bad—but not Gout——he made them carry him up-stairs however when I was Ill, 'spite of all Prohibition.

You say nothing of the Peace which I think is coming,[14] tho' the Comet does from his horrid Hair shake Pestilence and War.[15] Buonaparte will soon see that he cannot stop Commerce nor effect our Ruin without bringing on his own and that of this Family.[16] And If the Heir of Portugal does really mean to put his aged Parent on his Back as Rats are said to do when disposed to fly from a falling House, it will be a new Occurrence and much more wonderful than any Tricks the *Vagrants of the Sky* can possibly perform.[17] Adieu and give our best Love to the Dear Sisterhood and Compliments to Mr. Hoare believing me ever Most Affectionately Yours H: L: Piozzi.

I had forgotten the Brighthelmston Comet till you reminded me and I do not know the proper Direction for this Letter; but suspect Seven Oaks is *not* right.

Text: Bowood Collection. *Address:* Miss Thrale / Ashgrove Cottage / near Seven Oaks / Kent. *Postmark:* DENBIGH 224 E 19 OCT 1807.

1. Lord Kirkwall and his wife had separated. After years of complaint and countercomplaint, of general nastiness and probable paranoia, Lady Kirkwall was to sue for a divorce in 1817. The suit was still pending when Lord Kirkwall died, 23 November 1820.
2. According to *The Times*, 2 October 1807: "On Wednesday evening [30 September], a Comet made its appearance, visible to the naked eye, in the neighbourhood of London. Its place formed nearly a right angle with the bright star Arcturus, and the elegant constellation Corona, or the Northern Crown, and set almost due West about eight o'clock. Its appearance to the naked eye, was that of a star of the first magnitude, having a very distinguishable beam of light or nebulosity, extending to the left or south of its body, of about a foot or eighteen inches in length. The colour of the whole was very white." The comet was to remain visible for at least a month, taking much the same track in the evening as the sun does during the day.
Unlike more spectacular comets, this unnamed one disappointed HLP, who had hoped for a better view of the distinguishing "tail" (*caudatus*), "beard" (*barbatus*), or "long hair" (*crinitus*). The tail, though it "appeared sometimes extremely brilliant . . . at other times [seemed] almost to disappear" (*GM* 77, pt.2 [1807]: 972).
3. One invented by the optician Jesse Ramsden (1735–1800).
4. The following two papers by Herschel on the moon appeared in the *Philosophical Transactions*: "Astronomical Observations relating to the Mountains of the Moon," 70 (1780): 507–26; "An Account of Three Volcanos in the Moon," 77 (1787): 229–32. Both articles are included in *The Scientific Papers of Sir William Herschel*, 2 vols. (London: Published by the Royal Society and the Royal Astronomical Society and sold by Dulau and Co., 1912).
In his 1787 paper Herschel notes that he saw "three volcanos in different places of the dark part of the moon," only one of which was alit and its burning matter above three miles in diameter. "It is of an irregular round figure, and very sharply defined on the edges. . . . [It] exactly resembled a small piece of burning charcoal, when it is covered by a very thin coat of white ashes, which frequently adhere to it when it has been some time ignited."
5. Ashgrove Cottage was in the village of Knockholt, about twenty-two miles from London.
6. HLP uses Cumberland's description of Tunbridge Wells to identify the rural setting of Knockholt. According to the *Memoirs*, Cumberland "fixed [himself] at Tunbridge Wells. . . . It is not altogether a public place, yet it is at no period of the year a solitude. . . . Its vicinity to the capital brings quick intelligence of all that passes there" (2:178).
7. The beeches are 770 feet above sea level and create a dominant landmark.
8. Knole Park, just east of Sevenoaks, was but a few miles from Knockholt. Knole Park comprised an area of one thousand acres of heavily wooded and rolling country. In addition to the plane tree at Knole, HLT, when she visited the Sackville seat in 1777, would have seen great oak and beech trees, some said to date from medieval times.
9. Reynolds painted a half-length portrait of the musician and composer *Antonio* Maria Gaspero Gioacchino Sacchini (1730–86), a Florentine who lived in London from 1772 until 1782.
The portrait hung in the "Dining Parlour at Knole." See "A Copy of the Inventory of the Pictures, Statues, Busts, Household Goods & Furniture at Knole, Directed by the Will of the Late Duke of Dorset [John Frederick Sackville, 1769–99], to be left as Heir Looms. Taken by Thomas Clout, John Bridgman, & James Clout. August 12 &c. 1799." This is part of the manuscript catalog U29ES (C.R.O., Kent), a photocopy of which is in the National Portrait Gallery.
A cryptic entry among the nineteenth-century Knole notes reveals that the Sacchini portrait was purchased by the duke of Dorset in February 1787 for £36.15. Sometime in the next century it was bought for the Penrose Collection, Taunton, and in 1902 sold to Mrs. Joseph Drexel, United States.
10. The Gainsborough canvas, painted ca. 1772–74, now hangs in Bowood House. The painting depicts a herdsman driving cattle downhill before a seated couple. The landscape itself emphasizes a single tree and a hill beyond. SH was to retain the painting only until 1815, when it was sold at Philips's, 2–3 June. See John T. Hayes, *The Landscape Paintings of Thomas Gainsborough*, 2 vols. (Ithaca: Cornell University Press, 1982), 2:456–57.
11. A disciple of J. S. Bach, Karl Friedrich Abel (1723–87) was born in Cöthen. A composer and

viola da gamba performer, he migrated to England in 1759. There he was honored with the title of chamber musician to Her Majesty and an appointment of £200 per annum.

The Gainsborough painting was initially owned by Abel, who—according to a report—obtained it in exchange for a viola da gamba fancied by the painter. The painting remained in Abel's possession, being sold only after his death by John Greenwood (1727–1795), art auctioneer in Leicester Square, 13 December 1787, lot 47. (HLP became the next recorded owner.)

12. In the foreground of the painting a small spaniel stands before the seated rustic couple.

13. For Archibald Maclaine, who died in 1804, see HLP to PSP, 9 March 1800, n. 2.

14. The latest Coalition, only a year old, was virtually defunct. Prussia and Russia had both withdrawn; Sweden, remaining a nominal member until 1809, had in fact capitulated in September to the French. England was now without allies.

Moreover, by the terms of the treaty of Tilsit, the czar agreed to mediate with Great Britain in the search for a general peace, particularly over the issues of the return of France's former colonies and of the freedom of the seas. Ultimately, Napoleon wanted to be known as the "Pacificator" of Europe rather than its conqueror. HLP therefore assumed that he might conclude a peace treaty with England, if only to strengthen his image.

15. See *GM* 77, pt. 2 (1807): 972; *Thraliana* 2:1085 and n.3." Like the Red Star, that from his flaming Hair Shakes / down Diseases, Pestilence, and War." Pope, translation of the *Iliad* 19.413. Cf. Butler, *Hudibras*, pt. 1, canto 1, 11. 247–48; Hoole's translation of Tasso, *Jerusalem Delivered*, 1. 581.

16. On 20 June 1803 Bonaparte closed all French ports to British or British-transported colonial goods and, if landed, ordered their confiscation. He closed the ports also to neutral ships which did not either carry a certificate from the French representatives at their port of origin or undertake to carry back French goods of equal value.

In 1805 the victory at Austerlitz and the Peace of Pressburg allowed the French to extend the blockade to the Adriatic; to the German coast after the Prussian collapse at Jena (October 1806).

On 21 November 1806 the Berlin decree declared a blockade of the British Isles, imprisoned all British subjects in French-occupied territory, with confiscation of their property, and closed every port on the Continent to vessels coming from or calling at any port in England or its colonies.

On 7 July 1807 the treaty of Tilsit brought Russia into the blockade. The bombardment of Copenhagen alienated Denmark from England, making the Danes a member of the blockade. See HLP to LC, 21 November 1807, n. 1.

See *GM* 77, pt.2 (1807): 965–66; *The Times*, 7, 10, 17 October 1807.

17. During the months of September and October statements about the emigration of the court of Portugal to the Brazils were in the news.

More than a week after HLP's letter to Q, *The Times*, 26 October, "received *Paris* Papers to the 18th inst. One of these, the *Journal de l'Empire*, of the 17th inst. mentions [prematurely], on the authority of letters received from Bayonne, that the Prince Regent, his Son, and the whole Court, had sailed for the Brazils, with thriteen ships of the line."

See also HLP to LC, 21 November, 1 December; to Ly W, 31 December 1807.

TO MARGARET WILLIAMS

Brynbella
18 October 1807

My dear Miss Williams

I begin to grow Impatient for some News of our Bath Friends. Miss Sharpe left this Country long ago, and wrote as She promised from the midst of *Pleasure*, but She is now hindered by *Business*—a much more honourable excuse.

We have but little to do with either at Brynbella; the Comet serves us to look at, and Lord Kirkwall provided us Subjects of Prattle in coming down after so long an Absence without his Lady, and suffering us to *say* (how truly I know not) that they were parted for *ever*.

The Weather is always A country Topic of no small Interest; and these Storms, attended by a course of Warm dry Winds make it still more so this Year, when News from the Continent is so sought after.

Mrs. Mostyn took her Boys to Barmouth I forget how long ago, She has written me *one* Letter since and *but* one, and bid me direct my Answer to Kew Green without saying whether She was on a Visit or in Lodgings.

I am told she comes *home to Segroid* at Christmas. Perhaps Lady Newborough's aversion to England like Cecilia's to Wales, may expire with her Husband. Pretty Ladies are capricious Creatures, and 'tis a good Thing to be an Old Woman rather than a Young Man dependent on their Smiles and Frowns.

The Beaux and Belles of this Neighbourhood are preparing for Holywell Hunt—our Cousin Thelwall among the Gayest: He called here with the Squire of Vronew a while ago, and found me Ill enough,[1] and joked me for my Wan Looks: but I have been much worse since then.

Mr. Piozzi quite stout, only Chalk in his Foot; just as you predicted—and certainly not a Day older in Appearance for all he suffered at Bath. Let me hear as good an Account from you of our dear Mr. Gillon. The Siddonses—of whose Parting we all talked Nonsense for a Twelvemonth—have been living together in her pretty Cottage, very *closely united* I should suppose,[2] for there is no Room there to make separate Establishments, and I see her advertised as acting beauteous Zara to crouded Houses.[3] Indeed the Public have no Pretence for Quarrel with their *Amusers*—one dropping dead on a Race Ground, and one in an Orchestra and poor Mrs. Jordan put in a State of Expectation that can end only in Death[4]—from strong Exertion to divert her Audience. How thankful ought I to feel for Liberty to dye in my own Bed, and be buried with my own Folks!

As a Proof that 'tis the Sick who *live* always—and the Well who do *not*;[5] comes in while I am writing—Dear Doctor Thackeray: He was not expected to get on from Day to Day when we were first acquainted; now is he Father of a Family, fat, healthful and Rosy.[6] *He* however like us all, feels anxious about the present Crisis of Affairs, and says it is intended by Buonaparte in this Invasion of Portugal to destroy all the Vineyards:[7] that England may after the Peace be *forced*—willing or unwilling, to buy the French Wines at what Price he pleases. We have been too late in getting our Factory away from Lisbon; and no Small Ruin will be the Consequence. The People on this Occasion did not cry Fire time enough;[8] they were in too much haste at Sadlers Wells.

Well! now Adieu sweet Lady, and let me hear of you. We see Bodylwyddan from the Windows, and hear of Lady Williams dining at the Bishop's &c. but more than that I know not of them since I carried and left Miss Sharpe in their Protection: and brought home such a Toothach and Swelled Face, as yielded to nothing but Blisters.

Once more Farewell! and let nobody I love forget there is such a Person as *Your* / faithful H: L: Piozzi / at Brynbella / 18: October 1807.

Text: Victoria and Albert Museum Library. *Address:* Miss Williams / Upper Park Street / St. James's Square / Bath. *Postmark:* DENBIGH 224.

1. His mother having died in 1799 and his father—a suicide—in 1806, John Maddocks (1786–1837), M.P. for Denbigh Borough (1832–33), was the squire of Fron Iw. See HLP to Ly W, 10 February 1799, n. 13; and to Margaret Owen [ca. 12 February 1799], n. 2; Sir Walter James to HLP, 8 April 1806 (Ry. 555.114).
2. SS had purchased a small country house ca. 1804 at Westbourne, near Paddington.
3. On 15 October, SS took the role of Zara in Congreve's *Mourning Bride*. See HLP to PSP, 6 March 1804, n. 5.
4. Dorothea Jordan had fallen ill and reputedly suffered from a broken blood vessel. But on 17 October, *The Times* reported that she "took an airing yesterday, the first time since her indisposition, in her carriage, and is now able to resume her professional labours. We have heard with pleasure, that her illness did not arise from a rupture of a blood-vessel or any affection of the lungs."
5. One of HLP's favorite proverbs; see her letters to PSP, 1 June 1797 and [ca. 12 Dec. 1799].
6. The Chester physician William M. Thackeray had two daughters: Sarah Jane (1805–72) and Selina Martha (1806–35). See HLP to Q, 2 November 1805, n. 10.
7. In early September, news began to appear about the impending invasion of Portugal by Spanish and French troops. On 12 October, the *Courier* reported that a French army was assembling at Bayonne and on the 13th it announced "that all hopes of [Portuguese] accommodation with France have failed. . . . The entrance of the French, would, it was not doubted, be followed by the immediate desertion of the Royal Family for the Brazils.—The ships were all ready."
8. According to the *Courier,* 26 September 1807: "The English merchants, indeed the whole of those who compose what is called the English Factory at Lisbon have [upon news of invasion] naturally taken the alarm; and many of them have already made large remittances to this country, and much larger are expected by the next packet." On 14 and 15 October, the *Courier* reported that large numbers of British merchants in Lisbon were making "immediate preparations to embark with their property," that "Government have given orders for the departure of several ships for Lisbon. There is a great want of shipping in the Tagus to bring away British property."

TO THE REVEREND LEONARD CHAPPELOW

Brynbella
Saturday 21: November 1807.

I remember Dear Mr. Chappelow saying long ago that if we would live in Greenland we must not complain of Cold. Do tell me if London's Self is habitable this November, or whether the fashion of *Enjoying* our Country Seats till Spring, keeps it empty of every thing but Snow. My poor Trees are all torn, my Peafowl—(natives of a Softer Climate)—perishing under the Storm; and no *human* Creature within Call, if we were perishing too. Mr. Piozzi however *gains* health instead of losing,——and finds a wide Horizon better for his Cough, than ineffectual Draughts from Bath Apothecaries,——washing down heavy Fog.

Take Pity of our Ignorance tho', and want of Conversation: and tell us of these Princes the Dane[1] and Portugueze,[2] and what Services they will render Buonaparte, and what Salaries they will receive from him. The Decree for Stoppage of all Commerce too,—how will that agree with our Merchants?[3] so late the Princes, and the Proud Men of the Earth. You hear Sophia Thrale has married her old Sweetheart Mr. Hoare, and I think we were in Mourning for poor

Mostyn when we met last. So I have now Maids, Wife, and Widow Daughters; which do you think the happiest?

Write to me Dear Mr. Chappelow, and reflect how we are Shut up here to read Thomson's Winter and Cowper's Task for four or five Months;—and no Hope of a new Book—except from the Reading Society at Denbigh——*There* however is Improvement since You knew us. I saw one of the Young Gentlemen we met at Weston did I not? a Candidate for University Honours some time ago in the Newspapers which I think *teem with Horrors* this Year more than I can remember. New and prodigious Crimes, portentous Meteors—We had one *here,* an Arrow all of Fire;——Sudden Deaths—Suicides: or perhaps living alone and reading old Romances leads us to Dream of Murders &c. What went with that strange Story of the Hoddesdon Family?[4] Was it a Lye or Fable?—or having happened among *People that nobody knows*——has it been wholly forgotten? except by / Dear Sir / Your ever faithful / and Obliged / H: L: P.

Mr. Piozzi sends best Regards, and joins in my Request for a Letter. There is a *high Life Tale* concerning some Claimant that disturbs the Howard Race—What must I think of *that?*

Text: Ry. 561.136

1. England for several months early in 1807 tried to prevent the Danes from joining Napoleon's continental league. On 26 July 1807, Admiral James Gambier sailed for Copenhagen with a large fleet. His meeting with Lord Cathcart's troops evacuated from Swedish Pomeria permitted him to land twenty-seven thousand men near Copenhagen on 16 August. The Danes were offered an alliance and told to yield their fleet for the duration of the war. When they rejected this ultimatum, the British leveled large areas of Copenhagen. The Danes capitulated on 7 September, the British withdrawing with eighteen Danish ships of the line and many smaller vessels. Provoked by Britain's belligerent action, Prince Frederik (1768–1839), then regent, entered the war (30 October) on the side of France. See, e.g. *The Times,* 5 November 1807.

2. Prince João (1767–1826), regent of Portugal, wanted to remain neutral in the war between England and France even after the Berlin Decree of 1806. Nevertheless, on 19 July 1807, Napoleon demanded that the Portuguese join the continental bloc. Ten days later, he ordered a heavy concentration of troops under Junot around Bayonne. Portugal tried to placate both sides, refusing to confiscate British goods but closing ports to Britain and even declaring war on her. Portugal's compromise satisfied neither nation. In the middle of October the French troops set out for Portugal and marched through Spain. The Franco-Spanish convention of Fountainebleau (27 October) decreed a partition of Portugal.. See *The Times,* 6, 11, 12 November.

3. The attrition of British commerce was gradual but more real than HLP would acknowledge. Particularly costly to English merchants was the closure of Prussian and Russian ports (announced by *The Times,* 7 and 17 October).

On 10 November 1807 *The Times* reported: "A Proclamation is now, we understand, in readiness for his Majesty's signature, declaring France and the whole of her vassal kingdoms in a state of siege, and prohibiting all intercourse with her or them, all entrance of vessels into her or their harbours, except of such as have cleared last from a British port, either home or foreign. We shall be less surprized at the promulgation of such an edict, than at the length of time during which it has been suspended."

4. HLP refers to the multiple murders on 20 October 1807 in Hoddesdon, Herts. In a house were assembled Mr. Boreham, his wife, four daughters, and Mrs. Hummerstone, "who superintended the business of the Black Lion Inn at Hoddesdon. Thomas Simmons, aged 20, who had been servant in the family for about two years, but from which he had been recently dismissed . . . had paid his addresses to the servant, Eliz. Harris, who was many years older than himself; but the symptoms of a ferocious temper had induced his mistress to dissuade the woman from any connexion with him."

About 9 P.M. he entered the house, threatening all with a large knife. Some escaped but two had their throats cut and died. Mrs. Boreham was wounded, "and the old gentleman was found prostrate where he fell, with a poker by his side, which his feeble strength would not allow him to use." See *GM* 77, pt. 2 (1807): 970–71.

TO HESTER MARIA THRALE

Brynbella Sunday Night
22: November 1807.

I am delighted beyond all power of Expression that my dearest Girl will be so richly rewarded for all her numerous and various Virtues. I am delighted too that a *British Admiral* is to be made happy by accepting her pretty little White Hand;[1] and as for Mr. Piozzi, your Letter has put quite new Life in *him:* and he is at this Moment rummaging over Music which till today he has looked on— only with Disgust.[2]

So I shall have a dear Lady K——of *my own* now;[3] that will make me ample Amends for the true and unaffected Vexation poor Lady Kirkwall's perverse Conduct has given me: but the Boys and Girls marry too early I believe, and quarrel about cutting up their Apple Tarts. *They* have sincerely no serious Cause for Separation; and Some one told me the other Day, they were Coming home Hand in Hand.——Ay quoth I, like the Insurance Policy a Handinhand *Fire* Office I suppose.

So you all leave Susette in the Lurch! Poor Susette! But I think she will not stay starving in a Cottage this Weather without a Companion. Mrs. Mostyn sent word She was coming to Wales with three Children, not only *Sliding on the Ice* but ill of the *hooping Cough* beside. A Fine Pleasure! says Mr. Piozzi——who is confined here by Snow, and Symptoms of approaching Gout——and low Spirits too till your dear Letter came. Tell Mrs. Smyth I know *She* is happiest in the News next to myself, and She has Leisure to be happy now that her Son is got well:[4] and I think Mademoiselle you might have bespoke a correct Copy of Retrospection, that I might have had some Employment,——if you have not one already: the more So as Your Noble Husband's Name is in the Book.[5] I shall send for one at any Rate, and if not wanted for my dear Girl, shall present it to the *Reading Society at Denbigh* Set up by our Bishop Cleaver who has given them his Sermons.[6]

Nothing however can come now in Waggon or in Coach; I never remember so very deep a Snow——and quite an Alpine Prospect. Do you recollect laughing when I said that Mr. Moore—like Thomson's Bear in Winter—

Shaggy with Ice and dangling Snow
Stalk'd o'er the Wild forlorn——[7]

when we sent for him?—but 'tis worse now;—We cannot Send, nor can he come *at all;* and your Sweet Letter dated Wensday last arrived just 3 Hours ago; with one from poor Gillon who seems miserably ill and weak.[8] The Case is making for Sophia's Picture, and then we will wait her Orders,—and the Thaw.

Lord Newborough's Agents notified his Death to us with so much Form,[9] I feel *obliged* to wear the Black I hate so,—one Week longer; and then I'll throw it off, and think once more about Plumb Cake and Favours. Mr. Piozzi is very angry to see the Danes take some of our Ships,[10] he thought we had got *all theirs away*——and I had

qualche Speranza
in Casa Braganza[11]

but it dies off gradually. So Adieu dear Child! and be married, and be happy as is wished You / by Your ever Affectionate Mother / H: L: P.

Text: Bowood Collection. *Address:* Miss Thrale / Heath House / Bristol. *Postmark:* DENBIGH [with a brief and illegible postscript by GP in Italian].

1. For Admiral Lord Keith, see HLP to Q, 7 November 1796, n. 8; to LC, 22 July 1801, n. 4; to PSP, 3 December 1803, n. 11.
2. GP meant his own musical compositions to be his wedding present to Q, but in fact they became his bequest. Although not written into his will, his wishes were honored by HLP: namely, that Q was to have his traveling pianoforte and her choice of his music. See HLP to Q, 10 April 1809; P.R.O., Prob.11/1498/396, proved 2 May 1809.
3. Keith met Q in 1791. Their courtship covered sixteen years. Not once did she introduce him to HLP. Nor did Q invite her mother to the ceremony, which was held 10 January 1808, at Ramsgate. Q was forty-three, and the groom sixty-two.
4. See HLP to Q, 23 July 1805, n. 3.
5. Writing of British naval superiority in 1796 over the French, HLP went on to comment: "It was in happy consequence of this superiority, that Elphinstone captured rather than conquered the Dutch fleet near the Cape of Good Hope, and *their* possessions—if powers allied to France may be said to *possess* any thing; fell unresistingly into our hands" (*Retrospection* 2:526).
6. Cleaver provided the Denbigh Reading Society with an advance copy of his *Seven Sermons on Select Subjects* (Oxford: J. Parker, 1808).
7. Thomson, "Winter," in *The Seasons*, lines 828–29, ". . . the shapeless bear, / With dangling ice all horrid, stalks forlorn."
8. Gillon was suffering from a slowly spreading cancer. He died 14 December 1809, having admitted to HLP on 18 February 1809 (Ry. 579.153) that he was "so ill, and so weak, that it is with difficulty that I can migrate from one room to another." On 22 December 1809 (Ry. 579; end of folio), his friend Robarts wrote to HLP, saying "that exhausted as he was, and reduced to a mere skeleton, all medical aid proved unavailing . . . his death was un-accompanied by any particularly severe pain."
9. Thomas Wynn, Baron Newborough, was a Tory M.P. for various Welsh constituencies from 1761 until his death, serving as auditor of Wales and lord lieutenant of Carnarvonshire (1761–81); Fellow of the Society of Antiquaries (1774); colonel by brevet, in the army. He had married first in 1766 Catherine, née Perceval (1745/6–82), daughter of the second earl of Egmont. For his second marriage, see HLP to MW [ca. 11 April 1807], n. 10. He died 12 October 1807 at Nottingham Place, London.
10. See, e.g., *The Times*, 17 November: "The Danes, it seems, have begun to retaliate our attack upon Copenhagen, and with more success than we could have expected. Our Commanders in the Baltic were in such a hurry to return, that they forgot to leave a sufficient force for the protection of our commerce in that sea. Either from this, or from some egregious mismanagement on the part of some of the Masters of the vessels composing the last convoy, several sail have been captured, and carried into Elsineur. . . . To what purpose have we obtained possession of the Danish fleet, if it is not to be followed by the secure navigation of the Baltic?"
11. Braganza was the royal house of Portugal from 1640 to 1910.
On 24 November, *The Times* editorialized: "We may just remark . . . that if the [anti-French]

disposition of the people of Portugal is as is here represented, their Prince will have the less difficulty in executing his magnanimous project of retiring to the Brazils. We ought not, perhaps, to be severe upon this head, as we are under some obligation to his Highness, for suffering the whole of the British subjects and property to be embarked for this country."

TO JOHN STOCKDALE

28: November 1807.

Mrs. Piozzi sends her Compliments and desires the favour of Mr. Stockdale to send her a Copy of Retrospection[1] directed to Mr. Smyth Perfumer in Bond Street who will convey it with other Things he has to send to
   Brynbella near Denbigh N. Wales.
   Saturday 28: November 1807.

 Mrs. Piozzi means to be in London next March and settle her Account with Mr. Stockdale.[2]

Text: Osborn Collection. *Address:* Mr: Stockdale / Bookseller opposite Burlington house / Piccadilly / London. *Postmark:* DENBIGH 224; E DEC 1 1807.

 1. HLP wanted a fresh copy of *Retrospection* to emend for Q.
 2. HLP still owed Stockdale £10.13.6 for the frontispiece of *Retrospection:* the Bovi engraving of her portrait painted by Violet.

TO THE REVEREND LEONARD CHAPPELOW

Brynbella
Tuesday 1: December 1807.

Dear Mr. Chappelow
 did not *bid* me direct this to Lord Bradford No. 10 Hill Street, but I *will* direct it so; because my Lady was so kind in wishing a Continuance of our old Correspondence; that I think She will forward the Letter. I am glad She is well and happy: we want more such Ladies to give good Examples in this more than ever mad and wicked World. The *Elements* of Political Life have been sometime dissolved with the *fervent Heat* of these strange Times and People. The Elements of *natural* Life seem freezing in their Cases; and tho' Poetry tells us that *kind Nature the Embryo Blossom will save;*[1]Experience shows me my Torne Oaks, and bowed down Fir Trees, irrecoverably lost by these last Westerly Winds;——The like to which neither Thomson or Cowper ever witnessed I am sure——for they lived in Softer Climates.[2] What Winter 'tis! 30 Men have been *trying* all this last

Week to open the Road so that they may at least fetch Coals from the Pit—— and the Snow that fell Yesterday will fill all up again I suppose.³

Miss Thrales resolve however you see to keep warm in London like Yourself: I am glad the eldest marries my Lord Keith——if *any* body is safe, those are safe that anchor under Protection of a brave British Admiral. Sophia seems to like her Husband too as well as you like him, but there are so many Brothers I never know which is which.⁴

Lord and Lady Kirkwall are reconciled, and coming home together with a virtuous *Intention* to be happy;—and in such Cases good Intention is not nothing.

Mrs. Mostyn is at Segroid with her Children: They have the Hooping cough— *so I keep away:* but if She amuses herself as usual with painting Insects from Books of Natural History—She may perchance call to Mind that among the Hymenoptera are classed all those that wear Stings:—is not it *so?*

You never mention pretty Mrs. Clay; has She been *moulded* into a wife again? or do her Children fill up all her Cares? I used to love Mrs. Clay.⁵

But tho' you will not talk about Politics—*I will:* My heart is quite in a flutter to get the Prince Regent of Portugal safe away.⁶ Must we fight the Russian Fleet to save him? It would be a good Pretext to get the Russian Navy into our Hands, and *then* make Peace,⁷ which Buonaparte will certainly offer us; when Sugars at Paris come to five Shillings, and Coffee to 25 Shillings the Pound. We must not *give in* as the Boxers call it at any Rate, till the Antagonist is quite *cut down;* or we shall have another Challenge sent before we are recovered.⁸ The Comet was more like a Paradise Plume for the Head of a fair Lady than it was like a red Meteor Only ½ a Mile from the Earth. It *seemed* (the Comet did) at an immeasureable Distance;⁹ and how it could have occasioned those high Tides——I cannot guess: but the Astronomers lay much to his Charge. He shall at least never hinder me from being Dear Mr. Chappelow's faithful Servant whilst / H: L: P.

Mr. Piozzi sends all possible kind Words and Compliments.

Text: Ry. 561.137. *Address:* Rev: Mr. Chappelow / No. 13 Hill Street / Berkeley Square. *Postmark:* E DEC 5 1807; DENBIGH <224>.

1. Almost formulaic in the eighteenth century, the epithet "kind nature" connotes benevolence and protection, the guardianship of the vital principle. Both Thomson and Cowper utilize the concept, as in "Summer" (line 1540) and *The Task* (6.342). Both poets work out numerous optimistic variations; e.g.: Thomson celebrates "Nature's swift and secret-working Hand /. . . while the promis'd Fruit / Lies yet a little Embryo, unperceiv'd . . ." ("Spring," lines 95–100.) For Cowper, "some of nature's sweetest flow'rs, / Rose from a seed of tiny size" ("Epistle to Lady Austen," lines 94–95.)

2. HLP associates Cowper with Olney, Bucks., and Thomson, although a Scot, with London and Richmond.

3. Throughout the Midlands and the west of England, "the weather has been for the last week particularly severe, with deep snow, and dreadful hurricanes from the North-east. On Blackstone hedge, the Clayton heights, on Monday last [30 November], the snow lay in drifts 20 feet deep; and by Leek and Buxton travelling was almost prevented. Notwithstanding men were employed in cutting through the drifts, yet the after heavy falls so choaked up the road, as almost to prevent carriages from proceeding any distance. In many parts the stage-coaches could not be got on, though drawn by six or eight horses." See *GM* 77, pt.2 (1807): 1167.

4. Like HLP, LC had difficulty distinguishing among the Hoare brothers. Thus of SH's husband, he wrote on 26 November (Ry. 563.88): "Sophia has married the best man in the Kingdom—I know not so good a man—so accomplished a man, and so clever a Man as the Master of Stourhead—near Longleat.—Sophia must be the happiest.—" In short, LC confused Henry Merrik Hoare with Sir Richard Colt Hoare.

5. For Mrs. Jane Clay, see HLP to LC, 18 September 1797, n. 8

6. For the exile of the Portuguese prince regent and his court, see HLP to Ly W, 31 December 1807.

7. *The Times* on 27 November reported: "*Part of the Russian fleet had arrived in the Tagus:* two sail of the line arrived on the 9th, and three sail of the line and two frigates on the 11th, which, by some, were mistaken for English. . . .

"This last circumstance, of the Russian fleet having arrived in the Tagus, and . . . under English colours, is both a very singular and a very ominous one, with regard to the future relations between England and that Power."

The Times went on to argue that "the directing spirit of Buonaparte" prompted the Russian presence in the Tagus, and that the British had a "right" to prevent the Russian fleet from remaining there. See *The Times*, 28 and 30 November 1807.

See also *GM* 77, pt. 2 (1807): 1068, 1160, 1165 for Russia's diplomatic break with England and her proclamation of the principles of armed neutrality.

8. HLP matched LC's militaristic stance, who on 26 November had written: "I can say nothing about politics—The period is so eventful—that no conjecture can be made as to what is to follow.—Austria declares War against England.—The Infernal Corsican—dethrones the House Braganza.—foams at the mouth—because we have taken—not the *Danish* but *his* Fleet at Copenhagen.—We must declare War against every power upon the Continent of Europe, and take every Flag that flies—This will Light up a flame all over Europe—which must end either in Bonys—Destruction or in ours.—"

9. Late in November "the Comet was very near a small star in the Lyra, and about 2 ½ degrees from the bright star in the Lyra, in a line between these two stars; its tail has disappeared, and it is now only distinguishable from the small stars near it, by being hazy or fainter in light" (*GM* 77, pt. 2: 1072).

ADMIRAL BARON KEITH TO MRS. PIOZZI

Purbrook Park [Hants.] 1st December, 1807.

Madam,

By a letter from your Daughter I am informed she has communicated to you our intended Connexion. Therefore no reason exists from my withholding a duty any longer and to assure you, Madam, that the approbation of a parent is a matter of essential consequence to the General comfort of such a Union, and that I shall be happy to know it meets with your's. Our acquaintance is not of a late Date, and I hope I know and can appreciate her many Virtues as indeed I ought when I consider she condescends to become the companion of a man who has some Months past his sixtieth year, but whose study it will be to render her time as comfortable as it may be during his remaining life. Another consideration is that altho' I am well provided for as a Cadet of a Noble Family and an Industrious officer of the Country, yet I am not rich for the Rank to which I have been Raised but have enough for all the Reasonable Comforts of Life, and which I have fully explained to Miss Thrale and which has been approved of. I beg to offer my compliments to Mr. Piozzi and to assure you of the profound esteem with which I have the honor to be, / Madam, / Your most obliged faithful servant, / Keith.

Text: Broadley, p. 151.

TO SUSANNA ARABELLA THRALE

                                        Brynbella Thursday
                                        3: [December] 1807.[1]

And so my sweet *Susette* has lost her Christian Name—*without* being married; She is—or will be soon—*Miss Thrale*. When Palmer the Actor dropped down dead upon the Stage a Wag cried out—"and his Brother John has lost his *I* too"—The listeners begun blessing Themselves, and believed the poor Fellow struck with *Blindness;* but he was become Mr. Palmer.[2]

Well! I am something in your way myself: having lost by the Match—at least more than I have gained. Your eldest Sister and I having passed *Twenty* Years closely united, and never three Days out of each other's Sight.——Some Castles in the Air would now and then rise up in a Musing Hour,—as if we might *once more* meet in a like familiar Manner;—Those Misty Fabricks now are quite dissolved—and She has fixed *her* Castle—*in the Rock.*[3]

Dear Sophy seems enchanted with the Change; of Cecy I see nothing: but if her Sons recover happily in this Cold Climate—of which their Mama used to make *so many Complaints;* They must be stronger than She was at the Same Age, for Jebb[4] and Pepys[5] had a hard Task to bring *her* thro',—and they are far removed from such Physicians. Perhaps She is of Mr. Piozzi's Mind that it was the *Doctor's* Fault he was so ill at Bath;—perhaps they are both right: 'tis plain the Cough did never affect him at Brynbella as in the Smoky Towns.

How does Your pretty Cottage bear these tremendous Hurricanes? or do none blow except in North Wales? My Shrubs are all *broken quite down* with the vast Weight of Snows, and the very large old Oaks show their injured Dignity to the Thawing Atmosphere of this Morning with a truly affecting and impressive Appearance. I should not write about such Things to You though,—were you the Same Suzette who professed to prefer a *Ball-Room and Candles* to every rural Pleasure. But Opinions change, and so do Surrounding Circumstances.

Mr. Piozzi had written out his Music for your eldest Sister, and I had meditated to drop some Verses beside, inscribed to our dear Sophia into the Picture we are sending[6]—but *General Lake* as I call our Steward and Butler;[7] had packed up the Gainsborough with So much Care—and *he* thinks so much *Skill;* that *nothing* was to be admitted in the packing Case: and much do I hope, and with a trembling Hope too—that it will get Safely to her House *before next Year.*

Everything seems tedious—your kind Letter dated 27th: of November arrived *late last Night,* and all Denbigh told how Mrs. Mostyn and her Children were dragged by Horses borrowed from the Carrier, when they came thro' that horrible Snow and Ice to Segroid. But you are in London—like Juliets Family— *"culling such Ornaments as will be needful for your State tomorrow."*[8] God bless you all, and make you happy in your several Situations / prays your Affectionate Mother / H: L: P.

Text: Bowood Collection. *Address:* Miss Susanna Arabella Thrale / No. 5 Lower Seymour Street / Portman Square / London. *Postmark:* DENBIGH <224> S 6 DEC 1807.

    1. The letter, erroneously dated 3 November, was in fact written on 3 December, a Thursday; see the postmark.
    2. Two actors upon the stage at the same time were identically named. One John Palmer (d. 1768) was known as "Gentleman Palmer." After his decease, the more celebrated Palmer (ca. 1742–98) dropped the initial "I" (as in "John") from announcements of his name, and was known simply as "Palmer." The omission gave rise to Foote's joke that Jack Palmer had lost an "I". HLP cites the pun in *Thraliana* 2:772.
    3. HLP's double pun on the syllables of Elphinstone's name. See *Thraliana* 2:1087.
    4. Richard Jebb (1729–87) graduated M.D., 23 September 1751. A favorite of various members of the Royal Family, including George III, he was created baronet on 4 September 1778. His private practice was so large that in the period between 1779 and 1781, he is said to have earned 20,000 guineas in fees. In 1780 he was appointed physician to the Prince of Wales and in 1786 to the king.
    5. For Sir Lucas Pepys, see HLT to FB, 30 June 1784, n. 5.
    6. Just before ST's marriage HLP wrote four four-line stanzas, entitled "Lines addressed to— Sophia Thrale with a Present of a Padlock, Heart, Key and Chain." The poem begins, "Permit me Sophia the meaning t' explain. . . ." In the course of the poem the padlock represents prudence; the heart that of the giver; the chain suggests restraint; and the key all that can be given.
    7. Alexander Leak.
    8. Juliet to Lady Capulet, 4.3.7.–8; cf. 4.2.33–34. HLP has changed "our state" to "your state."

TO JOHN SALUSBURY PIOZZI SALUSBURY

                                Brynbella
                              Wednesday 30th: [December] 1807.

My dearest Boy
  has some Right to complain of *me* now: but indeed it has been too dreadful Weather for any one to encounter; much less your good Uncle, who though not put to Bed, is certainly in no Travelling Condition; and could not bear the Thoughts of your coming through that horrible Frost and Snow——in which, to speak the *Truth*—and without any Exaggeration, dear Mrs. Mostyn was much too near *to be lost*——She and her three Sons and Nanto were at last dragged home by the *Carrier's Horses* which met them on the Road, and the Man harnessed them on to her Chaise. You never saw such a Sight as poor Brynbella quite blockaded up:——we could not have sent to Denbigh had we been dying— no Horse Path was made for a full Week, and no Coals could be fetched from the Pits——so Hukin o'Go supplied us for the Kitchen for a while——and in

our own Apartments we burned Wood. The Thaw is come on now with heavy Rains, and I hear Lleweney is quite under Water: it rolls off *our* Grounds pretty well because we are on a Declivity. But our little River roars at a fine Rate and both the little wooden Bridges in the Shrubbery were soon carried away by the Stream. Peter whom you know very well, *Old Peter* that works in the Garden, says *he* cannot remember any Winter to equal it.

The Trees have been torne so, it half breaks my Heart:——That fine Oak with the Seat under, has lost its largest Boughs; and A Stone Pine over against the Sun Dial was snapt short in *Two*—so was my best Birch Tree by the Hurricane.

Mrs. Mostyn's eldest Son Salusbury is very ill with the Hooping Cough, and has spit Blood, and frighted his Mother cruelly—Harry is bad too: but She deserves to be frighted a little for setting out from London in such a Season—I was very angry with her you may be sure.

Miss Thrale is going to be married to Admiral Lord Keith.

So when I *do* write, I tell you News enough; and this is the last Letter I *shall* write with the date of 1807—and mind my dear Child that you begin your new Year with good Resolutions of increasing in Knowledge [and] Virtue: and when Mr. Shephard reads or talks to you seriously—listen to what he says,[1] and do not *try* to keep your Head upon something else. We have been talking about Travelling; and you may observe that *Years* are the *Mile Stones* of Life: every one that you pass, brings you nearer your *Journey's End*. And do not my good Boy believe that nobody dies except of *old Age*, as young folks are apt to suppose; every Newspaper brings accounts of Master *This*, and Miss *That* who are carried off when Children——nor can you guess how such Paragraphs make my Nerves flutter when they bring *Your possible Danger* to my Mind.

Be prudent my dear Salusbury, and do yourself all the Good you can, and gain all the Instruction in your Power, and give our best Regards to Mr. Shephard;—Mr. Charles is carrying on a Law Suit for us against Mr. Giles who will not pay what he owes us.[2] We had a Letter last Post, and he is better now——I mean Mr. Charles Shephard is better——not Mr. Giles—he is *bad* enough.

Shew this to the good Master of the House at Enborne and believe me / most Affectionately Yours / H: L: P.

Text: Ry. 585.3. *Address:* Master Salusbury / at The Rev. T. Shephard's / Enborne Cottage / near Newbury / Berkshire. *Postmark:* DENBIGH 224. [JSPS: "Answered/ / /Received/ / 3d/ / /January 1808"]

1. For the Reverend Thomas Shephard, headmaster of Enborne School, see HLP to Q, 22 April 1785, n. 27.
2. Peter Giles did not remain at Streatham Park for the time stipulated by his lease. The Piozzis sued him for the full payment of the rent as if he occupied Streatham Park for the time to which he had agreed. The litigation, after two years, was settled in the spring of 1808 when Giles paid what the Piozzis demanded of him. See HLP to Robert Ray, 20 April 1807, n.3.
Charles Mitchell Smith Shephard acted as the Piozzis' lawyer. See HLP to JSPS, 11 June 1808.

TO LADY WILLIAMS

Brynbella
31: December 1807.

My dear Lady Williams
 does me and my Daughters a great deal of honor by taking so tender an interest in our welfare. I hope they will begin a new year happily, another new year! Oh how the finishing of this reminds *me* of those Mile Stones which as one travels along shews one by their lengthening numbers from the place we set out from the approaching end of our journey. May your Ladyship's next Stage be a pleasant one; and may my amiable Sweetheart as I used to call him when a Child, continue long to increase the Comforts of his Mother.[1]
 Cecilia Mostyn's Children are still coughing, so We have not yet seen each other, and so dreadful are the Roads, So variable the Weather—we cannot wish a Friend far from their own Fireside. My poor Husband is chained fast to his, and the *big Finger* is threatening terribly.—Till the Storm burst however, it *may* blow off; and we live in Hope, and upon Hope as well as we can. His Loss of Appetite is what lowers his Spirits.
 Public news are pleasanter and the embarkation of that charming Prince Regent really filled my *Eyes* with joy, and its truest Symptom—tears. Poor soul! what nervous agitation must his have been when about to launch into a new Element, and leaving his native soil set boldly forward to a new Hemisphere; rather than lose sight of his honor and his Engagements.[2]
 That Buonaparte would revenge all upon *us* if he could do so—I doubt not; but he will be forced into a general Peace before that Attempt will be made. Were not you Ladies deeply interested in the unhappy Queen's recovery?[3] A strong imagination had driven her tender mind out of its Bias, a more forcible Reality drove it back like a dislocated Bone.
 I remember many years back, when there was an inundation at Perth in Scotland, occasioned by the melting Snows with a heavy Rain *at thaw*. The Mad House was in Danger of being carried down the Stream and all hands set to work to save the Patients—but strange to tell the very fiercest Lunatics among them clung round their Keepers promising obedience in return for protection—and being freed from their fetters etc., provided for their own and for each other's safety like the steadiest inhabitants of the Town.
 And now Adieu dear and lovely Lady Williams! present us respectfully and Affectionately to those nearest and dearest to You—believing Me ever with sincere and grateful Attachment / Your Ladyship's true Servant. / H: L: Piozzi.

Text: Ry. 3 (1807–11). *Address:* Lady Williams / Bodylwyddan / St. Asaph.

---

1. JW. See HLP to the Ladies of the Williams Family, 3 May 1797, n. 2.
2. On 19 December 1807, *The Times* reported: "Yesterday the very important intelligence was circulated in the City, that the Prince Regent and Government of Portugal had at length been driven to the expedient of emigrating from their country. The *Anne* armed ship, it was stated, had fallen

in with the Portuguese squadron, consisting of five sail of the line and one frigate, having the Royal Family on board."

The Times, however, remained dubious. Only on 21 December, in its leading article, did it confirm the fact that the Portuguese court had left Lisbon. It also reported the manifesto of the Prince Regent, wherein he stated his efforts to conciliate the government of France but that, unable to do so, "he had been reduced to the necessity of leaving the seat of Government, and of placing the Queen and family under the protection of their near ally the King of Great Britain;—that they were on the point of proceeding to Madeira, for the purpose of still leaving open the means of negociation; but that, should all access to these means be shut up, he had irrevocably resolved to transfer the Royal Family and the seat of government to the Brazils."

3. That Maria I was able to undertake the journey to the Brazils was true but that did not constitute "Recovery." She remained queen of Portugal only in name from 1777 until she died in 1816. See HLP to Q, 12 February [1799], n. 6.

TO WILLIAM WILSHIRE

> Brynbella near Denbigh
> N. Wales. Wensday
> 13: January 1808.

It seems long to *me* since I have heard of or from Mr. Wilshire,—and I suppose it seems still longer to Mr. Piozzi; who flattered himself that *something* was at *some* Time to come to his Wife from Hertfordshire. Nothing however *does* come: at least we hear of nothing being paid into Hammersley's—neither Sale nor Rent, neither Money nor Interest.[1]

Dear Sir let us at least have a letter, telling us good Tydings of the Arrears etc. for we shall certainly not come to London till the Spring is advanced, because this dreadful Winter has gone So very hard upon our Health. Mean While we wish You good Sir many happy Years and my heart now and then feels a silly hope of seeing once more the Spot where I spent my Maiden Days; when Hitchin and its beloved Environs were very familiar to Sir / Your obliged Servant &c. / H: L: Piozzi.

Text: Hitchin Museum, Paynes Park, Hitchin, Herts. *Address:* Mr. Wilshire Esq. / Hitchin / Hertfordshire / Hertfordshire. *Postmark:* JANUARY 15 1808; DENBIGH 224.

1. See HLP to Wilshire, concerning her "Hertfordshire copyholds," 26 April [1791].

TO JOHN SALUSBURY PIOZZI SALUSBURY

Brynbella
28: January 1808.

My dearest Salusbury
I was much pleased with your very agreeable Letter, and hope to be always pleased with you more and more. Mr. Shephard is very good to make you pass your Time so pleasantly, and Terence is such a diverting Book you cannot avoid liking it.

We are dismal enough here;—even the Beauties of this Place depend as *he* says somewhere of Rome, much less upon the Walls than on the Company. When Mr. Charles and you were here, we found Brynbella delightful. Now mind that this Compliment (however deserved) is a mere Common Place always quoted from Terence,[1] but you will have it again in Cicero,[2] and I do think 'tis to be found in Tacitus—where Otho harangues his Soldiers with much Elaboration—his own, or his Historians.[3]

At any Rate Dear Child get the common Classical Knowledge driven deep into your Head—*now* whilst you are young, and it will *stick* there. What one reads after 18 Years old glides out of the Mind much easier than what is sown in the early Season, and as to the Necessity of Classic Knowledge,—a Man who tries to go thro' Life without it, resembles one who sits all Night at a Whist Table, playing every hand against the Ace of Trumps turned up—Certain to lose the one grand Trick——and conscious that every body knows it.

Ask Mr. Shephard if I dont say true.

Meanwhile poor Uncle is poor Uncle indeed: not perhaps bad as he was last Year at this Time; but very bad, and very lowspirited, and goes to Bed at seven or eight o'Clock and leaves me all alone; and if I did not love Reading what would become of me? But "Eruditio inter Prospera Ornamentum; inter Adversa—refugium"—is a good old Saying, and so you will live to find it.[4]

We are under a heavy Snow still, and I have never Seen Cecilia Mostyn since *You did*,—Tho they are all at Segroid *under Snow too:* The Boys not yet well enough to return, nor the Weather fit for them to Travel in: Such a cruel Winter was never known in this Country. I do nothing all Morning long, but feed famished Robins at the Glass door; and you would be amazed to see how tame the Partridge are, and the Hares eat up poor Andrew's outer Garden without Mercy. Did I tell you how the Cow Man was blown over the Cliff into the Road, and came to no harm at all, only just hurt one hand. We have however raised all the five Pea-chicks and they are out of Danger now, at least as much as the old ones are.

Lord Kirkwall dined with us Twice, but went back to London; and staid away, and stays away still. Lady Keith sent us some of her Wedding Cake,[5] and I eat very little, yet it made me horrid sick, but here I am again alive and pretty well——Uncle knew nothing of the Matter, or he would have made a fine Ado: but Dunscombe is *so* discreet.

Young Williams is at home for the Holydays, but such is the Snow again, and such the Roads; he cannot ride over to see us. We are like the Egyptians during the Darkness *No Man rises from his Place*⁶—unless good Mr. Moore when I eat too much Plumb Cake.

Adieu dearest Boy, and be good; and mind Mr. Shephard: and be Dutyful to poor Uncle, and love your Affectionate Aunt / H: L: Piozzi.

Text: Ry. 585.4. *Address:* Master Salusbury / at The Rev. Thos. Shephard's / Enborne Cottage / near Newbury / Berks. *Postmark:* DENBIGH <224>.

1. The commonplace in Terence minimizes the worth of estates, possessions, and self-interest by underscoring the value of a shared humanity, the indispensable need of one person for another, the power of friendship to make all "Walls" common property. See, e.g., *Heauton Timorumenos,* 1.1.25; *Adelphoe,* 3.3.61, 5.3. 18.
2. See, e.g., *De Officiis,* 1.30; *Tusculan Disputations,* bk. 3.
3. See Tacitus's *Histories,* 1.54.
4. The aphorism, according to HLP "was a saying [of] old Lactantius [ca. 240–ca. 320] by Lord Verulam." See "Minced Meat for Pyes." Actually she found it not in Bacon or Lactantius but in Seward, *Anecdotes* 3:258–62. "The following letter of Lord Bacon is preserved in Sir Toby Mathews' collection of English letters. It is not inserted in the Folio Edition of Lord Bacon's Works; and is a striking instance of the resources of mind which this great though unfortunate man possessed; it is also an exquisite comment upon the celebrated sentence of Lactantius: / 'Eruditio inter prospera ornamentum—inter adversa refugium.'" What follows is the letter of "The Lord Viscount St. Alban's (Bacon) To The Bishop Of Winchester (Andrews), After His Fall. It Acquaints Him Both With His Comforts And His Writings."

The aphorism, as quoted by HLP and Seward, does not appear in Lactantius's collected works. It is, however, an apt summary of the *Divinarum Institutionum,* bk. 7, chap. 12, "De anima et corpore; atque de conjunctione eorum, et discessu ac reditu."

See *A Collection of Letters made by Sᵣ Tobie Mathews, Kt. . . . To which are Added many Letters of his own, to severall Persons of Honour, who were Contemporary with him* (London: Henry Herringman, 1660), pp. 36–39.
5. The Keith wedding took place on 10 January (1808) at Ramsgate.
6. The plague of darkness is in Exod. 10:21–23. The quotation is drawn from verse 23.

TO SAMUEL LYSONS

                                           Wednesday
                                     10: February 1808.

Dear Mr. Lysons

I have not written to you a long Time——and now I cannot *help* writing: I loved your Brother so much, and wished him happy so sincerely, his Change of Life affects me; and my Feelings will not permit me to tell *him* so.¹ Tell him yourself, my good Friend, and assure yourself that the Account of his Wife's Death in the Papers gave me a Sensation beyond what my Acquaintance with her called for.²——But She was pretty when we last met, and She was Young; and it seems so odd and melancholy to look in the Grave for those one used to see at the Tea Table!³

Well! you who live among the Records of past Life will bear these Things better;⁴ my Spirits are much depressed by Mr. Piozzi's miserable State of Health, nor can the Gayeties I hear of, draw my Attention from the Sorrows that I *see.* Mrs. Mostyn has politely taken a Weeks Share of them just now while her Sons are absent, and the London Winter not begun.— *Our* Winter commenced in November, and when it will end I know not: The Mountains are still covered with Snow, and such Tempestuous Weather did I never witness.

The Political Wonders have increased since the Suspension of our Correspondence so much, that we are all tired of wondering at Them—but this new Discovery of a Nest of Christians in Travancore must be considered as curious by every body who reads of it.[5]

Tell me the Price of Buchanan's Book and its Character,[6] I see nothing but Extracts—&c. those imperfect ones; and tell me some Literary Chat—remembering our Distance from all possibility of adding a new Idea to our Stock—except by the Voluntary Subscriptions and Contributions (to use an Hospital Phrase,) of the Nobility, Gentry, and others.

Hospital Phrases indeed best suit the Dwellers at Brynbella; but Doctor Johnson——never wrong——was right, *preeminently* right in this: That Chronic Diseases are never cured, and Acute ones if recovered from—cure themselves.[7] The Maxim has been confirmed by my experience every day since to me first pronounced; and I dare say the late unfortunate Event in your own Family, affords it no Contradiction.

Has your Brother many Children left him by his Lady? and is he living at Hempstead Court? He had better get to London and lose his Cares in the Croud.[8]

Dear Mr. Lysons do write to me, and in [the] Mean Time pity me, and my poor Husband, whose Sufferings one should believe on a cursory View of them wholly Insupportable; but God gives the Courage with the necessity of Exerting it.

Adieu and believe me / ever faithfully yours / H: L: Piozzi.

I hear all good of Mrs. Siddons.[9]

Text: Hyde Collection. *Address:* Samuel Lysons Esq: / Keeper of the Records in / The Tower of / London. *Postmark:* DENBIGH 224; E FE 12 1808.

1. In 1801 DL married Sarah, née Hardy. See HLP to DL, 3 September 1802, n. 1.
2. See, e.g., the *Bath Chronicle,* 4 February: "Sunday Se'nnight [24 January] died after a lingering illness [tuberculosis], in her 29th year, Mrs. Lysons, wife of the Rev. Daniel Lysons, of Hempsted-Court, near Glocester."
3. Joseph Farington, a friend of SL, described "the extraordinary fortitude & resignation of Mrs. Lysons previous to Her death. She talked of all circumstances respecting the care of Her family & gave directions for Her funeral &c. The day before Her Death she passed sometime in *knitting garters.* Her Lungs were wholly destroyed by an abscess, formed probably 12 months ago, but its progress suspended *during Her* pregnancy, a circumstance not uncommon." See Farington 9:3224.
4. SL became keeper of the records in the Tower of London in December 1803.
5. HLP first read of the newly revealed Christians in India in the November 1807 issue of *GM* 77, pt. 2: 1057–62. The account concerns Claudius Buchanan's "discovery" of the Syrian Christians who "inhabit the interior of Travancore and Malabar, in the South of India; and have been settled there from the early ages of Christianity." *GM,* which borrowed from the *Bristol Journal,* was confident that the discovery "cannot fail to excite the liveliest emotions in the bosom of every one, interested in the support and maintenance of the Christian Religion."

6. HLP referred to one or two of the books of Claudius Buchanan (1766–1815), best known as a Bengal chaplain and vice provost of the college of Fort William. The earlier work is *Memoir of the Expediency of an Ecclesiastical Establishment for British India*, published by Cadell and Davies in 1805.

This book was judged valuable in the *Monthly Review* 53 (May–August 1807): 40–41, because it discusses "the progress of the Christian faith in India, the particulars of Indian superstition, the political and religious differences which prevail among the natives, and the enormities of various kinds which are practised among them under sacred pretences, some of which seem capable of suppression."

By 4 January in the *Morning Post* another of Buchanan's books was announced as forthcoming: *An Account of the Christian Institution in the East*, also to be published by Cadell and Davies.

7. Cf. SJ to HLT, 19 April 1784, in *Letters* 2:362.

8. The dying Sarah Lysons "says she does not know that she has anything to blame in Her conduct except that Her fondness and anxiety abt. Her children may have been too great" (Farington 9:3204–5). She and DL had four children: Daniel (1804–14); Samuel (1806–77); Sarah (1802–33); Charlotte (1807–48).

According to SL, who on 25 February (Ry. 522.23) answered HLP's letter: "The children are at present with my youngest sister, whose husband is looking after his estate in Jamaica. My brother intends letting Hempsted Court for two years, and residing at his parsonage house at Rodmarton when he is in Gloucestershire; but we shall be travelling about thro' different Counties [a] great part of the summer making collections of our work."

9. SS had appeared thirty-nine times at Covent Garden in the 1805–6 season and thirty-four in the next. On 15 July 1807 she wrote a letter, probably to HLP, and it is to this that HLP primarily alludes.

"The houses are tolerably good. I can't expect to be followed like the great genius Master Betty, you know; but I hope to put about 1000*l*. into my pocket this summer. 'Tis better to work hard for a short time, and have done with it. If I can but add three hundred a-year to my present income, I shall be perfectly well provided for; and I am resolved, when that is accomplished, to make no more positive engagements in summer" (Campbell 2:319).

SS was performing only intermittently during the 1807–8 season and was able to visit her husband for six weeks in Bath, from late in December 1807 to February 1808. It was their last visit together.

TO MARGARET WILLIAMS

Fast Day[1]
17: February 1808
Brynbella

I thank you very kindly my very dear Miss Williams for your entertaining Letter; my poor Husband is at length set fast in his Bed, whence I have no hope or Notion of his rising up till towards May. Dear Mr. William Williams came over just before he was laid up, to see how we were all doing—he had once entertained Thoughts of going to Bath he said, but Things turned out perversely, and he could not. He met Dr. Myddelton here and Mrs. Mostyn;—*She* is here still. With Regard to Lord Keith I never saw him, or ever heard—but by common Report (which of Course always exaggerates)—any one Word spoken concerning his Fortune and Affairs.

We all heard when he captured the Dutch Fleet off the Cape of Good Hope:[2]—and some one Said he was a Widower,[3] whose Daughter had an Independant Estate of her own[4]—but I know precisely nothing beyond Mr. Piozzi's sick Room, and my own little Study—*How should I?* This I am sure of, that whoever seeks to get Dunscombe from me, must take Buonaparte for Ally before they succeed:

When I considered *myself*, and was considered by all around me—as on my Deathbed last October my Comfort was to think I left Mr. Piozzi Two such faithful *Carers* for his Person and his Fortune in our good upper Servants.

Poor Soul! his State of Dependance on *them* is mournful to reflect upon; and their quitting him would be an Act [of] Inhumanity of which I hope their Nature is not capable. He has now been in his Bed Eleven days, and scarcely moveable even *in it*—a Foot like that at Bath, and worse Ability to bear his Sorrows.

Cecilia *says* her Account from the Boys *to day* is unfavourable, and she looks lowspirited—and as if I should soon be deprived of her Company; They are at Streatham School: I understand She came here to escape the Loneliness of Segroid in their Absence, and probably She may think it right to follow them to Town.

The Newspapers relate the Death of my old Acquaintance Lord Thomond,[5] and I cannot help feeling for *old Friends*, tho' my *youthful Daughters* Presentations at court on their Marriages, ought perhaps to drive every melancholy Fancy far away.

Farewell dear Miss Williams! and may you never know the Sadness of attending the Sick Bed of the *last remaining* Friend who is bound by real Ties to desire the continuance of your own Existence. Such is my poor Husband to / his and Your / H: L: P.

Compliments to all who remember me.

Text: Ry. 3 (1807–11). *Address:* Miss Williams / Upper Park Street / St. James's / Bath. *Postmark:* DENBIGH.

1. "A Fast before Easter has been observed from the earliest Christian times; but the period of its duration varied in different countries and ages. . . . towards the middle of the third century, Origen speaks of forty days being consecrated to fasting before Easter. And at the Council of Nicæa this period was taken for granted, as if long in use.
"But however early the extension of the Lenten fast to forty days may have been, it is certain that they were reckoned in several different ways, though always immediately preceding Easter. By various Churches the forty days were distributed over periods of nine, eight, and seven weeks." *The Annotated Book of Common Prayer . . . of the Church of England*, ed. the Reverend John Henry Blunt (London, Oxford, Cambridge: Rivington's, 1866), pp. [28], 90.
Such fast days were commonly observed on Wednesdays and Fridays. 17 February 1808 fell on a Wednesday and Eastern Sunday on 17 April, i.e., almost nine weeks later.
2. For Lord Keith's occupation of the Dutch colony at the Cape of Good Hope (August–September 1796) and their trading center in Malacca, see HLP to Q, 7 November 1796, n. 6.
3. Lord Keith's first wife was Jane Mercer (d. 1789).
4. Lord Keith's only child from his first marriage was Margaret Elphinstone (1788–1867), suo jure Baroness Keith of Stonehaven Marischal in the peerage of Ireland (1793), as also Baroness Keith of Banheath (1803).
5. According to the *Courier*, 11 February: "We are sorry to state, that yesterday the Marquis of Thomond was unfortunately killed in Grosvenor-square. He was riding on horseback, and as he turned the corner of the Square from the east to the south side, he rode rather close to the railing, where the pavement is not so even. . . . The horse tumbled, and his Lordship fell upon his head. . . . Lord Sydney happened to be at home at the time, and ordered his porter and some others, to bring the unfortunate Nobleman into his house," where he was pronounced dead.

TO JOHN SALUSBURY PIOZZI SALUSBURY

Brynbella
Monday 22: February 1808.

My dearest Salusbury

You are a Letter in my Debt I *think*, but I will not be sure. *This* I am sure of, that Consolation is much wanted here at Brynbella; and that You should send me some. Poor Uncle has been confined to the Wing Room now just 16 Days; and when we shall have him on the Sopha again, *no Man can tell*. The Leg is all in a frightful Ulcer, and Chalk pouring out amain; The large Finger broken too, and discharging, and he is very low, and who can Wonder? He may *well* be low:—yet no Cough is come on hitherto, and good Mr. Moore walks in and out with his slow Pace and even Step, saying "I'll pledge my Life there's not an Atom of Danger." Had he made a *worse* Report we could have done nothing: for our Roads have been all snowed up, that Owen Hughes could not go even to Denbigh for Letters, nor could the Mail pass from Holywell to St. Asaph—— How then should we have been able to call Doctor Thackeray? Mr. Roberts found Difficulty in getting from his own house to Church upon the Fast Day—— Oh Such a Season sure was never known!

The young Mostyns are gone to School,[1] their Mother staid here a Week, but is returned to Segroid: Jones comes tomorrow[2]——It would be *too* hard upon me (would not it?) to live *quite* alone. We had a Ewe lambed under the Snow the dreadful drifting Night: Harry Hughes dug out Miss and her Mama both alive in the Morning—So we rear the young one and call her Agnes, and make a Pet of her. Poor Frisk has five Puppies, so She lives in the Stable and I lose even *her* Company: and Chancey is miserable because She does not go to London or Bath to see her Cousins and Aunts. Dunscombe takes very kind care of my Master, and is excessively attentive—and *General Lake* as we call him,[3] looks to the House and Grounds:—or we should be all overflowed now the Thaw is come again——Your Duck likes the dabbling very much and I give her a bit of Bread for your Sake now and then. No other News have I—nothing but Deaths I think——and a new North Wales Gazette to register them.[4]

Write to me soon Dear Love, for I want a Letter sadly, and give my Compliments to your good Friends at Enborne.

Harry Mostyn was sick again as soon as he got to Streatham, and went home to his Aunt Thrale. The Gentleman that took Care of the Boys *back*, a Mr. Davies of Denbigh and Student at Cambridge,—was taken ill on the Road, and died soon after he arrived at London, or is dying.[5] Oh how Lowspirited all these Things do make / Your ever Affectionate Aunt / H: L: P.

Text: Ry. 585.5. *Address:* Master Salusbury at The Rev. / Thos. Shephard's / Enborne Cottage / near Newbury / Berkshire. *Postmark:* DENBIGH 22<   >.

1. In 1808 CMM's three sons were ten, nine, and seven. Not handsome, they were very tall for their age. According to HLP they were "old men," always ailing with either colds or typical childhood diseases. They studied under RD at his school in Streatham.

2. Elener Jones had married the Denbigh apothecary Robert (Robin) Jones in 1806. See HLP to PSW, 29 August [1791], n. 8.
3. A favorite nickname for AL, derived from Gerard Lake (1744–1808), who rose steadily through army ranks until he became a general in 1802. In India he achieved his great fame as a military leader.
4. The *North Wales Gazette* was first issued on 5 January. It appeared initially on Tuesdays, but soon thereafter on Thursdays. The sixpenny newspaper was printed and published by John Broster in Bangor, Carnarvonshire. See *Thraliana* 2: 1090.
5. If HLP is accurate about the time of this event, no Mr. Davies of Cambridge fits the description. On the other hand, a David Davies of Ruthin, County Denbigh, had matriculated at Jesus College, Oxford, 17 May 1806, aged twenty-one. Far from dying in 1808, he received his B.A. in 1810.

TO JOHN GILLON

[ca. February 1808][1]

Dear Mr. Gillon's

heavy Roll of Papers came as you said they would:[2] had I dreamed of being engaged in Such Transactions, I had done better in my Youth to study Law than Grammar; for it is frightful to be made [to] Swear to what one cannot comprehend:[3]—The Gentleman who seems as if intending to elucidate Matters, only obscures them to *my* Eyes, which cannot read the light-written Characters delineated in red Ink upon the Margin. Your Expression of sending them for my *Approval* makes me Smile even in the midst of Trouble; for how can I possibly *approve* or *condemn* Transactions of which my precious Knowledge is precisely *Nothing*. All I can gather is that Mr. Joseph Cator[4] is mistaken in stating that Henrietta Sophia Thrale died before her father;[5] because I do know and can safely swear She died Two Years after him; and the last Annual Register will shew John Cator's Death in 1806—certainly before John Meredith Mostyn who we left *alive* in Bath the Spring of 1807.[6] I wonder these wise Men are not more accurate as to Dates——besides that one has been told about *Misnomers* in the Law; and it appears that the Names of Mr. Mostyn's Children (except the eldest) are set forth very differently from the names by which their Mother and Friends call them: She however is in Town, and the proper Person to adjust such Errors—if Errors they be—for as She never asked me to stand Sponsor to any of them, I have no Right to know—but will not *swear* till I *do* know—and *legally*.

There is a curious Marginal Note showing that the Trustees acted without my Concurrence in some early stage of the Business; but I was never anything but a writing-Machine in Mr. John Cator's hands, and that they all know.

The best is accusing me of Confederacy with the Ladies and their Husbands, whose very Persons I knew not; and who had never uttered a Word or Breath to me upon the Subject—Such Situations are very vexatious indeed:—but as Baretti used to say—Mondo!

I thought how Things were going with Abram Atkins Esq. but have no doubt of your knowing how to get the Money from him—colle buone o colle Cattive [*whether by good means or bad*].[7]

Spanish Affairs are going badly I fear, they have let the Tyrant in, and how shall we all get him out again?[8]

I doubt not Castillian Valour or British Bravery

> But the Strength of every other Member
> Depends upon our Belly Timber;
> And if I take this Matter right
> Pudding and Beef make Britons fight.
> Prior[9]

Now I greatly fear that the Pudding will be all *Malaga* Raisins—and *no Fat*—and John Bull when he is not fed will roar finely and the wretched Natives will soon find their Allies as great Devourers as the French Invaders——

Ah my heart is low now concerning the Spanish Power of opposing Buonaparte;[10] tho' *he* has shewn little Skill in leaving them so long to resolve on't. I am impatient for the result of a Battle against Sir John Moore, whose Name is dear to me for his Father's Sake, as well as his own incomparable Conduct in Ireland.[11]

Mr. Piozzi suffers quite beyond all telling, and sometimes beyond his own Powers of Endurance; but if he *does* faint from Excess of Pain—as sometimes happens——he recovers again, and hopes for the restoration of the Bourbons and Death of Buonaparte.

Adieu Dear Sir and believe me ever most sincerely Your faithful / and Obliged / H: L: P.

You must tell what the soda Water cost,—and you *must* coerce Mr. Atkyns.

What in the world is a Deed *Poll*?[12] I thought they meant Roll, till I saw it with a little p—in one of their Papers.

Text: Ry. 533.26. *Address:* John Gillon Esq. / No. 60. / Wellbeck Street.

1. HLP's letter can be dated late February, since it responds to Gillon's, dated 30 January (Ry. 579.150), and alludes to France's invasion of Spain in mid-February.
2. The "Roll of Papers" was sent to Gillon by John Cator's executor in July 1806. On the 23rd of that month Gillon informed HLP (Ry. 579.145): "I have received a Mahogany Chest from the Adelphi, at the Request of Mr. Joseph Cator, with all the Parchment Deeds, &c. belonging to the Estate of the late Mr. Thrale, among which I see there are Parchments relating to Bachygraig . . . and also your Contract of Marriage. Mr. Cator sent me a Box from Beckenham with other Papers; which I have not yet looked into. The Bottom of the *Chest* had come out; but I have had it compleatly repaired. And the whole are safe, here, in Welbeck Street, at your Disposal." Since GP's illness precluded HLP's visit to Wellbeck Street, Gillon sent the material to her.
3. The immediate issue of HLP's letter is spelled out by Gillon on 30 January: "The Debt and Costs, sued for by Mr. Lowndes, if the whole be recovered; and I fear it will, in the end, will amount to near £8000, of which each of your Daughters will have to pay one fourth. It is much to be regretted that Mr. Thrale ever entered into the Securities for his brother in law. But Regret is in vain now!"
Apparently, HT had guaranteed a loan made by Thomas Lowndes (1737–1828), of London and Hassall, Cheshire, to Arnold Nesbitt (ca. 1721–79), merchant, M.P., and first husband of Susanna Thrale (d. 1789).
4. Joseph Cator (1733–1818) of Ross, Hereford, and Bromley, Kent, was John's younger brother.
5. The youngest of the twelve Thrale children, Henrietta Sophia was born on 21 June 1778 and died 25 April 1783. HT died 4 April 1781.
6. John Cator had died 21 February 1806; John Meredith Mostyn 19 May 1807.
7. HLP is commenting on Gillon's statement of 30 January on difficulties with her Streatham Park tenant: "Having waited until to day, in vain, for an answer to my last letter to Mr. Atkins, I

have again written him, in a still more earnest Manner, to pay the money without further delay, and have said that, if he do not, I will not be answerable for the Consequences. He certainly behaves very ill! The Rent, however, is very safe; and you can always coerce payment, by distraining on his Effects: although it is an ungracious or rather a disagreeable measure to have recourse to, if it can possibly be avoided. But Mr. Piozzi is certainly mistaken as to the £13 for the Proportion of the Rent of the Garden; of which Mr. A:, by his Lease, was entitled to have Possession, with the rest of the Premises. He even threatened to be *off*, if he had not that possession, and it was considered as a favor, that he contented himself to receive a proportion of the rent from the 25th May to the 1st September; to which he is clearly entitled."

8. Napoleon had begun to move his troops into Spain in mid-February, although the Spanish government had already permitted French soldiers to enter all the key cities and communication centers of northern Spain in late 1807. To these troops were added three corps of the generals Pierre Dupont de l'Étang, Bon Adrien Jannot de Moncey, and Philippe Guillaume Duhesme.

9. HLP's variation of two separate passages in the third canto of Prior's *Alma*. See lines 204–5, 248–49.

10. As early as 1 April there was a riot against French troops in Madrid and another, more serious on 2 May so that martial law had to be imposed on the city. Between 20 and 27 May, the pro-French governors of Badajoz, Cartagena, and Cadiz were assassinated. Armies of Patriots were beginning to form so that by 10 June all provinces were arming. For further information on Spanish resistance, see HLP to Dr. Parry, 15 July 1808, n. 4.

11. General John Moore was the third but eldest surviving son of the apothecary. On 5 June 1798 he was present at the battle of New Ross and subsequently marched on Wexford, routing seven thousand rebels led by Father Roche. Moore remained in Ireland until 1799.

Only in July 1808 (after an unfortunate mission to Sweden in May) was he sent to the Peninsula.

12. Deed Poll: "A deed so called because it is cut evenly or polled at the top . . . and containing a single person's declaration to all of his act and intention, e.g. to grant a power of attorney or to change his name." *The Oxford Companion to Law*.

TO JOHN SALUSBURY PIOZZI SALUSBURY

Brynbella
Tuesday 1st: March 1808.

To me a melancholy St. David's Day; but better than yesterday, when my dear Boy's Letter arrived. Do not be frighted however, because tho' Mr. Piozzi's Situation is dismal enough: I hope, and pray;——and could almost say I *trust* he is in no present Danger.

These horrid Chalk Sores are indeed distressing, and that which is now beginning to heal, is certainly as bad,—worse I think if possible; than that he was plagued with at Bath. You could not at this Moment cover the open Place with the Lid of a common Teapot; and *that is the Truth* without any Addition whatever. Mean while he has no Cough, nor no Faintings as he had there, and the Pulse does not drop all away, as you and I have seen it when Bowen and Parry were frighted for him.[1]

But we have had a Misfortune you little think of, and for which I was wholly unprepared. Dunscombe taken *suddenly* and *dangerously* ill while attending his Master, who was greatly alarmed——and would bear nobody else about him. Oh what a Bustle and confusion were we all in! But the Fear is over, and the Man Safe—if *Safe* is a Word that Mortal *Man* may *use*.

Jones is very comfortable to me; Cæcilia Mostyn is planting, and improving her Son's Estate at Segroid:

She will go to London at Easter, and I suppose She will begin to enjoy herself towards May when her Mourning is over. The Williamses are well, and the Kirkwalls have got 1000£ o'Year by Death of poor old Lord Thomond.[2] I feel much obliged by Mr. Shephards carrying you into such good Company to amuse yourself so very properly. It is extremely desirable for young People to live early with genteel Society, and they will then keep clear of numberless vexations ill laid *on*: for vexed one *must* be; but 'tis better have one's fingers cut with a Razor, than rubbed hard with a Rasp: and I hate to owe my Pain to People who are incapable of giving me Pleasure.

I do not know now who Lord Caernarvon is:[3] My Aunt's Sister was Marchioness of Caernarvon when the name was Brydges, but that was in the late Kings Reign:[4] her Daughter married the Father of the present Admiral Stanhope,[5] but I have a Notion these People are no Relations to *them*.

The Aunt I speak of was such an Aunt as I am to *You*, my Uncle's Wife—She was Daughter to the Earl of Dysart, and married my Uncle Sir Robert Salusbury Cotton, and they built the long Gallery at Lleweney Hall.[6]

What a shocking Fate seems to follow Lord Nelson's Family!——but Young and Old are dropping so, and so oddly, as I never witnessed till now.[7]

Poor Lord Thomond at 85 Years of Age to expire in the Streets of London!—by mere Accident! for no Person of 40 could be more alert or healthy than he was.[8] But my Paper is out and I have scarce Room to say how much and how Affectionately I remain my dearest Salusbury ever yours / H: L: P.

I open my Letter to say that dear Uncle is better—a great *deal* better: and if no Relapse comes, we will have him on the Sofa tomorrow; and sing Jubilate, tho' it will be Ash Wednesday. Compliments to Mr. Shephard and his Family.

Text: Ry. 585.6. *Address:* Master Salusbury / at The / Rev: T: Shephard's / Enborne Cottage / near Newbury / Berks. *Postmark:* DENBIGH 22<   >.

1. The apothecary (Bowen) and physician (Parry) at Bath who attended GP during his last illness there. Within a week, GP had "weather'd the Storm" (*Thraliana* 2:1087).
2. The will of Murrough O'Brien, 1st marquess of Thomond [I.] and 1st baron Thomond of Taplow [U.K.], had been signed 1 July 1800 and proved at London 11 March 1808. See P.R.O., Prob. 11/1476/253.
What the Kirkwalls received from Lord Thomond was exaggerated by North Wales gossip. Thus: "And I give the following legacies to my affectionately loved daughter Mary Countess of Orkney one hundred pounds, to my dear grandson Lord Kirkwall, my silver mounted pistols, my pocket pistols, swords and <hangers>."
For more on Lord Thomond's will, see HLP to JSPS, 22 March 1808.
3. Henry Herbert (1741–1811) was created 17 October 1780 Lord Porchester of High Clere, county Southampton, and advanced to the earldom of the town and county of Carnarvon (1793). In 1771 he had married Elizabeth Alicia Maria, née Wyndham (d. 1826), daughter of the 1st earl of Egremont.
4. John Brydges (1702/3–27), marquess of Carnarvon, had married on 1 September 1724 Lady Catherine Tollemache (d. 1754), daughter of the second earl of Dysart.
5. The daughter of the marchioness of Carnarvon was Catherine (b. 1725), who married first William Berkeley Lyon, a captain in the horse guards; and second, Admiral Edwyn Francis Stanhope (1729–1807) of Stanwell, in Middlesex.
6. Robert Salusbury Cotton (d. 1748), third baronet of Combermere (1715), represented Cheshire in the first parliament of George II. He had married Lady Elizabeth Tollemache (d. 1745), eldest daughter of the second earl of Dysart.

7. Horatio Nelson (1788–1808), styled Viscount Trafalgar, was the only son and heir of William (1757–1835), second baron Nelson of the Nile and of Hilborough, etc., sole surviving brother of the admiral.

The boy had been educated at Eton and at Cambridge. By royal warrant March 1806, he accepted the order of Saint Joachim worn by his uncle. He died of typhus fever in London and was buried 25 January, in Saint Paul's Cathedral with his uncle.

8. According to *GM* 78, pt. 1 (1808): 180: "His Lordship was celebrated rather as a *bon vivant* . . . and for many years had the reputation of being a *six-bottled man*. . . . His Lordship . . . to his last hour enjoyed a most enviable state of health. . . . His Lordship's remains were removed on the 18th [of February] from Great George-street to Buckinghamshire, to be interred in the vault of the Church near his estate [Taplow Court]. The funeral procession was very plain; consisting merely of the hearse, the coronet borne on his Lordship's horse, two mourning coaches, and the carriage of the deceased."

TO WILLIAM SIDDONS

Brynbella
Monday 14: March 1808.

My dear Mr. Siddons
 will scarce believe that I received his very kind and entertaining Letter *but now*.[1] It would not have been longer coming from America, and I hope We shall soon hear of the Portuguese Court arriving there as Safely as my Box is at length come from Bath; but not with half such odd Drolleries on Board.

England possesses more Malice with less Merriment than any *other* Nation for the most Part; in these Character-Dialogues however, there is Sometimes a Strong Mixture of *both*, and I suspect the Writer to be *Irish* born. The Key was necessary to me in many Places, and I thank you a Thousand Times for it.[2] The Drafts upon Parnassus too are excellent[3]—and as Juliet says

"Joy comes well in such a needful Time."[4]

Mr. Piozzi has been many Weeks a suffering Inhabitant of his favourite *Wing Room* whence he begins now to be wheeled out in a Morning for a few Hours, but soon retires to Bed—though not to rest.

I am sorry for Miss Sharpe; Age and Infirmity should go together, and young Lasses like her should be free: but Miss Williams says that Mrs. Twiss's Daughter has gone through a great deal this Year, which has been a severe Season to all Conditions of Life.[5] Even the little dear Girl that Admired Your Beauty so—at Bodylwyddan, has been in no good way, and the Parents frighted enough for poor pretty Emma[6]—but I never told her Aunt—Miss Williams; She is of such an anxious Temper and so trongly attached to her family.

The Snows were really frightful a Short Time back, and our Shrubbery has suffered beyond all Imagination. Hardly a Primrose peeps out yet, and if a Thrush sings sweetly *one Day* he gets a sore throat for it like Miss Sharp I believe, and lies by again a whole Week.

Playhouse News never reaches *us* of Course, and I can only hear at a *Distance*, but always with Pleasure of Mrs. Siddons's Celebrity. I think the Actors escape surprisingly in this new School of Derision which so professes to reform People.

Dear Me! if Ridicule produced Reformation, I think we should be the best Folks in the World—and so perhaps we *may be* after all, bad as we are:—and that Terror of being hooked which prevents many Efforts, and rubs down many Prominencies in a Character; may keep away Enormities that would be much worse than our present Insipidity.——When the Pump room Conversations come out however, let all look to themselves,[7] and let the Author look to *himself,* that he make them as Witty as Dear Mr. Anstey's were; who hurt the Feeling of no Individual, and diverted all his Readers with innocent Pleasantry.[8]

Well! Adieu! and when You See any Friends who have not forgotten us, remember us to *them,* and at any Rate recollect that You have at 168 Miles Distance a / true Friend and *old* Acquaintance / in Yours sincerely / H: L: P.

Send me a Chit Chat Letter now and then, it would be a great Charity: we are quite Paupers in small Talk.

Text: Ry. 533.25. (In the hand of HLP, "never sent because the poor Man was dead".) *Address:* William Siddons Esq. / Henrietta Street / Bath.

1. William Siddons had written from Bath on 24 December 1807 (Ry. 574.26) what proved to be his last letter to HLP: he died unexpectedly on 11 March 1808 and was buried in the Bath Abbey on the 16th. See "Bath Abbey Burials, 1792–1812," C.R.O., Somerset.
Siddons's letter was chatty, steeped in Bath gossip. He discussed the satiric *Bath Characters* and decoded the names for her.
2. *Bath Characters; or, Sketches from Life,* by Peter Paul Pallet [i.e., the Reverend Richard Warner] (London: G. Wilkie and J. Robinson, 1807). The localized satire appeared first as a slim work, only 80 pages of text. It was enlarged with each edition, bringing the second in 1808 to 132 pages and the third in the same year to 162 pages. The introductions were also expanded from eight to twenty-four and finally to forty-four.
It became a Bath pastime to identify the real figures behind the significant names. And since some of the persons and names were obscure, several "keys" became available. William Siddons had sent HLP one such "key."
3. The reference goes back to the pretentious and usually bad poetry written for and read at Batheaston Villa, which its owners (Sir John Riggs Miller and his wife, Anne) liked to think of as "Parnassus." See HLP to Q, 23 February 1794, n. 6.
Now HLP refers to William Siddons' postscript. "Have you heard of two little Poems that everybody seems to be reading here,—one call'd the 'Peacock at home,' where all the birds are invited, and attend—the other the 'Butterflys Ball.' They are really playful things, and amuse 'children of a larger growth'—."
4. *Romeo and Juliet,* 3.5.105. See HLP to PSP, 27 February 1798.
5. For the elder Twisses, see HLP to PSP, [29] April 1798, n. 4.
From 1807, Mrs. Twiss, assisted by her husband and her three daughters, conducted a boarding and day school for girls at 16 Camden Place, Bath.
The three daughters were Amelia (d. 1852); Elizabeth (d. 1858); Frances Ann (d. 1804).
6. Emma Williams was now ten.
7. Siddons had written: "So much for the Bath Characters. Next are to appear 'Pump Room Conversations,' and I say to those that laugh at the characters—don't laugh to [sic] soon. Who knows who is to be plac'd in the Pump Room—."
8. See HLP to Q, 7 March 1805, n. 5.

TO JOHN SALUSBURY PIOZZI SALUSBURY

22: March 1808.

My dear Salusbury

I write from Uncle's Bedside; but though I say so, you need not fright yourself and think he *keeps his Bed*. We have had him out to Dinner Two or Three Times—just in the Drawing Room with Me or Jones who we kept with us a Night or So——Doctor Thackeray treats him just as the Bath Physicians—exactly——for when the Cough came on, I sent away to Chester *post haste* and delayed the Doctor here to sleep; so he watched him well: and prescribed accordingly, and left Dunscombe and me Orders how to go on in his Absence and so he did Mr. Moore, who has the best heart of our Patient of any among us. The Weather is horribly unfavourable as You say, both to sick and well. If we can get dear Uncle on to Spring and *Summer*, You will I hope have a happy Meeting here with him yet, and God send you may find him but little the worse since last July and August. Mean while Dr. Thackeray's Brother or first Cousin I forget which;[1] is one of the Masters at Eton School: and our friendly Physician hopes he may be of use to you, and direct your choice of a Dame as they call the Mistress of an Eton Boarding house. Pray ask Mr. Shephard if he remembers any of the Thackerays at School? I should fancy they might have been Cotemporaries.

Poor Mr. Siddons is dead, I think you will be sorry for it; and his Death which came on by sudden Suffocation, makes Uncle very lowspirited. The people in *his* Neighborhood are all in an Agony about an Illnatured Pamphlet called *Bath Characters:* making Sport of Miss Wroughton[2] and Doctor Gibbes[3] and little Sir George Colebrooke and Rauzzini[4] and a heap of Folks beside: Bowen the Apothecary beyond all.[5] There is more Malice than Wit in the Book, for ought I see; and more Mischief than common Sense.—But those who suffer it to prey upon their Health, and their Peace of Mind, will encourage the Writer to fling a little more Dirt at them, instead of leaving off where he is: and being forgotten as he Soon would be. Mrs. Glover sends her Love to you, John Octavius is gone to East India and is very happily settled there with his Brother[6]—Settling is not quite a proper Word tho' for a Soldiers Life—I only mean that he is to remain in India for some Time if untoward Accidents do not arise to change his Destination. Nobody in this World can know their future fate, yet are we bound in Duty to make Provision for what is to come, even in *this* World. Dunscombe is recovered. We write in considering him as a *principal Verb in The Sentence.* I should have no Leisure even as you say so comically to write additions to Beresfords Book of Miseries, was not Dunscombe able to attend on his poor Master by Night and Day.

Mrs. Mostyn will come to us on Thursday, and then She will take her Leave and take her Flight—My other Daughters write now and then, but mine is indeed a melancholy Life.

Do you remember a Silly Captain Somebody at Bath that used to sing Spring returns, and He pronounced it *Sprig*,[7] and the Girls laughed at him, especially Fanny Glover.[8] I think this Year we shall find *that Song* terribly out of *Season*.

Sir George Colebrooke (1729–1809), second baronet, long-time friend of the Piozzis. Portrait by Sir Joshua Reynolds from the collection at Wrotham Park; reproduced by the kind permission of the owners.

One Thrush to be sure I have heard, and one Primrose I have seen——a fine Vernal Equinox truly!!

The old Marquis of Thomond was Lord Kirkwall's Grandfather, but he left every thing to his Brother's Son now Earl of Inchiquin.[9] The Thousand Pound o'Year comes thro' Lady Orkney *his* Daughter, on whom it was settled; Lord K——will not touch it till her Death.

I write any Stuff to divert *your* Anxiety and my own: because I dread those horrid Spasms which come with the Cough upon poor wretched Uncle: He has had but *one* tho', and Doctor Thackeray was in the Room thank God, and Mr. Moore at the door, so we have all the help we *can* and pray for Heaven's Assistance—Be good and be happy dear Salusbury, and love and pity your Affectionate Aunt / H: L: P.

I have forgotten the Law Suit.[10]

My Letters are very costly. Mr. Shephard must be so good as [to] give You a Guinea to pay Postage——You will be able to read this I hope tho' written in so small a Hand. Mr. Moore bids me assure you *he* thinks Dear Uncle in no present Danger.

I open my Letter recollecting that I have never answered your Question about the Small Pox——but Uncle possesses an Account from your Mamma that you had Small pox naturally at two years old— besides Hooping Cough and Measles; and *now* She says, He is ready for the English Journey and may go when he will.

Text: Ry. 585.7. *Address:* Master Salusbury / at The Rev: T: Shephard's / Enborne Cottage / Newbury / Berks. *Postmark:* DENBIGH 22<   >; MARCH <   >8.

1. Dr. Thackeray's brother-in-law, the Reverend George Stevenson (1763–1825), had been a Fellow of King's College, Cambridge, and an assistant master at Eton. While he continued his interest in Eton, he had ca. 1796 been given the profitable living of Callan, county Kilkenny. He had married Dr. Thackeray's eldest sister, Lydia (1764–1851).
2. For Susannah Wroughton (Signora Rattana, "the cynosure of Bath circles," in *Bath Characters*), see HLP to PSW, 21 [November 1792]., n. 8.
3. Dr. Gibbes appeared in *Bath Characters* as Dr. Faddle.
Signora Rattana's dog had the colic. "'Send for Dr. Faddle instantly,' cried the distracted fair one.— 'Oh, my dear doctor, I am ruined for ever: behold the sick Fidel!' Faddle [aside]: 'Curse this little son of a bitch, this is the second time I've been call'd *out of my bed* to prescribe for him. Never distress yourself, my dear madam; a purge and a blister, a bleeding and clyster, a *solution* of silex, and a blast of phlogiston, will again set all to rights.'—'Ah! no doctor; 'tis too late, I fear. Even your skill is ineffectual . . .'" (pp. 30–31).
4. Sir George Colebrooke was ridiculed as Sir Gregory Croaker, and Rauzzini as Rosen.
5. In the prose text of *Bath Characters* Bowen as Mixum appears prominently in Dialogue the Third, wherein he speaks ignorantly and pretentiously with Dr. Borecat (Dr. Burkett) on the nature of medicine, pharmacology, and Bath ways in general. In the "Poetical Introduction to the Second Edition," Mixum presents himself as "the Apothecary beyond all."
6. John Octavius Glover (1789–1855) is identified by 6 July 1809 in the Army Lists as captain in the Royal Scots (First Foot) Regiment. Retiring as lieutenant colonel in 1837 or 1838, he died at Cambridge. See *GM* 44, n.s. (1855): 219.
His brother Frederick Augustus (d. 1865) also chose an army career, becoming by 1825 a captain in the Sixty-ninth Regiment of Foot.
7. "Elegy Written in Spring," by Michael Bruce (1746–67), a Scottish poet.
8. See HLP to MW, 21 May 1807, n.9.
9. With the death of Lord Thomond, the barony of Thomond of Taplow expired; but the Irish

honors devolved upon his nephew William O'Brien (d. 1846), sixth earl and baron of Inchiquin and second marquess of Thomond. According to Lord Thomond's will, all heirlooms, pictures, and furniture enjoyed by his wife during her lifetime should upon her decease be "sent to the then Earl of Inchiquin and to go as Heir Looms with the Title and Estate."

On the other hand, "Lord Thomond did all he cd. for [his wife] in the way of settlement. She has Her own fortune at her own disposal viz: £40,000 in the 3 per cents—£1000 a yr. on the Irish estate—all the personalty at Taplow & in town, including rents which were due—money in Bankers Hands and 5 or 600 guineas in Gold which His Lordship had at Taplow, making up altogether what will produce £2600 a year" (Farington 9:3258–59).

10. For the lawsuit against Peter Giles, see HLP to Robert Ray, 20 April 1807.

TO JOHN SALUSBURY PIOZZI SALUSBURY

Monday Morning or rather
Sunday Night 25: April 1808.

My dear Salusbury

will be glad and happy when I tell him that Uncle comes to the dining Parlour now everyday, and goes out—sometimes—as he used—in the Wheel Chair: Not quite well certainly, we cannot expect *that*; but Doctor Thackeray did the Cough good, and though some Spasms do attack his Stomach from Time to Time, they are quiet at this Moment, and he does not look ill in Proportion to what has been suffered.

So now let us be merry, and count the Weeks till Summer Holydays; and *wish* if not *hope* for Mr. Charles's Company; my Daughter Sophia and her Husband Mr. Hoare will be here in July, and pretty Mrs. Mostyn and her *Boys* who might as well be *old Men* I think—for they are always sick, and when I heard last were all down in the Measles. Poor Mr. Davies used to talk of *Troubles Troubles Troubles* if you remember; he *may* talk of Troubles *now*. All his Children ill at once, and their Mamas fainting away; and the Marchioness of Bath making *Interest* to lye on *The Floor* by *her* Son Lord Weymouth's Bedside:[1] *My* Cecy plaguing him night and Day to think of nothing but Harry Mostyn.—A fine House he has had of it!! Poor dear Mr. Davies! You should write him a Letter and comfort him, and poor Mrs. Plumer.[2]

We have had a White Winter here, and now we have a Black Spring. No Cuckoo come yet, no Swallows arrived from Palæstine and Ægypt,——for 'tis there they spend our coldest Months you know; and Ceylon is the Place they never leave at all. The Thrushes did try to sing once, but I fancy they got *sore Throats* for Bachygraig Wood was never so thin of Vocal performers, and our Plantations afford scarcely Six Songs in a Week.

Lleweney Forest fills with Rooks however: Lord and Lady Kirkwall are come home thank God, quite well and happy; but we could hardly hear one another speak for the Noise of those building Crows. Was not it very good of Uncle to let me go and spend a *Whole day* at dear Lleweney Hall? I have had but that one Holyday these 7 Months; never have stept into a [horse-drawn] Carriage, or

April 1808 185

dined at a Friends house since I carried Miss Sharpe to Bodylwyddan last October the first Week of the Month. And when Lord K—— heard Mr. Piozzi could eat nothing but Fish, they drew the Pond directly; and I brought him home some nice Perch, Tench &c. But he was *poorly* then and could not eat: I left Mrs. Jones of Pontriffeth[3] and Mr. Roberts the Vicar to keep him company, but they were all glad to see me come home at sunset, because he had a Spasm just as Dinner came on Table, and I fancy frighted them a little. He is expecting [a] Letter from *Your* Mr. Shephard soon——and a good Account of dear Salusbury and his Improvements. It is very pleasing to me that you feel yourself well-treated by every Body: I hope you will long find it so; but constant Kindness—deserve it how we will,—is no more to be hoped for than *Earthly* Immortality. Let us do the *best*, and enjoy the *most* we can with Innocence and a clear Conscience. I am no Cynical old Monitress as you may see, but my Dear Lad's ever Affectionate / Aunt / H: L: Piozzi.

Text: Ry. 585.8. *Address:* Master Salusbury / at the Rev: / T: Shephard's / Enborne Cottage / near Newbury / Berkshire. *Postmark:* DENBIGH 224.

1. The eldest son of the marchioness of Bath was Thomas Thynne (1796–1837), Viscount Weymouth.
2. Mrs. Plumer was the housekeeper at RD's school in Streatham.
3. "Mrs. Jones of Pontriffeth" [Pontruffeth] was Sarah Jones, wife of Joseph Jones.

TO MARGARET WILLIAMS

[ca. April 1808][1]

My dear Miss Williams's

Letters are always welcome and always desired. But we shall not reckon ourselves much among the *merry Ringers* till Mr. Piozzi's Health mends; and it is bad enough now.

Sir John and Lady Williams contribute very kindly to my very few Comforts. She lends my Sick Husband the Bed-chair, which was useful when her Ladyship lay in every Year, but She purposes putting that Exploit off for a while now, and your Brother says Three Couple and a Fidler suffice to make up a Domestic Ball: though I seem to think 8 necessary for a regular Cotillion. Joking apart, they are looking particularly well this Year, and I am Sure dear Sir John has taken no Crosses sincerely to Heart, or he would not grow fat as he does. We have Sickness round the Country tho', Sore Eyes and Typhus Fever; and my London Letters give no pleasant Bulletin of the Metropolis's State as to *health*.

With Regard to the unaccountable Passion entertained for Buonaparte there, it does not certainly confine itself to Booksellers: *They* poor Souls! would *sell* whatever Ladies, Lords, &c. would wish to *buy*.

For those who live to please; must *please* to *Live*——and charming Mrs. Lutwyche must have witnessed his preternatural Powers of fascinating Fools into his open Mouth—upon the Continent.[2]

I know no Person indeed more competent to converse upon such Subjects than *She* is, who saw the very *beginning* of this monstrous Revolution made in the Minds of Men. She is a Sweet Lady, and I am flattered by her kind Remembrance: *do* ask her what is become of Cornelia Knight? And whether She ever got a Pension or no.[3]

General Whitelock is also said to have owed much to a *fashionable* Fondness on this trying Occasion:[4] His Lady is sister to the Universal Favourite of Gay and Great,—Monk Lewis.[5]

Mr. Siddons has pleased *many* People by *his* Will, and nobody ever pleased *all:* I hear Complaints that he prefered his Widow to his Children; but as it is a Preference not likely to produce Imitation; The World will forgive, and her Family will be civil to her. I felt sincerely sorry for his Death.[6]

Your little Bunch of Primroses is a pretty, tasteful Mode of making us believe that spring is come, or coming. The East Winds keep all Effect of it away here: not a Gooseberry Leaf ventures out or if it does, is seen to curl *up* with the blight directly, and look like Parsley fried round a Dish of Soles. Soles however, or any Fish but Sparlings do we never see; and Mr. Piozzi can eat so few Things, and them with an Appetite made so capricious by Sickness, that 'tis dreadful. His Complaints are all slighter tho' than they were last Year; The Gout less painful, and the Cough less pertinacious: I often wonder *why he is so ill?*

Mrs. Mostyn leaves the Country next Week, so I believe does Dr. Myddelton——They used to call on me now and then, but I must depend on *Letters* for News of the living World: Yours are always charming—are the Pump Room Conversations come out? I saw private Memoirs of our British Court advertised, and suppose it will be in the Style of the Bath Characters——and *then* the London Booksellers——You shall see, will be hasty and liberal in their Purchases.[7] Fine Times to live in! But no Reading of any other Sort will go down.

In the mean Time Your dear Babies at Bodylwyddan study the Bible, and "I think Mamma—says my Godson to Lady Williams; that my Brother and I are very like Jacob and Esau,[8] he loves to sit and read with his Mother like Rebecca's favourite—but *for my Part* I am fondest of following Papa into the Fields."

Was there ever such a Darling in the World? ? And not five Years old? ? Do tell Mr. and Miss Wickens the Story, with my Compliments.[9] You never name our cousin Thelwalls, and my Paper will not hold half my good Wishes to my Dear Bath Friends. But believe me ever and every *Your* own / H: L: P.

Text: Victoria and Albert Museum Library. *Address:* Miss Williams / Upper Park Street / St. James's / Bath. *Postmark:* DENBIGH.

1. This letter may be dated ca. April 1808 on the basis of the following evidence: the guilt of General Whitelocke, decided 18 March, was sufficiently accepted to be a matter of gossip; William Siddons's will had been proved 2 April; *The Private History of the Court of England* was published ca. 6 April.
2. William Lutwyche (1745–1823) of 12 Marlborough Buildings, Bath, had married Mary, née Thomas (1753–1845). She had been and would be again a frequent traveler to France, where she had many friends among the royalists.

3. In 1805 Ellis Cornelia Knight had accepted an appointment as companion to Queen Charlotte. She was to hold this place until 1813, when she exchanged it for a similar position in the household of Princess Charlotte. See also HLP to SL, 1 March 1786, n. 9.

4. John Whitelocke (1757–1833) appears in the Army Lists as a colonel in the Sixth West India Regiment of Foot (1 September 1795); as a major general (18 June 1798); as a lieutenant general (30 October 1805), transferred to the Eighty-ninth Regiment of Foot. He is so carried in the lists in 1806 and 1807, but in the latter year his name was lined out with the notation "cashiered."

What is summed up here is Whitelocke's defeat at Buenos Aires and his subsequent court-martial. The news of his defeat began to appear, e.g., in *The Times*, 1, 3, 13, 14 September.

Whitelocke returned to England 7 November 1807 and his trial began 28 January at Chelsea. In the National Army Museum Archives (MS. 6807–275) there is a transcript of the proceedings against him for his part in the failed mission to Buenos Aires. Four charges ranged from inadequate planning to shameful surrender. The charges cover four full folio sheets plus an additional four lines of the fifth. The notes on the court martial proceedings consist of ca. 115 folio manuscript sheets.

See also *The Proceedings of a General Court Martial, Held at Chelsea Hospital, on Thursday, January 28, 1808, and continued, by Adjournment, till Tuesday, March 15, For the Trial of Lieut. Gen. Whitelocke, Late Commander-in-Chief of the Forces in South America*, 2 vols. (London, 1808).

5. Whitelocke's wife, Mary (1759–1832), was the daughter of William Lewis of Cornwall, Jamaica. Her brother Matthew was for a time deputy secretary at war and the father of the novelist, Matthew Gregory ["Monk"] Lewis (1775–1818). She was not Monk Lewis's sister but his aunt. See *The Bristol Cathedral Register, 1669–1837*, ed. C. R. Hudleston (1933), p. 54, in the Bristol City Record office.

6. William Siddons's will was signed 28 December 1804; a codicil was added 24 February 1806. He left his elder son, Henry, the property in Great Marlborough Street and his other son, George John, the property in Gower Street. To his only daughter, Cecilia, he left £2,000 (raised to £4,000 in the codicil) to be paid her at the age of twenty-one or the day of her marriage. He also bequeathed an investment of £2,000 in government or real securities, the interest to go toward her maintenance and education until she reached twenty-one or was married. All the residue of his estate and effects went to SS, whom he named sole executrix. See P.R.O., Prob. 11/1478/336.

7. In the *Monthly Literary Advertiser* (p. 27) for 9 April 1808 (also *The Times*, 6 April) appeared a notice of the following: *The Private History of the Court of England*, 2 vols. (London: Crosby and Co., 1808). The authorship has been attributed to Sarah Green, the novelist.

8. For the story of Jacob and Esau, see Gen. 25:29–34. For Esau the "cunning hunter, a man of the field," see Gen. 25:27, and for Jacob beloved by Rebecca, Gen. 25:28.

9. Son of the Reverend Thomas Wickins, Thomas (1767–1842) entered Rugby in 1782 and, at the age of seventeen, matriculated at Trinity College, Cambridge, where he received a B.A. (1789) and M.A. (1792). He died at Vaynol, Saint Asaph.

HLP knew him as MW's friend and a resident of Bath as early as 1805. In 1807 he moved to Park Street, for the first five years living at No. 11 and then at No. 43 until 1819, when his name disappeared from the "Walcot Parish Poor Rates," 1805–20, in the Guildhall, Bath.

His sister Martha (1762–1820) lived with him in Park Street and was therefore a neighbor of MW. Martha continued to live there until her death. She is buried in Saint Swithin's churchyard, Bath. See "Walcot Parish Burial Records," C.R.O., Somerset.

10. For the Thelwalls, see HLP Q, 6–7 March 1805, n. 2; to Robert Myddelton, 28 March 1805, n.5.

TO THE REVEREND THOMAS SEDGWICK WHALLEY

Brynbella Wednesday Night
11: May 1808.

It was very kindly and sweetly done of You Dear Mr. Whalley, to write me such a Letter; Your continued Friendship will bring Comfort to poor little Brynbella, which has so long been a *House of Mourning* for lost Health—it has nearly forgotten to be a *house of Feasting:* Such Company will at least revive our Spirits after this long, melancholy, Miserable Winter; which I thought would never have left us till the longest Day.¹ Our longest Nights were all past in Pain and Sorrow; yet I do think Mr. Piozzi bore the Torment of his Hands and Feet better than he does the Sicknesses and Spasms, which *now* from Time to Time affect his Stomach: We must not however choose our own Afflictions, but take with Patience those that are sent by Heaven.

Lord Keith is going to take his Wife a Tour through Scotland, when all the London Gayeties are over; Mr. and Mrs. Merrick Hoare will come here in July and August.

God grant us but Health to enjoy their Society, and *Yours* Dear Sir; than whose, none is more justly valued by my Husband, and by Your always Obliged and grateful and / faithful / H: L: P.

You shall have a good Bed, and Mr. Almon shall be well provided,² and the Footman will do well enough. Only come soon, and come well, and tell me the Day we may expect you——tho God knows we are never able to stir from home.

Text: Berg Collection +. *Address:* Rev: Thomas Sedgwick Whalley at / The Rev: George Warrington's / Wrexham / Denbighshire *Postmark:* DENBIGH <   >.

1. HLP responds to TSW's letter, dated from Wrexham on 10 May (Ry. 564.10): "You will easily believe that I cannot be within 25: Miles of you and Mr. Piozzi, without earnestly wishing to pay my respects to you, at your charming Bryn Bella. . . . it would be an high gratification, and cordial to my Spirits, to pass a Week under your friendly and hospitable Roof. *Yours* has been the House of Dance and Song, while *Mine* was the House of Mourning [caused by the death of Augusta Utica, TSW's second wife, in October 1807]. . . . I am wandering about, to recruit my Health and divert my Mind from sad Thoughts and useless recollections and regrets. . . .
"Can you receive me, my own Valet, and a Footman, about a fortnight hence?"
According to his letter of 14 May (Ry. 564.11), TSW planned to arrive on Wednesday, "the 25th instant . . . soon after four."
2. William Walter Slade Amans, or Amons (fl. 1780–1830), was TSW's confidential servant. According to the latter in a letter to Arthur Anstey, 17 January 1815, Amans was "reduced to service by a thoughtless and extravagant father. . . . he would have inherited a considerable estate, had not his unnatural grandfather, Mr. Slade, revenged his mother's refusal to marry her cousin, the Duke of Bolton—marrying Mr. Amans against his consent—on his grandson's Innocent head. Through some savings, and various handsome legacies . . . Amans is independent of me" (Wickham 2:389).

TO WILLIAM MAKEPEACE THACKERAY

By Dr. Norris[1]

Thursday
26: May 1808.

My dear Doctor Thackeray

has once or twice invited us to Chester; and *now* I shall like of all Things to go Thither: not to a Friend's House *on any Account* it will *not do* at all: I am very serious, and very sad about it; and by no means coquetting with Yours and Mrs. Thackeray's Kindness.²

That: shall if you please be exerted to procure us the following Apartments.

A good Sitting Room, and near it——on the same Floor—a large Bed Chamber with Two Beds for Mr. Piozzi and Dunscombe.

A Bed Room any where for me, and one not very far from me for my Maid.

Now if this can be found at a good Hotel where our Dinner will be provided by People of the House, and *no Stairs* for my Master can scarce bear even the Motion of being *carried* without fainting away—an Hotel will be *best,* because in Lodgings we shall have Dinner to provide &c., and that would be *Sad Work.*

He can bear a Post Chaise or the Garden Chair better than that sort of *Sedan* Motion of the Braces or Brancard;[3] and Mr. Shephard says that our Nephew shall be at Chester on the 21st.

We mean to come on the 14th if we can, and being *near your* will be an immense Comfort to *me:* so will the Sight of the Child, whom we shall bring hither for the Holydays.

Mr. Piozzi can be carried up Stairs *when we come* and down Stairs again *when we go away;* but that is all he *can* do: This Arthrital Syncope pursues him so very closely, and sometimes *Shortness* of *Breath* beside.

I hope we shall have *large* Apartments for that Reason, as he will feel *choked* in small ones——and Illness does bring on *so* much *Nicety!* and I am *so* desirous of help to bear our Calamitous Situation!

Dear Sir write to me! I am really much distressed tho' very glad that instead of *France, Spain,* or even *Italy* in these Days, Your Obliged and faithful Servant / H: L: Piozzi / is living at / *Brynbella.*

Text: Hyde Collection. *Address:* Doctor Thackeray / Chester. *Postmark:* DENBIGH 224.

1. Richard Wise Norris, who practiced surgery at Little Sutton near Chester. By 1826 he was a member of the Royal College of Surgeons and a licentiate of the Society of Apothecaries.
2. See *Thraliana* 2:1092.
3. Braces: straps for suspending carriage body from springs. Brancard: horse-drawn litter.

TO JOHN SALUSBURY PIOZZI SALUSBURY

Saturday
11: June 1808.
Brynbella

Nothing so necessary My dear Boy as to shew Politeness to such Friends: It is the way to *have* Friends, and to keep them; and I am desirous you should pay proper Compliments to all Your Acquaintances and ours *too.*

We shall rejoyce to see You again most sincerely; Uncle is certainly better just now, so we shall set off *next* Tuesday the 14: of June for fear of any thing stopping us.

Mr. Whalley who was here on a visit found Mr. Piozzi so *unwell* that he quite *pressed* us to go soon, and get Advice from Doctor Thackeray concerning the Bath Waters for next Winter, as the Complaint is now wholly in the Stomach.[1]

You once asked me about our Law Suit with Mr. Giles: he has submitted at last, and paid the Money, Mr. Charles Shephard managed *so* very nicely for us; Pray tell *Your* Mr. Shephard how much we feel obliged to his Son. I am happy to see your handwriting mend every Letter, it is not so trifling a Thing as many think it—to write a plain clear Character—because after all if People cannot make out one's Words, what signifies writing at all?

Our Master puts his *Veto* on the Post Chaise, You must come from Shrewsbury to Chester by the Coach——and as I said the longest day will be the happiest——So till then and ever God bless you, my dear Salusbury, assuring yourself that I am most truly / Your Affectionate Aunt / H: L: Piozzi.

Mr. Piozzi unites his Compliments with mine to All the Enborne Family.[2] Take Care of yourself dear child, and come to no Mischief before we meet. I shall be very anxious.——

Text: Ry. 585.9. *Address:* Mr. Shephard's / Enborne Cottage / near Newbury / Berkshire (In JSPS's hand, "Received the 14th of June. Does not require an Answer").

1. On 1 June, TSW was at Jackson's Hotel, Chester, writing "warm Thanks" for his Brynbella visit. As he continued: "I have seen Dr. Thackeray, who hopes that he may be able to drive the *Foul Fiend* from his Strong Hold in Dear Mr. Piozzi's Stomac and so far to renovate him, as to make his removal to Bath, in October, as safe, as it will, I trust in God!—be salutary. Between ourselves, I do not think the Apartment which Dr. Thackeray has chosen in this hotel [is] in unison with Mr. Piozzi's Taste, or the state of his Spirits. . . . they are sombre, at Mid Day, and their principal Object is a *Dunghill;* the fumes of which infect the air of the Bedchamber." He suggested four alternate rooms, still in Jackson's Hotel, concluding, "Mrs. Jackson *awaits your* decision; and whichever apartment Mr. Piozzi may prefer, write her but three Lines and she engages that it shall be made comfortable against the specified Day of your arrival" (Ry. 564.12). See *Thraliana* 2:1092.
2. Thomas Shephard had married Anne Parke Goddard (who died pre-1829). Apart from Charles Mitchell Smith, their only son, they had three unmarried daughters: Maria (d. ca. 1830); Elizabeth Charlotte Anne (d. 2 May 1861); Harriet Caroline Butler (d. ca. 1847). Information about the Shephards may be found in C.R.O., Berkshire, D/EX 360/14.

TO THE REVEREND THOMAS SEDGWICK WHALLEY

Jacksons Hotel
Wensday 15: June [1808].

I told Dear Mr. Whalley that I would write from Chester, and so I *do* write from Chester Wensday 15 June——and I do say that when we arrived Yester Noon—My Master's Pulse was better than mine:——and for that Fact Doctor Thackeray is good and Sufficient Authority—but then I have had a bilious Attack which begun Threatening whilst you were at Brynbella——and has not shewn Intention of retreating, till *just now*.

15 June 1808 191

Thanks—8000 for the 8 Dinner Pills: they will preserve me from future seizures, and the Prescription will be easily made up by good Mr. Moore.[1]

You bade me go see a Cottage, and Dr. Thackeray calls me to see a fine House, but I defy either to amaze *me* as did the County Goal in this old City. I hope you went to see how without any Exaggeration we may call it a Model of Simple Magnificence. The Cleanliness so perfect, the Chapel so impressive; The Baths and *Liveries*, to wash, and to *distinguish* the Prisoners so well judged.[2]—They are setting up a Statue of Britannia on the Front, and Dr. Thackeray asked me for a Motto. A Poet replied I has already made it in these Lines.

> Her Poor to Palaces Britannia brings,
> (is fit for)
> St. James's Hospital *may do for* Kings.[3]

It must have cost an Enormous Sum. It is true that The Author of Marmion has received from the Scotch Booksellers a Thousand Guineas for a Thousand Lines?[4]

Sure we are running over with Money!! yet that Fact was told me by no bad Authority, and I like Marmion very much *indeed*:[5] tho' the return to Gothick Architecture and Tales of the darker Ages may not perhaps evince true Taste—— but rather Weariness of that which long was deemed such——as poor Graham said of human Life, in his neglected Telemachus,

> Hence noble Souls
> Tir'd of the tedious and disrelish'd Good,
> Seek their Enjoyment in acknowledg'd Ill:
> Danger and Toil and Pain.[6]

Adieu dear Mr. Whalley; you are treading

> Old Caledonia Stern and wild
> Meet Nurse for a Poetic Child,
> Land of Brown Heath and shaggy Wood &c.[7]

I should not wonder if you met Lord and Lady Keith in your Rambles; they are gone Northward, and what Lady Kirkwall *told* and you so readily *believed*; I understand to be quite true.

Once more Adieu and a good Journey! And may you never hear worse Tydings of my good Husband than are now / reported by Your true / and faithful and Obliged / H: L: P.

He cannot walk, nor he cannot eat; yet he certainly < >, does not fright his Friends and his Wife as when you spent a Week with us.

Text: Berg Collection +. *Address:* Rev: Thos. Sedgwick Whalley / Kirkton House / near Bath Gate / West Lothian. *Postmark:* CHESTER JUN 15 1808 190; B JUN 17 1808; JUN 1808 20.

1. HLP responds to TSW's note of 3 June (Ry. 564.13): "The Rooms, my Dear Madam, will be ready for Mr. Piozzi, at the time appointed. Should he find it fatigueing to be carried up and down so many Stairs—tho they *are easy*—Mrs. Jackson will have the Bed taken down, in the front Chamber. . . . I will leave half a dozen of my Dinner Pills for you, with Mrs. Jackson and the Prescription for them. One taken when you have eaten about half your *great* Dinner, will be sufficient, to carry on Digestion fair and softly. . . . Dr <Tissot's> *Prescription for Antibilious Dinner Pills*

Of Aloes—One Ounce and a half.—
Of Mastic—Half an Ounce.—

Powder these Ingredients *finely* and separately, mix them with a sufficient Quantity of Syrup of Wormwood to make them into a *Paste,* and put three Grains of the Paste, to each Pill.—N:B:—Great care must be taken that the Aloes are *properly prepared* in a strong Tincture of Liquorice."

2. The county jail "is from the nature of the ground built on two levels. The upper line of building on the east side consists of the turnkey's rooms, the large and airy yard of the male debtors; on the west side the female debtors' rooms and court-yard, with the prison hospital adjoining. Both these yards, from their elevated situation, command a delightful view of the fine ruins of Beeston-castle, the Peckforton, Broxton, and Carden hills, &c. through the iron railing. . . . In the centre is the gaoler's house, projecting from the line of the upper level, so as to completely command a view of every part of the prison. The chapel of the prison is between the upper and lower level. . . . On the lower level . . . are the cells for solitary confinement and condemned criminals; also the very complete cold and warm baths, in which every prisoner committed, is made to wash himself, his clothes taken away, steamed and stoved, in an excellent apparatus for the purpose, himself clad in gaol dress, and his own apparel carefully preserved, to be put on the day of trial. In a semi-octagon arrangement of the lower level under the gaoler's house, are five large airy yards for felons [with suitable sleeping rooms] . . . inclosed by the thick and lofty exterior stone wall, forming the boundary of the prison. These useful and highly ornamental buildings, not only raise admiration of the architect, but must command the grateful thanks of the public to those county magistrates who selected the designs for them, and have granted the means of prosecuting and completing the expensive undertaking." See Joseph Hemingway, *History of the City of Chester, from its Foundation to the Present Time,* 2 vols. (Chester, 1831), 2:182–83.

3. See the Reverend James Bramston (ca. 1694–1744), *The Man of Taste. Occasion'd by an Epistle of Mr. Pope on that Subject,* in Dodsley 1:290. Substitute "may serve" for HLP's uncertain "May do."

4. In February 1808 *Marmion; a tale of Flodden field* (with introductory epistles to each canto and antiquarian notes) had been printed by the establishment of J. Ballantyne for A. Constable and Company.

The publication history of *Marmion* goes back to 1806, when Constable heard that Scott was writing it. The bookseller was prepared to pay a thousand guineas for it without having seen a line. Scott accepted the offer. But Constable could not raise the capital, and he allowed a half of the copyright to be shared by Miller and Murray. Not until 1811 (actually 1810) did the names of Miller and Murray appear on the title page. See Sir Herbert Grierson, *Sir Walter Scott, Bart.* (London: Constable and Co., 1936), p. 86.

5. HLP's pleasure in *Marmion* prompted her to write twenty-two lines of uncertain couplets, which begin:

> Oh Marmion! tho to Critic cold
> Thy Pegasus may seem too bold,
> When forth he bursts with broken rein,
> Snorting across th' ensanguin'd Plain
> My heart his flight pursues. . . .

See "Verses 1," pp. 106–7; *Thraliana* 2:1095.

6. The title page of this never-performed work (dedicated to Lord Lyttelton) indicates the following: "*Telemachus, A Mask.* By the Rev. George Graham [d. 1767], M.A., Fellow of *King's-College,* Cambridge (London: Printed for A. Millar, in the *Strand,* 1763)." The speech of Telemachus (p. 41) varies slightly from HLP's version.

7. See Scott's *The Lay of the Last Minstrel* (1805), canto 6, stanza 2.

TO THE REVEREND THOMAS SEDGWICK WHALLEY

Brynbella Wensday
29: June 1808.

My dear Mr. Whalley
 will not wonder to hear what a miserable Exploit our Journey to Chester turned out.—A fine Frolic truly! but Thanks be to God we are safe home again, and brought the Boy back much improved.

The Apartments were admirable, and one carrying up served for the whole Time; my poor hapless Husband never moved again till we came away, and now lies on His Back with a raging Foot—Two monstrous Wounds in it——and never touches Food: but the Spasms are gone, and We must be glad of *that*.[1]

You have fine Weather and good Health I hope, and are as happy as is wished / you by your ever Obliged / and faithful / H: L: P.

When we came home we found this Letter.[2]

Text: Hyde Collection. *Address:* Rev: Thos. Sedgwick Whalley / at Vans Agnew Esq. / Boness / West Lothian. *Postmark:* DENBIGH 224; JUL 1808.

1. *Thraliana* 2:1094.
2. TSW's letter, which prompted HLP's response of 29 June, is missing.

TO CALEB HILLIER PARRY

Brynbella Fryday
15: July 1808.

My Dear Sir[1]
 Tho' my Congratulations *do* come late, they are no less Sincere: My heart rejoyces in *Your* Happiness who have so often contributed to *mine:* and who knows whether your Skill has not enabled me to enjoy the Account of your Child's Felicity.[2]

But this is a Soliciting Letter, as well as a congratulating one; poor Maria Dore who brings it in her Hand, is a good Girl; and a Sick Girl: and wishes admittance into the List of those who receive help from Your Dispensary. I took her as a Kitchen Maid at Bath, the Winter before last, and thinking her merely *Chlorotic*, doubted not but that wholesome Food, change of Air, Sea Bathing and Aloetic Med'cines would restore her health. They have however all been tried, and tried in *vain* with regard to her Lameness: every thing else is as it should be, but how can She do my Work, or any one's else, with such a Knee as hers is? I shewed it Mr. Cam before we left Bath, and *He* said, (so did Mr. Bowen) that She had no Complaint except what *Time would cure*.[3] A long Time has elapsed however, and her Lame Leg continues. *Do* Dear Sir save the poor Creature from Destruction if you *can:* My Patience is worne out; and I must have efficient Servants in a House where the Master is a *confirmed Invalid* as at Brynbella whence I despair of moving any more. We tried a Jaunt to Chester 28 Miles a fortnight ago; but a fresh Abscess broke out in the Foot and sent us screaming back. How Mr. Piozzi bears the immoderate Discharges these Sores occasion, I guess not; but he is clear of Spasms on the Breast while they are open, and the Cough ventures not to attack him in this pure Mountain and Marine Air: He grows exceeding lean of Course, and has no Appetite, but sleeps better than one should expect——and tho' his Voice is *low* now in Conversation, his Spirits feel the general *Excitement* of all the human Race against Tyrannic Power so exercised, as in these latter Times by Buonaparte.

Well! now we shall see if he is indeed the Hero and the Statesman we have been so often told he was: Let him conquer one ill-appointed Mass of Men resolved to resist him—and he shall be a Mars, or an *Apollo* or an Appolyon—as he pleases. He never was resisted before; he was a mere Bowl among Ninepins.[4]

I see my old Acquaintance dropping round me—like Ninepins, and am sorry for good old Mrs. Quicke,[5] but Youth is not excused any more than Age. My poor Footman Richard, whom you *do* or rather who I suppose You do *not* remember, struck with Apoplexy or Palsy at the back of my chair, the day we came home from Chester died within the Week;[6] and affected my Spirits cruelly, and those of your Patient Maria:—he was her Townsman, and I believe She expected to be buried like him in Wales if She did not hasten to live or *dye* at Bath.

Accept Dear Sir the Compliments She brings you from me and mine presenting Mrs. Parry and Miss Parry their proper Share / and believing me most / faithfully yours / H: L: Piozzi.

Text: The Yushôdô Bookstore, Tokyo (compliments of Professor Susumu Kawanishi, University of Tokyo).

1. For Caleb Hillier Parry, see HLP to PSW, 1 September [1789], n. 7.
2. HLP had read that on 21 May at Bath, John Eardley Wilmot of Bruce Castle had married Elizabeth Emma Parry (d. 1818), the fourth daughter of the doctor. See, e.g., *GM* 78, pt. 1 (1808): 458.
John Eardley Wilmot, later Eardley-Wilmot (1783–1847), was created baronet in 1821.
3. Thomas Croxall Cam was to be long a surgeon of Bath, dying there at the age of eighty-four. He was buried on 10 February 1855 in Saint Swithin's churchyard. See "Walcot Parish Burial Records," C.R.O., Somerset. His son, Thomas (1816–1900), born in Bath, carried on the family tradition as Surgeon Extraordinary to the Hereford Infirmary (*Plarr's Lives of the Fellows of the Royal College of Surgeons of England,* 2 vols. [1930], 1:188–89).
4. HLP refers to the French invasion of Spain and the resistance it aroused among the Spanish patriots abetted by England.
On 11 June, the *Courier* announced that while "Great Britain is raising her mighty arm to sustain so great a cause, the flame of patriotism extends itself more and more over Spain; and that nation, which seemed to have sunk so low, presents a scene which must fill the mind of every man with respect, admiration, and love."
On 16 June the *Courier* reported, "We are most happy to hear that Biscay has joined the provinces of Gallicia and Asturias in the great cause of Freedom." It rejoiced further in "the declarations of his Majesty's Ministers . . . to afford the Patriots all possible assistance."
By 20 June the *Courier* reported the shipment of British arms to the Patriots and by the 27th the newspaper was convinced that French tyranny had to be defeated by them. On the 13th of July it

detailed in two reports the readiness of Sir Arthur Wellesley's expedition to sail to Spain and the departure of Sir John Moore's troops to the same place.

Many Britons toasted "'Success to the Spaniards'" on the assumption "that Bonaparte after such a tide of success & possessed of such immense power, might be supposed to feel that everything wd. bend before Him; and in this instance to have overshot His mark" (Farington 9:3308).

5. Jane, née Coster, of Bristol and widow of Robert Hoblyn of Nanswhyddon, had in 1759 married John Quicke of Newton Saint Cyres, high sheriff, Devon (1757).

6. In HLP's "Pocket Book" for 1808 (N.L.W., MS. 11099A), the footman is identified only as Richard. That he died unexpectedly on 4 July is indicated by the fact that on 8 May HLP had bought him "new livery." As recorded in the "Tremeirchion Parish Burial Register," 1761–1810, Richard Paget, "Footman of Brynbella," was buried 6 July 1808. See C.R.O., Clwyd; also, HLP to PSP, [ca. 28] August 1801.

TO THE REVEREND ROBERT GRAY

Brynbella Wednesday
10th: August 1808.

Everything changes round us, to say true; and my daughters, who spent two or three days here a week ago,[1] took from me all power of sleeping in the night by the strange tales they told of *London manners,* though I was beginning to quiet my nerves about poor dear Mr. Piozzi. Perhaps the town ladies have kindly resolved on compensating the civilians of Doctors Commons for their loss in no longer condemning Spanish prizes. The unexampled crowd of divorce causes will perhaps make them rich amends. Our three time o-week paper[2] gives us so many sudden deaths, so many accidents, so many thunder storms, it's like reading the casualties at the end of the old kings' reigns in a folio history.

Text: Hayward 2:267.

1. SH and her husband spent ten days at Brynbella and CMM visited for two or three. The three then left for a mountain tour of North Wales. See *Thraliana* 2:1097.

2. The *London Evening Mail,* established 2 March 1789, was published every Monday, Wednesday, Friday. Designed for country readers as a medium between daily and weekly newspapers, it was popular among the clergy and leisure classes. See *The Newspaper Press Directory* (London, 1846), p. 59. See also HLP to LC, 17 April 1801 and n. 2.

TO JOHN SALUSBURY PIOZZI SALUSBURY

Brynbella Saturday
20: August 1808.

My dearest Salusbury

I rejoyce in your kind and comfortable Letter from Enborne; that which was dated Shrewsbury, was full of *Miseries* like those enumerated by merry Mr. Beresford. The Acquaintance you have made with the Pemberton Family will I hope end in a long and lasting Friendship[1]——and indeed I *do* wish that you would be pleased to *Anglify* your Style a little, and not write as the Foreigners do that You arrived *to* Enborne instead of *at* Enborne: how is it possible meanwhile for you to find Difficulty in learning *French?* When adopting their mode of Expression——*Je me trouve si bien a Enborne;* and *vous allez donc a Enborne* is the same—on t'other Side the Water; but *here* The first Sentence must translate the a into *at;* The second into *To.* Here's Schooling enough however; I am as tired on't as you can be, and desirous to *call another Cause* as Mr. Charles Shephard would say: we had a kind Letter from him last Wednesday, I *think* he has half a Mind to see Wales once again.

I will now tell you exactly how your Uncle is. That violent Flux of Humours from the foot is certainly lessened very much—but by no means stopt: and I thought Mr. Piozzi so well on Monday that he and I both gave Dunscombe leave to go and see the Wheat Harvest at Bottom of the Park——We were alone; I writing to Miss Williams of Bath—he—reading a Pamphlet belonging to Mr. Hoare. On a sudden he cried out Ill, Ill; Giddy, giddy: and would have rolled from the Sopha upon the Floor, had I not held him up; and kept ringing the Bell as hard as I could——a foolish Face appeared at the Door——shut it, and disappeared directly.—Oh what an Agony I was in! but he grew better, and made it possible for me to leave him and get Brandy &c. so that all was perfectly safe before Robert[2] came back from fetching Dunscombe: when he saw his Master bad, the *tall* Goose with his head up—*like a Goose,* was frighted poor Soul; and left us to our Fate. There has been no return of the Complaint—— but Wednesday Morning a Spasm so alarmed him and Dunscombe too, that he did not come as usual to Breakfast. This *last* happened at 8 o'Clock in the Morning——The Man but just got up; I saw nothing of it, except the remaining Paleness——and *that* went away quietly; leaving him what I must call *pretty well,* and *better* than when you left us.

The Kirkwalls are at Abergeley for her to bathe: he sent us some Growse Yesterday, and they are returning soon to old Lleweney Hall for purpose of entertaining Mr. and Mrs. Hoare and Cecilia Mostyn a while, before they come back hither and finish their Visit to North Wales——meaning the *Londoners,* because 'tis most likely Mrs. Mostyn will stay at Segroid with her Sons—at least till their Holydays are over.

Mrs. Myddelton—*pretty* Mrs. Myddelton, has been very Ill;[3] but I hope will be well enough to meet the Party here on the 29th next Monday sennight; when you remember they promised to return from <Snowdon> &c.——and I hope Uncle will be pretty well too——he certainly appears *less* ill than whilst they were at Brynbella——a propòs You should have sent them Your Compliments. They like yourself were delighted with Warwick Castle; is it not a Grand Place?[4] You remember Dear Old Mr. Hamilton at Bath, who had the fine Picture; Lord Warwick is his Nephew.[5]

Tell me if *the way* is now to direct to Titmice such as yourself J: P: Salusbury *Esq.* instead of *Master* Salusbury——it seems to me very comical if it is so. I have written a long confidential Letter about You to Mr. Charles Shephard mentioning the private Tutor we talked of: I am more intimate with *him* you know than with Your Mr. Shephard: but I *will* write to him about it, and beg him to find me a proper Person against Christmas.

Uncle says *he* can't write, but insists on my bidding you mind what he said to you last. What *I* say is that / I am ever Dear Child your / Affectionate Aunt H: L: P.

Text: Ry 585.10. *Address:* Master Salusbury / at The Rev: T: Shephard's / Enborne Cottage / Near Newbury / Berkshire. *Postmark:* DENBIGH 22 <   >.

1. Anna Maria Emma Smythe (d. 1828) had in 1792 become the second wife of Captain Edward Pemberton (1762–1820), of Longnor, county Salop. At this time they had three children: one surviving son, Edward William Smythe (1793–1862); JSPS's future wife, Harriet Maria (1794–1831); Letitia Caroline (b. 1800). Also living with them was Frances (b. 1789), the only surviving child of Edward Pemberton and his first wife, Frances, née Yaldwin (d. 1790).
For information about the Pembertons of Longnor, see Florentia C. Herbert, "The History of Wrockwardine," *Transactions of the Shropshire Archeological Society*, 4th ser., 9 (1923–24): 81–117 (Shrewsbury: Printed for the Society, Hobson and Co., Wellington, Salop).
2. On 20 July 1808, "Robert a footman came in service." See HLP's "Pocket Book," 1808. He succeeded the late Richard Paget.
3. May Myddelton of Gwaynynog was frequently pregnant, producing eight children in ten years. For the Robert Myddeltons, see HLP to LC, 15 September 1794, n. 1.
4. For Warwick Castle, see HLP to SL, 9 September 1787, n. 6.
5. That is, the Reverend Frederick Hamilton, now ninety. For his nephew George Greville, second earl Brooke of Warwick Castle and earl of Warwick, see HLP to SL, 23 August [17]88, n. 3.

TO JOHN SALUSBURY PIOZZI SALUSBURY

Brynbella
Saturday 3: September 1808.

My dearest Salusbury

Your Letter was a good one and very kind, and deserves an explicit Answer, such as I always give; for Concealment is somewhat resembling Treachery, when used between You and Me. We are got more happily thro' our Company Week than I expected on Monday Morning——29th of August. The Hoares were then at Lleweney, and we had asked Dr. Myddelton and the Williamses to meet them; and Uncle passed a good Night Sunday, and I was preparing my household Matters: when Dunscombe sent for me to help put our poor Master back to Bed—so strong and so often repeated were the Spasms. Lake[1] galloped away for Mr. Moore, but Brandy, and that Mixture of Dr. Vaughan's recovered our Patient,[2] and he rallied up his Spirits, received his Company, eat a good Dinner, and did not quit the Drawingroom till 9 o'Clock at Night. On Tuesday came Spasm again at 5 or 6 o'Clock, and *we* left the dinner Table; and Mr. Hoare took *his* Place, and Cecilia took *mine*, when like Macbeth

> *We* had destroy'd the Mirth, broke the good Meeting
> With most admir'd Disorder.[3]

Since *then* all has gone on well, and even cheerfully; and he has been out every day in the Wheel Chair, and my Pulse rises—as the Stocks do,—upon *Good News*.[4] So much for Brynbella.

Let me now find that you consider Mr. Shephard as your *only Tutor:* he will be good to you (happen what will) and with him you will be safe and happy—— nor think of removal excepting from Enborne to Christ Church. Oh pray be diligent and study hard; and recollect that Knowlege is a Tree which if not planted young, will afford you no shade to sit under when old. The Comforts of Literature give such *Independance* to the Mind, no one can rob you of them. Do not lose Youthful Opportunities of storing your head with Knowlege; *pray* do not: and do not pretend like English Boys to scorn learning French; whilst you even spell the Word *Letter* in the French way—*Lettre!* how odd! you never could have seen it so spelt. English Misses do now and then mistake Plural Numbers for Genitive Cases as you do; And vice versa. But *Men* had better confine that Mode of Spelling to *Sign Boards* which I have seen exhibit Horse's and Coach's to *Lett* and *That* is no worse than your saying you love the *Pemberton's*.

Here comes dear Mr. Moore—for no Reason tho' thank God but to dinner; and bids me give his best Regards to you. I like Sir Richard Hoare very much indeed; he is a Man of no Foppery but most Gentlemanlike Manners;[5] and an indefatigable Spirit of Research for Antiquities of every kind——his Friend Mr. Fenton is agreable enough too.[6] Mrs. Mostyn—with one *Y* in her Name *no more;* left our Party to take her Children *to* the Sea and *from* the Sea; She never lets those Boys rest in a Place.

My Joke about the Tea Chest had good luck at Enborne indeed; Mr. Charles Shepherd sent me a better still made by a Westminster Boy. Did *your* Mr. Shephard ever see a Joke paraphased? I dare say not—but Lady Kirkwall[7] would have the *Tu doces* explained to her, so I sent her the following Verses which have no sense at all in them unless you tell how the Tea Chest was made out of a Weeping Willow Tree which Pope planted at Twickenham,[8] and Lady Howe cut down[9] (I *think* it was Lady Howe;)[10] a very few Months ago.

So God bless you, and farewell; and love your Affectionate Aunt / H: L: P.

> Thou Tea Chest! form'd from Pope's fam'd Willow,
> Which serv'd our Poet for his Pillow,
> When round his Head gay Visions rose
> Of bright Belinda and her Beaux;
> Torne from thy Thames to Scenes thus rude,
> How much of Life's Vicissitude
>   Thou teachest!
> Presented by a noble Dame
> From thee I hop'd inspiring Flame,
> But No; that Indian Shrub alone
> Which at thy Birth was scarcely known,
> In fragrant Fumes of fresh Bohea
> Is all I can inhale from thee
>   Thou Tea Chest.[11]

Text: Ry. 585.11. *Address:* John Piozzi Salusbury Esq.

1. The Piozzis' steward AL (Alexander Leak).
2. For Dr. Vaughan, see HLP to Q, [31 December 1804], n. 16.
3. *Macbeth,* 3.4.108–9.
4. But in *Thraliana* at this time HLP wrote: "M[r] Piozzi's Health declines rapidly, or People *think* it does: *I* am not so confident. . . . Doctors and Apothecaries we seem to have done with—& to confess the truth They did no Good: what Good is done, appears to be effected by Brandy. with Opium Draughts occasionally" (2:1098–99).
5. Sir Richard Colt Hoare began his research by discovering and writing about classical antiquities. But he also devoted himself to the history and antiquities of Wales and of his own county, Wiltshire. See, e.g., *The Itinerary of Archbishop Baldwin through Wales, A.D. 1188, by Giraldus de Barri, translated into English, and illustrated with Views, Annotations, and a Life of Giraldus,* 2 vols. (1806).
The reason for HLP's interest in Sir Richard Hoare and Richard Fenton is explained in her letters to LC, 24 September 1808; 3 October 1808.
6. Richard Fenton (1746–1821) was a topographer and poet. Born in South Wales, he moved at an early age to London. In time he entered the Middle Temple and, while there, came to know SJ, Garrick, Goldsmith, etc. After being called to the bar, he attended the circuits in Wales. From about 1800 onward he studied and wrote poetry, forming close friendships with William Lisle Bowles and Sir Richard Colt Hoare.
7. Perhaps Lady Kirkwall did not understand the joke but, according to *Thraliana* 2:1090 and nn. 2 and 3, she "has given me a Tea Chest made of Pope's Weeping Willow, The Willow he planted at Twickenham—Tis a great Curiosity." The entry is dated 1 May 1808.
8. One story has it that Pope watched Lady Suffolk unpack a gift wrapped in willow branches which had been sent to her from Spain. The poet saved a slip, planted it, and watched it become the famous willow at Twickenham. See *Notes and Queries* 3 (14 February 1863): 128–29.
9. In 1807 Pope's house at Twickenham was razed by Lady Howe even as she dug up the trees and gardens. Her "vandalism" was prompted by annoyance with the visitors who came to pay homage to the poet. See Maynard Mack, *The Garden and the City* (Toronto and Oxford: University of Toronto and Oxford University Presses, 1969), pp. 17n. , 266, 283.
Another legend has it that the willow died in 1801 and its bark was cut into relics, but the evidence is "ambiguous" (ibid., p. 266).
10. Sophia Charlotte Howe (1762–1835), suo jure Baroness Howe of Langar (1814), had married first in 1787 the Honorable Penn Assheton Curzon (d. 1797) and second in 1812 Sir Jonathan Wathen Waller (1769–1853), cr. baronet (1814).
11. The poem was written shortly after HLP received the tea chest. It appears as an addendum in *Thraliana* 2:1090–91, n. 3; and was written for preservation in "Verses 1," p. 104.

TO THE REVEREND ROBERT GRAY

Brynbella
Wednesday, 14th September 1808.

Sir Richard Hoare is an antiquarian you know, and was looking out for curiosities, but found nothing much worth his notice. Indeed the superficies of our earth exhibits at present matters more important than one could hope to find in its bosom; and Mr. Piozzi, troubled as he is with spasms on his stomach and cretaceous abscesses almost on every joynt, still feels a patriotic fervour at his heart, desiring life chiefly for the comfort of hearing that his lovely country has shaken off the yoke of Buonaparte.[1] He sees bright visions likewise, *ægri somnia*, of Austria and Russia joining to assist; but I remind him of an old book we saw in the library at Vienna, entitled 'Ung Livre des *Oysivetez des Empereurs*, souuerainement escrit *en Phroge.*'[2]

Text: Hayward 2:267

1. GP's *"ægri somnia"* could not wipe away the fact that Italy was in 1808 largely a French possession from the Italian Alps and Piedmont to Naples. Symbolic of what happened to Italy was the announcement in English newspapers on 25 June 1808 that Rome and the papal states had been annexed to the kingdom of Italy, that Tuscany, Parma, and Placentia had been joined to France. See also Farington 9:3304.

2. HLP's dismissal of wasted regal power—particularly in beaten, "idle" Russian and Austrian emperors—is aptly caught in the title of a book (ca. fifteenth century) she saw in Vienna. We have not been able to trace it. According to Dr. Otto Mazal, director of the Österreichische Nationalbibliothek in Vienna: "Die Recherchen der Katalogabteilung im Fonds der gedruckten Bücher verliefen negativ; ebenso ergab die Durchsicht des Kapitels 'Französische Literatur' in abendländischen Handschriften (im Katalog 'Tabulae codicum manuscriptorum Graecos et orientales in Bibliotheca Palatina Vindobonensi asservatorum. Wien 1864–1912) keinen Anhaltspunkt. Ich bedaure, derzeit nicht zur Lösung des Rätsels beitrangen zu können." ["Searches through the catalogues of printed books have proven negative; similarly a search of the section 'French Literature in Western Manuscripts' . . . has produced no evidence. I regret that I have been able to contribute nothing to the solution of the problem."]

TO THE REVEREND LEONARD CHAPPELOW

Brynbella
Saturday 24: September 1808.

Dear Mr. Chappelow

The Ladies of Llangollen get Letters from you, and we get none; *Indeed* now as We Cambrians say—that is ill done of you, *Indeed* it is *ill done*. They have a hundred Pleasures we have not, They have a hundred Talents we have not; and they have health to exert those Talents—and to enjoy those Pleasures: *Which We have not*. Come, now *do* write me a long Letter, and tell what Lord Bradford says, and Lady Bradford;——and how their beautiful Boys do: who *I* remember by Names of Little O and pretty Henry[1]——but now They are grown up the Honorable &c. Tell me how magnificent Weston is grown, and what you are all Saying about the Convention at Lisbon:[2] Tell me who set Covent Garden Theatre on Fire,[3] and what will become of the Play-going People when only one Place for that Amusement shall be open?[4] *I* thought the Crowds disagreeable enough when there were *Two*. Tell me—above all—that you have got the better of all your Ill Health, and that everybody we love is well and comfortable; particularly pretty Mrs. Clay, of whom I can enquire only thro' *Your means*.

Lord Lyttelton's Death[5] has closed——within one only—the List of Streatham Worthies.[6] Who would have thought that Doctor Burney, so very slight a Man, and born a *Twin too*; should have thus out-lived all his Contemporary Visitants at Mr. Thrale's Library;[7] where Lady Keith and I alone survive——at least we'll *hope* so; but it is very long since I heard from *her* at Cuper Angus in North Britain, and my last Letters said She was *unwell*.

Mr. Piozzi is no worse upon the whole—certainly no better, than when we parted last at the Hotel in Leicester Fields London, a year and half ago. I have had Two or Three rough Attacks, but still remain—in the *Minority*—Mr. and

Mrs. Hoare, and *his* Brother Sir Richard, came to see Wales this Year; and took us en passant. Till Buonaparte opens his Tuilleries to English People, visiting our Mountains and Cromlechs will be fashionable; and tis better spend your Money on us Barbarians here *within* the Island, than leave it in France to furnish future Navies.

Come now *do* send me a kind Letter, and say you have not wholly forgotten your / very Affectionate and very humble Servant / at Brynbella near Denbigh / Saturday 24th September 1808.

Text: Ry. 561.138.

1. HLP refers to two sons of Orlando Bridgeman, first earl of Bradford. "Little O" is the fourteen-year-old Orlando Henry, and "pretty Henry" is Henry Edmund, now thirteen.
2. British forces under the command of Sir Arthur Wellesley between 15 and 21 August defeated Junot's scattered troops in Portugal. Wellesley's rout of Junot and his thirteen thousand men near Vimiero was decisive. Junot then asked for an armistice, and Generals Sir Hew Dalrymple and Sir Harry Burrard, who assumed the command of the British expedition from a junior Wellesley, agreed to it. In the negotiations they allowed the repatriation of Junot, twenty-six thousand men, their weapons, etc., in return for complete French withdrawal from Portugal. The terms, therefore, established by the Convention of Cintra (signed 22 August) were favorable to the French. The British at home were so enraged that the government recalled Dalrymple and Burrard.

See, e.g., *The Times*, 19 September: "A curse, a deep curse, wring the heart and wither the hand that were base enough to devise and execute this cruel injury [the Convention of Cintra] on their country's peace and honour." The newspaper demanded the condemnation not only of Dalrymple, Burrard, and Cotton, but also of Sir Arthur Wellesley (who had indeed signed the armistice, but had not negotiated the convention). See also the *Courier,* 22 September.

While the *Morning Post,* 20 September, tried to suggest that attacks upon the signers of the convention were dictated by party politics, the paper itself was barraged by letters to the editor. One signed "Old Soldier" described the merchants at Lloyd's Coffee-house as "fired with rage, vexation, and indignation, at the base, shameful sacrifice of the honour of the Country."

3. At about 4 A.M. on 20 September, the Covent Garden theater, "which was erected in the year 1733, and enlarged with considerable alterations in 1792, was seen suddenly to be on fire" so that within three hours the whole interior was destroyed. The amount of destruction was estimated at £150,000. The number of victims "must have amounted to thirty! Many of them were dug out of the ruins in such a state that they could not be identified." The fire "was generally attributed to the wadding of a gun, that was discharged in the performance of *Pizarro*, having lodged unperceived in some crevice of the scenery" (Campbell 2:322–23).
4. Despite the destruction of their theater, the Covent Garden company managed to present a full season at King's and at the Haymarket, with SS, e.g., appearing forty times—her Lady Macbeth, Queen Katherine, and Mrs. Beverley outstripped all her other roles.

The new Covent Garden theater, designed by Robert Smirke, was to open 18 September 1810, with a performance of *Macbeth*.

5. Lord Lyttelton had died 14 September 1808, aged eighty-four.

He was William Henry Lyttelton, cr. baron Westcote of Ballymore, county Longford [I.] (1776) and baron Lyttelton of Frankley, county Worcester (1794). He had been governor of South Carolina (1755–60); governor of Jamaica (1760–66); envoy extraordinary and minister plenipotentiary to the court of Portugal (1766–71).

6. For the "Streatham Worthies"—the Reynolds portraits—see HLP to PSP, 1 June 1797, n. 4.
7. CB and his twin sister, Susanna (d. 1734).

TO JOHN SALUSBURY PIOZZI SALUSBURY

Monday
26: September 1808.

My dearest Salusbury
 I am glad you are so happy, and shall always desire that our Wishes may tend the same way. Much Vice and Folly will certainly be escaped by your not going to Eton; I hope you will gain Virtue and Knowledge where you are, and such a *Love* of both as will keep you out of Mischief when you enter into the World. Meanwhile you were speaking (when last at Home,) about being confirmed: and that is *another* Advantage you gain by staying with Mr. Shephard. He will instruct you in the Nature and Use of that Church Ceremony, by which a Man ratifies, and gives his *own* Consent, to his *own* Christianity—originally imposed on us in Infancy when we know not the Vow we are making. I shall be glad when you have been, by Imposition of a Bishop's hand,——*fixed* and *confirmed* in our *Anglican Church:* The superior Excellencies of which no one knows better than Mr. Shephard.[1]
 With Regard to dear Uncle I have never seen him so well since we left Chester, but his Appetite is not good; and the Disorder of his Stomach makes him cross enough at Dinner Time.
 Lake has had a late Crop of Hay on the Field by Hukin's House, and he is proud of that you may be sure: but we are now disposed to hate the very Name of *Hugh* and *Hukin,* ever since the silly Convention at Lisbon, when Sir *Hew* Dalrymple let his Covey fly away after having caught them safe in the Net; and the Wags cry *Eheu!*
 Your Friend Mrs. Mostyn keeps close at Segroid making *Improvements.* Her Son Harry stays at Prestatyn, making I fear *no* Improvement; but the other Two are gone back at last to Streatham School, where Mr. Davies says they would do very well if She would let them alone, and *She* says, Mr. Davies lets them *too much* alone.
 Mrs. Mostyn and Mr. Davies live in a constant Quarrel: and it is a sad thing upon the Boys when Parents and Tutor do not agree: I feel myself quite happy in Mr. Shephard, whose Fault it will *not* be I am sure if you are an Ignorant Fellow——for no Man has better right than *he* to despise so empty a Character. Dear Love! let me request you to read, and study; and do not perswade Yourself into a Silly Notion that you have a bad Memory—
 Every one *remembers* what *Interests* them; and I dare say the Boy that you say catches Butterflies, will never mistake an Orange-Tip for the Emperor; however he may forget the Names and Numbers of the Graces or Muses. I recollect a Gawkee-Lad that had run thro' Eton School, and did not know how many Weeks there were in a Year——he had forgotten it, he said——Can you (enquired I) remember how many Cards there are in a Pack? Yes, 52 *to be sure* was the reply: he had counted his *Cards* you see, tho not his *Time.*
 I am just Thinking how unlike my Letters to *you* are to those I write to my young Friend Marianne Francis;[2] who works at the Greek Verbs in *mi* till I am

forced to *beg* She will make Truce with Study, and go see a Play or something to divert Thought; and not fancy Scholarship the Sole Clue to Felicity, although Ignorance is the certain Road to Ruin.

We have warm Weather here still, and our Swallows have not left us: I have seldom observed them so late in the Season, and am glad on *that* Side my Head too, that you reside with Mr. Shephard: who would be as much disgusted as myself with a human Creature who should be contented not to know something of Natural History as well as Political History——something of the Men and Women who lived before us, and something of the Birds and Beasts that walk or fly about us. Farewell! Dear Salusbury; be good and be wise, and love your poor sick Uncle and your Affectionate Aunt / H: L: P.

Proper Compliments to all the Family.
Write to me soon again; This Letter is made up Sunday Night, to go early away in the Morning.

Text: Ry. 585.12. *Address:* John P: Salusbury Esq. / at The Rev: T: Shephard's / Enborne Cottage near / Newbury / Berks. *Postmark:* DENBIGH 224 (In JSPS's hand, "Received 29th Septr. Answered Oct. 5th 1808").

1. The only son of the Reverend Thomas Shephard, vicar of Speen, JSPS's headmaster at Enborne had not been ordained. Not until 1828 did he receive a D.D. from Cambridge. In his will, however, written 20 December 1841, he described himself as a "Clerk, a Doctor of divinity." See HLP to Q, 22 April 1785, n. 27; to JSPS, 11 June 1808, n. 2.
JSPS did not go to Eton because of his academic deficiencies.
2. Marianne Francis (1790–1832) was the younger daughter of FB's sister Charlotte Anne (1761–1838) and her first husband, Clement Francis (d. 1792). The girl and HLP first met at Bath in 1805 and began to exchange letters. Except for a random HLP letter to Marianne Francis, only the other side of the correspondence is extant (Ry. 582, 583, 584.1–185) and covers the period ca. 1806–20.
Marianne Francis—a *"prodige,"* according to CB—was drawn to evangelical piety. A few years later, as secretary to the blind Arthur Young, she had at Bradfield Hall "a table and a great chair filled with books in all languages, as she reads in every language every day to keep them up—Greek, Latin, Italian, Hebrew, Arabic, German, Spanish, French, Dutch, etc." See Amelia Defries, *Sheep and Turnips* (London, Methuen, 1938), p. 154; John G. Gazley, *The Life of Arthur Young, 1741–1820* (Philadelphia: American Philosophical Society, 1973), chaps. 11, 12.

TO THE REVEREND LEONARD CHAPPELOW

Brynbella Monday
3: October 1808.

Lady Bradford—Dear Mr. Chappelow—does me much honour to recollect there is such a Person in the World: She will remember me with far closer Interest when you tell her that *my* Attacks are like those of Mr. Bridgeman, and that the last of them left me with scarce a Hope of Life. Yet here I *am;* fearful of all I eat, lest it offend my Irascible *Inmates*—The *Bowels:* fearful of every Cold lest it strike to those outrageous *Prisoners*—whom no Convention can sufficiently cajole to give one lasting Peace.

I did conclude that our Generals in Portugal were trying to obtain one from Buonaparte when they acknowledged him Sovereign of that Nation—for so they *did* by calling Junot le Duc d'Abrantes[1]——as *Princes* only can confer Nobility—in *any* Country; and I see now no Reason why some other fav'rite Officer of his, should not be made Duke of Marlborough or Lord Bradford; while Weston Park and Blenheim are set up to Sale——Is he less King—by Choice or by Descent—of England than of Portugal? but there are strange Things occurring every day, not only in the Political, but in the natural World. Professor Vince of Cambridge said that we should in future have *Two* Seasons in our Temperate Zone,—*no more*:[2] His Words are coming strictly true——last Winter ceased not till the Month of May; and then followed an unexampled Heat——Now 'tis all Frost and Snow again like Christmas; and Spring and Autumn will be found only in Dictionaries——The Swallows however staid later this Year than ever, There were some seen this Morning——Now you *shall* tell me *why* that is, because 'tis *in your way* to tell; tho' I did expect better Reasons about the Covent Garden Fire, which has taken from your Pleasures more than from mine:—I only regret the Fire-mens Lives, and Dear old Handel's Organ,[3] on which I have myself seen him and heard him play.—

The Strange Productions of the Stage these late Years should all be burned together by my Consent, except a merry Quibble here and there, when "*Dulness blunders on Vivacities.*"[4] My Husband is very angry at Mrs. Siddons exhibiting herself before the Year is out.[5] *Our* pretty Widow Cæcilia turns a true *Black acre*, and sedulously sets herself to improve Segroid for her eldest Son, who She says dotes upon every Bush that his *Father* ever casually commended——The second Boy is sickly and condemned to Sea Bathing.

The Hoares staid a very short Time; Sir Richard indeed does Wales no small honour—leaving that heavenly Place at Stourhead, for a Cottage on the Black Lake of Bala, whence springs the River *Dee*——his Friend Mr. Fenton I saw too little of——but some of them in Conversation mentioned a young Lady, a Niece of *his* I *think*, as Author of a Romance called Ariel——The Writer 12 Years old:[6]——If I am *right*, and this Tale be *true* Buonaparte has done nothing more wonderful; his Passage over the Alps excepted. The Book is as far beyond common Powers at *that* Age, as his Exploits are beyond the common Powers of Man—at *his own* Age. But the World is so full of Wonders that our News Writer said in his last Paper, We are so crouded with *more Important Matter*, we have no Room to record the Particulars of an *Earthquake* in North Britain. I wrote to ask Lady Keith about it. Cecy says *She* is to spend the Winter at her Daughter in Law's Chateau—Micklour House Cuper Angus—[7] which my Lord prefers to his own beautiful Seat at Purbrook near the new Forest in Hampshire, altho' so *very* remote even from Edinburgh——but when I get Letters from her, there is *plenty of Wax and a large Coronet*, not like my poor Yellow Wafers and unpretending Cypher.

Well! concerning Dear Mr. Piozzi's Strength and Powers of Endurance you do speak most truly: never had Mortal Man so much to bear; and altho' since we parted at Sabloniere's Hôtel Leicester Fields he has past a Winter of *Agony*, and a Summer of *Sickness*; he is now what we must be contented to call *pretty well*:

better I think than he has been these Two Years——wholly bereft indeed of hands and feet; and subject to Spasms of the Breast and Stomach very difficult to recover from. He lies on his Sopha in the Drawing Room however, and sends you his best Compliments and hopes we shall all Live to see the end of Buonaparte; which whether we do or not, Dear Mr. Chappelow will for ever command the best Wishes of his old / Friend / H: L: P.

Swallows and Snow! Swallows and Snow! Was such a Union ever seen before?

Text: Ry. 561.139. *Address:* Rev: Mr. Chappelow.

1. HLP seethes over the designation of Junot as the duc d'Abrantès in the Convention of Cintra. According to LC, on 29 October 1808 (Ry. 563.89): "an intimate friend of Lord Castlereaghs, who has a place under the present Administration, and was here at Weston when the Gazette was read, and condemned Sir A.W.—for having given the Scoundrel Junot—the Title of D. of Abrantes."
The "Scoundrel" was Jean Andoche Junot (1771–1813), *général de division* (1801) and ennobled by Napoleon in 1807.
2. Samuel Vince (1749–1821) was Plumian professor of astronomy and experimental philosophy (1796–1821) at Cambridge. HLP thus interprets Vince's definition of the *"solar* or *tropical* year" in *A Complete System of Astronomy,* 3 vols. (Cambridge: At the University Press, 1797–1808), 1:50.
3. In the last year before his death (1759), though virtually blind, Handel played organ concertos.
4. Young, *Night Thoughts,* 8.1244.
5. HLP's dismissal of current "Productions of the Stage" and her mention of SS were provoked by the Covent Garden theater fire, 20 September 1808.
SS's husband had died on 11 March 1808 and for the remainder of the season she did not act. In the summer she made her usual visit to the Fitzhughs, at Bannisters. She then returned to the stage but she had acted only a few nights when the Covent Garden theater burned to the ground.
6. HLP refers to the anonymous *Ariel; or, the Invisible Monitor,* 4 vols. (London: Printed at the Minerva Press for William Lane, 1801). It was printed in 12mo. and sold for 18s. The work has since been attributed to a Mrs. Isaacs.
7. "Cuper Angus" is Coupar-Angus in Perthshire. For Q's daughter-in-law, see HLP to MW, 17 February 1808, n. 3.

TO LADY WILLIAMS

Wednesday
October 5. 1808

My Dearest Lady Williams
will read a note to say we are *alive* with Pleasure; We are *just alive!* My own Spirits have been low lately, and I have had Swelled Face and Sore Throat—and I have been *very sullen.* My poor Husband is on the Sopha where Your Ladyship left him;—some Times distrest with Giddiness and Faintness, sometimes with Spasms; which he describes as a Sensation totally different.——Let us hear that Things go better at Bodylwyddan, and that dear Mrs. Williams keeps heart-whole, and retains some degree of Appetite, which can alone give her Strength to combat the Disease.—My Daughter and her husband arrived safe in Town,[1] since when I have heard nothing concerning them: Lady Keith is in Scotland; and if *their* Mountains like ours are covered with Snow, making the Michaelmas

of 1808 look like a Christmas of any other Year;—I suppose She will soon be willing to try a warmer Climate.

Did Sir John Williams ever see Swallows in a *cold October* before *this?* or did he ever read such *Cold News* from a hot Country as ours from Portugal?

I am most angry with our People for having acknowledged Junot as Duke of Abrantes, They may as well call some other Favourite General of Buonaparte—Duke Hamilton: he has I trust the same right of creating Nobility in our Country as in Theirs.

But Adieu dear Madam! all this interests your Ladyship *but at a Distance;* permit me to send best Regards to all who have a *nearer* Claim to Your Attention: believing always that You have no truer / or more faithful Servants / than at / Brynbella.

Text: Ry. 3 (1807–11).

1. Sophia (Thrale) and her husband Henry Merrick Hoare.

TO JOHN SALUSBURY PIOZZI SALUSBURY

Brynbella Saturday
14–15 October 1808

My dearest Salusbury

I was just wishing for a Letter from Enborne, when yours and Mr. Shephard's arrived: it is delightful to me to find you are so happy; because I know that no one is happy but who is *good*——Angels are happier than Mankind because they are *better;* and with the Vice and Folly of Eton School, you will escape many an uneasy hour I do believe. You will escape one of their Whimsies too,—"That no Person of Genius or Talents ever could write a good hand."—I know it is an Eton Saying, but I know too that many a Person of very limited Talents and no Genius at all—writes a bad One.

Did you ever see Buonaparte's handwriting? I was glad to get a Fac Simile of it, tho' tis really scarce legible: a Man however who lives as he does in a Hurry, and had none but a mere Military Education may fairly stand excused. The best is to do every Thing as well as one *can;* every sort of Knowlege comes in Use one Time or other, and I dare say when you were at Aldermaston and saw those Statues;[1] it must have been a Pleasure to you to know *who they were* and whether well represented or not—because how can the Expression be judged of by a Person who knows not the Difference between Dido and Daphne, and is capable of mistaking Hercules for Harry the 5th. I have very little Patience with such Simpletons.

Congreve the Poet was I believe a proud Salopian;[2] it is constantly related of him that when the famous Voltaire paid him a Visit, and complimented him on his Dramatick Powers—he replied—"I wish Sir to be considered merely as an English Gentleman, and by no means as a professed Writer"—The French Wit answered with Truth and propriety:—"Had you been a mere Country Gentleman Mr. Congreve, I should not have troubled myself or you with this Intrusion"—and took a hasty Leave.[3]

There are some of his Name yet subsisting at Shrewsbury and we used to see a Miss Adelaide Congreve[4] about Miss Owen two or three years ago.—The Poet had his Education in Ireland.

When do your Christmas Holydays commence? The Days shorten so very fast now, I almost begin to wish they were at the shortest; and then our Time of the Meeting would be near. You will come down with your Shropshire Friends[5] well enough, wrapt in good Great Coats to keep out the Cold; and God send us a happier Vacation than the last was!

Poor Uncle is on his Sopha—less sick (just now at least) than Lowspirited;— but miserably depressed indeed, and in no Disposition to take Holydays himself or give them *me*. Since the Hoares went home I have never stirred a Step or seen a Friend.—Lady Kirkwall sends me Books sometimes, and I walk out, be the Weather what it will; the Storms are dreadful: We see the White Breakers foaming over Rhydland Castle very magnificently at this Moment, though the Spray is never tost up here in the manner I have known it on the Sussex Coast,[6] when with half as much Wind as we experience this very day—I remember the Wall Fruit being quite *Salt* 9 Miles off the Shore at Lewes:—We are not 4 *Miles* from the Sea Side *here* as the Crow flies; and I never knew an Instance of the Fruit or Leaves having a *Briny* Taste as *there:*—ask Mr. Shephard if he can guess the Reason, I am no good Naturalist myself.

My poor Poultry hate this windy Weather as much as I do; "But young and Old, and Cock and Hen, / All live in Aeolus's Den." The Gulls from Prestatyn cover our Park and Brick field, the Swallows staid till old Snowdon's *White Cap* frighted them away.—You never saw the distant Mountains covered with Snow I believe; you will see them this 1808.

I have no News to tell you may be sure——a Brynbella Gazette would contain few Incidents. For example—This Day Salusbury's favourite Duck was seen walking pensively by the Side of the Pond, and after a few waddling Paces— *flung herself in;*—The reason of this rash Action is not known. Yesterday Morning at 5 o'Clock a *Fire* was discovered—in old Peter's Tobacco pipe——but it was happily *got under* without further Damage.

So I think here is Nonsense enough for *one* Day: I will write to Mr. Shephard another Day, and request of him to Send his Account.

In the mean Time make our best Compliments to him, and assure him of our True Esteem; and of the tender Regard we feel to his Pupil John Salusbury— whose Affectionate / Aunt I shall ever remain / whilst H: L: Piozzi.

Compliments to the Ladies. Don't be too long without writing.

Text: Ry. 585.13. *Address:* John: P. Salusbury Esq. / at The Rev: T. Shephard's / Enborne Cottage near / Newbury / Berkshire. *Postmark:* DENBIGH 224.

1. Aldermaston in Berkshire is some nine miles from Reading. Specifically, HLP alludes to Aldermaston Court, built ca. 1636, and its high-mannered allegorical or mythological statues. The original house, which was partially burned in 1843, was pulled down and a new manor built in its place in 1847 or 1848.
2. Thinking of Aldermaston in 1808, HLP associated it with the name of Congreve, since the estate was then owned by a William Congreve (d. 1843).
The dramatist William Congreve (1670–1729) was not a Salopian, either by birth or choice. Born in Bardsley, near Leeds (Yorkshire), he was taken as an infant to Ireland, where he was educated at Kilkenny school and at Trinity College, Dublin.
3. See Voltaire, "Dix-Neuvième Lettre / Sur La Comédie," in *Lettres sur les Anglais* (*Lettres anglaises;* or *Lettres philosophiques*) (1734).
4. For Adelaide Sarah Congreve, see HLP to RD, 29 March 1800, n. 3.
5. For JSPS's schoolfriend, Edward William Smythe Pemberton, see HLP to JSPS, 20 August 1808, n. 1.
6. Rhuddlan Castle, portions of which predate Edward I, is now a ruin which sits on a rocky bluff above the Clwyd. Its main walls are of local red stone mixed with sandstone. Of immense thickness, they are complete in height and proportion. Still extant are the massive gate towers at every angle. The moat is visible all the way around. There is nothing left within the great space the walls enclose, the castle having been dismantled by Cromwell's order.

TO ELEANOR WILLIAMS

19 October 1808

It is very kind and very amiable in my dear Mrs. Williams to think so of her Neighbours, when She has so much to employ her Mind upon: but the less you and Mr. Piozzi dwell upon the Consideration of Complaints which cannot be removed,—the better; You have borne them long, and will have to bear them much longer: you have seen many healthy People go before you, and will see many more. One great Advantage that my dear Mrs. Williams has over Mr. Piozzi is that of a fuller Family, and more Variety of Chat, to take your Attention from *Self*. Sir John and my Lady—Dear Friends! will come home all alive, and full of Talk; will tell how happy their Brother is, and how prosperously all Things flourish at Liverpool, now the Spanish Ports are opened, and Portugal freed from her devourers the French.[1] We see so few People, and those few do so little towards driving Care away—that my poor husband has nothing to think or talk of but the diminution of his Powers.

Loss of Appetite is likewise an Increase of Sorrow, because the Spirits lower of Course; and the Voice gets weak and unwilling to exert itself.

These Evils have not assaulted *your* Peace *yet* I thank God; and we must hope they will long keep away.

Never fear the Ferry boat; Sir John will take Care of *yours* and his *own* Darling;—so justly loved by both: and if they get a little Splashed it will be only an Additional Incident for Conversation.

A Thousand Blessings and good Wishes wait my lovely Godson[2] and all the rest of a Family so deservedly Dear to, and respected by their obliged and / tenderly attached Friends and Servants / at Brynbella / Tuesday 19: October / 1808.

Text: Ry. 3 (1807–11).

1. HLP refers to the fact that by November 1805 all ports in the peninsula were effectively closed to British shipping. But military victories, e.g., at Bailen in July and at Vimiero in August, reopened Spanish and Portuguese ports to trading vessels from Liverpool and other English cities.
2. Hugh Williams.

TO THE REVEREND LEONARD CHAPPELOW

Brynbella
Thursday 27: October 1808.

This Letter Dear Mr. Chappelow—kind and comical as you are—I have written more for Lady Bradford's Sake than for yours.[1] I wish her to learn what is the *best* Remedy for these troublesome *Insides* of ours——and the best way is to rub the *outside:*—gentle Friction with soft Fleecy Hosiery dipt in Laudanum and Brandy when the Pain is *on:* rough Fleshbrushes when the Pain is *off* give more ease and safety than any Medicine we can swallow: at least so *my Lining* finds it.

Here is unparalleled Weather; we ascribe it to the Comet,[2]—though I think he may easily prove an *Alibi;* and joking apart, no Difficulty is greater than to believe that pale, nebulous, *distant* Star can affect our Atmosphere: but we *must* say something, so we cry *Comète:* Mr. Piozzi is still on his *Sophà* not *put to Bed* yet as we Females say; he is angry with Mrs. Siddons as well as you, but I question whether She is of a Constitution to enjoy Retirement——her honest old Husband was never Manager I believe, and as to her Brother who has more Influence, he must take every Method of filling his House—when he has one.[3] Harriet Lee writing Tales, and Sophia Lee Comedies after so horrible an Event in their own Family as poor Annette's Suicide, seems to me less excuseable.[4]

Public Affairs fright me cruelly: The Spaniards are no *longer* all of a Mind you see;[5] they quarrel, and Buonaparte will foment their Differences: like the Bully in Shakespear He seems to say "The World is Mine Oyster, which I with Sword will open."[6] Besides that the Patriots are fighting for an Invisible and Inefficient King, whose *Right* to give them away, themselves acknowlege.[7]—I have no Heart on't——they will be swallowed at last. For our own Boobies, (if only Boobies) they will suffer Punishment enough;——if they took Bribes *no* Punishment can be enough: to deter future Rascalities.[8] What is this Rumour about Captain Hogan and his Pamphlet?[9] Remember that we are out of the World completely, and let *us not burst in Ignorance.*[10]

The Ladies of Llangollen are all in Love with Sophia Hoare, and She with *them:* Madame de Genlis has written *Their History* 'tis said, but very incorrect, and they are of Course little pleased with it.[11] Of all Novels Ariel is the most surprizing—if written as I hear by a *Child*——but Children grow up out of one's Knowlege; and perhaps Mr. Bridgeman who is suffering as you describe[12]—was the beautiful Boy who was called *Little O* by his Brother Henry, when we were at Weston Park——Can it be *him* who is, or has been an Officer on Board the Repulse?[13]

Adieu dear Mr. Chappelow; and pray for better Weather: The People here cannot put their Wheat *into* the Ground, nor pull their Potatoes *out* of it: We shall have a Famine next Year, or *rather* the Year after. "Terrible Times to be expected Gentlemen! but I shall scarce live to see them" exclaimed at his own Table the Bishop of St. Asaph t'other Day. Most probably *not* my Lord——replied a Welsh Clergyman in Company; wholly absent, and little intending Offence.

Once more Adieu! present me most respectfully to Lady Bradford / and believe me / Dear Sir / Ever Yours / H: L: P.

Mr. Piozzi sends *his best.*

Text: Ry 561.140. Address: Rev: Mr. Chappelow.

1. HLP responds to LC's letter (Ry. 563.89) written at Weston, the Bradford seat.
2. "The Comet, which at this period last year first made its appearance, seems again to have directed its erratic course toward our sphere. It bears due east, and may be seen every clear evening soon after seven, somewhat below a straight line drawn between the planet Jupiter and the leading star in Ursa Minor, at about two thirds distance from the planet, and forming nearly a right angle with the 'Pleiades.' The tail is not so perceptible as last year, but its nucleus is visible to the naked eye" (*The Times*, 17, 20, and 25 October).
3. LC had asked in his letter; "Why does Mrs. Siddons continue to act?—When her husband was manager I supposed he was the instigator—surely it is high time to quit the stage—and enjoy retirement—before she quits the Last stage.—"

Her brother, John Philip Kemble, was manager of the Drury Lane theater.

4. According to LC's letter: "I have been reading 2 tales of our friend Harriet's Canterbury things—in her 5th vol:—but I could not get on—it Looks as if her old Novels had Kittened—These are poor Little squashing stones—as insipid as basins of water gruel without either butter or wine.—"

Since Anna Lee's death in 1805, Harriet Lee had completed *The Canterbury Tales* with volume 5, and Sophia Lee had written a comedy, *The Assignation*, produced at the Drury Lane on 28 January 1807.

5. In September 1808 the leaders of the Spanish insurrection tried futilely to achieve cohesion. On 25 September, e.g., in Madrid the Supreme Junta, made up of thirty-five provincial delegates, spent days debating constitutional issues but could not name a command-in-chief over the Spanish armies. Instead, it communicated separately with the leaders of the provincial armies, men diffuse in talents, experiences, ideologies, and even biases. "Thus the Supreme Junta controlled a very mixed bag of commanders [who]— . . . could not produce much in the way of an army between them." See Chandler, pp. 625–26.
6. HLP had just received a letter from Marianne Francis, dated 24 October, who wrote: "Buonaparte puts me in mind of——who is it?—in the Merry Wives of Windsor, that calls out—'The world's mine oyster! which I with sword will open.' And does he not do so?" (Ry. 582.27).

The words are Pistol's, 2.2.2–3.

7. Three men claimed the Spanish throne in October 1808: the two Bourbons, Carlos IV, now in exile at Compiègne, and his son Fernando, now in prison at Valençay; Napoleon's brother Joseph, one-time king of Naples and Sicily, now elevated to the crowns of Spain and the Indies. Most Spaniards, despite HLP's cynicism, were committed to Fernando.
8. The "Boobies" may be those who supported rumors of French peace overtures to the British through "a Russian Officer, and a French Messenger, who had landed . . . at Deal" and gone directly to London. See *The Times*, 22, 24, and 25 October.

The "Boobies" were more likely the men associated in British minds with the Convention of Cintra. So great was the frustration caused by it that many Britons began to suspect not only the motives of the three military leaders—Burrard, Wellesley, and Dalrymple—but to question the decision of those ministers responsible for the "inconsiderate act of firing the Park and Tower guns at ten o'clock at night, when the news of the Convention arrived"—a firing associated "with unusual symptoms of joy and exultation" (*The Times*, 13 October). As the clamor increased in the press—the *Sun, Globe, Pilot, Traveller, Star,* ("papers of all parties")—the government was forced to set up a court of inquiry, which first met on 14 November 1808. See also Farington 9:3348.

9. See Denis Hogan, *An Appeal to the Public, and a Farewell Address to the Army, by Brevet Major Hogan, late a Captain in the Thirty-second Regiment of Infantry, in which he resigned his Commission, in consequence of the Treatment he experienced from the Duke of York, and the System . . . respecting Promotions, etc.* (London J. M. Richardson, 1808).

The pamphlet, an early exposure of the behavior of the duke of York and Mrs. Clarke, was designed to prove how inequitable the system of promotion was and how often promotions were determined by Mrs. Clarke. The case was to become a *cause célèbre* in early 1809.

10. One of HLP's favorite quotations, from *Hamlet*, 1.4.45.

11. See a "Catalogue of Books at Brynbella 18 Oct. 1806, with additions to 1813" (Ry. 612). There is an entry in the "Catalogue"—"Genlis's Llangollen Ladies—called Souvenirs de Felicie, 2 vols. sm."; i.e. Stéphanie Félicité Ducrest de St. Aubin, Mme de Genlis (1746–1830), *Les Souvenirs de Felicité L***** (Paris: Maradan, an XII–1804).

12. LC had written of Lady Bradford in his letter: "she never forgets you.—The only difference between your 2 employments, is, that you are nursing a sick husband, and she is nursing a sick Son.—for alas! I cannot report progress—in Mr. B's convalescence, in such terms, and with such heart felt satisfaction, as I could wish.—He is now certainly better, his appetite is good, and so are his spirits—but he still continues in a recumbent posture—and is but able to get as far as the window in Lady B's Room.—neither is he at times, free from pain.—but he is resignation itself, and says he is happy, even under the continued state of confinement, he is necessitated to endure."

Because Lady Bradford had three sons still in England, we cannot determine which one was ill.

13. LC had written: "We expect every day [Lady Bradford's son], who has been 2 years in and about the Mediterranean—in the Repulse with Captain Legg Lord Dartmouth's Brother."

The *Repulse*, of seventy-four guns, had sailed from Gibraltar on 15 September "with a convoy from Malta" and landed at Portsmouth on 15 October. The ship was then quarantined. See *The Times*, 17 and 18 October.

Lady Bradford's son was Charles Orlando Bridgeman (1791–1860) who, after a brief stint at Harrow, entered the navy 18 June 1804 as a first-class volunteer on board the *Repulse*. By 1805 he had attained the rank of midshipman. He was to have a long career, becoming a lietenant by 1810, a commander by 1814, and ultimately a vice admiral. By 1827 he was on half pay.

TO JOHN SALUSBURY PIOZZI SALUSBURY

Saturday
7: November 1808.

My dear Salusbury

I have received your second agreeable Letter, and am very glad you are happy. It is good to *see* as many Things, and *know* as many Things as we can; and my only reason for regretting our State of Retirement, is the Reflexion that whilst I am feeding my Chickens——(as poor Dr. Johnson used too say)—I am Starving my Understanding.[1] If however we cannot see People who know and can tell us what passes in the World, We must even converse with our Leather-coated Friends upon the Shelves; who give good Advice, and yet are never arrogant and assuming.

Do you understand *that* Figure of Speech? It does not lie *deep* like the Joke of your own Duck drowning herself in the *Pond*——how should a Duck drown herself? Dear Salusbury will you never be able to take a Silly Joke?

You know I said you should have Paragraphs from the *Brynbella Chronicle*—and because we could not chronicle any but *such* Occurrences; I made up a *true*

Tale of the Old Man's Tobacco Pipe, and the Duck waddling by the Side of the Water; in Imitation of Newspaper Paragraphs—who when a drunken Wench flings herself into the River commonly add—*"That the Reason of this rash Action is not known."* Can't you understand it yet Salusbury?—can't you *indeed*?

Dear Uncle is still on his Sopha, and pretty well, when he does not neglect taking the night-draughts—otherwise very bad: and complaining of Pain in his Stomach—want of Appetite &c. but we have had no Fits of Giddiness lately, nor no Strong Spasms; so I keep my Spirits up tolerably——his Fingers being all lost is a melancholy Thing; because it is so excessively difficult for him to move a Paper, or open a Book, or handle a Spoon or any thing.

Lord Kirkwall has had a Fall from his horse and is a good deal hurt.[2] Sir John and Lady Williams have been to the Musick Meeting at Liverpool,[3]—my Lady's Mother is excessively Ill, and not likely to live long.——Lord de Blaquiere has been Weather-bound in Anglesea this Month past;[4] not daring to cross the Irish Channel for Fear of these late Storms——and poor Old Peter! who was so well when I wrote last, that I was trying to *Strike Fire* of Amusement for you out of his Tobacco Pipe; dropt down dead in the Tool house in our Kitchen Garden; without one Word of Complaint, or previous Expression of ill health. This is dismal, and I confess affected me very deeply——but 'tis better *prepare* for Death than be frighted with the *Sight* of it. See how courageously the Spaniards defy it in the Field[5]——They are like the Boxer I read of in our Paper 'tother Day, who lamented that they took him home *not half-beaten*. Peace and Capitulation said the French General Lefevre; War and Death replied Count Palafox:—That is true Castillian Spirit: is it not?[6]

Mr. Shephard gives a kind and partial Account of you to us: Make his Words good my Dear Soul; and love your Book; and learn to know Jest from Earnest: and do not be such a mere *Matter of Fact Fellow*, though I shall ever rejoyce in your Spirit of Virtue and Prudence. Everybody asks kindly for you, and nobody can love their own Son better than you are loved by / Uncle's and *Your* ever Affectionate / H: L: Piozzi.

Text: Ry. 585.14. *Address:* John P: Salusbury Esq. / Rev: Mr. Shephard's / Enborne Cottage / near Newbury / Berks. *Postmark:* DENBIGH 22 <   >.

1. *Anecdotes*, p. 265.
2. Lord Kirkwall frequently fell from his horse; see, e.g., HLP to LC, 17 September 1801 and n. 1.
3. The Liverpool annual subscription concerts began on 11 October, "at the Music Hall, during which, six of ten performances were given in the first style of excellence,—Mrs. Billington, Mr. Harrison, and Mr. Bartleman, were never heard to greater advantage—enrapturing the audience with their unrivalled talents. Of the instrumental performers it is needless to expatiate, their merits being so well known and acknowledged. The receipts (though not to the amount that might have been expected from such a combination of merit) will, however . . . leave a handsome surplus in the hands of the managers, after paying every attendant expence" (*Chester Chronicle*, 21 October).
4. For John, Baron de Blaquiere, see HLP to Ly W, 24 February 1800, n. 9.
5. HLP refers to the siege of Saragossa, which began on 15 June 1808 when Charles Lefebvre-Desnouëttes (1773–1822) with six thousand men attempted to occupy the city. He expected little trouble from José Palafox, who had only about fifteen hundred patriots to defend it. But the Frenchman made no headway, pulling back and besieging the city while he awaited reinforcements. Late in June they arrived under the command of Verdier, who only on 4 August established a bridgehead in the city's streets. He called to Palafox to surrender. The Spaniard answered, "Hasta la ultima

tapia" ("until the last wall"). An engagement followed, but on 5 August Spanish reinforcements arrived with news of the victory at Bailen. By mid-August, Verdier broke off the siege.

6. The hero of Saragossa was José Palafox y Melzi (1780–1847). As an officer of the Spanish Royal Guard, he accompanied Crown Prince Fernando to Bayonne in 1808 but escaped when the latter was imprisoned. Palafox returned to Aragón, in the vicinity of his birthplace and raised it against the French invaders. He is best known for his courageous conduct during the two sieges of Saragossa (1808, 1809). After the fall of that city, he was imprisoned in France, returning to Spain in 1814, when he was made captain general of Aragón and later duke of Saragossa.

TO MARGARET WILLIAMS

Brynbella
18: February 1809.

My Dear Miss Williams
 will think me ungrateful, but it is not so: The Bath Newspaper entertained me exceedingly; if we can call by the name of Entertainment such a Sensation as your long List of Calamities must afford. The long list of Subscribers to the Suffering Set, with our kind Cousin Thelwall's Name prefixed,[1]—is however no small Compensation for such uneasiness as general Sorrow causes—but how shall be compensated to any feeling Mind the general Disgrace which Mrs. Clarke's Examination is bringing upon such numbers of Names and Families?[2] I never heard so complicated a Tale of Dupery and Falsehood, and Folly and Rascality unravelled in my Life before; and am almost happy at finding myself so far distant from a Theatre of such horrible Absurdities and Crimes. Meanwhile our own Country exhibits some silly Conduct, and some sorrowful Consequences of it. Doctor Thackeray, who was called to Mr. Piozzi this Day fortnight; told us that old Lleweney was on Sale, and Sir John Williams who with his Lady called here Yesterday, said they had heard the same unpleasing Report.[3] Lady Williams is much altered since her Illness—*not thinner;*—the *Reverse* I think; but her Complexion changed, her Face covered with Pimples &c.—tho' She makes few Complaints.

We did not see the Young Squire, he is returned to his Studies,—so is *our* Boy;[4] so will shortly be—Dr. Myddeltons—They are now Tall Youths: but at Gwaynynnog there is *once more* good hope of a Second Son—and I should be very sorry, were they *once more* disappointed.[5]

The Season has been less cold than last Year, but more Noisy if possible: I never heard the Winds so loud and high. Lady Keith's Letters tell of a Scotch Earthquake, and those from Naples speak of four foot snow in the Streets: a Phænomenon equally out of its *natural Place*.—The paragraphs should have been changed to make them credible:——but odd Things are no longer to be called odd;—They happen so often and so commonly.

Mrs. Williams and Mr. Piozzi are among the strange Instances of Strength, to endure Illness and Agony difficult of Description: Lady Williams says Her Mama is ulcerated by this spreading Cancer in such a Manner, that as King David Says—"There is no whole part in her Body."[6] The Throat is greatly affected with large Lumps, yet She dresses, dines at Table &c.—so does Mr. Piozzi: whose Torments I *trust,* even more than equal hers—but Doctor Thackeray relieved them this last Visit by some Alteration to the Draughts.

Take Care of your own Health and write me some Chat from Bath, for we are very lonely and very dull. Mrs. Hoare says there was a pretty Mrs. Bruce near to be burned in Pallmall with her Children;[7] Was it the Lady You and I visited in or near St. James's Square? at whose house I was so astonished by the incomparable Dancing of a Baby? *She* was extremely handsome I remember, and the Child quite out of the common Way:—a Prodigy of Power!!

Remember me to all Friends Dear Miss Williams and believe me / ever Yours / H: L: P.

Text: Ry. 8 (1808–12).

1. For the Reverend Edward Thelwall, see HLP to the Reverend Robert Myddelton, 28 March 1805, n. 5.
2. Mary Anne Clarke (1776–1852) used her intimacy with the duke of York to promise promotions to army officers, who paid her for a recommendation. On 27 January, the matter was presented by Gwyllym Lloyd Wardle (M.P., Okehampton) to the Commons, which referred it to a select committee. For the resulting actions of the committee, see HLP to Q, 19 March 1809, n. 11.
3. For Llewenny Hall, see HLP to PSW, 6 October 1792, n. 2.
Lord Kirkwall had inherited Llewenny Hall when he was only fifteen. At the time of this letter—some seven years after his unhappy marriage to Anna Maria De Blaquiere—he contemplated the sale of Llewenny and in 1810 sold it to the Reverend Edward Hughes of Kinmel (owner of the Parys copper mines in Anglesea). It was eventually razed.
4. The "Young Squire" was John Williams II, and *"our Boy"* his brother Hugh.
5. May and Robert Myddelton had their fifth daughter, Augusta (1809–1823).
6. Ps. 38:7, a morning prayer for the eighth day in "The Psalter" *(Book of Common Prayer).*
7. The wife and a daughter of Alexander Bruce (d. 1817), an army agent of 5 Pall Mall Court (later 47 Parliament Street) and Streatham. See P.R.O., Prob. 11/1588/2; the "Army Agents" in the *Law List* from 1802 until his death; *Boyle's Court Guide* from 1805 to 1812.
For the fire which had broken out on 2 February "at four this morning," see GM 79, pt. 1 (1809): 175.

TO THE WILLIAMS FAMILY

[3 March 1809]

I thank You very sincerely my very dear and kind friends. Poor Mr. Piozzi has much to endure——and in another Way *So have I.* I saw him sleep quietly at 3 and 4 o'clock this Morning; but he has been sometimes *restless,* sometimes *torpid* ever since Dr. Myddleton left him.

Never out of Bed, and the Heat of his Face like *Fire.* Mr. Moore speaks well of the Pulse, or I should send for Dr. Thackeray directly.

We go at present by his *written* Directions—miserable enough certainly: yet happier than some Dukes,[1] Earls,[2] Deans,[3] and Theatrical Proprietors[4]—*They* perhaps would be glad to change even with H: L: P.

I am an Object of *Envy,* when 'tis known how kind Sir John and Lady Williams and Mr. W: Williams have always been to their / true Servant at Brynbella.

Text: Ry. 3 (1807–11). *Address:* Bodylwyddan.

1. HLP is alert to the scandal involving the duke of York and Mrs. Clarke and to the persistent gossip concerning the duke of Clarence's seduction of one of Mrs. Jordan's daughters (Farington 9:3399).
2. The noblemen specifically alluded to are the earls of Westmorland and Uxbridge. The former's daughter Augusta, married to Lord Boringdon, was divorced by an act of Parliament on 14 February. Two days later she married Sir Arthur Paget, Lord Uxbridge's son. See *GM,* 79, pt. 1 (1809): 181.

Far more notorious was the conduct of Henry William Paget, the eldest son of Lord Uxbridge. See HLP to Q, 19 March 1809, n.15.

3. The dean was William Davies Shipley (see HLP to LC, 30 September 1796, nn. 9 and 10). He was made unhappy by his son Robert John. See HLP to Q, 19 March and 10 April 1809.
4. Theater proprietors were victimized by fires: the Covent Garden burned in September 1808 and the Drury Lane on 24 February 1809.

TO JOHN SALSUBURY PIOZZI SALUSBURY

Sunday Evening 5: March 1809.

My dearest Salusbury

Our Bulletin of Health here goes on very Ill; but you charged me to write, and conceal nothing from You. Poor Uncle has been delirious now a whole Week, Doctor Myddelton came here this Day sennight to pray and preach for Mr. Roberts; and we thought my Master was not in his right Mind then, tho' he got up and dined at Table as usual— —The hand looking—Oh horrible! all red and inflamed with fierce Gout, but he—complaining of no Pain at all, rather making odd Preparations for a Journey *in Italy,* for I understood he considered himself as now at *Milan.* The Attack on his Senses remitted however in due Time, and he conversed rationally with Mr. Oldfield the Attorney on *Wednesday* Morning[1]——The Gout furious as when he was 48 Years Old. *That* Night, notwithstanding we laid aside much of the Wine and Brandy; was passed wholly in delirious Raving: So was *last* Night; and when I came down at Two O'Clock this Morning—waked by some unusual Noise:—Dunscombe protested *he* had felt the Shock of an Earthquake while his wretched Master was spitting at Flies and Birds—which had no Existence, and quarrelling with the Man for not driving them away. Meanwhile Mr. Moore keeps on in his cold slow manner; assuring me there is *no Cause* of *Alarm;* and *pledging his Life* there's *not an Atom of Danger.* But I have written for Doctor Thackeray again, and if *I* have not Cause of Alarm—I wonder who *has?*

The best News of today is that he complains of his Back-Bone coming thro' his Skin; I greatly fear he has disregarded it too long, and whilst he was seeing Sights of Ladies, Processions, and I know not what Stuff——we shall have a shocking Place *there*——especially as the Supplies of Wine and Brandy *must* be cut off, or he must lose his Wits forever. Shew this Letter to Mr. Shephard, he will tell you what to hope and fear better than I can; who trust only to God's Mercy for help and Consolation.

Dunscombe is fatigued to Death; we put him to Bed in another part of the house tonight, while Leake takes his Post, and I sit in the little Dressing Room.

Nothing that *can* be *done* shall be left *un*done / by your poor Affectionate Aunt / H: L: Piozzi.

Send me word you get this safely, and I will let you hear what Doctor Thackeray says. *He* must have been mistaken about Water on the Breast; an Hydropic Patient could not have thrown out *half* this fiery Gout, which surprizes all who see it.

Don't you remember my saying that Uncle would have his Annual *Set-fast* as I called it: and the Doctors laughed at my thinking it possible——he was too weak and low they replied: but here is such a Set-fast as I never saw. Gout and Inflammation to a prodigious Degree, and *those Discharges* almost stopt—in Comparison of what you have known them.——He is as different as if he was another Man.

Was there an Earthquake? or was Dunscombe delirious too? "The Fellow is distract, and so am I; and here we wander in Illusions"[2]—says Antipholis of Syracuse in your Comedy of Errors.

Text: Ry. 585.17. *Address:* John P. Salusbury Esq. / at The Rev. Mr. T. Shephard's / Enborne near / Newbury / Berkshire. *Postmark:* ST.ASAPH 218 (In JSPS's hand, "Received March 9th Answered March 10th 1809").

1. John Oldfield (1760–1841) appears in the *Law Lists* under "Country Attornies." As early as 1800 he was practicing at Bettws Abergele, Denbighshire, with his brother Edward (1782–1850). By 1815 they are listed as attorneys at Farm, near Abergele. In 1820 they were joined by Thomas Oldfield, the firm continuing as such until 1842. In this latter year, only Edward and Thomas Oldfield are listed, and in 1844, Thomas alone.

Of the two elder Oldfields, John was the Piozzis' attorney; see, e.g., his name as witness to GP's will, 27 November 1802.

See the "Bettws yn Rhos Burial Register," C.R.O., Clwyd.

2. Spoken by Antipholus, 4.3.42–43.

TO JOHN SALUSBURY PIOZZI SALUSBURY

Fryday 10: March 1809.

Well! dearest Salusbury!—

Here is Fryday Night March 10: I thought not to have written till Sunday Evening, that you might have The *Weekly Bill of sad Mortality* more regular. But The dreadful Symptom having disappeared, and Mr. Moore protesting there is no present harm; and the Back being better, and in less Danger of a Gangrene, I write with steadier Fingers——*or I flatter myself.* We have had a sad Time on't, and today when we did get him to change his Things, ventilate his Room &c. he fainted almost away from Weakness and Fatigue.

Mean Time The Thrushes sing delightfully; and Dunscombe's Tree, as we call the Tacamahac by his Area Steps is coming out in Leaf; and with a Strong Perfume. One of the Kitchen Garden Walls—by the Toolhouse and Rabbet Hutches, is all full of Peach-Bloom; and we have Misty Mornings, warm Noonday Suns &c.

Sir Philip went for sixpence o'Pound rough and smooth—and Leak got £17.17s.6d. for him, so you may calculate his Weight.—We dine off him tomorrow, and I feel no Regret, he was so very vicious and violent——Old Daisie was forced to go with him to Denbigh, and I must own he has been a Three Years Torment to us all. Venus and Brunette the Two Young Heifers, must make us some Amends. I think you hit off Lady K——'s Case exactly; My Lord went to London and took no Leave; and if she ever was Shrewish, which I never saw, She will soon grow Tame I trust as Shakespeare's Katharine——The Servants will offer her Mustard without the Beef I warrant them, as Grumio did;—when their Master's Behaviour authorizes their Insolence.[1]

Poor Jones just trotted her Mare over here one Day to see Mr. Piozzi, but her own Husband's Health is very Ill thought on by the Doctors, and She has enough to do at home, and looks miserably.

Poor Uncle never looked so ill as today I think; but the Fever is gone which gave him a *Colour,* and now We see him as he *is.*

Mr. Roberts is returned; and when I gave him back the Books *you said* he lent you——he had wholly forgotten the Transaction—The Sale of Lleweney Hall would vex me cruelly, if there was nothing nearer me to vex about; it was the Scene of my *first happy Days*—in my poor Uncle's Time:[2] There is some Talk of keeping it in the *present* Family by making other Sacrifices instead, but I fear they are awkward Contrivers——no Neighbours will ever be to me what these have been, may I *but* keep them! Sweet Lady Kirkwall is really Ill—of an Ague however, and fancies the Place lying too low to be wholesome after these heavy Rains.

I shewed poor Jones what you wrote to me about *her* and She cried, and thanked you; and bid me give her Duty, Love &c. her Husband has an Asthma and Dropsy.

How shall I get through so many Perplexities?——But Mr. Piozzi is free from all Spasm now, and Sickness; only agonizing Pain, and he knows the worst *that* can do; and we hope to have no more Delirium. The Back is the worst Thing at present, because it is *not* a Chalk Sore like the others: The Chalk Sores are never dangerous, though always horrible and odious—but here comes Mr. Moore says Lady Kirkwall wont perhaps live 12 Hours—The Servants have sent for Dr. Currie to her from Chester.[3] And here's my poor Piozzi with a Diarrhaea in Addition to all his Weakness and Misery and here in Affliction on every Side her heart / sits poor / H: L: P.

Saturday Morning

Late at Night. I *must* go to Bed when Owen takes this.

Text: Ry. 585.18. *Address:* John P: Salusbury Esq. / at the Rev: T: Shephard's / Enborne near Newbury / Berkshire. *Postmark:* DENBIGH 224 (In JSPS's hand, "Received 14th March 1809——Answered March 19th 1809").

1. *The Taming of the Shrew,* 4.3.30.
2. HLP is remembering Llewenny Hall when it belonged to her maternal uncle, Robert Cotton, third baronet. For Lord Kirkwall's intention to sell it, see HLP to MW, 18 February 1809, n. 3.
3. William Currie, M.D. (ca. 1749–1834), of Boughton Hall, Chester. See HLP to LC, 19 March 1799, n. 20.

TO JOHN SALUSBURY PIOZZI SALUSBURY

[Brynbella]
Monday 13–14 March 1809.

I receive your second Letter this Moment dearest Salusbury—Monday Morning 13 March, but tho' I sit down to write now, I shall not *send* my Answer till Wednesday the 15th when Lake goes to Denbigh, and by that Time Things *may* mend——we must pray to God and trust in him for Comfort.

Poor Uncle *was* so well—(of his Head,) and so collected when Dr. Thackeray was here *Saturday*——the Day before Yesterday—that he shewed a *faint* Hope of his Restoration—but the Hope was dimmed with *Tears* for his old Friend—who he protested had been preserved these last Two Years by *Miracle;* "and who *has*—added he, in the Course of these last Two Years, suffered what would have killed any Two Men I ever saw in the Flower of Youth and Strength." So he left a Blister to be applied to the Nape of his Neck if the Delirium should return, and he gave Directions about that *vile Back* of which I live in perpetual Terror—— and went home to little Selina who has got the Measles.[1] Meanwhile News came that Lady Kirkwall had survived her 12 Hours, and was *not* struck——as they expected—with the Palsy——her Disorder was *Cholera Morbus* the same I had last October Twelve-month, brought on by Agitated Spirits. My Lord left her without Money, or Friend, or a kind Word to comfort her; and they expected Creditors to come and seize all; and She began Vomiting and *T'other thing;* and lay at last for dead: while I was chained by Duties superior even to Gratitude or Friendship—far from her miserable Couch. The Servants however *did* send for Mr. Anwyl,[2] and he for Doctor Currie; and I have got Three Lines under her poor Staggering hand to thank me for my affectionate Anxiety——and who knows but *She* may live and see happier Hours?—Forsitan et hæc olim meminisse juvabit.[3] She is very young——If *we* were only *Twice* her Age, I would hope happier hours for *us too:* She is scarce 28 Years old—a few Months more or less——and that is too early to be wretched. Yet what after all are Lady Kirkwall's Sorrows or mine to those of 13 poor Women whose husbands were all destroyed at once Yesterday in the Coalpit at Mostyn!![4] Poor Creatures! I warrant they are made of the same Flesh and Blood as *we* are—created and Redeemed by the same Almighty Power: in whose Sight they are as *good*—perhaps *better* than we, who have more Words to lament our Fate with.

But you had rather hear about Uncle, and I am more able to tell you *his* Sufferings than theirs. He throws out *too much* Gout into those poor mangled Hands of his, and the Pain drives him frantic. We were unwilling to lay on a Blister on the *only* sound part of his Distempered Body; and put it off till last night when with a *loud strong Voice* he cried out that I had pulled half his House down—and filled his Room with People till he could not breathe. That Mrs. Mostyn was poisoned by a Rascal he must prosecute—that it would cost him 1000£ but no matter &c. Mr. Moore was frighted then himself—cool as he is; and we put on the Blister, and I sate with Dunscombe till the Dawn of Day and then put *my* half-crazed Head to sleep. Mr. Moore has been again this Morning and will come at Night to comfort us; Piozzi dozes in the Day Time, but begins these ranting Fits just as Candles are lighted. I will write no more till *Tuesday.* Adieu.

Here is Tuesday 14:—and all *quiet;*—after a Night's good sound Sleep without delirious Dreams: but *such* a Back! Oh I am sure it must end in a Sphacelus and Gangrene——It *must;* for there is no Chalk there to hinder Putrefaction as in the Cretaceous Abcesses; and it has ran through Sheets, Blankets every thing in the Course of the Night. Mr. Shephard will tell you what a Sphacelation is, and whence derived; σφαίχελος——I can neither write Greek nor read it; but my Heart told me this Misery was coming forward long ago—he used to cry out of his Back when on the Sopha you remember, how much more now he has lain so long in Bed irritating those Parts——There is *another* Misery, now the Delirium is done with:——which to express delicately we must use a Greek Word for; *Dysury.* The Diarrhæa was stopt perhaps *too soon* with Port Wine and powdered Sugar on Toasted Bread——and poor Nature (worne down on every Side) now refuses to disburthen herself *any way*——The last Blister never rose at all, and we cannot get him *to the Place* since Fryday Night, when he went *too much,* and this is *Tuesday.* He is now raving for Mr. Moore, who has been fetched from us to a Woman in Labour, and the other Denbigh Apothecary—Robin Jones; is Ill *himself.* What shall I do? Oh here comes Mr. Moore——and now they are to give Mr. Piozzi Caster Oyl, and he *won't touch* it——and we are at our Wits End. Be a good Boy and God bless you, and tell Mr. Shepherd how miserable is your / truly Affectionate Aunt H: L: P.

We all slept last Night, so we are fresh to bear *this.* It will be a *bad* one I fear—but I must make up my Letter now, because of going to Bed in the Morning when Leake goes to Denbigh—but on Saturday I will write to you again. <Vales>

Text: Ry. 585.19. *Address:* John P: Salusbury Esq. / at The Rev: Mr. T. Shephard's / Enborne near / Newbury / Berkshire. *Postmark:* DENBIGH 224 (In JSPS's hand, "Received March 18th 1809. Answered March 19th 1809").

1. For Thackeray's daughters, Sarah Jane and Selina Martha, see HLP to MW, 18 October 1807, n. 6.
2. The Reverend Robert Anwyl (b. 1741) who received an Oxford B.A. in 1763. He was, according to "Harvard Piozziana" (3:113), "the chaplain of Lleweney hall."
3. *Aeneid*, 1.203.
4. According to the *Chester Chronicle*, 17 March 1809: "On Friday the 10th instant, a melancholy catastrophe occurred in the collieries in Sir Thomas Mostyn's Park, owing to a fire-damp, which instantaneously destroyed fifteen unfortunate workmen, and severely burnt twelve others, seven of whom are since dead, and we are sorry to add many have left wives and large families.—We blush to state that the lessee of the works, who was nearly on the spot at the time of the fatal accident, neither sent for medical assistance, nor afforded any relief to the unfortunate sufferers. . . . This is the second calamity which has taken place at the same pit.—In April 1807, twenty-five industrious colliers experienced a similar fate."

See also the "Whitford Parish Register," and its list of nineteen "Persons" who "were on the 10th day of March 1809 burnt to death in Mostyn Colliery by a noxious Vapor called the Damp." The mass burial took place two days later.

TO JOHN SALUSBURY PIOZZI SALUSBURY

sent Saturday Morning
18: March 1809.

My dearest Salusbury
I continue according to Promise my melancholy Narrative——He would *not* take the Caster oyl; so they administered something else which answered before Two in the Morning—Wednesday; and every body lay down—and *some*—slept; My Master the best among us, and waked quiet at Breakfast hour—The Delirium *gone*, so far as one could perceive; but he said himself that his Head was *not at home*. The Back was dreadful. An open Sore below the lowest of the Vertebræ; Surgeons call it the Os Coccygis. You might have buried a Small Phial Bottle in the Place, and the Discharge nearly insupportable to us all——Our Patient speaking in a firm and angry Tone; his natural Voice clear and strong—and eat his dinner, and quarreled with the Cooking of it, *as usual*—and passed no bad Night.

On Thursday Mr. Moore came early and saw—to his own Amazement—healthy Granulations springing up in the Wound—and all Tendency towards Gangrene disappeared. So I began thinking how to be happy and was sitting near 3 o'Clock The Paper in My Hand——when Dunscombe called me suddenly to his Bedside—I'll come said I, and read the News to him. News! cried the Man—*look* at him. Mr. Moore had not left the House a Quarter of an hour—— I saw him *shivering* and as if all convulsed with Cold: Black Clouds as it were wandering over his Face, and Death as I *believed* in every Feature——It *was a Rigor*. And by dint of Cordials, warm Blankets, and a long Et cætera—Life and Warmth came again with a profuse Sweat, and *critical,* he has been mending ever since: tho' some delirious dreams injured his Night's repose. We have had him in his Dressing-Room this Morning to shave and change Linen, because there was now not only Fœtor, but Danger; from the Number of putrid Ulcers—*all going;* and we have burned Camphor and Cascarilla Bark, and flung the Aromatic Vinegar about most liberally; and instead of any Fainting or Rigor—soon as he was put to Bed—he *stormed* away with Anger, directed chiefly against *me* who he said had always used him very Ill, and worse now than Ever, so he fell asleep: and waked in an hour, and eat his Dinner with Appetite——not Chicken which he quarreled with before; but Calves foot fricaseed White, and *French Beans;* beautiful ones. I think it a fine Thing for *my* Part to *have* young Chickens at this Time of Year, and I have six yet fit to kill, and Numberless Hens *sitting.*

Well! Now Dear Love be merry, and let none be sad except / Your Affectionate Aunt / H: L: P.

I hear our poor old Friend Gillon is not likely to live;[1] Lady Kirkwall gains no Strength, but does not die: and Allen's Husband Jones of Pontriffeth has a tedious but Incurable Disease on him. The Lleweney Affairs I am told are mending, The pecuniary Matters I mean. Farewell and be good. I consider Uncle now—and so may *you,*—as recovering: I mean recovering to the wretched State he is in when at his best. He is the Strongest Man ever under the hand of a Physician, and Mr. Moore says that Ill Humour and *Crossness* such as *his,* are certain Pledges that he will get well.

Adieu! and give my *best* to Mr. Shephard and his Family, and your Friends; and Good Night: for I am half dead and hope for Sound Sleep Myself This Fryday Night / 17th March 1809.

Text: Ry. 585.20. *Address:* John P: Salusbury Esq. / At The Rev. T: Shephard's / Enborne / near Newbury / Berks. *Postmark:* DENBIGH 22< >.

1. John Gillon, who had been ailing for the last two years, was to die on 14 December 1809 "in Welbeck-street, Cavendish-square." See *GM* 80, pt. 1 (1810): 89.

TO LADY KEITH

(Brynbella) Sunday Night
19: March 1809.

It is very kind in You to write so my Dearest, and very obliging to provide me some Amusement for purpose of withdrawing my Thoughts from *such* Scenes as none but a Hospitaliere Nun ever witnessed—Doctor Thackeray protests no English Hospital exhibits anything as bad—and his Eyes filled with Tears, prove both His Feelings and Veracity.

Mrs. Smith must have died 20 Deaths had She heard her Son's Agony expressed as her own was when She brought him into the World; and to cry out as Mr. Piozzi is doing *now,* would kill a Consumptive Patient on the Spot—My Situation most resembles that of your Footman in the Sea, half despairing of his own Life, and listening to the Death Shrieks of his Companions. Quelles Horreurs! And I feel Sorry for the favourite Dog too, they *might* have thrown him overboard poor Fellow! and given him a Chance——I am sure I would have leaped into the Sea myself had I been refused the Boat.¹ Oh pray never more make Apologies for your *Hand Writing;* Mr. Moore who saw it on the Table—and who has billets from me five in a Day—said *how like mine* it was! God bless the People!

When moulting Season arrives, I will endeavor to Secure You Pek's cast-off Finery:—he and his Cousin a Black Japan Peacock are both just now in full Beauty but your Dress was more a decided Blue—and so much the more elegant—than my Bird's Feathers.

> He glistneth *Purple,* and he glistneth Gold,
> Now in bright Green, now Blue himself arraying:
> —So doth thy Beauty bright, all other Beauties
>   swaying.²

Now tell me where those Verses are, and whose? Did I tell you that a Reading Society in England sent me a Letter requesting to be informed where this often-quoted Line was to be found? Men are but Children of a larger Growth;³ and who was the Author of it—I deemed it Doctor Young's, and looked the Night Thoughts over, Line by Line; feeling that it *must* be Blank Verse by the last Word. When however all their Enquiries of other Literary Characters failed—pretty Lady Derby sent them *Chapter and Verse*—⁴ The Line is in Dryden's All for Love, and *She* has not forgotten her *Book* it seems—I was delighted with her for it. Ah Me! what a Source of Comfort is Reading! and what a dead Wretch should I be now—if I did not love it? Is Coelebs pretty? And is it Hannah More's? I must have Coelebs.⁵

Poor Lady de Pilar! Her destruction will precede that of all Spain.⁶—When Loretto was pillaged, the People all turned Atheists because they concluded She could not defend her Worshippers——and had of course no Existence—but in false Records: so they dismissed all Creeds, all Bibles—all Belief in God and Christ——⁷

> Religion blushing veils her sacred Fires
> And unawares Morality expires.⁸

Apropos to Morality are you not sorry for my Neighbours here? Lord Uxbridge⁹ and the Dean of St. Asaph?¹⁰ Unlike in their Political Opinions, they are sad Partners in Domestic Sorrow—and our good King too must grieve I trust to hear the Reports which buz around him;¹¹ for altho' Parents will not give Credit—and should not—to malicious Tales—*Something will* force through the thick Fog we wrap around us, to keep Idea of Danger at a Distance.

My Friends and Servants are even now enraged because they see *I think* my husband will recover—yet he has recovered so often! and by Recovery I only mean a Power of being wheeled out to Breakfast in one Parlour, and to Dinner in the other, retiring at 8 o'clock to Sleep as he has done for Two Years pretty nigh.—and *that* too much Felicity! Well! so perhaps it *is:* and I transcribed your Interesting Account of the Czarina[12] for your Namesake Lady K——— by which I hope She and I shall both of us Edify—and not fancy with old Shylock that there are no Sighs but of *our* breathing, no Tears but *our* Shedding.[13] Tell me whose Daughter Lady Charlotte[14] is who ran away with our Anglesea Hero,[15] and what Relation her husband is to Sir Arthur Wellesley.[16] Remember I live completely out of the World; and Newspaper Intelligence—like the Westminster Grammar,[17]—sets out by supposing People acquainted with the Præcognita, and already skilled in the Rudiments.

Farewell! and be happy *as* you can and *while* you can; and remember dear old Dr. Johnson's saying

> Wear the Gown and wear the Hat,
> Snatch thy Pleasures while they last;
> Hads't thou nine Lives—like a Cat,
> Soon those nine Lives would be past.[18]

My last is passing rapidly away; yet am I ever—*one* Sweet Lady K's true Friend;— and the other's Affectionate Mother / H: L: Piozzi.

Make my proper Respects acceptable to Lord Keith, and Love to your Sisters when you see them.

Text: Bowood Collection.

1. The incident is lost with Q's missing letter.
2. HLP alludes to a description of a peacock in William Mason's "Musaeus: a Monody to the Memory of Mr. Pope. In Imitation of Milton's Lycidas," stanza 4, in Dodsley 3: 307–8.
3. Spoken by Dolabella in *All for Love,* 4.43.
4. For Lady Derby, see HLP to LC, 3 February 1796, n. 8.
5. Published in 1808, Hannah More's *Coelebs in Search of a Wife* is essentially a series of social sketches and moral precepts fictionalized by the hero's search for a wife who embodies all virtues and values insisted upon by his deceased parents.
6. The church of Nuestra Señora del Pilar (Iglesia Metropolitana del Pilar) in Saragossa was conceived in the grand style by Francisco Herrara (second half of the seventeenth century) and remodeled by Ventura Rodriguez Tizón (second half of the eighteenth century). The church owes its name to one of the most adored objects in Spain—the "pillar" of jasper on which the Virgin is said to have rested when she manifested herself to Saint James, who was traveling through Saragossa.
7. According to tradition, the Holy House of the Virgin in Nazareth was brought to Loreto (in the province of Ancona) by angels at the end of the thirteenth century. Around it was built the Santuario della Santa Casa, begun in 1468. In the course of time the church acquired the mosaics of Domenichino and Guido Reni, etc.; the frescoes of Melozzo da Forli and Luca Signorelli; the treasure room of sixteenth-century majolica. The church was pillaged by the French in 1797.
8. *The Dunciad,* 4.649–50.
9. HLP refers to Henry Paget (1744–1812), tenth baron Paget of Beaudesert (1770), third earl of Uxbridge (1784). Significant in the Tory political scene in North Wales, he had married on 11 April 1767 Jane, née Champagné (d. 1817). Their "Domestic Sorrow" was caused by their sons Henry William (1768–1854) and Arthur (1771–1840).
10. As HLP was to explain in her next letter to Q, dated 10 April: the dean was "under some Pressure of Vexation from" a son's behavior. Whatever it was, it was mentioned only as a bit of North Wales gossip and never described.

The dean deliberately omitted from his will the name of a single son, Robert John. On presumptive evidence, he is the culprit. The context would suggest sexual misconduct. For Shipley's will, signed 19 August 1820 and proved 23 June 1826, see P.R.O., Prob. 11/1713/348.

11. On 17 March, "Two Divisions having . . . taken place in the House of Commons on the Duke of York's investigation," there was consensus "that He ought not to be continued in Office" (Farington 9:3422). At the same time he was acquitted of any corrupt practices by a vote of 278 to 196. The following day he resigned his post as commander in chief of the army. Public reaction against the duke was harsh despite attempts to impute the accusations to the Jacobins.

12. Alexander I had married 28 September 1793 Elisaveta Alexeievna, formerly *Luise* Marie Auguste (1779–1826), third daughter of *Karl* Ludwig, hereditary prince of Baden.

13. *The Merchant of Venice*, 3.1.95–96.

14. Charlotte Wellesley (1781–1853), the wife of Sir Henry Wellesley, was the daughter of Charles Sloane Cadogan (1728–1807), first earl Cadogan (1800).

15. Henry William Paget, cr. first marquess of Anglesey three weeks after he commanded Wellington's cavalry at Waterloo, began his military career in 1793, becoming a major general in 1802, a lieutenant general in 1808, a general in 1819. As Lord Paget, he distinguished himself in the campaigns (1794, 1799) of the duke of York and later (1808–9) when commanding the cavalry at Corunna under Sir John Moore.

In 1809 he abandoned his wife Caroline Elizabeth, née Villiers (1774–1835), and eloped with Charlotte Wellesley, a mother of four children whom he allegedly seduced.

On 10 March, *The Times* reported "that on Monday [the 6th] Lady C. W. wife of the Hon. H. W. eloped with Lord P.: this has been generally affirmed, but what has been further added, viz. that Sir A. W. the brother of the injured husband, pursued and overtook the fugitives, and that a duel between Sir A. W. and Lord P. took place, in which his Lordship was mortally wounded, is contradicted."

16. Henry Wellesley (1773–1847) was the youngest brother of Sir Arthur Wellesley (1769–1852), later first duke of Wellington (1814). Young Wellesley was already a distinguished diplomat who was to be created Baron Cowley in 1828.

17. *Rudimentum grammaticae latinae metricum, in usum Scholae Regiae Westmonasteriensis* (1770); *The Construction of the Latin Verse-Grammar. For the use of the lower forms in Westminster School* (1774).

18. See *Anecdotes*, p. 165. SJ's impromptu lines were called forth by Q's discussion with a friend about "a new gown and dressed hat she thought of wearing to an assembly."

TO LADY WILLIAMS

Sunday
March 26th 1809

Nothing *can* be exaggerated Dearest Madam: Mr. Piozzi's Sufferings far exceed whatever can be *said*.

I will bear mine how I can: Thankful to my Friends; and Submissive to God's Will——but we are best alone; at such Times there is no Consolation but from above.

We hope his Sufferings begin to remit now: Nature is nearly exhausted.

I can scarce say / how much I am / Your Ladyships / H: L: P.

Mr. Piozzi expired at 2 o'Clock.

Text: Ry. 3 (1807–11). *Address:* Bodylwyddan.

TO LADY KEITH

Tuesday
[4] April 1809[1]

My dearest Girl
has written very kindly—so have you *all*; *all* very good and very amiable; and I have less *Right* and *Claim* to my little Hoard of Sorrow than I *wish* for in my present State of Mind—but to part as I did yesterday *for ever* from the Man who has engrossed my heart for so long a Course of Years, must cost a cruel Pang—*You know* it must. He hapless Creature knew nothing nor nobody for many dreadful Days; Frantic with unexampled Anguish, he lived till the slow-spreading Gangrene reached his Spinal Marrow;—The Medical Men praying incessantly for his Release—as force only could make him swallow either soothing Opiates or Supporting Food: nor had Nature performed any of her Functions for 66 Hours. I can say nothing else and will now say no more except that I will leave this Theatre of Horror and lie forgotten for 3 or 4 Weeks among the Crouds of London. Bath would not *do*—my *Friends* would be my Scourge; at an Hotel I can shut out even my Children, unless as mere *droppers-In:* one at a Time, or *Two* at most, dear Creatures! when they have a Leisure Hour—*nothing more.* I will not enter a House belonging to any human Creature—but an *Inn* keeper, like Shenstone:[2] and I will try to get good Seabathing in the *hot Summer* Months. A November Dip would now kill your poor Nerve-shaken but ever Affectionate /
H: L: P.

Text: Bowood Collection.

1. Misdated 3 April, the letter was written on the day after GP's interment in the Dymerchion (or Tremeirchion) church.
2. Shenstone's famous poem, "Written at an Inn," was a favorite of SJ, who also thought of the public house as a seat of human happiness, a retreat from daily care and deception. See *Boswell's Johnson* 2:452; *Johns. Misc.* 2:253.

TO LADY KEITH

Brynbella Monday
10: April 1809.

I thank you my dear Creature,—*heartily* for your last Letter,—for *all* your Letters. You were always wise, and I was always willing so to deem you.—

The Earl of Kent in Shakespeare's King Lear said not more truly that *You* say——

> He *hates* him;
> That would upon the Rack of this tough World
> Stretch him out longer——

Yet Kent's next Speech and his *last* come closer to my Heart, perhaps my Destination.[1]—Well! no Matter: I must have Man Maid and lodging whilst I *do* live. Indeed I did say to Cecilia Mostyn that She should do me the favour to hand Sophia Daniel and her Welsh Richard out of the Window for Patterns; tho' your Quondam Servant Mr. William that I remember in Cumberland Street, would be a good Model for my *Upper* Man; to be above the Country Servants——and below *General Lake* as we call our Steward and Factotum: he must therefore wear a Livery, or he would (like Johnson whom you recollect perhaps) refuse to walk home with a female Friend——unless he *lent her his* Arm. I warrant your tenacious Memory has not let Slip that Silly old Stuff.

With Regard to Modern Matters, 'tis the Dean, not the Bishop of St. Asaph who is under some Pressure of Vexation from a Son who seems to have cruelly enough by his Conduct increased the Regret which his honourable Brothers brave Death caused to his Family.[2] Cecilia can explain.

I shall be very desirous to take when I am able an Interest in passing Scenes— my Wishes are for *escaping* Sorrow, not encouraging. And the Young Men I sent for to assist me thro' my Business here—Poor Piozzi's Nephew Salusbury, and his Friend; give me full Credit for endeavouring to recall my Senses,—scattered as they were by Grief and Horror. Did Doctor Myddelton call on any of You in London? He read the Commendatory Prayer over my wretched Husband a full Week before his Release—but whether he *quite knew* what past—Poor Soul! I have never felt convinced. He administered the Sacrament to us all in our Drawing Room about a *Twelvemonth* ago, when Mr. Piozzi was in full Possession of his mental Powers[3]—made his Will &c.[4]

Apropòs he bade me request Dear Lady Keith to accept his little Piano Forte made in Form of a Coach Seat by Pohlman, and of most elegant *Tone*.[5] I meant to bring it up with me to London but the Construction of Carriages is altered, and it does not fit my Chaise—it must abate its *Dignity* poor Dear! and travel in a Waggon some Time, when you have done it the honour to promise it house Room and Patronage. You are to have Choice of Musick whatever you like best.

I never could tell anyone but you what Mr. Piozzi endured these last five or six Weeks;—for Cecy would disregard the Narration as a Dream: and Sophy would be sick and faint away.

It is however strictly true that four of the lower Vertebrae were *visible,* and that Two of them *Sphacelated* and cracked with Torture. May we all find easier Exits from this World to the next! So painful a one was surely never passed since the Days of Martyrdom.[6] Present me properly to your Noble Husband and believe me ever / Your Affectionate Mother whilst / H: L: Piozzi.

I fancy you will all be contented to set me down at Warrens.[7] 'Tis my favourite Hotel, but Cecy offered first, so She will direct me.

I think I shall see London this Day fortnight Monday 24: April. Perhaps the Noise of Coaches in the Street will make me Sleep—This Death-like *Stillness* hinders my Resting somehow; nor can I here close my poor Eyes till Morning's Dawn sets all the Birds o'Singing.

Somebody write—and tell me where to drive to. I gave Mrs. Hoare to understand A *few* of my Distresses which you never knew of—The Danger was greater I now see, than that which I apprehended—but God Almighty delivered me from all—as you say—I ought to be thankful and so says Mr. Shephard!!!

Text: Bowood Collection. *Address:* R: H: Baroness Keith.

1. *King Lear,* 5.3.314–16. Kent's next speech is about Lear himself.

> The wonder is he hath endur'd so long,
> He but usurp'd his life.
> (lines 318–19)

Kent's last speech is simply,

> I have a journey, sir, shortly to go:
> My master calls me, I must not say no.
> (lines 322–23)

2. Dean Shipley's second son was Mordaunt James, who died on 27 November 1806 at Russel's Rest, in the island of the Nevis, aged twenty-six. A member of the Council there, he succumbed to a fever indigenous to the island where he had lived for six years.

Another son, Conway (b. 1782) was in command of the *Nymphe* frigate when in a cutting-out expedition on the Tagus he was killed in April 1808.

3. GP had earlier been converted to Anglicanism ca. Jan. 1807 in Bath. According to "Harvard Piozziana" 3:101–2: "When however [GP] was not expected to live four and Twenty hours, and I had requested of him to send over the Way for some or all of a Whole Army of Romish Priests attending on Mrs. Fitzherbert's Mother——when to this Request he replied No No No—with Quickness——My Heart began to feel Hope of a new and heavenly Kind——would you *like* then said I, to see a Clergyman of our Church?—and communicate in *our* Perswasion. Certainly; was his Reply:—with Mr. Leman if possible.—I sent for him Instantly, and whilst they conversed—did truly myself give God the Glory, for having led him out of Error by *his own hand*—for I never dared trust the Subject between us; lest I might entangle my *own* Conscience and distress *his.*"

4. GP's final will was signed at Brynbella on 28 November 1808 with John Oldfield as the consulting attorney. A codicil was added 11 January 1809 with Charles Mitchell Smith Shephard of Gray's Inn, Charles Kirkwell, and Alexander Leak as witnesses. GP died 26 March and was buried on 3 April "at Dymerchion, Flintshire, in a vault which he had constructed in that church, when it was repaired and beautified some years ago at his expense, and under his direction" (*Shrewsbury Chronicle,* 7 April). For the will, proved 2 May 1809, see P.R.O. Prob. 11/1498/396.

5. Johannes Pohlman (fl. 1760–1807), of German extraction, was an English harpsichord and piano maker. He worked in London, first in Compton Street, Soho, and later at 113 Great Russell Street, Bloomsbury. See *Journals and Letters* 12:801, n. 3.

GP's traveling pianoforte was made in 1784, shortly before he and HLP went to the Continent.

6. HLP's "Pocket Books" tersely notes the onslaught of GP's last illness (N.L.W., MS. 11099A [1808] and 11100A [1809]). From 3 September 1808 onward HLP begins to repeat her references to GP's bad health, his constant pain, giddiness, loss of appetite, and ill temper. By February 1809 he was often delirious, and Dr. Thackeray was called from Chester. On 23 March 1809, HLP writes that GP suffers from gangrene of foot and hand, that he "sleeps perpetually, Life ebbing out." On 26 March, "All hope extinguished. All *Life* extinguished." On 31 March, "Good Fryday all dismal!!" and on 2 April, "Sent the Chester Paper [obituary] Paragraph." On 3 April, "The dismal Day—last,

last, last" and four days later, "Blank Sorrow. Thankful for Salusbury's Company and Shephard's." By the 10th they had left and she writes simply, "All alone." By 13 April, she remarks, "Packed up the Travelling Pianoe forte for Lady Keith; put Dear Piozzi's Sonatas *in* it, and his Song in un Marditante Pene."
7. HLP left Brynbella for London on 19 April.

TO JOHN SALUSBURY PIOZZI SALUSBURY

Chester Wensday
19: April 1809.

My dearest Salusbury
will be glad now to hear *of* and from me. I am so far safe on my Journey; and under Doctor Thackeray's Care how can I come to harm? A swelled face is my worst Complaint at present, and the wise Men say that even *that* is caused merely by relaxation and the long Torment my poor Nerves have suffered. Oh how the *Poor* Folks came Yesterday round the Carriage we set out in!——You would have expected me to have been devoured! And Robert (the Tall Footman's Mother) *crying* because her *little Boy* was leaving Wales, and *sure enough* he would never, no *never* come back alive. Leak was finely enraged with them.

It was such dreadful Weather on Sunday none of the Servants could go to Church;—still less durst I venture, and God forgive me I felt half glad to escape the black Pew &c. So I called my Family and read Prayers to them in the Drawing Room at Night;—to beg a Blessing both on the goers away and the Stayers-behind.—It was a Melancholy Meeting—all in our dismal Dresses so, but I got through it somehow; and Allen-Jones and I had a good Hysterical Cry after all was over.——Her poor Husband gets gradually worse and worse, Dr. Thackeray fears it's scarce possible he should recover. What do You think Mr. Moore's Bill was for these last Two Years? Guess first, and then I'll tell you.

Mr. Charles Shephard wrote very goodnaturedly from Oxford, he met another *blind Cupid* I understand, that made you a World of Sport: Dr. Thackeray says you had no Sport *here*, the Weather was so wretched. He gives one good Advice to eat and drink, and take *no* Medicine; but use Exercise and endeavour to raise my miserable Pulse to a better State: and to get good Nights by *Fatigue* rather than *Opiates*——he is raving mad after the new-fashioned *Schools*——in Lancaster's Method brought from India and seems to expect Dulness—like the Small Pox—is to be quite eradicated by Modern Improvement.[1]

The *Ladies* as we call *my Daughters*, expect me in London on Monday 24. Warren's Hôtel, Charles Street, St. James's Square. Thither you must direct, and tell me how good you are, and how well you are;——These are Inn Pens—I cannot make them mark the Letters;—and tell me when Your Summer Holydays are, that I may know whether we shall pass them in North or South Wales——

whether at Brynbella, or Tenby in Pembrokeshire; as I mean to bathe in the Sea there, upon my Way to Bath.

Give my *best* Regards to Mr. Shephard, and Compliments to his Family: and believe my Dearest Boy, that you have an Affectionate Aunt and a true Friend in Your / H: L: P.

Text: Ry. 585.21.

1. "Modern Improvement" in education was represented by Joseph Lancaster (1778–1838) and by Andrew Bell (1753–1832). Working independently—Lancaster in a London school and Bell in Madras—both men became proponents of the "mutual" or "monitorial system" of public education. In 1803–4 each acknowledged the work of the other, but within a few years each claimed to be the originator of the system and each had his adherents.

TO MARGARET WILLIAMS

                                     Morin's Hotel Duke Street
                                     Manchester Square
                                     London Wensday
                                     26 April 1809.

My dear Miss Williams
pursues me with Kindnesses; If I live long enough I will pay her my personal Thanks next Winter:—Will *This* Winter ever have an End? I thought *Spring* was arrived at Brynbella, where we left Asparagus and Cucumbers and Forest Trees in full Leaf; but travelling southward were amazed by Snow-Storms, Floods and every frightful Description of Weather.

Doctor Thackeray detained me but a short Time at Chester—he said my Health would mend upon the Journey and so it *does* mend; but much is yet wanting to make it tolerable. Kind Mr. Bowen, and dear Doctor Parry shall try what they can do with me next November. Ah—little do they know what my poor Nerves have suffered—from the Contemplation of Disease, Delirium, and Inevitable Death for Three sad Melancholy Moons—all in a solitary Country Seat too—and no comfort even of Lady Kirkwall, whose Life hung by a Thread the whole Time: and Allen-Jones of Pontriffeth expecting *her* husband to accompany mine.—Other Matters tormenting me beside; Kitchen-Griefs as I call them—but 'tis all over; all my Sorrow! and *all my Joy* of this World to which my last Link, of my last Chain is broken.

Does Dunscombe go home to his Wife now? or *is* She his Wife after all? He has got all he *could* get, and his Dismission from Brynbella—The People there said he was married to my Maid Chancey—She too is leaving Me, but there are Plenty such in this Gay Town.

My poor dear Valuable old Friend Mr. Gillon goes to his long home latest of the four Invalids that we lamented at Bath Two Years ago; Mostyn, Piozzi, Siddons, and Gillon will be all off the Stage now in Two or Three Months Time.

Dear Miss Williams let us remember we are to follow! Mr. Piozzi left me sole Executrix, and sole Legatee—only some trifling Remembrances to Friends in Italy. He never named his Nephew in the Will; which This Day I go to prove at Doctors Commons: of such Men there are *not* Plenty, and so said dear Mr. Lemon whose Kindness I shall for ever gratefully remember, and I hope to see *him* next Winter.[1]

Oh tell all my dear Friends, it is because I love them *too well* I did not come to Bath this Spring: I dared not trust my Spirits among you—at such a Moment. *Here* nobody has Time for Feeling, nor is the Expression of it at all fashionable: I have *all that suits me best,* Civility:—and Tenderness would only oppress. Miss Wroughton is ever Angelic and I know she loved my Husband.[2] The amiable Lutwyches are well schooled in Affliction and have weathered *their* Storm as I wish to weather mine.[3] The Thelwalls' compassionate Hearts I am sure are in the right Place—Oh give my truest Regards to all who recollect Your own poor /
H: L: P.

They told me at Chester you were leaving Bath, but I hope it is not true.

Text: Ry. 8 (1808–12).

1. For the Reverend Thomas Leman, see HLP to Thomas Pennant, 24 December 1798, n. 3.
2. For Susannah Wroughton, see HLP to PSW, 21 [November 1792], n. 8.
3. For Mary and William Lutwyche, see HLP to MW [ca. April 1808], n. 2.

TO JOHN SALUSBURY PIOZZI SALUSBURY

London
Wednesday 26: [April 1809]

My dearest Salusbury

I have got your Letter, and am happy as you say to feel our Distance from each other so shortened: Mr. Charles Shephard and I are going tomorrow to prove poor Uncle's Will at Doctors Commons—he frighted me so about dying before the *Probate* that I was quite ill upon the Road—with *that* Apprehension——because I have now no other; but my Nights are mended with the London Noise and rattle.

Dunscombe staid at Denbigh ten Days, and kept writing to me for more Money; he followed us to Chester, but I hope We are rid of him at last. I shewed Mr. C: Shephard his Letters, and he agrees with me that We had a happy Escape of that very dangerous Fellow. Mr. Merrick Hoare says so too: *He* had such Apprehension of his ill Conduct that he would have come down to take Care of me, but that *the Ladies* as we call them, kept him away; and said they were sure I should *run directly to Bath.*

Well! here I am, and not at Bath at all: nor at Warren's Hôtel—which could not take me in—but at Morin's Hotel—a French house, Duke Street, Manchester Square, and the Droppers-*In* are already numerous enough. I tell them all they must be very agreeable to compensate the Beauty of Brynbella were we left Spring to come *Southwards,* and find Winter. I hope they will prove so agreeable as to detain me in Town till it may suit you to *come home* and then we will *go together:* and Mr. C: Shephard (my Oracle—and *St. Januarius*)¹ says it will be *the best way.*

He brought me *Your* Mr. Shephards Account yester Morning, and I discharged it by Checque upon Hammersley—tell him so, and shew him this Letter; and give my best Regards. Mr. Moore's Bill was 168£——The Undertakers 157£ The Taylors 36£——I forget odd Shillings;—and Mr. Charles Shephard says Tommorrows Exploit cost 90£. In the Apothecary's Account were included the Attendance on some poor Neighbours—and it was of Two Years Standing——All is paid however; and Miss Edgeworth's pretty Popular Tale bears witness that

Out of Debt is out of Danger.²

I receive kind Letters from Absent Friends all the Day long, and Visits innumerable: if the Weather was better, I should mend faster; but some sour Wine that I put in my Gruel at Jackson's Hotel, Chester made me terrible Ill indeed, and Dr. Thackeray had to tye me up for the Journey with Bottles of Stuff &c. &c. Fear no Colours however; I shall get into Harbour like the disabled Ships on *Jury* Masts—Apropòs Why *Jury* Masts? unde derwatur? is it not from the French—Mâts de durer?³ I think so: like the Fellow's Mistake who called The Lemon Juice—Lemon *Duce* so deliberately.

Well! God bless my dear Child, and be very good, and very wise; and a lasting Comfort to your truly / Affectionate Aunt / H: L: Piozzi.

I have seen Streatham Davies, who asks much for you; He says the Mostyn Boys are so *sharp* that he wishes them—and so do I; *better Looking.*

Text: Ry. 585.22 Address: John P: Salusbury Esq. / at the Rev. Thomas Shephard's / Enborne near Newbury / Berks. Postmark: AP 26 1809 (In JSPS's hand, "Received April 27 1809. Answered Do Do")

1. A kindly allusion to Shephard's loyalty. Saint Januarius (San Gennaro), fl. end of the third century, had endured several cruel tests of his constancy. Martyr and bishop, he is the patron saint of Naples.
2. HLP alludes to Maria Edgeworth's *Out of Debt, Out of Danger,* the third tale in the first volume of *Popular Tales,* 3 vols. (London: J. Johnson, 1804).
3. The origin of the term is unknown, and HLP's etymological solution simply attests to her interest in verbal derivation.

TO LADY WILLIAMS

> Mayday 1809.
> Morin's hôtel Duke Street
> Manchester Square
> London

My dearest Lady Williams
 will not now get the amazing Letters She used to love from her poor H: L: Piozzi—who sits in her hôtel hungry for Amusement *herself*, but fully resolved not to quit it for any House but of the sick and sorrowful. I was at dear Mr. Gillon's Bedside yesterday however; his *Deathbed* side as 'tis supposed, but I rather think he has yet much to Suffer. The other Faces which shew themselves to my weak Eyes, appear bursting with Enjoyment:—only poor Lady de Blaquiere, who seems low enough; her unmarried Daughter is grown *quite a Beauty* though, and very good and dutyful; and that is a choice Comfort.[1]

I hear pretty Mrs. Pennant is in Town and near me,[2] but we never visited, your Ladyship knows, and as to being near me, *every*body is near me; we are in the midst of the Gay World, and I like the Rattle and Noise well enough. There will be much on't *by and by* indeed—when The Earl of Dundonald's Death[3] shall call Lord Cochrane to a Seat in the upper House;[4] for then Mr. Wardle and Mrs. Clark will be borne about the Streets in Triumph 'tis supposed,[5]—as an Inducement for the Westminster Electors—to choose him Member.—I expect fine Rioting if this happens.

But dear Sir John and my sweet Lady, and Mrs. Williams will like to hear how I get on as to health. My Nerves did certainly use me ill enough upon *the Road:*—and the first Time I went to Church here at London, feeling myself one Solitary Soul among a *Thousand* human creatures assembled for Service at St. Martin's large spacious Temple[6]—The loud Organ pealing in my Ears, who have not heard a Musical Note or seen 25 People together for 25 Months; affected me too strongly: and I was very near fainting away.

These delicate Feelings will however wear down by Degrees, and leave my Mind dull and *blunted* as an old Woman's *ought to be:* and when I return to Brynbella in July, I hope your Ladyship will do me the honour to come and *witness the Improvement.*

My Daughters give me as much of their Time as I could *possibly expect*,—— more perhaps; and the Husbands of the married ones are exceedingly civil and polite.

My Apartments are wretched hitherto, but I wait for very handsome ones in the *same house*, and hope to get fixed there on Wensday next—day after Tomorrow. Spring seems backwarder about here than at home this Season; I never saw such melancholy Weather, and we had a severe Snow-Storm at Lichfield.

I hope all the dear Young People are well, and that the Sore Eyes Cockneys are plagued with round London, have not yet reached our remote Regions:

There never were seen such Numbers of blind Folks about since the Memory of Man.

The foreign News is rather good than bad I believe,[7] but there is a general disposition to like *bad* news best, and there are ugly Papers stuck against the Walls everywhere; and serious Thinkers do not think Well of the Times at all. I am however sick of Men's affected Fears of an Invasion from an Enemy who has no Ships.

Adieu dear Friends: and sometimes write a Line to say You have not forgotten / Your Obliged and Attached H: L: P.

Text: Ry. 3 (1807–11). *Address:* Lady Williams / Bodylwyddan near / St. Asaph / Flintshire N: Wales. *Postmark:* MA 1 .809.

1. The youngest child of Lord and Lady de Blaquiere was Eleanor (1794–1867). On 8 January 1822 at Saint George's, Hanover Square, she was to marry Joseph Knight. See *GM* 92, pt. 1 (1822): 82.
2. For Louisa Pennant, see HLP to Thomas Pennant, 2 June 1795, n. 3.
3. Archibald Cochrane (1747/8–1831), ninth earl of Dundonald (1778), abandoned a short military career in both the army and navy for scientific pursuits which earned him very little money during his own lifetime. He died impoverished in Paris.
4. Thomas Cochrane (1775–1860), styled Lord Cochrane, tenth earl of Dundonald (1831).

While admiring Cochrane's naval skill and courage for which he was invested as a knight of the Bath, 26 April, HLP distrusted his political position, which became evident in his behavior as M.P. (Radical Reformer) for Honiton (1806–7) and for Westminster thereafter. As the member for Westminster, he was told by Lord Mulgrave that a vote of thanks to Lord Gambier (for his action against the French navy, April 1809) would be proposed. Cochrane stated that he would oppose the motion, that Gambier "had neglected to destroy the French fleet in the Aix roads when it was clearly in his power to do so." This was one of Cochrane's many parliamentary attacks on the admiralty.

5. HLP associated Lord Cochrane and Gwyllym Lloyd Wardle (ca. 1762–1833) for several reasons. Both had strong military ties; both were M.P.s; both, as HLP assumed, used their political power to undermine the military.

Wardle as M.P. for Okehampton had exposed the duke of York's liaison with Mary Anne Clarke late in January 1809. His victory over the duke made him so popular that the freedom of London was voted to him on 6 April, and congratulatory addresses were made to him by several corporations throughout the country. In the spring of 1809 (although all was to change by summer) Wardle— like Lord Cochrane—seemed destined for political fame by frustrating authority.

See *GM* 79, pt. 1 (1809): 163, 348, 373, for the adulation he enjoyed.

6. St. Martin's in-the-Fields.
7. After the news of demoralized British troops at Corunna, English newspapers, like the *Morning Post* on 13 April, announced "that advice was yesterday received at the Admiralty of the surrender of Vigo to the Spanish Patriots, and his Majesty's frigates the *Lively* and *Venus*.—The French garrison consisted of 1500 men, and 50 Officers, who were all compelled to surrender at discretion, and lay down their arms to Capt. M'Kinley, of the *Lively* frigate, and the whole of them are now on their way to England. The military chest of the enemy, and about 450 horses, were at Vigo when it surrendered, and of course fell into the hands of the captors . . . on the 28th ult. [March] and on the following day the whole of the French prisoners were embarked on board our ships for England. . . .

"We have also the happiness to be informed . . . that the garrison of Villafranca had surrendered to the army under [marquis de Romana's] command [25 March]. . . . Thus does the prospect of affairs in Spain begin once more to brighten, and to afford the most happy presages of the issue of the contest in which, with the powerful aid of Britain, [Spain] so gallantly perseveres against the common enemy of all legitimate sovereignty and of civilized man."

Moreover, *The Times* on 1 May suggested that the Austrian army under the command of Archduke Charles had taken the offensive against France.

TO JOHN SALUSBURY PIOZZI SALUSBURY

Monday Morning
May Day 1809.

My dearest Boy
  will believe me when I say that Mr. Shephard's Letter and yours were very pleasing to me. Oh No! no; Things do not go on half so rapidly as Young Fellows fancy: The Lawyers throw a Thousand Rubs in the Way of this Denizenation Business;[1] and our Friend Mr. Charles Shephard will go out o'Soldiering as we call it tomorrow Morning. We must get forward as fast as we *can*, not as fast as we *will* in this World, where scarce any thing *but* Study is sure to produce the desired Effect——A man may try to be *wise*, or *happy* or *rich*—and miss his Aim at last; but he who resolves to study, will be *Learned*; and he who prays for Grace will rarely fail of being *good*.—"since but to *wish* more Virtue is to *gain*."[2]
  Meanwhile all you say about Chancey is right enough, and *wise* enough; but it is difficult for me to suit myself, as I want a Lady's Maid and Housekeeper *united*—Poor Old Mrs. Ray at 75 Years old, has a Right to repose; She must be put upon the Yellow List like our Superannuated Admirals who retire on half pay——and I think I have seen a Woman likely to do very well—if *General Leak*—can form her into an *Adjutant*, and not drive her by severe Looks into *Mutiny*.
  My Apartments are *Miserable*; but Happiness always comes *après Demain*; and the old Frenchman whose Hôtel we Inhabit, protests that *après Demain*—(Wednesday,)—I shall have the very good ones which Mr. Darell leaves that Day.[3] The same Direction will do: Morin's, Duke Street, Manchester Square.
  You remember Lord Deerhurst; he will be Earl Coventry in a Week or two:[4] That old Nobleman has done writing Latin Verses—almost—Two Months; and the young ones say he *must die now*——he is close on 88 Years of Age, and has enjoyed Vigorous Faculties of Mind and Body.—His Son is exactly like him, and laments his being Stone-blind of both Eyes——because he can't look into a *Gradus*. If you tell Mr. Shephard this Stuff, I think it will make him laugh and it will lead him into an Error too, making him believe how *well* I am, and I am not well at all.
  Mr. Charles Shephard set me a hard Task yesterday—writing all that long Will and Testament over again——and making a Duplicate beside for fear it should be *lost*—and no attested Copy.[5]——So now *he* Mr. Charles, is joined in the Executorship with Sir Walter James and Mr. Ray;[6] and my Nerves were So hurried I thought I should die before *next* Sunday; so I went to Church to Day—to St. Martin's because they administer the Sacrament *There* every Sunday thro' the Year on Account of Gentlemen who come to qualify for Offices of State &c.[7] and the loud Organ and the large Church, and the full Congregation seemed so awful to me who have not made one among more than 25 human Creatures at once for 25 Months——That altho no *Whimperer* as you well know,—I burst

out o'Crying; and was happy only in the Consciousness that nobody there knew me—or could possibly care.

Well! now I dare say better Nights will come, and quieter Spirits—and my Friends come about me kindly, and Lady de Blaquiere particularly so: and Sir Walter James said he had seen you and believed you would be a good Boy— and Mr. Shephard says so—*Your* Mr. Shephard: and *his* Assurance of it is a Cordial to your truly / Affectionate Aunt / H: L: Piozzi.

This is written in the Night Sunday 30.

Text: Ry. 585.23. *Address:* John P: Salusbury Esq. / at The Rev. Mr. Thos. Shephard's / Enborne near / Newbury / Berkshire. *Postmark:* MA 1 1809 (In the hand of JSPS, "Received May the 2nd Answered May the 4th 1809").

1. For JSPS's letters of denization, see Ry. Charter 1250. He became a "faithful liege Subject" of the British monarch on 30 June 1809.
2. A variation of the axiom "Virtue is its own reward." Beginning as a commonplace of Stoic philosophy, it was early christianized. See, e.g. Lactantius, *Divine Institutes,* particularly 7.10: "De vitiis et virtutibus, atque de vita et morte." In the eighteenth century HLP might have found parallels of sentiment and language in Young's *Night Thoughts,* 6.477–82; (George Lyttelton), "To Mr. Poyntz, Ambassador of the Congress of Soissons, in the Year 1728," in Dodsley 2:31–34, lines 11–14; "An Epistle to the Right Honorable the Lord Viscount Cornbury," in Dodsley 2:207.
3. Edward Darell (fl. 1777–1830) of Colehill in Kent.
4. HLP was premature; the sixth earl of Coventry died on 3 September 1809, in Piccadilly. He was eighty-seven.
For George William Coventry, the sixth earl, see HLP to Q, 19 March 1799, n. 17.
5. HLP's 1809 will is missing, but it undoubtedly makes JSPS a principal beneficiary along with her daughters. Q, e.g., makes no objection to the will but is concerned about those named as trustees. See HLP to Q, 1 June [1809]: "Mr. Ray made me a very polite Visit, explanatory of all Lord Keith and You said one Day concerning the nomination of Trustees &c. He is a worthy and wise man, and I think You are very happy in his Friendship" (Bowood Collection).
6. For Sir Walter James, see HLP to PSP, 27 March 1798, n. 2; for Robert Ray, the lawyer, see HLP to Q, 7 July 1787, n. 2.
7. That holders of political office came to Saint Martin's is verified by Lord Campbell, as cited by Wheatley 2:479.
"I well remember the time when barristers who had not been at church for many years, on being appointed King's counsel, used to go to *St. Martin's Church* (appropriated for this purpose), pay their guinea, and bring away a Certificate of their having taken the Sacrament of the Lord's Supper according to the rites and ceremonies of the Church of England."

TO THE REVEREND LEONARD CHAPPELOW

Tuesday May 2nd 1809.

If dear Mr. Chappelow

will call upon an Old Friend tomorrow at Morin's Hôtel Duke Street, Manchester Square, he shall hear her Expressions of Astonishment that the Ladies of Llangollen knowing as it seems they did—her afflicting Situation—should be just the *only* People who have appeared wholly to forget her.

Lady Bradford's pious and delicate Mind is always ready to receive awful and useful Impressions: I pray God She may long be spared as an Example to a World which wants such Ladies.

Adieu Dear Sir for a Day only at furthest and then make me among the Droppers-*In* who kindly seek to console and amuse your much grieved, but ever Obliged—H: L: P.

Text: Ry. 561.141.

TO JOHN SALUSBURY PIOZZI SALUSBURY

Saturday Night
6: May 1809.

My dearest Salusbury

You are quite right about the Mourning: do not have any *Thought* of changing till the End of the Year—Autumn at soonest. *My* Motions will be regulated very much by what *your* Mr. Shephard shall say when he comes up to celebrate the Eton Anniversary——Tell me when that is; I do not yet read it advertised in any News paper.[1] He will be the properest Person alive to sign our Memorial Mr. Windle says;[2]—and Mr. Windle is Mr. Charles Shephard's *Pronoun* as I call him:—he is his *Substitute* and *Representative*——but what say you is our Memorial? Why our Memorial is the Memorial and Petition of Hester Lynch Piozzi to the Secretary of State Lord Liverpool,[3] in behalf of an Infant John Salusbury Piozzi, known by the Name of John Piozzi Salusbury; whose request it is That the King will give him leave (altho born an Alien) to enjoy the Privileges of English Birth, for the Preservation of his Property; and to entitle him to accept, receive, and enjoy whatever Land or Money may be given or bequeathed him by the Memorialist—Hester Lynch Piozzi——Now you see this Memorial or Request must be drawn up, and it must be *Engrossed;* and then it must be witnessed—attested by Three at least Men of Character who will lend their Names to say that they know the Aforesaid Hester Lynch Piozzi and her husband's Nephew John Salusbury; and that they do believe he has been bred up in the Church of England and that he will prove a Loyal Subject to King George &c. &c. deserving this Favour of being made a Denizen of Great Britain.

Mr. Shephard's Name is above all Names desirable as he knows the Truth of the Memorial—so does Streatham Davies; and if Sir Walter James comes to Town quickly I will make *him* sign it; and I will write a Letter to Lord Liverpool besides—urging our Request, and pleading my old Acquaintance with his good Father[4]——and after all this——it will lye a good while in the Secretary of State's Office without doubt——and Fees to pay at last. *So much for Business.*

Health gets rather better than worse I believe; but when Sir Lucas Pepys has examined me, it will be better ascertained. The sudden Seizures of Trembling and consequent Languor are less frequent, and People say my Looks are less bad than they *counted* on;——I suppose they *expected* a little old Hag upon a Broomstick like the Witches in Macbeth.

Poor Lady Kirkwall did come to see me at Brynbella—She has *seen* nothing since. Her Eyes have been so inflamed and injured with this horrid Opthalmia that *goes about;* Lady de Blaquiere can hardly read her Letters. Mrs. Mostyn's sick Children have had it; they are always having something to keep them away from School. She looks exceeding well her*self,* so does Mrs. Hoare. Robert is *too little* frighted at the Town, instead of too much: I can hardly keep him at home *now* that Leak is in Norfolk seeing his Friends——except by telling him I shall complain to the General,—*General Lake* on his Return.

Dunscombe has refered a Cheshire Baronet to me for his *Character* as *Butler and Valet*——Oh what frontless Impudence! Write to me Dear Child, and tell me when this Eton Anniversary is, for then I shall see *both* Mr. Shephards; and indeed I am impatient enough, especially when in a low-spirited humour—lest I should leave anything undone which could tend to prove how truly / I am your Affectionate Aunt / H: L: Piozzi.

Read this Letter to Mr. Shephard and make him tell you when he comes to Town.

The Apartments are comfortable enough; The new *Lady-Maid* as poor dear Uncle used to call such Damsels; is I fear more Lady than Maid:—but we shall do somehow——any thing better than as we were.

Text: Ry. 585.24. *Address:* John Piozzi Salusbury Esq. / at The Rev: Thos. Shephard's / Enborne near Newbury / Berkshire. *Postmark:* MA 8 1809 (In JSPS's hand, "Received May 9th 1809.——Answered May 11th 1809").

1. According to the *Courier,* 15 May, "The Eton Anniversary will be held at the Crown and Anchor Tavern, in the Strand, on Saturday, the 20th instant. / General Sir Alured Clarke, K.B. President."
2. Thomas Windle (d. 1818) described himself in his will as an attorney of John Street, Bedford Row, and of Wirk Hill, near Bracknell, Berks. His name as a pleader before the King's Bench and Court of Common Pleas appears in the *Law Lists* as early as 1789. His office was consistently given as 21 Bartlett's Buildings, Holborn. See P.R.O., Prob. 11/1611/592.
3. Robert Banks Jenkinson (1770–1828), Baron Hawkesbury (1803), second earl of Liverpool (1808). A staunch Tory and confirmed anti-Catholic, he held and was to hold several significant political offices: that of home secretary, 1804–6 and 1807–9; secretary for war and colonies, 1809–12; first lord of the treasury, 1812–27.
4. Charles Jenkinson (1729–1808), Baron Hawkesbury (1786), first earl of Liverpool (1796). HLP knew him as Mr. Jenkinson who visited Streatham Park in 1780 (*Thraliana* 1:456).

TO SAMUEL LYSONS

Morin's Hotel
Monday Noon [8: May 1809].

Mrs. Piozzi is broken-hearted to think She lost the Visit from Dear Mr. Lysons and his amiable Brother.

She never *can* (on account of her Dress and Situation) go out at all except early in a Morning when fashionable People are *in their first Sleep:* and She took that opportunity today of seeing the Exhibition of Drawings at Spring Gardens[1]——a miserable Compensation for *their Visit,* which She hopes they will repeat in Compassion to their old / Friend and faithful Servant / H: L: Piozzi.

Text: Hyde Collection. *Address:* Sam: Lysons Esq: / Kings Bench Walks / No. 7. / Temple. *Postmark:* 8 o'Clock MY 9 1809; MA 8 1809.

1 According to *The Times,* 21 April 1809, "The Fifth Annual Exhibition of the Society of Painters in Water Colours . . . will Open on Monday next, April 24, at the Great Room, Spring-gardens at 10 o'clock. On each succeeding Morning the Room will be open at eight o'clock and continue so till dusk." The exhibition was to close 17 June, more a social than an artistic success.

TO JOHN SALUSBURY PIOZZI SALUSBURY

Wednesday
17: May 1809.

Well! *now* dearest Salusbury

I have performed *my* Part towards making you a British Subject. Mr. Windle—the Man Mr. C. Shephard recommended, has drawn up the Memorial of your *Merits* and *Request,* we have had it properly engrossed; and I have got it signed by the truly respectable Names of Lord Deerhurst, Lord Kirkwall, Sir Walter James, Doctor Robert Gray, Prebendary of Durham, Author of the Key to the Old Testament &c. and Reynold Davies *the Reverend* who best can answer for your early Instruction in the Anglican Church Principles as by Law established. Lord Liverpool;—to whose Office this Memorial will be certainly presented in Course of this Week—will I dare say expedite the business so sharply pressed upon him by *such Solicitors,* much more quickly than he would have done in the common Course and Routine of Affairs; for tho' Government is grown very shy of admitting Foreigners to enjoy Privileges of a British Subject, yet they will have no Scruples when they see the names of *our Friends* at the Bottom: and kind Lord Deerhurst has written a Letter to Lord Liverpool *besides* to quicken him if he should be tardily disposed.

Leak is this Moment gone to Mr. Windle with this Important Packet, which I would trust to *no other* hand: and then he takes his Place in the Stage for dear Brynbella, where the Cows and the Sheep require his Care——and I consign myself to Robert—and the new Maid—who is more Lady than Maid I fear, but never mind! All I can do is done I believe. And whether H:L:Piozzi lives or dies, *You* must be a good Boy till you are a good Man.

Mrs. Glover of Bath has lost one of her two eldest Sons——John Octavius I *fear*,¹ but have no certain Intelligence. Pallida Mors æquo pede pulsat &c. &c.² Old and Young——rich and poor; nobody escapes; and the Physicians say this last Season has been strangely fatal——Indeed those who frequent public Places observe more black among the Dresses than usual.

Whilst I write comes in Doctor Myddelton, who professes himself sorry *he* did not call Time enough to sign Your Memorial——so you see There is such a Thing as Friendship in the World, bad as it is:——Mr. Apreece was with him—— he was Your Schoolfellow at Streatham.³ I want to go to Streatham Park, but Mr. Gillon says I had better wait till Atkins has paid his Rent, lest he should step out and beg me to stay for my Money a while; which would not suit me at all just now, as I spend more than I like every Day: and these Letters of Denizenation will cost no Trifle.

Adieu and tell Mr. Shephard how things are going / on, and write soon to your Affectionate Aunt / H: L: P.

<Two lines of indecipherable marginalia.>

which the Heat gives animation to, are my greatest Scourge.—

And I want nothing to irritate me Body or Mind.

Text: Ry. 585.25. *Address:* John P: Salusbury Esq. / at the Rev. T: Shephard's / Enborne near / Newbury / Berks. *Postmark:* MA 17 809.

1. An unfounded rumor. See HLP to JSPS, 22 March 1808, n. 6.
2. For the impartiality of death, see Horace, *Odes*, 1.4.13–14.
3. For Apreece, see HLP to RD, 5 April 1799, n. 5.

TO JOHN SALUSBURY PIOZZI SALUSBURY

Tuesday
30: May [1809].

My dearest Salusbury.

I am expecting to see you now every day: Our good Friend Mr. Windle——The Pronoun—says he can do every thing for us if you will but *come up:* and I have an encouraging Letter from Lord and Lady Deerhurst giving me hope that all will be soon settled.[1]

I am very tired of Town, and if this Affair was once over, and my Carriage ready for Travelling I would soon slip away from The Heat and Dust and Bugs——and monstrous Expence of a London Hôtel. Mr. Shephard must decide for us whether you will come home *with me* for six Weeks and then return to *him;* or wait as usual for the Pembertons.

God bless my dear Child; and be good and wise: and love Your / Affectionate Aunt / H: L: P.

Text: Ry. 585.27.

1. According to Lady Deerhurst, 29 May 1809 (Ry. 554.56): "The dinner was on the table at the Moment your letter with its enclosure, arrived or I should not have delayed an immediate answer.

"Lord Deerhurst begs to know the age of your young relation, and will obtain from his friend Mr. Reeves, who is at the head of the Alien Office every information requisite, for the completion of the business in question."

Two days later HLP received the following (Ry. 554.57): "Lord Deerhurst has called on Mr. Reeves superintendant of the Alien Office who Informs him that Mr. Capper conducts the Dennization business in the Secretary of States department to whom he will speak in order to forward the forms requisite and will also contribute on his Part to the Completion of the desire Object. It will be necessary for the youth with a companion to wait upon Mr. Reeves at the Alien Office, Crown Street, Westminster between one and two o'clock and Lord Deerhurst will give him a note to Mr. R. as already arranged."

TO JOHN SALUSBURY PIOZZI SALUSBURY

Tuesday
7: June 1809.

My dearest Boy

has cost me so much Money and Care in these Dozen Years of his British Life, that a little more may be willingly *thrown in.* I will dine at Speen hill the *old Castle* on Monday next if it please God[1]——It *does* please St. Januarius;[2] because when I told my *Reasons* for wishing to leave *this House,* he found them solid and good;—and advised me to be gone as soon as possible. On Monday then 12th of June expect me to Dinner at Speen *hill,* and if it is within a Walk of you, call there; and secure us our old Apartment. We will drive the next Day to Woodstock; where—to make you amends for travelling *slowly* with Aunt and her Maid——I shall show you Blenheim House and Park——and so on by gentle Stages home. *You* standing in Place both of *Protector* and *Protegé* united / towards your truly Affectionate / H: L: Piozzi.

Give my truest Regards to Mr. and Miss. Shephard.[3] I go to Streatham Park on Saturday in the new Carriage to try it.

Text: Ry. 585.28.

1. When HLP visited JSPS at Enborne, she stayed at the Castle Inn, Speen Hill, Bucks. The inn, established in 1758, stands today as three houses, to which it had been converted in the nineteenth century. See C.R.O., Berkshire (D/EB 833 T62).
2. "St. Januarius": Charles Shephard. See HLP to JSPS 26 April 1809, n. 1.
3. Mr. Shephard: Rev. Thomas Shephard. Miss Shephard; probably Shephard's eldest daughter Maria (Shephard) Mackenzie, who died c. 1830 at Crux Eaton; but possibly Elizabeth Charlotte Anne (d. 2 May 1861) or Harriet Caroline Butler (d. *c.* 1847). See C.R.O. Berkshire for the wills of Maria (D/EX 360/15) and Elizabeth Charlotte (D/EX 360/20).

TO LADY KEITH

Brynbella Tuesday
20: June 1809.

I make haste to write that your Freed Cover may enclose the Thousand kind Wishes which wait on *all* my Dear Girls; and to you who have been my dear Girl *longest,* a sincere Hope that Lord Keith's anxiety and your own concerning the Nomination of new Trustees may be speedily ended in the Manner you most wish.

For me and *my precious Health;* every day, and by every Accident becoming of less Value to myself and every one else:—I rather incline to Think *we mend,* rather than grow worse. Our Journey consisted only of short Airings; and I stopt at Blenheim and Worcester and Coalbrook on purpose to shew my young Companion Places of such Curiosity as might make Compensation for going on an Old Lady's sober Trot instead of being happily dashed to Pieces like Mr. Churchill on the Pavement of St. James's Street from A Situation every young Man must have been envying five Minutes before he fell.[1]

Our Newspaper tells too of Mrs. Boehm's Ball, and altho' London is emptying every hour without doubt, there are still gay Days and Gala Nights:[2] I hope your own 14th: produced upon the whole more Pleasure than Fatigue. Lord Keith you said, would not remain a Week in Town after his Return to it, and you will then retire to Purbrook, of which and its numerous Beauties, I have heard So much.

Meanwhile there will be a general Exchange made from that *Rill* of Rhenish Wine and Water and Sugar Talk, that trickles rather than flows thro' the crouded Assemblies of a crouded Metropolis; to a no less Insipid, but more solid and nutritious Calves-foot Conversation, held at Gentlemens Country Seats during the Venison Season—when the Crops of *Hay* and *Corn* are discoursed about, and each congratulates other upon the Show of Wall Fruit, and the Improvement of those vile Roads that used to fright the Ladies at such and such a Turning where the Quarter was particularly high.

Our Neighbours have been happily furnished indeed from higher Subjects, Mr. Wardle and Mr. Maddocks[3]—whose Names will be echoed among our Mountains, long after London has forgotten to repeat them. Susan Thrale promised me some *Pages of Inanity*, pray make her keep her Word; Mrs. Hoare has some bad Verses of mine which might have been made tolerable, but She caught me in the Fact, and finding *She* liked them, my Fancy was deceived and I let her take them uncorrected, and for a Moment liked them well enough myself, *but am wiser now.* Living alone does make one wise for a *while,* and after a while it makes one foolish, for want of Contradiction. If anything very curious comes out, coax Cecy to bring it me; Oh if I get to London next Year, I will be acquainted with Miss Joanna Baillie, Shee the Painter, and Walter Scott;[4] and when I have Spent an Evening or Two in *their* Company—(but not before;) I will compare these Times with past Times, and if those were really better—for Chat I mean—how highly! and with what encreased Reverence shall I regard them!

Mr. Rogers said that Dear old Cumberland would come to see me, but at that Instant came out his Review[5] censuring some Stuff of mine—and then he was ashamed to come—how silly![6] Why his Review censures *Marmion!!*[7] Surely my Synonymes might be happy to be ill spoken of, in such Company. In Peter Pindar's last *funny* Thing about Mrs. Clarke,[8] there are two Lines would make a capital good Motto for Cumberland's Review, while he begs Assistance from Horace Twiss—who has *just done growing,* and Mr. Crowe who has so lately begun feathering his Nest.

> *Young Magpies,* with *old Ravens,* Choughs and *Crows,*
> Spit in our Face and pull us by the Nose.[9]

These however are merry Jests only; If that very elegant, very classical, and what is better, very *pious* Writer Cumberland, ever comes to Want five or Ten Guineas; mine shall be at his Service:[10] with Ill Will enough to Those who Suffer such a Man to be distressed—It is a Shame to Opulence and Liberality.[11]

Adieu. Write when you are at Leisure and beg Letters from your Sisters in the mean Time: presenting my best Affections to them all and assuring them that I am still theirs / and Your own (like Posthumus)[12] increasing / in Love / H: L: Piozzi.

Text: Bowood Collection.

1. According to the *Morning Post*, 16 June: "The Earl of Sefton met with a serious accident on Wednesday afternoon [the 14th]. As his Lordship was driving his lofty barouche at a great rate, with four blood bays with Mr. Churchill sitting on the box, on turning from Arlington-street into St. James's-street, the spring of the box broke; his Lordship fell upon the horses, but continued to hold the reins, and was thus by a great exertion, enabled to restrain their speed. He received no material injury; but Mr. Churchill was thrown on the pavement, on the near side of the carriage, with great violence, and remained for a short time nearly senseless; he was conveyed in a sedan to his house at the corner of Park-lane."

The victim was Charles Spencer-Churchill (1794–1840), who was to become an army officer and M.P. The Earl of Sefton was William Philip Molyneux (1772–1838), second earl.

2. See the *Morning Post*, 16 June: "Mrs. Boehm saw masks on Wednesday evening at her magnificent house, in St. James's-square, which was fitted up for the occasion with great taste, and illuminated by diamond-cut Grecian lamps of uncommon beauty and perfection. . . . Although the masks were not numerous . . . Mr. Champneys was there as a French dancing master of the old school, and led off *Lady Coventry's Minuet* most admirably with Mrs. Boehm. . . . [He] was extremely well dressed in a white satin coat, embroidered with roses, &c. The Ladies were all extremely anxious to take a lesson, not even excepting her Grace of Grafton. This party for upwards of two hours supported their several characters with great spirit, when, on the motion of Mrs. Boehm, the company ordered their carriages and departed for the Argyle Masquerade."

Dorothy Elizabeth, née Berney (d. 1842), was the wife of Edmund Boehm (d. 1822). See her will signed 17 February 1837 and proved 4 February 1842 (P.R.O., Prob. 11/1957/68).

3. According to the *Morning Post*, 6 May 1809: "The public were prepared to expect something important in last night's Debates of the House of Commons, and truly important did they prove to be." The newspaper went on to liken the debates to the demagoguery in "the Revolutionary Halls of France."

"A notice from Mr. Maddocks . . . stood on the Orders 'For an examination into the conduct of Ministers with regard to the sale of Seats in Parliament,' and upon this *general* notice, Mr. Maddocks stood up in his place and denounced, in the most vague terms, *two individuals*, guilty of gross corruption." The charges were directed against Perceval, chancellor of the exchequer, and Lord Castlereagh, colonel secretary of state.

The Times on 13 May reported that "Mr. Madock's motion, upon the corrupt practices imputed" to the above two ministers was "negatived by a great majority."

HLP's villain was William Alexander Madocks (1773–1828), a second-generation Welshman. An Oxonian, he was M.P. for Boston (1802–20) and Chippenham (1820–26). "Mr Wardle" was Gwyllym Lloyd Wardle (ca. 1762–1833), M.P. for Okehampton, 1807–12.

4. HLP mentions three names which circulated widely among London intellectual circles in 1809.

In 1806 Joanna Baillie and her sister Agnes (1761–1861) rented a house near Hampstead Heath. Here they entertained writers, scientists, and painters; here many of the intellectual controversies of the day were debated.

The portrait painter Martin Archer Shee (1769–1850), knighted ca. 1830, published in 1809 *Elements of Art*, a poem "very highly spoken of." See Farington 9:3477–78, 3483.

Sir Walter Scott had been lately so lionized in London that he "was weary of the intercourse He had [there], viz. dining & being perpetually in Society.—'I have dined with them till I am weary of it, I now want them to dine with me, in my domestic quiet state.' sd. He" (ibid. 10:3514).

5. The *London Review*, conducted by Richard Cumberland (London: Samuel Tipper, Leadenhall-Street, 1809), vol. 1 (Feb.-May 1809), vol. 2 (Aug.-Nov. 1809). Although it was designed "To be continued Quarterly," it lasted for only two issues.

6. The *London Review* (1:282–302) printed a critique by the philologist Daniel Boileau of J. A. Eberhard's *Versuch einer Allgemeinen Deutschen Synonymik*, etc. (6 vols.), and of its translation, *Dictionary of German Synonymous Words*. The review at length finds HLP's *British Synonymy* faulty in the distinctions it makes among certain synonyms: e.g., now, at present, and this instant; or openness, candour, purity of mind, ingenuity, and sincerity. The "intention" of the review is to dismiss HLP's work and "to point out the advantage which future English synonymists will derive from consulting Mr. Eberhard's work."

7. Horace Twiss reviewed Scott's *Marmion* for the *London Review* 1:82–121.

Twiss complained that the style which Scott introduced in *The Lay of the Last Minstrel* and repeated in *Marmion* had lost its "novelty: and unfortunately it is in itself so faulty, that, when it loses this, it loses its only charm." Twiss laments further: "every reader, when he beholds [Scott's] imagination so vigorous and so fertile wasted on this injurious style, must feel a degree of indignation mingled with his regret; and while he laments to see the rich treasure sinking to the bottom of the deep, he cannot chuse but blame the careless owner, for having trusted such a cargo to a vessel that was not sea-worthy" (pp. 93, 94).

8. HLP refers to Peter Pindar's *A Solemn Sentimental and Reprobating Epistle to Mrs. Clarke* (1809) in *The Works of Peter Pindar, Esq.*, 4 vols. (London: F. C. and J. Rivington; J. Nunn; Cadell and Davies; Longman, etc. 1816), 4:33 ff. The lines are as follows:

> The small pert Tenants of the Hedge rush out,
> To put the solemn Trav'ller to the rout;
> Magpies and Jays, and Ravens, Rooks and Crows,
> Spit in his face, and pull him by the nose.

9. HLP knew that Horace Twiss was a regular reviewer, appearing in the first volume with an attack on *Marmion*, and with an evaluation of Malthus on population; in the second with a statement on Thomas Campbell's *Gertrude of Wyoming*.

G. W. Crowe appeared as a reviewer in the second number and regularly thereafter during the short life of the journal.

10. When Cumberland died in 1811, he left his daughter Frances Marianne Jansen (with whom he lived) all his property, which amounted to less than £450. Two volumes of his posthumous works were to be published in 1813 for her benefit.

11. HLP genuinely admired "Poor old Cumberland! he is dead, and will be buried in Westminster Abbey at last; I am glad he is to be in his own odd Phrase, so well *located*. He was a Champion of the Church in this Infidel Age, and a good man too——for aught I ever heard—Poor old Cumberland!" ("Harvard Piozziana," vol. 4).

See HLP to Q, 17 October 1807, n. 6.

12. *Cymbeline*, 3.2.46.

TO JOHN SALUSBURY PIOZZI SALUSBURY

Thursday Morning
17: August 1809.

My dearest Salusbury

You can hardly believe how glad I was to see Your Letter from Mold [Flintshire] with the Key inclosed; It came on the Day after you went—Tuesday; and I have *lived* upon it quite comfortably till this Morning, when Owen brought home the Shrewsbury Letter directed by myself, but filled with truly agreeable Contents. That from Oxford is however the most *desireable,* on Account of the odious Stage Coaches, and their overturns so often celebrated in otherwise Empty Newspapers:[1]—but just *now* Sir Arthur Wellesley has given us something else to think about.[2]

Pray write from Enborne too, and tell Mr. Charles Shephard that my 700£.3s.7d. at length is safely lodged in Hammersley's hands—and that Mr. Merrick Hoare cries Peccavi; and that his Wife sends *you* a Thousand Compliments, and Invitations——to put *me* in good humour——Comical enough! but when Spring Season comes, we will take due Advantage of her Tenderness, and make our Debût at their Assemblies in York Place. Mean while be good dear Salusbury, and study as hard as you can perswade yourself to do: and *help me* to make them all believe You are the cleverest Fellow in the World. Young Myddelton[3] is come home a *Shadow,* My Mother's *Son* Sir, as Feeble says to Bardolph; and my Father's *Shadow:*[4] The Doctor hopes however to make him a *prædicable Substance* very soon, and then no hopes *for* Caroline, or *of* Caroline.⁵ I fancy Mr. Shephard must translate this Joke for you; indeed my Wish and desire is, that you may get as much of *his Conversation* as possible before other Claimants come to divide his Care. You know I am always wishing for you *That which you like best.*

We have begun Harvest by cutting the Vetches; and I see nothing that even Lake can fret about, except that too many Wood Pigeons are eating up all our Pease. Mrs. Mostyn is here, but I think *not* in high good humour; The Gardenhouse goes on rapidly, and our After Grass in the Park looks like an Emerald. Shall we make the old Cottage a Rabbet-Place instead of pulling it down?—The poor Bunneys are all put to the Rout by breaking the new Doorway, and they would like such a Habitation of all Things——It won't do for Pigeons, or else its Fate would be fixed at once.

The Road to Mold is always very bad—We must pray for a dry day and a clear Frost the last Week of November. Miss Williams says We shall live at a good House (all our own) in Queen Square Bath, quite a Central Situation; and capital Room for Mr. Charles Shephard and You: and we will have please God! a chearful Christmas.

Make him understand that the Money was not paid *at last* by Virtue of a Power of Attorney granted to Hammersley; but by Mr. Hoare, receiving it Himself and paying it into the Bankers——at least so Sophia writes word, tho' I know not how her Husband could receive it——if he is not a Trustee, perhaps She meant his Brother. Oh heavens! the Paper *does* bring News of Lightning terrifying some Stage Coach Horses and a Man struck Dead.⁶ I shall not sleep till I see Accounts from you with the Oxford Post Mark. God preserve my dearest Boy, and send us a happy Meeting in old King Bladud's Country.⁷ Glover goes on as usual—— Poor little Thing! Poor little *Thing!*⁸ My Face is *bad* enough still: When was it a *good* one? say you and Your Enborne Friends—Twenty Years ago Sauce-Box— replies Your / ever Affectionate Aunt / H: L: Piozzi.

Text: Ry. 585.29. *Address:* John Piozzi Salusbury Esq. / at The Rev: T: Shephard's / Enborne / near Newbury / Berkshire. *Postmark:* ST ASAPH < > (In JSPS's hand, "Received the 21st Augst 1809 / Answered Augst 23d 1809").

1. So numerous had stagecoach accidents become that efforts were made to alter the construction of the vehicle. The proposed new design (only reluctantly tried) "by keeping the centre of gravity extremely low, makes an overturn next to impossible; and, by having small supplemental wheels, properly attached, prevents all danger from the loss of a wheel; or even all the principal wheels," etc. See *GM* 79, pt. 2 (1809): 1104–5.
2. HLP alludes to Wellesley's victory at the battle of Talavera, 27–28 July.
His description of the battle's major events was reprinted as an *Extraordinary Gazette* and was to be "read by every lover of his country, with mingled emotions of admiration and pride, as affording a decided proof of the unconquerable valour, discipline, and enthusiasm of the British Army." See *GM* 79, pt. 2: 766, 772.
3. Young Robert Myddelton had returned from Harrow.
4. *The Second Part of Henry the Fourth,* 3.2.126–29.
5. The joke has to do with Caroline May Myddelton (1796–1850), the eldest daughter of the Reverend Robert Myddelton of Gwaynynog.
6. "This night [26 July], as a Bath coach was travelling near *Colnbrook,* the leaders took fright at the lightning, and became unmanageable; the consequence was, the animals started off at full

speed, and the vehicle was upset, and literally shattered in pieces. Nine persons were seriously hurt, and a female passenger died of her bruises, on being conveyed to Hounslow.—About two miles from the same spot a poor man was killed in a lane by a cart turning over, the animal also having plunged out of the road." Such accidents were commonplace during the summer storms. See *GM* 79, pt. 2: 775–76.

7. That is, Bath.

8. Ann Glover (b. 1783), already widowed, was to marry Alexander Leak on 9 October 1813.

TO JOHN SALUSBURY PIOZZI SALUSBURY

Brynbella Saturday
9: September 1809.

I fix on this Day to express my very true and tender Sense of Dear Salusbury's dutyful and Affectionate Promises, to whom my heart wishes every good Thing, that *this* Life—and the *next* can afford.[1] The Letters from Enborne are capricious Visitants—Yours and Mr. Charles Shephard's came by the same Post. I shall be happy to receive Mr. Pemberton as your Friend, and shew him every Civility in my Power;[2] but this unexpected Pregnancy of Lady Keith throws a momentary Gloom over my Prospects of a chearful Winter——She *may* find her Life endangered; and She *may* (possibly) feel her Tenderness rekindled towards a Mother who so long adored her: and She *may* request my Presence at her Delivery—— If She *does*——Imperious Duty will bear down every Consideration, and I shall quit Friends, Pleasures,——Social Comforts, and my *dearest Salusbury;* for a Sick Room: and Shrieks that will shatter my newly restored Nerves to Death——You know I *ought* to do it,——and your Mr. Shephard will say so too.[3]

Meanwhile you may hope and trust nothing of all this will happen——There is a vast deal of Falsehood in the World; I am *now* perswaded that Cecy Mostyn saw how Things were standing——Weeks, ay and Months before I was informed of it:—She looked so odd and so particularly sullen—just like the Weather I think—and She was so warmly solicitous that I should give her Son the odd old curious Christening Bason that was bought for Catherine de Berayne's Baptism, and had remained 309 Years in the Family——Thin as a sixpence; and worth not 5 Guineas except for its Antiquity——She was afraid I should give it Lady Keith!! Ah! says Mr. Charles Shephard, "Why these Girls were all born at *Chislehurst.*"[4]

Well! now for something better. Doctor Gray—who Wrote the Key to the Old Testament, and who signed your Memorial; sent Me a very Affectionate Letter the other Day, and asked after young Salusbury very kindly,—hoping he would *do Credit to the Name* &c. Mrs. Cleaver is even *comically* partial to you, said She should not do Justice to *your pretty Answer* about some Trifle I forget what—— but I do think Mr. Roberts' Welsh Eyes saw further than we thought they did. Lord Deerhurst is at last become Earl of Coventry, so we have a Sure Friend in the house of Peers, if on any Occasion we should want one——Sir Walter James says there can be no Opposition from the Crown to our Enclosure Bill:[5] Mr.

Oldfield is not diligent, and the People are refractory, but I am resolute, and the Work shall be done. Suaviter in Modo if you please; sed *fortitur in re.*[6]

Now for something worse——The Harvest: no harvest can be worse than ours—except our Neighbours. All the Standing Corn lodged and growing into the Ground again—All the cut Corn spoyling of Course;—and my Pease which were such a beautiful Crop—lying there to be ruined. Pray tell in earnest how it is about Berkshire; our Wheat and Barley will bear tremendous Prices, but General Lake will have none to sell.

Martha is pronounced a confirmed Lunatic:——What can I do with her? No Friends or Brothers come to take her away, and the Expense and Plague of her here at home is insupportable——but Duty must be done in *this* Case too, and I must turn Matron of a Madhouse in my latter Days.

Pray for *me* now dearest Salusbury, that I may do my Duty in this Life, so as to escape beating with *very many Stripes* in the next. See St. Luke 12th Chapter 47th Verse.——All that I do for *You* is prompted by *Affection* and will be compleatly rewarded in *this* World by your good Conduct, and continued Esteem. Make my truest regards to lovely Lady Kirkwall; She is well and happy I am told; She never writes to me and I wonder at her Silence. There was such a Ringing of Bells the other Day at Denbigh——and *our* little wretched Thing at Dymerchion answering them; that my Heart felt half angry: I thought the Boobies were rejoycing that Lord Kirkwall was come home without his Wife.

> Lord! sayd I
> How they toil at that Rope still unsparing of Pain
>   While my Nerves with their Nonsense they vex;
> I think they will never be quiet again
>   Till 'tis twisted round some of their Necks.[7]

There was however a Cause I dreamed not of for their ridiculous Joy: My thrice noble Cousin Sir Robert Salusbury——my *Heir at Law* had I never possessed Husband or Children——was arrived at Denbigh forsooth, on a pretended Visit;[8] but with a View no doubt to purchase poor dear old *Lleweney Hall,* or *Bachŷgraig,* or any of the Old Stuff that he could lay hold on. This was the Relation who got the Offley Estate from me which Mr. Charles Shephard is securing the *Dregs* of for you. A good 3000£ o'Year it was 40 Years ago——He has nothing to do (except distant Kindred) with my *first* Cousin Sir Robert Salusbury Cotton lately dead, who sold Lleweney to Lord Kirkwall's Father.[9]

Cecy Mostyn will be mad enough at the Ringers. She is not here now, but will return next Week when her eldest Son is gone to Streatham, and Harry returned with his Sore Head to Prestatyn. Cecy is *not* admirable as a Companion to keep one from thinking of Illness: She is admirable for her *Ingenuity* in all *Manual Arts;* can bind Books incomparably, make Shoes excellently, and has painted a Toothpick Case so exquisitely upon Ivory——I know not what Miniature Painter can go beyond Her——Yet one Hour of Lady Keith's Company (who can do none of these Things) is worth a Week of her Sister's——the *full Mind;* from the Plenitude of which, Conversation drops out as if by Chance, is the desireable Thing in a Companion——Whoever plays a Trick is annihilated when the Trick has been once plaid and finished——and your Jack Bannister would be found the dullest Fellow breathing I dare say—after the Third Night's exhibition.[10]

Mean while Mimickry is a most entertaining Power—*in a Pantomime;* so much so, that The Mimic seems to be

> Not *One,* but all Mankind's *Epitome.*

As Dryden says of some Man[11]——The Mock Bird is the Jack Banister of India; he imitates all other Animals, but has no Original Note of his own.

But you are tired of my *holding one Note* so long I suppose; and 'tis Time to give over——even the Rainy Weather must have done *Sometime,* and I hope the Change—the favorable Change will be upon your Birthday. Long may that prove a Red Letter Day to *You;* and while it does do so, it shall be *blest* by my dear Salusbury's affectionate Aunt, and truly careful Parent / H: L: Piozzi.

I will write to Mr. Charles Shephard on Monday next——Will the Letters come together to Enborne?

Mind that I do not yet know at all *when* this extraordinary Event is to take Place; so that there is no need to suppose it will affect our Holydays. God forbid that it should!—I have had *so few happy Days!* for so long a Time!!—Make my best Compliments to your *friends*—All *your* Friends must be *mine.*

Text: Ry. 585.32. *Address:* John Piozzi Salusbury Esq. / at the Rev: T: Shephard's / Enborne / Near Newbury / Berkshire. *Postmark:* DENBIGH <224> (In JSPS's hand, "Received 12th Septr 1809. Answered 14th Sepr 1809").

1. The letter anticipates JSPS's birthday, on 12 September.
2. For Edward William Smythe Pemberton, see HLP to JSPS, 20 August 1808, n. 1.
3. Q's daughter was born on 12 December 1809; HLP was not present at the delivery, although she offered frequently to be there. Q wished no more than did CMM to have her mother's attendance.
4. An accusation of cheating or fraud by HLP's daughters is implicit in Shephard's cruel pun. "Chisel" was a recent addition to English slang words.
5. Although the "Land Tax Assessments" for Flintshire are missing, we can assume that HLP had in mind the common land called the Bryn, or "Mountain," adjacent to the Bachygraig Estate. In her "Pocket Book" for 1809, she wrote on 27 August and again on 3 September: "Mr. Oldfield set the Notice up of our Enclosure and the Neighbors tore it down." Despite their displeasure, she noted further, "The enclosure is determined" (N.L.W., MS. 11100A). The enclosure act, however, was longer in coming than HLP expected. See her letter to Q, 31 January 1810; to JSPS, 16 July 1810 and n. 4.
6. See HLP to SL, 30 April 1785, n. 17.
7. Probably HLP's.
8. For Sir Robert Salusbury, see HLP to Q, 20 September 1803, n. 8; HLP to Q, 23 July 1805.
9. Sir Robert Salusbury Cotton, aged seventy, had died 24 August at Combermere Abbey. See *GM* 79, pt. 2 (1809): 889; and HLP to PSW, 6 October 1792, n. 2; to Q, 17 September 1794, n. 5.
10. John Bannister (1760–1836) had been a talented student at the Royal Academy. But he abandoned it to become an actor in 1778. Although he appeared in tragic roles, he was best known for his comic performances and imitations. He was to retire from the stage in 1815.
11. In the first part of *Absalom and Achitophel,* line 546, Dryden uses this epithet to describe "Zimri," i.e., George Villiers, second duke of Buckingham.

TO LADY WILLIAMS

Monday Morning
11: September 1809.

I will come to my dearest Lady before the Month is out, but cannot Yet fix the day: when I know my own Power over myself I will exert it.

This World is full of Brambles, and as one walkes on thro' Life They will now and then cling to one's Petticoats.—We must rid ourselves of them as gently as We can, *without tearing the Gown.*

One of my Maids has been seized with Lunacy in a Strange Manner, and for some Time greatly disordered the Family, She went home to her Friends however last Saturday Thank God.

Lady Keith's Pregnancy being announced is likewise an Interesting Event—it may serve to amuse Dear Mrs. Williams, to whom I beg Your Ladyship will present me with most Affectionate Respect, I will not leave Wales without seeing her.

Dear Salusbury writes tender and Dutyful Letters which I have reason to think come from the heart—he is a good Child and knows himself honoured by Your Ladyship's obliging Enquiry. Mrs. Mostyn dines with me to day, and I *must* go to Segroid—or lose my Legacy, but I will go no where else except to Bodylwyddan tho' the dismal ½ year will be up now in Ten or Twelve Days.—

Dearest Madam Adieu! and be chearful.

I am ever more and more Your Ladyships and Dear Sir John's / Obliged and Grateful / H: L: P.

Salusbury and Shephard have got sweet Lady Kirkwall at *Speen*—but Three Miles from *Enborne;* They must take Care of her.

Text: Ry. 3 (1807–11).

TO LADY WILLIAMS

Brynbella
26 October 1809.

My Dear Madam

I can live no longer without hearing some Account of Dear Bodylwyddan: how is poor Mrs. Williams?—and how is my charming Lady Williams? Not in her Bed yet![1]

Lady Keith goes to London *on* her Business the Week after next: I suppose the Admiral is in a hurry to be giving Orders to his little *Cabin-Boy* and they begin expecting before the Time.

How went the Jubilee off at St. Asaph?[2] I hear nothing, and can say nothing but that five Weeks more will see the Departure of Your Ladyship's true, and tenderly attached humble Servant / H: L: Piozzi / from Brynbella.

Text: Ry. 3 (1807-11).

1. Now the mother of three sons and four daughters, Ly W would in November bear Ellen (d. 1876).
2. The jubilee of George III's accession was celebrated throughout Great Britain on 26 October 1809. See *GM* 79, pt. 2 (1809): 975-76, 995, 997, 1002, 1070; for the Royal Family's celebration at Windsor, see Olwen Hedley, *Queen Charlotte* (London: John Murray, 1975), pp. 233-34; Denis Gray, *Spencer Perceval: The Evangelical Prime Minister, 1762-1812* (Manchester: At the University Press, 1963), pp. 286-87.

TO THE REVEREND LEONARD CHAPPELOW

Brynbella Saturday
28: October 1809.

I am sorry my Dear Mr. Chappelow that you are not well, and *very* sorry that you cannot conveniently come here and tell me so: but we who remember our good old King's Coronation,[1] must be contented to say we have likewise seen his Jubilee: it was a grateful Sight in my Eyes, and gave me a Momentary Pleasure such as I had not hoped to enjoy. Depend upon't he is at this Instant a happier Man than Buonaparte, who probably recollects the Verses we read upon the Gates of Bologna, among which these only come back to my Head.

> Si tibi pulchræ Domus, si splendida Mensa,—quid inde?
> Si species auri, argenti quoque Massa,—quid inde?
> Si faveat Mundus, si prospera cuncta;—quid inde?
> Si Prior, aut Abbas; Si Dux, Si Papa—quid inde?
> Si felix annos regnes per Mille:—quid inde?
> Si rota Fortunæ se tollit ad astra;—quid inde?
> Tam citò, tamque cito fugiunt hæc—ut nihil inde.
> Sola manet Virtus——&c. &c.[2]

The Ladies of Llangollen have been fortunate—*in their way:* Miss Ormsby's Mother, my Cousin Owen of Porkington left them an Annuity and now this Legacy which I heard not of before.[3] Poor *Poor* Lady Clarges![4] made wretched by her Sons vehement aspirations after Intellectual Excellence——and both of them to possess—or be possessed of a like Passion![5] I perfectly remember her Lying In of Sir Thomas, and its being told about the Town how Lady Clarges when She *first* saw her *first*-born, cried out—Oh the pretty Creature! how happy he will make me when I see him in *Pink Satten Breeches*, the sweetest Fellow in the Pit of the Opera!——and then he goes and cracks his Crown, while his Brother breaks a Blood Vessel—for Love of the Æolic Digamma. Mondo! as poor Mr. Piozzi used to say.[6]

Lady Keith will not bring *her* Baby till next Month is over, as her Sisters tell *me*. Cecilia Mostyn's Boy is my *Great* Grandson; I never saw so *large* a Child of his Age, not healthy tho',—nor yet his Brothers, who are always Sea Bathing. Good Mr. Gillon neither dies nor lives; but our Contemporaries are mostly dropping round us; and as I was looking over old Magazines that tell of this Time 49 Years and the Shows and the Galas of those Days——I can see only The Duchess of Marlborough and Lady Pembroke alive—of the whole Set.[7] How old is the *Young* Dutchess of Devonshire?[8] and what does Lady Bradford think of this worthless World? Taught by *her* Example, we will hope her Young People will help to mend it—*a little:* but it seems to *me* quite ripening for Destruction. I shall be glad of some Chat with pretty Mrs. Clay;[9] The Waters of Bath would give you an Appetite, but the Air is certainly oppressive, compared to beautiful Weston Park;——or perhaps even to *Hyde* Park which always agrees with *You*. The Theatre appears to be a compleat Bear Garden—for ought I hear or read:[10] It amazes me that any decent People, Women especially, can think of going to such A riotous Exhibition of Obstinacy on one Side, and Perverseness on the other. Why do they not all stay at home? till the Prices please them better. The Managers as *Managers,* will lose nothing by letting the Town act *their own* Farce instead of seeing *them* act *theirs.* And Kemble may learn that it was not his Attractions which carried them there before;[11] but the Desire of seeing each other, and getting rid of so much Time—*To ease the Anguish of a torturing Hour."*[12]

Dear Mr. Chappelow Adieu: If this Nonsense was to cost you anything I would not send it——but if it would coax you out of *one more Letter* before the last Week of the next Month—(— for then I pack and go;) it would be kind: and I should have the honour of hearing once again how very graciously our charming Lady Bradford accepts the true and respectful Compliments of Dear Sir Your old and sincere Servant / H: L: Piozzi.

Text: Ry. 561.142. *Address:* Rev: Mr. Chappelow.

1. George was crowned in Westminster Abbey on 22 September 1761.
2. These lines were inscribed on a marble tablet in memory of "la dottoressa Laura Bassi" and placed over the door of the Specola. HLP recorded and translated them in "Harvard Piozziana" 2:48–50.
   Laura Maria Bassi (1711–78), the wife of Dr. Giuseppe Viratti, was born in Scandiano, received her doctorate from the University of Bologna in 1732. She was at first a professor of philosophy and later of physics at the university.
3. Margaret Ormsby, née Owen (d. 1806), stipulated in her will: "I give and devise to Lady Eleanor Butler and Miss Ponsonby during their joint lives . . . one Annuity or yearly rent Charge of one hundred pounds" (P.R.O., Prob. 11/1446/591; signed 5 February 1805 and proved at London, 18 July 1806).
   LC summarizes in his letter of 27 November (Ry. 563.91) the other legacies that the Ladies of Llangollen received: "£500 Legacy Left them by Lady Clarges. . . . It cannot rain &c. &c. &c.—for they also tell me that the Duke of Richmond has granted them--for this year on the Irish Pension List £100 per Annum—and next year it will be doubled to £200 per Annum."
4. Louisa Clarges, the widow of the third baronet Clarges, had died on 5 August "at her house on Richmond-hill, Surrey, of a dropsy." See *GM* 79, pt. 2: 788. Her will, in which she had written her bequest to the Ladies of Llangollen, had been signed 13 January 1809 and proved 31 August (P.R.O., Prob. 11/1501/613).
   For Sir Thomas and Lady Clarges, see HLP to Elizabeth Gray, 20 July 1799, n. 10.
5. Lady Clarges's elder son was Thomas, who succeeded to the baronetcy upon coming of age,

25 December 1802. He had matriculated at Christ Church, Oxford, in 1799 and received his B.A. in 1802. Of Lady Clarges's three children, he was the only one to outlive her. For the death of her second son, William, also of Christ Church, see HLP to MW, 21 May 1807, n. 8.

6. HLP uses the "Aeolic Digamma," like Pope, as a symbol of useless, if recondite, knowledge. See *The Dunciad*, 4.217–18.

7. Of the seven ladies-in-waiting to Queen Charlotte at the coronation, HLP recalls the two survivors.

The duchess of Marlborough was Caroline (d. 1811), only daughter of the fourth duke of Bedford. In 1762 she had married George Spencer (1739–1817), fourth duke of Marlborough.

Lady Pembroke was Elizabeth (1737–1831), a daughter of the third duke of Marlborough, who in 1756 had married Henry Herbert (1734–94), tenth earl of Pembroke (1750) and seventh of Montgomery.

8. The fifth duke of Devonshire took as his second wife on 19 October the widowed Lady Elizabeth (Foster), née Hervey (ca. 1760–1824), a daughter of the fourth earl of Bristol.

For the duke and his first wife, Georgiana, see HLP to FB, [24] June 1784, n. 3.

9. Mrs. Clay was coming to Bath with her daughter Catharine Charlotte. See HLP to LC, 18 September [1797], n. 8.

10. "The new Theatre at Covent-garden opened" on Monday, 18 September, and almost immediately the O.P. riots began. These were organized and prolonged public demonstrations against the raising of admission prices. The upheaval lasted throughout the season. Thus, on 23 September, "The catcalls, accompanied by rattles, trumpets, whistles, &c. proceeded in full chorus during the play and farce. . . . During the interval, a number of placards were displayed, suspended principally from the first tier of boxes, with inscriptions favourable to the public cause." See *GM* 79, pt. 2; 882; *AR*, "Chronicle" 51 (1809): 346 ff.

11. As manager of the Covent Garden theater and one of its proprietors, Kemble became a target of the O.P. rioters. On opening night, when he played the role of Macbeth, he attempted to address them. But his address and his performance were drowned out.

12. *A Midsummer Night's Dream*, 5.1.37.

TO LADY WILLIAMS

Sunday
29: October 1809.

God send my Sweet Lady Williams a happy Minute——If I *can* come for a Morning before my Packing Season, I *will*.

*Every*body seems to have behaved well on the Jubilee Day,[1] and there are reports of Peace; and I incline to believe them.[2]

Poor Dear Mrs. Williams! She will see the domestic Cotillion completed, and perhaps—a general Cessation of Arms thro' out the World, after so much Bloodshed.

Adieu! Mrs. Mostyn is here. She overstays me in the Country: Indeed the Weather is such as to perswade anyone's Stay, but that Miss Williams has probably engaged my House before now, and fixed the Time for the 1st of December as I took the Liberty to give her Commission.

Adieu my Dear Lady—and do not treat us with a Pair of Twins this Time, because odd Numbers are never staid at:—We shall then be wanting *another*. Lady Keith seems in better spirits by her Letters. There is nothing so good in such Cases as Chearfulness. It carried through 13 hard Struggles / Your Ladyship's / ever true and faithful / H: L: P.

Every kind and respectful Wish attend Your whole Household.

Text: Victoria and Albert Museum Library. *Address:* Lady Williams / Bodylwyddan.

1. In summarizing the events of the jubilee, GM for November 1809 pointed out that "It is utterly impossible to do adequate justice to the scenes of general festivity and loyalty, by which this ever-memorable event has been distinguished. We are, however, happy to observe that all accounts uniformly agree in describing the order and decorum with which the whole went off" (79, pt. 2: 1070).
2. There was evidence of peace negotiations throughout Europe. Thus, "Advice [had] been received, through a channel which is considered authentic, that Peace between Austria and France was concluded on" 5 October. Furthermore, the French were willing to enter into discussions with Great Britain "on the subject of neutral commerce," whereby all blockades would cease. Sweden and Denmark were working to negotiate a peace, Russia and Sweden having already achieved one. HLP apparently interpreted these various incidents as the advent of a "general Cessation of Arms." See *GM* 79, pt. 2 (1809): 971–74.

TO JOHN LLOYD

Saturday
11: November 1809.

My dear Mr. Lloyd[1]
who never hears the Cause of a poor Body without redressing it, and never turns a deaf Ear that it may not be heard—will excuse my sending him my Compliments by a wretched Girl who had a Child 7 Years ago by an unfeeling Fellow that deserted her, and married a *worse Wench*. The Parish are tired of maintaining the Boy of *Course*: and wish him to be put under his Father's Care—whose Wife will use him ill—of *Course*. I want the Man to pay on till the Lad is 10 Years old, and then I will take Care of him myself—but Mr. Roberts (who crosses me at every Turn)[2] perswades the People to be perverse and give him up to his Father.

I put her Cause in Your hands, and am ever with True Regard and just Esteem / Dear Sir / Your most Obedient / H: L. Piozzi.

I wish you would send my Blazonry and Pedigree Stuff home by her. She would take Care of it.

Text: National Library of Wales MS 12421D.

1. John ("Philosopher") Lloyd of Wigfair.
2. The tax assessor in Flintshire was John Roberts of Denbigh. By occupation an ironmonger, he died in 1829. See P.R.O., Prob. 6/205.

TO JOHN SALUSBURY PIOZZI SALUSBURY

Monday Night
20: November 1809.

I do my dearest Child give you full Credit for having done Your Business *as if* you understood what you were about; and I give dear Mr. Shephard Credit for his kind Instructions and Care——and I *will* give Doctor Randolph Credit for his Friendship towards me on that happy Day when he recommended you to Enborne.[1]

If Leak can get his Business settled; and the Tenants Money paid in, and the Cattle safe in the Straw Yard, and the Manure carted out properly, and the Field ploughed for Fallow &c. I will set out for Bath this Week; if *not* I will stay till the next, because I am convinced he does what is best for *our Advantage,* and I will not put him out of his Way.

The Ring will be more necessary this Year than ever to conjure the Flies away: for a Horse stinger fastened on my Face no longer ago than last Week, and swelled my Eye Lid up frightfully as if it was Summer, *and* Cecy has a Pear Tree in Blossom at Segroid now:—but sharp Frosts are coming, and will do our health good and brace my wretched Nerves that shook at sight of Mr. Shephard's hand this Morning.

Can you believe how ill Mr. Roberts has used me, and how angry I am? If he does not mend his Manners, and behave very differently *indeed* on the 12th of December when there will be another Meeting——My Welsh Blood will boil over I fear. I am ashamed to think how much his bad Behaviour has vexed me.[2]

My Paper is out, I have outstayed all my Things—My Candles are out, my Coffee is out, and I wish myself for once in my Life out of Brynbella. When you are *Out* of Cash, call on Mr. Shephard: whatever he does is well done. Mean Time tell him I once shewed the Abraxas Gem to Doctor Burney of Greenwich[3]——and he knew no more about the matter than my Chamber Maid—not so Dear Dr. Gray—who wrote the Key to the old Testament and signed your Memorial like a true Friend as he is: He was *au fait* of it at once.

I have not the new Chambers's Dictionary,[4] and Scott's Supplement did I never see.[5] Mosheim tells about the Æons and the Pleroma,[6] and how Miss *Achamoth* tumbled out of the Pleroma (like Hebe in the old Mythology;)[7] and Beausobre in his Histoire Critique de Manichèisme gives *all* the Gnostic Tales I believe.[8]

So God bless my dearest Salusbury and lament the Pens, Ink, and Paper of / Your truly Affectionate Aunt / H: L: P.

Miss Williams has let all the Houses slip thro' her fingers—so that I must go to the White Lyon and choose for myself. Did you never read the Fable of the Farmer and the Larks? They were not likely their Mother said to be unroosted, till the Master took the Field in Hand to *reap himself.*[9] Old Prance is dead. Adieu for a short Time only.

Text: Ry. 585.38. *Address:* John Piozzi Salusbury Esq. / Enborne.

1. For Francis Randolph, the proprietor and Minister of Laura Chapel, Bath, see HLP to PSW, 29 August [1791], n. 9.

2. HLP had written to JSPS on 13 November (Ry. 585.37): "A meeting of the Freeholders was called on the 7th of this Month up at Dymerchion (Hill), and Sir Edward Lloyd was wonderfully polite, and drove the Business forward chiefly because he thought it would please me—for you can recollect very well that he flung Cold Water on the Project at the beginning. David Lloyd attended for his sick Father T. Lloyd of Denbigh, and Oldfield and Leak attended as my Representatives. There were 30 Proprietors to the Thousand Acres, but mine and Mr. Lloyd's Shares were the largest: and though Some of the very small Landholders were unwilling, none were perverse; and All would have gone forward without Opposition but for one Enemy—Can you guess who?—*Mr. Roberts*. There must now be more Expence incurred, and more Meetings called, and more Vexations—all from that Man's—what shall I call it? Malice or Idiotism? Tell Mr. Shephard his Objection is to giving up his Tythes for two Years—Tythes of the Rock! The uncultivated Mountain! When there is anything to *decimate* he will have his *Tenth*, in Addition to what he has already:—but no: he will resist, he is resolved—and he will go away from us—and complain of Persecution. A good Joke indeed! why he has been persecuted by Kindness and *good Luck* They are however all enraged at him."

3. See HLP to Q, 12 February [1799], nn. 8 and 9.

4. Ephraim Chambers's *Cyclopaedia; or, an Universal Dictionary of Arts and Sciences* (1728); among the many editions, the latest would probably have been that of 1795.

5. *A Supplement to Mr. Chambers' Cyclopaedia; or, Universal Dictionary of Arts and Sciences*, completed and edited by George Lewis Scott, 2 vols. (1753).

6. HLP refers to John Lawrence Mosheim's *An Ecclesiastical History, Antient and Modern*. See HLP to PSP [ca. 20 July 1801], n. 3.

Mosheim points out that oriental philosophers in the early years of the Christian church were "unanimous in acknowledging the existence of an eternal nature" that was perfect. "This great being was considered by them, as a most pure and radiant *light*, diffused through the immensity of space, which they called *pleroma*, a Greek word which signalizes fullnes"; that the pleroma "'produced, at length, from *itself*, two minds of a different sex. . . . From the prolific union of these two beings others arose . . . so that, in process of time, a celestial family was formed in the *pleroma*. This divine progeny . . . was called by the philosophers *aeon*,' a term which signifies, in the Greek language, an eternal nature. How many in number these *aeons* were, was a point much controverted among the oriental sages" (1:38–39).

7. Mosheim points out various heretics in the second century A.D. who plagued the Christian church. One of these heretics was Valentine, the Egyptian, who placed in the pleroma "'thirty *aeons*, of which one half were male, and the other female. . . . The youngest of the *aeons*, called *Sophia* (i.e. wisdom), conceived an ardent desire of comprehending the nature of the Supreme Being, and, by the force of this propensity, brought forth a daughter, named *Achamoth* [who], being exiled from the *pleroma*, fell down into the rude and undigested mass of matter, to which she gave a certain arrangement; and, by the assistance of Jesus, produced the *demiurge*, the lord and creator of all things'" (1:115).

8. HLP refers to Isaac de Beausobre (1659–1738) and his *Histoire Critique de Manichée et du Manicheïsme*, 2 vols. (Amsterdam: chez J. Frederick Bernard, 1734, 1739).

9. La Fontaine, *Fables*, 4.22: "L'Alouette et ses Petits avec le Maître d'un Champ." See also Aesop, "The Lark and Her Young Ones," with its conclusion. Said the mother lark to her young ones who had reported the farmer's plan to reap the field: "'Then, my dears, it is time for us to go indeed, for when a man undertakes to do his business himself, it is not so likely that he will be disappointed.' She removed her Young Ones immediately, and the corn was reaped the next day by the old man and his son."

TO JOHN SALUSBURY PIOZZI SALUSBURY

No. 6 Pultney Street Bath
Saturday 2d: December 1809

My dearest Boy
 will be glad to hear I am safe housed at Bath, and nice Apartments ready for you and your Friends Mr. Pemberton and Mr. Shephard. I wrote to London last Night to Mr. Charles; and told him how happy his and Your Company will make me. The Journey went off exceeding well, and Glover was not *Hill* upon the Road:—only broke her Shins the first Day with the Tin Dressing-Box and Medicine Chest; because She had not Power and Ability to move them out Of her Way; but I packed her up neatly at Ellesmere——and then—*She slept better a great Deal.*
 The Weather has been beautiful, but I saw no Corn forwarder nor no Calves handsomer than my Own thro' all the Country I crossed over. We drove to the White Lyon[1] here at the Market Place and got an agreeable House enough—directly.
 The best News from Wales is that Allen-Jones of Pontriffeth brought a nice baby with very little Pain, and *certainly* no Danger:[2] The Father is better too, but it is Supposed he has the Tenia—Tape Worm; and if so: Recovery is difficult indeed. Mr. Roberts pretends to be ashamed of having used me so Ill concerning the Enclosure; everybody has scolded him so:—but We must see how he behaves the next Meeting, for I am loth to trust much upon Methodist *Honour*. He professes to think that Quality *Superfluous,* so that one has no hold on him except as Interest or bounden Duty helps one: And with regard to Interest he mistakes——and Duty he explains away. Well! 'tis a fine Thing at last to have to do with *Gentlemen*—and not with Such low Fellows. Mrs. Mostyn is well, and the Cousin I told you of—James Henry Cotton—has got a Living of 600£ o'Year.[3]
 What have I else to tell you? nothing but that nobody on Earth can love You half as well as does / Your ever Affectionate Aunt / H: L: P.

Write and say when I may expect You.

Text: Ry. 585.39.

 1. "White Lyon" [Lion]: a Bath inn that became fashionable toward the end of the 18th c.
 2. On 25 March 1810 was baptized Dorothy, daughter of Elener, née Allen, and Robert Jones of Llŷs. See "Bodfari Baptismal Register," C.R.O., Clwyd.
 3. James Henry (1780–1862) was the second son of George Cotton, dean of Chester. Educated at Rugby and Trinity College, Cambridge, he was ordained in 1803. In 1809 he became rector of Derwen, Denbighshire. He was to move steadily upward in the ecclesiastical hierarchy, becoming dean of Bangor Cathedral in 1838. He was to identify himself as early as 1810 with every aspect of church work in the diocese of Bangor, to make Welsh a part of divine service, and to integrate the cathedral with its national culture.

TO LADY WILLIAMS

Bath
6: December 1809.

My dear Friends Sir John and Lady Williams will be glad to hear I am safe *housed*. It was both right and kind to let me chuse my own Dwelling, of which there are but too great Plenty vacant—never being so bad a season known at Bath; no Music in the Pump Room, and one set of Rooms quite shut up. My friends however who lie chiefly among the Inhabitants are clustering round me very kindly;—and I hope to have a little social Comfort after so long Seclusion. We dwell on dismal Topics though, Very dismal indeed; Public affairs certainly never did bear so bad an Appearance, and the approaching election at Oxford sours People's Tempers towards one another.[1]

The Idea of Lord Gr[en]v[il]le's favouring the Catholic bill is much against him;[2] and to say true, the Romanists were scarcely prudent in making such a pompous show here last week—last Sunday it was; with the Consecration of their new Chapel,[3] where Catalani sang and the people ran in crowds to hear her and see the Glories of High Mass performed.[4]

I think people go no where Else—Some of my Servants went to the Play, and told me the house was all but empty and Laura Chapel where we used to struggle for seats and pay high terms besides, looks like a Desart.

The Gaming Tables alone are *full:* and there is a ruinous game Marco or Mark Ho—or some strange name that destroys the young men and their fortunes at a fine rate.[5]

Old women are however safe enough, so I shall make my Winter out very comfortably. No News from Lady Keith yet—Salusbury says he is coming to me, and will bring his Schoolfellow young Pemberton of Condover near Shrewsbury, so then I shall have *Beaux of my own*. Dear Miss Williams is in excellent Looks; She is an Oracle to her Friends here, but here Heart lies toward old Rhudland Castle, and her Enquiries are all about the Loves and Darlings at Bodylwyddan.

I hope Mrs. Williams does not get worse, and I am sure Lady Williams *does* [tear] better.

I am *very* sure that I have the honour and Happiness to be most faithfully theirs and Sir John's ever Obliged and Obedient / H: L: Piozzi.

Text: Ry. 3 (1807–11). *Address:* Lady Williams / Bodylwyddan / near St. Asaph / N. Wales.

1. The election, which took place on 13–14 December, was ostensibly to choose the chancellor of the University. But since Lord Grenville was one of the candidates, what was at stake was his support of the Catholic Bill. Involved too was the fact that the king in March 1807 dissolved the Ministry of All the Talents and appointed the duke of Portland first lord of the treasury, to succeed Grenville. All this lay behind Grenville's run for the chancellorship of the University of Oxford in 1809.
2. On 13 November, *The Times* wrote: "The canvass for the Chancellorship of Oxford is now carried on very warmly. It has been erroneously stated that the Archbishop of York favours the

Duke of Beaufort. His Grace, together with the Bishops of London, St. Asaph, and Oxford, are all strenuous Advocates for Lord Grenville. The majority of Christ Church is certainly in favour of his Lordship. . . . The Vice-Chancellor, with the whole of University College, St. John's, and Worcester College, are the Patrons of Lord Eldon. The Duke of Beaufort has a very considerable party in most of the other Colleges."

The results of the election were as follows: 406 votes for Lord Grenville; 393 for Lord Eldon; 288 for the duke of Beaufort.

As *The Times* editorialized on 16 December: "We shall not here attempt to fathom a subject of so much profundity as the Catholic question, which is supposed by many to be so intimately connected with the result of this Election . . . but barely observe, that the advocates of Emancipation . . . do certainly consider themselves as having gained a step towards the attainment of their project, by the distinguished honour just conferred upon the firmest friend of that measure."

3. The Catholics in Bath had assembled for many years in a large, old house in Bell Tree Lane, where a room had been set aside for their use. Their numbers increasing, "some opulent members of the Romish Church erected a spacious chapel near St. James's-parade." But this was destroyed by fire during the riots of 1780. "A building, not far distant, but in a less conspicuous situation, was afterwards erected in Corn-street; where the service of this church was continued nearly thirty years; but on account of the great increase of the city of Bath, and the consequent increase of the Catholic congregations, the old Theatre in Orchard-street, was in the year 1809, converted into a neat, spacious, and convenient chapel." See *The Original Bath Guide, Considerably Enlarged and Improved* (Bath: Meyler and Son, 1815), pp. 54–55.

4. Angelica Catalani (1780–1849) had a concert engagement at Bath between 11 November and Christmas. She had agreed to sing at the consecration of the Roman Catholic chapel in Orchard Street on 26 November. See *Bath Journal,* 13 November; *Bath Chronicle,* 16 November.

5. HLP had in mind the card game Macao, which was Hungarian in origin and analogous to Vingt-et-Un.

TO THE REVEREND LEONARD CHAPPELOW

Bath is enough Direction
Wensday 13: December
1809.

Dear Mr. Chappelow
is very good not to forget his old Friend, and Lady Bradford's Kindness—shall be deserved better, when my health mends, and I can write pretty Letters again——At present I am suffocating with a Cough, Cold and Sore Throat; The Words will not come out even *on Paper.*

Lady Keith has a Daughter[1]—The Son stays till next Year. Poor old Gillon is on His Deathbed,[2] and Lady Elinor's Mary—*gone.*[3] Something like our White Hart Inn here at Bath, where some arrive, and whence some depart, every hour of the Day almost.

You remember the Horse-Race. Here they come, here they come, here they come; There they go, There they go, There they go. But anything is better than too long Delay at *the Inn.* Do you recollect a Doctor De Chair long a Showy Man upon the Town?—King's Chaplain, and well known to the Musical World and to all *nous autres Gens de Talents.* He drank Tea here Yesterday—Oh! what a Wreck![4]

> White his Locks, his visage wan,
> Strength and Ease and Hope are gone;

13 December 1809 259

Bending with Disease and Cares
All the Load of Life he bears—[5]

Let us make Interest to go by the next Diligence *rather than so*.

You say nothing of Mr. Bridgeman now he is got well; Is he still at Weston? and does he use my Prescription The Flesh Brush? It is far superior to Medicine.

Do you care about Lord Grenville and Lord Eldon? The People here are raving Mad about them.[6] And do you care about Mrs. Clarke and Mr. Wardle? My Newspaper is filled with nothing else, and yet I can't find out who has carried the Cause. That Wardle was carried by the Mob is all I comprehend.[7]

Covent Garden Riots seem to entertain all Europe—Effodiuntur ⟨ OPs / opes Irritamenta Malorum is the best Joke I have heard upon the Subject.[8] I forget whether Mr. Nicholls was an Acquaintance of yours—*Abbè* Nicholls they called him: he was a Clergyman with a good Estate in Suffolk—a Show Place— Blumston or Blumstead—He is dead however:[9]—We were very, *very* old Friends indeed; had played together when Children and never forgot each other.—C'est un Ami de moins—but never mind—*Sequor*——and that so soon as I believe, that one need not care very deeply. My Heart is naturally a light one—and it is *Empty* now, and so is even lighter than usual. Mrs. [Jane] Clay is not well, and I am worse; and cannot go to see her. Is Miss [Catherine Charlotte] with her here? Bath grows a bad Place now for Young People; There is but one Set of Rooms open, and nobody goes even *there*——Mr. King says that there are 4000 Strangers fewer than last Year:[10] and Bills on all the houses. Rainy Weather besides, and Talk of a Flood they had 10 Months ago.[11]

Strange Talk too for and against Mrs. Siddons,[12] and for and against some Lord and Lady Avermore, of whom I never heard till last Week, and now hear of little else.[13]

Write to me again Dear Mr. Chappelow, and tell me you *hope* we shall meet in London about Easter. And Farewell till then, and lay me at charming Lady Bradford's Feet; and believe me ever yours while / H: L: Piozzi.

Text: 561.143.

1. Georgiana *Augusta* Henrietta Elphinstone was born 12 December in the Harley Street home of her parents.
2. Gillon died the next day. See HLP to JSPS, 18 March 1809, n. 1.
3. The servant Mary Carryll, closest of all people to the Ladies of Llangollen, began to ail in February 1808. Preparing for her death, she left to Sarah Ponsonby Aber Adda field, which she had bought with her life's savings. By the end of 1810, Miss Ponsonby still grieved over "the dreadful vacancy made in Our family and our comfort by the fatal event of November 22nd. 1809." See Mavor, p. 172; also HLP to PSP, 5 April 1801, n. 9.
4. A Londoner, John De Chair (1729–1810) matriculated at Oriel College, Oxford, in 1747, where he received his B.A. in 1750, M.A. in 1753, and B. and D.C.L. in 1758. The Reverend De Chair, who would die in Bath, was rector of Little Rissington, Glos., vicar of Horley and Hornton, Oxon., and "one of His Majesty's chaplains in ordinary" (*GM* 80, pt. 2 [1810]: 394).
5. See John Hawkesworth, "Life. An Ode," *GM* 17 (1747): 337. The lines, correctly quoted, are not in proper order: the present second couplet should precede the first.
6. HLP refers to William Wyndham Grenville; John Scott (1751–1838), first baron Eldon (1799) and first earl of Eldon (1821). She could also have mentioned Henry Charles Somerset (1766–1835), sixth duke of Beaufort (1803), and their race to be elected chancellor of Oxford.

With the defeat of Eldon, the government lost the Oxford election, the last bastion of "No Popery." In a straight fight Eldon, the ministry's candidate, would probably have won, but Beaufort's involvement split the anti-Catholic vote.

The election of Grenville was interpreted as giving the death blow to the "No Popery" slogan, to Toryism and rigid conservative thinking. See the *Courier*, 15 December; Denis Gray, *Spencer Perceval, The evangelical Prime Minister, 1762–1812* (Manchester, 1963), pp. 285–86.

7. Apparently Gwyllym Lloyd Wardle, in return for Mrs. Clarke's exposure of the duke of York, agreed to furnish a house for her and provide her with an income. But they soon quarreled. An upholsterer named Wright, who had furnished her house, brought an action against Wardle on 3 July for the cost of the furniture. Wright won his case, whereupon Wardle brought an action for conspiracy against Mrs. Clarke and the two Wright brothers. This action was tried on 11 December, Lord Ellenborough charging the jury in a way unfavorable to Wardle. The jury took but five minutes to return a judgment against him.

Nevertheless, Cobbett and others stood up for him, and on 31 January 1810 he was to receive "from the Chamberlain of the City of London, the thanks and freedom of the City in a gold box of the value of 100 guineas." See *AR* 80, pt. 1 (1810): 175–76; Farington 10: 3588.

8. Just as the first spate of O.P. riots began to subside, Henry Clifford (1768–1813), a barrister of Lincoln's Inn, "appeared in the pit, with the letters O.P. in his hat." Riots began anew. "Brandon, the box-keeper, got Mr. Clifford apprehended as a rioter, and carried before a magistrate at Bow-street; by whom he was immediately discharged. Mr. Clifford now indicted Brandon for an assault and false imprisonment, in which indictment Brandon was cast." The judgment of the jury was applauded by the spectators in the courtroom. See *AR*, "Chronicle" 51 (1809): 406.

Thereupon a dinner took place on 14 December at the Crown and Anchor with Clifford in the chair. Kemble realized that compromise was essential. He asked permission to attend the dinner, where he presented his compromises. After some debate and counterproposals, "the customary routine" of the theater was "restored" by the middle of December. See Farington 10:3587–88.

9. HLP refers to the Reverend Norton Nicholls (b. ca. 1742) of Blundeston, Suffolk. He had died 22 November. See HLP to PSP, 11 May 1795, n. 1.

10. For James King, Bath master of ceremonies, see HLP to PSP, [ca. 21 April 1800], n. 3.

11. In February 1809, as the result of a thaw, "at *Bath* the flood rushed with such velocity as to threaten destruction to whatever impeded its progress. The inhabitants have been great sufferers. Houses, unable to withstand the torrent, fell, and buried their inmates under the ruins. Several have been drowned, and others lost their property. Timber to a great amount, cattle, horses, carts, &c. have been carried away. The flood has been greater than known in the memory of man." See *GM* 79, pt. 1 (1809): 173.

12. HLP refers to Catherine Galindo, self-styled as SS's "wretched victim," and to the publication of *Mrs. Galindo's Letter to Mrs. Siddons: Being a Circumstantial Detail of Mrs. Siddons's Life for the Last Seven Years*, an eighty-page pamphlet published in November. In it Mrs. Galindo attacks SS for alienating her husband's affections seven years earlier. The *Letter* is a prolonged accusation of SS—her wantonness and dishonesty, her cruelty to a young wife whom she professed to love, etc. See particularly pp. 35–38 of the *Letter*.

13. That is, William Charles Yelverton (1762–1814), second viscount Avonmore (1805), principal registrar of the Court of Chancery. On 1 September 1787 he had married Mary, née Reade (d. 1834), and at this time he had three sons and two daughters.

Whatever the gossip, it remained oral and sufficiently intermittent so that HLP could mistake the title created only in 1795.

TO JOHN SALUSBURY PIOZZI SALUSBURY

Wednesday
13: December 1809.

My dearest Salusbury

will be most welcome to Dinner next Monday—The happy 18th of December as I shall be sure to deem it. We will dine at 5 o'Clock: and it is a very good

Thing that you go to Mrs. Wynch's Rout.¹ My Desire is to see You always in the *best* Company, and my hope is that you will never delight in any other. Vice and Vulgarity begin with a Letter—was an old Line in my Copybook ½ a Century ago, or rather much more; but I really have always found it a most true Saying:— *My* heart and Mr. T. Shephard's, agree in abhorring *both*. Mrs. and Miss Parkes came to dinner Yesterday²—and the Good Girls sung to me all Evening—We had only six People in the Room—I have not Health for large Parties if I wished it: The Cold and Oppression upon my Breath is very bad just now, but Maria Parke's Lungs were in high Order; She sung like an Angel: and I shall make her amends by taking Tickets for her Benefit Concert,³ which I hope you will come Time enough to enjoy; and treat your Friend besides. I can go no where of Course but to Mrs. Thelwall's or such houses—Mrs. Glovers &c.⁴ but Lord Carrington is here whose Family wish me to be more with them than Health and Propriety permit:⁵ The house will however be a good House for You and Mr. Pemberton—There are *Eleven* Daughters, nice Partners for the Ball.

I expect Mr. Charles Shephard too, and have kept Leak from Brynbella for purpose of talking with him about the Enclosure &c.: he must go back after Christmas greatly as I shall want him to help me take Care of Glover—Poor little Thing!⁶ but She is desirous to see *you* again, and I love anything that loves my Titmouse. Poor Piccolino! left to *my* Care alone. Oh how I sate and cried last Night when Miss Parke (foolishly perhaps) sung the new Ballad which I had never heard before—

> Here's the bower he lov'd so much,
>   And here's the Tree he planted!!
> Here's The Harp he *used to touch*,
>   Oh! how that *Touch enchanted*!!
> Roses now unheeded die
>   For here's no hand to wreathe them;
> Songs in wild Disorder lie
>   Here's now no *Lip to breathe them*.⁷

God bless you my Dear Child and come soon; and shew me all that is left of all that was *passionately* loved / by your poor Affectionate Aunt / H: L: Piozzi.

Tell Mr. Shephard how much of my true Regard he possesses, and mind what he says, and take his Advice in everything. I wrote him word I was far from well, and it is but too true; I am very glad you come so soon.

Text: Ry. 585.41.

1. Mary, the wife of George Wynch (d. 1823) of 15 Burlington Street, Bath. The Wynches, who kept the Bath house from 1809 to ca. 1813, had also a town house at 26 Grosvenor Place, London, as well as a country seat in Glamorganshire.
Wynch himself had entered the East India Service as a civil servant in 1772 and had a successful career until 1795 when, for an unspecified cause, he was "suspended from the service." By 1800 he was "at home" and by 1805 "out of the service." See Charles C. Princep, *Record of Services of the Honourable East India Company's Civil Servants in the Madras Presidency. From 1741 to 1858* (London, 1885).

The Wynches had three children: Henry, John, and Florentia. The first of these—Henry—was a pupil at Enborne and a classmate of JSPS.

2. Hannah Parke was the wife of the oboist. For her two daughters, see HLP to Q, [25 January 1806], n. 13.

3. Maria Parke performed in Rauzzini's Second Subscription Concert on 6 December 1809 in the New Assembly Rooms. According to the *Bath Journal* (11 December), "The chief attraction of the evening was Miss Parke, who made her first appearance this season, and never was in finer voice. . . . Miss Parke looked extremely well, and was honoured with the most rapturous applause." Her benefit concert took place on Wednesday, 27 December. See the *Bath Journal*, 25 December 1809 and 1 January 1810.

4. Mrs. Thelwall lived in Burlington Street and Mrs. Glover in Pulteney Street, Bath.

5. Robert Smith (1752–1838), first baron Carrington, of Upton, Notts. (1797), was at this time married to Anne, née Barnard (d. 1827), his first wife, by whom he had nine children: Robert John (1796–1868); Harriet (d. 1856); Catharine Lucy (d. 1843); Charlotte Elizabeth (d. 1811); Esther (d. 1854); Jane (d. 1837); Louisa Mary (d. 1830); Georgiana (d. 1875); Emily (d. 1869).

6. The Salopian Ann Glover, more "Lady than Maid," was given to hysterics. In her "Pocket Book" for 8 February 1810 (Ry. 616), HLP wrote: "Glover sick and weeping all the Way—very dismal." On 9 February, "Miss Williams came; Says She has heard that Glover pines for Leak. But why should she cry so." Almost a year later, on 9 October, HLP commented, "Glover very Ill, and shrieking in Hysterics."

7. See the advertisement in the *Morning Post*, 4 March 1811: "Miss Parke's celebrated Ballad, 'The Kiss and the Tear,' is at length published by Golding and Co. The Words by Mr. Dimond, are beautiful, and worthy the charming music that is set to them."

TO LADY WILLIAMS

Bath Saturday
16: December 1809

My dear Lady Williams
will be glad, having said and thought so kindly on the Subject—to hear how safely my eldest Daughter is put to Bed with her *Female* Baby. She was but five Hours in Labour; with every favourable Symptom, and every possible Comfort——Her Lord and Sisters all attending—except Mrs. Mostyn, who is I suppose still in Wales.

Sir John's Chimney Piece of Verd Antique must be admired by all the World—my Anglesea Specimen is as truly fine as any from Ægypt and you know I said it was very surprizing—but on Reflection I am well convinced that the Green has taken its richly-tinted Hue from the Copper-Mine.

How is poor Mrs. Williams? not I hope materially worse; and the young Creatures! all well, and lively, and dancing away: Miss Williams is never well I think, but keeps her Looks, and keeps her Friends, and keeps her Spirits.—She also keeps her Kindness for my dear Lady Williams's / ever obliged and / Faithful H: L: P.

This Town never was so empty, nor the Inhabitants *ever so low*. Rooms shut up—Concerts thinly attended, Theatre—a Desart—Nothing but Routs at private houses, and those but a few.

I made myself Ill by *drinking too freely* at the Pump—but am better now. A bad Account of a Lady's Complaints—a'nt it?

Text: Ry 3 (1807–11). *Address:* Lady Williams / Bodylwyddan / near St. Asaph / N. Wales.

TO LADY KEITH

>Wednesday
>Night
>31. January 1810.

I am really flattered at hearing that my Letter amused Lord Keith and your dear Self: It was a comical Scene enough, The Lady's Name—Holford. They called her Miss Holford all Evening, but I knew not a Bit the more that She was Author of Wallace—and one of them said she had read that Poem to them the Evening before—to which I only bowed, and Wondered why her Eyes darted fire at *me* so.[1]

We have now more Serious Subjects of Melancholy talk. Poor Lady Glenbervie could hardly quiet her Spirits to entertain even a small Party of us last Night[2]— on Account of this dreadful Disappearance of Mr. Eden, and the equally dreadful tho' senseless Reports in every News Paper—*all which* her *private* Letters continue to contradict—he has never been heard of.[3]

Sir Charles Turner too, whose Gouty Hand I gently pressed on Monday, and kissed his faithful Dog that sate by him in the Wheel Chair—is gone this Morning[4]—Parry and Crawford and Bowen and Gibbes could not retard, or turn the Scythe of Death;—who I thought was only shaking his Hour Glass.[5] But 'spite of all these Warnings, all these Threats; We build and plant,[6] and court and marry as did the Antediluvians—and though I fondly hoped my Claim to Manorial Rights had no Competitor when I saw Grants made by Edward 6th., by Queen Elizabeth, and even by their Father in my own Possession—when I have long received Chiefties and taken Strays as Lady of the Manor of Bachygraig—— This Day brings me a Letter to inform me that Mr. Pillar says *I must wave my Claim* and so 'tis sure I must:[7] The King is Lord of the whole County of Flint in right of his Earldom of Chester, and would *justly* withhold his Royal Assent, even if the Bill passed both Houses of Parliament. My Proofs were presumptive merely, I had no *specific* Grants out of his Majesty's Rights——So is your poor H: L: P sunk into a Landholder, and a Landholder only—and so is every Mountain and Hill laid Low. But still am I desirous of passing the Enclosure Bill, because I am certainly the principal Landholder;—and I shall keep Annoyance from my Door by it; and I do verily believe not much will be lost, and the Expence will be lessened and Mr. Shephard says there is still Time enough—— I have taken the Liberty—a very great one—of enclosing A Note to *him*, requesting him to call in Harley Street, and see Lord Keith or you if permitted— You will find him *talkable*—not like poor Oldfield, who if he does get to London, will be lost perhaps between Piccadilly and Cavendish Square; or lose his Wits with Wonder when arrived there; "Never before stood he in such a Presence" as Young Norval says.[8] It will be better speak to Mr. Shephard whom You have seen with me at Morin's Hôtel.

Miss Susan Arabella Thrale's Note is full of reproaches; instead of Thanks for her Letter telling me a Tale that all the World knows— and telling it wrong too. Well! nothing ailed her Letter after all, except the *Direction*——had I been living at *Brynbella* I should have studied it and got it by heart.

Your Letter told me *Something;* it told me Lady Kirkwall had a useful and noble Friend sprung up; the Thought of it rejoyces my heart. If your Delight is in frivolous Chat as a *Rill* to *wash down* Salt and Sour Politics—come to Bath.—We discuss Mr. Coutts's Buttons[9] and Mrs. Panton's *Head* Dress; (She wears no *other* Dress) all the day long.[10] Mr. Coutts' Buttons are sometimes said to be Rubies, sometimes Diamonds; and the Boys and Girls are all a Gape to see when Mr. Coutts will act Romeo, and how he will act as President—of I know not what Society.—But Mr. Coutts plays all the Play, and leaves no one Silent for want of an Immediate Subject of Conversation. Who he is—nobody seems to care; he makes fine Sport, and will make finer, when taking the whole Theatre he will exhibit himself either as Lover or Tyrant.

Lady Nelson—The Admiral's Widow, always enquires for you——I dare say She will be among the Titterers—serious as She seems[11]—when Lady Hamilton comes forward with her new Conquest. I wonder when that *Wellsorted* Union is to be perfected!—We have heard on't a long Time.[12] Lady Saxton talks *no Latin* now, but tells me what a Charmer She has in her youngest Son[13]—such a Scholar! such a Figure! such a Every Thing——You will know what Sincerity there is in *that* Language very soon——I think Susan feels some of it towards your Ladyships beautiful Daughter. I have no Joy meanwhile in young Mostyn's Gyantism; nor can make myself of our Countryman Fluellin's mind in Shakespeare's Play, that Great and *Pig* are Synonymous—"Alexander the Pig, and the huge, and the Magnanimous &c."[14] He is however 'tis plain no degenerated Progeny of *Meyrick Meredith* Colossus of the 3 Counties as they called him.[15]

Well now Adieu! *Pelted* as my Nephew Salusbury and myself are with Invitations, and seduced into Society on every Side by every Creature—I think it is very pretty to Sit at home and write Letters about nothing in the World so. Apropòs to Letters, Miss Seward's are going to be published;[16] I wonder how they will be liked![17] She was a dazzling Creature. Suffice it for me if I can contribute a Moment to yours or your dear Lord's Amusement and believe me ever his and Your Affectionate and / Obliged H: L: Piozzi.

Lord and Lady Kilmorey are here,[18] living at the Whitehart:—yet going into Company perpetually. I thought of Count Manucci[19] and the *Fully Moon.*

Text: Bowood Collection. *Address:* R: H: Baroness Keith.

1. HLP alludes to Margaret Holford (1778–1852), afterward Hodson, and her metrical romance *Wallace; or, The Fight of Falkirk* (London: Cadell and Davies, 1809).
Behind this allusion lies an anecdote. On 25 January, HLP had written to Q: "I went to a *Blue* Party for Purpose of mending my Amusements, and getting some what for the Money I fling away: There however I made so bad a figure I shall be afraid even of Greys in future. They asked me what

I thought of *Wallace* a new Poem. I think little about it, quoth I; 'tis one of those Imitations of Marmion which Walter Scott's Merit is sure to fill the Kingdom with—he has set a new Fashion, and everybody will follow it I suppose—They do the same by Braham's Music—Miss Such a one's Dress—and Abee Sieyes's Politics. There *Sate* the Lady who wrote the Book—encircled with admirers, not one of whom I was acquainted with—so I sneaked home with a fresh Cold *caught* in the Cause of Literature! ! !" (Bowood Collection).

2. The wife of Sylvester Douglas (1743–1823), cr. first baron Glenbervie (1800), was Catherine Anne (1760–1817), daughter of Frederick North, second earl of Guilford.

3. On 19 January 1810 William Frederick Eden, the son of the first baron Auckland, disappeared. On 24 February the body was found in the Thames. The coroner's inquest held on 14 March concluded: "*Found drowned in the river, but by what means it came there, there was no evidence before the jury.*" See AR, "Chronicle," 52 (1810): 328–29.

Young Eden had been born in 1782. At the time of his death he was one of the tellers of the exchequer and a lieutenant colonel in the Westminster Volunteers.

4. Charles Turner (1773–1810), second baronet (1783), died issueless on 1 February 1810, when the title became extinct.

5. HLP refers to the medical greats of Bath. For Caleb Hillier Parry, see HLP to PSW, 1 September [1789], n. 7; for Stewart Crawford, HLP to PSP, 6 August 1802, n. 7; for William Bowen, again to PSP, 14 April 1803, n. 2; and for George Smith Gibbes, HLP to John Roberts, 20 March 1807, n. 6.

6. See HLP to PSP, 24 March 1795, n. 5.

7. HLP had written to JSPS, [19 September 1809], (Ry. 585.33): "Tell Mr. C. Shepard that I was forced to be very smooth indeed with Mr. Oldfield, who persists in saying how the Crown sets its Face resolutely against *Welsh Grants* since the Dean of St. Asaph's Triumph over the King at Rhyddlan; and that Enquiry will be made at the Land Revenue Office whether our Grants are recorded there or no. There is a Mr. *Pilar* at head of that Department, and I must get him spoke to in our Favour."

James Pillar (1764–1833), a resident of Lambeth, was an official of the Land Revenue Office, Westminster (and later of the Office of Woods, Forests, and Land Revenues). For his will, proved 10 December 1833, see P.R.O., Prob. 11/1825/776.

8. See *Douglas. A Tragedy* (1756). Written by Mr. Hume [John Home]. Taken from the Manager's Book at the Theatre Royal, Covent Garden (London: Cadell, 1798).

Norval, who is in fact Lord Douglas, has saved Lord Randolph's life. The latter acknowledges his gratitude:

> Next to myself and equal to Glenalvon,
> In honour and command shall Norval be.

Norval responds:

> I know not how to thank you. Rude I am
> In speech and manners: never till this hour
> Stood I in such a presence. . . .
> (act 2)

9. Robert Coates (1772–1848), known as Romeo Coates, was rich and owned a large collection of diamonds. About 1808 he set up a lavish establishment in Bath. His carriage, shaped like a kettledrum, was drawn by white horses. Across the bar of his curricle was a brass cock displaying his motto, "Whilst I live I'll crow." On 9 February 1810 he made his debut in the Bath Theatre Royal as Romeo, wearing diamond buttons on his coat and waistcoat. See *Macready's Reminiscences*, ed. Sir Frederick Pollock, 2 vols. (London: Macmillan, 1875), 1:112, 114–15.

10. Probably Mary Panton, née Gubbins (fl. 1770–1824). Her husband, Thomas (d. 1808), was a large property owner in and around Newmarket. After his death, she went to Bath, residing first at 2 Widcombe Terrace and after 1820 at 5 Cambridge Place. Her social activities were frequently reported in the newspapers. Thus, the *Morning Post* of 5 January quoted the *Bath Chronicle* on "the elegance and taste" of her entertainments "in the circle of fashion" at Bath. On this occasion she beguiled her guests with a juvenile theatrical in her home.

11. The widowed Frances Herbert (Nisbet), née Woolward (1758– 1831), married Horatio Nelson on 11 March 1787 at Nevis in the West Indies. Their relationship seemed firm through 1798, when reports of her husband's intimacy with Lady Hamilton in Naples reached her. They separated early in 1800, Nelson providing her with a financial settlement.

See Farington 8:3067–68 for the alleged cause which broke up the Nelsons' marriage.

12. For Emma Hamilton, see HLP to Ly W, 10 February 1799, n. 11.

According to Bath gossip, Lady Hamilton was to marry Sir Harry Featherstonehaugh; see HLP to LY W, 9 February 1810, n. 9.

13. Charles Saxton (ca. 1730–1808), cr. baronet (1794), had married on 11 July 1771 Mary, née Bush (d. ca. 1823). They had three sons: Charles (1773–1838), second baronet, at this time an undersecretary (1808–12) to the viceroy of Ireland; John, said to have been "a Captain of Dragoons"; Clement, the youngest son. The last two were not mentioned in the wills of their father and their brother, Charles.

14. See *Henry the Fifth,* 4.7.14–18.

15. An allusion to the young Mostyns' great-grandfather Meyrick Meredith (Meurig Maredydd) of Pengwern, county Flint, whose vast property spanned three counties in North Wales. See Lloyd 4:382–83.

16. *Letters of Anna Seward Written between the Years 1784 and 1807,* 6 vols. (Edinburgh: Archibald Constable; London: Longman, etc., 1811).

17. When Miss Seward's *Letters* appeared in 1811, HLP wrote in "Harvard Piozziana," vol. 4: "And her rancorous Hatred of Johnson, and his Insults on my Character and Conduct—and Boswell—Impudent Lyar! telling *her* that Johnson had been really in Love with *me,* are all so new to me and so diverting I can read nothing else. Her keeping Copies too of her own Letters! how astonishing! Copies of one's own Letters! She might well complain for want of *Time* when She wrote every Trifle so,—Twice over.—Mr. Samuel Lysons could have informed her how little I weeded Doctor Johnson's correspondence—and how certain it was, that had not *he* preserved my *Letters,* they would not ever have been seen by Lysons or Cadell."

18. See HLP to MW, [11 April 1807], n. 9.

19. For Giovanni Tommaso Mannucci, see HLP to SL, 14 June 1785, n. 10.

TO LADY WILLIAMS

[Marlborough] Friday
9: February 1810.

My dear Lady Williams
  will wonder at this Letter, if She looks at the Post Mark;—but the Truth is I had been too long plagued with a Cough which I well knew would yield to nothing but Change of Air; so when Salusbury's Vacation Time was up, I resolved to accompany him to Speen; and am now at Marlborough on my Road back to Bath where he passed gay holy days, and took his first Taste of Worldly Pleasure—Balls, Concerts, Ladies &c. But though petted and flattered, he was not spoiled; but glad as ever to rejoin the Society of Mr. Shephard of Enborne—Father of the Tall Young Man to whom Your Ladyship was so polite when in Wales.
  What famous News you tell me thence! Famous News truly; so Mr. Biddulph has bought poor old Lleweny Hall[1]—I wonder how much Estate went with it![2] Lady Kirkwall's last Letter to *me* Impressed me so I could not sleep for thinking on't—her tender Regrets, and grateful Remembrances of sweet Bodylwyddan! her forcible Appeal against Lord K's Cruelty in suffering her to sit at his Door in London—her Child in her Arms—and be refused Admittance, his Instructions to the Servants he set about her at Speen to obey her Commands only so far, and upon such and such Occasions——his Severity in having a Table spread for his Dinner at Speen—separate from hers—at which the very Waiters and Chambermaids of the Inn over against her Ladyship's habitation—cryed

Shame.——And after all this, her Willingness to forgive everything and be reconciled rather than live apart.

Lady Keith's last Letter however afforded me some Consolation: She says the Duke of Portland has taken up our amiable Friend's Cause, and will see Justice done her.[3] But I am sure the World in General is on t'other Side, Lady Bellmore[4] and Miss Caldwell,[5]—but chiefly Miss Caldwell and I pleaded the whole Story out to good old Lady Elizabeth Garnier[6] last Thursday Evening at Lady Wilmots Assembly, and got quite a little Audience round us.[7] It is astonishing how some Women obtain,—some lose the World's Good Will, without seeming in any particular Manner at having endeavoured to procure, or fling it from them. When the great Admiral Nelson was supposed to afflict his deserving Wife by superior Attachment shewn to Lady Hamilton—no one condemned, and few censured the Proceeding—though Gratitude and Justice were offended by such Conduct,—but People said that was the Triumph of Talent. Poor Lady Kirkwall has Talent enough: I know not why People are against her.

Sir Matthew—no; Sir *Harry* Featherstonehaugh is going to lead Lord Nelson's Favourite from Prison to the Altar.[8] Wonderful Luck at her advanced Age! tho' it is whispered that the Young Baronet himself has a damaged character.[9] We have a flaring Man at Bath that makes the Town stand a gape at his oddities— wearing Diamond Buttons, and Broches of Rubies, and platting up his Hair like a Woman with a Comb at Top. I understand he is to play Romeo tonight,—by his own Particular Desire, and a fine Riot I expect to be the Consequence; I shall make haste home to hear about it.

The *large Stomach* Your Ladyship tells me of, is a natural Consequence of Visits to Liverpool—I should think She would go back thither—'tis a famous Place for such Damsels, it was *there* Lady H⸺ received her Education.

Mrs. Mostyn has written me a most polite Letter, saying She heard I was *terribly lowspirited* and that She would come with her Sons, and pass a fortnight with me, tho' Bath *had no Charms for her.* The People I am living with praise my *good Spirits;* but certainly such a Visit must be extremely desireable, I shall expect her soon. Meanwhile I am wishing to say something of poor dear Mrs. Williams, but what can I say?[10] that I sincerely grieve for her Sufferings and admire Dr. Cumming's Power of alleviating *any* of them.[11] That I pity my dear Lady Williams from my Soul, *her* Feelings are so completely in unison with what my own were; and with what they *are* too, losing the Company of her *eldest Boy*[12]—Well! what God sends, let us bear; and keep our *eldest Boys* out of Evil, and nothing shall *quite* break our hearts—but poor Lady Auckland will deserve Praise if She keeps her Wits—her most intimate Friend told me that Mr. Eden had been busy at his Desk all day, that he drank Tea with his Family at 6 in the Evening—said he would be home in an hour to dress for his Mama's Party—went out for that hour, and was seen no more.[13] Adieu dear Lady! and write when you want another Letter / from your H: L: P.

Text: Ry. 3 (1807–11). *Address:* Lady Williams / Bodylwyddan / near St. Asaph / Flintshire / N: Wales. *Postmark:* MARLBOROUGH.

1. Robert Biddulph of Ledbury, Herefs., and Cofton Hall, Worcs., might well have been interested in the purchase of a North Wales seat ever since 24 December 1801, when he married Charlotte Myddleton of Chirk Castle. He did not, however, buy Llewenny. For the Reverend Edward Hughes's purchase of it, see HLP to MW, 18 February 1809, n.3.

2. The sale of Llewenny was important to HLP, who associated it with the Salusbury name. In "Harvard Piozziana," vol. 1, she wrote: "Henry Salusbury's Name long stood recorded on an Obelisk, which stood placed upon the Spot where Edward the 4th in 1471 won the Battle of Barnet from the King-maker Earl of Warwick:—Here Henry Salusbury having shewed Mercy in the Fight, to an old Acquaintance that prostrated himself--'Satest prostrasse Leoni' at his feet——took those remarkable Words for *Legenda*. He built Lleweni Hall.—The old Territorial Name of the Place, was Weithian, where dwelt *Mars* Weithian in the Year 720—third of the 15 Princes of N. Wales. This Henry Salusbury set his old Bavarian Lyon on the top of the new House, which he called Lleweny—*Llew* for the Lyon,—an *ny* for us——and the Scrowl in his Paw bore the Motto."

3. William Henry Cavendish-Scott-Bentinck (1768–1854), fourth duke of Portland (1809).

4. Juliana Butler (1783–1861), a daughter of the second earl of Carrick, had married in 1800 Somerset Lowry-Corry (1774–1841), second earl of Belmore (1802).

5. See HLP to Q, 14 March 1806, n. 16.

6. Lady Elizabeth, née Howard (d. 1813), sister of the fifth earl of Carlisle, was the widow of Charles Garnier, captain of H.M.S. *Aurora*, who drowned 16 December 1796 in Yarmouth while attempting to return to his ship. See *GM* 66, pt. 2 (1796): 1062.

7. On 15 March 1795 Mary Anne, née Howard (1776–1862), became the second wife of Robert, second baronet Wimot (1772) of Osmaston. (His first wife had been Juliana Elizabeth, née Byron, who had died in 1788.)

8. HLP confused two generations of Fetherstonhaughs.

Matthew Fetherstonhaugh (ca. 1715–74), cr. baronet (1747), purchased the estate of Uppark and in 1767 that of Ladyholt, both in Sussex. An M.P. for various constituencies (1755–74), he had married in 1746 Sarah, née Lethieullier (d. 1788).

Their only son was Henry (1754–1846), second baronet, M.P. for Portsmouth (1782–96).

9. Sir Harry, hardly young, was eleven years older than Emma, Lady Hamilton, who had been born in April 1765.

Their association began in 1780, when he brought Emma to Uppark as his mistress. In 1782 she had become pregnant, believing the child to be his and expecting his protection. Instead he banished her. After Nelson's death, the breach between them was lessened: he lent her £500 in 1806 and was available whenever she needed rescue from her gambling debts and extravagances. They agreed to forget their earlier intimacy but were openly friends in 1810.

10. Eleanor Williams was to die of cancer on 13 May 1810.

11. George Brownlow Cumming (1782–1863) received his M.D. from Edinburgh in 1802, becoming in 1812 a licentiate of the Royal College of Physicians in London. In 1804 he was appointed physician to the Chester Infirmary. Diffident because of his youth, he resigned in 1806 and retired to Denbigh, where he lived and practiced until his return to Chester in 1823. He would come back to Denbigh in 1835 and resume his practice there.

12. See HLP to Ly W, 31 December 1807 and n. 1.

13. William Eden, first baron Auckland, had married 26 September 1776 Eleanor, née Elliot (d. 1818). They had three sons and eight daughters. The Edens were made anxious by the disappearance of their eldest son on 19 January 1809.

TO JOHN SALUSBURY PIOZZI SALUSBURY

Bath Monday Night
19: February 1810.

Now dearest Salusbury I beg of you to make your old Aunt welcome at Enborne——Everybody says how perfectly it resembles me, and I can myself perceive that it is an admirable Miniature of my *Black Bonnet*.[1] So here is the Talisman presented—the Mystery explained; and pray accept the Writing Box you have so often saved from Ruin. I have bought one for my own Use two Sizes larger, and this will be a clever Thing for you to keep Your Letters and Papers in.

The frozen Snow and Rain make our Town quite dangerous for Walkers; Sir John Callender fell at his own Door an hour ago, and hurt himself severely.[2] As for Gay Street, the Sight of that sharp hill, and Coal Carts going up it——The wretched Horses falling at every Step, and the brutal Fellows bawling after them: shocked a Gentleman so, that in running to avoid them *he* slipt and fell, and broke his Leg almost as I was passing. Virgil's Tartarus came in *my head*

> Hinc exaudiri Gemitus, et sæva Sonare
> Verbera; tum Stridor ferri—tract æque Catenæ[3]

How dreadful must it be just by the Lyon Inn Shrewsbury! When I am there in Winter, I always *do* shut my Eyes.[4] Take Care dear Soul! and do not come to any hurt, Body or Mind——I verily think any bad Accident to you would kill me; I think too that poor Doctor Law[5] is more to be pitied than his paltry feeble minded Son[6]——Tho' Temptations are terrible Things and those who *set the Snares* are the wickedest of all Creatures. It was Bowen told me the Tale in Confidence and said the Boy was too ill as yet to be reprimanded.

Leak says no Lambs are dropt yet at Brynbella—but poor *Agnes* my favourite Ewe, is expecting every hour. She was herself born under a heavy Drift of Snow two years back, and was dug out with her Mother Two Days after her Birth.

The *Topes* and *Jungles*—as Lord Valentia's Book calls the Groves and Woods,[7]—are in very pretty Forwardness I hear; and tho' I do not cry for Dear Wales as poor Miss Williams does—my Heart feels a longing Desire to see it again and applaud our numerous Improvements. Apropos I saw a Letter to her from her eldest Nephew Your Friend John; he sends True Love to Salusbury if at Bath and says how Ill he has been *himself*, and that he thinks poor Lady Williams's Mother "his dearest Grandmama" he calls her——will not be alive Three Weeks.

Here comes Robert with your Box to pack——He looks *Hunappy* still, and coughs dreadfully. I must make haste I suppose, and finish this Empty Letter. My Heart however is full enough——various petty Vexations about these odious Servants, and some Uneasiness at not hearing from Charles Shephard about our Money Stuff:[8] but nothing to affect my Health or Peace of Mind whilst my dear Salusbury keeps *well, wise* and *good*.

That I consider you as my Comfort on all Occasions, and that I have a firm Trust in your Virtue diligently prayed for by us both——You *well know*; but will receive further Marks of my Approbation on opening your Writing Box, which as you did not expect it will be the more Welcome from / Your truly Affectionate Aunt / and Sincere old experienced / Friend / H: L: Piozzi.

Tell me what you all think of the Talisman.[9]

Text: Ry. 585.46.

1. The miniature of HLP wearing her black bonnet was painted by John Jackson (1778–1831). The original may be seen at the Johnson House, Gough Square, London. See also Clifford, facing p. 408.
2. John Callender, or Callendar (1739–1812), of Westertown, Stirlingshire, cr. baronet (1798). He had been an army colonel and M.P. for Berwick-upon-Tweed (1795–1802, 1806–7).
3. Aeneas's descent into the underworld is described in bk. 6 of the *Aeneid*. The lines quoted are 557–58.
4. The Lion Inn (or Hotel, as it is now called) is at the top of Wyle Cop and thus vulnerable to the weather. But then—as now—it was surrounded by buildings.
5. Occasionally preaching at Laura Chapel in place of Dr. Randolph (HLP's "Pocket Book" for 1810, Ry. 616), George Henry Law (1761–1845) was educated at Charterhouse and Queen's College, Cambridge. A vicar of several churches, he served as bishop of Chester (1812–24) and bishop of Bath and Wells (1824–45). A conservative in ecclesiastical matters, he opposed the Test and Corporation Acts and other reform measures.
6. That is, James Thomas Law (1790–1876), at this time a student at Christ's, Cambridge. He was to reform, enter the church, and become in 1821 chancellor of the diocese of Lichfield.
7. George Annesley (1770–1844), styled Viscount Valentia (1793–1816), second Earl of Mountnorris (1816). He had traveled extensively from 1802 to 1806, publishing an account of his experiences in *Voyages and Travels to India, Ceylon, the Red Sea, Abyssinia, and Egypt, etc.*, 3 vols. (London: W. Miller, 1809).
8. See HLP to JSPS, 22 February 1810, nn. 6, 7.
9. Talisman: The miniature of HLP.

TO JOHN SALUSBURY PIOZZI SALUSBURY

Thursday
22: February 1810.

Whilst I sit expecting my Dear Child's Letter from Newbury, and whilst I hear the Post Man knocking at every Door except poor No. 6, I must tell what Conversations I have had concerning You with Friends that are mine chiefly because I hope they will be Yours. Good old Tall Townsend—Husband to Lady Clerke[1]——says "Oh now for Pity do not put that fine-pure hearted Boy to Christ Church; it is the wickedest College in Oxford——any other College, Oh *any* Place but Christ Church, although my dear Doctor Hall[2] does purpose a restoration of that Discipline and an Encouragement of those good Morals, which the late Dean *wholly despaired of,* and by so doing, helped drive them away.[3]

I am confident Sir—(was my Answer,) that Salusbury will be thrown into dreadful Temptations at Christ Church;—but when he and I saw the Porcelain Manufacture together at Coalbrook Dale, we saw that when they had turned the Plate, and shaped it elegantly—and painted a beautiful Figure of *Virtue* or *Religion* on it——The Man was at last obliged to put it in a *Furnace* and *burn it in* before the Plate was fitted for use.——

Aye (replied Townsend) in a *Furnace,* but Christ Church when my Son was there, might be considered as a *Crucible* that would melt down Gold itself.[4] If however he does go thither, and if the College does reform under its present Head, I will give him Letters of Strong Recommendation to my Friend Doctor Hall who will be glad of a *good Boy,* and give him every Encouragement—but remember the *Loadstone of Vice* he will be within the Attractions of—Day and

Night——Meanwhile dear Madam I *must* add one Word, just to say that as your Connection with that Child is founded on Duty and Honour; I feel strongly perswaded that The *Almighty will bless it.*
So much for this Tender Talk.
Mr. Byng says that his Brother in Law has set his Heart on reforming the Follies and Excesses of his Gentlemen Commoners;[5] and that Good Behaviour is the surest Road to Notice and to Favour at present.

Good Heavens! but here's the Post gone by—and no Letter from Newbury— Why surely my Dear Salusbury's hand could never have been stopt by any Accident from letting me know his Box was safe arrived, with the Writing-Thing—and my Picture in its private Drawer; and all the Cravats, Books, Guetres [i.e. gaiters], Trowsers and Trumpery making a *large* wooden Box, which I directed myself; and Robert saw *booked* and is sure it went safely.

And now instead of a Letter from my Darling from Newbury—comes a heap of *Italian* Letters full of Stuff and Nonsense—and calling aloud for the other 2400£.[6] Charles Shephard is very kind, and has Infinite Trouble with *Them* and with *me*:[7] but *Dear* now for Mercy's Sake, write directly; and say you are alive; and that you like the Picture, and that you love your / too Affectionate Aunt / H: L: Piozzi.

Oh tell Pemberton and Mr. Shephard what an Agony I am in; and make *them* write if anything ails *you* which God forbid.

I am going to dine at Mrs. Lutwyche's but shall not eat a Morsel for anxiety.[8] Oh Salusbury! have you no Pity?

Write only two words—*Alive* and *Well*

Text: Ry. 585.47. *Address:* John Piozzi Salusbury Esq. / at The Rev: Thomas Shephard's / Enborne near Newbury / Berks. *Postmark:* <   > (In JSPS's hand, "Received Febry 23rd 1810, Answered Do 25th Do").

1. A geologist, Joseph Townsend (1739–1816) was educated at Clare Hall, Cambridge, graduating B.A. in 1762 and M.A. in 1765. He took orders, showed sympathy for the Methodists, and occasionally preached in Lady Huntington's chapel in Bath. After serving as chaplain to the duke of Atholl, he became rector of Pewsey, Wilts., where he died. He was twice married: in 1773 to Joyce, née Nankivell (d. 1785); in 1790 to Lydia Hammond (d. 1812), widow of Sir John Clerke.
2. Charles Henry Hall (1763–1827) had matriculated at Christ Church, Oxford, in 1779, receiving his B.A. in 1783, M.A. in 1786, and B.D. in 1794. He stayed on at Christ Church to become subdean in 1805, dean from 1809 to 1824. At one time regius professor of divinity (1807–9), he also held several curacies and in the last three years of his life served as dean of Durham.
3. The late dean of Christ Church was Cyril Jackson (1746–1819), who in 1779 was created canon of Christ Church and in 1783 dean of the college. He was celebrated as a dean, enforcing discipline, improving the buildings and grounds. He was often offered high ecclesiastical preferments but rejected them all. In 1809 he left Christ Church and retired to the manor house at Felpham, near Bognor, Sussex.
4. Henry Townsend (b. 1782) had matriculated at Christ Church in 1797. Not remaining for a degree, he entered the army and was to drown in the Red Sea.
5. Edmund Byng (1774–1854) was a son of the fifth viscount Torrington and a commissioner of the colonial audit office. His sister Anna Maria Bridget (d. 1852) had on 29 August 1794 married Dr. Hall.

6. According to GP's will, he left £4,000 for his eleven surviving Italian relatives. ". . . said Sum of four thousand pounds I order and direct my said Wife to pay and distribute among such of my relations as she shall think most worthy." The specific bequests, such as £2,000 to his brother Giambattiata and £1,000 to his nephew Pietro, along with smaller ones, first appeared in a codicil written on 11 January 1809.

7. HLP had wanted to honor GP's bequests as quickly as possible, despite the depressed state of securities in the year following his death. In February she wrote in her "Pocket Book" for 1810 (Ry. 616): "Gave Authority to Mssr: Hammersley to sell out my little Stock and Savings and transmit to Shephard and Angelo Levy [a merchant] for Purpose of Sending to Italy.—" The transaction actually cost £6,000 and was handled largely by Charles Shephard as her lawyer.

8. Mary Lutwyche of 12 Marlborough Buildings, Bath.

TO JOHN SALUSBURY PIOZZI SALUSBURY

Fryday 2: March 1810.

My dearest Salusbury has I hope long since recovered that Good Humour which our Italian Letters recently disturbed. Relations always *do* disturb one's Good humour: I have often wished myself as far removed from *mine* as Providence has placed Yours from *You*—and what think you of poor Miss Williams? who plagues all of us, and herself *most* of all, with those unhappy family Differences &c. Let us pay these People to the last Penny, and then wash our Heads clear of them. Tell Mr. Pemberton I know how kindly he has spoken of the Time passed here at No. 6—and tell him how much I feel obliged.—*He* too will one Day have his Share of the Trouble given by *Kinsffolk* I doubt not.

But I must tell you of a Mr. Ball, The Gentleman who rides up and down all Day with an important Face and nothing to do——and People call him Knight of the White Horse. He visited me two Days ago to learn Mr. Shephard's Terms—I answered 150£ per Annum boldly.—"But this (says he) is for my *only Son*, the finest Crater in the World perhaps;—14 Years of Age and he is in Ovid *now*"—with a sharp Irish Accent. Where was he bred Sir? At Westminster; was the reply;——but it is too near London, and he has nothing he can *ate* at Mr. Smedley's the head Boarding house. I fear my serious face could last no longer, and I got rid of further conversation by assuring him that I *thought* the House at Enborne was full, but he might be assured I would not fail to make proper Enquiry. Mr. Charles Shephard will say this is one of my *picked Men* but upon my honour the Dialogue was as I state it here.[1]

Doctor Randolph was greater than ever on the Fast Day; my Spirits were very low, and he half broke my heart with his pathetic Eloquence. I have no Skill in making People weep but I can make *him* and Mrs. Siddons too burst into fits of unexpected Laughter after they have been drawing Tears from every Eye. Poor Mr. Eden is found at last, but Lord Glenbervie staid not in Bath to tell us any thing—he left the Town in eight and forty hours after arriving. Could I have caught his Lordship he should have franked some of my expensive Letters to

Hammersley, Levy,² Shephard & c. I am dying to learn the full and final Statement of all that the Correspondence has cost.

Glover does not know where She left my Parasol—I fancy 'tis at Speen Hill: She *only just* recollects my having it when I walked up the Mount at Marlborough—and that was as we *went*—not on my *return*. Ask for it someday when you want excuse for a long Walk.

Well! Dr. Randolph says that the Nation like its Individuals has spent its Youth in Prodigality—its mature Age in Pride——that it even now dotes on the Dregs of Vice, and depends at last upon a *Death Bed* Repentance. This is bad News indeed—and is so near to true, It frights one. Keep *your* self Dearest Salusbury an Exception to this general Corruption, and make *my Name* quoted as an Example of Excelling Virtue. Can there be a greater *honour* either to you or Me?—or can the Person live, who could have a keener Sensibility of such Happiness than myself? *This* Happiness 'tis in your Power to *bestow*, on her who *I will say* best deserves it *from* You, even your old Aunt H:L:P.—who when She has seen her own Family *forced* to confess that her favours to You have been all well deserved,—will die content, and sing *Nunc dimittis*.³

It came into my head once, that the Praise one receives from Friends is sweet like Vegetable Fragrance—Roses and Honey Suckles in a Garden——The Approbation we are able to *extort* from *Enemies*, resembles the Scent of Plants under Distillation;——Hungary and Lavender Water: it is forced out by *Fire*.

Lady Keith has never so much as said She should be glad to see me, and shew her Child to me; and Sophy scarce thanked me for my fine Presents—but they rave all about the Princes and the Royal Dukes &c. "Thrones, Dominations, Princedoms Virtues, Pow'rs."⁴ Pride, Pride, as dear Doctor Randolph says—and I do think that for Profligacy, poor Lady de Blaquiere's Son George will soon exhibit himself against *anyone*.⁵ He has been caught in criminal Intercourse with a married Woman whose Husband sues him for Damages, and he has not a Guinea in the World; so must make his wretched Mother pay for his vicious Frolic out of the Money tied up for her own Subsistence and her Daughters— or She must see him disgracefully fly the Country his Profession calls him to defend——and *fly from his Bail too*, a Species of Rascality which Mr. Shephard will explain to you viva voce, better than I can by Letter. Ah my sweet Friend! my poor Lady de Blaquiere! how my Heart bleeds for *her* Heart, which will I fear prove too soft on this Occasion to hold firm *her Duty*—and drive the worthless Fellow from her Sight.

My dearest Salusbury is a *wise Child;* and God Almighty will I hope preserve him to *be*, and me to *see* him, a virtuous and honourable Character. Your *Opinion* of Glover is very rationally founded; and what will confirm you in it, is the *finding of the Knife*——*in her Possession*. Robert foams with fury, and coughs himself black in the Face with Illness and Anger. Never mind. We called in a Welsh Harper, and made merry on St. Davids Day—'spite of all.

The Toast was	Leeks	—	Cakes	—	Pudding and Potatoes.
	Wales,	—	Scotland,	—	England and Ireland.

Lady Nelson, Lady Lambart,⁶ Lady Bulkely Hughes⁷ came in the Evening; so did just 45 People more, among the rest Miss Wroughton who has been confined by Tooth ach. "I had *such* a *Face* said She as nobody ever saw but my own." So you always had replied I:—and Colonel Barry observed that even Miss Wroughton never had a finer Compliment paid her than *This*.

So you see some promptness of Expression is yet left to my Dearest Boy's most truly Affectionate Aunt / H:L:P.

Write to me soon again, your Letters are very pleasing to me: and you will learn Composition by Practice.

Text: Ry. 585.50. Address: John P. Salusbury Esq. / at the Rev: Thos: Shephard's / Enborne / near Newbury / Berks. *Postmark:* BATH (In JSPS's hand, "Received March 3rd 1810.—Answered Do. 4th Do.").

1. HLP refers to Thomas Ball (1751–1825) of Cullyhanna, county Armagh, and Sidney Place, Bath. His son was Thomas Prideaux Ball (1797–1869), who had entered Westminister School in 1809 and left the following year. He matriculated in 1814 at Trinity College, Oxford, and was called to the bar at the Inner Temple on 12 February 1819. For the elder Thomas Ball, see his will, dated 6 October 1824, codicil 7 March 1825, and proved 27 June 1825; also the "Newton St. Loe Burial Register," C.R.O., Somerset.

2. Angelo Levy (fl. 1770–1816) was a London merchant of 16 Trinity Square, Tower Hill, and later of 12 Devonshire Square. (He disappears from the London directories of 1817.) In the "Commonplace Book" under *Distress of Nations with Perplexity,* dated 14 July 1814, HLP identifies "a Jew gentleman (Angelo Levy a Diamond Merchant)."

3. See HLP to SL, 17 September 1784, n. 9. HLP perhaps remembered Bacon's *Essay II,* "Of Death," wherein he wrote; "But above all, believe it, the sweetest canticle is, *nunc dimittis;* when a man hath obtained worthy ends and expectations."

4. *Paradise Lost,* 5.601.

5. An army officer, George de Blaquiere had distinguished himself at Corunna. See HLP to Q, [ca. 23 September 1800], n. 7.

According to the *Chester Chronicle,* 22 June 1810: "Lee v. Blaquiere.—This was an action brought by the plaintiff, a Clergyman, against the Defendant, Captain Blaquiere, for criminal conversation with the plaintiff's wife.—Damages were laid at 10,000 *l.*—it appeared that the lady had left her husband, having also forsaken a child she had by him, and had co-habited with the defendant for the last two years. There was no difficulty, therefore, in making out the case on the part of the plaintiff.

"On the part of the defendant, many circumstances in mitigation of damages were stated by the Counsel, (Mr. Parke) particularly that the lady was 16 years of age at the time of her marriage, while the husband was upward of 45; that he dressed up the servant for the purpose of acting as her father on the occasion of the marriage ceremony; that they had uniformly used separate beds; and that the defendant had left his wife in an unprotected state for several months.

"Lord Ellenborough conceived the present not to be an aggravated case, and the Jury found for the plaintiff.—Damages 500 *l.*"

6. HLP, who sometimes confused the form of titles, probably had in mind Lady Alicia Lambart (d. 1818), a daughter of Richard (1763–1837), seventh earl of Cavan.

7. William Bulkeley Hughes (1766–1836), of Plâs Coch, high sheriff of Anglesey (1803), knighted on 4 May 1803, had married on 2 July 1792 Elizabeth, née Thomas (d. 1839).

TO LADY WILLIAMS

Too fine Weather.—
Monday 5: March 1810.

My dearest Lady Williams
  may assure herself of my heart's true Sympathy—every Sentiment that Swells Your Veins—once flowed through mine; and every Day and hour has convinced me, that one may have other Husbands and other Children——Objects of *our* Affection; but that the Parent to which *we* were each of us the *Sole Object* can be had but once.

When pretty Lady Nelson the Admiral's Widow, told me the other day of her Titles, her Income, her Coronets and her *Miseries*—I said to her—Yes; they took your Bread and Butter and Tea away from You, and gave You Turtle and Venison and Claret for Compensation: but I see *it does not do*——and She burst out o'crying.

So it was with *me* when my dear Mother died, and left me to admire the happy Lot of a fortunate Family which She had placed me in; and which continues, (I thank God) to be prosperous:——But still I have lost my Friend and my Companion—to whom I could have talked of their Prosperity. Let us after all recollect that few People have had as long Enjoyment of that Comfort as dear Lady Williams and her Neighbour at Brynbella; and that when everything is said and done——God has been most gracious in sparing Us to console *them* in their Affliction. My hope is that the State of your Ladyship's Mind will not sink into languid Acquiescence, but rise to active Vigilance: that you may *watch* your new Governess, instead of *confiding too much* in her—be She who She may.

And above all things I delight in the Thought of Your Eldest Son's Accomplishements and pleasing Character. I saw a Letter from him to his Aunt which quite charmed me. Our Boys are really Creatures to be justly proud of; Salusbury was so petted here and fondled by the Bath ffolks, it would have spoiled any Young Man almost; but he returned to his Studies quite willingly, and I shall give him a little London at Easter.

Indeed My Excursions into the living World are chiefly for Purpose of Setting him *afloat* on't. Your Ladyship and Dear Sir John know my Intentions for him, and we must make early Friends and good Connexions as soon as we can; but as Lord Glenbervie said when I told *him* my Plans——There must be a little Christ Church first; and he cannot get in before next Year.

May I *but* live to launch him! He will in *me* lose a Parent, let my departure be soon or late.

Young Mr. Williams's Expressions of Tenderness to his Grandmama were beautiful, I really could not stand Them.

Miss Williams has bad health, but does not give up to it. We shall eat our Morsel together today and She will add all that *can* be added of Affection and Regard to Dear Bodylwyddan.

Lady Kirkwall is not out of hot Water yet, I fear by my London Letters; but there is Talk of her own Family affording her and poor Lady de B―――― fresh Cause of Sorrow. How cruel in those who afflict the already broken-hearted. Ever My dear Kind Lady's Truly Faithful and Obedient / H: L: P.

If Mrs. Williams can yet care about my best Wishes—present them to her. I hope Sir John busies himself about the Mine.

Text: Ry. 3 (1807–11). *Address:* Lady Williams / Bodylwyddan / near St. Asaph / N: Wales. *Postmark:* BATH.

TO JOHN SALUSBURY PIOZZI SALUSBURY

Bath Wednesday
14: March 1810.

My dearest Salusbury's last Letter was quite *lovely;* I ran to Mr. Townsends with it, but the house was too sick and sorrowful to admit me, and if you would only remember that *were* is A Verb, and *where* is an adverb; you never could mistake and spell the last without the Aspirate.—How the Women manage who *never* know one part of Speech from another,—They must tell; but certain it is, the Well-bred ones never miss.

You are a dear Creature with your comical Allusions to my old Damask Table Linen; but indeed they were originally of a *Strong* Fabric, tho' a *fine* one: and the *Cross* Threads which make the figures on them, helped the Preservation. Charles Shephard has sent me a very kind—but a very reprehensory Letter for wearing myself out by unnecessary Agitation—So, like the Men who are reprimanded by the House of Commons, *I am reprimanded accordingly;* and will be good as long as ever I can. If Flattery could keep one alive, *You* and *he,* and Mr. Byng and Mr. Leveson[1] cum multis aliis, would do much towards it; and *so you do:* Yet

1.
Who can preserve their best earn'd Praise,
With every Talent aiding?
The Flow'rs that crown'd our Vernal Days,
What Care can keep from fading?
2.
Even Fruits, of early Toil the Price
From Autumn's Warmth demanded;
Look Melancholy *kept in Ice,*
Or by cold Winter *candied.*
3.
Whilst far our busy Vale beyond,
Bright Virtue more assuming;
Lives with *Immortal* Fruitage crown'd,
And Wreaths *for ever* blooming.

4.
Then *that* Way let us turn our Sight
And make no more Digression,
The Scripture Path, pure, plain, and white,
Leads surest to Possession.

The Story I promised is more true than pretty, at least I find it so upon Revision; but it relates to our late Subject of Temptation.

Sir Edward Walpole a gay Man of the World when I was younger than you are *now,* meant to seduce his Mother's Maid—whose Beauty had seduced *him* but without any Intent on *her Part*; who was a Girl virtuously brought up, and of good Principles. Well! She withstood all his Intreaties, all of his Offers;—and finally forbore to accept a *Thousand Pounds o'Year*, when She considered it as a Compensation for lost Honour.—At her Request he now left off his Visits; and She *believed* herself secure from his Attacks, but Sir Edward enlisting in his Cause a Gossiping Woman of the Girl's Acquaintance, suborned *her* to shew his favourite from a good Station. The Ladies going to Court upon the next grand Birthday—and take Advantage *there* of her Simplicity——A Green and Gold Petticoat passed by—worne as I recollect, by the Dutchess of Bedford.[2] Oh how beautiful! exclaims the Maid! and how *happy* must the Wearer be! The next Morning a Dress perfectly resembling it was brought her by the female Friend— (or you may take out the *r* and read *Fiend*)——and followed by Sir Edward Walpole; who obtained for a *Petticoat* the poor Creature *never could wear*, in a Place to which She never *could be admitted;* what his 1000£ per Annum could not procure for him. She lived his Mistress, brought him Three Daughters, and died in Obscurity of a broken heart.[3]

The Tale is true, and the Duke of Gloucester is her Grandson—ask Mr. Shephard if he knows the Story.[4]

He will see some of our fine *Mocha* Coffee very soon, I have written for it to be packed and sent to Newbury—*Raw* Coffee, because we always roast ours *at home*; and if you do not roast Yours enough—it will be good for nothing. The Berries are much smaller, and less oily than those of Martinico; and a very strange Thing it is, and worthy of Observation; that the Animals, Vegetables, ay and *Minerals* of the new found Hemisphere, are every one of them inferior to what we find in the East——But Phœbus is partial to his Birth Place I suppose.[5]

I have heard nothing of our travelled Friend Mr. Byng, since he left Bath to wait upon Lord Torington, who may be very sick perhaps, but not dying.[6] He is very little disposed to go abroad again; Said to me in Confidence that he would rather *starve* here than live well in any of their fine Climates——*Memorandum* he calls 3 or 400£ o'Year *starving;* and it *is* very little certainly for a Man of such Extraction.

Mousey Mostyn has never written since I told you——She then asked civilly after by *dear blossoming Thorn*; who *will* I hope *flourish*, and be a famous *Plant* after all. You are a wise Boy in thinking me too much alone,—and unless one has a Party, or goes to a Party—One must be *Sola, Solissima;* tho' the Hubers sent to beg me for their *Fireside* last Night, and I liked it of all Things.[7]

Mr. Ball will never be so much of a Hibernian surely—as not to call on Me for *Commands* when he is going to Enborne, but I have seen nothing more of him since I wrote you word. This is Wednesday! Oh what a melancholy Marketing! When they offer me Things I used to buy for *you,* Eggs or Fish—I turn away *so foolish-looking*——but the Lutwyches call me to dine with them tomorrow: Mr. Lutwyche has made a tolerable Epigram on Buonaparte's Marriage;[8] I will send it you (if you remind me on't) in my next Letter. What more shall I cram into *This?* Loves, Blessings, Prayers! and truly affectionate Wishes from the truly Affectionate Heart of Dearest Salusbury / yours ever while / H: L: P.

Mousey Mostyn will forget her Cares in the Crouds of London—unless Lady Keith should bring a Boy next Year——*That* Event would indeed affect her Good humour no little. I hope She is comforting Lady de B. and I partly hope the Husband will be pacified without <Prosecution:> for if great Damages are awarded——my poor Friend will be undone. God bless and preserve *my* Dear and honourable Boy from such Disgrace, and such well-earned Detestation.—Compliments to the Family—kind Remembrances to Pemberton.

Text: Ry. 585.53 *Address:* John P. Salusbury Esq. / at The Rev: Thos. Shephard's / Enborne / near Newbury / Berks. (In JSPS's hand, "Received March 15th 1810. Answered Do 18th Do")

1. Granville Leveson-Gower (1773–1846), Viscount Granville (1815), first earl Granville (1833). He had matriculated at Christ Church, Oxford, in 1789 and was created D.C.L. in June 1799. He was elected M.P. for Lichfield, 1795–99, Staffs., 1799–1815. He served as ambassador to Russia from 1804 to 1805 and again in 1807; as ambassador to France from 1824 to 1828, 1830 to 1841.
2. Lady Anne Egerton (d. 1762), a daughter of the duke of Bridgewater, had married in 1725 Wriothesley Russell (1708–32), third duke of Bedford (1711).
3. HLP transforms the anecdote of Sir Edward Walpole (1706–84) and his mistress into a moral lesson for JSPS. Sir Edward's mistress was Dorothy Clement (fl. 1715–39), the daughter of a postmaster in Darlington, county Durham. Their liaison began ca. 1730, when she was working in a second-hand clothes shop in Pall Mall.
According to Lady Mary Wortley Montagu in a letter to Lady Bute, 24 June [1759], regarding Maria Walpole (1736–1807), an illegitimate daughter of Sir Edward and Dorothy Clement, who in 1759 married James (1714/15–63), second earl Waldegrave (1741): "I am not surpriz'd at Lady Waldegrave's good fortune; Beauty has a large Prerogative. Her mother was the most remarkable I have ever heard of. Being taken notice of by Mrs. Secker [Catherine, née Benson, d. 1748] (who told it me) when she was in the humble position of sitting on a Dust Cart before the Bishop's door, that Lady had the Curiosity to call her in, meerly to see her nearer, and assur'd me that, in all her rags and Dirt, she never saw a more lovely Creature. Some time after, she heard she was in the hands of a Covent Garden Milliner, who transferr'd her to Neddy W[alpole], who doated on her till the Day of her Death." See *The Complete Letters of Lady Mary Wortley Montagu* 3:213.
4. The widowed Lady Maria Waldegrave married his Royal Highness William Henry, first duke of Gloucester, (1743–1805) by whom she was the mother of William Frederick, second duke (1776–1834); Sophia (1773–1844); and Caroline Augusta Maria (1774–75).
5. HLP refers to Apollo, about whose place of origin there are two principal theories: he comes from Delos; he is Asiatic, associated with Lycia. HLP is inclined toward the second theory.
6. George Byng, fourth viscount Torrington, was Edmund Byng's uncle.
7. Barthélmy Huber (1748–1837), originally of Vevey, Switzerland, came to England in 1769 and married Lydia, née Strutt (1759–1813). He was a banker with financial interests on the Continent and a one-time director of La Compagnie des Indes. In 1802–3 he actively helped to effect a peace between France and the Allies.
8. See the report, dated 17 February, in the *Courier,* 12 March 1810: "A notice has been circulated with respect to the ceremonies which are to be observed previous to the marriage of the Archduchess

[Marie Louise]. The Prince of Neufchatel, who is to arrive on the 2d of March, will reside at the War Chancery. The following day he will be presented at Court, and make the demand. . . . On the 5th, the ceremony of marriage [by proxy] will take place in the Church of the Augustins, in the same form as observed in the marriage of the Emperor. . . . On the 8th the Princess will set out for France." The dates were in fact altered. The marriage by proxy took place in Vienna on 11 March; two days later the bride went to France, where she arrived on the 27th. On 1 April at Saint Cloud a civil ceremony was performed, a religious service at the Louvre on 2 April, and the whole month of May was given over to national festivities.
  Marie Louise (1791–1847) was the second daughter of Franz I, emperor of Austria.

TO JOHN SALUSBURY PIOZZI SALUSBURY

Bath Tuesday
20: March 1810.

I feel much *pleased* my Dearest Salusbury, and something *flattered* too, that my Letters are so welcome at Enborne. Flattery is a nauseous Thing *per se;* but one is delighted, and not unreasonably, when People flatter us, because it shews we are of Consequence enough—to make them take so much Trouble. Your Observation concerning the Picture is perfectly correct, and shews a Knowlege of the World which I wonder how you have attained. The Joke is a tolerable good Joke too, if the Household Stuff sold was belonging to a *Public* House:— if it was *Farming* Stock, The Sinners had little to do with it. Leak writes Word that he has done Wonders in Wales on our little Farm &c.——We shall see some of these Days, and I feel half Impatient. Mean while I am to *study to be quiet,* and mind *grave* Counsellors, *Shephard* and *Salusbury;* but Hammersley's People must be more accurate in their Accounts, before I *can* sit down quite contented:[1]——They are really so negligent it amazes me; but you know Cecy Mostyn says that "Nobody *does* understand his own Business."
  Mr. Ball will go to London to see if his Son will *choose to move,*——for else Says he—how can I move him? If the Boy resembles his Papa—I think you will have a fine Fellow of him——and Mr. Shephard has already undertaken *Oddities* if all I hear is true. You saw Sir Godfrey Webster's Exploits in the Newspaper— when the Riot was made in the Opera house[2]—but now for our Friend Lutwyche's *Anti* Epithalamium on Buonaparte's Nuptials

> By bridal Bed ne'er shalt thou know
> 'Spite of thy deep designing Mind;
> T'*entail* on humbled Europe Woe
> And forge new Fetters for Mankind.
> No; Tyrant! learn, and learn with awe
> That Bounds are set to Powr's Abuse;
> Immutable is Nature's Law
> That *Monsters never reproduce.*

Now you see without some Acquaintance with Natural History—the point of this Epigram loses all Sting; but Mr. Shephard will tell you that the Fact is as he states it: Mules,—Monsters of every kind are incapable of carrying forward that deviation which is permitted to Individuals—Were it otherwise, Man would deform the Work of Creation itself; so steadily is he *bent* on Mischief, or so perpetually is he *tempted* to it.

I'm glad you like my Stories, and my Stuff; and am very happy in your Observations on them. You are a *good* Child, and to me a truly *Dear* one; Tall Townsend has seen your Letter, and loves you with all his heart. A Mr. and Miss Peele[3] who dined with you at Bathurst Pye Bennet's likewise, always ask after you; and seem much interested in your Welfare:[4] but the Bath People are very amiable. I have a long Letter from Mr. Scrope Davis[5]—who *will absolutely* keep up an Acquaintance with me, and makes you the Excuse for our Correspondence—*he* says there is *no Admittance* at Christ Church till this time next Year, and Mr. Townsend says he hears the same Account and that the Work of Reformation goes on prosperously, under his Friend Dr. Hall: and that you shall command Letters of strong Recommendation *from him* when the Time comes——I told you Mr. Byng had already written, and I told you *true*. I did not perhaps tell you that he wrote the Letter from my own Desk here in Pultney Street, That he spoke of you as his *own very particular Friend,* and as Nephew to Mrs. Piozzi;[6] who would most willingly allow you——as Gentleman Commoner—whatever *he* Doctor Hall, thought fit for you to spend. To this Letter if any Answer was *sent,* I could not see it; for Mr. Byng directed his Brother to send his Reply to London:[7] and in Twelve hours *our* young Friend was summoned to his Uncle Lord Torington's sick Bed at Long Leat, and while Scrope Davies has been writing—*he* is *silent*. There may however be reasons for *this* too. *One* is bred a Scholar, and likes to shew off with a *clever Letter* to H:L:P. the *other* has been like Old Neptune in the Iliad striding from Island to Island instead of minding his Book[8]—so he does not *seek* Correspondence but prefers *oral* Communication.

General Donkin's[9] Son is come home from Spain and Portugal. He is A fine shining Fellow indeed,—and excessively entertaining;[10] and he has given Me a *Latin Charade* which You shall have in my next Packet of Nonsense. Make Miss Shephards show you some English and French Charades that you may be a good Critic of this *queer Performance.* You remember mine I dare say.

> My *first* annoys from Cottage Doors,——
> My *second* from the Stage:
> My *Third* in Youth is always sour,——
> But sweetens with old Age

<The> Word is a Currant——read the Lines *long wise.*

And now my Darling Boy, be well, be good, and be happy. ½ as well, ½ as good, ½ as happy as I *wish* you, and you will exceed in Health, Virtue, and Felicity any Young Man ever yet seen by Your / Affectionate Aunt / H: L: P.

Give my best Regards to Mr. Pemberton and Mr. Shephard; and the Family: and keep Blessings Loves and Prayers for your dear Self.

Text: Ry. 585.54 *Address:* John P: Saulsbury Esq. / at The / Rev: Thos. Shephard's / Enborne / near Newbury. *Postmark:* BATH (In JSPS's hand, "Received March 21st 1810. Answered Do 22nd Do")

1. HLP still fretted about the delay in distributing GP's bequests to his Italian relatives.
2. Godfrey Vassal Webster (1789–1836), fifth baronet (1800), M.P. for Sussex (1812–20). See the *Morning Post*, 27 November 1809, under the heading "Bow-Street / Covent-Garden Theatre."
On "Jubilee Night" (Saturday the 25th), so-called to celebrate the re-opening of Covent Garden, "a grand *row* was expected to take place." There was, indeed a *"row"* with Sir Godfrey as a participant.
He "made a complaint of his having been violently assaulted by a man at the door of the office."
Despite attempts to dissuade Sir Godfrey from making a charge, he "persisted in conceiving himself violently assaulted and ill-treated." He therefore "pointed out William Blackman, one of the patrole, who he said assaulted him, and repeated his former statement, of being collared and pushed off the steps of the Office." Thereupon followed charges and countercharges; apparently Sir Godfrey changed his mind and dropped the indictment.
3. Probably William Yates Peel (1789–1858) and his sister Elizabeth (d. 1828), the issue of Robert Peel (1750–1830), cr. baronet (1800), one of the most successful cotton manufacturers in Great Britain.
4. For Elizabeth Bathurst Pye Benet, see HLT to Q, 1 July 1784, n. 16.
5. Scrope Berdmore Davies (1782–1852) took his B.A. and M.A. from King's, Cambridge. Distinguished as an athlete and a wit, he was also a friend of such poets as Tom Moore and Byron.
6. In her "Pocket Book" for 1810 (Ry. 616), HLP had written on 5 March: "Mr. Byng came, wrote to Doctor Hall for Salusbury—*in my Sight*. Spoke highly of him."
7. Probably John, who was to die in 1811, although there were three other brothers: George (1768–1831); Henry Dilkes (d. 1860); Frederick Gerald (d. 1871).
8. Pope's *Iliad*, 13.32–33.
9. HLP knew General Robert Donkin (1727–1821) as a neighbor who lived at 2 Laura Place, close to her residence at 6 Pulteney Street, Bath.
10. Rufane Shaw Donkin (1773–1841) began his army career as an ensign in the Forty-fourth (East Essex) Foot Regiment. By 31 May he became a captain, a major on 1 September 1795, a lieutenant colonel on 24 May 1798, and a colonel by 25 April 1808. The following year he had been appointed assistant quartermaster general with the army in Portugal; he also commanded a brigade on the Douro and at the battle of Talavera. He rose steadily in rank to become a lieutenant general (1821), after having been made a K.C.B. on 14 October 1818.

TO LADY KEITH

Bath Thursday
22: March 1810.

Your Letters my dearest Lady Keith are always delightful, and I am always delighted to receive them—Tho' You have no Chance for any *Replies* but such as are made by the *Echo*. I can however tell you who Mr. Byng is without any Difficulty—he is Nephew to Lord Torington, and was called to his Uncle's sick Bed a Week ago.—He is particularly agreeable, about Three or four and Thirty Years old in Appearance, has seen a Vast Deal, and I have a Sad Loss of him; but every body meets in London, where You will permit me to introduce him to you—with his young Friend.[1]

Politics I always studiously avoid, for fear of giving Offence; but a Joke endured at Paris, may perhaps be permitted at London.

William Hogarth, *The Lady's Last Stake*, 1759, oil on canvas, Albright-Knox Art Gallery, Buffalo, New York, Seymour H. Knox Fund through special gifts to the fund by Mrs. Marjorie Knox Campbell, Mrs. Dorothy Knox Rogers and Seymour B. Knox Jr. 1945. Reproduced by the kind permission of the Gallery.

A Brodeuse had formed for the *Nuptials* of Buonaparte, a very beautiful Canopy—or Baldanquin, intended to appear in some Part of the Procession:—The Ground Scarlet; the Device a large Spreading *Oak* with Branches hanging downwards perfectly natural. A Wag observed "que la Chêne s'élève vraiment jusqu'aux Cieux; mais *au fonds* Mademoiselle, ce sera tousjours ⟨ Sans Glands Sanglant." I think indeed no one Seems to expect Issue from the Marriage—They may tell me why.² Now do just say in your next, if this merry jest be new to you.

We have had Meuler here the Tyrolese Chief and we went after *him* stare, stare, *stare.* ³ Too much Fool indeed, but he did *not say so.* You remember in Cyrus's Time the Persians were taught to sit their Horse, draw their Bow—and *Tell Truth.* ⁴ His drinking Champagne and Burgundy will draw those Truths out.

I *thought* Mr. Beckford was not dead; and I thought very rationally that a Man of such an overgrown Fortune could not die unnoticed by the veriest Rustic in the Island⎯⎯⎯ He is of a Character which *ought* to be *Singular;*⁵ but I told Doctor Randolph ten Minutes ago, that I met my own Butcher's Boy walking in the Crescent on Sunday last, *rouged* in as elegant and in as visible a Manner, as any Lady I have seen in the Pump Room.

My first Cousin's Widow, *Tall* Lady Cotton is my near Neighbour;[6] her daughter Viscountess Killmorey is the very Image of her: Mrs. Clough of Glan o' Werne lives at my next Door too[7]——but Bath is a perpetual *Come and go* Place. Alas! For the Thelwalls! that fine Estate goes to another Family of the same Name—not Mostyns's and *my* Relation.[8] The beautiful Fonthill *we saw* together 26 Years ago, has furnished our Bath Theatre with Finery:[9] and the Chevalier Casali's lovely Picture of Gunhilda rejecting her penitent Husband—which he painted for the *first* British Exhibition[10]—and which *I saw there* when H: L: Salusbury, is now at the Top of the Dome here in Beaufort Square, and has a very fine Effect. I wonder who got dear Hogarth's Picture of the Lady's last Stake?[11] which he intended as a Present for *me* to keep me from being a Gamester he said; [12] but dying before it was quite finished,[13] I lost what now would have been invaluable, but tho' no Gamester—I was always a good Loser.[14]

There was also at Fonthill a Portrait of one of my Uncles—Cotton King: Son to my Grandmother Cotton by her second Husband, I guess not where that went.[15]

Did you ever among the Ladies' Riddle Books—See a Latin Charade? I had one sent me Yesterday, and will copy it for you. It came as I was sitting down to Dinner with a Friend; so I only sent the Author back a Verbal Message, that if he would call next Day—We would pluck a Crow together. A Witticism quite in Unison with the Charade.

> Te *primum* incauto nimium proprius que tuenti,
> Laura! mihi furtim surripuisse queror.
> Nec tamen hoc furtum tibi condonare recusem,
> Si pretium simili solvere merce velis.
> Sed quo plus Candoris habent tua Colla *Secundo,*
> Hoc tibi plus *Primum* frigoris intus habet.
> Jamque sinistra Câva cantabit ab Ilice *Totum*
> Ominà, et audaces spes vetat esse ratas.[16]

Now if these Nonsens*es* are really new to you, I have *more* and in a Third Language; but of an older Date made by an Italian on poor Pius Sextus's Journey to Vienna; a regular Sonnet, and in my Mind very comical.[17]

Adieu and accept my best Loves, Wishes, everything worth, or not worth acceptance: and convey the Overplus in a Kiss to *la jolie Georgette,* who is a Beauty to *my own Taste* I am confident;[18] because everybody says She is so like her Dear pretty Mama, whose I am ever most Affectionately / H: L: P.

Give my kindest Respects and Remembrances to Lord Keith.

Another Word about Mr. Byng—he is Brother to Mrs. Hall and Mrs. Hopwood and Mrs. Herbert and Mrs. Morris[19]—and was here with his Sister The Widow of that Son of Lord Caernarvon's, who was crushed or drowned, between the Ship and Boat, or between the Boat and the Shore—some shocking Accident—and the Lady left quite inconsolable; tho' She has a Daughter six Years old excelling in beauty any Child I ever saw except one.[20] Mr. Byng's Father and

Mother have had 18 Children, of whom a Dozen *yet live.*[21] I believe Lord Torington—his Uncle—is o'Dying now; I believe so.

Text: Bowood Collection. *Address:* R: H: Baroness Keith.

    1. In a previous letter [February 1810] to Q, HLP wrote: "My Conquest of Mr. Byng deserves to be recorded. We met one morning at Lady Glenbervie's and he would *wait on me home* (I had no Young Man with me) because he was so pleased with my Conversation—in good Time!—The Plot then thickened of Course, and he informed me that he had seen the Sun rise from the heights of Aetna, had climbed Mount Olympus, had inscribed his Name on the uppermost Stone in the great Pyramid of Giza; had crossed Caffraria on foot just above the Cape of Good Hope: and navigated his canoe on Lake Hurons in North America. It is agreed that he is to finish his Exploits by dining at Dolly's Chophouse with H: L: Piozzi in her 70th: year. Our Continuation of Intimacy is no Wonder—he found Sheppard and Salusbury agreeable Companions, but I always tell them, that I won him *Singlehanded"* (Bowood Collection).
    2. Napoleon's marriage with Marie Louise did in fact produce a son, *Napoléon*-François-Joseph-Charles (1811–32), styled king of Rome from his birth, recognized as emperor of the French after his father's second abdication (28 June 1815), and deposed (3 July 1815), cr. duke of Reichstadt in Austria (1818).
    3. Under the treaty of Pressburg (1805), all of Tyrol had been awarded to Napoleon's ally, Bavaria. But when in 1809 war broke out between France and Austria, the Tyrolean peasants, led by Andreas Hofer, the "Tyrolean Chief," resisted the French and Bavarian forces. (Hofer was betrayed to the French and executed at Mantua, 21 Febaruary 1810.)
HLP's allusion is to Major Joseph Christian Müller (b. 1775 in Bludenz, Vorarlberg), whose arrival in Bath was reported in the *Journal,* 19 March. Since August 1809, Müller, accompanied by a prominent "Innsbrucker Schiffsmeister," John Georg Schenacher, or Schönnacher, or Schoenacher (1773–1821), had been in England, deputized to raise funds on behalf of the Tyrolean and Vorarlberg insurgents. They were received favorably by officers of the Bank of England, the East India House, members of Parliament, and the general public (*The Times,* 8 November 1810).
See "Landesarchive," Innsbruck, and "Vorarlberger Landesarchive," Bregenz, Austria; Josef Hirn, *Englische Subsidien für Tirol und die Emigranten von 1809* (Innsbruck, 1912), pp. 3, 6.
    4. See Herodotus, 1.136: "[The Persians] educate their boys from five to twenty years old, and teach them three things only, riding and archery and truth-telling."
    5. When William Beckford, alderman and twice lord mayor of London, died in June 1770, he left his son—after a long minority—about £1,000,000 and £100,000 annually.
The young William Beckford (1759–1844), educated by tutors and widely traveled, began late in the eighteenth century to rebuild the family mansion, Fonthill, in Wiltshire. No sooner was it completed than he had it pulled down and a more lavish building set up on another site. Similarly, the expensive furniture was sold off to make room for even more costly furniture. The lavish grounds were enclosed by a high wall to discourage intruders. Although HLP did not know this, Beckford was to become a virtual recluse at Fonthill for the last twenty years of his life.
    6. For Robert Salusbury Cotton, fifth baronet, and his wife, Frances, née Stapleton, see HLP to PSW, 6 October 1792, n. 2; to Q, 17 September 1794, n. 5.
    7. For Patty Clough, née Butler, see HLP to PSP [ca. 28 August 1801], n. 13. For her husband, Richard Clough, see HLP to Q, 3 April [1795], n. 5.
    8. When Ann Lloyd, née Thelwall, died in 1810, the estate of Blaen Ial in the parish of Llantysilio passed to her son John Lloyd, later Salusbury. This family, as HLP observes, was unrelated to her own relatives, the Thelwalls, or—at the time—to the Mostyns. In the following June, however, John Lloyd married the sister of John Meredith Mostyn, Anna Maria. See HLP to John Meredith Mostyn, 14 June 1795, n. 5.
    9. For the Theatre Royal, Bath, and its paintings by Casali, see HLP to Ly W, 29 December 1805, n. 6.
The Casali pictures were given to the Theatre Royal not by Beckford, who had sold them, but by Paul Cobb Methuen (1752–1816) of Corsham, who bought them. They were removed in 1839.
See Walter Ison, *The Georgian Buildings of Bath from 1700 to 1830* (London: Faber and Faber, 1948), pp. 92–93.
    10. Andrea Casali (1705–84), called "The Chevalier," was an Italian painter and engraver. In 1741 he came to England to work and remained there until 1766, after which he lived for some years in Rome.

In 1760 he exhibited for the first time in the Society of Artists his painting *The Story of Gunhilda* for which he won the second prize of fifty guineas. See the National Portrait Gallery's annotated "Catalogue[s] of the Pictures, Sculptures, Models, Drawings, Prints, &c. of the Artists. Exhibited in the Great Room of the Society for the Encouragement of Arts, Manufactures, and Commerce."

11. "The Lady's Last Stake" was finished in 1759 for James Caulfeild, first earl of Charlemont, and it remained in his family until 1874. Sold several times since then, it is now in the Albright-Knox Art Gallery, Buffalo, New York.

According to Hogarth, "The story I pitched upon was a young and virtuous married lady, who by playing at cards with an officer, loses her money, watch and jewels; the moment when he offers them back in return for her honour, and she is wavering at his suit, was my point of time." See John Ireland, *Hogarth Illustrated from His Own Manuscripts*, 3 vols. (London: Boydell and Company, 1812), 3:191–92.

12. HLP mentions her association with "The Lady's Last Stake" several times: in this letter to Q and in another to the same recipient on 28 March 1812 (in both she reports only that Hogarth intended the picture to be his gift to her). On four other occasions, with slightly varying details of age and place, she maintains that she sat for the portrait of the lady. See her "Commonplace Book" under the entry "Fortune"; her letter to JF, 30 October 1815; her "Autobiographical Memoirs" (Hayward 2:28); her conversation with EM (Mangin, pp. 11–12). See also EM's letter to "Mr. Urban" in *GM* 92, pt.2 (1822):486–87.

There is no doubt that HLP knew Hogarth, "that he was a close friend of John Salusbury . . . who was the only subscriber for *Sigismunda* (1761) to refuse the refund Hogarth offered when he failed to secure an engraver." See Ronald Paulson, *Hogarth: His Life, Art, and Times*, 2 vols. (New Haven and London: Yale Unviersity Press, 1971), 2:291. Whether she actually sat for the portrait has been a matter of inconclusive debate. See Paulson, *Hogarth* 2:292–93, 454, n. 13; Clifford, pp. 23–24 and n. 2; "The Great Hogarth of the Morgan Collection," *The Connoisseur* (Jan. 1936), pp. 41–42.

13. Hogarth died in 1764, about five years after the picture was completed.

14. In this paragraph HLP suggests that "The Lady's Last Stake" was once at Fonthill. Although it was never there, she repeated this detail to JF, 30 October 1815. The discrepancy may probably be explained by the fact that there is a "copy of the picture, which has sometimes been mistaken for another version painted by Hogarth." This copy, continues Paulson, "is at Goodwood [the Sussex seat of the Dukes of Richmond], and may have been at Fonthill some time" (2:292, 454, n. 13). JF's endorsement at the end of HLP's letter to him (30 October 1815) indicates that he saw the painting at Goodwood in 1851.

15. HLP's grandmother Philadelphia Cotton was widowed at the age of thirty-four, and she soon remarried, this time "an Irish Officer one Captain [Thomas] King" (*Thraliana* 1:277). As Philadelphia King, she had several offspring, the eldest being Cotton King (d.1761).

16. The charade was given to HLP by Colonel Donkin and its solution by Charles Shephard. Both appear in "Minced Meat for Pyes." The solution:

> Pectora faemineo sperat quam grata voluptas
> Cor nimium incanti surripuisse Viri.
> Quum *Nix* alba cadit, lachrymas fit et ipsa videntem
> Pectora quod superant candidiora Chloes.
> Aspice qua summa tristis sedet ilice *Cornix*
> Complet et incautum rauca timore sinum.
> Da mihi *Cor* raptum Nive meus et < pr   > alba
> Expectata mihi Munera certa dabit.

17. What prompted the pope's journey to Vienna were the policies of Joseph II: his edict of toleration, his secularization of contemplative orders, his claim to the right of presenting the Milanese benefices. Hopeful of easing the differences between them, Pius VI left Rome on 27 February 1782 and reached Vienna on 22 March. The differences were debated for a month, and they parted cordially. See Pastor 39:449–59; Giuseppe Gorani, *Mémoires* (Paris, 1944) 2:45–46.

18. HLP cites the opinion of others because she was to see her granddaughter only in April, when the baby was five months old.

19. Cecilia Byng (d. 1843) had married on 31 December 1805 Robert Gregge Hopwood (1773–1854), of Hopwood Hall, Lancaster.

Lucy Juliana Byng (d. 1881) had married on 5 October 1809 John Morris (d. 1855), second baronet (1819).

For Anna Maria Bridget Hall, née Byng, see HLP to JSPS, 22 February 1810, n. 5.

20. Bridget Augusta Forrest Byng (d. 1876) had married on 9 July 1806 Captain Charles Herbert, who died by drowning on 12 September 1808.

Their daughter was Augusta Elizabeth (d. 1876), who on 10 May 1824 was to marry Francis Vincent (1803–80), tenth baronet (1809).

21. John Byng (1743–1813), who succeeded his brother as fifth viscount Torrington (1812) had married in 1767 Bridget, née Forrest (d. 1823). Of their twelve surviving children, only John was to predecease his father.

TO JOHN SALUSBURY PIOZZI SALUSBURY

Bath Tuesday
3: April 1810.

I write now to my dearest Salusbury to ask whether he will be picked up and taken *home*—(meaning to London)—*with* me; next Tuesday or Wednesday—(meaning this Day Sennight)—or whether he will make the Passion Week and Easter Sunday with Mr. Shephard at Enborne and follow me Easter Monday Morning to No. 54—not Holles—but Wellbeck Street Cavendish Square—close to where poor old Gillon lived and died. The Houses in Holles Street were all catched up and gone, before Leak could be *refitted* and *careened* as the Seaman's Phrase is; and *pressed* out upon a *new Cruize*. He is come back this Morning barely alive, and poor Miss Williams very bad indeed but *I think* going to London to Lady Callender.[1]

Leak left a Letter for you at Newbury as he passed and I expected a Line from You by todays Post. Be *well*, my sweet Child, and be *good*——You would not be well if you were *not* good—no not a Day: I know you so perfectly my heart is sure Your bodily Welfare depends on a free conscience

> For Health consists with Temperance alone,
> And Peace—Fair Virtue!—Peace is all thy own.[2]

These Verses are Pope's too, and if you gain an early Taste for his Writings—— Frivolous Authors will be apt to disgust you. The Mind accustomed to *his* forcible Style, loves to read nothing but what leaves strong Impression behind it.

The Essay on Criticism is all borrowed however from Horace and Boileau, Poets of the same kind with himself: yet has he ornamented his little Work with two Passages to which I know nothing superior. The Comparison of false Eloquence to the Glare of a Prism,[3] and the Parallel between a Young Student and a Traveller going over the Alps.[4]

Adieu, I hate to be writing without *you answer me*. "Faites au moins Monsieur, quelque Signe que vous m'entendez"—says a Frenchman to his English Companion: I never leave you a Day without Reply. So now tell me whether you will come to Town with me, or follow with Pemberton. I leave it to your own Taste and your own Discretion; but write directly—That is as soon as you have determined—to dear Love / Your Affectionate Parent and Friend / H: L: P.

I dine at Mrs. Lutwyche's on Sunday next to meet Mr. Whalley and shall set forward the Day after on my London Journey.

Text: Ry. 585.58.

1. Lady Callender: Margaret (née Romer), widow of Bridges Kearney and wife (1786) of John Callander, or Callendar, first baronet (cr. 1798).
2. *An Essay on Man*, 4.81–82 (slightly misquoted).
3. The comparison between "False Eloquence" and "Prismatic Glass" may be found in lines 311–12.
4. For the image of "fearless Youth" and the traveler over "the tow'ring *Alps,*" see lines 220–28.

TO JOHN SALUSBURY PIOZZI SALUSBURY

Salthill   Wednesday Evening
11: April 1810.

> You bid me write to You my Dear!
> And tell you all the News I hear.
> Why;—Grief and Anger, Hope and Fear,
> Disturb our *Loyal Spirits here:*
> Blue-ribbon'd Fellows, mad as queer,
> Pour Tales of Terror on our Ear,
> Of Soldiers borne on Sable Bier
> And Posted Troops at each Barrier:
> While London mourns her Lot severe,
> And claims from each true Friend—a Tear.
>
> Yet if *my* Course I can but steer
> 'Twixt levell'd Gun, and pointed Spear,
> I trust we yet may make good Cheer,
> When my young Enborne Friends appear;
> And pray for brighter Prospects,—'ere
> We close this ill-commencing Year.

Will you have any more Rhymes to the same Word—*Pug?* You may remember I began at the Coach Door, whence my heart wished you a pleasant Walk, and a happy Meeting on Easter Monday at No. 54 Wellbeck Street Cavendish Square. I will write again from thence, but I sincerely believe that the Town is not only quite tranquil, but likely to continue so. The Oppositionists have (in my Mind) completely overshot their Mark, and by hastily blaming Ministers for not acting more *energetically,* have unintentionally themselves strengthened the hands of Government, and given more Force to the Executive Power.[1] Whatever Struggle may result from *this,*—will not be immediate, and we shall enjoy our Holydays together comfortably enough. There will be *one general Topic* of Discourse, which keeps *Family Chat* at a Distance:[2] just as a General Mourning precludes unbecoming Colours in Female Dress——Altho' in itself a bad Thing all the Time.

And so here I sit sullen and dismal, after reading the Debates—*dry;* and picking the boiled Fowl's bones, till my Inside turns into a perfect *Hen Coop,* never tasting any other Food so long——Here I sit, counting the Days till Dear Easter Monday, when I shall expect to see You at six o'Clock—No. 54 Wellbeck Street—like Sylvester Daggerwood, whose Benefit was fixed &c. &c.[3]

Now dearest Salusbury, do not you believe because I write *cheerfully,* that I think *seriously well,* either of the Times, or of my own Powers of Duration to observe their goings *on.* The Times are horrible; and my harrassed Frame wearing out gradually like the Resources of the Country.—And Yet, *After Dinner,* I do certainly feel something of a *renewed* hope, that both may last till you are One and Twenty——and *then* You must act *Your* Part on the Stage of Life— whilst I conclude mine, and turning to *You* like Augustus in *his* last Moments— cry Plaudite.[4] My most earnest Desire is, that *You* may Say for 60 Years ensuing— Well! certainly I did possess a most / Affectionate Aunt, / and a most faithful Friend in / H: L: Piozzi.

Pray make my best Compliments to Mr. Pemberton, and hope he did not at all increase his Cold by walking home to Enborne: Pray make my proper Compliments to Mr. Shephard, and tell him that Hannah Wyat seems very good and happy: and *Pray* Write to me soon to London.

Text: Ry. 585.60.

1. The Tory party in the winter of 1809–10 faced several problems. It was itself split, with George Canning standing aloof, when Spencer Perceval became prime minister and completed the formation of his ministry on 2 December 1809. Almost immediately the ministry experienced flimsy victories or outright defeats on several issues: the composition of the finance committee; the conduct of the war, etc. The Opposition took advantage of dissension in Tory ranks, and London became an embattled city. See HLP to JSPS, 14 [–15] April 1810 and n. 5.

See Denis Gray, pp. 287–89, 297–304; Spencer Walpole, *The Life of Spencer Perceval,* 2 vols. (London: Hurst and Blackett, 1874), 2:88–102.

2. "*One general Topic* of Discourse" had to do with Sir Francis Burdett, a consistent leader of the attacks on the ministry. Early in April a motion accusing him of breach of privilege passed without division. Thereupon Sir Robert Salusbury "moved that Sir F. Burdett should be committed to the Tower," which was carried.

According to the *Courier,* 6 April: "As soon as [the parliamentary decision] was known, about two hundred persons assembled near Sir Francis's house in Piccadilly, which number increased considerably during the course of the morning. About 300 persons were collected near the Tower about eleven o'clock waiting to see the Baronet conveyed thither. The number increased rapidly. There were groups in other parts of the town, and occasionally cries were heard of Burdett for ever." Sir Francis was arrested on 9 April and brought to the Tower.

3. *Sylvester Daggerwood; or, New Hay at the Old Market* (1795) was a farce by George Colman the Younger (1762–1836).

The protagonist, when the play opens, has "slept . . . for five mornings in his old arm chair" waiting to see the manager, and in the first scene he says twice to Fustian: "Sir, I'm your most respectful servant to command—whose benefit is fixed for the eleventh of June, by particular desire of several persons of distinction."

4. See Suetonius, *De vita Caesarum,* bk. 2, sec. 99.

TO JOHN SALUSBURY PIOZZI SALUSBURY

Saturday
14 [–15] April 1810.

My dearest Salusbury's Letter was quite charming, and *So* welcome! I wrote the very Evening of my Arrival and found at my new home a Message from Charles Shephard to say all was safe.

Never was Country Village more tranquil than London at this hour, no Soldiers to be seen, no Writing on the Walls;[1] no Bluster about Death and Liberty, all quiet as Pultney Street Bath; and I have written to dear Mr. Davies to beg he would make up our *no Quarrel*, and say he will dine with me Next *Wednesday Sennight*——The Wensday in Easter Week; when his Answer comes, I shall send out Cards for those who are to meet him: Chappelow above all, who used to hoot *Bold face* and *White face* as he called you and Young Salusbury Mostyn—Cæcilia has agreed to be of the Party, and I suppose—her Sons which are in Town,——I wish they were better looking. Lady Keith's Baby is very pretty—The Mob tore Lord Keith off his Horse, because having forgotten where Sir Francis lived, he rode thro' Piccadilly and Stared up at the Windows thinking it a Gaming house where the Merry-Men were kicking up a *Row;* finding himself assaulted however, he sternly asked them what They meant——Why Sir (said two of the Ringleaders) we mean to make you pull off your Hat to Burdett, and cry Long live Sir Francis &c. *Not I truly,* replied the Admiral, so they pelted him and His Servant till a Gentleman of their own Perswasion came up; and cried "Let Lord Keith alone, he is a *Friend,* he is a *Friend,* he hates the Ministers"—and at that Word they let him go. But everybody has some Story to tell——Mine is, that I see no *present* Trace of Confusion. The last Letter told you What a comfortable Bed, and Bed Chamber I have got here, much better than Bath; our Dining Parlour *longer,* and the Drawing Room perhaps a little bigger,—not *less;* but I have as yet no Forte Piano in it, which takes up Room. The People were uneasy all *round* London long after they were quiet within: if you throw a Stone into Water, The Sides are not affected at first, but by the Time it is got smooth in the Middle—you observe a beating against the Shores—I hope Easter will pass peaceably, and that the People—when they see all Nature renovating her Green Appearance in honour of her Saviour's Resuscitation from the Earth——will think seriously for *one* Week or two in the Year, of the Blessings We enjoy, and the grand Purchase that was paid for us.

Mr. Charles Shephard and his intended dine with me today[2]——and her Brother Clement Francis, if he can get Time.[3] He sate with me Tête a Tête Yester Evening and is a wonderfully Intelligent Boy; full of Literature, replete with Knowledge; but unpolished, coarse; and I fancy——by no means *clean-minded.* It is a strange Thing to me that *Science* should not act as a Preservative from Vice, and a dismal Thing when it fails to do so——because then the Centaur is not fabulous at all——where the Beast gallops away with the Man.

Well! here is Sunday, and I have heard The famous Sydney Smith preach,[4] he took no Notice of the Times—(which indeed every body seems to have forgotten—)—but told us we must not hope for Salvation without *compensating* every Wrong, every Injustice we had done our Neighbours. I expected to see my Table covered on my Return with *Parchments,* and *penitential Letters,* but tho' his Person and Eloquence are popular—his Doctrines *are not.* How would Sir Francis Burdett *compensate* the Mischief *he* has done, I wonder![5]

Mr. Davies has written, and I believe Peace is proclaimed between him and me. It ought to be so; for I begged Pardon, tho I had really committed no Offence——he quite misunderstood me: so we will have a fine Day's Merriment and I am very sorry You are to come so *late* on Monday 8 o'Clock!! God bless you and Pemberton? and tell him how welcome he will be.

But a good Boy is *such* a Treasure! And Those who possess such a Treasure have a Right to be *so* proud and *so* happy! Oh how proud and how happy of Course is my own dear Salusbury's / Affectionate / H: L: P.

Every Day shews me more and more <mauvais> Sujets, and tho' our Preacher said to day that <th   > be miserable even in *this* World They go on!!——

Text: Ry. 585.62. *Address:* John P. Salusbury Esq. / At the Rev: Thos: Shephard's / Enborne / near Newbury / Berks. *Postmark:* <   > 16 <   > (In JSPS's hand, "Received April 16th 1810. Answered April 21st 1810")

1. HLP's play on political graffiti scrawled on walls, and on a biblical verse (Dan. 5:5).
2. The perpetual matchmaker, HLP hoped in vain for the marriage of Marianne Francis with almost anyone, in this case with Charles Shephard. For Marianne Francis, see HLP to JSPS, 26 September 1808, n. 2.
3. Clement Francis (1792–1829)had in 1809 been forced to defer his university career. As his sister wrote HLP on 11 October 1809, Clement "will . . . soon be engaged with some Merchant. . . . For what could Clem do at College with 100 *l* a year?—a Sum that would not keep him in 'Green Books'—and as he is not Erasmus, he must have *'cloathes'* too" (Ry. 582.49).
He was, however, able to matriculate at Caius College, Cambridge, in November 1811. A studious mathematician, he was to graduate in 1817 as eighth wrangler, to be ordained deacon in 1820 and priest in 1821.
4. Sydney Smith (1771–1845), an Oxonian, had been ordained in 1794. Eight years later, he helped to start the *Edinburgh Review* and would occasionally preach at Charlotte Chapel in that city. Dugald Stewart declared that Smith's pulpit manner suggested "a thrilling sensation of sublimity never before awakened by any oratory."
About 1804 he and his family moved to London, where he preached at the Foundling Hospital, at Fitzroy Chapel, and Berkeley Chapel, where he was "much in fashion in High Life." By 1809 they moved to Foston-le-Clay, Yorkshire, but not until 1813 or 1814 did Smith settle in there.
HLP heard him preach (15 April) on one of those relatively rare times at the Foundling Hospital. She admired his thunderous pulpit manner leavened by wit. See Farington 10:3618–19.
5. On 2 February 1810, when the Commons was about to go into committee on the Walcheren expedition, Charles Yorke moved the standing order which excluded all strangers from the House. On the 6th, Sheridan, with Burdett's support, proposed that in the future all motions to clear the public galleries should be put to a vote. On 12 February, the British Forum Society, a radical debating group, attacked Yorke's standing order as a violation of a free press. Its members then decided, and placarded all over Westminster, that at its next weekly meeting Mr. Yorke's motion would be debated.
On 19 February, the Commons decided to summon the Forum's secretary, John Gale Jones, to the bar of the House. Two days later, he appeared and apologized, but nevertheless was committed to Newgate. On 12 March, Burdett, who had been ill, moved for Jones's release. The motion was defeated, and Burdett wrote an open letter (*Political Register,* 24 March) to his constituents which denounced the tyranny of the Commons. Almost immediately after the warrant for his arrest was signed on 6 April, the capital was virtually in the hands of the mob. See the *Sun,* 6 April.

TO THE REVEREND THOMAS SEDGWICK WHALLEY

Brynbella
1st: July 1810.

Dear Doctor Whalley has certainly behaved *beautifully* with regard to our lamented Friend Mrs. Holman; Was it not the first Time She had ever been talked to on the Subject? I fear so. See how good God Almighty is to us all! affording *her* such a long Time for Reflexion with her Senses all bright and keen to the last Minute of Temporal Existence[1]—while the poor Countess of Rothes was called away at less (as I understand), than 12 Hours Warning. Her Death affected me Strongly, my Mind was prepared for the other; but dear Sir Lucas's Lady had been once my *Friend*—once my Enemy, and of late Years scarce my Acquaintance.[2] She had however written me a kind Letter——something like *making up* as we call it—which I answered even *eagerly;* —expressing my never-forgotten Veneration of *her* Virtue and Abilities——She was a truly noble Creature when I lived in Habits with her,—and had such firm-fixed Principles, that I am confident She must have died as She lived. Her Husband was ever—like your kind Self—good to me on all Occasions *never swayed with Doubt or sagged with Fear* as Shakespear says.[3]

Miss Thrale writes me Word that our sweet Siddons is with *her* at Ashgrove Cottage Kent—a heavenly Country when I saw it last towards 20 Years ago—— But this last Rain has really made my own Brynbella so lovely I can care for little else, except the Dear Lad of my heart as you so obligingly,—so *truly* call him: and I am tying up the Honeysuckles that they may look smart when he comes home, and fretting that the Strawberries will all be gone &c.——You know exactly how. He is really an exemplary Child: when we were in Town young Mr. Byng—*Edmund,* the Nephew of Lord Torington with whom Salusbury had formed a Friendship—asked my Leave to let them go on an Excursion together, thro' Scotland and Ireland; and meet me here in August. I told my Boy that I would not deny him such a Jaunt *if he wished it;*——but said he, "Aunt you know, if I am to go next March or April to Christ Church, it would be bad for me to shake all these Greek Choruses out of my Head that are but just *putting in;* and I'm sure *You* think it would be better for me to stay and study hard with Mr. Shephard who reads and explains the Greek Testament to us every Sunday—than run dashing about with dear Mr. Byng whom I like the Company of exceedingly, notwithstanding my Refusal of his Offer."

Now tho' I have passed a full Period of 50 Years since I was capable as now of judging Characters; and tho' in the Course of that ½ Century I have seen Young People turn out exactly the Reverse of what their Friends hoped from them—I cannot help forming good Expectations of *this* Creature; and with *your* Blessing, which I receive as you bestow it, in all true Kindness:——I am strong in the <Per>swasion he will be every thing his dear, *dear* Uncle wished.

I am very glad that Malvern Water does you good,[4] if *my* Nerves fail thro' the heat of this Weather, I will strengthen them in my own blue Sea Six Miles off, and go no further till *London* Season calls. What a Mercy it was not made a

Scene of Distraction when Sir *Francis Burdett* was liberated!⁵———The *frantic Disturbers* which is the Anagram of his Name—were preparing for an absolute Saturnalia as it appears by the News Paper⁶———and what a frightful Business is the Assassination of a Prince of the Blood in St. James's Palace!⁷—an Event since we parted. Ah dear Doctor Whalley—you *know better* I am confident than to believe Sellis was the guilty Person. *You know* that a *Bravo* of his Country will never use a *Sword* while there is a *Knife* to be found; and surely no Man of *any* Country who had just tied up his Master's head him*self* with a thick Bandeau and Tassel, would go flourishing a Sabre directly on the *defended Part.*⁸ The Dreadful Deed seems to me completely the Act of a *Soldier* whose first Idea is, Cut him down. An Assassin used to such Work would have struck him to the Heart. And an Italian to sever his *own* Head from his own Body almost!! how unlikely!!—and for what? *You* know that Men of that Description will commit any Crime but Suicide, which no Dread even of *Torture* ever led one to———here there was nothing to apprehend,—but hanging:—scarcely *that*———and how firm his Nerves were grown all on a sudden; he could not kill the Duke, but he could cut his own head almost off!!

Oh write to me dear Sir, and write soon; and say that *Your* Mind is of *my* Mind's *opinion.* Can there be a greater Compliment to her who is Your much obliged and faithful Servant and will be *ever* while / H: L: Piozzi.

Text: Berg Collection +. *Address:* Rev: Doctor Thomas Sedgwick Whalley / Mendip Lodge / near / Bristol. *Postmark:* DENBIGH 224.

1. HLP responds to TSW's letter of 18 June 1810 (Ry. 564.17), in which he talks of Jane Holman dying of cancer.
Requested to go upstairs to see the dying woman, he wrote, "I found poor Mrs. Holman much sunk and changed. The dimness of Death was in her Eyes and his shadows were on her cheek. But her Intellects were clear and her Mind firm. She smiled on me, held out her emaciated hand to grasp mine, and said, that as she almost despaired of recovery, it would be a great kindness in me to write down a few requests she had it at Heart to make to her dear, and ever indulgent Father, which she knew he would comply with . . . when she was no more.—I thought this the *fair moment* for pressing a more important concern. . . . 'My dear Mrs. Holman, I replied, you may command my ready and best Services. . . . But in turning your attention to earthly objects, I am confident you will not forget heavenly ones.' . . . 'I am willing, my Dear Sir, to do every thing you advise as far as my fluttered Spirits and debilitated Body will permit. I know I am a wretched Sinner.' 'Yours my Dear Mrs. Holman have been the Sins of *omission* than of *commission.*' . . . 'What act expressive of my Devotion and Faith would you recommend?' 'The receiving of the holy Sacrament, which includes all points of Devotion.' . . . 'But I fear my attention would fail, and my spasms interrupt the sacred Service.'—'Fear it *not.* God will support you. . . .' [She] shewed an edifying devotion through the *whole impressive* Service and Ceremony, with scarcely any interruption from agonizing Pain.—The Service ended, she thanked me with fervor; assuring me that it was a great comfort to her Mind and that the best Father could not have done more for her, than I had done."
Jane Holman, separated from her husband and largely ignored by her family, died on 11 June 1810 in Mortimer Street, Cavendish Square.
2. For Jane Elizabeth Leslie, suo jure countess of Rothes, see HLP to LC, 30 September 1796, n. 6. For her second husband, Sir Lucas Pepys, see HLT to FB, 30 June 1784, n. 5.
3. *Macbeth,* 5.3.10.
4. In his letter of June 18, 1810 TSW wrote: "The Malvern Air and Water have done wonders for me in *fifteen days!* Such a sudden renovation of Health and Spirits I had not the presumption to hope for, at my Age, and with my infirm Constitution. Before I left Malvern, I could climb the Mountain like a goat, and eat like an Hound. This will induce me to pass the month of November there, to strengthen me for my winter Campaign in London" (Ry. 564.17).

5. Burdett's constituents planned a triumphal procession to celebrate his release from the Tower, and riots were feared. On 21 June 1810 the *Courier* announced the "Liberation of Sir Francis Burdett."

"About twelve this morning, a party from St. Anne's Parish, set off with banners bearing the words 'Magna Charta'—'Trial by Jury'—'Constitution'—'Burdett for Ever.'—They came down the Strand, and were met on this side Temple Bar by the 12th Regiment of Light Dragoons from Romford, about 700 men.

"A detachment of the Queen's Dragoons is stationed near the Asylum.

"The day being so fine, all the lower orders are making a Jubilee day of it. Ribbons are displayed in profusion, and carts, waggons, hackney coaches, are all in requisition."

But Burdett did not allow himself a triumphal procession and was rowed down the Thames to Wimbledon.

On 23 and 25 June 1810 the *Courier* expressed relief similar to HLP's.

6. See the *Courier*, 18 June 1810: "Anagram. / Sir Francis Burdett— / Frantic Disturber."

7. Ernest Augustus (1771–1851), duke of Cumberland (1799), later king of Hanover (1837). In 1810 he was suspect to Whig leaders and to radicals, who, overlooking his earlier military career, now concentrated on his Tory partisanship and strong Protestant bias.

On the night of 31 May, he was found in his apartments in Saint James's Palace with a head wound. His valet Sellis was found dead in his bed with his throat cut. A coroner's jury returned the verdict that Sellis had committed suicide after trying to assassinate the duke. There was no apparent motive or hard evidence to account for the widely discussed affair.

8. Democratic journalists were highly critical of the coroner's verdict. They accused the duke of dreadful crimes and even hinted that he had murdered Sellis. HLP, who questioned the coroner's verdict, found herself in strange political company and sought reassurances from conservative friends.

In a letter postmarked 6 July 1810, Marianne Francis sufficiently vindicated the official judgment for HLP to abandon her suspicions. "There is one curious circumstance belonging to the affair— Sellis cut his own throat . . . *from ear to ear:* You know Rapin says, that when Lord Essex, (who had been taken up on pretence of the rye-house plot because he was inimical to the *Catholic Court*) was found with his throat cut by a razor from ear to ear in the Tower, the People clamoured against Charles 2, and the Duke of York, and swore *they* had done the deed, because, said the Men of those times, no person could cut *himself* in that manner. A *mistake* it seems, and the King and his Brother perhaps deserve to exculpated. I only lament that *Our* good old King will fret for his Son—as for the Duke, it will do him no harm, as there is no danger, to have a little time to be sober" (Ry. 582.56).

TO JOHN SALUSBURY PIOZZI SALUSBURY

Monday
16: July 1810.

Your Letter Dearest Salusbury interested me quite deeply for that poor Horse it told of—*more* deeply than wise People approve of one's being Interested; but I cannot help thinking that Animals have a *Claim* upon us. A good Man Solomon says is Merciful to his Beast, and we may observe that *their* Maker, who is also *ours*; respects his own Creation:[1] when sparing the Threatened City Ninive he urges as a Reason that it contained not only senseless Infants—but also *much Cattle,* which cannot in *that* Place be cared for as useful to *Man*; because they were to accompany their Masters in Destruction——but on *their own* Accounts:[2] Our Saviour also says that not a Sparrow's Feather falls to Ground without Observation of the Almighty[3]——how then can People practise Cruelty on these poor Things committed to their Care,—Yet fancy themselves Innocent?

You will be very kind I am sure to Your new Steed—Browney—Leak says he has no Fault—I see he has one;—but it is neither Starting nor Stumbling—my

Umbrella furled in his Face gives him no Concern tho' his Eyes are bright; and with those Legs—Stumbling were Impossible.

When shall you see, and show him Pemberton?

These Mondays begin to glide rapidly on before I have done half what I intended should be completed against your Arrival: but Maughan the Commissioner and Oldfield dined with me on Saturday after examining the Claims of 22 People to our Mountain.[4] I hope my Hertfordshire friend Mr. Maughan will feel *some* thing besides Contempt—and Pity is like it in such Cases;[5]—for your poor Aunt who has really been *too* ill used——tho' the Man laughed and well he might, when I shewed him a Letter in my Father's hand-writing to say that *he* bought, the very Land I am *soliciting*.

Miss Bridge brought me the Paper having heard of the Enclosure, it was directed to her Father who purchased it for mine, in the Year 1758.[6] But Mr. Thrale *scorned such Trifles;*—and to say true had no Thought of the Place coming to me perhaps, hearing all was entailed on my Uncle who had just married a Young Wife after promising me the Hertfordshire Estate 20 Times over——so he thought not of it, and the Place tho' purchased never was fenced in—and ½ a Century has elapsed that it has lain Waste——and If I will have it now—Why I must pay all Expences. On the first Day of August they meet again, and so as they make out the Allotments in Time for Planting, fencing et cætera, I will be *content*—I must *perforce* as Lady Percy says:[7] yet some Quantity of Good humour is necessary *too*. Let me thank God I am able to beg and battle for what is of Right and Equity my own. You are perfectly correct in considering the Uncertain Tenure of human Reason as much more dangerous and dreadful, than the Uncertainty of human Wealth—and one of these often includes the other. Poor Mrs. Williams was according to the true tho' vulgar Phrase—not *herself:* The Torturing Pain, and the Opium taken to still it, kept her Mind in strong Delirium or melancholy Stupor—till Death cut the Cords and set the Soul free of its Exuviæ.

From such an Exit may God preserve Your poor Affectionate Aunt, who while any Consciousness remains, will love *you* for Your Dear Uncle's Sake, and for *your own*. Charles Shephard and Edward Pemberton *both* know and witness,—morally if not legally, my Intents towards *You;* and if they ever change—unless provoked by your own ill Behaviour—will be convinced There has been foul Play; so will Windle:—who is a legal Witness to my Will, made when possessed of my right Wits most surely.[8]

Mrs. Mostyn has written, says She sets out for Segroid the 18th. Her Letter's dated from her Sister's Cottage; tells that her eldest Son will get removed into the 4th Form at Westminster next Christmas; and *then* fagging is to be over.[9] He and his Brother will come down in August: Harry remains ever by her Side—— She mentions Mrs. Smythe Owen as having visited Miss Thrale while *She* did;[10] and says *She* comes to Shropshire very soon to see her Friends who are related to Mr. Pemberton. Those are her Words; but not a Syllable of *Salusbury*—who *knowing* there are Snares set for him on every Side, must look sharp and not *fall in:* no one can have more Warnings. I am *so* glad your Friend comes with You: he can give Counsel as to *these* Matters with better Grace and with less Scruple

16 July 1810

than I could——he will advise you, so will Mr. Shephard, to take all *four Wings* Duty, Fear, Interest and Affection and fly the Moment Illness seizes me, to the Bedside of Yours in / all true Esteem and Tenderness / H: L: P.

I am very well at present however; and eat Cherry Pye without any Apprehensions, except of all being gone before you come. We carry Hay tonight as long as we can see to work.

I really believe that my Attachment to you does me good; keeps me on the *Alert* and hinders Lethargic Drowsiness from taking Place—as it does with poor old Mrs. Ray—7 Years my Senior.[11] I should care for none of the Nonsense you will read about the Mountain—was it not for my dearest Salusbury. So give my true Regards to all who love you and Farewell.

Text: Ry. 585.72. *Address:* John P: Salusbury Esq: / At The Rev: Thos: Shephard's / Enborne / near Newbury / Berkshire. *Postmark:* DENBIGH 224 (In JSPS's hand, "Received July 19th 1810. Answered Do 20th Do")

1. Prov. 12:10.
2. Jon. 4:11.
3. Matt. 10:29.
4. HLP first heard about the claimants to the Bryn—"the mountain," as she called it—on 6 January 1810, although difficulties about its enclosure had begun earlier. See her letter to JSPS, 9 September 1809, n. 5.

Her efforts, written up in her "Pocket Book" (Ry. 616), were arduous. After her initial entry on 6 January 1810, she noted on 15 January, "Wrote to Lloyd of Denbigh concerning the Moors and the Mountains." And on the 18th she wrote another "Letter about the Mountain."

On 14 July, she recorded that "Mr. Oldfield [came] to dinner, and Mr. Maughan; and Mr. Moore: it was the Day of Claims at the Bryn." Four days later, on the 18th, she learned from a Mr. Parry that "the Commissioners will delay the award." Apparently, she had to wait a about a year and a half to secure "the mountain." See her letter to JSPS, 12 February 1812.

5. John Maughan or Maugham (fl. 1777–1830) was an estate agent and surveyor. The term "Commissioner" may refer to the work he did as an enclosure commissioner. In 1798–99, he worked, e.g., on behalf of the Tower family to settle their disputes with tenants and was also "attending, surveying and taking a Ground Plan of the [Tower] House at Gadebridge [Hemel Hempstead, Herts.] with a view to alter and amend it" (C.R.O., Hertfordshire).

Working as a surveyor, he is recorded as being in residence at Luton, Beds., in 1798 and at various times during 1815–29; at Hitchin, Herts.; at Oswestry in Salop in 1821; and at Burnt Green, Worcs., between 1812 and 1830. In 1821 he gave evidence to the parliamentary committee concerned with the depressed state of architecture. (From the records at the library of the Royal Institution of Chartered Surveyors, London.)

6. Frances Bridge (b. 30 June 1743) of Aberwheeler. On 11 July HLP wrote in her "Pocket Book": "Miss Bridge brought me a Letter from my poor Father to hers—proving the Mountain I *solicit* is my own." For this document HLP paid her £1, but on 2 August, "Miss Bridge called—wanted Twenty Pounds of me,—Likely Stuff."

For the Salusbury steward, Edward Bridge, see John Field to HLP, 28 December 1791, n. 4; also the "Bodfari Baptism Register, 1731–51," C.R.O., Clwyd.

7. The remark is made by Clarence in *Richard the Third* (1.1.117).
8. For Thomas Windle, who witnessed HLP's will in 1809, see HLP's letter to JSPS, 6 May 1809, n.2.
9. CMM's oldest son, Salusbury, and her youngest son, Bertie, were to matriculate at Westminster in 1810. For their subsequent careers, see HLP to LC, 18 January 1814.
10. Nicholas Owen (Smythe) Owen (1769–1804), of Condover, assumed, according to the will of his great-grandmother Letitia (Mytton) Barnston, née Owen (d. 1755), the surname and arms of Owen. He married Henrietta Jemima, née Townsend (d. 1814). Prior to his death, he devised his estates to his nephew Edward William Smythe Pemberton (JSPS's "Pem").

11. Elinor Ray of Brynbella, born in 1732, was in fact nine years older than HLP. She was to be buried on 12 August 1814. See "Drymerchion Parish Registers" (C.R.O., Clwyd).

TO JOHN SALUSBURY PIOZZI SALUSBURY

Brynbella Fryday
27: July 1810.

If my dearest Boy had been the Child of my Body, instead of the *Son of my Soul* I should have feared he might have participated in my Anxiety of Temper, and then the freed Letter to Mr. Shephard would have frighted him, because 'tis so unusual for me to procure a Frank. But the *Bishop's Lordship*[1] after no small ado, prevailed on himself to give me an Envelope for You, and I would not burthen him with a longer Direction for the little News I have to Send.

Do you remember my distant Relation Maria Boycott at Bath—playing at Cards with Lord Glenbervie, and with my much nearer Cousin Lady Kilmorey? I told You She had been handsome, and you would not believe it:——She is married to the Earl of Guildford!!! And do you Remember Sophia Boycott her Sister, a very tall large showy Woman? She is married to Bowen the Apothecary!![2]

These are the Facts on which we may all make our own Reflections. Mine is that if you and Your Friend do not choose *Your* Wives in a ——but I won't finish the Sentence; you may fill up the Blanks your own Way.—

I never passed a duller day at the Palace[3]——only myself and "Martha, Martha, come Martha"—for *Ladies;* the rest—dependant Clergymen of which a little round Man the Examining Chaplain was most agreable.——He asked me very seriously if I had ever been in Company with Madame D'Arblaye——cy devant Fanny Burney: "Oh Yes Sir, I had the honour of Miss Burney's Company as an *Inmate,* and an *Intimate* for Three or four Years."[4] The Bishop then turned to *me,* and said "I made acquaintance with *her* Brother last Month at Oxford; Pray is not Doctor Charles Burney an exemplarily good Man Mrs. Piozzi?"—"An Exemplarily *great Greek Scholar* I believe My Lord"[5]—"Ay, but he has abridged Pearson on the Creed—and to that he could have had no Inducement but Virtue"[6]——I am perswaded My Lord that Dr. Charles Burney cannot avoid having a high Value for Virtue, and I am confident he is a Man well convinced of religious Truths. Could I say less evil (so called upon) of a Man well known to be a habitual Drunkard? living all but openly with a Woman in his own *house*[7]— and who made his Magazine when he had the Conduct of one: a Vehicle of such Abuse upon *me* as no other Literary Repository would receive and publish.[8] I think I will be praised for my Candour. Oh come! let me in the same Spirit of Candour repress my Feelings of Ridicule concerning Lord Guildfords Marriage: He is not the Young Man I took him for——a Boy 19 or no more at most than 20 Years of Age:—*That* poor Fellow died it seems; and the Title reverted back to his Uncle a Companion well enough chosen by and for Maria Boycott[9]—but what Luck those Women have! I suppose neither of them under 40 Years old, and *Starving* till now! Bowen's Purse is rated at 100,000£.—Cecy Mostyn said—Lord! how Sophia will but stink of the Shop!——It will replied I, have no Need to supply her with *Bark* for an *Appetite* at least——Oh they have been living like the Lady who boyled Her Rabbet in the Chocolate Pot. Cecy Mostyn's Place at Segroid is really quite a Show-*Thing*—exquisite Taste She has displayed in it, yet The Pleasure Ground *there* is perhaps too much in Unison with her London Drawing Room and *dining* Parlour, from which I think *you* were excluded. I watched on Monday to see if She would ask for you, but as there was no Sign of an Enquiry, I said slowly on purpose—"so You *never ask how* my *Mountain* goes forward." Before The marked Word came out, She turned with a stern Air towards me: and recalling the Look—replied—Oh I know the Mountain is good for nothing—every one can tell what a silly Project *that* is. Ay truly was the Answer—Silly enough! and so I would have *her* think it——no need of exciting *more* Jealousy or Malice.

But her Son will one Day see that the Money spent in adorning Segroid was the foolish Project; because the Estate will not be increased an Acre in Size by all her playful Devices——nor improved in Value half a Crown——Whereas if We can plant 10000 Trees, we know that they *must* be worth 10000£ by the Time Your Son's of Age; besides an Extent of Territory, which is good at *any Rate;* and I hope Mr. Maughan will be coaxed to allot us some good Turnep Land beside; and that the General may be flattered into a Fancy of cultivating it him*self*. But see My Darling! what a World it is; and how many Briars are sticking in poor H:L:P's Petticoats, and Thorns piercing her Side. The Claims must be adjusted,—a general Survey of the Mountain must be made; and Then every Claimant's present Possessions must be valued, that the Allotment may keep just Proportion to our Estates in the Neighbourhood—an Award will then be made, and if I live till that wished for hour——I will pay all Expences, and begin planting, fencing &c. like Fury——and you will come in to the Profits (of the Arable) in Seven Years,—*My* purse standing in Lieu of *Your* empty one to discharge all Costs.

Lord Bless us! here is News of Mrs. Jones's Death of Rhialt—Mother to the mad Lady who is so large a Fortune. She was well, and at Church last Sunday:—complained on Monday Evening and died last Night. A Stout healthy Woman 54 Years old or 56 perhaps—certainly not 60.[10] Remember this is written Thursday——and then reflect how very necessary it is to keep the White Plumage in full Gloss ready for *sudden Flight.*

I will not say a Word about the Hay, or the Apples—or about Browney's only Fault. Have we not all of us more faults than one? You my Dearest have but ½ of One, that I know of; And It will be eased by seeing how Expert an Angler our Adversary is——Self Confidence is the Fault, (if a Fault;) For you all know Security Is Mortals chiefest Enemy as Say the Witches when tempting Macbeth.[11]—May He who *only* did resist Temptation when clad in Human Form, preserve my best and dearest Boy ultimately for himself; <now> for your *Affectionate* Aunt / H: L: P.

Text: Ry. 585.74. *Address:* John Piozzi Salusbury Esq: / at the Rev: T: Shephard's / Enborne / near Newbury / Berkshire. *Postmark:* DENBIGH.

1. William Cleaver.
2. HLP refers to two daughter of Thomas Boycott (d. 1798) of Wrexham and Rudge Hall, Salop. Maria (d. 1821) was to marry on 19 July Francis North (1761–1817), fourth earl of Guilford (1802). Sophia (d. 1830) married William Bowen of Bath. For the latter, see HLP to PSP, 14 April 1803, n. 2.
3. That is, the residence of the bishop of Saint Asaph.
4. By 1779 the friendship between HLT and FB was close. Indeed, according to FB's "French Exercise Book," "elle insista que je comptasse Streatham comme un autre chez moi. . . . Elle m'arranga une chambre à coté de *sa Dressing room* pour que nous puissions toujours être près l'une de l'autre." See *Journals and Letters* 7:528–29. For the breakup of their friendship, see HLP to FB, 6 August 1784.
5. For the Reverend Charles Burney's reputation as a Greek scholar, see HLP to Q, 23 August 1801, n. 5.
6. By 1808, the Rev. Charles Burney seemed to concentrate his efforts on becoming a bishop. According to Marianne Francis on 21 November 1808, "People have already settled that [he] is to be a *Bishop:* and when I questioned him on his intentions, he pleaded the profoundest ignorance of his destiny; but that to please me he *would* try to be a Bishop as fast as he could" (*Journals and Letters* 7:108).
In 1810, he produced *The Exposition of the Creed, by J. Pearson* [Bishop of Chester] . . . *Abridged for the Use of Young Persons.*
7. HLP refers to Sabrina Bicknell, called Sidney (ca. 1757–1843), who began life as an unnamed orphan in a foundling hospital in Shrewsbury. Named, educated, and trained to be a wife by Thomas Day (1748–89), she eventually became the ward of Richard Lovell Edgeworth.
About 1784, she married John Bicknell (d. 1787), a writer and barrister. When he died, she and two infant sons were left without money. She became at that time housekeeper and general manager of the younger Burney's schools at Chiswick, Hammersmith, and Greenwich. She continued to live in his rectory at Deptford.
8. For the source of HLP's hostility toward Burney, see her letter to Sophia Byron, 8 June 1788, n. 6.
9. HLP is inaccurate.
George Augustus North (1757–1802), third earl of Guilford (1792), had two sons: with his first wife, Maria Frances Mary, née Hobart (d. 1794), he had George Augustus (1791–92), styled Lord North; with his second wife, Susan, née Coutts (d. 1837), he had Frederick (1801–2), styled Lord North.
In 1802, the barony and earldom of Guilford devolved on the male heir, Francis (1761–1817), a brother of the third earl.
10. There is no record of a burial in 1810 of Mrs. Jones. HLP may have heard a rumor of the lady's death and passed it on to JSPS as a fact. There is, however, a Cwm burial on 4 August 1812, which is pertinent: "Mary Jones, relict of the late John Jones, Esq. of Rhualt." See "Parish Registers of Tremeirchion, Cwm, and St. Asaph" (C.R.O., Clwyd).
11. *Macbeth,* 3.5.32–33.

TO CLEMENT FRANCIS

Brynbella
28: July 1810.

My dear Young Friend's
Letter gave me infinite Pleasure;—it is so contradictory to all one hears of the Impossibility a Woman of my Age must necessarily find in gaining the Attention

of a Person no older than yourself. Marianne is another Instance. She does right to keep out of London, and you do right to keep *in* it¹—'Tis the only Mart for Industry; and its consequent Comforts. Leisure and Independance will as surely follow, as you exert your Powers to obtain them—*Half* the Powers you possess—ay a *tenth* Part, might make You the *first* Character on the Commercial Side of Temple Bar; but then you must keep them bright and keen by *not* sitting nine hours at a Feast, till after nine and Twenty Years old; and by that Time such sort of Appetites will I hope be blunted.

The Bishop of St. Asaph asked me last Week if I knew your Uncle Charles? I bowed Assent—Well and do you not think him Madam! an *exemplarily* good Man? An astonishingly great Greek Scholar my Lord! I have often heard he was; replied H:L:P. Ay; but he has abridged Pearson on the Creed, for which he could have had no Motives (as I can see) except *pure Virtue*——My Lord, A Man of Dr. Charles Burney's Talents, if there are any more such Men—must necessarily set the highest possible Value upon *pure Virtue,*—and his Religious Opinions are I believe perfectly Orthodox. Was this Candour?—or what was it? *Justice;* so far as I could call up Words to express it at the Moment.²

With regard to your Oxford Frolick it was a pretty one: You do very well to keep alive the Delight in Literature to which you will one Day devote yourself entirely——and in hope of which enjoyment you are now contented to toil: as many Men are, in hope of the favrite, the Future Wife——still looking forward toward Tomorrow.

> The Soldier wearied with his Wintry March
> Still sees Tomorrow dress'd in Robes of Triumph;
> Still to the Lover's long-expecting Arms
> Tomorrow brings the Visionary Bride.³

I am at present watching for Tomorrow *sennight* when Salusbury's Weeks of Absence will be over, and he and his Friend will be coming home immediately. Next Wednesday they set out for Longnor Hall The Seat of Mr. Pemberton's Father and Mother near Shrewsbury.⁴

Our Chester Bank has distressed many Individuals hereabout,⁵ but the Story in your kind Letter is really very affecting. If I had Money and Opportunity now I would lay all out in Land; though Your Rich Men in London *are* holding up the Consols so with both hands.

How does Mr. Kingstone⁶ bear the Stones thrown at him by the Reviewers?⁷ I hope he has the Art like Dean Swift's Conjurer of making them fall upon his head like so many Pillows⁸—but he must have known what would follow such a Publication, and the *Ancients* of whom he speaks,—never went to War without a <Shield.> His 7th and 8th Pages are exquisitely beautiful—I cannot meddle with the verbal Criticisms,—<&c.> the general *Truths* are in my Mind *undeniable*⁹——It is a *feminine* Objection of the Scotch Critics, to say that an Englishman's sole Occupation from seven Years old to 24—is learning *Latin* and *Greek.*——It is *not* so: They are learning *Language;* and those who never study Language in its Construction, by persing &c., never do learn it at all—but as an advertising Gouvernante learns it. Classical Literature is an Englishman's Common Field—and these new Enclosures which may fertilize *North* Britain, will only confine *him,* and take from the general Dignity of the whole, by their numerous Intersections.

How does Your dear Mama do? and little Dolph?[10] Pray give them my best Regards—and say if your Grandfather keeps well, and enjoys the temporary Depression of the Democrates?

Adieu Dear Sir, and never forget that charming Mr. White you were so fond of;[11] and continue Your very valuable Esteem and Kindness for yours / and your Family's very faithfully / H: L: Piozzi.

[Two lines obliterated.]

Text: Berg Collection, m.b. *Address:* Clement Francis Esq. / No. 10 Chenies Street / Bedford Square / London. *Postmark:* DENBIGH 224; E 30 JY 30 1810.

1. While Clement Francis worked in "a Merchant's house in the City," Marianne Francis lived in Richmond with her mother and stepbrother Dolph. See below, n. 10.

2. Clement Francis responded with a letter postmarked 9 August. "What the Bishop of Asaph can mean, by Burney's being an exemplary good man, I can't divine. Not even in the sense the world may apply that no little title can it belong to him, I fear. To be sure, he may place his name next to the Duke of Norfolk's in a charity list. If such a man can be called a Grace to one. All these Sums so subscribed are more than half either through ostentation, through desire to be thought rich or not imagined stingy after a dinner, from drunken profusion or from the unhappy desire to be great. However poor Man, though we can't grant him praise he may be allowed Peace, for, that unfortunate Cambridge business has weighed hard down upon him through life. And indeed I almost think it might be buried in Silence. But it sticks to him like a leech" (Ry. 584.165).

For the "Cambridge business," see HLP to Q, 25 March 1811, n. 4; and *Journals and Letters* 7: 57–58, n. 4, and 88, n. 1.

3. SJ, *Irene*, 3.2.28–31. HLP has slightly altered the first line from "The Soldier lab'ring through a Winter's March." She had perhaps seen and recollected an unpublished draft of *Irene* with the reading "The weary Soldier . . ."

4. For Captain Edward Pemberton and his wife, Anna Maria Emma, see HLP to JSPS, 20 August 1808, n. 1.

5. In July people in various parts of England distrusted the reliability of country banks. As a consequence of this and "the scarcity of small change," several such banks, including the one in Chester, suffered considerable runs on cash payments so that temporarily all business was "at a stand." See *GM* 80, pt. 2 (1810): 81.

6. HLP mistakenly writes Kingstone for Edward Copleston (1776–1849), an Oxonian, who from 1802 to 1812 was professor of poetry at the university. In time he was to serve as provost of Oriel (1814–28), dean of Chester (1826), bishop of Llandaff and dean of Saint Paul's (1828–49).

In his *Advice to a Young Reviewer* (1807) he parodied the method of criticism associated with the *Edinburgh Review.* Between then and 1809 the magazine maintained a steady attack against Oxford, berating its dependence on Aristotle and its neglect of modern mathematics, censuring its system of classical education (see, e.g., nos. 22 and 28).

In 1810 Copleston rose in defense of the university, writing *A Reply to the Calumnies of the Edinburgh Review against Oxford.* (In all, he wrote three *Replies,* the third in 1811; and each was attacked by the *Review.*)

7. In art. 7 of no. 31 (April 1810) the *Edinburgh Review* answered Copleston without mentioning his name. A twenty-nine page article attempted to establish the fallacies upon which *A Reply* was grounded. It concluded with a personal attack upon the author as "an envious pedant."

8. See the first voyage, chap. 3, in *Gulliver's Travels* wherein Flimnap (Sir Robert Walpole), straining too far on the tightrope, fell and "would have infallibly broke his neck, if one of the King's cushions, that accidentally lay on the ground, had not weakened the force of his fall." The cushion was a metaphor for the duchess of Kendal, one of George I's mistresses.

9. HLP has in mind pp. 7–9 of Copleston's first *Reply,* wherein he defends all individuals who

labor to fulfill their God-given gifts and, conversely, urges critics to understand their proper purpose: their skill in analysis "should be reserved for offences of deeper guilt and more serious mischief, for the grovelling reptiles of quackery and obscenity, for the foul deformed monsters of malice, sedition, and impiety. Against these let the indignant Spirit of criticism bare his red right arm, and hurl his thunders; against these let him send forth the fierce ministers of vengeance, with their viper hair and sounding lash."

10. Charlotte Ann Burney had married first Clement Francis and had three children: Charlotte (1786–1870), Marianne, and Clement. She married secondly Ralph Broome (1742–1805) and had an only child, Ralph or "Dolph" (1801–17). The precocious boy was subject to respiratory ailments, eventually dying of tuberculosis.

11. John White (1786–1851) had been admitted to Caius College, Cambridge, on 26 April 1804. He received his B.A. (fourth Wrangler) in 1808, his M.A. in 1811. He was made a fellow at Caius in 1808 and served as dean from 1812 to 1817. Ordained a deacon on 18 December 1808, he became a priest in 1810.

TO LADY KEITH

Brynbella Monday
31 July 1810.—

My dearest Lady Keith

has been free from my Letters now a very decent Time;[1] The Tooth Ach and swelled Face has employed my Leisure, and served my Correspondents very obligingly. It is surprizing to think How ill one behaves to People without any bad Intentions: You have repeatedly mentioned those agreeable *Coxes* in your Letters to me, and I have as often failed to say how much I like, and how sincerely I respect them.[2]—We used to meet frequently at the now deserted House of Mrs. Holroyd, Sister to Lord Sheffield; a Bath Inhabitant in Bath's better Days.[3]—And it was there I first learned poor Mrs. Lyon's truly interesting and half romantic Adventures.[4] Our old Acquaintance William Coxe the Traveller, brought *his* Wife to Mrs. Holroyd's too;[5] where a very unaffected chearful Society used to meet,—of which the present Bishops of Waterford and Meath were the solid Dishes;[6] while *nous autres diseurs & diseuses de petit Mots a rire* served for the

> Tulip Leaves and Lemon Peel
> Brought only to adorn the Meal.[7]

I am in gross Fault too towards the most faultlessly correct of all Characters, who made my Acquaintance Solely that he might be talking about you. I mean Sir Edward Leslie, who made me his Chargée de Complimens all last Winter— and I never unpacked them till today.[8] Pray assure yourself that He feels deeply indebted to you and Lord Keith for some favours shewn to Some Mr. and Mrs. Halliborton[9] of whom likewise he delights to talk, but of whom I am unfortunate enough to know nothing.

Dear! Dear! what an exemplary Creature that Sir Edward Leslie is—by the by—Sitting at home to read with his sick Lady, and refusing all Amusements she cannot share[10]—but there are some charming People certainly, scattered up and down the World, and one meets and parts with them, and then—(those who live to my Age) hear some dismal End befalling the major Part of what once formed desirable Society. E: G: Princesse Pauline; who was so *very* obligingly kind to me in my happy Days at dear Brussels—burned to Death! a Disfigured Corpse! the Paper says.[11] Doctor Whalley will feel as sorry as myself—he was writing the Verses which Mr. Piozzi set and sung in *her* Praise, and her lovely Mother's:[12] Ah poor Princesse Pauline! It was at her Father's house—The reigning Duc D'Arenberg[13]—that I did *not* kiss Christina's White hand,[14] because She had broke the Custom, and when the Dutchess *presented*,— She *embraced* us. And how like a Dream it all is! The Duke was Stoneblind like Lord Coventry and his Wife danced Country dances with him, was his Partner at Whist &c.[15] Well! those Figures are all moved off the Magick Lanthorn, and I am looking for My Mountain *now*—Canvassing Lord Keith to get the Bill through the House, and courting the Commissioner Slyly with good Dinners to allot me—What I have just found out—my own Father purchased and paid for; and I am to beg and purchase the favour—*of buying it over again.* What clever Management! It was an Old Woman—older even than poor H: L: P— who brought me my Father's Letter, written to *her* Father Mr. Bridge[16] in the Year 1758–four Years and ½ after the Date of which, I married into an opulent Family, that scorned (naturally enough) my poor Skin and Bone Country: so it fell into Waste Land, and must this Year be reclaimed by a Bill of general Inclosure. But it does not matter *a Pin* as the Clown says and sings for

> A great while ago the World begun
> With heigh Ho! The Wind and the Rain;
> But that's all one, when *our Work's done*
> And the Rain it raineth every Day.[17]

'Tis incredible how little I care concerning it—only just enough to kick Life along: The Appearance of Plenty for the Poor interests me much more nearly, and they will *not* want Bread for themselves, or Feed for their Beasts thank God, 'spite of the Prophetess.

The Newspapers are filled with Thunder-Storms, but I have seen none in the Sky.[18] Cecy Mostyn says I read nothing but Accidents and Offences, and truly *they* were never more frequent, or more *Black:* She will tell you that Lady Kirkwall is at Abergeley.—They cannot bear to be out of Wales 'tis plain.—I know not who will give me anything out of poor dear Lleweney, Lord K―― presented Catherine de Berayne's fine Portrait painted by Lucas Van Heere[19] to the Hugheses 7 Years ago—I was very angry, and very sorry, but all laughed; and said it was a Joke.[20] It was no Joke however when I begged Rebecca who worked at Kinmel to copy it,[21] and he never could gain Access to the Room where it hung. Cecilia's Sister in Law is married to a distant Cousin of mine and of Sir Robert Salusbury;[22] I went to pay the Wedding Visit, and saw my frightful Ancestors reared up against the Wall with their Mottoes and Coat Armour very curious. Maria, cy-devant Mostyn seemed to view them with *no Partiality*, and her House is to be all new done by some of these fine Surveyors—so perhaps Old Bachygraig will get enriched by the Cast offs of Modern Improvement—*somewhere*.

Cecy has made her Place really *quite a Gem*. I never saw anything nearer than the Leasowes—or Ilam, more truly beautiful than the Grounds about Segroid. Did you see a Journey thro' Caernarfonshire advertised?[23] The Traveller has done poor little Bodvel my Birthplace, the Honour to write Verses on it;[24] and as he sent me several Copies I will enclose one if it will not overweight the Frank. The Author is unknown to me,—Doctor Thackeray says his Name is Hall.[25] But it is high Time to sign my own Name to all this Nonsense. Could it indeed have been written by anyone except Dear Lady Keith's Affectionate Mother / H: L: Piozzi.

If Susette is with You—kiss her for *me*, and beg her to write soon: She owes me a Letter, and will I hope tell me in it That the Fair Lady of Purbrook Park like Empress Louisa *is in blessed Circumstances of Body*.[26]

No Ill Will to *Baby* tho'—for Baby is a good Dear; and never cries like her old Grandmother except for the *Tooth ach*—which would really make the very Saints cry, I'm sure it would.

Give my best Regards to Lord Keith.

Text: Bowood Collection. *Address:* R: H: Baroness Keith.

1. HLP had last written a short letter to Q on 6 July 1810, concluding: "Farewell! and tremble at the Thoughts of writing to her who has no Occupation but to read and think; and who is never happier than to say what She thinks of what She has lately read—The Lady of the Lake for Example; but it does not interest or animate me as Marmion did. Walter Scott felt perhaps like Fontenelle who when he published his second Dialogues des Morts said 'L'Indulgence du Public pour la première Partie, m'a donné presque autant de Crainte que de Courage'" (Bowood Collection).
2. For the Reverend George Coxe, see HLP to SL, 4 November 1785, n. 7.
3. For Sarah Martha Holroyd, who lived at 3 Queen's Parade, Bath, see HLP to PSP, 7 March [1803], n. 1.
4. Mary Lyon, née Hamilton (1754–1843), was now the wife of the Reverend George Coxe. She was the widow of Captain James Lyon, killed at the battle of Bunker Hill. Their son James Frederick Lyon (1775–1842), later lieutenant general and K.C.B. (1815), was born posthumously on board a transport returning to England from America. See *GM*, n.s., 20, pt. 2 (1843): 107.
5. For the Reverend William Coxe, see HLP to SL, 17 November 1787, n. 3. In 1803 he had married Eleanora (Yeldham), née Shairp (1759–1830).
6. In 1810 Joseph Stock, bishop of Killala, was translated to the bishopric of Waterford and Lismore, where he died in 1813. See also HLP to LC, 30 July 1803, n. 15; to John Roberts, 2 March 1807, n. 6; to Q, 11 August 1807, n. 11.
For Thomas Lewis O'Beirne, bishop of Meath (1798–1823), see HLP to PSP, 16 December 1802, n. 3.
7. Matthew Prior, *Alma*, 1.381–82.
8. Edward Leslie (1744–1818), of Tarbert, county Kerry, was an Oxonian who became a barrister at the Middle Temple in 1777. As M.P. for Old Leighlin (1787–90), he assisted in quelling disturbances there. For this action he was created baronet on 3 September 1787. In 1802–3 he raised a cavalry corps from among his tenants at Tarbert, appointing himself captain commandant.
9. There is no reference to the Halliburtons in the Elphinstone Muniments deposited at the Scottish Record Office, Edinburgh. They probably are, however, the Scottish-descended William Hersey Otis Haliburton (d. 1829), a justice in Nova Scotia, and his wife, Lucy Chandler, née Grant. They would have become acquainted with Elphinstone when as a young naval officer he sailed in American waters.
10. In July 1773 Edward Leslie had married Anne, née Cane (d. 1825), of Dowdstown, county Kildare.

11. Pauline d'Arenberg, who had married Karl Philipp (1771–1820), prince of Schwarzenberg, perished in a fire in July 1810 at the Austrian embassy in Paris. The fire gutted the embassy during a ball given to celebrate the marriage of Napoleon and Marie Louise.

12. TSW met the duc and duchess d'Arenberg with their daughter Pauline when they visited Brussels in 1786–87.

13. Louis-Engelbert-Marie-Joseph-Augustin (1750–1820), duc d'Arenberg (also duc d'Arshot and de Croy), had married in 1773 Pauline-Louise-Antoinette-Candide (d. 1812), daughter of the duc de Brancas-Lauraquais. HLP had met them early in 1787 in Brussels.

14. For Marie Christine, see HLP to Q, 10 July 1796, n. 7.

15. The duc d'Arenberg, who had been born in Brussels, entered military service, when not quite twenty-four, he was blinded by a friend's gun, which misfired during a hunt.

16. Edward Bridge, once steward of Salusbury properties. See John Field to HLP, 28 December 1791, n. 4.

17. HLP's improvisation of the Fool's song in *King Lear,* 3.2.74–77.

18. There were localized thunderstorms through much of July. On the 26th, e.g., "a tremendous storm of thunder and lightning happened this afternoon, in the neighbourhood of *Norwich.* At *Swainsthorpe,* a large timber oak, on the premises of Mr. Mayes, was shivered to atoms; some of the pieces flew fifty yards, and what is very remarkable, the body of the tree was completely wrung round, and the earth on each side clear away full four feet." See *GM,* 80, pt. 2 (1810): 82.

19. Lukas de Heere (1534–84), a poet and painter born in Ghent. He probably did the portrait of Katheryn of Berain in 1576 when he was in England, having been exiled from Ghent.

20. A little more than six years before or earlier, Lord Kirkwall intended to give the portrait of Katheryn of Berain as a wedding present to Charlotte and William Lewis Hughes of Kinmel Park. See HLP to MW, 5 July [1807], n. 10.

21. Biagio Rebecca (1735–1808) was elected an associate of the Royal Academy in 1771. With Cipriani and later John Francis Rigaud he acquired a large practice in decorative painting, especially in the imitation of antique basso-relievos on ceilings, staircases, etc., in large houses of the nobility and gentry.

22. For Anna Maria Mostyn, who had married John Lloyd Salusbury of Galltfaenon, see JMM to HLP, 14 June 1795, n. 5; HLP to Q, 22 March 1810, n. 8.

23. HLP knew about the "Journey" from Dr. Thackeray's letter, dated 22 March [1810]: "My friend Mr. Hall who is publishing the His[tory] of Carnarvonshire, which I believe will be a valuable book, has lately been in Chester; he was much surprised to find that you were born in the County, and promised me that he would pay particular attention to the place of your Nativity." Enclosed in the letter are Hall's verses on "Bodfel Hall / The Birth place / of / H: L: Piozzi."

24. Hall's "Lines on Bodfel Hall" consists of six Spenserian stanzas; each ends with the refrain "To Bodfel ye the pleasures owe." The verses celebrate HLP's literary achievement from *The Three Warnings* to *Retrospection.* Preserved in "Minced Meat for Pyes" and the "Commonplace Book," they also appeared in the *North Wales Gazette,* 24 May 1810.

25. See *A Description of Caernarvonshire (1809–1811),* by Edmund Hyde Hall, edited from the original manuscript in the Library of the University College of North Wales, by Emyr Gwynne Jones, M.A. (Caernarvon: Printed by Gwenlyn Evans, 1952).

Although *A Description* remained unpublished until 1952, it is possible that Hall produced a briefer, anonymous publication in either 1810 or 1811.

Hall, a native of Jamaica, probably attended Harrow and subsequently the Middle Temple (until 1796) but without evidence of being called to the bar. Visiting Carnarvon, in 1796 and again in 1809, he expected to publish his travel manuscript. He even issued a printed prospectus on the assumption of publication by Cadell and Davies. The prospectus was printed by Broster of Bangor and a subscription list of ca. two hundred names was put together. Nothing demonstrable came of this effort, and Hall died obscurely in Dublin on 17 October 1824.

26. The Lady of Purbrook Park was Q. She, contrary to HLP's wishes, was not pregnant, while the Empress Marie Louise was.

TO [JESSÉ FOOT][1]

Brynbella, 29: August, 1810.

Sir,—I feel glad to be told that Mr. Woodhouse yet lives, who certainly was made the excuse of bringing Dr. Johnson to my acquaintance. My own book tells the story *truely*.[2] I am confident—yours has not reached me—and I have nothing here at present to refer to: but thus called on, I will try my recollection.

Poor Mr. Murphy was an intimate of my first husband's, and soon after our marriage, expressed an eager desire that we should know the great writer, of whom we were always speaking. Our residence was in the borough of Southwark; yet I *could bring* him here, says he, only we must seek an ostensible reason for his coming. That reason was found in Mr. Woodhouse's celebrity.[3] The day was appointed, and passed so agreeably, that the *same* day in the *next* week was fixed for our meeting again—but I think, Mr. Woodhouse came but once. Johnson's injunction to him about the Spectators struck me very forcibly—'Give days and nights, sir, to the study of Addison.'[4]

Your letter, saying *Mr. Murphy is dead,* struck me forcibly too; but of friends we were living with forty-six years ago, who is left alive? The portraits painted for Mr. Thrale at Streatham, by Sir Joshua Reynolds, have *all* lost their originals, except Dr. Burney of Chelsea College, and her, who has the honour to be, / Sir / Your very obedient humble servant / H: L: Piozzi.

Text: *Blackwood's Magazine* 26 (November 1829): 754–55.

1. The letter was undoubtedly addressed to Murphy's executor, Dr. Jessé Foot, whose *Life* of Arthur Murphy was to be published by Faulder early in 1811. See HLP to LC, 14 November 1805, n. 11.
2. In the *Anecdotes,* pp. 232–33, HLT dates her first meeting with SJ as 1764. In *Thraliana* 1:158–59, however, "it was on the second Thursday of the Month of January 1765." SJ's pocket diary for 1765–78 (Hyde Collection) reads "[Jan.] 9 Wedn. At Mr Trails."
3. James Woodhouse (1735–1820), the shoemaker-poet, who had "been asked to some Tables, should likewise be asked to ours, and made a Temptation to Mr Johnson to meet him: accordingly he came, and Mr Murphy at four o'clock brought Mr Johnson to dinner. We liked each other so well that the next Thursday was appointed for the same company to meet—exclusive of the Shoemaker" (*Thraliana* 1:159).
4. *English Poets* 2:150.

TO JOHN SALUSBURY PIOZZI SALUSBURY

Brynbella
15: October 1810.

Accept Dear Salusbury these collected Trifles, put together to pass Time which glides too slowly in your Absence; and to convince you of my fond Esteem by throwing into your Hands the favoured Follies of my Youth, joined here to those you have so often witnessed—as kind Companions to my declining Years.

The Book will at least excite one useful Reflexion:[1] That since our Original Taste in Amusement never quits us, tis happy when safe and honourable ones are chosen; for if I feel ashamed even of this empty Employment—and at 70 Years of Age confess an Apology necessary for copying out Nonsense never worth much regard; What must become of those who pass in vicious Pleasures their Sunshiny Day, when lengthening Shadows shew it near a Close?

That the Friend of my Choice, and the Child of my Soul may be the Providence of God 'scape *such* Calamity, will be the parting Prayer, and firm perswasion of / His truly Affectionate Aunt / Hester Lynch Piozzi.

Text: Harvard MS Eng. 1280 (bound into "Harvard Piozziana").

1. HLP had enclosed in this letter several poems and anecdotes which she used to preface the "Harvard Piozziana." Begun on the very day this letter was written, the five manuscript volumes (ca. 285 folio sheets) ended on 2 May 1814. She entitled the whole "Poems on Several Occasions with Anecdotes, &c., introductory to the *Poems, Piozziana* and *Scrap and Trifle Book.*"

TO JOHN SALUSBURY PIOZZI SALUSBURY

Brynbella Monday
21: October 1810.

Why My Dearest Salusbury—
   Thou art like Hamlet's Ghost—coming

   "To whet my almost blunted Purpose"[1]

but I am like Hamlet who never felt his Purpose *blunted at all.* You saw the Letter I wrote to Doctor Hall's Lady,[2] who never answered it. You would have made yourself a stronger Interest in her Memory, could I have kept you at home half an hour that Morning in Wellbeck Street when Mr. Byng had told us She intended to call. But what can be done—on *my* Part—shall not be neglected. I have written to the Doctor himself, and I have written to Tall Townsend of Bath to coax him to write to his old Acquaintance—he professes Intimacy you know with the Dean of Christ Church.[3] As for Byng, I have no Notion where he *is*—— In his joking way he said when we parted, that if he did not come to see the reigning Dutchess of Brynbella——She might assure herself He was gone to pay his Compliments to the Queen of The Hottentots—meaning he would be sent to his Duty at the Cape of Good Hope. I do not however believe he is gone thither, and if I can light on any Direction by which to find him out, I will shoot A Letter at him, which may or not reach according to my Skill at taking Aim: so this leads me to Your other Wish about the Gun. Leak seems very surly about it, and considers the Expence of fetching and carrying the Box as wholly unnecessary, not seeing why the Gun may not accompany Its Master home again. I *do* see why: because I wish You to come home through Llangollen, and call on the Ladies there——and win *their* hearts; and Secure *their* good Liking: It is worth more than one is aware of, to stand well with the Ladies of Llangollen.

Lady Kirkwall canvassed them divinely, and they are now *all on her Side*—— and I am *so* glad.

Mrs. Mostyn has been with me Three or four Days——and the Rain has kept us *constantly close together*, yet has Your Name nor Lady K———'s ever passed her Lips or mine.[4] Harry must certainly find it a dull Visit—Yet here they are, and Sophia Daniel with them[5]——*She* will from our Servants hear all the Gossip no doubt, and make a famous Report.——Our Folks all seem quite doating on them.

Marianne writes me word of a New Acquaintance *She* has made of a *good* Young Man Frederick Doveton by Name:[6] who was frighted from the University by its *Wickedness*.[7] I trust it is like the World where as Your Old Greek Proverb says The Majority is Wicked.[8]

By the way I am in ill Thoughts of your intended Servant *Bill*——and wish you could pick up a Shropshire or a Berkshire Boy——You may remember I did not look pleased when *he was recommended*——and I am *not pleased now*.

Here is my Letter to *Dr.* Hall

Presuming an Old Acquaintance with dear Mrs. Hall I took The Liberty about Six Weeks ago to trouble Her with a Letter concerning my Nephew Mr. Salusbury who is Impatient to be entered as Gentleman Commoner at Christ Church: but I feel it was a foolish Thing to plague *her* about it, and as Mr. Edmund Byng was kind enough to apply himself as long ago as last May, when he shewed Me a Letter He had received in Return from You Sir—with undeserved Expressions of Polite Attentions towards Me; I take the Liberty of reminding you that there *are* such Persons as Myself and My adopted Son; who solicit Your Patronage, and will endeavour to deserve the honour of Your Protection. Will it be too much to request a Line of Information whether in February, March, or April. This Youth may present himself as Candidate for a Happiness so eagerly solicited by Sir / Your most Obedient / humble Servant / Hester Lynch Piozzi.

Well! and now I have done this Feat I suppose I may hang myself, but Indeed I have Many more Feats to perform before I can go to Sleep under the Stone Night Cap with a quiet Mind.

Mr. Maughan and Mr. Oldfield never come near me, and here is good Planting Weather, and I shall get my Trees in high Order to put out, if there was Hope of fencing or doing any Thing—except subscribing to the Pillar on Moel Vamma in honour of our 50 Years Reign;[9] concerning which Dear Doctor Myddelton will certainly go raving mad, and never for A moment Think of Those School Lands,[10] or of anything else Projected by your poor H: L: Piozzi.

Farewell dearest Child—and I *would fain* say don't be too *anxious*, but that so saying I should reproach myself for *living* in Anxiety——Sure, Sure, I shall not die thinking of this Vile World its Cares and Affections—Oh that would be *too* bad after 70 Years continuation in it.

Give my very best Regards to Pemberton——and to the Flock not of Sheep but of Shephards.

Text: Ry. 585.78. *Address:* John Piozzi Salusbury Esq. / At The Reverend: Thos. Shephards / Enborne / near Newbury / Berkshire. *Postmark:* DENBIGH 224 (In JSPS's hand, "Received Octr 25th. Answered Octr 26th Do")

1. *Hamlet*, 3.4.110–11.
2. Anna Maria Bridget Hall, née Byng.
3. Dr. Charles Henry Hall.
4. HLP believed CMM to be jealous of Q's baby and JSPS as potential rivals of her sons.
5. CMM's housekeeper at Segroid.
6. In a letter postmarked 5 October 1810 (Ry. 583.65), Marianne Francis wrote: "Frederic Doveton was here today—an Oxford Scholar, and a very religious young man, who like You, reads nothing but his Bible, though he has not, like you, read every thing else."
7. Frederick Doveton (1788–1871), of Blackheath, Kent. He had matriculated at Corpus Christi College on 26 April 1807, receiving his B.A. in 1809 and M.A. in 1813. In 1819 he became rector of South Normanton, Derbyshire.
8. HLP read the proverb in *Rambler* 175, SJ attributing it to Bias. For SJ's sources, see the *Greek Anthology*, 9.366, and Diogenes Laertius, *Lives*, "Bias," 1.5 (paragraph 88).
9. Thomas Harrison (1744–1829) designed the obelisk erected on Moel Vammau, Denbighshire, to commemorate the golden jubilee of George III.
10. At this time the Reverend Robert Myddelton of Gwaynynog was actively raising money to buy land on which to build a Blue Coat school in Denbigh. It was founded in 1816 and continued to flourish well into the nineteenth century.

TO JOHN SALUSBURY PIOZZI SALUSBURY

Brynbella
1: November 1810.

My dearest Soul—

I *live* but to keep you out of *Ill*, and put you into *Good* so far as my Powers are able: Get Mr. Shephard to procure you such a Servant as he approves—and let him settle the Wages. He and you both know I care for Money *only for your Sake*——so does Hammersley——He writes me Word that he has done what's right about our *mutual* Transactions at the Bankers——I apply now always to George Hammersley himself[1]—since last Year that the *Clerks* transfered Mr. Shephard's Money to me, instead of mine to him, which by the Way Leak was the Man to find out. He, *Leak* is very acute; and very honest, and very useful—nay necessary to us, and does best for your Interest I *am confident* with regard to the Farming Concern——Oh dearest Salusbury! do you think I would *endure him an hour* if I was not so perswaded?——Let us but see these next four Years out[2]—together,—and *then*——We will turn over a new Leaf never doubt it: and in the Mean time your Determination to be *civil* and *distant,* is like all your Determinations, founded in good Sense.

> Good Sense! which only is the Gift of heaven
> And though no Science—fairly worth the Seven.[3]

Well! here is the desired Letter come from Doctor Hall, as kind as one *can* desire; and so your Fortune is fixed, and my Child must be launched into Life, The second Week after Good Fryday next——I feel all over Goose-Skin at the Thought on't——knowing as I do, how sharp Folks are looking to see whether You make Slips or no,—That they may be ready to push You quite down. As for the Letter I will copy it on the other Side—Tho' I could have written as good a Letter myself, *without* University Education.

Christ Church
27: October

Madam

Mrs. Hall would certainly have answered the Letter She had The pleasure of receiving from You some Time ago if she had not been Ill at the Time, and ever since She has been with her Sister at Hopwood.[4] I beg now to inform you that I shall be happy to receive Mr. Salusbury here, at The Time I originally mentioned to my Brother in Law Mr. Edmund Byng, the beginning that is of Easter Term. That will be the second Week after Good Fryday. I will take Care however to let you know in proper Time the precise Day on which he ought to be here. I have the honour to be / Madam / Your faithful and Obedient Servant / Charles Henry Hall.

So now dismiss all Anxiety excepting for your own *Scholarship* and *Virtue* and *Honour* for they alone are necessary to your well being at *Oxford*—in *Heaven,* and in *this Life.*

A little Anxiety for Your poor H:L:P I will permit you though: because *She* too is necessary to your Well being these four Years—and then——what then?—A merry Dinner Dear Aunt say you, and a happy Day. *Be it so.*

Pemberton's Letter is charming——I half believe *that* Rogue does love us; but how can You or he be such *Pugs* as to suppose I would send you to the Ladies of Llangollen without a *fine Letter* from Mrs. Piozzi, written with her *best Pen,* and in her *finest hand.* Not *like this:* but I am in a hurry to send this to St. Asaph, where I shall order Horses for a Visit to Bodylwyddan tomorrow;[5] Yes indeed, and stay till Monday; and dine that Day at the Bishop's Palace and home at Night. Here's Raking for you!

Have no Thought about *Bill;* he will do *me* no harm—if his Propensities *are* as I suspect——and his good old honest Father is dying; and I would not for the World hurt the Wretch, if he *is* the Wretch I fear he is inclined to be. My Duty must be done you know; come Good, come Evil; because *My* Accounts must *soon* be shewed up at any Rate, and I must keep the Page clean.

The Duke of Argylle is not of that Mind I trust——After living almost *openly* as even *you know* with Lady William Russel for many years,[6] he will marry no one but *her Sister*—the deserted Lady Paget[7]—whose husband is wild to wed his *own* favourite, Lady Charlotte Wellesley for whom he neglected his Wife.[8]

But the virtuous Doctors of Civil Law in England will not grant the Divorce——so they apply to the Scotch Legislature which says If they will all four kneel down on the bare Stones before an Open Bible and swear they do not each get rid of the other for the Sake of marrying some one else, and if they will solemnly call down upon Themselves, Their Offspring, and their *Cattle* all the Curses in that Book if they have any *unowned Meaning* in requesting this Divorce;——why Lord and Lady Paget shall be parted, and it shall be lawful for all Parties then to do *how they like*. Lady Charlotte was separated from Mr. Wellesley at the Beginning of this Affair, but Lord Paget could not marry because his Wife had done nothing for which he could divorce her. Here *will* be Enormity, if you talk of Enormity: but it is not yet committed—and I hope Some thing will happen to hinder it. I work at my Task, and intolerable as the Paper is, have finished 100 Pages in the Month.[9]

Mrs. M_____ hindered me three Days—Oh *Six* Days She hindered me. Her inviting Harry Hughes to Segroid was curious enough—Andrew of *course* because of the Garden Things: The old Man (Nancy says) never had such a *Welcoming* in all his Life—Leake *roughed* them at last, and bid them mind their Employers, and not be dangling after Mrs. Mostyn so. I watch them *all* as narrowly as I can, and wish my Spirit higher, and my Nerves Stronger for your Sake——but four Years will fly away——May I *but* last till Then!

October never passes without affronting me—I had a Bilious Attack but it was trifling; *only* a Menace: *Your* good Conduct will keep me alive to hear of it. The poor pretty Greyhound is very Ill—of the Distemper as they call it: Owen is in Despair. The Horses quite well,—and the Gun arrived,—and I hope every thing as *you wish it*. Write *soon* and say so. Say you are well and happy for that is the true Cordial to your H: L: P.

Why will Pem. and you write by the *same* Post? Give my best Regards to him.

Text: Ry. 585.79. *Address:* John Piozzi Salusbury Esq. / at The / Rev: Thos. Shephards / Enborne / near Newbury / Berkshire. *Postmark:* ST. ASAPH <218> (In JSPS's hand, "Received Novr 4th 1810. Answered Do 6th Do")

---

1. Educated briefly at Harrow, George Hammersley (1785–1835) became a member of [Thomas] Hammersley and Company, 76 Pall Mall. After the death of Thomas Hammersley in 1812, the bank changed its name to Hammersley, Brooksbank, Greenwood, and Drew. In 1840 it was absorbed by Messrs. Coutts.
2. In four years JSPS will have come of age.
3. Pope, *Epistle IV. To Richard Boyle, Earl of Burlington*, lines 43–44.
4. Mrs. Hall was visiting her sister Cecilia Hopwood at Hopwood Hall, Lancashire.
5. HLP was planning a weekend with Sir John and Lady Williams at Bodelwyddan, only four miles from the bishop's residence in Saint Asaph.
6. For Lady Charlotte Anne Villiers (d. 1808), eldest daughter of the fourth earl of Jersey, who in 1789 had married Lord William Russell, see HLP to Q, 13 November 1793, n. 3.
7. George William Campbell (1768–1839), sixth duke of Argyll (1806), was on 29 November 1810

to marry Caroline Elizabeth, a younger daughter of the fourth earl of Jersey. Her previous marriage with Henry William, Lord Paget, had been dissolved in Scotland at her request. See HLP to Q, 19 March 1809, n. 15.

8. Lord Paget, shortly after his wife divorced him, married in 1810 Charlotte, previously the wife of Sir Henry Wellesley, G.C.B. (later first baron Cowley), and daughter of the first earl of Cadogan. See HLP to Q, 19 March 1809, n. 14.

9. That is, on "Harvard Piozziana."

TO CLEMENT FRANCIS

Brynbella
13: November 1810.

My Dear Sir

I thank you for your nice Letter——and would have You ask that Clever Mr. Frey if any of the Jews are good Genealogists,[1] and can count back their Families for seven Generations—it would facilitate our Computation of the Time's Approach.—For I nothing doubt but that as from Abraham to David were 14 Generations,—from David to the carrying away Captive 14 Generations, and from that Time to the Birth of Jesus Christ 14 Generations; (see the 1st Chapter of St. Matthew—)[2] so from Messiah's human Birth to his coming again in Glory will be 14 Generations.—Every Thing going as it does, by *Sabbaths* and *Septenaries*.—Abraham was *One and Twentieth*,—Three *Sevens* from Adam you know: and the Idea of a Seventh Son being a wise Man, is hardly yet out of the World. One would think you were a 7th Son yourself—so thoughtful as You are.[3]

We are on *Tiptoe* here listening after Guns at a Distance which we hope are firing at Liverpool for the good News.[4] Lord Wellington must needs know that *his* Countryfolks never look at the Merits of a General but by the strong and splendid Light of a Victory:[5] He will be therefore much in Earnest——and Massena must fight or be *undone*.[6] It is a critical Moment.[7] The good it would do our best beloved Sovereign makes it still more important—his poor Nerves have Been *so* shattered; yet something tells me he will yet recover——a Victory in Portugal would save him——Godspeed the Account.[8]

Well! you were right enough about that odious Mr. Atkins;[9] Those Rumours like the swelling of a West Indian Sea—portended a coming Hurricane—He is now I suppose safe in the Kings Bench—drunk and happy——Charles Shephard and Mr. Windle must squeeze the dirty Orange—and then fling it away.

Marianne continues at Richmond—Give my true Love to her, and best Regards to Mr. and Mrs. Barrett:[10] I will write soon—but have a little Task in hand just now which takes up all my Time.

This is a *black Letter* Performance like your own,—never say Mrs. Piozzi writes *well* any more:—but assure Yourself that tho' I am going out of the World, I do not feel unconcerned for you that remain in it——My heart has long told me that Serious Times are coming forward—and *that*,—rapidly.

Jacob wandered 19 Years[11]—Mr. White will tell you; and arrived at *home* just at their Close; his last Boy was born on the *Confines*—Son of my Sorrow—said his Mother who expired—as I suppose Judaism will, when 19 Centuries are nearly elapsed, Annus pro die imputabitur.—But his Father called him Son of *his right Hand*[12]——and I have a Notion that these latter Jews will be highly favoured of Heaven in some way—a *double* Portion of Prosperity——Well! you will see how it is, You that are so young: and if a Precursor Prophet starts up to instruct them &c. *You* will not wonder; but something more striking will certainly be seen than a Subscription from *Penny Societies* among the low Classes of our crouded Metropolis——altho' this may be the noise of the Water under the Ice, roaring before a general and Apparently-sudden *Thaw*—which if a Skaiter,—You must have observed.[13]

Adieu dear Sir and give my Love to Mama and Dolph, and Dolph's Niece little Julia[14] and accept the same Yourself from / Your Obliged / and faithful / H: L: Piozzi.

Salusbury goes to Christ Church Oxford immediately after Easter. And Then I shall come to London but not before: he is at Enborne *now.*

Write sometimes and tell what is going forward and whether Stock rises or falls with these reports of Victory and Defeat—and Sickness and Sorrow.

Text: Berg Collection, m.b. *Address:* Clement Francis Esq. / No. 10: / Chenies Street / Bedford Square / London. *Postmark:* DENBIGH 224; E 16 NO 16 1810.

1. Joseph Samuel Christian Frederick Frey (1771–1850) was an authority on Judaica and on Hebrew grammar. A popular lecturer, he spoke often on the subject of Christ as Messiah.

2. Matt. 1:17: "So all the generations from Abraham to David, are fourteen generations; and from David until the carrying away into Babylon, are fourteen generations; and from the carrying away into Babylon unto Christ, are fourteen generations."

3. Alongside of "Enoch walked with God" (Gen. 5:24), HLP wrote in her 1770 Bible: "Well! he was 7th from Adam and was *perfect.* . . . Quere have not we fancied peculiar Vertues in a 7th Son ever since?

"Seven is the perfect Number sure enough; composed of 4 and 3: and set apart as Sabbatical. 7 Millenaries of Existence are probably destined to our little Planet, 6 laborious—and the 7th Sabbatical."

4. The Liverpool guns were being fired in response to information cited by a Falmouth newspaper which "states, with confidence, 'that the French are Retreating, and that Massena *had already begun to remove his heavy baggage and his advanced guards before the packet sailed.* . . . it was understood Ld. Wellington did not mean to follow with his whole army, but to annoy his retreat by cavalry and light troops only. Massena had attempted to cross the Tagus, by throwing a bridge of boats over from Santarem, but these have been completely destroyed by our gun-boats and artillery. [The large number of deserters] represent the French army as suffering the extreme of want and wretchedness. It was rumoured that Massena had offered terms to Lord Wellington; but this was not ascertained. . . . The British army were in high health and spirits, and confident that Massena's army must be almost all destroyed in their wretched retreat through a deserted country, in this rainy season.'" See the *Courier,* 13 November.

5. Arthur Wellington had been created Baron Douro of Wellesley, Somerset, and Viscount Wellington of Talavera and Wellington, Somerset, 4 September 1809.

6. General Masséna was associated in HLP's mind with the Army of Italy, whose command he held intermittently from 1800 to 1808, being appointed maréchal in 1804 and created duc de Rivoli in 1808. In April 1809 he took over the Fourth Corps of the Army of Germany and fought so successfully that in January 1810 he was made prince d'Essling.

By April 1810 he was in command of the Army of Portugal, only to be repulsed by Wellington's Anglo-Portuguese Army at Bussaco on 27 September. News of the Allied victory at Bussaco reached

England in a *London Gazette Extraordinary,* 14 October, which contained Wellington's account, dated Coimbra, September 30.

7. Following the battle of Bussaco, British anxiety mounted as people questioned Masséna's new strategy in Portugal.

See, e.g., in the *Courier* for 29 October a report from a Dublin paper: "'We have it in our power to extract an important fact from intelligence, which we give with the fullest confidence of its authenticity, and which is dated at the head-quarters of the allied army in Portugal, on the 16th instant. . . . On the day just stated, it was understood in Lord Wellington's army . . . that Masséna would not delay his grand attack more than three or four days. The Allies expected it with feelings that strongly anticipated victory, and therefore wished it.'"

The *Courier,* however, on 10 November admitted that no news from Wellington had been received in nearly a month and the newspaper—rightly so—was "inclined to believe no battle had been fought up to the 22d of last month."

8. On 30 October, the *Courier* reported that the king had a cold, but it soon altered its statement to one which indicated that he was emotionally affected by the imminent death of Princess Amelia and by one incident in particular, which involved her giving him a ring with her hair worked into it and with the inscription, *"Remember me when I am gone."* See the *Courier,* 2 November 1810.

The king could not take in her death on 2 November. Dr. Henry Revell Reynolds, the king's physician in ordinary, saw him on 3 November and ordered that he be restrained.

On 9 November, however, a remission occurred so that he could understand that Amelia was dead. He did not attend her funeral on the 13th. Two days later, he experienced a second paroxysm; this was succeeded by a third and fourth before the year's end.

9. As recorded in her "Pocket Book" for 1810: "22 May, Arrived at home—heard of Atkins's Bankruptcy. A melancholy meeting with Atkins who disputes the Taxes." (Actually, Abraham Atkins's bankruptcy "as merchant, dealer, and chapman" of Finsbury Square was not reported in the newspapers until 3 December 1810. See the *Courier* and *The Times* for that date.)

The difficulties with Atkins continued. On 11 June 1810 she wrote: "Terrible News from Hammersley. Atkins has paid nothing: and no Letter from Windle who assured me I might at least depend upon the *Balance* from Streatham, tho' my Tenant refused paying the Taxes. And now Nothing." And on 12 November, she concluded: "Mr. Atkins already in Prison. What can become for poor Streatham Park?" (Ry. 616).

10. HLP refers to Clement Francis's elder sister Charlotte, who had married Henry Barrett (1756–1843). At this time they had one child, Julia Charlotte (1808–64). For Charlotte Barrett, see HLP to Clement Francis, 28 July 1810, n. 10.

11. In Gen. 31:38 Jacob says to Laban, "This twenty years have I been with thee." There is a biblical tradition of using the closest round number for a specific figure. Perhaps this is how HLP arrived at nineteen years for Jacob's wandering. However it was arrived at, the figure nineteen was essential to her belief in the Jews' conversion to Christ after wandering for nineteen centuries. See her gloss in the Imperial Family Bible (which she owned) for Dan. 12:7: "Before the Second Coming can occur, the Jews must be called home: Oh! that will happen in the 19th Century I doubt not. Rebekah was barren 19 Years before She brought Jacob and Esau: and Jacob wandered 19 Years before he could get home."

12. Rachel, at the cost of her own life, gave birth to Benjamin, her second son, while on the way from Bethel to Ephrath. Just before she died, she called this son Ben-oni (Son of my Sorrow) but Jacob later named him Benjamin, i.e., "son of the right hand." See Gen. 35:16–19, 48:7.

13. In her Imperial Bible, HLP was to gloss Gen. 48:7.

"Yes, Rachel died upon the Confines of the promised Land, and was not laid in the Family Burial Place.

"Judaism will perhaps so expire, just before Christ's 2d. Coming.

"Jacob wandered 19 Years before he got home, and perhaps his Progeny may wander 19 Centuries in Darkness and Distress.

"It is *now* [1820] not long till then, only 80 Years, and

"*Then* perhaps; or soon after, they shall look on him of whom Joseph was a Type; their merciful, their forgiving *Saviour.*"

Similar ideas are expressed in the marginalia of her copy of William Dodd, *A Commentary on the Books of the Old and New Testament,* 3 vols. (1770); i.e., Gen. 32:25; Isa. 49:22, 66:7; Jer. 23:5–6.

14. For "Dolph" Broome, see HLP to Clement Francis, 28 July 1810, n. 10; for Julia, see above, n. 10.

TO JOHN SALUSBURY PIOZZI SALUSBURY

> Brynbella written Tuesday—
> Sent Wednesday 13: November 1810.

My dearest Salusbury *did* send me a Cordial in his last welcome Letter; I had just been complaining of your Silence and Lady Kirkwall's, when the Post came—and told me I ought *never* to complain with *such* a Child and *such* a Friend.

Enclosed you receive a Letter for Mr. Shephard breaking the Ice——and begging the greatest possible favour *for You* and *from him*.[1] What Profession You will pitch upon remains to be seen, but mine will be that of a *Solicitor* during whats to come of *my* Life I perceive.—Ah poor Salusbury! There was a Time when *that* Part was easier to me, and more likely to be successful—You are just arrived to *tilt the Cask,* and get the *Dregs* of what would have been *Thrale's Intire* had the *Ladies been Less severe.*

Mr. Charles Shephard is pacifying them as well as he can concerning Atkins's Depredations.[2] I shall have a fine Expence with that shocking Fellow, who is already in Prison it seems; you will perceive therefore that My Income will cut short in the Place least expected,—for I have no Tenant now, and Repairs to pay and all. Said I not well that 'tis on *You*—I depend for Consolation? Charles Shephard approves of my Task—which indeed goes on worse than I *wish*—but I dare say better than You *hope:*——The Old Pantaloon in a Harlequin Farce, that runs *with all his Speed,* and makes *no Way,* is a true Emblem of Your H:L:P.[3] but we make huge Way with our Farm-Yard Improvements—The Barn has got good Doors and the Place is walled in neatly, and We have made a Hovel for the Horses to shelter in——and People will say how wrong that is, but we must not mind *sayers of Speeches,* or we shall do nothing at all. The People were always telling Me how to manage my Children—*when* to put them to School, and *where* to put them, but in a *resolute Mind* is as *necessary* as a soft manner is *pleasing.*

Suaviter in Modo, fortiter in Re is my Motto.[4] The Plantations are Thinning too, just opposite the back Drawing-Room Windows——and I feel my Heart bleed under the Ax: but nothing shall hinder my doing what will benefit your tiny Wood by strengthening our few—our *very* few Timber Trees; none of them as old as Yourself.

When Louis quatorze went to visit Le Duc d'Antin he admired the Place excessively—but said I wonder Monsieur le Duc that you should suffer that fine Avenue of Oaks to keep out the Beauties of the surrounding Country——no Reply was made, and Preparations for amusing his Majesty filled the Day and Night. Next Morning the King walked out with the Master of the Mansion. The Avenue was gone——How's this? said Louis amazed. "Nothing can *live* Sire under Your Condemnation, The Oaks are no more." This was agreeable Flattery.[5]

But I have not told you about Bodylwyddan; They all ask for *you* there, and all speak highly of You—and they have asked You and I to celebrate John Williams's Birthday and Hughey's;[6] they are the 8th and 9th of next January, and there will

13 November 1810 315

be Dancing and crouding and Music and Suppers, and All the pretty Misses—and Masters *too* within 20 Miles of the Place. I have no Room for *both:* but I have something pleasing *besides* to tell you, and something *Di*spleasing: I think I will keep the one and the other for my next Letter——and then there will be *Balance.*

Greyhound is got well; *I* cured him with Hasty Pudding and Laudanum; poor Wretch!——he wanted no James's Powders; he had a desperate Diarrhæa. The King has Hæmorrhoids and Dysentery—very bad *indeed,* and A temporary Brain Fever beside—but my Trust is he will yet recover. Robert Sayer has got *his* senses again, why should not his Betters do so too?

> Unless Misfortune makes The Throne her Seat,
> And none to be unhappy but the Great.[7]

Oh I am confident our Prayers saved George the 3rd in the Year 1788 and surely he is of more Consequence to us now than he was *then:*[8] my Heart feels warm *hope* of his getting well again.

And who do you think has got 1200£ Prize in the Lottery? Why your old Friend Plummer, Mr. Davies of Streatham's House-keeper—a 16th of the 20000£.

Dear Salusbury! I hope Good Luck will follow all who love You, and Above all your / truly Affectionate Aunt / H: L: Piozzi.

Give my true Regards to Pem. I have a strange Tale to tell him of his Namesake William Edward FitzMaurice.[9] *Write soon.*

Text: Ry. 585.80. *Address:* John Piozzi Salusbury Esq. / at The Rev: Thos. Shephard's / Enborne / near Newbury / Berkshire. *Postmark:* DENBIGH 224 (In JSPS's hand, "Received Novr 17th. Answered 18th Do").

1. HLP's letter to Thomas Shephard is missing but she apparently had asked the schoolmaster to write on behalf of JSPS and to send his recommendation to Dean Hall of Christ Church.
2. HT had left HLP a life interest in Streatham Park and complete possession of the contents. After her death, however, the estate was to go to his daughters. HLP knew, therefore, that she was responsible for the house and its maintenance, not merely for herself but for her children.
In response to Q's questions about Streatham Park, HLP wrote on 12 November: "I have meanwhile done my Duty towards counteracting the Evil [stemming from Atkins's bankruptcy and his abandonment of Streatham Park]; I have commenced an expensive Process against Mr. Atkins—that so, however I may suffer, no Injury shall befall my fair Reversionaries" (Bowood Collection).
On 29 November HLP was again to write to Q concerning Streatham Park: "Mr. Shephard has put a Man into Streatham Park in whom he has particular Confidence; and I hope no more Mischief will be done. The Gardens are in good Order he tells me. . . . Atkins must have made monstrous Advantage,—but like Dr. Goldsmith's *knowing-one* he is gone to Goal; and his old Landlord *Farm*borough will die in nobody's Debt notwithstanding" (Bowood Collection).
3. A traditional pantomime figure, Pantaloon is the old man—later Columbine's father, guardian, or husband—in the harlequinade where he is the butt of the clown's practical jokes. For this stock movement—running in place—performed by Pantaloon, see James Messink's *The Elopement* (1 October 1776).
4. See HLP to SL, 30 April 1785, n. 17.
5. HLP repeats a well-known anecdote concerning Antoine de Pardaillon de Gondrin (ca. 1665–1736), duc d'Antin, the archetype of a perfect courtier (Larousse, *Grand Dictionnaire universel du xixe Siècle* [1866], 1:446). HLP has embroidered her earlier version, *Retrospection* 2:264.
6. John Williams was now sixteen and his brother Hugh eight.

7. See the prologue of *The Fair Penitent* (1703): "As if misfortune made the throne her seat, / And none could be unhappy but the great."
8. For the king's first bout of mental illness, in early June 1788, and the struggle over the nature of the regency, see HLP to Sophia Byron, 29 June 1788, n. 9; to SL, 15 November [1788], n. 17; to TSW, 5 January [1789], n. 3.
9. Lady Kirkwall's younger son, now five years old.

TO JOHN SALUSBURY PIOZZI SALUSBURY

Thursday 6th: December 1810.

I think Dearest Salusbury—That Enborne is the Place whence I am to look for Kindness: Pem's Letter was very obliging—and Mr. Shephard is good natured in the Extreme: You must help me to Thank him for us both. Davies of Streatham has sent me an Epistle I can in no *way,* and in no *wise* decypher: whether in Jest or Earnest however, it is completely offensive and disgusting—I dispatched it to Charles Shephard who will tell a plain Tale and make others tell it—against any Man I know. "When will you come and see the *Park in Ruins?"* are Mr. Davies's last Words—but he uses some Expressions concerning the Difference between my *present Management* and that of *the old Regime* alluding to Mr. Thrale's Time; that I do not easily swallow down—without help of a Whalebone and Spunge. It was *He* who set Lord and Lady Keith upon me I perceive: but perhaps it may yet be long before his Lordship is entitled to what he is so zealous about—meaning the 4th Part of the Profits of poor dear Streatham, *after my Demise. You* must keep me alive by your good Conduct at Oxford and every where else. I *know* how *keenly* it will be watched. I *know* too that Superfluous Attention is the only Way I shall ever take to injure You: and even *that* shall be moderated if it can possibly do you the least Prejudice.

We shall surely meet soon now, and talk the whole *Talk* thro'. I have much to *Say* that is not so well to *write*——but do not let every Word of every Friend sink deeply in Your Mind. Many Words (as I once observed to You about Advice concerning Servants Children &c.) are said to shew the Importance of the Adviser,——or to fill up Time;—or 20 Reasons. Let us resolve to hear *gracefully,—* to reply *politely;—*to behave *steadily*——and to keep in Scripture Phrase, our *Souls unspotted* by *the World.*[1]

I am going for a few Days to Bodylwyddan to comfort the Dear Williamses. My Task is done; and laid by for your *Admiration.* After Duty comes Pleasure.——

Will you have a Baronets Daughter without a Guinea—five Years hence? She will be *good,* and *pretty;* and *take place* of Mrs. Hoare and Mrs. Mostyn in every Assembly room——but I don't know how She'll contrive to *purchase The Ticket.*

No Time to add more Nonsense, I am very well: and shall put this in the Post at St. Asaph as we go along——If you do not come home to conclude the Old Year with me; you will not deserve half the Blessings and Prayers with which I am wearying Heaven to procure You a happy 1811. Adieu! and rest perswaded that *my* Affection——perhaps mine *alone;* is *wholly* disinterested. While you are good and wise and kind—*That* Affection you do most positively command / from Yours and Your *only* / H: L: Piozzi.

I have *two* Projects in hand, but shall disclose neither of them till We meet—God send it a happy Meeting!² Glover is calling me to be dressed. Farewell.

Make my proper Compliments, Thanks &c. &c. We shall have A Gay Time on the 7th 8th and 9th of January notwithstanding *les Maux po<da>gres.*³

Text: Ry. 585. 83. *Address:* John P: Salusbury Esq. / At The / Rev: Thos. Shephard's / Enborne / Near Newbury / Berks.
Postmark: <3M>.

1. James 1:27.
2. HLP's projects were to make JSPS the heir to her property and to get him a baronetcy.
3. *Maux podagres:* gout in the foot.

TO LADY WILLIAMS

Tuesday Night
December 11th 1810

My dear Lady Williams

Will kindly rejoyce that I got home safe thro' a famous Snow indeed. I found more letters on my Table at returning to the old Green Room—one from Miss Williams with *not a Word* concerning her *other Brothers;* but numberless tender Enquiries about Bodylwyddan. She seems to write in good Spirits, says every one is kind to *her*—that Sir John's health mends &c. with a heap of Chit Chat which She begs me to *burn as Important,* but which can*not* be important to any human Creature, at least I think not;—for what has Lady Callender's Rouge box to do with any one but herself and her Maid?

When I examined Sweet Lady K's Letter more minutely, I found still more Tender Friendship towards myself, and a Resolution to insist on my residing with her when in London. She has got a new House in Manchester Street—and tho' a Nutshell She says—I shall command it &c. This is an offer I never had—no nor a *Hint* of any such Offer from any of Mr. Thrale's Daughters in Town or Country—Tho' I have slept I suppose six Times in my Life at *Segroid;* but I mean the two Married Ladies in London, or Susan Thrale who has a Country Seat 16 miles off.

Well Dear Madam! but you would rather hear how my Cold does—The Voice, Smell, and Taste are *all gone;* so if any one says Mrs. Piozzi has lost *her Senses* it will be a truer Report than many which have been raised upon her. The Throat is less sore however; and The Sickness less troublesome, but I must eat no more *Pattès* made by dear little *Willy's own Receipt.*

Weak plain Mutton Broth is all I have lived on since we parted, no need to covet kind Lady Williams's excellent Cook. Adieu Dear Madam! and continue as happy as you *are*, as happy as you *deserve*, and as happy as You are *wished* to be by / Your Ladyship's and Dear Sir John's / most exceedingly Obliged / H: L: Piozzi.

Text: Ry. 3 (1807–11). *Address:* Lady Williams / Bodylwyddan / St. Asaph. *Postmark:* DENBIGH 22<4>.

TO JOHN SALUSBURY PIOZZI SALUSBURY

         Brynbella
         Wednesday 15: December 1810.

My dearest Salusbury
 had better pay Sixpence more, than not have his Letter for the Ladies; It will be always an Introduction to them, come what may.[1] When others are lowspirited they sit *still*. When I am *happy*, I sit *still:* but when lowspirited I begin looking round me to see what is wanted that it may be done before I'm called away. Perhaps this Lesson was learned in the Year 1781 or 1782—when Mr. Cator called to make me sign over my Whole Estate in Mortgage to *The Miss Thrales* because I wanted Money to pay Lady Salusbury—and *they* were to take all possible Advantages of my poor Empty Purse.[2] "My Mistress is ill in her Bed Sir," exclaimed the Maid. "*I'll* say you! replies Cator; Shew me to her *directly* then; and let's make her sign over the Deed, before *She slips thro' our Fingers*." I rose and signed——and by God's Mercy have lived to *see it Cancelled;* and my Land *my own* again——Poor Cator *gone too* to answer for his unprovoked Severity.[3] When I think how many People will be in danger of Punishment for having used me ill in this Life——it makes my very heart sick——but you were sent to compensate me for all.
 Doctor Gray—Author of the Key to the Old Testament has not forgotten me; he writes—*very* kindly—and hopes *his* Nephew and *mine* will continue *our* Friendship thro' the next Generation.[4] I have had some true Friends—Dear Lady Kirkwall a cordial one:——She was within a Hair's Breadth of Death—or a fractured Skull The other Day.—Lay senseless and speechless for many hours—but waked in Lady de Blaquiere's Arms—Mrs. Mostyn is at Cheltenham.——*Her* Sister in Law (Married to Garthvrino,) is ready to lye in; So She will have another *Salusbury* to guard against.[5] Mrs. Wynne has her Estate wholly in *her own Power,* like myself:[6] whether She will be *as* scrupulously attentive to do Good to those who *despitefully* use her— I know not:——If She *is*; it will be the better for young Mostyn.
 Your Agnes de Sorel is as rough, and as playful as a Colt——a true *Sorèl:* did I ever tell you why they call a Yellow Horse a *Sorrel* Horse? It is because the Name of a Fawn the second Year is *Sorèl* in French: We had all our *Stag hunting* Terms from France; and all our Military, and all our *Culinary* Terms. For Example,

The Ox in the *Field* turns *Beef Bœuf* upon the Table;—The Calf is Veal from *Veau:* The Sheep is *Mouton* and so on. Your Spatter-dash Things are Guêtres because worne by the *Watch*—le *Guest:* or leaving out the *s*, le *Guêt*—with a Caret or Circumflex over——to denote that there is a Letter *wanting*. What Profundity of Knowlege!! yet few People dig as deep.

Dear Love! when will you come home? I am very tired of sitting *alone* and find the *Caret* in every part of my Study or Establishment whilst you are away——Going out makes me sick——Their Dinners are to me so dreadful! I can starve at home upon a *Carrot* if I like it, unless Mr. Moore comes to eat *Could* Beef and *Ould* Cheese with me.[7] He will come today.

Everyone is on Tiptoe for News from Portugal;[8] That from Italy is not good. Charles Shephard has a Letter saying that Count Fenaroli—Your Godfather—is dead,[9] and our Japan China—no longer to be hoped for;——seized among Bankrupts Effects.—The Family *se portent bien, pour vous Servir.*

Well! we always expected such News as This you know; It was quite a natural Event. What I did *not* expect was Miss Williams's silly Heroism of offering *her* Bankrupt Brother *all her Fortune*[10]——"Many Thanks! exclaims Lady Williams: and then Sir John may have her to keep I suppose"—I have helped to prevent his *lending his Name* as Security for such a Scape Grace. They know not as I do, how Mr. Fleetwood kept a Mistress, and a House and a Carriage for the Mistress——Oh let him pay for his own Frolicks:—and not ruin a worthy Man and his virtuous Family!

God bless my dearest Boy, and keep *him* from Vice and from *Remorse:* The fatal Egg, which Folly lays in Pleasure's Nest;—but which when *hatched*, is *horrible*. Adieu! and fail not to love Your / Affectionate H: L: Piozzi.

I begin now to Think Davies should be *confined*, whilst his Ushers and his Nephew dispute the *Regency* of Streatham School.[11] I sent his first Letter for Charles Shephard to decypher, who took the *Straight Road;* and made him pay fourscore Pounds which he owed me[12]——he has written me a *second* Letter which would baffle all the Wise Men retained of old by Nebuchadnezzar for purpose of Interpreting Dreams and Difficulties.[13] *I will never have a 3d. from him.*

Give my *best* to *Pem.* true Regards and Compliments to Mr. Shephard and his Ladies: This will be my last Letter directed to Enborne—Won't it? What a pretty Paper is that in Johnson's Idler—concerning *The last!* read it[14]—I give you all my Books; so can't direct you to the Page.

I have just read a pretty Thing in French. "Je remplies ma jeunesse pour que ma Viellesse ne puisse pas me reprocher."[15] Remember it Dearest! "remember thy Creator in the days of thy Youth."[16] I wish you a Merry Christmas.

Text: Ry. 585.85. *Address:* John P: Salusbury Esq: / At the Rev: T: Shephard's / Enborne Near Newbury / Berkshire. *Postmark:* DENBIGH 2<24> (In JSPS's hand, "Received Decr 1810. Answered Do. Do.")

1. On his way to Brynbella, JSPS was to visit the Ladies of Llangollen.
2. See HLP to Sophia Byron, 1 September 1788, n. 2.

3. For Cator's death on 26 February 1806, see HLP to John Gillon [ca. February 1808], n. 6.

4. That is, Robert Gray (1788–1838), the son of RG's half-brother Thomas, of Saint James's, Middlesex. The young Gray had matriculated at Oriel College, Oxford (RG's college), where he received his B.A. in 1809 and his M.A. in 1813. He served as rector of Sunderland from 1819 until his death.

5. CMM's sister-in-law Anna Maria was the wife of John Lloyd Salusbury. See HLP to Q, 31 July 1810, n. 22.

6. Anna Maria Wynne, (or Wynn) had several estates which she inherited from her parents, the Merediths of Pengwern. From her second husband Edward Watkin Wynn[e], she inherited Llewessog Lodge, Llwyn, Denbighshire. See HLP to Q, 25 October 1796, n. 10; and to PSP, 10 January 1798, n. 2.

7. HLP's facetious reference to John Moore's Cumberland accent.

8. As early as mid-November 1810 the English believed that the French army under Masséna was in retreat in Portugal.

The *Courier*, 1 December, reported news brought by a Bristol vessel, which left Lisbon 17 November: that "the French army had broken up, and it was in full retreat towards Spain; and that Lord Wellington's cavalry and light troops were continually harassing them."

By 2 December, the *Courier* confirmed the fact of Masséna's retreat. Two days later the newspaper debated with itself as to Masséna's intention: did his retreat mean that he was to leave Portugal or was he "only retiring to be nearer his reinforcements?"

To HLP the dearth of hard news concerning Masséna was pleasurable, allowing her to believe with the *Courier*, e.g., on 8 December: "We are still without any intelligence, official or unofficial, from our Army. . . . But we anticipate, even from the articles in the *Moniteur*, that it will be good. They seem to be preparing the people of France for the abandonment of the Expedition against Portugal.— . . . [Napoleon] knows that the failure of the attack upon Portugal will render his affairs in Spain more desperate—and he feels and fears that the lesson which these two countries have taught may not be lost upon the rest of Europe."

9. For Conte Luigi Fenaroli, see HLP to LC, [ca. 6 or 7 January 1799], n. 4.

10. That is, Roger Hesketh *Fleetwood* Williams (1777–1826), Sir John's youngest brother. See P.R.O., Prob. 11/1719/612. Dying at Grophwysfa, near Bangor, he had been a New Bond Street wine merchant.

11. RD precipitated his problem by discussing the future ownership of the school in Streatham. In 1820 the school was to pass to his sister's son, later known as the Reverend David Jones (1791–1825), who had been born at Ystrad-vellte, county Brecon. He had begun his university career at Trinity College, Cambridge, but apparently at his uncle's urging, he migrated to Jesus College, Oxford, in 1811 (where RD had once been a student). Jones received his B.A. in 1813 and M.A. in 1816. He died in Streatham, having inherited his uncle's school and property there. See "Streatham Land Tax Assessment," 1822–25 (C.R.O., Surrey).

12. In 1802 Davies rented a field in Streatham owned by the Piozzis. On it he built an extension to his school.

On 15 June 1802 (Ry. 573.37), he wrote to HLP: "Last Night in bed did I settle the Field-business. Lest I should be suspected of proceeding in a mercenary way I hereby engage to give *six and twenty* pounds per annum for the said field for a period of twenty seven years from Michaelmas next."

His suggested rent was raised to £34 and in 1806–7 to £55 yearly. He continued to rent the land until his death.

See "Streatham Land Tax Lists" (C.R.O., Surrey).

13. Dan. 2:1–13.

14. *Idler* 103 was the concluding essay of the series, printed 5 April 1760. HLP was at this time particularly sensitive to "the horror of the last."

15. The line is virtually a commonplace of French poetry in the sixteenth and seventeenth centuries. See, e.g., François Villon, *Testament*, 22–23; Pierre de Ronsard, *Quatre premiers livres des Odes*, 4.10; Henri Estienne, *Les Prémices*, 4; Jean de la Fontaine, *Fables*, "Le vieux chat et la jeune souris," 12.5.

16. Eccles. 12:1.

TO JOHN SALUSBURY PIOZZI SALUSBURY

> Brynbella
> Fryday Night
> 21: December 1810.

Although the Shortest Day is past dear Salusbury,—or it *will* be when you read This.—

Leak goes tomorrow by the Morning Moon to Chester to take those Notes of Morshall's—dreadful Sorrow! and see what can be got from the Assignees. We were *obliged* to accept the Notes in Payment, and now the Man's a Bankrupt, God knows what we shall get for them.[1]——*He* takes this Letter, which he says I *must* write to prevent Your *trying* to come home by Bachegraig. These Rains and melted Snows render *that* Road Impassable. Come by *Bodvari;* alias Potfarry—Thro' poor Lleweney Grounds; it is A Mile shorter than t'other way, and I *do* long to hear the Carriage Wheels.

We have So much to *Say* to one another—So little that can be *written*! *One* Thing you may tell the Friends with whom you are passing Time away—it seems to me So pretty. *Private* Letters have told how at the Battle of Busaco, General Crawfurd (a Scotchman)[2] rode up to the 58th Regiment, and begged them to behave well.—Remember said he our *dear dead Sir John Moore:* he's looking on us *now,* I'm *sure* he is;[3] The Men could hardly give Three Cheers for Weeping—— but *drove* forward like Lyons;—and were in the Engagement *Irresistible:* This was heroic Feeling: and I *know* the Fact to be a true one.

You are right in saying that the Marriage of Lady Pa[get] with the Duke of A[rgyll] revolts against every Sentiment of honesty and honour: Incest, Perjury, and Sacrilege—Tria juncta in uno! as says the Motto to the order of the Bath. Let us see if Lord Paget will lead Lady Charlotte Wellesley to the Altar!—His Father is dying of a broken Heart[4]—and then she will be Countess of Uxbridge——These are at the *Top* of our Nobility[5]—The *Bottom* of Society never was known so foul: and Newgate complains that the Year 1810—sees her Annals polluted with Crimes unknown before. Let us Thank God who placed *us* in the *Middle* Class of Humanity.—"Medio tutissimus ibis.[6] Said Apollo to Phaeton— and *He* had *looked* on this Earth a good while even *Then.*

Lady Kirkwall has had Fever and Confinement enough, but forgets not her Friends. She was not trained or Disciplined to Sorrow; So all is new to her Unhappy Soul!

Young Trees should be fenced in while *Young* with *Thorns:* and so perhaps Young *Minds* should. What will become of Dearest Salusbury—when the Cattle begin to browze—The Weather to beat *hard* on him!—will he blame my Care to keep all Thorns away? I hope not.

God bless you, and send us a happy Meeting. Was my Letter a large Folio Sheet filled *up,* It would contain nothing else, but vary'd (I should write *varied*) Expressions of the Self same Thing, like Monsieur Jourdain's Love Letter—"Belle Marquise! vos beaux Yeux me font mourir d'Amour,'"[7] So if I can find nothing else to laugh at, You See I can laugh at your foolish old Aunt / and Affectionate H: L: Piozzi.

Make my best Compliments to the Amiable Family of which I trust you are making A merry Part—at Longmore.

You will wonder to see Chester on the Post Mark but the Inside will explain all.

This has been an Unlucky year about the Money Stuff—Streatham Park worst of all. Do you remember *that* funny Story? I'm like the foolish Master of the Yacht now. Come into the *Wessle* I wants you.

Text: Ry. 586.87. *Address:* John P: Salusbury Esq. / At Edw: Pemberton Esq. / Longmore near / Shrewsbury. *Postmark:* CHESTER 21 DE 21 1810.

1. As a creditor of Thomas Morshall, banker of Chester and Shrewsbury, HLP was desperate to salvage what she could from a loan to him. Morshall and his partner, William Rowton, had been declared legally bankrupt on 26 September.
By 5 January 1811, their creditors assembled at the Shrewsbury Town Hall, having previously "furnish[ed] the Amount of their Debts, and the Particulars of the Notes they hold, at the Bank, in order that their Depositions may be prepared with Expence to the Creditors."
But only on 29 June 1811 was the matter settled, for after the adjudication of claims on the partners, 1 June, the commissioners of bankruptcy set a meeting at the Guildhall (London) for the affairs of Morshall alone; i.e., convening on 29 June "in order to make a Dividend of the Separate Estate and Effects of that erstwhile Banker." See the *London Gazette*, 25–29 December 1810; 8–12 January 1811; 29 January–2 February; 7–11 May.
2. HLP refers to Major General Robert Craufurd (1764–1812), known as "Black Bob." He had first gained recognition in the Indian wars against Tippoo Sahib when he was a captain. Promoted to lieutenant colonel in 1797, he served in Ireland during the revolt of 1798. In 1807 he commanded the light brigade during the campaign against Buenos Aires and later served under Moore during the Corunna campaign. Active in the Peninsular War, he was killed at the storming of Ciudad Rodrigo.
3. For General Sir John Moore, see HLP to PSP, 17 October 1799, n. 2; to Q [23 May 1801], n. 3.
He died on 16 January 1809 at Corunna where an important rearguard battle was won by the British under his command against Soult.
4. That is, Henry Paget, third earl of Uxbridge, died in 1812. See HLP to Q, 19 March 1809, n. 9.
5. The marital peccadilloes of Lord Paget shocked many even in relatively liberated circles, Farington (11:3950) remarking, "Thus are morals & principles disregarded."
6. Ovid, *Metamorphoses*, 2.137. See also HLP to Q, [25 January 1806], n. 6.
7. Molière, *Le Bourgeois Gentilhomme* (1670), 2.4.

TO LADY WILLIAMS

Brynbella
21: December 1810.

Dearest Lady Williams wishes to hear how my cold does? The voice, taste, smell are all gone so if anyone says Mrs. Piozzi has *lost her Senses* it will be a truer report than many which have been raised upon her. The throat is less sore however, the sickness less troublesome.

The King will recover—but to what will he be restored? To the sight of his Son enjoying his place and power and to the necessity of saying gracefully—

that such a sight is all a fond Parent can desire &c.—and so he will go home and eat his Gruel as old Folks should—dont we see the young Laurels push the last years leaves away every hour of our lives?[1] Those dear, honest, honorable Physicians all agree that the Kings is a Green Old Age—no matter! The Laurel is an Evergreen but it must give place. Adieu Dear Madam. These are melancholy reflections I will add no more.— / H: L: P.

Text: Ry. 3 (1807–11). *Address:* Lady Williams / Bodylwyddan / St. Asaph.

1. The king began to ail toward the end of October 1810 but from then through December he would improve and relapse. In the latter month, his physicians were examined by select committees of the Lords and Commons. They admitted bafflement. See Brooke, pp. 382–83; *GM* 80, pt. 2 (1810): 472–73.

At the same time, the government began to test reactions to a regency bill with restrictions on the model of 1788, which were to be set aside if the king failed to recover in twelve months. On 5 February 1811, the Regency Act was passed, which made the Prince of Wales regent by hereditary right.

Index

Abel, Karl Friedrich, 153, 154–55 n.11
Ablett, Joseph, 106, 108 n.8
Achamoth (daughter of Sophia), 254, 255 n.7
Adams, Jane, née Owen (fl. 1758–1810) (mother of Susan), 140, 141 n.8
Adams, Susan (ca. 1786–1804), 140, 141 n.8
Addington, Henry, first viscount Sidmouth, 95, 97 nn. 2 and 3
Addison, Joseph: *Spectator*, 305
Address to the Public containing a review of the Charges . . . against . . . Melville, 109 n.20
Adolphus Frederick, duke of Cambridge (1774–1850), 119, 121 n.4
Aesop: *Fables*, "The Lark and Her Young ones," 254, 255 n.9
Agar, Louisa, née Talbot, 96, 97 n.14
Agar, William (husband of above), 97 n.14
Albani (or Albano), Francesco, 61, 63 n.17
Alexander I (czar of Russia), 110, 111 n.5, 112 n.8, 128 n.4, 224 n.12
Allen, Elener (HLP maid), 91, 94 n.15. *See also* Jones, Elener, née Allen
Allen, Rev. Joseph, 119, 121 n.7
Almon. *See* Amans
Althorpe. *See* Spencer
Amans (or Amons), William Walter Slade (TSW's confidential servant), 188 and n.2
Amelia, H.R.H. Princess (daughter of George III), 313 n.8
Andrew (Brynbella gardener), 169
Andrews, Miles Peter, 92, 95 n.31
Anglesey. *See* Paget
Annesley, George, viscount Valentia (later, 1816, second earl of Mountnorris): *Voyages and Travels . . . in the Years 1802–6*, 269, 270
Anstey, Christopher: *New Bath Guide*, 60, 62 n.5, 180 and n.8
Antin, Antoine de Pardaillon de Gondrin, duc d', 314, 315 n.5
Antiparos (Cyclades island), 61, 63 n.19
Anwyl, Rev. Robert, 218, 220 n.2

Apreece, Thomas George, 239 and n.3
Arblay, Mme d'. *See* Burney, Frances
Ardkill. *See* De Blaquiere
Arenberg, Louis-Engelbert-Marie-Joseph-Augustin, duc d', 302, 304 nn. 12, 13 and 15
Arenberg, Pauline-Louise-Antoinette-Candide, duchess d' (d. 1812), 302, 304 nn. 12 and 13
Argyll. *See* Campbell
Arias Montanus, Benedictus: *Biblia Herbraica*, 148, 150 n.15
Assheton, Ralph (father of Anne, née Assheton, Cleaver), 144 n.3
Atkins, Abraham (Streatham Park tenant), 135–36 n.1, 138, 175–76, 176–77 n.7, 239, 311, 312 n.9, 314, 315 n.2
Auckland. *See* Eden
Augusta, duchess of Brunswick and Wolfenbüttel, 87, 89 n.5
Aurelian (Lucius Domitius Aurelianus), 148, 150 n.16
Austin, William (supposed illegitimate child of H.R.H. Caroline, Princess of Wales), 114 n.5
Avonmore. *See* Yelverton

Bacon, Francis, first baron Verulam, 170 n.4; *Essay II*, "Of Death," 274 n.3
Bagot, Rev. Lewis, bishop of St. Asaph, 72, 73 n.1
Bagot, Rev. Richard, bishop of Oxford, 132 n.8
Baillie, Agnes (sister of Joanna), 243 n.4
Baillie, Joanna, 242, 243 n.4; *Miscellaneous Plays*, 110, 112 n.9
Baird, Maj. Gen. Sir David, 100 n.7
Baker-Holroyd (formerly Holroyd), John, first earl of Sheffield (brother of Sarah Martha Holroyd), 301
Baldwin, Thomas (designer of Laura Chapel, Bath), 132 n.4
Ball, Thomas, 272, 274 n.1, 278, 279

Ball, Thomas Prideaux (son of above), 272, 274 n.1
Bannister, John (actor), 248 and n. 10
Baretti, Giuseppe, 31, 175
Barns, Mrs. (HLP cook), 113, 116
Barnston, Letitia, née Owen (Mytton) (grandmother of Nicholas Owen, formerly Smythe), 295 n.10
Baronius, Cardinal Caesar, 93 n.7
Barrett, Charlotte, née Francis, 311, 313 n.10
Barrett, Henry, 311, 313 n.10
Barrett, Julia Charlotte (daughter of Charlotte and Henry above), 312, 313 nn. 10 and 14
Barrett-Lennard, Anna Maria, née Pratt, baroness Dacre, 67 n.2
Barrett-Lennard, Thomas, seventeenth baron Dacre (husband of above), 67 n.2
Barrington, George (pickpocket), 120, 122 n.15
Barrington, Rev. Shute, bishop of Durham, 80 n.5, 119, 120, 121 n.11
Barry, Col. Henry, 139, 274
Bassi, Laura Maria, 250, 251 n.2
Bates, Ely: *Christian Politics*, 101, 103 n.12
Bath. *See* Thynne
Bathurst, Rev. Henry, bishop of Norwich, 120, 122 n.16
Bayle, Pierre, 94 n.27
Beardmore, John (husband of Maria Hester, née Parke), 108 n.1
Beattie, James: *Life of* by Sir William Forbes, 147, 148 n.2
Beaudesert. *See* Paget
Beaufort. *See* Somerset
Beausobre, Isaac de: *Histoire Critique de Manichée et du Manichéisme*, 254, 255 n.8
Beckford, William (d. 1770), 284 n.5
Beckford, William (1759–1884) (son of above), 282, 284 nn. 5 and 6
Bedford. *See* Russell
Beechey, Sir William (artist), 138 n.2
Beethoven, Ludwig van, 97 n.8
Bell, Andrew, 229 n.1
Belmore. *See* Lowry-Corry
Benet (or Bennet), Elizabeth Bathurst Pye, 280, 281 n.4
Bennet, Charles, fourth earl of Tankerville, 96, 98 n.24
Bennigsen, Gen. Levin A.T., 128 n.2
Bentinck, William Henry Cavendish, third duke of Portland, 133 n.4, 257 n.1, 266, 267 n.3

Beresford, James: *Miseries of Human Life*, 117, 118 n.6, 181, 195
Beresford, Col. William Carr, 118 n.5
Betty, William Henry West ("Young Roscius") (boy actor), 59, 60, 61–62 n.3, 72, 84, 86 n.13; 88, 89 n.7, 91, 94 n.19, 172 n.9
Bible: Japheth, 104, 105 n.3; Jared, 104, 105 n.3; Jehoshaphet, 104, 105 n.6; Jehova, 105; Jephthah, 104, 105 n.7; Jethro, 104, 105 n.8; Job, 105, 106 n.9; Joel, 105, 106 n.9; Jopheth, 104, 105 n.3; Joseph, 104, 105 n.6; Joshua, 104, 106 n.6; Judah, 104, 105 n.7
—books of: Daniel, 148, 150 n.13; Ecclesiastes, 124 and n.5, 319, 320 n.16; Exodus, 170 and n.6; James, 316, 317 n.1; Jonah, 293, 295 n.2; Luke, 247; Matthew, 293, 295 n.3; Numbers, 99, 100 n.6; Proverbs, 148, 149 n.10, 293, 295 n.1; Psalms, 213, 214 n.6; Revelation, 90, 93 n.6
Bicknell, John, 298 n.7
Bicknell, Sabrina (called Sidny) (wife of above), 296, 298 n.7
Biddulph, Charlotte, née Myddleton, 268 n.1
Biddulph, Robert (husband of above), 266, 268 n.1
Bill (proposed servant for JSPS), 307, 309
Bingham, Lady Elizabeth, née Belayse (Howard), countess of Lucan, 62 n.9
Bingham, Gen. Richard, second earl of Lucan (husband of above), 60, 62 n.9
Blackman, William, 281 n.2
Boehm, Dorothy Elizabeth, née Berney, 241, 243 n.2
Boehm, Edmund (husband of above), 243 n.2
Boileau, Daniel, 243 n.6
Boileau-Despréaux, Nicholas, 286
Bonaparte, Caroline, 59 n.1
Bonaparte, Elisa Bacciocchi, princess of Lucca, 59 n.1, 111 n.6
Bonaparte, Jérôme, 59 n.1
Bonaparte, Joseph, 59 n.1, 103 n.7, 111 n.6, 210 n.7
Bonaparte, Louis, 59 n.1
Bonaparte, Lucien, 59 n.1
Bonaparte, Napoleon, 176, 201; achievements of, 204; advancement and titles for family members of, 59 and n.1; and battle of Austerlitz and treaty of Pressburg, 88 n.3, 98 n.19; and British expedition to Sicily, 66, 67 n.4; British fascination with, 185–86; and capture of Cape of Good Hope, 99, 100 n.7; and Convention of

Cintra, 204; facsimile of handwriting of, 206; and general peace proposals, 167; and Italy, 111n.6, 199, 200n.1; letter from to Friedrich Wilhelm III, 128 and n. 4; marriage of to Princess Marie Louise, 278, 278–79n.8, 281–82, 284n.2, 304n.11; and naval blockade of Great Britain, 153, 154n.16; numerology applied to name of, 90, 92, 94n.27; and peace overtures to Great Britain, 65–66n.2, 95, 99, 108n.8, 120, 122n.17, 162; and Peninsular War, 156, 157n.7, 163n.8, 175–76, 176n.1, 177nn. 8 and 10, 194, 194–95n.4, 209, 210n.5, 320n.8; and plans to invade England, 65–66n.2, 68n.1, 233; and regents of Portugal and Denmark, 157, 158nn. 1 and 2; victories of 1805 of, 83, 85n.3; vs. George III, 250; in Warsaw, 128 and n.2; and war with Prussia and its Russian allies, 96, 98n.19, 120, 122n.18
Bonaparte, Pauline, 59n.1
Boreham, Mr., and his wife, 158–59n.4
Borgia, Caesar, 83, 85n.6
Borgia, Rodrigo, 85n.6
Boringdon. *See* Parker
Boswell, James, 266n.17
Bourbon. *See* under names or titles of individual family members
Bouverie, William, first earl of Radnor, 97n.14
Bovi, Marino: engraving of Violet's portrait of HLP for frontispiece of *Retrospection*, 161n.2
Bowen, William (Bath apothecary), 11, 12, 34n.10, 84, 85n.10, 134, 135n.3, 136, 138, 141, 142, 177, 178n.1, 181, 183n.5, 193, 229, 263, 265n.5, 269, 296, 297, 298n.2
Bowles, William Lisle, 199n.6
Boycott, Maria: marriage of to Francis North, fourth earl of Guilford, 296–97, 298nn. 2 and 9
Boycott, Sophia: marriage of to William Bowen, 296, 298n.2
Boycott, Thomas (father of Maria and Sophia), 298n.2
Bradford, Mary, née Wharton, 144n.11
Bradford, William Mussage Kirkwall (husband of above), 143–44 and n. 11
Bradford. *See also* Bridgeman
Brahms, Johannes, 265n.1
Bramston, Rev. James: *Man of Taste*, 191, 192n.3
Brancas-Lauraquais, duc de (father of Pauline, duchess d'Arenberg), 304n.13
Brandenburgh-Anspach. *See* Christian Frederick, margrave of; Elizabeth Berkeley (Craven), margravine of
Brandon, Mr. (box keeper at Covent Garden theater), 260n.8
Breadalbane. *See* Campbell
Bridge, Edward (steward of Salusbury properties), 294, 295n.6, 302, 304n.16
Bridge, Frances (daughter of above), 295, 296n.6, 302
Bridgeman, Charles Orlando (1791–1806) (son of Orlando Bridgeman, baron Bradford of Bradford), 209–10, 211n.13
Bridgeman, Elizabeth, née Simpson (1735–1806), dowager Lady Bradford (widow of Henry Bridgeman, baron Bradford of Bradford), 73, 84, 85n.10, 111n.1
Bridgeman, Henry Edmund (b. 1795) (son of Orlando Bridgeman, baron Bradford of Bradford), 200, 201n.1, 209
Bridgeman, Lucy Elizabeth, née Byng, baroness Bradford of Bradford (wife of Orlando Bridgeman, baron Bradford of Bradford), 73, 119, 120, 161, 200, 203, 211n.13, 235–36, 251, 258; illness of son of, 209–10, 211n.12, 259
Bridgeman, Orlando (1762–1825), baron Bradford of Bradford (later first earl of Bradford) (son of Henry Bridgeman, baron Bradford of Bradford), 73, 109, 117, 119, 120, 161, 200, 201n.1
Bridgeman, Orlando Henry (b. 1794) (son of Orlando Bridgeman, baron Bradford of Bradford), 200, 201n.1, 209–10
Bridgewater. *See* Egerton
Bristol. *See* Hervey
Britton, John, 112nn. 1 and 2; letter to, 112
Brooke of Warwick Castle. *See* Grenville
Broome, Charlotte Ann, née Burney (Francis) (wife of Ralph Broome), 203n.2, 300, 301n.10, 312
Broome, Ralph (1742–1805), 301n.10
Broome, Ralph (or "Dolph") (1801–17) (son of above), 300, 301n.10, 312, 313n.14
Broster, John, 175n.4
Bruce, Alexander: wife and daughter of, 214 and n.7
Bruce, Charles Andrew (governor of Prince of Wales Island), 102, 103n.15
Bruce, James (the African traveler), 102, 103n.15
Bruce, Michael: "Elegy Written in Spring," 181, 183n.7
Brunswick. *See* Augusta, duchess of Brunswick and Wolfenbüttel; Friedrich Wil-

helm, duke of Brunswick; Karl Wilhelm Ferdinand, duke of Brunswick

Brydges, Lady Catherine, née Tollemache (d. 1754), marchioness of Carnarvon (wife of John Brydges, marquess of Carnarvon), 178 and n.4

Brydges, Lady Catherine (b. 1725) (daughter of John Brydges, marquess of Carnarvon; married first William Berkeley Lyon; married second Adm. Edwyn Francis Stanhope), 178 and n.5

Brydges, John (1702/3–27), marquess of Carnarvon (husband of Lady Catherine, née Tollemache), 178 and n.4

Buchanan, Claudius: accounts of Christians in India, 171 and n.5, 172 n.6

Buchner, Rev. John, bishop of Chichester, 132 n.10

Buckingham. See Grenville; Villiers

Bulkeley (later Warren-Bulkeley), Thomas James, viscount Bulkeley of Cashel and baron Bulkeley of Beaumaris, 110, 112 n.13

Buller, Elizabeth, née Yorke (first wife of John Buller), 115 n.5

Buller, Harriet, née Hulse (second wife of John Buller), 115 n.5

Buller, John, 114, 115–16 n.5

Bunnell (or Bunhall), Mrs. (Lady Orkney's housekeeper-companion), 138, 139 n.6, 142 and n.2, 143; husband of, see Gough, Mr.

Burdett, Sir Francis, fifth baronet, 141 n.6, 288 n.2, 289, 290 and n.5, 292, 293 nn. 5, 6

Burke, Edmund, 86 n.11

Burkett, Dr. (Bath physician), 183 n.5

Burney, Charles (1726–1814) (father of Rev. Charles Burney; grandfather of Clement Francis) (CB), 108 n.11, 124 nn. 1, 3, 4, and 6, 125, 127 n.3, 200, 201 n.7, 300, 305; Reynolds' portrait of at Streatham, 126 (reproduced); letter from 123–24; letter to, 125

Burney, Rev. Charles (1757–1814) (son of CB), 125 n.1, 254, 296, 298 nn. 5, 6, and 8, 299, 300 n.2; abridgement of J. Pearson's *Exposition of the Creed*, 296, 298 n.6, 299; letter from, 127 n.3; letter to, 125

Burney, Frances "Fanny" (in 1793 Mme d'Arblay) (FB), 25, 35 n.65, 203 n.2, 296, 298 n.4

Burney, Susanna (twin sister of CB), 200, 201 n.7

Burrard, Gen. Sir Harry, 201 n.2, 210 n.8

Burroughs (formerly Salusbury), Jane, née Offley, 77 n.14

Burroughs (formerly Salusbury), Rev. Lynch, of Offley, Herts. (brother of Sir Robert Salusbury, first baronet; husband of above, 60, 62 n.6, 77 n.14

Butler, Lady Eleanor. See Llangollen, Ladies of

Butler, Henry Thomas, second earl of Carrick (father of Lady Juliana, née Bulter, Lowry-Corry), 268 n.4

Butler, John, seventeenth earl of Ormonde, 69 n.2

Butler, Samuel: *Hudibras*, 110, 112 n.10

Byng, Anna Maria Bridget. See Hall, Anna Maria Bridget, née Byng

Byng, Augusta Forrest. See Hall, Augusta Forrest, née Byng

Byng, Bridget, née Forrest (wife of John Byng, later fifth viscount Torrington; mother of Edmund Byng), 284, 286 n.21

Byng, Cecilia. See Hopwood, Cecilia, née Byng

Byng, Edmund (son of John Byng, later fifth viscount Torrington; brother-in-law of Charles Henry Hall) (friend of JSPS), 271 and n.5, 276, 277, 278 n.6, 280, 281 n.6, 281, 283, 284 n.1, 291, 306, 307, 309; brothers of 281 n.7

Byng, Frederick Gerald (brother of Edmund Byng), 281 n.7

Byng, George (brother of Edmund Byng), 281 n.7

Byng, George, fourth viscount Torrington (uncle of Edmund Byng), 277, 278 n.6, 280, 281, 284

Byng, Henry Dilkes (brother of Edmund Byng), 281 n.7

Byng, John (brother of Edmund Byng), 280, 281 n.7, 286 n.21

Byng, John (later, 1812, fifth viscount Torrington) (father of Edmund Byng), 271 n.5, 283–84, 286 n.21

Byng, Lucy Juliana. See Morris, Lucy Juliana, née Byng

Byron, George Gordon, Lord, 281 n.5

Cadell, Thomas, 266 n.17

Cadogan, Charles Sloan Cadogan, first earl), 224 n.14

Cadogan, William: *A Dissertation on the Gout*, 125 and n.1

Calder, Adm. Sir Robert, 68 n.1

Caldwell, Amelia Alice (ca. 1765–1841), 103 n.16

Caldwell, Elizabeth, née Hort, Lady (wife of Sir James), 103 n. 16
Caldwell, Elizabeth Frances (1767–1854), 103 n. 16
Caldwell, Sir James (ca. 1720–84), fourth baronet, 103 n. 16
Caldwell, Mary Anne (eldest daughter of Sir James), 102, 103 n. 16, 267, 268 n. 5
Callender (or Callendar), Sir John, first baronet, 269, 270 n. 2, 287 n. 1
Callender (or Callendar), Margaret, née Romer (Kearney), Lady (wife of above), 286, 287 n. 1, 317
Cam, Thomas (Bath surgeon), 194 n. 3
Cam, Thomas Croxall (Bath surgeon) (father of above), 193, 194 n. 3
Cambridge. *See* Adolphus Frederick, duke of Cambridge
Campbell, George William (1768–1839), sixth duke of Argyll, 310, 310–11 n. 7, 321; wife of, *see* Paget, Caroline Elizabeth, née Villiers
Campbell, Mary, née Turner, countess of Breadalbane, 138 n. 2
Campbell, Thomas: *Gertrude of Wyoming*, 244 n. 9
Canning, George, 288 n. 1
Capel, Arthur (1631–1683), earl of Essex, 293 n. 7
Capper, Mr., in Secretary of State's department, 240 n. 1
Caracci (Carracci) school, 63 n. 17
Carlisle. *See* Howard
Carnarvon. *See* Brydges; Herbert
Caroline Amelia Elizabeth, Princess of Wales, 113, 114 n. 5, 114 Caroline Augusta Maria, Lady (daughter of William Henry, first duke of Gloucester), 278 n. 4
Carrick. *See* Butler
Carrington. *See* Smith
Carryll, Mary (servant to Ladies of Llangollen), 258, 259 n. 3
Casali, Andrea ("The Chevalier") (Italian painter): *The Story of Gunhilda*, 283, 285 nn. 9 and 10
Castlereagh. *See* Stewart
Catalani, Angelica (Italian soprano), 134, 135 n. 5, 257, 258 n. 4
Catherine the Great (czarina of Russia), 112 n. 8
Cator, John (d. 1806) (Thrale daughter guardian), 16, 31, 101, 102 n. 6, 175, 176 nn. 2, 4, and 6, 318, 320 n. 3
Cator, Joseph (1733–1818) (brother and executor of John Cator), 175, 176 nn. 2 and 4
Caulfeild, James, first earl of Charlemont, 285 n. 11
Cavan. *See* Lambart
Cavendish, Lady Elizabeth, née Hervey (Foster), duchess of Devonshire (second wife of the fifth duke), 251, 252 n. 8
Cavendish, Lady Georgiana, née Spencer (first wife of the fifth duke), 16, 252 n. 8
Cavendish, William, fifth duke of Devonshire, 252 n. 8
Ceres (asteroid), 60, 61 n. 1
Chamberlayne, Cecil, née Talbot (d. 1832) (daughter of George Talbot), 96, 97 n. 14
Chamberlayne, Edmond John (husband of above), 97 n. 14
Chambers, Ephraim: *Cyclopaedia*, 254, 255 n. 4
Champneys, T.S., 243 n. 2
Chancey, Mrs. (HLP servant), 136, 229, 234
Chappelow, Rev. Leonard (LC), 69–70 n. 2, 289; anecdotes, 119, 121 n. 2; health problems, 118–19; on international affairs, 120, 121 n. 18, 163; *Magna Britannia*, 101, 103 n. 14; "The Sentimental Naturalist" (his poem on animal kingdom), 84, 85 n. 12; letters from, 69–70 n. 2, 118–21, 151 n. 23, 163 nn. 4 and 8, 205 n. 1, 210 nn. 3 and 4, 211 nn. 12 and 13, 251 n. 3; letters to, 18, 30, 33, 34 n. 35, 35 nn. 84 and 97, 36 n. 98, 72–73, 83–84, 109–11, 117, 157–58, 161–62, 200–201, 203–5, 209–10, 235–36, 250–51, 258–59
Charlemont. *See* Caulfeild
Charles, Archduke of Austria (1771–1847), 233 n. 7
Charles I (king of England, Scotland, and Ireland), 77 n. 12, 86 n. 11
Charles II (king of England, Scotland, and Ireland), 72, 73 n. 6, 293 n. 8
Charles IV (king of Spain), 210 n. 7
Charlotte Augusta, Princess (1796–1817) (daughter of the Prince and Princess of Wales), 95 n. 32, 187 n. 3
Charlotte Augusta Matilda, Princess Royal and duchess of Württemberg, 94 n. 21
Charlotte Sophia (queen of Great Britain), 134 n. 6, 187 n. 3, 252 n. 7
Chesterfield. *See* Stanhope
Christian Frederick, margrave of Brandenburgh-Anspach and Bayreuth, 91, 94 nn. 20 and 22
Churchill. *See* Spencer-Churchill
Cicero, Marcus Tullius, 169, 170 n. 2

Cipriani, Giovanni Battista (Italian painter and engraver), 304 n.21
Clarence, duke of. *See* William Henry, H.R.H. duke of Clarence
Clarges, Louisa (daughter of the third baronet), 92, 95 n.29
Clarges, Louisa, née Skrine, Lady (wife of the third baronet), 95 n.29, 136, 250, 251 n.4, 251–52 n.5
Clarges, Sir Thomas (1751–82), third baronet, 95 n.29, 100 n.15
Clarges, Sir Thomas (ca. 1780–1834), fourth baronet (son of the third baronet), 250, 251–52 n.5
Clarges, William (son of the third baronet), 95 n.29, 99, 100 n.15, 136, 137 n.8, 250, 252 n.5
Clarke, Mary Anne, née Thompson (mistress of Frederick Augustus, duke of York and Albany), 211 n.9, 213, 214 n.2, 214, 215 n.1, 224 n.11, 232, 233 n.5, 242, 244 n.8, 259, 260 n.7
Clay, Catharine Charlotte (daughter of Jane Clay), 162, 252 n.9, 259
Clay, Jane, née Musgrave (wife of William Clay), 162, 163 n.5, 200, 251, 252 n.9, 259
Clay, Musgrave Knightly (son of Jane Clay), 162
Cleaver, Anne, née Assheton (wife of William Cleaver), 143, 144 and n.3, 147, 246
Cleaver, Rev. Euseby (later bishop of Dublin) (brother of William Cleaver), 132, 133 n.2
Cleaver, Rev. William, bishop (successively) of Bangor and St. Asaph, 117, 118 nn. 2 and 4, 119, 121 n.5, 131, 132, 133 nn. 1 and 2, 143, 144 and nn. 1 and 3, 147, 156, 210, 258 n.2, 296, 298 nn. 1 and 3, 299, 300 n.2, 309, 310 n.5; *Seven Sermons on Select Subjects*, 159, 160 n.6; letter to, 131 (copy)
Clement V (pope), 59 n.2
Clement, Dorothy (mistress of Sir Edward Walpole), 277, 278 n.3
Clerke, Sir John, 271 n.1
Clerke, Lydia, née Hammond (wife of above; later wife of Joseph Townsend), 270, 271 n.1
Clifford, George (suitor of HLS), 107, 108 n.12
Clifford, Henry (barrister of Lincoln's Inn), 260 n.8
Clough, Patty, née Butler, 283, 284 n.7
Clough, Richard (husband of above), 283, 284 n.7

Coates, Robert, 264, 265 n.9, 267
Cobbett, William, 260 n.7
Cochran, Mrs. (companion of Thrale daughters), 29
Cochrane, Archibald (1747/8–1831), ninth earl of Dundonald, 232, 233 n.3
Cochrane, Thomas (1775–1860), styled Lord Cochrane (later, 1810, tenth earl of Dundonald), 141 n.6, 232, 233 nn. 4 and 5
Cole, Rev. William, 119, 121 n.7
Colebrooke, Sir George, second baronet, 181, 183 n.4; portrait of by Reynolds, 182 (reproduced)
Collingwood, Vice Adm. Cuthbert, baron Collingwood of Coldburne and Hethpoole, 84, 85 n.7, 148, 150 n.21
Colman, George, the Younger: *Sylvester Daggerwood*, 288 and n.3
Comenius, Johann Amos: *Lux e Tenebris*, 94 n.27
Congreve, Adelaide Sarah, 207, 208 n.4
Congreve, William, 206–7, 208 n.2; lines about Edward Young, 62 n.4; *Mourning Bride*, 156, 157 n.3
Constable, Archibald, 192 n.4
Conway, Francis Charles Seymour, styled earl of Yarmouth (later marquess of Hertford), 122 n.17
Conway, William Augustus, 34 n.43
Cooke, George Frederick (actor), 61 n.3
Cooper, Mrs. (seller of greens in Bath), 16
Copleston, Edward (called Kingstone in error by HLP): *Advice to a Young reviewer* and three *Replies to the Calumnies of the Edinburgh Review against Oxford*, 299–300 and nn. 6 and 7, 300–301 n.9
Cornwallis, Adm. Sir William, 68 n.1
Correggio (Antonio Allegri), 61, 63 nn. 17 and 18
Cotton, Lady Elizabeth, née Tollemache (d. 1745) (wife of Sir Robert Salusbury Cotton, HLP's uncle), 178 and n.6
Cotton, Elizabeth Abigail, née Cotton, Lady (1713–77) (wife of Sir Lynch Salusbury Cotton), 71 n.2
Cotton, Frances, née Stapleton, Lady (d. 1825) (wife of Sir Robert Salusbury Cotton, fifth baronet), 283, 284 n.6
Cotton, Rev. George, dean of Chester, 256 n.3
Cotton, Rev. James Henry (1780–1862) (son of above), 256 and n.3
Cotton, Sir Lynch Salusbury (ca. 1705–75), fourth baronet of Combermere (uncle of HLP), 71 n.2, 90, 93 n.11

Cotton, Philadelphia, née Lynch (maternal grandmother of HLP). *See* King, Philadelphia, née Lynch (Cotton)
Cotton, Sir Robert Salusbury (d. 1748), third baronet of Combermere (husband of Lady Elizabeth, née Tollemache, Cotton; uncle of HLP), 178 and n.6, 217, 218 n.2
Cotton, Sir Robert Salusbury (1739–1809), fifth baronet (father of Frances, née Cotton, Needham), 135 n.9, 247, 248 n.9, 283, 284 n.6
Cotton, Sir Stapleton, first viscount Combermere, 202 n.2
Cotton, Lt. Gen. Sir Willoughby Cotton: marriage to Lady Augusta Maria Coventry, 96, 98 n.18
Coventry, Lady Augusta Maria (1785–1865) (daughter of George William Coventry, seventh earl of Coventry): marriage to Lt. Gen. Sir Willoughby Cotton, 96, 98 n.18
Coventry, George William (1722–1809), sixth earl of Coventry, 234, 235 n.4
Coventry, George William (1758–1831), viscount Deerhurst and (1809) seventh earl of Coventry, 98 n.18, 234, 238, 239, 240 and n.1, 246
Coventry, Peggy, née Pitches, countess of Coventry (second wife of above), 240; letter from, 240 n.1
Cowper, William, 161, 162 n.2; "Epistle to Lady Austen," 162 n.1; *The Task*, 18, 158, 162 n.1
Coxe, Charles Westley (d. 1806), 101, 102 n.5
Coxe, Eleanora, née Sharp (Yeldham) (wife of Rev. William Coxe), 301, 303 n.5
Coxe, Rev. George, 301, 303 nn. 2 and 4
Coxe, John Hippisley (d. 1782), 102 n.5
Coxe, Mary, née Hamilton (Lyon) (wife of Rev. George Coxe), 301, 303 n.4
Coxe, Rev. William, 301, 303 n.5
Craufurd, Maj. Gen. Robert, 321, 322 n.2
Crawford, Stewart (Bath physician), 263, 265 n.5
Crowe, G. W., 242, 244 n.9
Crutchley, Jeremiah (Thrale daughter guardian), 16, 91, 94 n.24
Cumberland, duke of. *See* Ernest Augustus
Cumberland, Richard, 242, 243 n.6, 244 nn. 10 and 11; *Memoirs*, 96, 98 n.21, 101, 110, 112 n.11, 153, 154 n.6; *The West Indian*, 106, 108 n.7; daughter of, *see* Jansen, Frances Marianne, née Cumberland

Cumming, George Brownlow (M.D.), 267, 268 n.11
Currie, James (M.D.) (1756–1805), 82, 83 n.9
Currie, William (M.D.) (ca. 1749–1834), 217, 218 n.3, 218
Curzon, Hon. Penn Assheton (d. 1797) (first husband of Sophia Charlotte Howe), 199 n.10
Cyrus II, the Great, 282

Dacre. *See* Barrett-Lennard
Dalrymple, Gen. Sir Hew, 201 n.2, 202, 210 n.8
Dance, George, 89 n.6
Daniel, Sophia (CMM's housekeeper), 226, 307, 308 n.5
Darby. *See* Stanley
Darell, Edward, 234, 235 n.3
Dartmouth. *See* Legge
Davies, Mr., of Denbigh, 174, 175 n.5
Davies, D., vicar of Penegoes, 132 n.8
Davies, David, of Ruthin, co. Denbigh, 175 n.5
Davies, Rev. Reynold (RD): school of at Streatham, 20, 32, 33, 102 n.2, 174 n.1, 184, 202, 231, 236, 238, 289, 290, 316, 319, 320 nn. 11 and 12; letter from, 320 n.12
Davies, Scrope Berdmore, 280, 281 n.5
Dawson-Damer, George Lionel (husband of "Minny" Seymour), 114 n.6
Dawson-Damer, John, first earl of Portarlington (father of above), 114 n.6
Day, Mr. (witness to HLP's 1809 will), 15
Day, Thomas (1748–89), 298 n.7
De Blaquiere, Eleanor (1794–1867) (daughter of John de Blaquiere, first baron of Ardkill; later wife of Joseph Knight), 232, 233 n.1, 273
De Blaquiere, Eleanor, née Dobson (1756–1831), baroness of Ardkill (wife of John de Blaquiere, first baron of Ardkill; mother of Anna Maria Fitzmaurice, viscountess Kirkwall), 81, 84, 86 n.17, 89, 99, 100 n.14, 110, 232, 233 n.1, 235, 237, 273, 276, 318
De Blaquiere, Elizabeth: marriage of to John Bernard Hankey, 138, 139 n.4, 142, 273
De Blaquiere, George (ca. 1782–1826) (son of John de Blaquiere, first baron of Ardkill), 273, 274 n.5
De Blaquiere, John (1732–1812), first baron of Ardkill (husband of Eleanor, née Dobson), 84, 86 n.17, 89, 110, 212 and n.4, 233 n.1

332   *The Piozzi Letters*

De Chair, Rev. John, 258, 259n.4
Deerhurst. *See* Coventry
De Luc, Mrs., of Bath, 16
Derby Peak, near Castleton, Derbyshire, 61, 63n.19
Devonshire. *See* Cavendish
Dimond, Mr.: words to ballad "The Kiss and the Tear," 262n.7
Dinorband. *See* Hughes
Diodatti, Giovanni: *La Sacra Bibbia* (Italian translation of the Bible), 148, 149n.14
Domenichino: mosaics by in Loreto church, 223n.7
Donkin, Gen. Robert (1727–1821), 280, 281n.9
Donkin, Lt. Gen. Rufane Shaw (1773–1841) (son of above), 280, 281n.10, 285n.16
Donoughmore. *See* Hely-Hutchinson
Dore, Marie (servant of HLP), 193, 194
Dorset. *See* Sackville
Douglas, Lady Catherine Anne, baroness Glenbervie, 263, 265n.2, 284n.1
Douglas, Sylvester, first baron Glenbervie (husband of above), 265n.2, 272, 275, 296
Doveton, Frederick, 307, 308nn. 6 and 7
Dryden, John: *Absalom and Achitophel*, 248 and n.11; *All for Love*, 222, 223n.3; *Aureng-Zebe*, 64n.6
Duhesme, Gen. Philippe Guillaume, 177n.8
Dundas, Henry, first viscount Melville, 97n.12, 107, 109n.20
Dundas, Lady Jean, née Hope, viscountess Melville (second wife of above), 96, 97n.12
Dundonald. *See* Cochrane
Dunscombe (GP's valet), 127 and n.1, 136, 141, 169, 172, 174, 177, 181, 189, 196, 197, 215, 216, 217, 219, 229, 230–31, 237
Dupont de l'Étang, Gen. Pierre, 177n.8
Dutton, Honoria (or Honor), née Gubbins, 129, 130n.3
Dyer, John (poet), 108n.8
Dysart. *See* Tollemache

Eardley-Wilmot. *See* Wilmot
Eberhard, Johann August: *Dictionary of German Synonymous Words*, 243n.6
Eddowes, Joshua (printer and bookseller, Shrewsbury), 69, 70n.7
Eddowes, William (son of above), 70n.7
Eden, Eleanor, née Elliot, baroness Auckland, 267, 268n.13
Eden, William, first baron Auckland (husband of above), 265n.3, 268n.13

Eden, William Frederick (son of above), 263, 265n.2, 267, 268n.13, 272
Edgcumbe, Adm. George, earl of Mount Edgcumbe, 90, 93n.8
Edgcumbe, Richard (d. 1758), first baron Edgcumbe, 93n.8
Edgcumbe, Richard (d. 1761), second baron Edgcumbe, 93n.8
Edgeworth, Maria: *Castle Rackrent*, 88, 89n.9; *Out of Debt, Out of Danger*, 231 and n.2
Edgeworth, Richard Lovell, 298n.7
Edinburgh Review: attacks on Edward Copleston and Oxford University, 299–300 and nn. 6 and 7; review of Baillie's *Miscellaneous Plays*, 110, 112n.9
Edwards, Charlotte, née Mostyn, 116n.10
Edwards, Rev. Samuel (husband of above), 116n.10
Edwards, Thomas Mostyn (son of above), 115, 116n.10
Egerton, Scroop, first duke of Bridgewater, 278n.2
Egmont. *See* Perceval
Egremont. *See* Wyndham
Eldon. *See* Scott
Elisaveta Alexeievna (czarina of Russia), 223, 224n.12
Elizabeth Berkeley (Craven), margravine of Brandenburgh-Anspach, 91, 94n.22
Ellenborough. *See* Law
Ellis, Charles Augustus, baron Howard of Walden, 149, 151n.23
Ellis, Charles Rose (later baron Seaford) (father of above), 151n.23
Ellis, Elizabeth Catherine Caroline, née Hervey (first wife of above and mother of Charles Augustus Ellis), 151n.23
Elphinstone, Adm. George Keith, baron Keith (later, 1814, viscount Keith), 173n.2; first marriage of, 172, 173nn. 3 and 4; in HLP's *Retrospection*, 159, 160n.5; and HLP's trustees, 235n.5, 241; marriage of to Q, 29, 30, 159, 160 and nn. 1 and 3, 162, 163, 164, 165n.3, 166, 169, 170n.5; and Q's pregnancy, 249, 262; relationship with HLP, 19, 30, 172, 223, 226, 232, 263, 283, 302; in Scotland with Q, 188, 191, 204, 241–42; letters from, 30, 35n.84, 163–64
Elphinstone, Georgiana Augusta Henrietta (daughter of above by Q), 30, 258, 259n.1, 262, 264, 273, 283, 285n.18, 289, 303, 308
Elphinstone, Hester Maria "Queeney," née

Thrale, baroness Keith (second wife of Lord Keith) (Q), 301, 303, 304 n.26; pregnancy of and birth of daughter, 30, 33, 246, 248 and n.3, 249, 251, 252, 257, 258, 259 n.1, 262, 273; and Streatham Park, 241, 315 n.2, 316; in Scotland with Lord Keith, 188, 191, 204, 205 n.7, 205, 241–42; letters to, 35 nn. 82 and 83, 221–23, 225, 225–27, 235 n.5, 241–42, 263–64, 264–65 n.1, 281–84 and n.1, 301–3, 303 n.1, 315 n.2. *See also* Thrale, Hester Maria "Queeney" (daughter of HLT and HT) (later Lady Keith) (Q)

Elphinstone, Jane, née Mercer (d. 1789) (first wife of Lord Keith), 172, 173 n.3

Elphinstone, Margaret, *suo jure* baroness Keith of Stonehaven Marishal and baroness Keith of Banheath (daughter of Lord Keith by his first wife), 29, 30, 172, 173 n.4, 204

Enghien, Louis-Antoine-Henri de Bourbon, 91, 94 n.18

Ernest Augustus, duke of Cumberland (later king of Hanover), 292, 293 nn. 7 and 8

Erskine, Thomas, first baron Erskine, 114 n.5

Essex. *See* Capel

Evans, Mr. (Denbigh undertaker), 14

Evans, Evan (b. 1743), 132 nn. 8, 10, 11

Exposure of the Persecution of Lord Melville, 109 n.20

Faber, Rev. George Stanley: *Dissertation on the Prophecies*, Bampton lectures, *Dissertation on the Mysteries of the Cabiri*, 96, 98 nn. 22 and 23, 123 n.1; *Supplement to the Dissertation on the 1260 Years*, 122, 123 n.2

Fane, John, tenth earl of Westmorland (father of Lady Augusta, née Fane (Parker) Paget, 214, 215 n.2

Farington, Joseph, 171 n.3, 184 n.9, 322 n.5

Fell, Mr., of Nornaville and Fell (London booksellers and stationers), 15, 138, 139 n.7

Fenaroli, Conte Luigi (JSPS's godfather), 319, 320 n.9

Fenton, Richard (1746–1821), 198, 199 nn. 5 and 6, 204

Ferdinand (crown prince of Spain, 1808, and later Ferdinand VII, king of Spain), 210 n.7, 213 n.6

Ferdinando IV (king of Naples and Sicily, 1759–1825; styled Ferdinando I of the Two Sicilies, 1816–25), 91, 111 n.6, 117, 118 nn. 9 and 10

Fesch, Joseph (French prelate), 111 n.6

Fetherstonhaugh, Sir Henry (1754–1846), second baronet, 266 n.12, 267, 268 nn. 8 and 9

Fetherstonhaugh, Sir Matthew, first baronet (father of above), 267, 268 n.8

Fetherstonhaugh, Sarah, née Lethieullier, Lady (wife of above), 268 n.8

Fingal. *See* Plunkett

Fingal's Cave, 61, 62 n.13

Fitzherbert, Maria Anne, née Smythe (Wild) ("wife" of Prince of Wales), 113, 114 n.6, 128

Fitzmaurice, Anna Maria, née De Blaquiere (1780–1843), viscountess Kirkwall (wife of John Hamilton Fitzmaurice), 138, 142, 178 n.2, 191, 247, 307; children of, 64 and n.4, 73 n.2, 84, 86 n.18, 89, 92 n.2, 99, 100 n.13, 316 n.9; godson of, 88, 89 n.8; and HLP, 30, 81, 83 n.4, 130, 184, 198, 199 n.7, 207, 223, 317; illnesses of, 72, 81, 196, 217, 218, 221, 229, 237, 318, 321; marital problems of, 87, 88 n.2, 154 n.1, 155–56, 159, 162, 214 n.3, 218, 266–67, 275–76; travels of, 110, 196, 249, 302

Fitzmaurice, John Hamilton (1778–1820), styled viscount Kirkwall (husband of above), 81, 83 n.4, 86 n.18, 97 n.17, 144 n.11, 152, 169, 178 and n.2, 183, 184, 185, 196, 212 and n.2, 238, 304 n.20; children of, 64 and n.4, 89 n.2, 96, 99, 100 n.13; marital problems of, 87, 88 n.2, 152, 154 n.1, 155–56, 159, 162, 214 n.3, 218, 247, 266–67; and sale of Llewenny Hall, 213, 214 n.3, 217, 218 n.2, 247, 302; travels of, 72, 74, 110, 142, 143, 169

Fitzmaurice, Mary, née O'Bryen or O'Brien, *suo jure* countess of Orkney (daughter of Murrough O'Brien, marquess of Thomond; wife of Thomas Fitzmaurice; mother of above) 90, 100 n.14, 110, 144 n.11, 178 n.2, 183

Fitzmaurice, Thomas (1742–93) (husband of above), 144 n.11, 247

Fitzmaurice, Thomas John Hamilton (b. 1803) (first son of Lord and Lady Kirkwall) (later fifth earl of Orkney), 73 n.2, 83 n.4, 84, 86 n.18, 89, 92 n.2, 96, 99, 100 n.13, 144 and n.12

Fitzmaurice, William Edward (b. 1805) (second son of Lord and Lady Kirkwall), 64

and n.4, 72, 73 n.2, 83 n.4, 84, 86 n.18, 89, 92 n.2, 99, 100 n.13, 266, 315, 316 n.9
Fitzroy, Elizabeth, née Wrottesley, duchess of Grafton (second wife of Henry Fitzroy, third duke of Grafton), 243 n.2
Flaxman, John (sculptor), 138 n.2
Fontenelle, Bernard Le Bovier de, Sieur: *Relation de l'île de nouveau dialogues des morts*, 303 n.1
Foot, Jessé: *Life of Arthur Murphy*, 84, 85–86 n.11, 305 n.1; letter to, 305
Foote, Samuel, 165
Forbes, Sir William: *Account of the Life and Writings of James Beattie*, 147, 148 n.2
Fox, Charles James, 66 n.4, 73 n.4, 97 n.2, 98, 100 n.3, 117, 118 n.7, 122 n.17
Francis, Charlotte (sister of Clement Francis), 301 n.10. *See also* Barrett, Charlotte, née Francis
Francis, Charlotte Ann, née Burney. *See* Broome, Charlotte Ann, née Burney (Francis)
Francis, Clement (d. 1792) (father of Marianne Francis), 203 n.2, 301 n.10
Francis, Clement (1792–1829) (brother of Marianne Francis), 289, 290 n.3, 300 n.1, 301 n.10, 311 n.10; letter from 300 n.2; letters to, 298–300, 311–12
Francis, Marianne, 202, 203 n.2, 289, 299, 300 n.1, 301 n.10, 307, 311; letters from, 210 n.6, 290 n.3, 293 n.8, 298 n.6, 308 n.6
Franz (or Francis) II (1768–1835) (Holy Roman Emperor, 1792-1806; emperor of Austria, as Franz I, 1804–35; king of Bohemia and Hungary, 1792–1835), 83, 85 n.5, 279 n.8
Frederick (prince regent of Denmark; later Frederick VI, king of Denmark), 157, 185 n.1
Frederick Augustus, duke of York and Albany (1763–1827), 119, 121 n.4, 211 n.9, 214 n.2, 214, 215 n.1, 224 nn. 11 and 14, 233 n.5, 260 n.7
Frey, Mr. (preacher), 123 n.10
Frey, Joseph Samuel Christian Frederick, 123 n.10, 311, 312 n.1
Friedrich Wilhelm (1771–1815), duke of Brunswick, 120, 122 n.20
Friedrich Wilhelm III (1770–1840) (king of Prussia, 1797–1840), 120, 122 n.19, 128 n.4
Friedrich Wilhelm Karl (1754–1816), elector of Württemberg, 91, 94 n.21

Gainsborough, Thomas: landscape of given by HLP and GP as wedding gift to SH, 153, 154 n.10, 154–55 n.11, 155 n.12, 164

Galindo, Catherine: *Mrs. Galindo's Letter to Mrs. Siddons*, 260 n.12
Gambier, Adm. James, first baron Gambier, 233 n.4
Garnier, Capt. Charles, 268 n.6
Garnier, Lady Elizabeth, née Howard, 267, 268 n.6
Garrick, David, 61 n.3, 199 n.6
Genlis, Stéphanie Ducrest de Saint-Aubin, comtesse de: *Le Souvenirs de Felicité L*****, 209, 211 n.11
George II (king of Great Britain), 178
George III (king of Great Britain), 23, 86 n.11, 87, 89 n.5, 100 n.8, 115 n.3, 119, 122 n.17, 165 n.4, 168 n.2, 222, 236, 293 n.8; coronation of, 250, 251 and n.1, 252 n.7; jubilee of coronation of, 249, 250 n.2, 250, 252, 253 n.1, 308 n.9; madness of, 311, 313 n.8, 315, 322–23 and n.1; and Parliament, 97 n.2, 141 n.6
George IV (king of Great Britain), 136 n.6
George Augustus Frederick, Prince of Wales (later George IV, king of Great Britain): and "Minny" Seymour, 114 n.6, 115 n.3, 165 n.4; as prince regent, 322–23 and n.1
Giants Causeway, county Antrim, North Ireland, 61, 63 n.19
Gibbes, George Smith (M.D.), 133, 133–34 n.6, 181, 183 n.3, 263, 265 n.5
Giles, Peter (Streatham Park tenant), 112, 113 n.3, 135–36 n.1, 138; GP/HLP litigation against, 166 and n.2, 183, 184 n.10, 190
Gillon, John (HLT/HLP family advisor), 33, 72, 73 n.3, 102, 103 n.15, 109 n.19, 129, 129–30 n.2, 134, 135–36 n.1, 136, 138, 142, 156, 160 and n.8, 176 nn. 1, 2, and 3, 221 and n.1, 229–30, 232, 239, 251, 259, 260 n.2, 286; letters to, 175–76, 176–77 n.7
Glenbervie. *See* Douglas
Gloucester. *See* Maria, née Walpole (Waldegrave), duchess of Gloucester; William Frederick, second duke of Gloucester; William Henry, first duke of Gloucester
Glover, Ann (HLP servant), 237, 256, 261, 262 n.6, 273, 317
Glover Anna (daughter of Lt. Col. John Jackson Glover), 137 n.9, 245, 246 n.8
Glover, Frances, née Cook (or Cooke) (wife of Lt. Col. John Jackson Glover), 137 and n.9, 181, 239, 261, 262 n.4
Glover, Frances (daughter of Lt. Col. John Jackson Glover), 137 n.9, 181
Glover, Frederick Augustus (son of Lt. Col.

John Jackson Glover), 137n.9, 181, 183n.6
Glover, Henrietta (daughter of Lt. Col. John Jackson Glover), 137n.9
Glover, Lt. Col. John Jackson, 137n.9
Glover, John Octavius Augustus (son of Lt. Col. John Jackson Glover), 137n.9, 181, 183n.6, 239 and n.1
Glynne, Sir Stephen Richard, eighth baronet, 142, 143n.4
Godwin, William: *Caleb Williams*, 62n.7; *Damon and Delia*, 62n.7; *Fleetwood*, 60, 62n.7; *Imogen*, 62n.7; *Italian Letters*, 62n.7; *St. Leon*, 60, 62n.7
Goldsmith, Oliver, 199n.6, 315n.2
Gorani, Joseph (Giuseppe): *Mémoires . . . des cours . . . de l'Italie*, 118n.10
Gough, Mr. (upholsterer) (husband of Mrs. Bunnell), 142 and n.2, 143
Gouvion-Saint-Cyr, Gen. 94n.25
Grafton. *See* Fitzroy
Graham, Rev. George: *Telemachus, a Mask*, 191, 192n.6
Granville. *See* Leveson-Gower
Gray, Robert, the elder (d. 1788) (father of RG), 121n.13
Gray, Robert (1788–1838) (son of RG's half-brother Thomas), 318, 320n.4
Gray, Rev. Robert "Old Testament" (1762–1834) (RG), 119, 120, 121n.13, 123n.10, 130, 131n.2, 238, 246, 254, 318; *Key to the Old Testament and Apocrypha*, 73, 80n.4, 122, 123n.3, 254, 318; letter from, 123n.3; letters to, 10, 18, 34nn. 2 and 36, 59, 79–80, 122, 127–28, 195, 199–200
Gray, Thomas (half-brother of RG), 320n.4
Greatheed, Richard Wilson, 60, 62n.11
Green, Matthew, *The Spleen*, 71, 72n.4
Green, Sarah: *Private History of the Court of England*, 186 and n.1, 187n.7
Greenwood, John (art auctioneer), 155n.11
Grenville, George, second earl Brooke of Warwick Castle and earl of Warwick, 196, 197n.5
Grenville, George, third earl Temple and first marquess of Buckingham (afterwards Nugent-Temple-Grenville), 121n.10, 133n.2
Grenville, William Wyndham, baron Grenville, 73n.4, 95n.31, 97n.2, 114n.4, 119, 121n.10; and election of chancellor of Oxford University, 257 and n.1, 258n.2, 259, 259–60n.6
Grey, Charles, Lord Howick (later, 1807, earl Grey), 133n.3

Grey of Sheerness, Commissioner, 86n.16
Grinfield, W. (proprietor and minister of Laura Chapel, Bath), 131n.4
Guilford. *See* North

Hall, Anna Maria Bridget, née Byng, 271n.5, 283, 285n.19, 306, 307, 308n.2, 309, 310n.4
Hall, Charles Henry, dean of Christ Church College, Oxford (husband of above), 24, 25, 270, 271nn. 2 and 5, 280, 281n.6, 306, 308n.3, 309, 315n.1; letter from, 309 (copy); letter to, 307 (copy)
Hall, Edmund Hyde: "Lines on Bodfel Hall" in tribute to HLP, 303, 304n.24; travel MS. on Carnarvonshire, 303, 304nn. 23 and 25
Halliborton. *See* Halliburton
Halliburton, Lucy Chandler, née Grant, 301, 303n.9
Halliburton, William Hersey Otis (husband of above), 301, 303n.9
Hallifax, Robert (M.D.), 114, 115n.3
Hamilton, Elizabeth: *Agrippina*, 60, 62n.8
Hamilton, Emma Hart, Lady, 264, 265n.11, 265–66n.12, 267, 268n.9
Hamilton, Frances. *See* Madden, Frances, née Hamilton
Hamilton, Rev. Frederick, 196, 197n.5
Hamilton, Hugh, bishop of Ossory (father of Isabella Hamilton), 71n.1
Hamilton, Isabella, 71n.1, 75, 77n.17, 102, 104n.17; letter to, 71
Hamilton, Isabella, née Wood (mother of above), 71 and n.1
Hammersley, George (Pall Mall banker), 308, 310n.1
Hammersley, Thomas (Pall Mall banker), 244, 245, 272n.7, 273, 279, 310n.1
Handel, George Frideric, 204, 205n.3
Hankey, John Bernard: marriage to Elizabeth de Blaquiere, 138, 139n.4
Hankey, John-Peter (uncle of above), 138, 139n.5
Hannibal, 64 and n.2
Harris, Elizabeth, 158–59n.4
Harrison, Thomas (designer of obelisk in Denbighshire commemorating jubilee of George III), 308n.9
Hawkesbury. *See* Jenkinson
Hawkesworth, John: "Life. An Ode," 128 and n.5, 258–59 and n.5
Hay-Williams. *See* Williams, John Hay
Heaton, John (son of Richard Heaton), 76n.6, 141n.4

Heaton, Richard, of Lleweny Green, 76 n.6, 141 n.4
Heaton, Sarah, née Venables (widow of Richard Heaton?), 87 n.22
Heberden, William, the elder, 119, 121 n.12
Hebrides, 61
Hely-Hutchinson, John, baron Hutchinson (later second earl of Donoughmore), 129, 130 n.4
Herbert, Augusta Elizabeth (daughter of Captain Charles Herbert), 283, 286 n.20
Herbert, Bridget Augusta Forrest, née Byng (mother of above), 283, 285 n.20
Herbert, Capt. Charles, 283, 285 n.20
Herbert, Lady Elizabeth, née Spencer, countess of Pembroke, 251, 252 n.7
Herbert, Elizabeth Alice Maria, née Wyndham, countess of Carnarvon (wife of Henry Herbert, earl of Carnarvon), 178 n.3
Herbert, Henry (1734–94), tenth earl of Pembroke and seventh earl of Montgomery, 252 n.7
Herbert, Henry (1741–1811), earl of Carnarvon, 178 and n.3, 283
Herrara, Francisco (architect of Saragossa church), 223 n.6
Herre, Lukas de (artist): portrait of Katheryn of Beraine by, 302, 304 nn. 19 and 20
Herschel, Sir William: *Scientific Papers of . . .* , 153, 154 n.4
Hertford. *See* Conway; Seymour
Hervey, Frederick Augustus, fourth earl of Bristol, 252 n.8
Hervey, Frederick Augustus (d. 1803), fifth earl of Bristol and *de jure* Lord Howard of Bristol (father of John Augustus Hervey), 151 n.23
Hervey, John Augustus (d. 1796), styled Lord Hervey (father of Elizabeth Catherine Caroline, née Hervey, Ellis), 151 n.23
Hesketh, Maria, née Rawlinson, 137 n.6
Hesketh, Robert (husband of above), 136, 137 n.6
Hinde, Mary, née Ball (wife of Robert Hinde), 93 n.10
Hinde, Mary Elizabeth (daughter of above), 90, 93 nn. 9, 10, and 11; letter from, 93 n.9
Hinde, Robert (father of above), 93 n.10
Hoare, Arabella Penelope Eliza, née Green (wife of Peter Richard Hoare), 146 n.3
Hoare, Charles (brother of Henry Merrik Hoare), 145, 146 n.4
Hoare, Frances Anne, née Acland (second wife of Richard Hoare; mother of Henry Merrik Hoare), 145 n.2
Hoare, Frances Dorothea, née Robinson (wife of Charles Hoare), 145, 146 n.4
Hoare, Henry Hugh (later third baronet) (brother of Henry Merrik Hoare), 146 and n.3
Hoare, Henry Merrik (husband of SH): brothers of, 145, 145–46 n.3, 146 n.4, 162, 163 n.4, 245; at Brynbella with SH, 146 and n.2, 184, 188, 195 and n.1, 196, 197, 200–201, 204, 207; and HLP, 19, 231, 232, 245; and JSPS, 244; at Llewenny Hall, 196, 197; London residence of, 145, 146 n.5, 205, 206 n.1; marriage of to ST, 28, 33, 145 and nn. 1 and 2, 146 n.6, 146 and n.1, 147, 149 n.6, 157, 162, 163 n.4
Hoare, Maria Palmer, née Acland (wife of Henry Hugh Hoare), 146 n.3
Hoare, Peter Richard (brother of Henry Merrik Hoare), 146 n.3
Hoare, Sir Richard, first baronet (father of Henry Merrik Hoare), 145 n.2, 163 n.4
Hoare, Sir Richard Colt, second baronet (half-brother of Henry Merrik Hoare), 145 and n.3, 198, 199 nn. 5 and 6, 199, 200, 204; *Itinerary of Archbishop Baldwin through Wales*, 199 n.5
Hoare, Sophia, née Thrale (daughter of HLT and HT; wife of Henry Merrik Hoare) (SH), 316; at Brynbella, 146 and n.2, 184, 188, 195 and n.1, 196, 197, 201, 204, 207; and GP's final suffering, 226, 227; and HLP, 19, 30, 214, 242, 245, 317; and JSPS, 244; and Ladies of Llangollen, 209; at Llewenny Hall, 196, 197; London residence of, 145, 146 n.5, 205, 206 n.1; and Q, 164, 262. *See also* Thrale, Sophia (daughter of HLT and HT) (later Mrs. Hoare) (ST)
Hoblyn, Robert (first husband of Jane, née Cox (Hoblyn) Quicke), 195 n.5
Hochkins, Eleanor (mistress of John Gillon), 103 n.15
Hoddeston, Herts.: murders at, 158, 158–59 n.4
Hofer, Andreas, 284 n.3
Hogan, Denis: *Appeal to the Public, and a Farewell Address to the Army*, 209, 211 n.9
Hogarth, William: *The Lady's Last Stake*, 282 (reproduced), 283, 285 nn. 11, 12, 13, and 14; *Sigismunda*, 285 n.12
Holford, Margaret (afterwards Hodson): *Wallace; or, The Fight of Falkirk*, 263, 264–65 n.1

Holman, Jane, 291, 292 n.2
Holroyd. *See* Baker-Holroyd
Holroyd, Sarah Martha, 301, 303 n.2
Home John: *Douglas,* 263–64, 265 n.8
Hop ("Hope") family (Dutch mercantile and political dynasty), 107, 108–9 n.13
Hope, John, second earl of Hopetoun, 97 n.12
Hopetoun. *See* Hope
Hopwood, Cecilia, née Byng, 283, 285 n.19, 310 n.4
Hopwood, Robert Gregge, 285 n.19
Horace, 286; *Ars Poetica,* 119, 121 n.1; *Epistles,* 151, 152 n.4; *Odes,* 99, 100 n.11, 239 and n.2
Horsley, Frances Emma, née Bourke (wife of Heneage Horsley), 100 n.4
Horsley, Rev. Heneage, 98, 100 n.4, 119, 121 n.6
Horsley, Rev. Samuel, bishop (successively) of Rochester and St. Asaph, 72, 73 n.1, 98, 100 n.4, 117 and n.1, 118 n.2, 119, 121 n.6
Hort, Josiah, archbishop of Tuam (father of Elizabeth, née Hort, Caldwell), 103 n.16
Howard. *See* Hervey, Frederick Augustus
Howard, Bernard Edward, twelfth duke of Norfolk, 62 n.9
Howard, Frederick, fifth earl of Carlisle, 268 n.6
Howard, Henrietta, née Hobart, countess of Suffolk, 199 n.8
Howard, Thomas, thirteenth duke of Norfolk, 75, 77 n.10
Howard of Walden. *See* Ellis
Howe, Sophia Charlotte, *suo jure* baroness Howe of Langar, 198, 199 nn. 9 and 10
Howick. *See* Grey
Huber, Barthélmy, 277, 278 n.7
Huber, Lydia, née Strutt, 278 n.7
Hudson, Thomas (portrait artist), 75, 77 n.15
Hughes, Charlotte Margaret, née Grey (wife of William Lewis Hughes), 143, 144 n.10, 302, 304 n.20
Hughes, E., of Caerwys, 132 n.8
Hughes, Rev. Edward, of Kinmel Park, Denbighshire, 99, 100 n.5, 115, 116 n.8, 129, 130 n.5, 214 n.3, 268 n.1
Hughes, Elizabeth, née Thomas, Lady (wife of Sir William Bulkeley Hughes), 273, 274 n.7
Hughes, Harry (Brynbella farmhand?), 174
Hughes, Hugh (d. 1810), 89 n.9
Hughes, Owen (GP/HLP servant), 174, 217, 244
Hughes, Robert (fellow of Jesus College, Oxford), 132 nn. 8 and 10
Hughes, Sir William Bulkeley (husband of Elizabeth, Lady Hughes), 274 n.7
Hughes, William Lewis (later first baron Dinorban), 144 n.10, 302, 304 n.20
Hulse, Sir Edward, third baronet (father of Harriet, née Hulse, Buller), 115 n.5
Hummerstone, Mrs., 158–59 n.4
Humphreys family: and Bodelwyddan estate, 79 n.8
Hussey, Thomas, Catholic bishop of Waterford and Lismore, 85-86 n.11
Hutchinson. *See* Hely-Hutchinson

Inchiquin. *See* O'Brien
Io (priestess of Hera), 104, 105 n.5
Ion (Greek poet), 104, 105 n.5
Isaacs, Mrs.: *Ariel,* 204, 205 n.6, 209

Jackson, Mrs., of Jackson's Hotel, Chester, 190 n.1, 192 n.1
Jackson, Cyril, dean of Christ Church College, Oxford, 24, 270, 271 n.3
Jackson, John (artist): copies of the Reynolds portraits at Streatham Park, 112 n.2; miniature of HLP by, 268, 269, 270 nn. 1 and 9
James II (king of England, Ireland, and Scotland), 75; as duke of York, 293 n.8
James, Sir Walter, 66, 67 nn. 2 and 3, 68, 125 and n.2, 234, 235 and n.6, 236, 238, 246
Jansen, Frances Marianne, née Cumberland (daughter of Richard Cumberland), 244 n.10
Janssens, Gen. Jan Willem, 100 n.7
Jaswant (or Jeswant, or Jeswut Row) Ráo Holkar, 65 n.1
Jebb, Sir Richard (M.D.), baronet, 164, 165 n.4
Jefferson, Thomas, 150 n.20
Jenkinson, Charles, baron Hawkesbury and first earl of Liverpool, 236, 237 n.4
Jenkinson, Robert Banks, baron Hawkesbury and second earl of Liverpool (son of above), 22, 97 n.2, 133 n.4, 236, 237 n.3, 238, 239
Jersey. *See* Villiers
Jervis, John, earl of St. Vincent, 138 n.2
John (Joao), prince regent of Portugal (later King John VI), 153, 155 n.17, 157 n.7, 157, 158 n.2, 160, 161 n.11, 162, 163 nn.6 and 8, 167, 167–68 n.2, 179

Johnson, John, 226
Johnson, Mary (HLP maid) (wife of above), 101, 103 n.10
Johnson, Samuel (SJ): circle of, 70 n.3; and Richard Fenton, 199 n.6; and Thomas Hussey, 86 n.11; and William Maxwell, 130, 131 n.3; and Q, 27; relationship with and advice to HLT/HLP, 15, 18, 20, 34 n.33, 79 n.4, 108 n.7, 266 n.17, 305 n.2; relationship with HT, 20, 79 n.4; and Anna Seward, 266 n.17; and Shenstone's "Written at an Inn," 225 n.2; and Dr. Tattersall, 92
—opinions of: on chronic vs. acute disease, 171, 172 n.7; on knowledge and the commonplace, 147–48 and n.9, 211; on public houses, 225 n.2; on source of Greek proverb, 308 n.8; on study of classics, 35 n.45; on women's conversation vs. their letters, 71 and n.2
—Works: *Dictionary*, 105 n.2; *Idler*, 25, 35 n.62, 319, 320 n.14; impromptu verse on Q's gown and hat, 223, 224 n.4; *Irene*, 299, 300 n.3; *Lives*, 305 and n.4; "Preceptor," 20–21, 34 n.42
Jones, Ann (housekeeper and mistress of Peter Giles), 136 n.1
Jones, Rev. David (nephew of RD), 319, 320 n.11
Jones, Dorothy, 256 and n.2
Jones, Elener, née Allen (HLP servant) (wife of Robert Jones and mother of above), 15, 137, 142 n.3, 174, 175 n.2, 177, 181, 189, 217, 221, 228, 229, 256 and n.2; letter from, 142 n.3
Jones, Rev. Gervas, of Offley (uncle of Ann, née Jones, Tench), 90, 93 nn. 9 and 12
Jones, John (1717–1806), 89, 93 n.3, 117, 118 n.11, 120
Jones, John, Esq., of Rhualt, 298 n.10
Jones, John Gale, 290 n.5
Jones, Joseph, of Pontruffeth (husband of Sarah), 185 n.3
Jones, Mary, of Rhualt, 297, 298 n.10
Jones, Robert ("Robin") (pharmacist) (husband of Elener, née Allen, Jones), 15. 16, 33, 81, 83 n.5, 91, 94 n.15, 142, 175 n.2, 217, 219, 221, 228, 229, 256 and n.2
Jones, Sarah, of Pontruffeth (wife of Joseph Jones), 185 and n.3
Jordan, Dorothea (actress), 156, 157 n.4, 215 n.1
Joseph II (Holy Roman Emperor), 285 n.17
Joseph Bonaparte. *See* Bonaparte, Joseph

Junot, Jean Andoche, duc d'Abrantès, 201 n.2, 204, 205 n.1, 206

Karl Philipp, prince of Schwarzenberg (husband of Pauline, daughter of duc and duchess d'Arenberg), 302, 304 nn. 11, 12, 13, and 15
Karl Wilhelm Ferdinand, duke of Brunswick, 122 n.20
Katheryn of Beraine (wife of John Salusbury), 246, 302, 304 nn. 19 and 20
Kearney, Bridges (first husband of Margaret, née Romer (Bridges) Callender), 287 n.1
Keith. *See* Elphinstone
Kemble, John Philip (actor) (brother of SS), 61 n.3, 209, 210 n.3, 251, 252 n.11, 260 n.8
Kilmorey. *See* Needham
King, Cotton (d. 1761) (son of Philadelphia, née Lynch (Cotton) King by her second husband), 283, 285 n.15
King, James (Bath master of ceremonies), 259, 260 n.10
King, Philadelphia, née Lynch (Cotton) (HLP's maternal grandmother), 283, 285 n.15
King, Sarah, née Burrows. *See* Salusbury, Sarah, née Burrows (King)
King, Capt. Thomas (second husband of HLP's maternal grandmother Philadelphia, née Lynch, (Cotton) King, 283, 285 n.15
Kinglake, Dr. Robert: *A Dissertation on Gout*, 110, 112 n.12
Kingstone. *See* Copleston
Kirkwall. *See* Fitzmaurice
Kirwell, Charles, 227 n.4
Knight, Cornelia, 186, 187 n.3
Knight, Joseph (husband of Eleanor de Blaquiere), 233 n.1
Kotzebue, August Friedrich Ferdinand von: *Menschenhass und Reue* of translated and adapted as *The Stranger*, 95, 97 n.9

Lactantius, Lucius Caecilius Fermianus: *Divinarum Institutionum*, 170 n.4
La Fontaine, Jean de: *Fables*: "L'Alouette et ses Petits avec le Maître d'un Champ," 254, 255 n.9
Lake, Gen. Gerard (later first viscount Lake of Delhi and Laswarree), 65 n.1, 175 n.3
Lambart, Lady Alicia (daughter of Richard Lambart, seventh earl of Cavan), 273, 274 n.6

Lambart, Richard, seventh earl of Cavan, 274 n.6
Lancaster, Joseph, 228, 229 n.1
Lansdowne. *See* Petty-Fitzmaurice
Laud, William, archbishop of Canterbury, 86 n.11
Lauderdale. *See* Maitland
Law, Edward, first baron Ellenborough, 114 n.5, 260 n.7, 274 n.5
Law, George Henry, 269, 270 n.5
Law, James Thomas (son of above), 269, 270 n.5
Leak, Alexander ("General Lake") (HLP steward) (AL): 136, 137 n.5, 164, 165 n.7, 174, 175 n.3, 197, 199 n.1, 202, 216, 218, 219, 226, 227 n.4, 228, 234, 237, 239, 245, 246 n.8, 247, 254, 255 n.2, 261, 269, 279, 286, 293, 297, 306, 308, 321
Lee, Mrs. (actress) (mother of Anna, Harriet, and Sophia Lee), 85 n.2
Lee, Anna (Ann), 16, 83, 85 n.2, 209, 210 n.4
Lee, Harriet, 85 n.2; *The Canterbury Tales*, with Sophia Lee, 209, 210 n.4
Lee, Sophia: *The Assignation*, 209, 210 n.4
Lefebvre-Desnouëttes, Charles, comte, 212, 212–13 n.5
Legge, Sir Arthur Kaye, 211 n.13
Legge, George, third earl of Dartmouth (brother of above), 211 n.13
Leman, Rev. Thomas, 12, 227 n.3, 230 and n.1
Lennox, Charles, fourth duke of Richmond, 251 n.3
Leo, Daniel, of Llanerch Park, 99, 100 n.16
Leslie, Anne, née Cane, Lady, 301–2, 303 n.10
Leslie, Sir Edward, baronet, 301–2, 303 nn. 8 and 10
Leveson-Gower, George Granville, second marquess of Stafford (later, 1833, duke of Sutherland), 138, 139 n.3
Leveson-Gower, Granville (later, 1815, viscount Granville and, in 1833, first earl Granville), 276, 278 n.1
Levy, Angelo (London merchant), 272 n.7, 273, 274 n.2
Lewis, Matthew (brother of Mary, née Lewis, Whitelock), 187 n.5
Lewis, Matthew Gregory ("Monk") (son of above), 186, 187 n.5
Lewis, William, of Cornwall, Jamaica (father of Mary, née Lewis, Whitelock), 187 n.5
Linois, Admiral Charles-Alexandre-Léon Durand, comte de, 70 n.5, 110, 111 n.4

Liverpool. *See* Jenkinson
Llangollen, Ladies of (i.e. Lady Eleanor Butler and Sarah Ponsonby), 69, 69–70 n.2, 71, 72, 84, 117, 118 n.13, 200, 209, 211 n.11, 235, 250, 251 nn. 3 and 4, 258, 259 n.3, 307, 309, 318, 319 n.1
"Llewenny family". *See* Fitzmaurice
Lloyd, Ann, née Thelwall, 283, 284 n.8
Lloyd (later Salusbury), Anna Maria, née Mostyn (sister of JMM; wife of John Lloyd Salusbury), 284 n.8, 302–3, 304 n.22, 318, 320 n.5
Lloyd, David (son of T. Lloyd of Denbigh), 255 n.2
Lloyd, Sir Edward Pryce, 143 n.4, 255 n.2
Lloyd, Evan (first husband of Anne, née Perceval (Lloyd) Salusbury), 77 n.8
Lloyd, John (later Salusbury) (son of above; husband of Anna Maria, née Mostyn, Lloyd), 284 n.8, 302, 304 n.22, 320 n.5
Lloyd, John ("Philosopher"), of Wigfair (or Wickwor), 133; letter to, 253
Lloyd, T., of Denbigh, 255 n.2, 295 n.4
Lloyd family of Blaen Ial, 283, 284 n.8
Londonderry. *See* Stewart
London Review, 242, 243 nn. 5 and 6, 243–44 n.7, 244 n.9
Louis XIV (king of France), 94 n.27, 314
Lowndes, Thomas, 176 n.3
Lowry-Corry, Lady Juliana, née Butler, countess of Belmore, 267, 268 n.4
Lowry-Corry, Somerset, second earl of Belmore (husband of above), 268 n.4
Lowth, Robert: *Isaiah. A New Translation*, 147, 148, 149 n.1, 150 nn. 17 and 19
Lucan. *See* Bingham
Lutwyche, Mary, née Thomas, 185–86 and n.2, 230 and n.3, 271, 272 n.8, 278, 287
Lutwyche, William (husband of above), 186 n.2, 230 and n.3, 278, 279
Lyon, Capt. James (first husband of Mary, née Hamilton (Lyon) Coxe), 303 n.4
Lyon, Lt. Gen. James Frederick (son of above), 303 n.4
Lyon, William Berkeley (first husband of Catherine, née Brydges (Lyon) Stanhope), 178 n.5
Lysons, Charlotte (daughter of DL), 171, 172 n.8
Lysons, Rev. Daniel (brother of SL) (DL), 18–19, 170, 171 and nn. 1, 2, and 3, 172 n.8, 238
Lysons, Daniel (son of DL), 171, 172 n.8
Lysons, Mary (sister of DL and SL). *See* Tyre, Mary, née Lysons

Lysons, Samuel (1763–1819) (brother of DL) (SL), 107, 171 n.4, 266 n.17; letter from, 172 n.8; letters to, 19, 34 n.37, 170–71, 238

Lysons, Samuel (1806–77) (son of DL), 171, 172 n.8

Lysons, Sarah (1802–33) (daughter of DL), 171, 172 n.8

Lysons, Sarah, née Hardy (d. 1808) (wife of DL), 17–18, 170, 171 and nn. 1, 2, and 3, 172 n.8

Lyster, Susanna (aunt of Margaret Owen), 70 n.3

Lyttleton, George, first baron Lyttleton of Frankley: "To Mr. Poyntz" and "Epistle to . . . Lord Viscount Cornbury," 235 n.2

Lyttleton, William Henry, baron Westcote of Ballymore and baron Lyttelton of Frankley, 200, 201 n.5

Mackay, Lucy, née Jones, 89, 92 n.1

Mackenzie, Maria, née Shephard (daughter of Thomas Shepard), 190 n.2, 241 and n.3

McKinley, Capt. George, of Lively, 233 n.7

Maclaine (or Maclean), Rev. Archibald, 154, 155 n.13

McPherson, James: Ossian, 28

Madden, Frances, née Hamilton (sister of Isabella Hamilton), 71, 72 n.5, 75, 77 n.17, 102

Madden, Michael Dodgson (husband of above), 72 n.5

Maddocks, William Alexander, M.P., 242, 243 n.3

Madocks (or Maddocks), John Edward, squire of Fron Iw, 16, 156, 157 n.1

Maharbal (commander of Hannibal's cavalry), 64 n.2

Maitland, James, eighth earl of Lauderdale and baron Lauderdale of Thirlestane, 99, 100 nn. 8 and 9, 122 n.17

Malherbe, François de: *Épitaphe d'un Gentilhomme de ses Amis*, HLP's translation of, 89–90, 93 n.4, 118 n.11

Malthus, Thomas Robert, 244 n.9

Mannucci, Giovanni Tommaso, 264, 266 n.19

Maria, née Walpole (Waldegrave), duchess of Gloucester (wife of H.R.H. William Henry, first duke of Gloucester), 278 nn. 3 and 4

Maria I (queen of Portugal) (mother of John VI), 153, 155 n.17, 157 n.7, 160, 161–62 n.11, 163 n.8, 167, 168 nn. 2 and 3, 179

Marie Caroline (queen of Naples) (sister of Marie-Antoinette), 91, 111 n.6

Marie Christine Johanna Josephine Antonie (joint viceroy of Hungary and governor general of the Netherlands), 302, 304 n.14

Marie Louise of Austria, Princess (wife of Napoleon Bonaparte), 278, 278–79 n.8, 279, 281–82, 284 n.2, 303, 304 nn. 11 and 26

Marlborough. *See* Spencer

Marmontel, Jean-François: *Mémoires*, 96, 97 n.11, 98 n.20

Marshall, Andrew (M.D.), 134, 135 n.1

Martha (HLP maid), 247, 249

Mason, Mrs. (CMM's maid), 32

Mason, William: "Museaus," 222, 223 n.2

Masséna, Maréchal André, duc de Rivoli and Prince d'Essling, 103 n.7, 311, 312 nn. 4 and 6, 313 n.7, 320 n.8

Mathews, Sir Toby: *Collection of Letters*, 170 n.4

Mathias, James (merchant) (uncle of Thomas James Mathias), 106-7, 108 n.11

Mathias, Thomas James, 106, 107, 108 n.10; *The Pursuits of Literature*, 107, 109 n.17

Mathias, Vincent (father of above), 107, 109 n.14

Matilda; or The Adventures of an Orphan, 101, 103 n.13

Maughan (or Maugham), John (estate agent and surveyor), 294, 295 nn. 4 and 5, 297, 307

Maxwell, William, 130, 131 n.3

Mazzola (or Mazzolina or Mazzuola), 61, 63 n.18

Melozzo da Forli, 223 n.7

Melville. *See* Dundas

Meredith, Meyrick (Meurig Maredydd), of Pengwern (great-grandfather of John Salusbury Mostyn), 264, 266 n.15

Methuen, Paul Cobb, 284 n.9

Miles, Jane ("Jenny") Mary, née Guest, 92, 95 n.32

Miller, Anne, née Riggs, Lady, 180 n.3

Miller, Joe: *Jest Book*, 121 n.2

Miller, Sir John Riggs (husband of Anne, née Riggs, Miller), 180 n.3

Miller, William (joint publisher with Murray and Constable of Scott's *Marmion*), 192 n.4

Milton, John: *Eikonoklastes*, 103 n.8; *Paradise Lost*, 273, 274 n.4

Möllendorf, Field Marshall Richard J.H. von, 120, 122 n.21

Mohammed ibn 'Abd al-Wahhab, 101, 103 n.9
Molière: *Le Bourgeois Gentilhomme*, 321, 322 n.7
Molyneux, William Philip, second earl of Sefton, 243 n.1
Moncey, Gen. Bon Adrien Jannot de, 177 n.8
Monson, Lt. Col. William, 65 n.1
Montgomery. *See* Herbert
Moore, John (Denbigh surgeon and apothecary), 10–11, 13, 14, 15, 95, 116 and n.2, 139, 141 n.2, 142 and n.3, 153, 159, 170, 174, 176, 177 n.11, 183, 191, 197, 198, 214, 215, 216, 217, 219, 220, 221, 222, 228, 231, 295, 319, 320 n.7
Moore, Gen. Sir John (son of above), 10, 176, 177 n.11, 195 n.4, 224 n.15, 321, 322 n.3
Moore, Tom, 281 n.5
More, Hannah, 77 n.18; *Coelebs in Search of a Wife*, 222, 223 n.5; *Hints towards Forming the Character of a Young Princess*, 80 and n.6
Morichelli-Bosello, Anna (Reggio Emilia), 101, 102 n.10
Morley. *See* Parker
Morris, John (later, 1819, second baronet), 285 n.19
Morris, Lucy Juliana, née Byng (wife of above), 283, 285 n.19
Morshall, Thomas (banker of Chester), 321, 322 n.1
Mosheim, John Lawrence: *Ecclesiastical History, Antient and Modern*, 254, 255 nn. 6 and 7
Moss, Charles, bishop of Oxford, 258 n.2
Mostyn, Anna Maria (sister of JMM), 133. *See also* Salusbury, Anna Maria, née Mostyn
Mostyn, Cecilia Margaretta, née Thrale (daughter of HLT and HT) (CMM), 16, 226, 279, 316; attitude toward Wales, 156, 164; in Bath, 87, 88 n.2, 91, 133, 267; in Cheltenham, 318; children of, 91, 94 n.16, 101, 102 n.2, 115, 137 nn. 3 and 4, 156, 164, 171, 174 n.1, 175, 177, 196, 198, 199; education of children of, 32, 102 n.2, 152, 173, 174, 202, 231; and GP's final suffering, 226; and her sisters, 26, 33, 136, 137 n.1, 146 n.2, 262, 294, 308 n.4; HLP on vs. Q, 247; illness of children of, 159, 162, 166, 167, 184, 237, 251; and JMM's illness and death, 109 n.19, 120, 137 and nn. 3 and 4, 138 n.1, 140, 142; JSPS, Q's baby, and sister-in-law's child as threats to her sons, 33, 34, 307, 308 n.4, 318; at Llewenny Hall, 196; in London, 171, 186, 278, 289; relationship with HLP, 30, 32, 33, 35 n.97, 140, 142, 147, 152, 156, 164, 227, 242, 246, 248 n.3, 256, 267, 277, 317; relationship with JMM, 26, 30, 32, 72; and Segroid, 30, 33, 101, 110–11, 137 nn. 3 and 4, 138 n.1, 156, 159, 162, 165, 166, 169, 177, 196, 202, 204, 254, 294, 297, 302, 317; servants of, 91, 101, 226; visits of to Brynbella, 84, 172, 173, 174, 181, 184, 195 and n.1, 196, 197, 245, 247–49, 252, 297, 302, 307. *See also* Thrale, Cecilia Margaretta
Mostyn, Edward (later, 1823, seventh baronet), 138 and n.1
Mostyn, Henry ("Harry") Meredith (second son of CMM and JMM), 91, 94 n.16, 101, 102 n.2, 136, 137 n.3, 166, 174, 184, 202, 204, 247, 251, 289, 294, 307
Mostyn, John, of Segroid (first husband of Anna Maria, née Meredith (Mostyn) Wynn; father of JMM), 78 n.19
Mostyn, John Meredith (JMM): at Bath (1805–1806), 32, 60, 72, 87, 88 n.2, 91, 111; children of, 101, 102 n.2, 204; final illness and death of, 16–17, 33, 36 n.97, 91, 92, 95, 107, 109 n.19, 117, 118 n.12, 120, 129, 133, 136, 137 nn. 1, 3 and 4, 138 n.1, 140, 141, 157–58, 175, 176 n.6, 230; relationship with CMM, 26, 30, 32, 72; relationship with HLP, 32; and Thrale daughters, 26
Mostyn, John Salusbury (eldest son of CMM and JMM), 101, 102 n.2, 136, 137 n.3, 166, 175, 202, 204, 247, 251, 264, 289, 294, 295 n.9, 297
Mostyn, Roger (father of Charlotte, née Mostyn, Edwards), 116 n.10
Mostyn, Sir Thomas: colliery of, 218–19, 220 n.4
Mostyn, Thomas Arthur Bertie (third son of CMM and JMM), 101, 102 n.2, 136, 137 n.3, 143, 144 n.9, 202, 251, 289, 294, 295 n.9
Mount Edgcumbe. *See* Edgcumbe
Mountnorris. *See* Annesley
Müller, Major Joseph Christian, 282, 284 n.3
Muhammad (Mahomet) (founder of Islam), 94 n.27, 99, 101, 103 n.8
Mulgrave. *See* Phipps
Murat, Marshal Joachim, 128 n.2

Murphy, Arthur, 305 and n.1; Jessé Foot's *Life of*, 84, 85–86 n.11
Murphy, Jane, née French (mother of above), 86 n.11
Murray, John (joint publisher with Constable and Miller of Scott's *Marmion*), 192 n.4
Myddelton, Augusta (daughter of Robert and May Myddelton), 214 n.5
Myddelton, Caroline May (eldest daughter of Robert and May Myddelton), 245 and n.5
Myddelton, Louisa Dorothea, 64 n.3
Myddelton, May, née Ogilvie (wife of Robert Myddelton), 64, 196, 197 n.3, 213, 214 n.5
Myddelton, Rev. Robert, D.D. (1751–1815) (husband of above), 14, 113, 115, 116 n.9, 140, 172, 186, 197 n.3, 197, 213, 214 n.5, 214, 215, 226, 239, 244–45 and n.5, 307, 308 n.10; letter to, 63–64
Myddelton, Robert (1795–1876) (son of above), 63, 64 n.1, 115, 116 n.9, 140, 141 n.5, 213, 244–45 and n.3

Naples, royal family of. See Ferdinando IV; Marie Caroline
Napoleon Bonaparte. See Bonaparte, Napoleon
Napoleon II (François-Joseph-Charles Bonaparte) (son of Napoleon I and Marie Louise), 284 n.2
Neale ("Neild"), Edward (son of George Vansittart), 95, 97 n.7
Needham, Frances, née Cotton, viscountess Kilmorey, 134, 135 n.9, 264, 266 n.18, 283, 296
Needham, Robert, eleventh viscount Kilmorey (husband of above), 134, 135 n.9, 264, 266 n.18
Nelson, Frances Herbert, née Woodward (Nisbet), duchess of Bronté (wife of Adm. Horatio Nelson), 264, 265 n.11, 267, 273, 275
Nelson, Adm. Horatio (1758–1805), baron and viscount Nelson, duke of Bronté, 67, 68 n.1, 72, 73 n.5, 78, 79 nn. 5 and 7, 99, 178, 264, 265 n.11, 267; death and funeral of, 84, 85 n.7, 86 nn. 14, 15, and 16, 91, 94 n.17, 268 n.9
Nelson, Horatio (1788–1808), styled viscount Trafalgar, 178, 179 n.7
Nelson, William (1757–1835), second baron Nelson of the Nile (father of above; brother of Adm. Horatio Nelson), 179 n.7

Nesbitt, Arnold (brother-in-law of HT), 27, 35 n.70, 176 n.3
Nesbitt, Susanna, née Thrale (wife of above; sister of HT), 176 n.3
Newborough. See Wynn
Nicholls, Rev. Norton, 106, 108 n.5, 139–40, 259, 260 n.9
Norfolk. See Howard
Normanby. See Phipps
Norris, Richard Wise (surgeon at Little Sutton), 188, 189 n.1
North, Francis, fourth earl of Guilford (brother of the third earl; husband of Maria, née Boycott, North), 296–97, 298 nn. 2 and 9
North, Frederick, second earl of Guilford, 265 n.2
North, Frederick (1801–2), styled Lord North (son of third earl of Guilford), 298 n.9
North, George Augustus, third earl of Guilford, 298 n.9
North, George Augustus (1791–92), styled Lord North (son of third earl of Guilford), 298 n.9
North, Maria, née Boycott, countess of Guilford. See Boycott, Maria
North, Maria Frances Mary, née Hobart (d. 1794), countess of Guilford (first wife of third earl of Guilford), 298 n.9
North, Susan, née Couts (d. 1837), countess of Guilford (second wife of third earl), 298 n.9

O'Beirne, Thomas Lewis, bishop of Ossory and Meath, 92, 95 n.28, 301, 303 n.6
O'Brien (or O'Bryan), Mary, née Palmer, marchioness of Thomond (second wife of Murrough O'Brien, marquess of Thomond), 184 n.9
O'Brien (or O'Bryan), Murrough, baron Thomond of Taplow, Bucks., fifth earl of Inchiquin, marquess of Thomond (husband of above), 173 and n.5, 178 and n.2, 179 n.8, 183, 183–84 n.9
O'Brien, William, baron and sixth earl of Inchiquin, second marquess of Thomond (nephew and heir of Murrough O'Brien), 183, 184 n.9
O'Connor, Roger (Irish nationalist), 95, 97 n.4
Oldfield, Edward (1782–1850) (attorney), 216 n.1
Oldfield, John (1760–1841) (HLP and GP attorney), 13, 102 n.4, 215, 216 n.1, 227 n.4,

247, 255n.2, 263, 265n.7, 294, 295n.4, 307
Oldfield, Thomas, 216n.1
Orkney. *See* Fitzmaurice
Ormonde. *See* Butler
Ormsby, Margaret, née Owen, 101, 102n.3, 108n.4, 250, 251n.3
Ormsby, Owen (husband of above), 106, 108n.4
Ormsby-Gore, Mary Jane, née Ormsby (daughter of Margaret and Owen Ormsby), 106, 108nn. 3 and 4, 250
Ormsby-Gore, William (husband above), 108n.3
Ovid: *Metamorphoses*, 95, 97n.6, 321, 322n.6
Owen. *See* Hughes, Owen.
Owen, Elizabeth, née Lyster (mother of Margaret Owen), 70n.3
Owen, Henrietta Jemima. *See* Smythe-Owen
Owen, John (brother of Margaret Owen), 70n.3
Owen, Letitia. *See* Barnston, Letitia, née Owen (Mytton)
Owen, Lewys (father of Margaret Owen), 70n.3
Owen, Margaret ("Peggy") (Shrewsbury relative of HLP), 71, 207; letter to, 69
Owen, Nicholas, of Condover. *See* Smythe-Owen
Owen, William, of Porkington, 108n.4

Pacchierotti, Gasparo, 124 and n.4
Paget, Sir Arthur (son of Henry Paget, third earl of Uxbridge; second husband of Lady Augusta, née Fane (Parker)), 215n.2, 223n.9
Paget, Lady Augusta, née Fane (Parker) (wife of above), 215n.2
Paget, Caroline Elizabeth, née Villiers (wife of Henry William Paget; later wife of George William Campbell, sixth duke of Argyll), 224n.15, 310, 311n.7, 321
Paget, Lady Charlotte. *See* Wellesley, Lady Charlotte, née Cadogan
Paget, Henry, tenth baron Paget of Beaudesert, third earl of Uxbridge, 214, 215n.2, 222, 223n.9, 321, 322n.4
Paget, Henry William (later first marquess of Anglesey) (son of Henry Paget, third earl of Uxbridge; husband of Caroline Elizabeth Villiers; later husband of Lady Charlotte, née Cadogan, (Wellesley) Paget), 215n.2, 223n.9, 224n.15, 311nn. 7 and 8, 321, 322n.5
Paget, Jane, née Champagné, baroness (wife of tenth baron Paget), 223n.9
Paget, Richard (HLP footman), 194, 195n.5, 197n.2
Palafox y Melzi, José, 212, 212–13n.5, 213n.6
Paley, William, 80n.5, 119, 121n.13; *Natural Theology*, 79, 80nn. 1, 2, and 3
Pallet, Peter Paul (pseud.). *See* Warner, Rev. Richard
Palmer, John (1742–98) (actor), 164, 165n.2
Palmer, John (architect of Bath theater), 89n.6
Palmer, John ("Gentleman") (d. 1768) (actor), 164, 165n.2
Panton, Mary, née Gubbins, 264, 265n.10
Panton, Thomas (husband of above), 265n.10
Parke, Mr. (London attorney), 274n.5
Parke, Frances Margaretta (daughter of John Parke), 95, 96, 97n.13, 261, 262n.2
Parke, Hannah (wife of John Parke), 261, 262n.2
Parke, John (oboist), 97n.13, 108n.1, 262n.2
Parke, Maria Hester (daughter of John; later wife of John Beardmore), 95, 96, 97n.13, 106, 108n.1, 261, 262nn. 2, 3, and 7
Parker, John, viscount Boringdon of North Molton and first earl of Morley, 63n.15, 215n.2
Parmigiano, Il. *See* Mazzola, Gerolamo Francesco Maria
Parr, Rev. Samuel, 117, 118n.7
Parry, Mr., 295n.4
Parry, Caleb Hillier (Bath M.D.), 137, 229; attends GP and HLP, 11, 12, 17, 60, 127n.2, 177, 178n.1, 193, 194n.1, 263, 265n.5; attends Lady Bradford, 84, 85n.10; letters to, 34n.29, 193–94
Parry, Elizabeth Emma (daughter of above), 193, 194n.2
Parry, Sarah, née Rigby (wife of Caleb Hillier Parry), 194
Pauline, Princess (daughter of duc and duchess d'Arenberg; wife of Karl Philipp, prince of Schwarzenberg), 302, 304nn. 11 and 12
Pedro I (emperor of Brazil) (son of John VI of Portugal), 155n.17, 157n.7, 160, 161–62n.11, 163n.8, 168n.2, 179
Peel, Elizabeth, 281n.3

Peel, Sir Robert, baronet (father of above), 281 n.3
Peel, William Yates (son of above), 280, 281 n.3
Pemberton, Anna Maria Emma, née Smythe (second wife of Capt. Edward Pemberton), 197 n.1, 299, 300 n.4
Pemberton, Capt. Edward (husband of Frances, née Yaldwin, and later husband of Anna Maria Emma, née Smythe), 197 n.1, 299, 300 n.4
Pemberton, Edward William Smythe (son of Anna Maria and Capt. Edward Pemberton) (school friend of JSPS), 23, 197 n.1, 208 n.5, 246, 248 n.2, 256, 257, 261, 272, 278, 280, 286, 288, 290, 294, 295 n.10, 299, 308, 309, 310, 315, 316, 319
Pemberton, Frances, née Yaldwin (first wife of Capt. Edward Pemberton), 197 n.1
Pemberton, Frances (daughter of above), 197 n.1
Pemberton, Harriet Maria (daughter of Anna Maria and Capt. Edward Pemberton), 23, 197 n.1
Pemberton, Letitia Caroline (daughter of Anna Maria and Capt. Edward Pemberton), 197 n.1
Pemberton family of Longnor, 195, 197 n.1
Pembroke. *See* Herbert
Pennant, Louisa, 232, 233 n.2
Penrice, Anna Maria. *See* Salusbury, Anna Maria, née Penrice
Penrice, Sir Henry (father of Anna Maria, née Penrice, Salusbury), 75, 77 n.16
Pepys, Jane Elizabeth, née Leslie (Evelyn), *suo jure* countess of Roth, 291, 292 n.2
Pepys, Sir Lucas, baronet (M.D.), 31, 164, 165 n.5, 236, 291, 292 n.2
Perceval, Anne (daughter of Thomas Perceval of North Weston, Somerset), 77 n.8
Perceval, Bridget, countess of Egmont (wife of the fourth earl), 75, 76–77 n.8
Perceval, John, second earl of Egmont, 160 n.9
Perceval, John, fourth earl of Egmont, 77 n.8
Perceval, Spencer (son of second earl of Egmont), 243 n.3, 288.1
Perceval, Thomas, of North Weston, Somerset (father of Anne Perceval), 77 n.8
Perkins, Amelia (daughter of John Perkins, the younger), 91, 94 n.26
Perkins, Amelia, née Mosely (Bevan) (second wife of John Perkins, the elder), 91, 94 n.26
Perkins, John (1730–1812), 91, 94 n.26, 102 n.6
Perkins, John (1755-ca. 1818) (son of above), 94 n.26
Perkins, Sarah Anne (wife of John Perkins, the younger), 94 n.26
Perry, Dr. William: *A Dialogue in the Shades*, 112 n.12
Peter (gardener at Brynbella), 166, 207, 212
Petty-Fitzmaurice, Henry, third marquess of Lansdowne, 96, 97–98 n.17
Phillips's (auction house), 154 n.10
Phipps, Sir Henry, third baron Mulgrave, first viscount Normanby, first earl of Mulgrave, 65 n.2, 233 n.4
Piazzi, Giuseppe, 60, 61 n.1
Pillar, James, 263, 265 n.7
Pindar, Peter: *Solemn . . . Epistle to Mrs. Clarke*, 242, 244 n.8
Pink (HLP calf), 113, 114 n.4, 115
Piozzi, Gabriel (second husband of HLT) (GP): anti-Bonaparte feelings of, 176, 194, 199, 200 n.1, 205; conversion of to Anglicanism, 12–13, 14, 226, 227 n.3; death and burial of, 14, 224, 225 and n.1, 227 n.4, 227–28 n.6; and JSPS, 21, 34 n.10, 152 and n.1, 291; as "proper" English squire, 17; proposed trip to Italy with HLP (1789), 31; and Reynolds' portraits at Streatham Park, 112; and SS's return to stage (1808), 204, 209; and Thrale daughters, 26, 29–30, 31, 32, 231
—illnesses of: at Bath, 63, 87, 102, 125, 127 n.2, 127–28, 129, 164; bedridden, 172, 173, 174, 179, 181; at Chester, 191, 193; compared with Mrs Williams', 213–14; costs of, 14, 231; demands of on HLP, 184–85; Elener Jones on, 142 n.3; final days of, 214, 216, 217, 218, 219, 220–21, 224, 225, 226, 227 n.6, 230; gout, 59, 70 n.4, 74, 78 n.1, 81, 83 n.3, 92, 136, 143, 151, 159, 215-16; symptoms of and treatments for, 10–12, 13–14, 19, 60, 78, 82, 102, 113, 114 n.14, 134, 153, 181, 186, 188, 190, 196, 197, 199 and n.4, 202, 205, 207, 215, 219, 220, 221; ups and downs of, 72, 84, 141–42, 145, 157, 167, 169, 170–71, 176, 177, 184, 187–88, 200, 204–5, 212, 222–23
—as musician: compositions of, 159, 160 n.2, 164; effect of his illness on, 106; and imitation of Pacchierotti's singing style, 124 and n.4; musical setting for

TSW's verses, 302; traveling pianoforte of, 29–30, 226, 227 n.5, 228 n.6
—will of, 14, 216 n.1, 226, 227 n.4, 230, 231; bequests of to his Italian relations, 23, 269, 270 n.8, 271, 276 nn. 6 and 7, 272, 273, 279, 281 n.1; bequests of to Q, 29, 226, 228 n.6

Piozzi, Hester Lynch, née Salusbury (Thrale) (HLP):
—and agriculture at Brynbella, 9, 71, 72, 152 n.3, 203, 279, 291; cattle and sheep, 82, 174, 217, 239, 254, 269; crops, 78, 110, 196, 210, 229, 242, 295; fall harvest, 245, 247; pea-fowl, 157, 169, 222; poultry, 174, 207, 221; trees, 153, 157, 161, 164, 166, 297; wood pigeons and rabbits, 245; veterinary medicine at, 315; vs. England, 256
—on art, music, and literature: aphorisms and proverbs, 91, 156, 157 n.5, 169, 170 n.4; Edgeworth's *Castle Rackrent*, 88; epitaphs, 89–90; Exhibition of the Society of Painters in Water Colours (1809), 238; Godwin's novels, 60; and GP's illness, 9; Edmund Hyde Hall's lines in tribute to HLP, 303, 304 n.24; Elizabeth Hamilton's *Agrippina*, 60; Lukas de Heere's portrait of Katheryn of Beraine, 302; her love of reading and sources of books, 101, 158, 159, 169, 211, 222; Hogarth's "The Lady's Last Stake," 283, 285 nn. 12 and 14; "literary chat" with SL, 171; Malherbe's poetry, 89–90; malignity of reviewers, 110; Marmontel's vs. Cumberland's memoirs, 96; miniature of by John Jackson, 268, 269, 271; new Bath theater, 88; organ concerts by Handel in London, 204; paintings of Robert Andrew Riddell and Frances Talbot, 60–61; portraits of HLP's ancestors at home of John Lloyd, 302–3; Reynolds' portraits at Streatham Park (including one of HLP), 112, 200, 305; satires on Bath society and the British Court, 179, 180, 181, 186; Scott's *Marmion*, 191, 192 n.5; Anna Seward's *Letters*, 264, 266 n.17; viewing of Marquess of Stafford's art collection, 138; visit to Somerset House Exhibition (1807), 138 and n.2
—business affairs: catalogue of library and paintings at Streatham Park, 138; as creditor of Thomas Morshall, 321, 322; financial problems, 17; as GP's executrix and sole legatee, 230, 269, 270 n.8, 271, 272 nn. 6 and 7, 272, 273, 279, 281 n.1; Hertfordshire copyholds, 168 and n.1; her 1809 will, 15, 234, 235 n.5, 241, 294–95, 295 n.8, 297; and HT's estate and his attitude toward HLT's Welsh properties, 175, 302; lease of Streatham Park and lawsuit against Peter Giles, 9, 106–7, 135, 135–36 n.1, 138, 166 and n.2, 175, 176, 176–77 n.7, 183, 184 n.10, 190, 239, 311, 312 n.9, 314, 315 n.2, 316; management of Brynbella and bill of enclosure, 9, 246–47, 248 n.5, 254, 255 n.2, 256, 261, 263, 265 nn. 6 and 7, 294, 295 and n.4, 297, 302, 307, 308, 309, 310 n.2; property rights and HLP's Salusbury inheritance, 9, 60, 62 n.6, 75, 77 nn. 9, 14, and 16, 82 n.2, 106–7, 294; rent from RD for land for his Streatham school, 319, 320 n.12
—character traits of: complex personality, 17–18; good breeding, 17, 23; independence and resiliency, 9, 17; melancholia, 10, 19; morbidity, 10, 15, 16–17, 18, 33, 91, 110, 166, 167, 212, 224, 225, 226, 239, 258–59, 263, 288, 302, 305, 307, 309, 311; self-assurance, sociability, and witty gregariousness, 9, 17, 70 n.6, 71, 211–12
—health of, 63, 156; coughs and colds, 87–88, 258, 261, 265 n.1, 266, 317, 322; effect of GP's death on, 227, 228, 229, 230, 232, 234–35, 236–37; food poisoning, 139, 142, 153; gastro-intestinal attacks, 169, 190–91, 192 n.1, 200, 203, 262; neuroses, 17, 19; swollen face, 205, 228, 245; toothache, 156, 301, 303
—interests in and attitudes toward: Abraxas stone, 254, 255 n.3; agriculture, 210; Americans, 78, 79 n.7; astronomy, 60; biblical philology, 148; biblical prophecy, 147, 148, 150 nn. 18 and 19; cave of iron in Siberia, 114, 115 n.4; Chester county jail, 191; conversation vs. letter writing, 71; criticism of her published works, 17, 92, 94 n.27, 107, 242, 243 n.6; cruelty to animals, 293; education for boys, 63–64, 206; eschatology, 99; family relationships, 148; flattery, 279; food, 160, 170; gaming in Bath, 257, 258 n.5; genealogy, 253; Gnosticism, 254, 255 n.6; letters of to SJ, 266 n.17; letter writing, 9, 18; living alone, 242; living past one's intellectual powers, 125; medical remedies and health treatments, 11, 12, 65, 66, 67, 74, 78 and n.1, 81, 90, 110, 127, 129, 139, 140 n.1, 142, 157, 197, 199 n.4, 209, 214, 218, 219, 220, 221, 228, 231, 259, 291; memory, 202; newspapers for current

events, 18, 174, 195; numerology, 90, 94 n.27, 311–12 and nn. 2 and 3, 313 nn. 11, 12, and 13; parenting and scandalous behavior of offspring, 222; phonetics, foreign pronunciations, and roots of English words in French, 104–5 and n.2, 318–19; pomp and showiness of funerals, 91; praise from friends vs. enemies, 273; religion, 65, 130; restoration of the Jews to Palestine, 122, 123 nn. 1 and 10; social life, 60, 69 n.1; study of the Bible, 64, 122; study of Hebrew, 80 and n.8, 82 n.2, 101, 103 n.11, 104–5 and n.1, 130, 148; style and fashion, 17, 60; vice and folly at Eaton, 202, 206; Warwick Castle, 196, 197 n.4; the Welsh Bible, 131; word games and word play, 280, 282, 283, 285 n.16, 290, 292, 293 n.6, 297

—and international events: America as ally of Napoleon, 99; armistice between Austria and France (1805), 88; battle of Talavera, 244, 245 n.2; battle of Trafalgar, 83–84, 85 n.7; British actions in Calabria, 117, 118 n.8; British naval bombardment of Boulogne, 84, 86 n.15; capture of British ships by the Danes, 160 and n.10; capture of Buenos Aires by Britain, 117, 118 n.5, 120; capture of Cape of Good Hope by Britain, 99, 100 n.7; capture of Naples by France, 101, 103 n.7; Christian settlement in India, 171 and n.5; Convention of Cintra, 200, 201 n.2, 202, 203–4, 205 n.4, 206, 209, 210–11 n.8; defeat of Massena's army at Bussaco by Wellington, 311, 312 nn. 4, 5, and 6, 313 n.7; effect of French Revolution on taste and learning, 109 n.17; effect of war on British merchants, 157, 158 n.3; entry of Denmark into war, 157, 158 n.1; events leading to War of 1812, 148, 150 n.20; French buildup in West Indies, 72, 73 n.3; French emigrés in England, 99; French naval blockade of Britain, 153, 155 n.16, 157, 158 n.3; invasion of Portugal by France, 156, 157 nn. 7 and 8; invasion of Spain by France, 175–76, 176 n.1, 177 nn. 8 and 10, 194, 194–95 n.4; Jewish sanhedrim at Paris (1807), 149, 150 n.22; journey of Pius VI to Vienna (1810), 283, 285 n.17; mission of Lord Hutchinson to Prussia and Russia, 129, 130 n.4; Napoleon's arrival in Warsaw, 128 n.2; Napoleon's letter to Friedrich Wilhelm III, 128 n.4; Napoleon's second marriage, 278, 278–79 n.8, 279; Napoleon's threat to India, 110, 111 n.7; Napoleon's victories in 1805, 83, 85 n.4; opening of Spanish and Portuguese ports, 208, 209 n.1; peace negotiations with France, 65–66 n.2, 95, 99, 100 nn. 8 and 9, 120, 122 n.17, 162, 167, 209, 210 n.8, 252, 253 n.2; Peninsular War, 319, 320 n.8, 321, 322 nn. 2 and 3; pillaging of Loretto, 222, 223 n.7; Portuguese royal family's exile to Brazil, 160, 160–61 n.10, 162, 163 n.6, 167, 167–68 n.2, 179; role of Austria and Russia in war, 199, 200 n.2; Russian fleet at Lisbon, 162, 163 n.7; Russian troops return home from Prussia, 97; Russo-Turkish wars, 110, 111 n.5, 112 n.6; siege of Saragossa, 212, 212–13 n.5, 213 n.6, 222, 223 n.6; slaves in West Indies, 77 n.18; Spanish insurrection and king of Spain, 209, 210 nn. 5 and 7; threat of French invasion of Britain, 110, 233; Toulon fleet, 67; Tyrolean and Vorarlberg insurgents, 282, 284 n.3; uprisings in India, 65 and n.1; Wahhabis movement, 101, 103 n.9

—and local events and natural phenomena: autumn, 203, 254; birds at Brynbella, 169, 183, 184, 203, 204, 206, 207, 217; boy in care of Denbigh parish, 253; caves, 61; comets and meteors, 18, 153, 154 and n.2, 155, 158, 162, 209; earthquake in Scotland, 204, 213; fire at Mostyn colliery, 13, 218–19; postal rate increase, 72; St. David's Day celebrations, 177, 273; snow storms, 159–60, 161–62, 164, 165, 205–6, 321; spring, 181, 183, 184, 186, 217, 229, 231, 232; stagecoach accidents, 244, 245; storms, 207, 302, 304 n.18; unhealthfulness of London, 164; weather, 9, 18, 72, 101, 110, 115, 151, 152 n.3, 156, 157, 204, 269, 321; winds, 213; winter of 1807–8, 165–66, 167, 168, 169–70, 171, 174, 269, 321

—and national events: arrest of Sir Francis Burdett and riots concerning, 287, 288 n.2, 289, 290 and n.5, 292, 293 nn. 5 and 6; assassination attempt on Duke of Cumberland, 292, 293 nn. 7 and 8; British expedition to Sicily, 66, 67 n.4; British naval affairs, 69, 70 n.5; Catholic Emancipation Bill, 92, 257, 258 n.2; Catholic emancipation in Ireland, 72, 73 n.4; Mary Anne Clarke scandal, 211 n.9, 213, 214 n.2, 214, 215 n.1, 224 n.11, 232, 233 n.5, 242, 244 n.8, 259, 260 n.7; consecration of Catholic chapel at Bath, 257;

coronation of George III, 250, 251 and n.1, 252 n.7; day of thanksgiving for victory at Trafalgar, 84, 86 n.14; death of Pitt and formation of new government, 95, 97 nn. 1 and 2; election of chancellor of Oxford University, 257 and n.1, 257–58 n.2, 259, 259–60 n.6; election riots in London, 115; fires at Covent Gardens and Drury Lane theaters, London, 200, 201 nn. 3 and 4, 204, 205 n.5, 214, 215 n.4; illness and epidemics in London and Wales, 87, 98, 140, 185, 232–33; Irish attitudes toward Napoleon, 92; jubilee of George III's accession, 249, 250 n.2, 250, 252, 253 n.1; mad dogs running loose in London, 133 and n.5; madness of George III, 311, 313 n.8, 315, 322–23 and n.1; Ministry of All the Talents, 98, 100 nn. 2 and 3; parliamentary elections and formation of new government, 85, 86 n.14, 133 and n.4, 140, 141 n.6, 142, 143 n.4, 232; parliamentary politics, 65, 287–88, 288 n.1; political graffiti in London, 289, 290 n.1; possible war with U.S. over impress of U.S. seamen, 99, 100 n.12; rebellion in Ireland, 176, 177 n.11; rising food prices, 162; Roman Catholic Army and Navy Service Bill, 133 and nn. 3 and 4; run on Chester bank, 299, 300 n.5; theaters in Bath, 88, 89 n.6, 283, 284 n.9; theater ticket price riots, 251, 252 nn. 11 and 12, 259, 260 n.8, 279, 281 n.2

—personal life: described in 1805, 87 n.22; first meeting with SJ, 305 and nn. 2 and 3; gossip mongering in re marriage to GP, 28; and grandchildren of, 16, 184; hostility of toward Charles Burney, the younger, 125 and n. 1, 296, 298 n.8; on kinsfolk and family differences, 272, 275; marriage to HT vs. marriage to GP, 17; memories of youth at Llewenny Hall, 217, 218 n.2; mourning for GP, 14–15, 19, 230, 236; on personalities of her daughters, 26–27, 31–32; pet dogs "Greyhound," "Frisk," and "Chancey," 174, 310, 315; and second pregnancy for Q, 303, 304 n.26; wedding anniversaries of with GP, 11, 16, 78, 113

—servants of, 9, 13–14, 15, 69, 81, 82, 83 n.12, 91, 101, 103 n.10, 127 and n.1, 136, 172–73, 193–94, 195 n.5, 222, 226, 228, 229, 237, 239, 241, 257, 269, 307, 308; the "dying cook," 113; HLP's relationship with, 15. *See also* Allen, Elener; Andrew; Barns, Mrs.; Chancey, Mrs.; Dore, Marie; Dunscombe; Glover, Ann; Hughes, Owen; Johnson, Mary; Jones, Elener; Leak, Alexander; Martha; Mason, Mrs.; Paget, Richard; Peter; Ray, Mrs.; Robert; Watkins, Ruth

—travels and visits: to Abergele, 70 n.4, 83 n.3; to Bath for annual winter-spring residence, 11, 12, 18, 34 n.10, 60, 65, 66, 69 and n.1, 70 n.4, 71 n.1, 79, 80 n.1, 82, 84, 87, 105 n.1, 116 and n.5, 117, 124 n.1, 190 and n.1, 245, 248, 250, 251, 252, 254, 255, 256 and n.1, 257, 258, 259, 262, 263, 264 n.1, 265, 266, 269, 275, 282–3, 284 n.1; to Bodelwyddan, 309, 310 n.5, 314–15, 316; to Chester, 11, 12, 113, 115, 188–89, 189–90, 190–91, 193, 194; as escape from sorrow, 225, 226; to Ladies of Llangollen, 69, 69–70 n.2, 71, 72; to Llewenny Hall, 81, 83 n.4, 184–85; to Llyn, Carnarvonshire, 116 and n.3; from London to Wales with JSPS, 24, 240, 241; to London and back to Brynbella, 15, 18, 26, 134, 135, 138, 139, 141, 142, 225, 226, 227, 228 n.7, 228, 259, 275, 286, 287, 288; to Margaret Owen, 69, 70 n.3, 71; to Prestatyn, 70 n.4, 74, 76 n.1, 78, 79 n.3, 81, 82–83 n.3; to Sackville seat, 154 n.8; to Segroid, 30, 249, 317; to Speen, 240–41, 266; on tourism and travel to Wales, 201

—minor works: epigram on gift of pens from CMM, 76, 78 n.20; "Epitaph on old Mr. Jones of Cavendish Square," 118 n.11; "Lines addressed to Sophia Thrale," 164, 165 n.6; "Minced Meat for Pyes," 170 n.4; "Pocket Books," 34 n.23, 248 n.5, 262 n.6, 272 n.7, 281 n.6, 295 n.4, 313 n.9; "Poems on Several Occasions with Anecdotes, &c." (i.e., *Harvard Piozziana*), 305–6 and n.1, 310, 311 n.9; Sunday-school hymn by, 115; translation of verses in memory of Dr. Laura Bassi, 250, 251 n.2; unedited verses by in possession of SH, 242; verses by for JSPS (1810), 276–77, 287; verses on Scott's *Marmion*, 192 n.5; verses on tea chest formed from Pope's willow, 198, 199 n.11; verses on twenty-second anniversary of marriage with GP, 16; verses on tolling bells at Denbigh and Dymerchion, 247, 248 n.7

—works: *Anecdotes*, 17, 212 n.1, 224 n.4, 305 n.2; *British Synonymy*, 23, 242, 243 n.6; *Florence Miscellany*, 70 n.2, 107; *Retrospection*, 17, 92, 93 n.7, 94 n.27, 107, 109 n.17, 159, 160 n.5, 161 and nn. 1 and 2, 304 n.24, 315 n.5; *The Three Warnings*,

304 n.24; *Thraliana*, 11, 12–13, 14, 15, 16, 20, 26–33, 34 nn. 5, 7, 10, 11, 19, 26, 27, and 41, 35 nn. 69, 70, 73, 74, 76–79, 81, and 88–97, 79 n.3, 83 nn. 4, 6, 11, and 13, 116 n.3, 127 n.2, 137 n.1, 146 n.2, 152 nn. 1 and 3, 178 n.1, 199 nn. 4 and 11, 237 n.4, 305 nn. 2 and 3
Pitt, William, 66 n.4, 72 n.4; death of, 16, 95, 97 nn. 1, 2, 3, and 5
Pius VI (pope), 283, 285 n.17
Pius VII (pope), 59, 111 n.6
Plummer, Mrs. (housekeeper at RD's school), 184, 185 n.2, 315
Plunkett, Arthur James, eighth earl of Fingal, 73 n.4
Pohlman, Joannes (English harpsichord and piano maker), 226, 227 n.5
Ponsonby, Sarah. *See* Llangollen, Ladies of
Pope, Alexander: *Dunciad*, 222, 223 n.8; *Epistle IV. To Richard Boyle, Earl of Burlington*, 309, 310 n.3; *Essay on Criticism*, 286, 287 nn. 3 and 4; *Essay on Man*, 85 n.11, 286, 287 n.2; *Iliad*, 280, 281 n.8; willow of at Twickenham, 198, 199 nn. 7, 8, and 9
Popham, Com. Sir Home Riggs, 118 n.5
Portarlington. *See* Dawson-Damer
Porteus, Beilby, bishop, successively, of Chester and London, 75, 77–78 n.18
Portland. *See* Bentinck
Portuguese court. *See* Maria I; John (Joao), prince regent of Portugal; Pedro I
Prescott, Miss (London quack), 127, 128 n.1
Prior, Matthew: *Alma*, 176, 177 n.9, 301, 303 n.7
Pye, Bathurst, 16

Quicke, Jane, née Cox (Hoblyn), 194, 195 n.5
Quicke, John (second husband of above), 195 n.5

Rackstraw's Museum, London, 147, 149 n.3
Radnor. *See* Bouverie
Ramsden, Jesse (optician), 153, 154 n.3
Randolph, Rev. Francis (proprietor and minister of Octagon and Laura chapels, Bath; prebendary of Bristol), 22, 92, 101, 130, 131 n.4, 254, 255 n.1, 270 n.5, 272, 273, 282
Randolph, Rev. John, bishop of London, 25 n.2
Rapin de Thoyras (or de Rapin-Thoyras), Paul: *The History of England*, 293 n.8
Rauzzini, Venanzio (Italian operatic singer and composer), 95 n.32, 95, 181, 183 n.4

Ray, Mrs. (HLP servant), 234
Ray, Ann, née Barker, 107
Ray, Elinor, 295, 296 n.11
Ray, Robert (lawyer) (husband of Ann, née Barker, Ray), 107, 234, 255 nn. 5 and 6; letter to, 135
Rebecca, Biagio (artist), 302, 304 n.21
Reeves, Mr., of the Alien Office, 240 n.1
Rendlesham. *See* Thelluson
Reni, Guido, 223 n.7
Reynolds, Dr. Henry Revell, 313 n.8
Reynolds, James (Bath perfumer), 134, 135 n.6
Reynolds, Sir Joshua: portrait of Dr. Charles Burney, 126 (reproduced), 305; portrait of Sir George Colebrooke, 182 (reproduced); portrait of Sacchini, 153, 154 n.9; portrait of HLT, 305; portraits by at Streatham Park, 112 and n.2, 113 n.4, 200, 201 n.6, 305; statue of by Flaxman, 138 n.2
Richmond. *See* Lennox
Riddell, Sir James, first baronet (d. 1797), 61, 62–63 n.14
Riddell, Sir James Milles (1787–1861), second baronet (grandson of the first baronet), 63 n.14
Riddell, Mary, née Milles, Lady (first wife of Sir James Riddell, first baronet), 63 n.14
Riddell, Robert Andrew (watercolorist), 60–61, 62 n.12, 63 n.14
Riddell, Sarah, née Burdon (Swinburne), Lady (2nd wife of Sir James Riddell, first baronet), 63 n.14
Rigaud, John Francis (artist), 304 n.21
Robarts, Mr. (friend of John Gillon), 160 n.8
Robert (HLP footman), 196, 197 n.2, 228, 237, 239, 269, 271, 273
Roberts, Rev. John (HLP's Hebrew tutor), 103 n.11, 105 n.1, 117, 118 nn. 3 and 4, 119, 131 nn. 2 and 3, 132 nn. 8 and 10, 185, 215, 217, 246; HLP's letter on his behalf to Rev. William Cleaver, 131; letters to, 104–5, 130–31, 132–33, 174
Roberts, John, of Denbigh (ironmonger and tax collector), 253 and n.2, 254, 255 n.2, 256
Roche, Father Philip, 177 n.11
Rogers, Samuel (poet), 242
Romilly, Sir Samuel, 114 n.5
Roscoe, William: *The Life . . . of Leo the Tenth*, 80 and n.7
Roth, *suo jure* countess of. *See* Pepys, Jane Elizabeth, née Leslie (Evelyn)

Rowe, Nicholas: *The Fair Penitent*, 315, 316 n.7
Rowton, William (banker), 322 n.1
Russell, Lady Anne, née Egerton, duchess of Bedford (wife of the third duke), 277, 278 n.2
Russell, Lady Charlotte Anne, née Villiers (eldest daughter of fourth earl of Jersey; wife of Lord William Russell; later wife of George William Campbell, sixth earl of Argyle), 310 and n.6
Russell, John, fourth duke of Bedford, 252
Russell, Lord William (youngest brother of Francis Russell, fifth duke of Bedford), 310 and n.6
Russell, Wriothesley, third duke of Bedford, 278 n.2

Sacchini, Antonio Maria Gaspero Gioacchino (musician and composer): Reynolds's portrait of, 153, 154 n.9
Sackville, John Frederick, duke of Dorset, 154 nn. 8 and 9
Saint-Cyr, Gen. Laurent de Gouvion, 103 n.7
Saint Januarius, 231 and n.1
St. Vincent. *See* Jervis
Salt, Henry, 103 n.15
Salusbury, Mr. (paternal great-grandfather of HLP), 75
Salusbury, Anna Maria, née Penrice, Lady (1715–59) (first wife of Sir Thomas Salusbury, d. 1773, uncle of HLP), 75, 77 n.16
Salusbury, Anne, née Perceval (Lloyd) (wife of Col. Thomas Salusbury, d. 1700), 77 n.8
Salusbury, Catherine, née Van (or Vanne), Lady (d. 1836) (wife of Sir Robert Salusbury), 75, 77 n.13
Salusbury, Rev. Sir Charles John (1792–1868), third and last baronet (son of Sir Robert Salusbury), 77 n.13
Salusbury, Charlotte Gwendolen (daughter of Sir Robert Salusbury), 77 n.13
Salusbury, Elizabeth, née Williams, of Tynewydd, Denbighshire (wife of Norfolk Salusbury, the son of Col. Thomas Salusbury), 77 n.10
Salusbury, Gwendolen, née Davis (d. 1790) (wife of Robert Salusbury, d. 1776; mother of Sir Robert Salusbury, 1755–1817), 75, 77 n.11
Salusbury, Henry (builder of Llewenny Hall) (ancestor of HLP), 268 n.2
Salusbury, Henry, of Llanrhaiadr (father of Catherine, née Salusbury, Wynn), 135 n.11
Salusbury, Henry Vanne (son of Sir Robert Salusbury), 77 n.13
Salusbury, Hester Lynch (HLS): marriage of to HT, 15, 17, 24, 32, 176 n.2. *See also* Thrale, Hester Lynch; Piozzi, Hester Lynch
Salusbury, Hester Maria, née Cotton (mother of HLP), 15, 275
Salusbury, Jane, née Offley. *See* Burroughs (formerly Salusbury), Jane, née Offley
Salusbury, Jane, née Thelwall, of Plas y Ward (wife of Norfolk Salusbury), 75
Salusbury, John (1707–62) (father of HLP), 15, 75, 77 n.9, 106, 285, 294, 295 n.6, 302; portrait of, 75
Salusbury, John (husband of Mary, née Pennant, Salusbury, of Bychton; brother of Col. Thomas Salusbury, d. 1700), 77 n.8
Salusbury, John Lloyd. *See* Lloyd (later Salusbury), John
Salusbury, John Salusbury Piozzi Salusbury (adopted son of HLP and GP) (JSPS): annual holidays with HLP and GP in London, Bath, and Wales, 20, 27, 143, 189, 190, 193, 240, 241, 245, 248, 257, 260–61, 264, 266, 275, 284, 287, 288, 293–94, 299, 316, 318, 319, 321; baronetcy for, 317 and n.2; and choice of wife, 296; conversion of to Anglicanism, 22, 202; friendships of and social connections for, 23, 24, 189, 195–96, 207, 269, 275, 284, 291; as heir of GP and HLP, 9, 19–20, 26, 28, 33, 235 n.5, 244, 273, 294, 295 n.8, 314, 316, 317 and n.2; and Lady Kirkwall, 249; and Alexander Leak, 306–7, 308–9; memorial for and denization of, 20, 22–23, 234, 235 n.1, 236, 238–39, 240 and n.1, 246, 254; personality and character of, 18, 20, 21, 22, 152 n.1, 212, 261, 269, 273, 286, 319; post-Oxford career for, 21, 24, 34, 314; servant for, 307, 308, 309; and societal rank, 21–22, 24, 151, 178; visit to Aldermaston Court, 206, 208 n.1; visit to Ladies of Llangollen, 307, 309, 318
—education of: and admission to Christ Church College, Oxford, 20, 24–25, 35 n.61, 198, 270–71, 275, 280, 291, 306, 307, 309, 314, 315 n.1; and admission to Eton, 22, 24, 202, 203 n.1, 206; HLP as supervisor of and course of study for, 20, 21, 24, 151, 169, 196, 198, 202–3, 206, 211, 286, 291; and facility in English grammar,

spelling, and conversation, 23–24, 196, 198, 245, 276; at Thomas Shephard's school, *see* Shephard, Thomas: school of and JSPS as pupil at; study habits of, 21, 24, 152, 166, 198, 202
—and GP, 34 n.10, 152 and n.1, 230, 236; at Brynbella after GP's death, 14, 226, 228 n.6; and reports from HLP on GP's condition, 13, 20, 151, 169, 174, 177, 178, 181, 183, 184, 189–90, 196, 197–98, 202, 207, 212, 215–16, 217, 218, 219, 220–21
—and HLP, 20, 25, 249, 266 n.17, 288; and death of GP, 24; and gifts for at school, 270, 271; HLP as model for, 22; JSPS as her reason for living, 308; her visit to at Enborne, 24, 240–41 and n.1
—letters to, 13–14, 15, 17, 18, 21–25, 33–34, 34 nn. 12–14, 16, 22, 23, 30, 32, 34, 44, and 45, 35 nn. 46–57, 59, 61, 63, and 64, 36 nn. 99, 100, and 101, 151–52, 165–66, 169–70, 174, 177–78, 181–83, 184–85, 189–90, 195–97, 197–99, 202–3, 206–7, 211–12, 215–16, 216–18, 218–19, 220–21, 228–29, 230–31, 234–35, 236–37, 238–39, 240, 240–41, 244–45, 246–48, 254, 255 n.2, 256, 260–61, 265 n.7, 268–69, 270–71, 272–74, 276–78, 279–81, 286–87, 287–88, 289–90, 293–95, 296–98, 305–6, 306–8, 308–10, 314–15, 316–17, 318–19, 321–23

Salusbury, Lucy, née Salusbury (ca. 1667–1745) (wife of Thomas Salusbury, d. 1714; paternal grandmother of HLP), 75, 77 nn. 8 and 9

Salusbury, Rev. Lynch. *See* Burroughs (formerly Salusbury), Rev. Lynch

Salusbury, Mary, née Pennant, of Bychton (wife of John Salusbury), 77 n.8

Salusbury, Norfolk (not son of Col. Thomas Salusbury), 75

Salusbury, Norfolk (d. 1736) (son of Col. Thomas Salusbury; great-uncle of HLP), 75, 77 n.10

Salusbury, Robert (d. 1776) (son of Norfolk Salusbury; husband of Gwendolen, née Davis), 77 n.11

Salusbury, Sir Robert (1756–1817), first baronet (great-grandson of Col. Thomas Salusbury), 60, 62 n.6, 75, 76 n.7, 77 nn. 13 and 14, 247, 248 n.8, 288 n.2, 302

Salusbury, Sarah, née Burrows (King), Lady (ca. 1721–1804) (second wife of Sir Thomas Salusbury of Offley), 60, 62 n.6, 75, 77 n.14, 82 n.2, 106–7, 294, 318

Salusbury, Sarah Katherine (daughter of Sir Robert Salusbury), 77 n.13

Salusbury, Rev. Thelwall (d. 1803) (younger son, or grandson?, of Norfolk Salusbury), 75, 77 n.11, 90, 93 nn. 12 and 13

Salusbury, Col. Thomas (d. 1700) (great-grandfather of Sir Robert Salusbury, 1756–1817) (HLP's great uncle), 75, 76 n.7, 77 n.8

Salusbury, Thomas (d. 1714) (paternal grandfather of HLP; husband of Lucy Salusbury), 75, 77 n.9

Salusbury, Sir Thomas, of Offley (1708–73) (husband of Anna Maria, née Penrice, Salusbury; later husband of Sarah, née Burrows (King) Salusbury; HLP's uncle), 9, 15, 60, 77 nn. 9, 14, and 16, 294; portrait of by Hudson, 75

Salusbury, Sir Thomas Robert (1783–1835), second baronet (son of Sir Robert Salusbury, 1756–1817), 75, 77 nn. 13 and 14

Salusbury, Col. William (d. ca. 1660), 75, 76 nn. 7 and 12

Salvador, John Lovell (at Laura Chapel, Bath, 1807), 130, 132 n.5

Saville, John, 62 n.10

Saxton, Sir Charles (ca. 1730–1808), first baronet, 266 n.13

Saxton, Sir Charles (1773–1838), second baronet, 266 n.13

Saxton, Clement (brother of the second baronet), 264, 266 n.13

Saxton, Capt. John (brother of the second baronet), 266 n.13

Saxton, Mary, née Bush, Lady (wife of the first baronet), 264, 266 n.13

Sayer, Robert, 315

Schenacher (or Schönnacher, or Schoenacher), John Georg, 284 n.3

Scott, George Lewis: editor of *Supplement to Mr. Chamber's Cyclopaedia*, 254, 255 n.5

Scott, John (1751–1838), first baron Eldon (later, 1821, first earl of Eldon), 133 n.4, 258 n.2, 259, 259–60 n.6

Scott, Sir Walter, 242; *The Lady of the Lake*, 303 n.1; *Lay of the Last Minstrel*, 192 n.7; *Marmion*, 191, 192 nn. 4 and 5, 242, 243–44 n.7, 244 n.9, 265 n.1, 303 n.1

Seaford. *See* Ellis

Secker, Catherine, née Benson, 278 n.3

Sefton. *See* Molyneux

Sellis, valet to Ernest Augustus, duke of Cumberland, 292, 293 nn. 7 and 8

Sévigné, Marquise de (née Marie de Rabulin-Chantal), 28

Seward, Anna, 60, 62 n.10, 67 n.1; *Letters*, 264, 266 nn. 16 and 17
Seward, William: *Anecdotes*, 170 n.4
Seymour, Lady Anne Horatia, née Waldegrave (daughter of Maria Walpole; mother of "Minny" Seymour), 114 n.6, 277
Seymour, Francis, first marquis of Hertford (father of Adm. Lord Hugh Seymour and Lord Francis Seymour), 114 n.6
Seymour, Lord Francis (uncle of "Minny" Seymour), 114 n.6
Seymour, Adm. Lord Hugh (father of "Minny" Seymour), 114 n.6
Seymour, Lady Isabella (aunt of "Minny" Seymour), 114 n.6
Seymour, Mary ("Minny") Georgianna Emma (later wife of George Lionel Dawson-Damer), 114 n.6
Shakespeare, William: *Antony and Cleopatra*, 95, 97 n.10; *Comedy of Errors*, 216 and n.2; *Cymbeline*, 242, 244 n.12; *Hamlet*, 73, 74 n.11, 209, 211 n.10, 306, 308 n.1; *Henry IV, Part 2*, 244, 245 n.4; *Henry V*, 264, 266 n.14; *King Lear*, 226, 227 n.1, 302, 304 n.17; *Macbeth*, 197, 199 n.3, 237, 291, 292 n.3, 297, 298 n.11; *Measure for Measure*, 106, 108 n.9; *Merchant of Venice*, 223, 224 n.13; *Merry Wives of Windsor*, 209, 210 n.7; *Midsummer Night's Dream*, 251, 252 n.12; *Much Ado About Nothing*, 147, 149 n.7; *Richard II*, 91, 94 n.23, 101; *Richard III*, 294, 295 n.7; *Romeo and Juliet*, 165 and n.8, 179, 180 n.4, 264, 265 n.9; *Taming of the Shrew*, 217, 218 n.1; *Winter's Tale*, 107–8, 109 n.21
Sharp, Elizabeth ("Betty") (Bath singer and pianist), 95, 98, 102, 106, 108 n.2, 113, 114, 152 and n.6, 155, 156, 179, 185
Shee, Martin Archer (portrait painter), 242, 243 n.4
Sheffield. *See* Baker-Holroyd
Shelley, Frances, née Winckley, Lady (wife of sixth baronet), 140, 141 n.7
Shelley, Henry, of Lewes (cousin of HLP), 91, 94 n.24
Shelley, Sir John, fifth baronet, 140
Shelley, Sir John, sixth baronet (son of above), 140, 141 n.7
Shelley, Philadelphia, née Cotton, 94 n.24
Shenstone, William: "Written at an Inn," 225 and n.2
Shephard, Anne Parke Goddard (wife of Thomas Shephard), 190 n.2, 308
Shephard, Charles Mitchell Smith (son of Thomas Shephard, the younger), 190 n.2; at Brynbella, 14, 143, 144 n.2, 151, 169, 184, 226, 227, 228 n.6; education of, 152 n.2; as HLP and GP's lawyer and personal friend, 166 and n.2, 190, 196, 198, 227 n.4, 231, 234, 236, 237, 238, 240 and 241 n.2, 244, 245, 246, 247, 248 and n.4, 254, 255 n.2, 256, 261, 263, 264, 265 n.7, 266, 269, 271, 272 n.7, 272, 273, 276, 279, 285 n.16, 294, 308, 311, 314, 315 n.2, 316, 319; and JSPS, 152, 228, 229, 284 n.1, 289
Shephard, Elizabeth Charlotte Anne (daughter of Thomas Shephard), 190 n.2, 241 and n.1
Shephard, Harriet Caroline Butler (daughter of Thomas Shephard), 190 n.2, 241 and n.3
Shephard, Maria (daughter of Thomas Shephard), 190 n.2, 241 and n.3
Shephard, Rev. Thomas (vicar of Speen), 203 n.1, 241 and n.3
Shephard, Thomas (son of above): education of, 203 n.1; family of, 190 n.2, 241 n.3; school of and JSPS as pupil at, 20, 21, 22, 24, 144 n.2, 166 and n.1, 169, 170, 178, 181, 183, 185, 189, 190, 197, 198, 202, 203, 206, 207, 212, 215–16, 219, 221, 231, 234, 235, 236, 237, 239, 240, 241, 245, 246, 249, 254, 261, 266, 271, 272, 273, 277, 279, 280, 286, 288, 291, 295, 296, 308, 314, 316, 319
Sheridan, Richard Brinsley, 66 n.4, 290 n.5; translation (with B. Thompson) of Kotzebue's *Menschenhass und Reue* as *The Stranger*, 95, 97 n.9
Shipley, Conway (son of Rev. William Davies Shipley), 22, 227 n.2
Shipley, Mordaunt James (son of Rev. William Davies Shipley), 226, 227 n.2
Shipley, Robert John (son of Rev. William Davies Shipley), 215 n.3, 223–24 n.10, 226
Shipley, William (son of Rev. William Davies Shipley), 143 n.4
Shipley, Rev. William Davies (dean of Saint Asaph), 98, 100 n.2, 142, 143 n.4, 214, 215 n.3, 222, 223–24 n.10, 226, 227 n.2
Siddons, Cecilia (daughter of SS), 186, 187 n.6
Siddons, George John (son of SS), 186, 187 n.6
Siddons, Henry (son of SS), 186, 187 n.6
Siddons, Maria (daughter of SS), 61 n.3
Siddons, Sarah, née Kemble (actress) (SS), 84, 87, 101, 259, 260 n.12, 272, 291; HLP on acting techniques of, 91; on Master Betty, 60, 61 n.3; marriage and family of,

68, 88 n.2, 156, 157 n.2; performances of, 156, 157 n.3, 171, 172 n.9, 180, 201 n.4, 204, 205 n.5, 209, 210 n.3; and will of William Siddons, 186, 187 n.6; letter from, 172 n.9

Siddons, William (actor) (husband of SS), 61 n.3, 68 and n.4, 87, 88 n.2, 102, 156, 172 n.9, 180 and nn. 1 and 2, 186 and n.1, 187 n.6, 205 n.5, 209, 210 n.3, 230; letters from, 85 n.2, 180 nn. 3 and 7, 181; letter to, 179–80

Sidmouth. See Addington

Sieyes, Emmanuel Joseph (Canon of Tréguier), 265 n.1

Signorelli, Luca, 223 n.7

Simmons, Thomas, 158–59 n.4

Skurray, Rev. Francis, 120, 121 n.14

Smirke, Robert (theater designer), 201 n.4

Smith, Anne, née Barnard, baroness Carrington (first wife of the first baron), 261, 262 n.5

Smith, Catharine Lucy (daughter of first baron Carrington), 261, 262 n.5

Smith, Charlotte Elizabeth (daughter of first baron Carrington), 261, 262 n.5

Smith, Emily (daughter of first baron Carrington), 262, 262 n.5

Smith, Esther (daughter of first baron Carrington), 261, 262 n.5

Smith, Georgiana (daughter of first baron Carrington), 261, 262 n.5

Smith, Harriet (daughter of first baron Carrington), 261, 262 n.5

Smith, Jane (daughter of first baron Carrington), 261, 262 n.5

Smith, Louisa Mary (daughter of first baron Carrington), 262, 262 n.5

Smith, Father Richard, 16, 113, 114 n.3

Smith, Robert, first baron Carrington, 262, 262 n.5

Smith, Robert John (son of above), 261, 262 n.5

Smith, Rev. Sydney, 289–90 and n.4

Smith, Sir William Sidney (British naval commander), 84, 86 n.15

Smyth, Sir Hugh, third baronet of Ashton Court (son of Thomas Smyth), 74, 76 n.3, 82, 83 n.7, 159, 160 n.4,

Smyth, James, and Nephews (London perfumers), 15, 134, 135 n.7

Smyth, Jane, née Whitchurch (wife of Thomas), 74, 76 n.3, 81, 82 n.1, 82, 83 n.4, 159, 160 n.4

Smyth, John (son of Thomas Smyth) (later fourth baronet of Ashton Court), 74, 76 n.3, 159, 160 n.4

Smyth, Sir John Hugh, second baronet of Ashton Court, 76 n.3, 83 n.7

Smyth, Thomas (husband of Jane), 76 n.3

Smythe, Mary, née Errington (mother of Maria Anne Fitzherbert), 128 and n.3, 227 n.3

Smythe-Owen, Henrietta Jemima, née Townsend), 294, 295 n.10

Smythe-Owen, Nicholas, of Condover (husband of above; uncle of Edward Pemberton), 294, 295 n.10

Solomon ben Isaac (or Shelomoh ben Yizhak) (Rabbi), 104, 105 n.4

Somerset, Henry Charles, sixth duke of Beaufort, 258 n.2, 259 n.6

Sophia, H.R.H. Lady (daughter of William Henry, first duke of Gloucester), 278 n.4

Southey, Robert: *Madoc*, 73, 74 n.9; *Thalaba*, 73, 74 nn. 9 and 10

Spencer, Lady Caroline, née Russell, duchess of Marlborough, 251, 252 n.7

Spencer, Charles, third duke of Marlborough and fifth earl of Sunderland, 525 n.7

Spencer, George, fourth duke of Marlborough, 121 n.7, 252 n.7

Spencer, George, marquess of Blanford (son of the fourth duke of Marlborough), 121 n.7

Spencer, George John, second earl Spencer, 114 n.5, 119, 121 n.8

Spencer, Henry (son of the fourth duke of Marlborough), 121 n.7

Spencer, John Charles, styled viscount Althorpe (later third earl Spencer), 119, 121 n.9

Spencer-Churchill, Charles, 241, 243 n.1

Staffa (Hebrides island), 61, 62 n.13

Stafford. See Leveson-Gower

Stanhope, Lady Catherine, née Brydges (Lyon), 178 and n.5

Stanhope, Adm. Edwyn Francis (1729–1807) (second husband of above), 178 and n.5

Stanhope, Adm. Sir Henry Edwyn, baronet (d. 1814) (son of above), 178

Stanhope, Philip Dormer, fourth earl of Chesterfield, 20, 71 and n.3

Stanley, Elizabeth, née Farren, countess of Darby, 222, 223 n.4

Stephenson, Edward, 97 n.15

Stephenson, Mary Cecilia, née Strickland (wife of above), 97 n.15

Stephenson ("Stevenson"), Mary Eliza (daughter of Edward), 96, 97 n.15
Stephenson, Rowland (husband of Mary Eliza Stephenson), 97 n.15
Stephenson ("Stevenson"), Rowland (later Standish) (son of Edward; brother of Mary Eliza), 96, 97 n.15
Stevenson, Rev. George, 181, 183 n.1
Stevenson, Lydia, née Thackeray (sister of William Makepeace Thackeray; wife of above), 183 n.1
Stewart, Dugald, 290 n.4
Stewart, Robert, viscount Castlereagh (later second marquess of Londonderry), 205 n.1, 243 n.3
Stock, Joseph (successively bishop of Killala, and of Waterford and Lismore), 301, 303 n.6; *The Book of the Prophet Isaiah*, 130, 132 n.6, 147, 148, 149 nn. 8 and 11, 149–50 n.12, 150 n.18
Stockdale, John, 161 n.2; letter to, 161
Strickland, Cecilia, née Towneley, 96, 97 n.16
Suetonius: *De vita Caesarum*, 288 and n.4
Suffolk. *See* Howard
Sutherland. *See* Leveson-Gower
Swift, Jonathan: *Gulliver's Travels*, 299, 300 n.8
Sydney. *See* Townshend
Synge, Edward: *A Gentleman's Religion*, 79, 80 n.3

Tacitus, Publicus Cornelius: *Histories*, 169, 170 n.3
Talbot, Lady Anne, née Bouverie (wife of George Talbot), 96, 97 n.14
Talbot, Charles, first baron Talbot of Hensol, 97 n.14
Talbot, Frances (later second wife of John Parker, viscount Boringdon), 61, 63 n.15
Talbot, Rev. George, D.D. (third son of Charles, first baron Talbot of Hensol), 97 n.14
Talbot, Thomas (surgeon at Wymondham), 63 n.15
Tallyrand-Périgord, Charles-Maurice de, 122 n.17
Tankerville. *See* Bennet
Tattersal, Dr., 92, 95 n.30
Temple. *See* Grenville
Tench, Ann, née Jones (wife of Rev. Thomas Tench), 90, 93 nn. 9 and 11
Tench, Edward (son of Rev. John Tench), 93 n.11
Tench, Edward (son of Rev. Thomas Tench), 90, 93 n.11
Tench, Elizabeth (daughter of Rev. John Tench), 93 n.4
Tench, John (son of Rev. John Tench), 90, 93 n.11
Tench, John (son of Rev. Thomas Tench), 93 n.11
Tench, Rev. John, 93 n.11
Tench, Mary, née Cotton (wife of above), 90, 93 n.11; letter to, 93 n.11
Tench, Philadelphia (daughter of Rev. John Tench), 93 n.11
Tench, Rev. Thomas (son of Rev. John Tench; husband of Ann, née Jones), 90, 93 n.11
Terence (Publius Terentius Afer), 169, 170 n.1
Thackeray, Eliza, née Wilson (Jones) (wife of Dr. William Makepeace Thackeray), 73, 83 n.10, 188
Thackeray, Jane Townley (sister of Dr. William Makepeace Thackeray), 84, 87 n.22
Thackeray, Martin (brother of Dr. William Makepeace Thackeray), 73 and 73–74 n.8, 87 n.2
Thackeray, Sarah Jane (daughter of Dr. William Makepeace Thackeray), 82, 83 n.10, 84, 87 n.21, 220 n.1
Thackeray, Selina Martha (daughter of Dr. William Makepeace Thackeray), 83 n.10, 157 n.6, 218, 220 n.1
Thackeray, William Makepeace (M.D.) (grandfather of the novelist), 11, 12, 13, 73, 82, 83 n.10, 84, 87 n.22, 156, 157 n.6, 174, 181, 183 and n.1, 184, 190 and n.1, 190, 191, 213, 214, 215, 216, 218, 221, 227 n.6, 228, 229, 231, 303; letter from, 304 n.23; letter to, 188–89
Thelluson, Peter Isaac, Baron Rendlesham of Rendlesham, 119, 120 n.4
Thelwall, Bevis (son of Rev. Edward Thelwall), 64 n.5, 136, 137 n.7
Thelwall, Rev. Edward (d. 1814) (cousin of HLP), 60, 61 n.2, 64 and n.5, 108 n.8, 113, 114, 115 n.1, 116 and n.1, 136, 186, 187 n.10, 213, 214 n.1, 230
Thelwall, Edward (1781–1870) (son of above), 64 n.5, 156
Thelwall, Mary Elizabeth, née Baldwyn (wife of Rev. Edward Thelwall), 64 n.5, 186, 187 n.10, 230, 261, 262 n.4
Thelwall, Miles John (son of Rev. Edward Thelwall), 64 n.5

Thelwall, Richard (son of Rev. Edward Thelwall), 64 n.5
Thomond. *See* O'Brien (or O'Bryan)
Thompson, Benjamin: translation (with R. B. Sheridan) of Kotzebue's *Menschenhass und Reue* as *The Stranger*, 95, 97 n.9
Thomson, James, 161, 162 n.2; "Summer" in *The Seasons*, 162 n.1; "Winter" in *The Seasons*, 18, 158, 159, 160 n.7
Thrale, Cecilia Margaretta (daughter of HLT and HT) (CMT): HLP on personality of, 31–32; marriage of, 30; relationship of with GP, 31; relationship of with her sisters, 30–31; relationship of with HLP, 26, 27, 31–32. *See also* Mostyn, Cecilia Margaretta
Thrale, Henrietta Sophia ("Harriet") (1778–1783) (youngest child of HLT and HT), 31, 175, 176 n.5
Thrale, Henry (husband of HLT) (HT), 70 n.3, 92; business affairs, will, death, and estate of, 27, 102 n.6, 175, 176 nn. 2, 3, and 5, 294, 314, 315 n.2, 316; relationship with HLT, 15, 17, 24, 32; Reynolds' portraits commissioned by, 126 (ill.), 305; and *Thraliana* notebooks, 14; travels with HLT, Q, and SJ to North Wales (1774), 79 n.4, 116 n.3
Thrale, Henry ("Harry") Salusbury (d. 1776) (son of HLT and HT), 20
Thrale, Hester Lynch, née Salusbury (wife of Henry Thrale) (HLT): death of children of, 15; death of HT and financial problems, 15, 318; Q as heir of, 27–28; relationship with Thrale daughters, 15, 145 n.1, 152, 317, 318; and travels with HT, SJ, and Q to Wales (1774), 79 n.4, 116 n.3. *See also* Piozzi, Hester Lynch; Salusbury, Hester Lynch
Thrale, Hester Maria "Queeney" (daughter of HLT and HT) (later Lady Keith) (Q), 95 n.32; GP's wedding gift and bequests to, 159, 160 n.2, 164, 226, 228 n.6; and her sisters, 27, 28, 30–31, 31–32, 33, 247, 307; inheritance of and HT's and HLP's wills, 101, 102–3 n.6, 235 n.5, 241, 316; marriage of to Lord Keith, 29, 30, 159, 160 and n.3, 162, 163, 164, 166, 169, 170 n.5; portrait of by Reynolds, 200; relationship with HLP, 15, 25, 26, 27–28, 29, 30, 35 n.65, 159, 160 and n.1, 164, 267, 273, 317; travels to North Wales with HT, HLT, and SJ (1774), 79 n.4; letters from, 25; letters to, 24, 33, 34 nn. 5, 17, 21, and 31, 35 nn. 67 and 75, 60–61, 74–76, 77 n.14, 81–82, 82 n.2, 83 n.4, 85 n.11, 89–92, 95–96, 101–2, 102–3 n.6, 106–8, 147–49, 152–54, 159–60. *See also* Elphinstone, Hester Maria "Queeney," née Thrale, baroness Keith
Thrale, Ralph (1773–1775) (son of HLT and HT), 20
Thrale, Sophia (daughter of HLT and HT) (later Mrs. Hoare) (ST), 28, 96, 138; Gainsborough landscape as wedding gift from GP and HLP, 153, 154 n.10, 160, 164; and her sisters, 28, 30, 32, 145; marriage of to Henry Merrik Hoare, 28, 33, 35 n.97, 145 and nn. 1 and 2, 146 n.6, 146 and n.1, 147, 148, 149 n.6, 157, 162, 163 n.4, 164, 165 n.6; relationship with HLP, 26–27, 28–29, 30, 32, 75–76, 134, 136, 137 n.1, 164, 165 n.6, 242; letter from to GP, 145; letter from to HLP, 146. *See also* Hoare, Sophia, née Thrale (daughter of HLT and HT; wife of Henry Merrik Hoare) (SH)
Thrale, Susanna Arabella (daughter of HLT and HT) (SAT): Ashgrove cottage of, 153, 154 n.5, 159, 291, 317; birthday of, 107, 109 n.18; and her sisters, 30, 32, 145, 262, 264, 317; LC talk with (1806), 111; relationship with HLP, 26, 27, 28, 264, 273, 303; relationship with William Frederick Wells, 27, 28, 140, 141 n.3, 164; letters to, 29, 35 n.81, 164–65
Thrale daughters, 223; attitudes of toward JSPS, 9, 18, 22, 23, 25, 26, 33, 273, 294–95, 297, 314; HLP on personalities of, 26–27, 28, 29, 33; and HLP's management of Streatham Park, 314, 315 n.2, 316; and HT's will, 102–3 n.6, 175, 176 n.3, 314, 315 n.2, 316; marriagability of, 27, 158; relationship with HLP, 9, 14–15, 15–16, 18, 19, 20, 25–34, 84, 136, 138, 142, 176 n.3, 228, 232, 241, 242, 246, 248 nn. 3 and 4, 317, 318; relationships among themselves, 246, 248 n.4; letters from, 181; letters to, 10, 34 n.3, 139–40
Thynne, Isabella Elizabeth, née Byng, marchioness of Bath (mother of viscount Weymouth), 184, 185 n.1
Thynne, Thomas, second marquis of Bath (husband of above), 120, 121 n.14
Thynne, Thomas, viscount Weymouth (son of above), 184, 185 n.1
Tizón, Ventura Rodriguez, 223 n.6
Tollemache, Lionel, second earl of Dysart, 178 nn. 4 and 6
Torrington. *See* Byng

Index   355

Townsend, Henry (son of Joseph Townsend), 270, 271 n.4
Townsend, Joseph, 270–71 and n.1, 276, 280, 306
Townsend, Joyce, née Nankivell (first wife of Joseph Townsend), 271 n.1
Townsend, Lydia, née Hammond (Clerke) (second wife of Joseph Townsend), 270, 271 n.1
Townshend, John Thomas, viscount Sydney of St. Leonards, 173 n.5
Turner, Sir Charles, second baronet, 263, 265 n.4
Turner, Joseph Mallord William (painter), 138 n.2
Twiss, Amelia (daughter of Francis Twiss), 179, 180 n.5
Twiss, Elizabeth (daughter of Francis Twiss), 179, 180 n.5
Twiss, Frances, née Kemble (sister of SS; wife of Francis Twiss), 179, 180 n.5
Twiss, Frances Ann (daughter of Francis Twiss), 180 n.5
Twiss, Francis (father of above), 180 n.5
Twiss, Horace (son of Francis Twiss), 101, 102 n.1, 242, 243-44 n.7, 244 n.9
Tyre, Charles Brandon, 172 n.8
Tyre, Mary, née Lysons (sister of SL and DL; wife of above), 172 n.8

Ungern-Steinberg, Baron Edward (second husband of Maria Stella Petronilla, née Chiappin (Wynn) Ungern-Steinberg), 135 n.10
Uxbridge. *See* Paget

Valentia. *See* Annesley
Valentine, the Egyptian (Christian heretic), 255 n.7
Vansittart, George, of Calcutta (father of Edward Neale), 97 n.7
Vaughan, Henry (M.D.), 134, 135 n.2, 197, 199 n.2
Verdier, Jean-Antoine, comte, 212–13 n.5
Vernon (afterward Harcourt), Rev. Edward Venables, archbishop of York, 257–58 n.2
Verulam. *See* Bacon
Villeneuve, Admiral Pierre-Charles-Jean-Baptiste Silvestre de, 68 n.1, 110, 111 n.3
Villiers, George, second duke of Buckingham, 248 n.11
Villiers, George Bussy, fourth earl of Jersey, 310 n.6, 311 n.7
Vince, Samuel: *Complete System of Astronomy*, 204, 205 n.2

Vincent, Sir Francis, tenth baronet, 286 n.20
Violet, Pierre (artist): engraving of his portrait of HLP used for frontispiece of *Retrospection*, 161 n.2
Viratti, Dr. Giuseppe, 251 n.2
Virgil (Publius Virgilius Maro): *Aeneid*, 84, 85 n.8, 218, 220 n.3, 269, 270 n.3; *Bucolica*, 147, 149 n.4
Voiture, 28
Voltaire: *Lettres sur les Anglais*, 206–7, 280 n.3

Waldegrave, James, second earl Waldegrave (first husband of Maria Walpole), 278 n.3
Waldegrave, Maria, née Walpole, countess Waldegrave, 278 n.3
Wales, Prince of. *See* George Augustus Frederick, Prince of Wales
Waller, Sir Jonathan Wathen (second husband of Sophia Charlotte Howe), 199 n.10
Walpole, Sir Edward, 277, 278 n.3
Walpole, Maria (illegitimate daughter of Sir Edward Walpole and Dorothy Clement), 277, 278 n.3. *See also* Waldegrave, Maria, née Walpole, countess Waldegrave; Gloucester, Maria, née Walpole (Waldegrave), duchess of
Wardle, Gwyllym Lloyd, 214 n.2, 232, 233 n.5, 242, 243 n.3, 259, 260 n.7
Warner, Rev. Richard: *Bath Characters*, 179, 180 nn. 2 and 7, 181, 183 nn. 2, 3, 4, and 5, 186
Warren, Mr. (Bath cheesemonger), 16
Warren, Sir John Borlase, 111 n.4
Warwick. *See* Grenville
Watkins, Ruth (HLP housekeeper), 82, 83 n.12
Webster, Sir Godfrey Vassal, fifth baronet, 279, 281 n.2
Wellesley, Sir Arthur, baron Douro of Wellesley, viscount Wellington of Talavera and Wellington, later duke of Wellington, 195 n.4, 201 n.2, 204, 205 n.1, 210 n.8, 223, 224 nn. 15 and 16, 244, 245 n.2, 311, 312 nn. 4 and 5, 312–13 nn. 6 and 7, 320 n.8
Wellesley, Lady Charlotte, née Cadogan (wife of Sir Henry Wellesley; later wife of Henry William, Lord Paget), 223, 224 nn. 14 and 15, 310, 311 n.8, 321
Wellesley, Henry (later baron Cowley) (brother of Sir Arthur Wellesley), 223, 224 nn. 14, 15, and 16

Wellington. *See* Wellesley, Sir Arthur
Wells, William Frederick: and SAT, 27, 140, 141 n.3, 164
Werff, Adriaen (or Adriaan) van der (painter-architect), 61, 63 n.16
West, Benjamin (painter), 138 n.2
Westall, Richard (artist), 138 n.2
Westcote of Ballymore. *See* Lyttleton
Westmorland. *See* Fane
Weston, Jacob (HLP steward), 137 n.5
Weymouth. *See* Thynne
Whalley, Augusta Utica, née Heathcote (second wife of TSW), 66. 67 n.5. 69. 188 n.1
Whalley, Rev. Thomas Sedgwick (TSW), 61, 66, 67 n.1, 92, 96, 189-90, 287, 304 n.12; letters from, 10, 24, 188 n.1, 190 n.1, 192 n.1, 193 n.2, 292 nn. 1 and 4; letters to, 10, 24, 34 n.2, 35 n.60; 66, 67–68, 187–88, 190–91, 193, 291–92
White, John, 300, 301 n.11, 311
Whitelocke, Gen. John, 186 and n.1, 187 n.4
Whitelocke, Mary, née Lewis (wife of above), 186, 187 n.5
Wickins, Martha (sister of Thomas Wickins), 186, 187 n.9
Wickins, Rev. Thomas (father of Thomas and Martha), 187 n.9
Wickins, Thomas (son of above; brother of Martha), 186, 187 n.9
Wilberforce, William (M.P.; philanthropist), 66 n.4
Wilkes, John: *Correspondence of the Late J.[ohn] W.[ilkes]*, 130, 132 n.7
Wilkinson, Patty (companion of SS), 61–62 n.3
Wilkinson, Tate, 61 n.3
William, Mr. (servant of Q's in London), 226
William, prince of Orange (later William III, king of England), 75, 77 n.12
William Frederick, second duke of Gloucester, 277, 278 n.4
William Henry, H.R.H. duke of Clarence, 214, 215 n.11
William Henry, first duke of Gloucester (second husband of Maria, née Walpole, Waldegrave), 273, 278 n.4
Williams, Eleanor, née Hughes (wife of Hugh Williams; mother of Ly W): at Brynbella, 143; death of, 16, 78 n.2, 268 n.10; family of, 78 n.2, 89 n.2, 144 n.4, 269, 275, 294; friendship with HLP, 249, 276; illness of, 13, 78, 88, 99, 205, 212, 252, 257, 262, 267, 269; letters to, 78, 209
Williams, Ellen (daughter of Sir John Williams and Ly W), 84, 86 n.19, 250 n.1
Williams, Emma (daughter of Sir John Williams and Ly W), 84, 86 n.19, 99, 100 n.17, 143, 144 n.6, 179, 180 n.6
Williams, Hanbury, 16
Williams, Harriet (daughter of Sir John Williams and Ly W), 84, 86 n.19
Williams, Hugh (husband of Eleanor Williams), 78 n.2, 89 n.9
Williams, Hugh (later third baronet) (son of Sir John Williams and Ly W; godson of HLP), 84, 86 n.19, 143, 144 n.8, 186, 208, 209 n.2, 213, 214 n.4, 314–15 and n.6
Williams, Sir John, of Bodelwyddan, first baronet (husband of Ly W), 78, 206, 262, 276, 317; Bodelwyddan described, 79 n.8, 87 n.20; at Brynbella, 143, 197, 213; family of, 79 n.8, 86 n.10, 100 nn. 1 and 17, 114, 115 n.2, 208, 319, 320 n.10; friendship with HLP, 24, 129, 185, 215, 232, 249, 257, 275, 309, 310 n.5, 314–15, 316, 318; gift of heifer calf to HLP, 113, 114 n.4, 115; travels of 134, 135 n.8, 136, 208, 212
Williams, John Hay (later second baronet; eventually Hay-Williams) (son of Sir John Williams and Ly W) (JW), 84, 86 n.19, 144, 145 n.5, 167 and n.1, 169, 213, 214 n.4, 267, 269, 275, 314–15 and n.6
Williams, Margaret (sister of Sir John Williams; sister-in-law of Ly W) (MW), 88 and n.1, 156, 269; at Brynbella, 87; family of, 115 n.2, 143, 179, 186, 208, 272, 317, 319; friendship with HLP, 87, 98, 100 n.1, 114, 129, 134, 196, 212, 249, 252, 254, 317; health of, 257, 262, 275, 286; travels, 208, 212; letters to, 12, 13, 19, 26, 30, 34 nn. 9, 15, and 39, 35 nn. 68 and 85, 114–15, 116, 127, 134, 136–37, 138, 141–42, 143–44, 155–57, 172–73, 185–86, 213–14, 229–30
Williams, Margaret (daughter of Sir John Williams and Ly W), 84, 86 n.19, 143, 144 n.6
Williams, Margaret, née Williams, Lady, of Bodelwyddan (wife of Sir John Williams) (Ly W): at Brynbella, 143, 197, 213; family of, 79 n.8, 84, 86 n.19, 87 n.20, 88, 89 n.8, 100 n.17, 113, 143, 144 nn. 5 and 6, 167, 249, 250 n.1, 319; friendship with HLP, 24, 129, 185, 215, 232, 257, 309, 310 n.5, 316, 318; letters to, 11–12, 14, 16, 19, 24, 30, 34 nn. 4, 6, 8, 18, 28, 38, and

40, 35 nn. 58 and 87, 65, 78, 87–88, 98–99, 113, 129, 167, 205–6, 224, 232–33, 249, 249–50, 252–53, 257, 262–63, 266–67, 275–76, 317–18, 322–23
Williams, Mary Elizabeth (daughter of Sir John Williams and Ly W), 84, 86 n.19
Williams, Peter (editor of 1807 edition of Welsh Bible), 132 n.9
Williams, Roger Hesketh Fleetwood (brother of MW), 114, 115 n.2, 317, 319, 320 n.10
Williams, William (son of Sir John Williams and Ly W), 84, 86 n.19, 88, 89 n.8, 143, 144 n.8, 186
Williams, Sir William (1634–1700), 79 n.8
Williams (later Williams-Edwards), Rev. William (brother of MW), 114, 115 n.2, 143, 144 n.5, 172, 215, 317
Williams family of Bodelwyddan, 115, 178, 186; letter to, 214–15
Wilmot, Elizabeth Emma, née Parry, 193, 194 n.2
Wilmot, John Eardley (later (Eardley-Wilmot) (husband of above), 194 n.2
Wilmot, Juliana Elizabeth, née Byron, Lady (first wife of Sir Robert Wilmot, second baronet), 268 n.3
Wilmot, Mary Anne, née Howard, Lady (second wife of Sir Robert Wilmot, second baronet), 267, 268 n.3
Wilmot, Sir Robert, second baronet, 268 n.3
Wilshire, William: letter to, 168
Wilson, Robert: *Coblers Prophesie*, 147, 149 n.5
Winckley, Thomas, of Brockholes, Lancs. (father of Frances, née Winckley, Shelley), 141 n.7
Windle, Thomas (attorney), 236, 237 n.2, 238, 239, 240, 294, 295 n.8, 311, 313 n.9
Wölfl, Joseph ("the Stranger") (pianist and composer), 95, 96, 97 n.8
Woodhouse, James (shoemaker-poet), 305 and n.3
Wotton, Sir Henry, 103 n.8
Wright, Mr. (London upholsterer), 260 n.7
Wroughton, Susannah, 181, 183 n.2, 230 and n.2, 274
Württemberg. *See* Charlotte Augusta Matilda, Princess Royal and duchess of Württemberg; Friedrich Wilhelm Karl, elector of Württemberg
Wyat, Hannah, 288
Wyatt, John (barrister), 64 n.3

Wyatt, Mary, née Burberow (wife of above), 64 and n.3
Wynch, Florentia (daughter of George Wynch), 262 n.1
Wynch, George, 261–62 n.1
Wynch, Henry (son of George Wynch), 262 n.1
Wynch, John (son of George Wynch), 262 n.1
Wynch, Mary (wife of George Wynch), 261, 261–62 n.1
Wyndham, Charles, first earl of Egremont, 178 n.3
Wynn (or Wynne), Anna Maria, née Meredith (Mostyn) (widow, successively, of John Mostyn of Segroid and of Edward Watkin Wynn; mother of JMM), 32, 75, 76, 78 n.19, 133, 318, 320 n.6
Wynn (or Wynne), Anne, née Dod (Sobieski) (wife of Robert Watkin Wynn), 76 n.4, 102 n.4
Wynn, Catherine, née Perceval, baroness Newborough (first wife of Thomas Wynn, baron Newborough), 160 n.9
Wynn, Catherine, née Salusbury (wife of Hugh ap John Wynn, of Bodvil), 135 n.11
Wynn (or Wynne), Charles (son of Robert Watkin Wynn), 26, 74–75, 76 nn. 4 and 6
Wynn (or Wynne), Maj. Edward Watkin, of Llewessog (second husband of Anna Maria, née Meredith (Mostyn) Wynn), 78 n.19, 320 n.6
Wynn, Hugh ap John, of Bodvil (husband of Catherine, née Salusbury, Wynn), 135 n.11
Wynn (or Wynne), John (son of Robert Watkin Wynn), 26, 74, 76 nn. 4, 5, and 6
Wynn (or Wynne), Julius (son of Robert Watkin Wynn), 74, 76 n.4
Wynn, Maria Stella Petronilla Chiappini, baroness Newborough (self-styled Marchesina of Modigliana) (second wife of Thomas Wynn, baron Newborough; married secondly baron Edward Ungern-Steinberg), 134, 135 nn. 10 and 11, 156
Wynn (or Wynne), Robert (son of Robert Watkin Wynn) (died young), 76 n.4
Wynn (or Wynne), Robert Watkin, of Plasnewydd and Garthmeilo, 16, 26, 66, 67 n.3, 68 and nn. 5 and 6, 74, 76 nn. 4, 5, and 6, 98, 100 n.3, 101, 102 n.4, 140
Wynn (or Wynne), Sarah Anne, née Parr (wife of John Wynn), 74, 76 n.5
Wynn, Spencer Bulkeley (son of Thomas

Wynn, baron Newborough, and his second wife), 134, 135 n.11
Wynn, Thomas, baron Newborough (husband of Catherine, née Percival, Wynn, and later of Maria Stella Petronilla Chiappini Wynn), 135 nn. 10 and 11, 156, 160 and n.9
Wynn, Thomas John (son of Thomas Wynn, baron Newborough, and his second wife), 134, 135 n.11
Wynn (or Wynne), Watkin (son of Robert Watkin Wynn), 26, 74–75 76 nn. 4 and 6
Wynn (or Wynne), Sir Watkin Williams, fifth baronet (son of Sir Watkin Williams Wynne), 115, 116 n.7

Yarmouth. *See* Conway
Yelverton, Mary, née Reade, viscountess Avonmore, 259, 260 n.13
Yelverton, William Charles, second viscount Avonmore (husband of above), 259, 260 n.13
York. *See* Frederick Augustus, duke of York and Albany
Yorke, Charles, 290 n.5
Yorke, Rev. James, bishop of Ely (father of Elizabeth, née Yorke, Buller), 115 n.5
Young, Edward: *Love of Fame*, 60, 62 n.4; *Night Thoughts*, 204, 205 n.4, 222, 235 n.2
Young Roscius. *See* Betty, William Henry West